"When we met in LA he showed me his sketch book and it was completely filled with drawings from cover to cover... every single inch of it.
I remember thinking that, for him, to draw is to live. "

「LA で会った時に見せてもらったスケッチブックには
裏も表も関係なく、びっしり絵が書き込まれていて、、、
本当にびっしりと、、、それは、描く事は生きている事と
同じレベルなんだな、とおもった」

– TAKASHI MURAKAMI

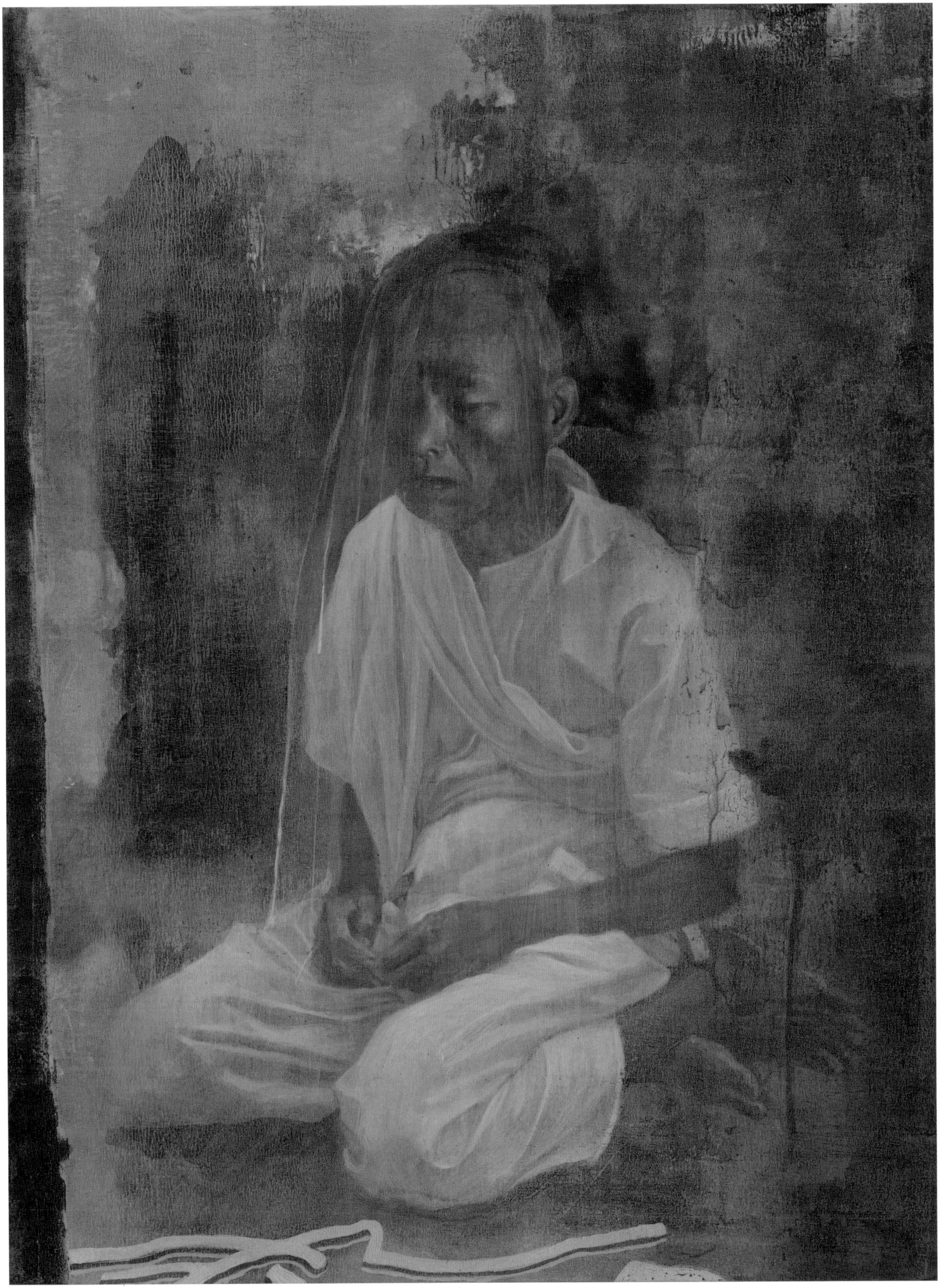

JAMES JEAN

PAREIDOLIA

パレイドリア

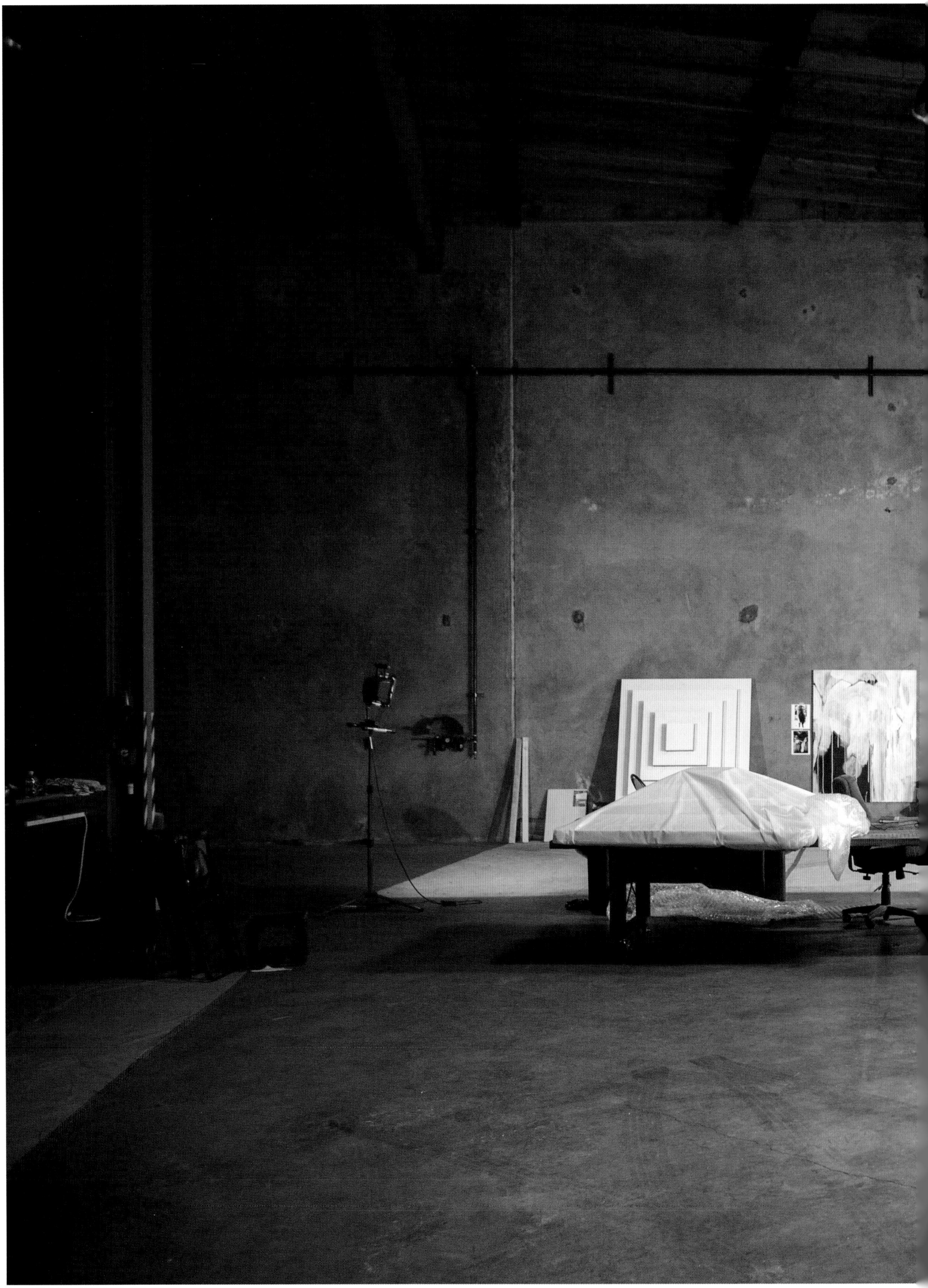

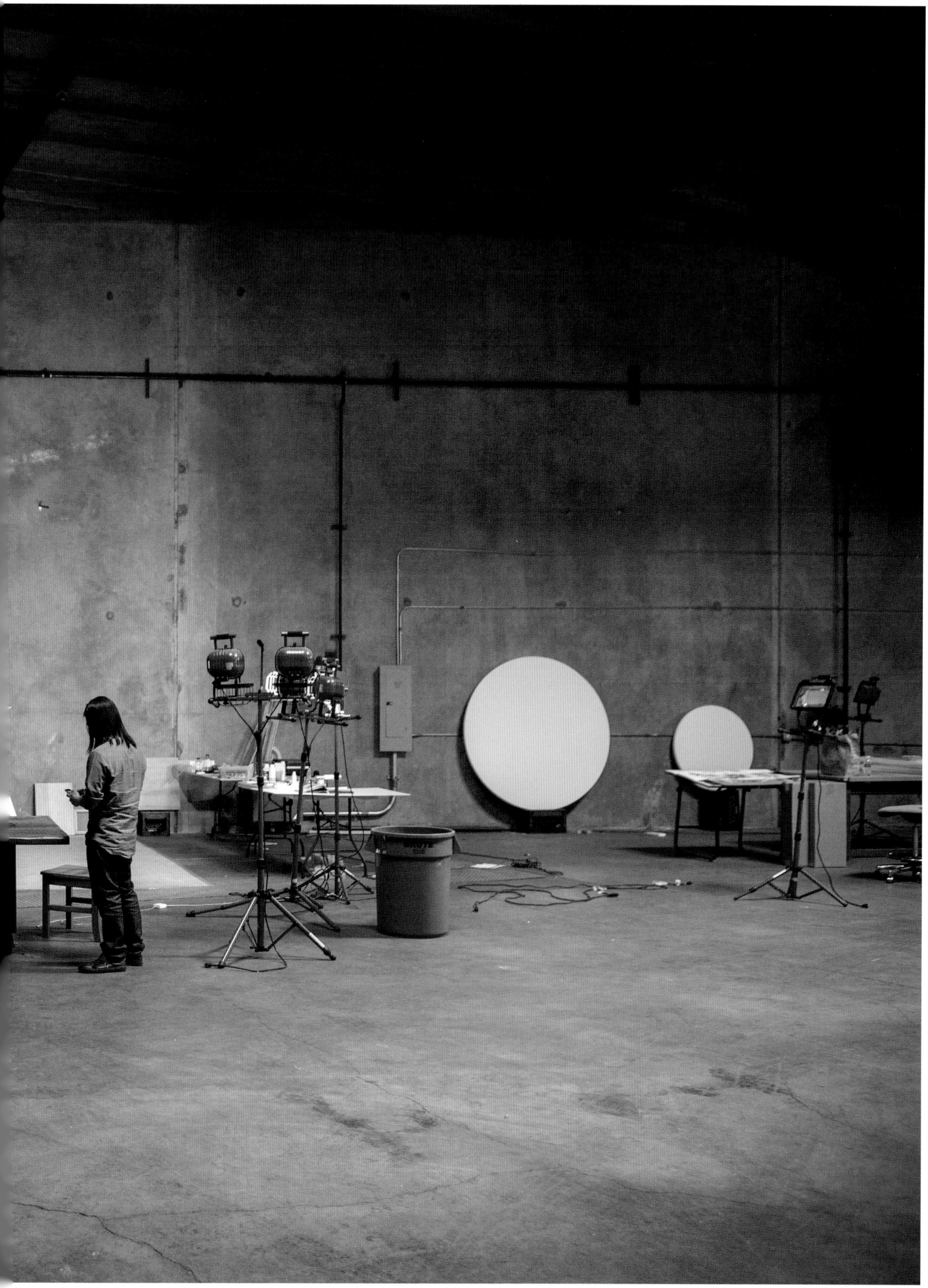

"James Jean's art is supple, fluid, and full of grace. Redolent of baroque friezes but tinged with lysergic abandon, his compositions are meticulously planned and yet supple and alive. His mastery of form and color connects him to deeper roots than pop culture and suffuses his images with emotion and immediacy."

「ジェームス・ジーンのアートは、圧倒的な流線美をもち、しなやかで気品に満ちている。バロック建築の浮き彫りを彷彿とさせるが、より幻惑的で奔放。そのコンポジションは計算しつくされていながらもなお、やわらかで生命感に溢れている。その「形」と「色」への精通は、ポップカルチャーを超えて、彼を世界の深層に結び付け、そのイメージを興奮と緊迫感で満たす」

– GUILLERMO DEL TORO

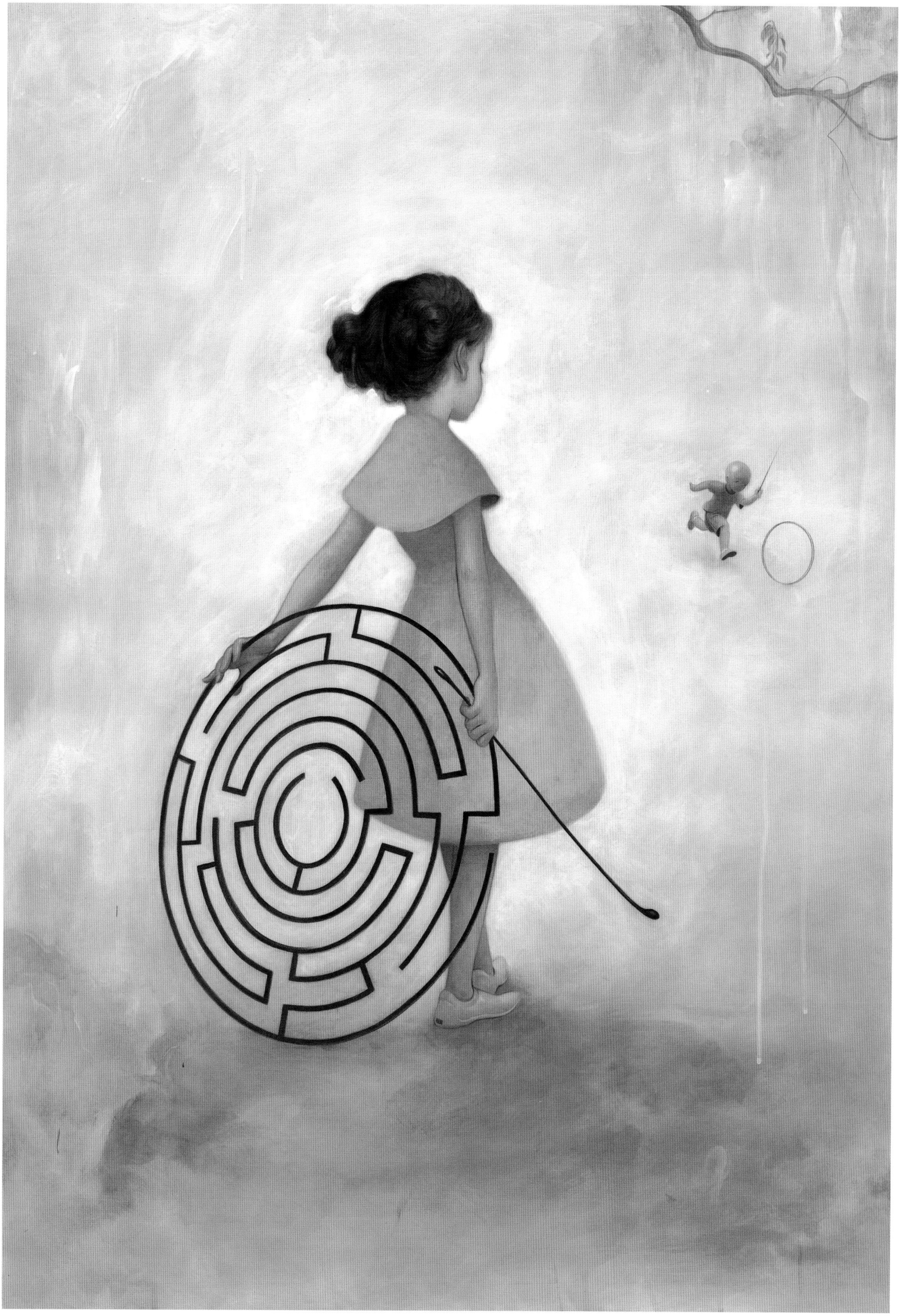

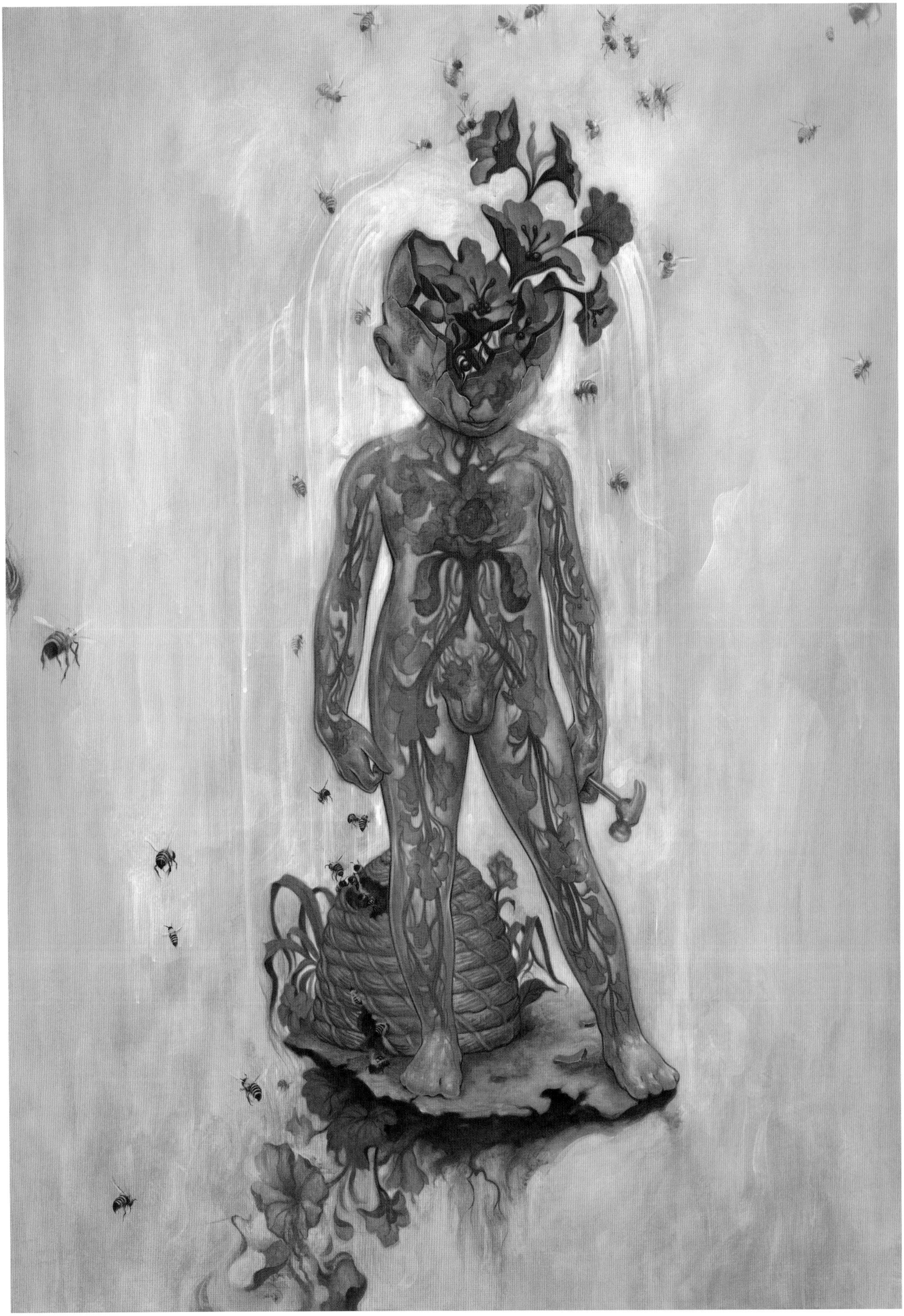

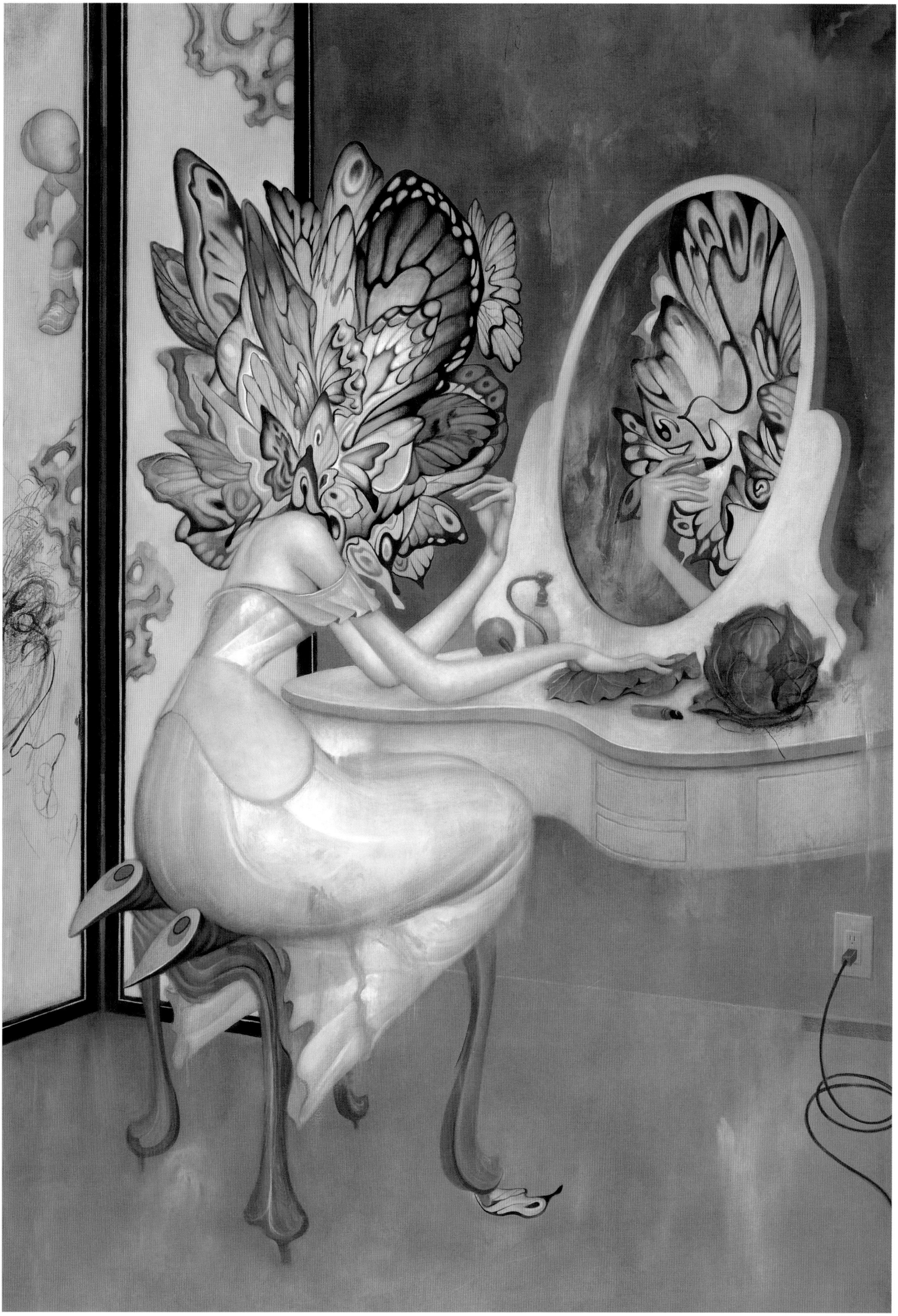

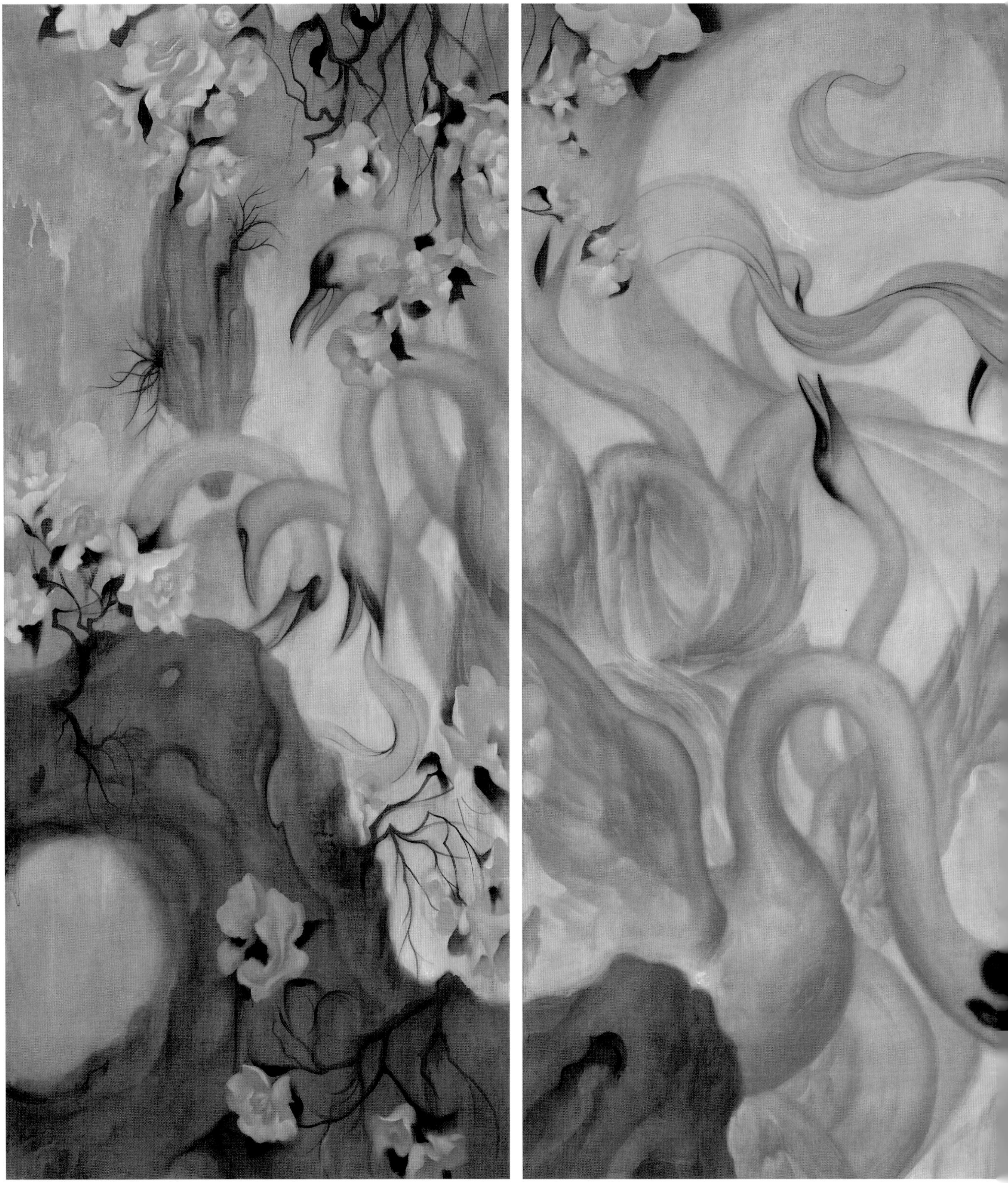

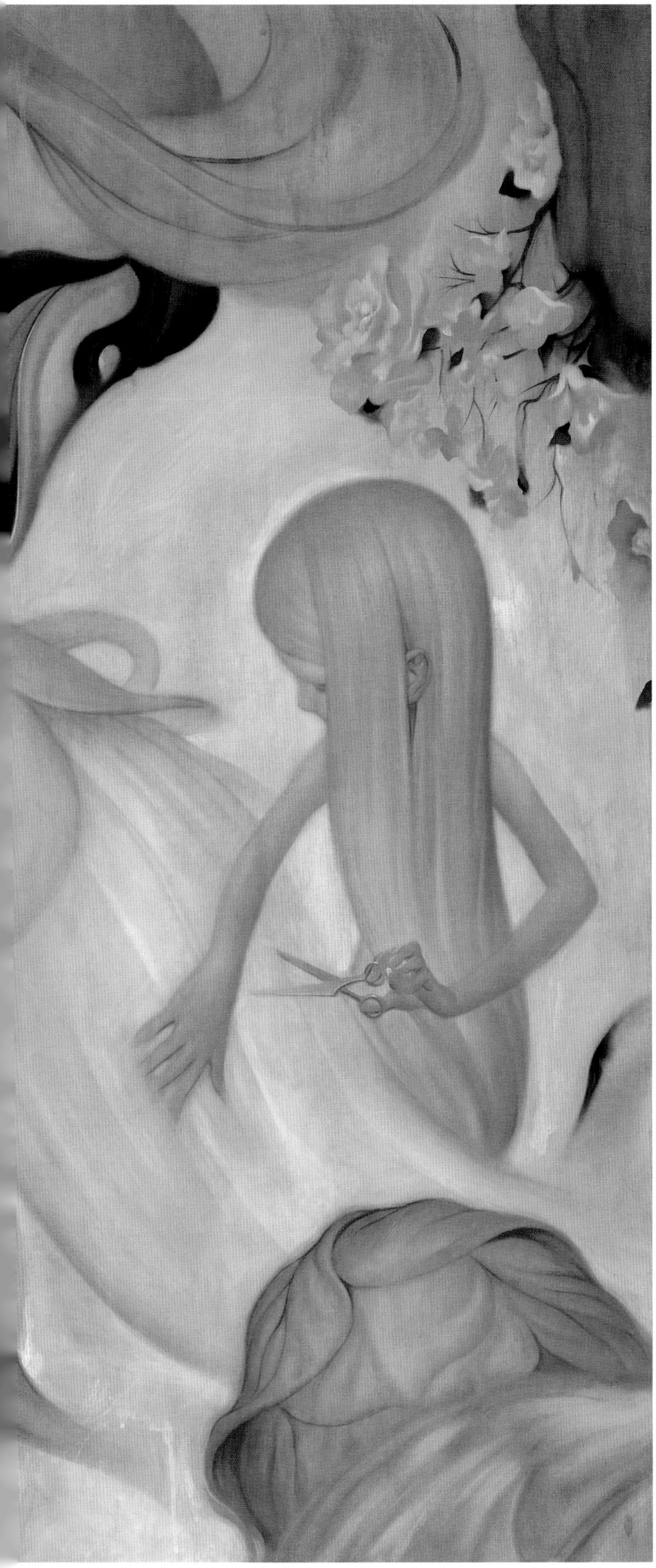

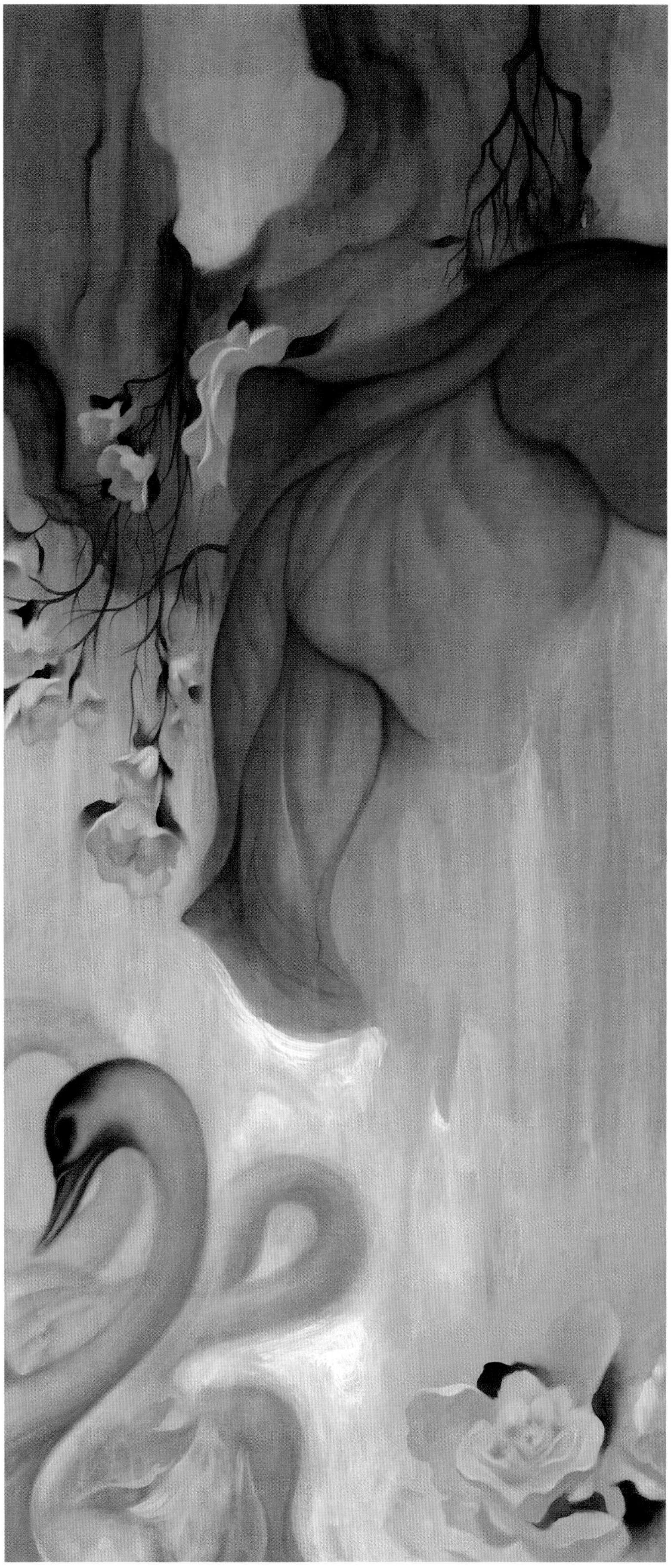

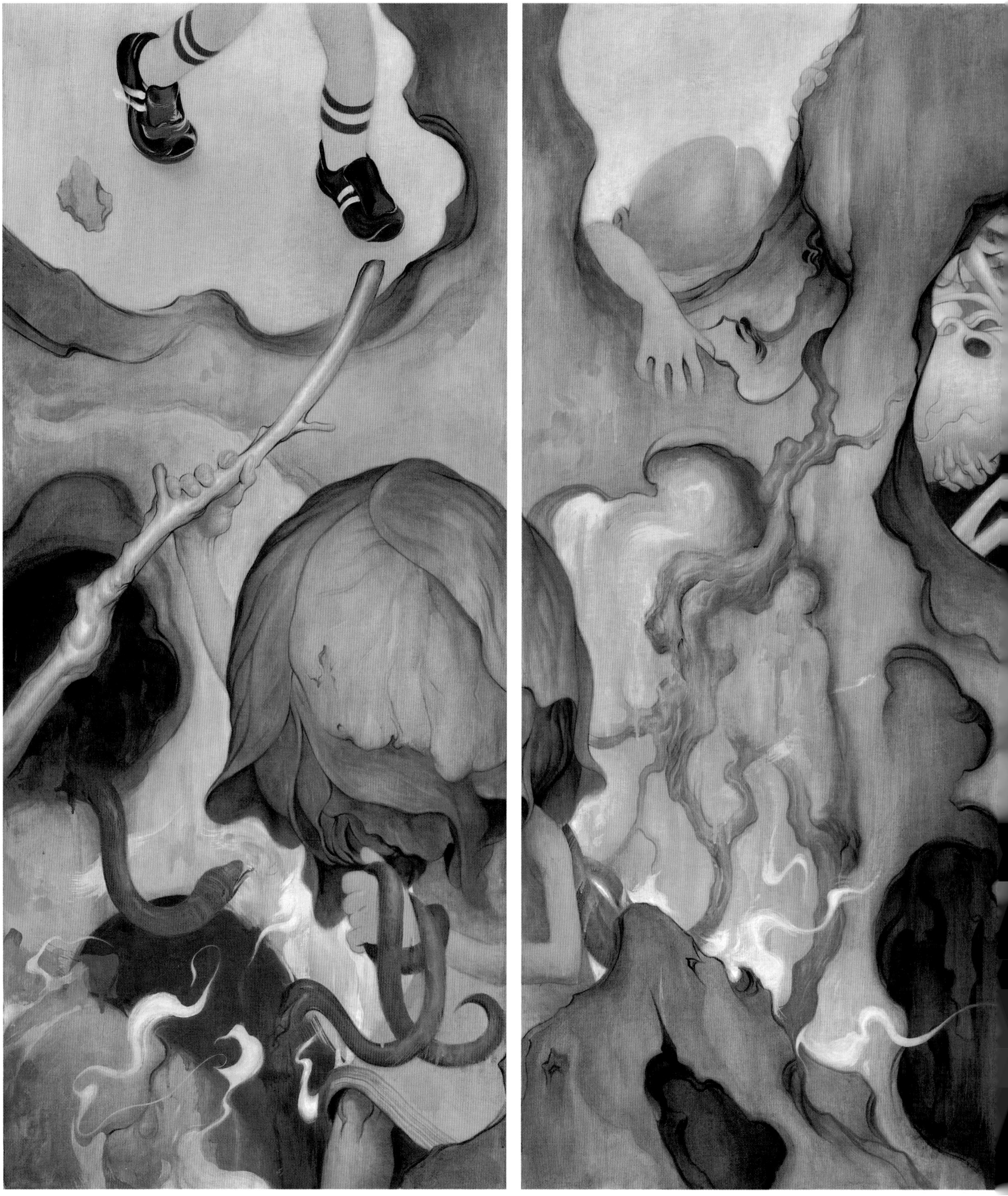

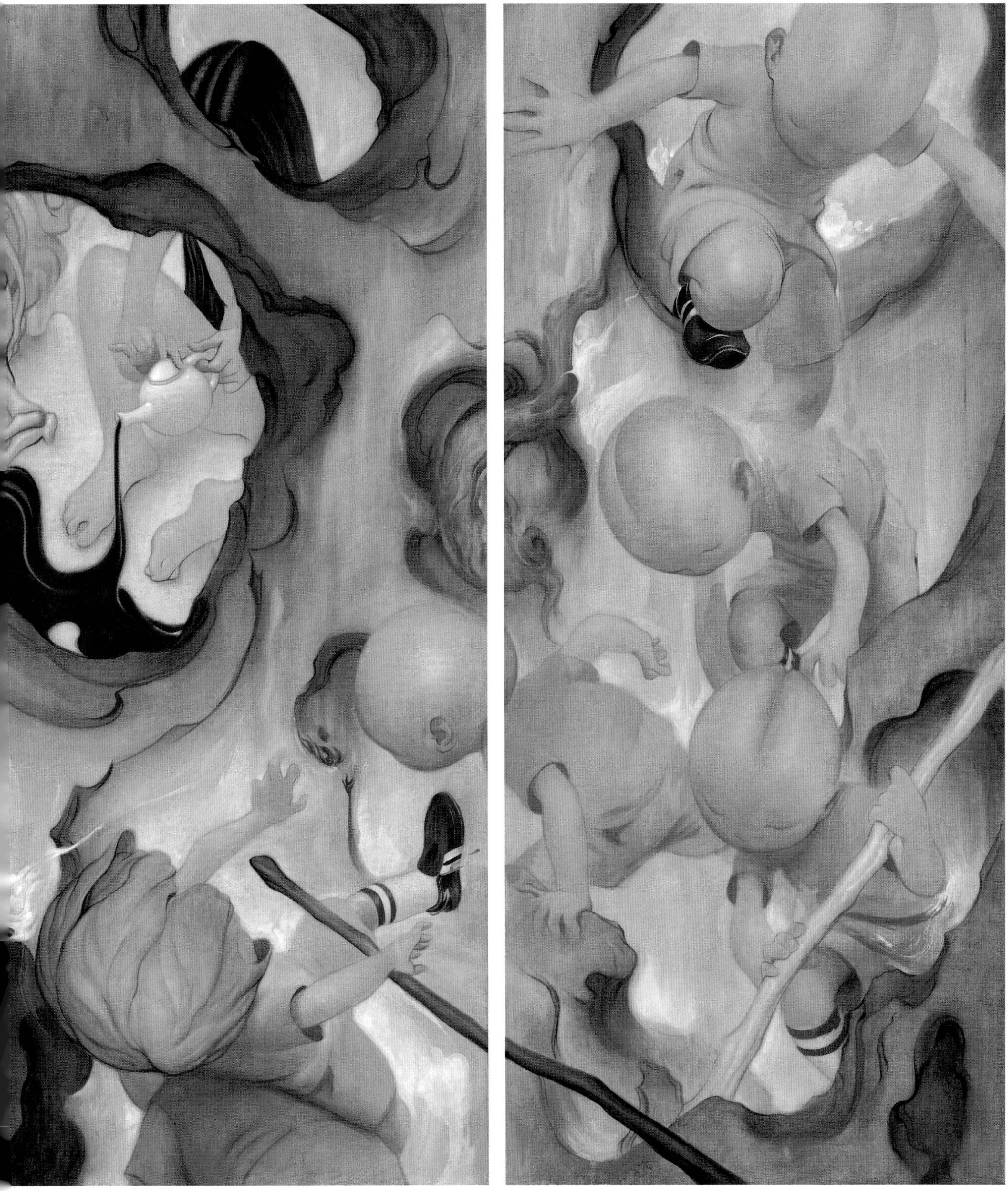

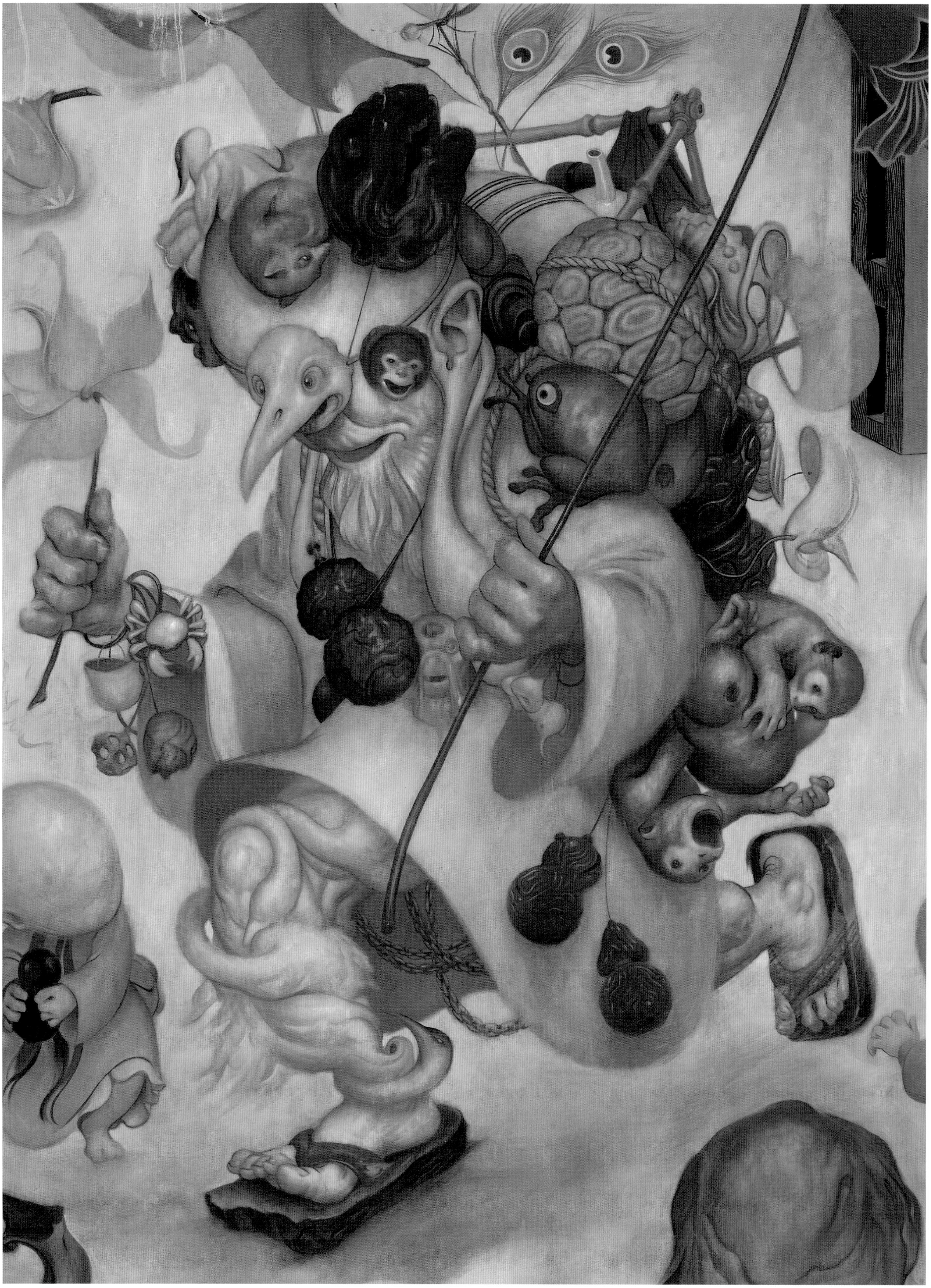

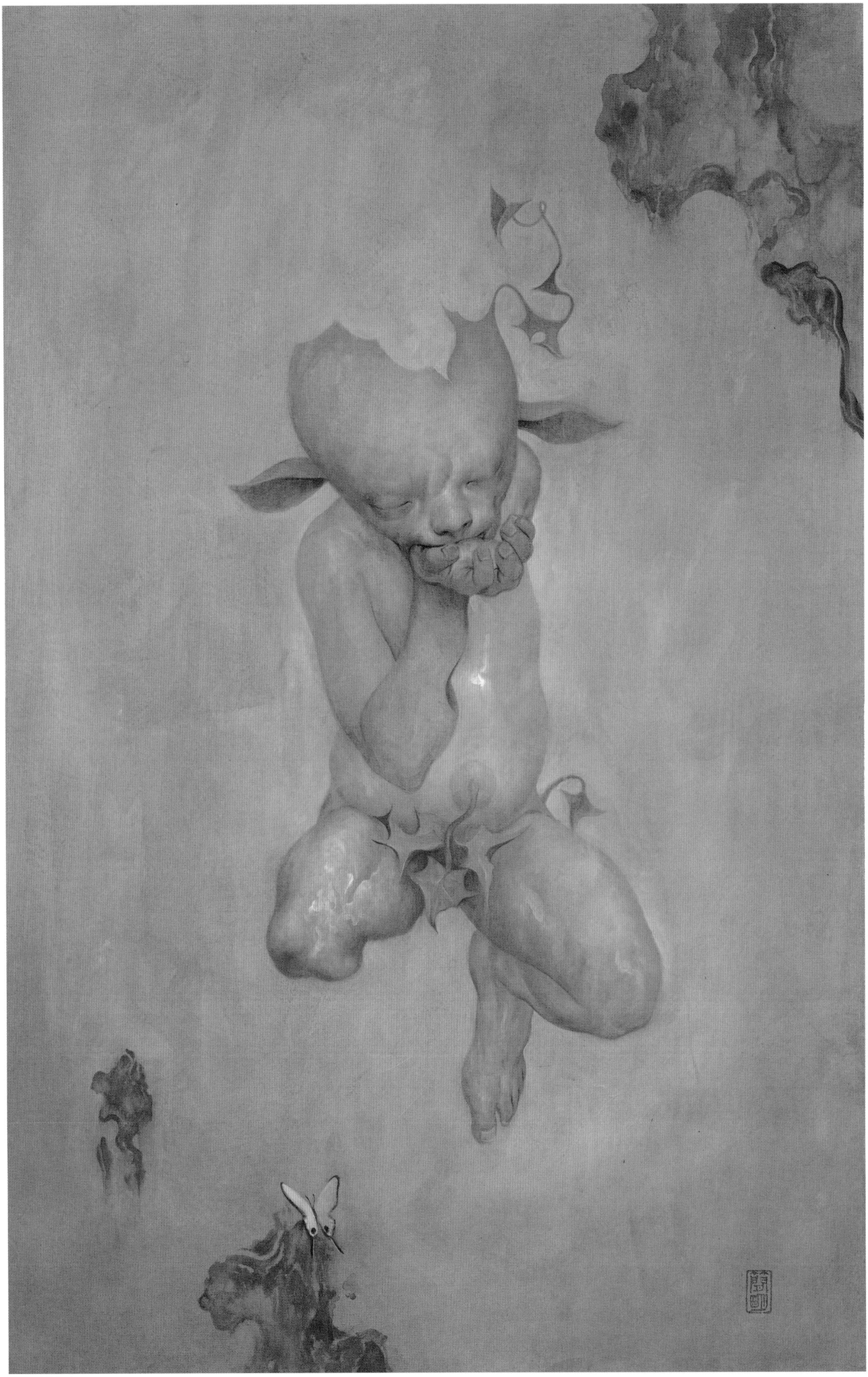

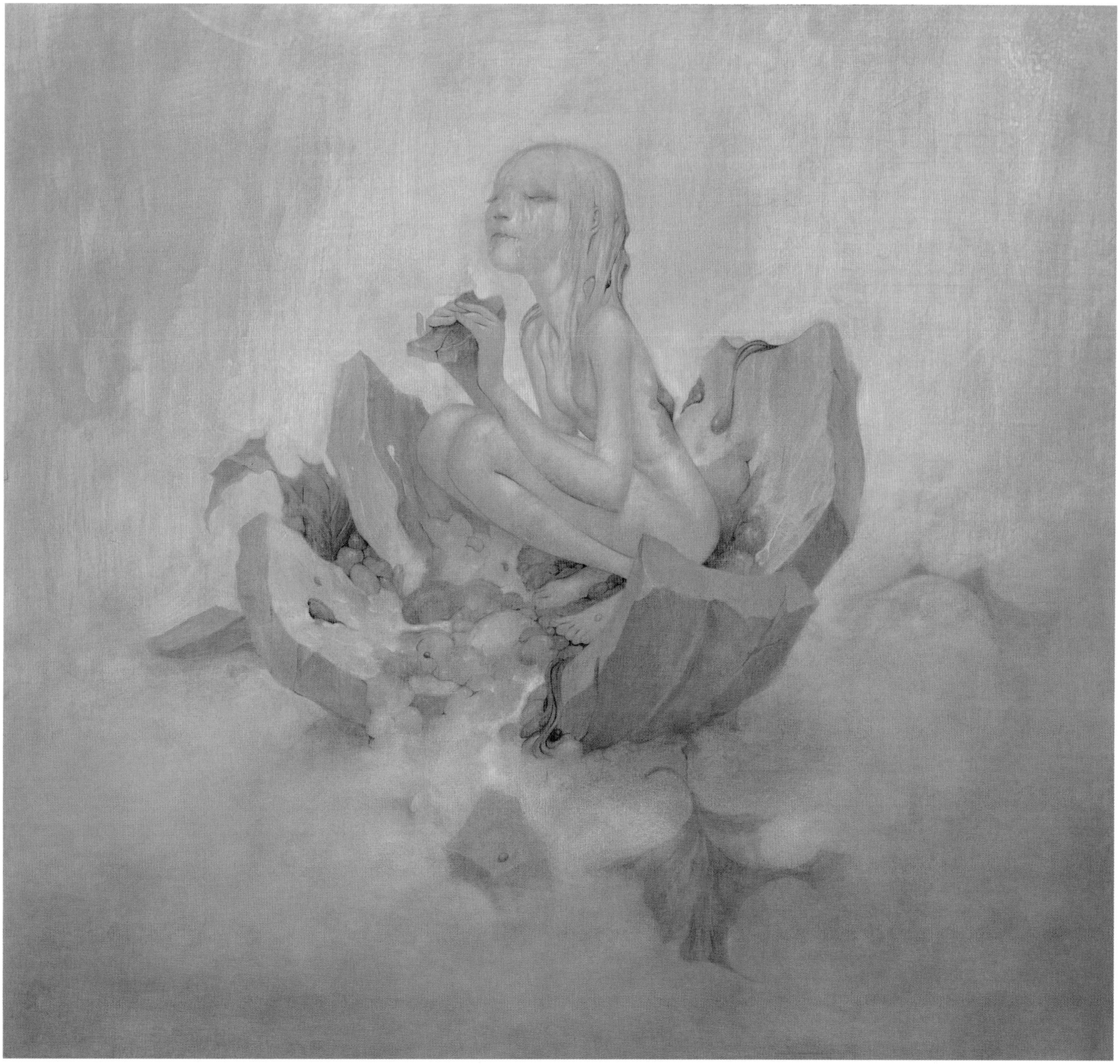

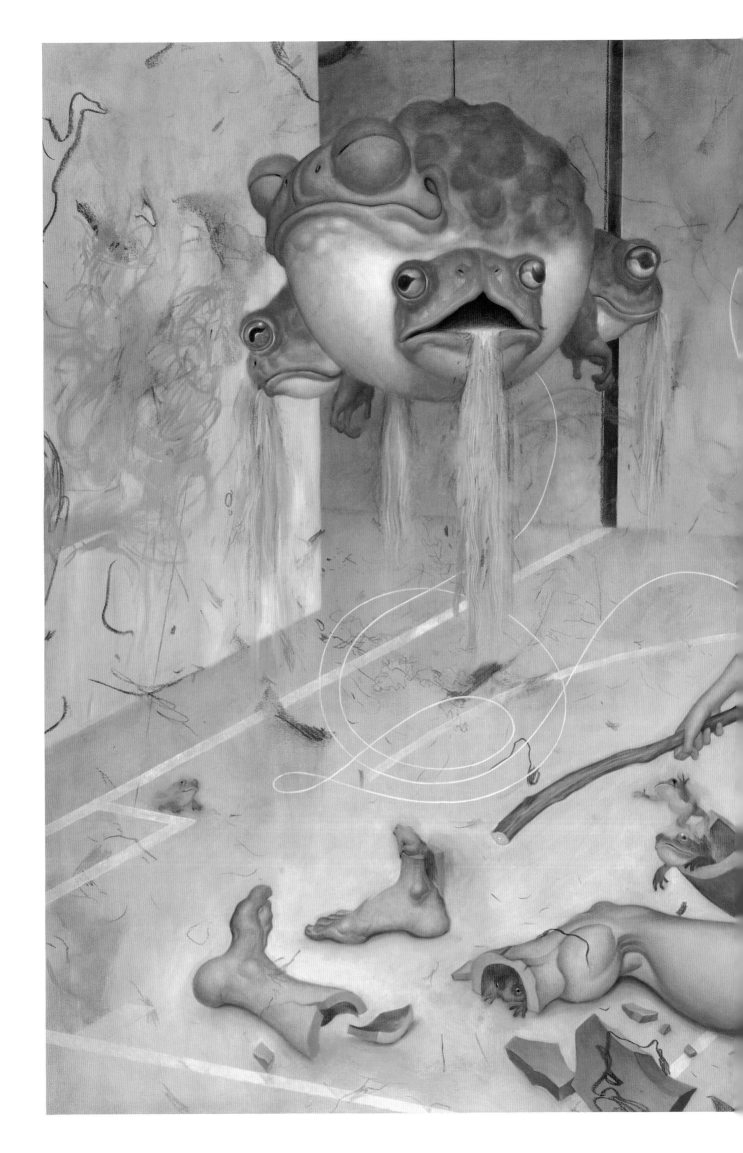

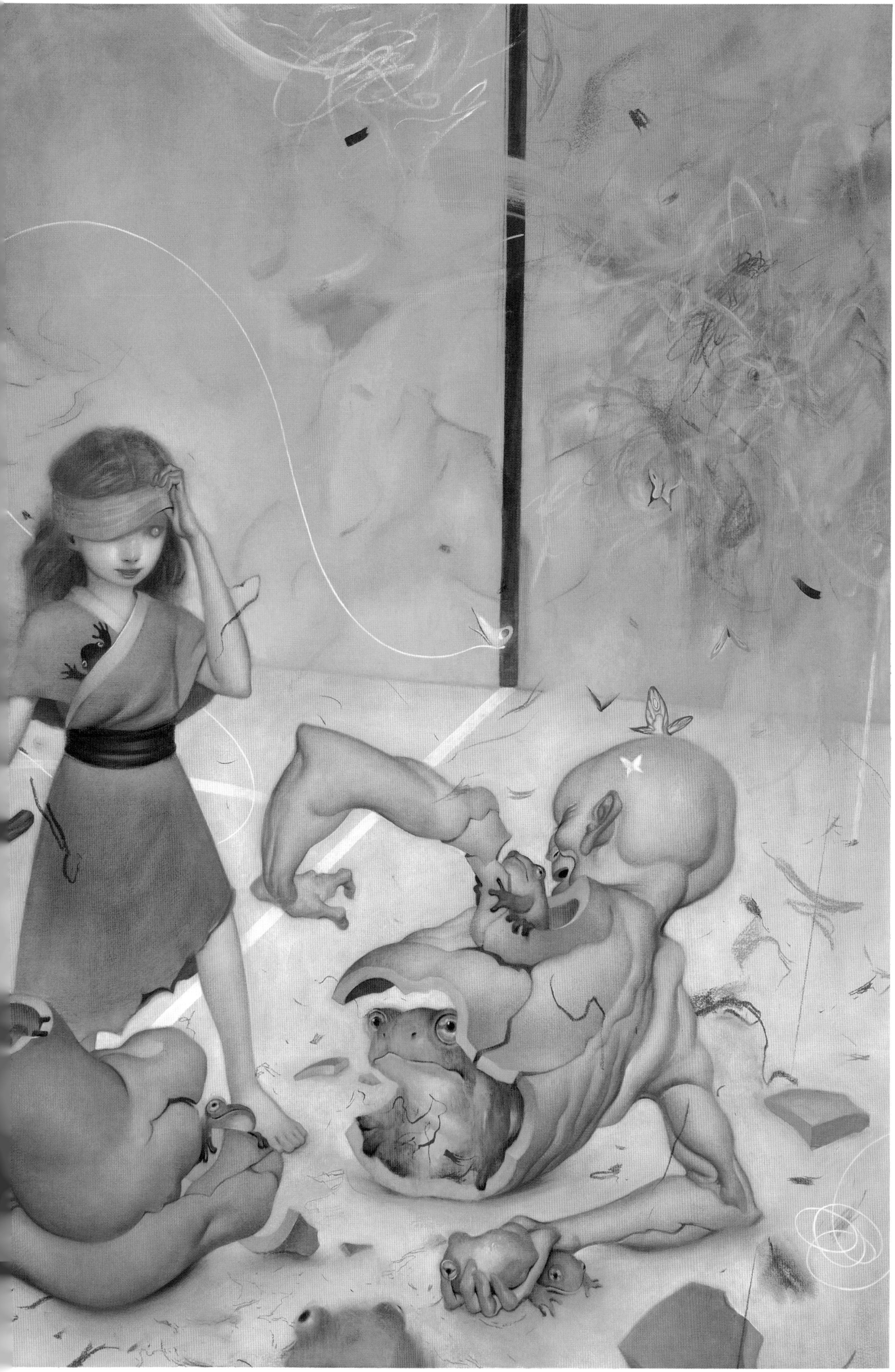

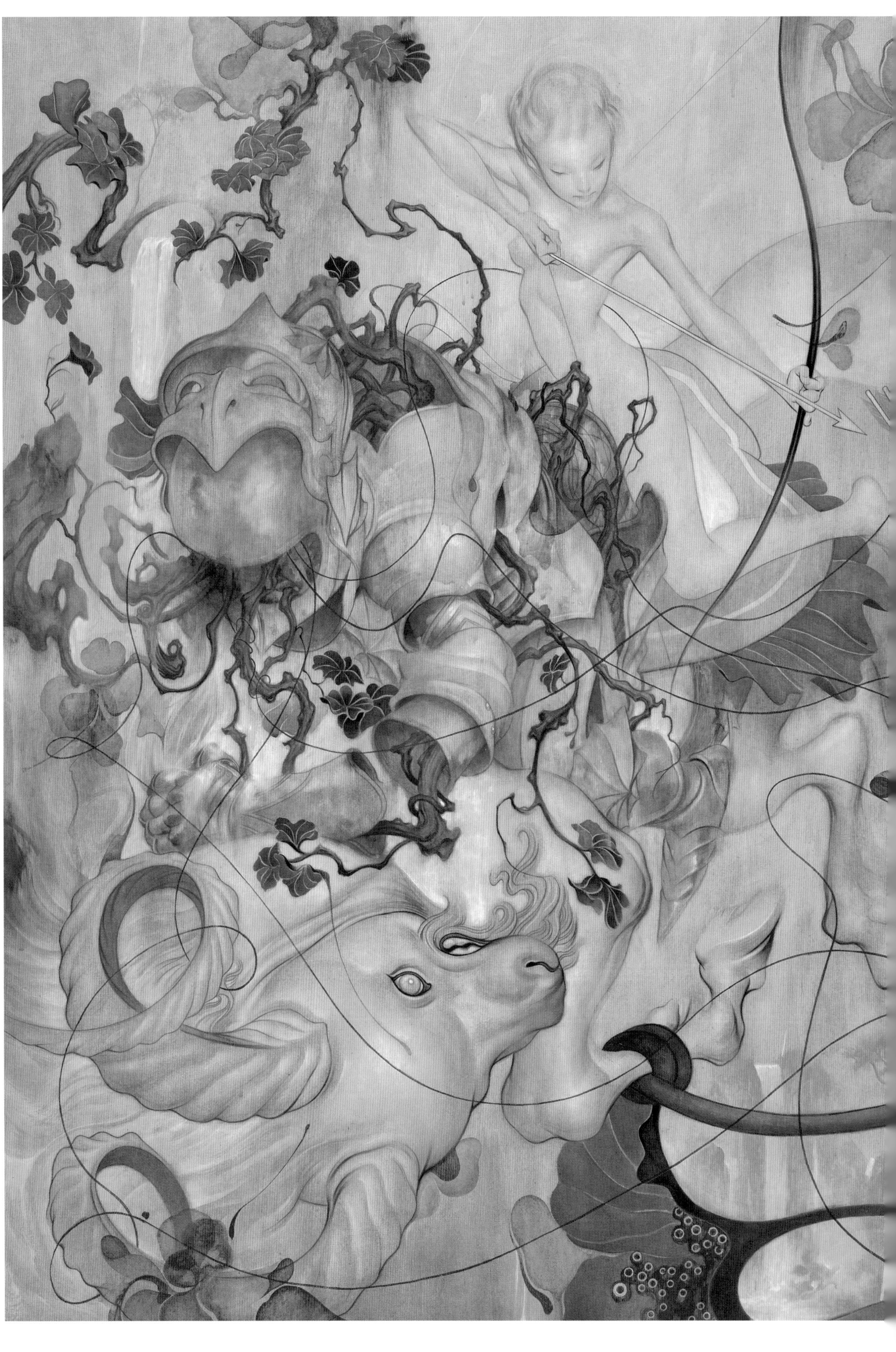

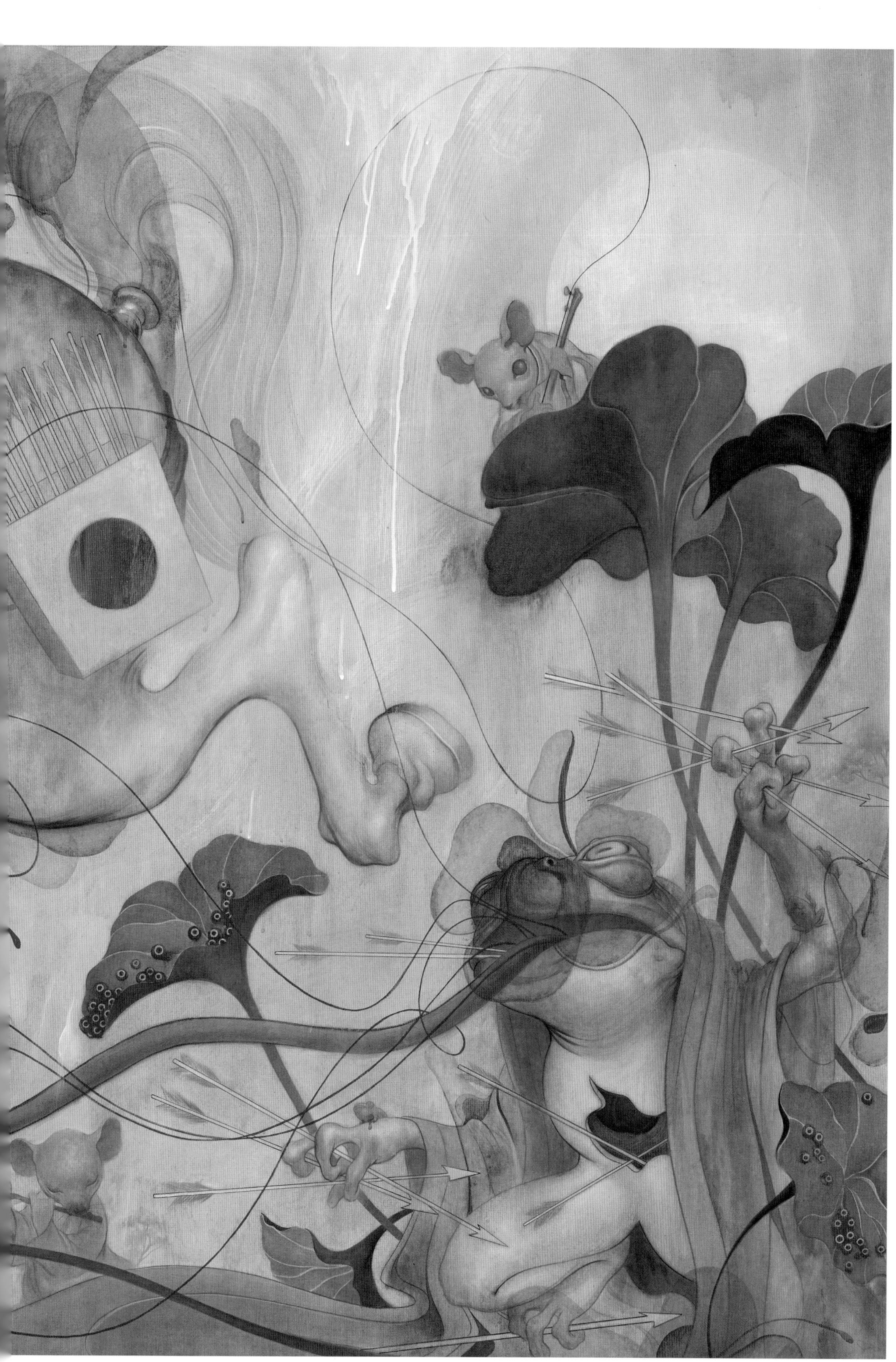

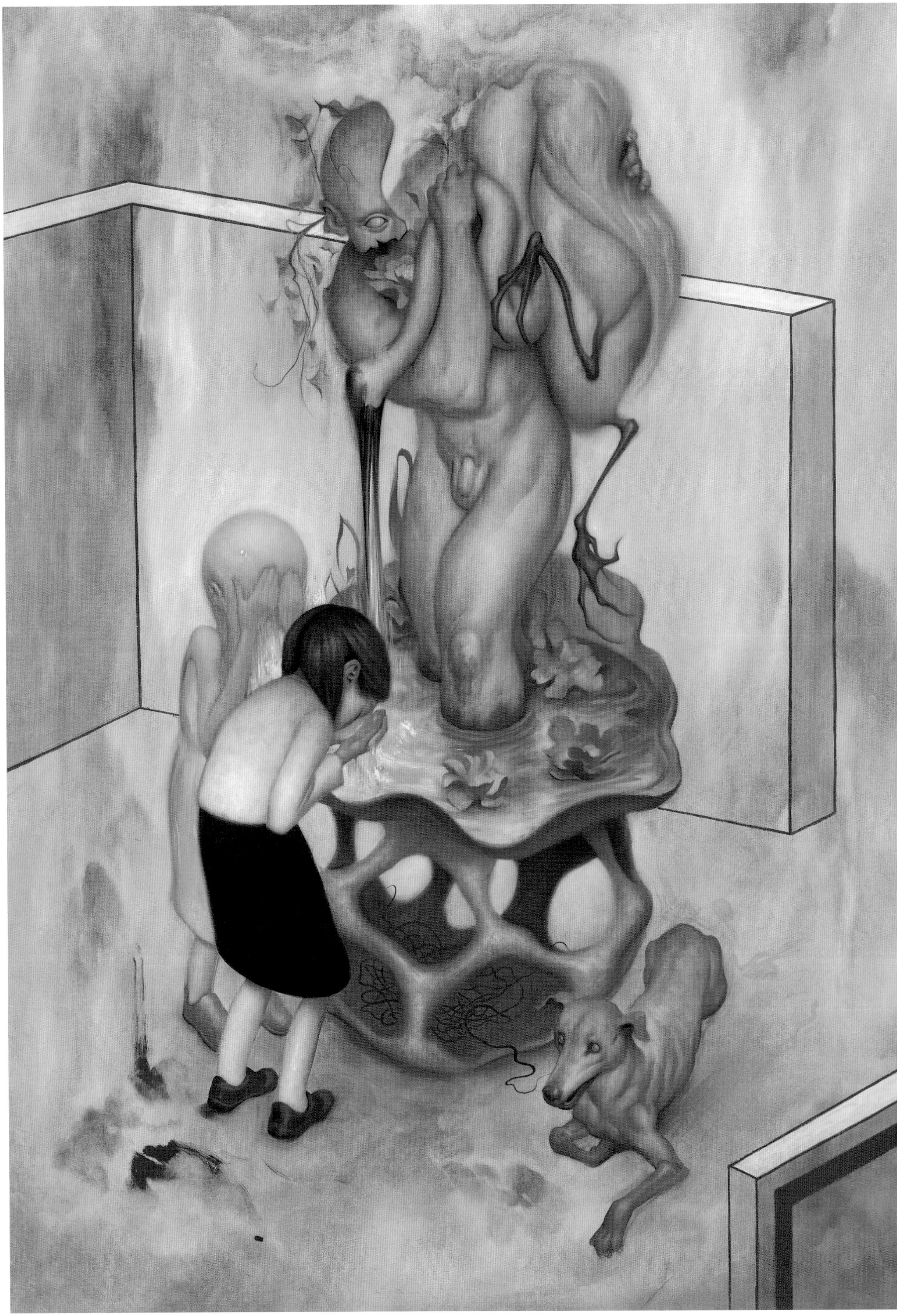

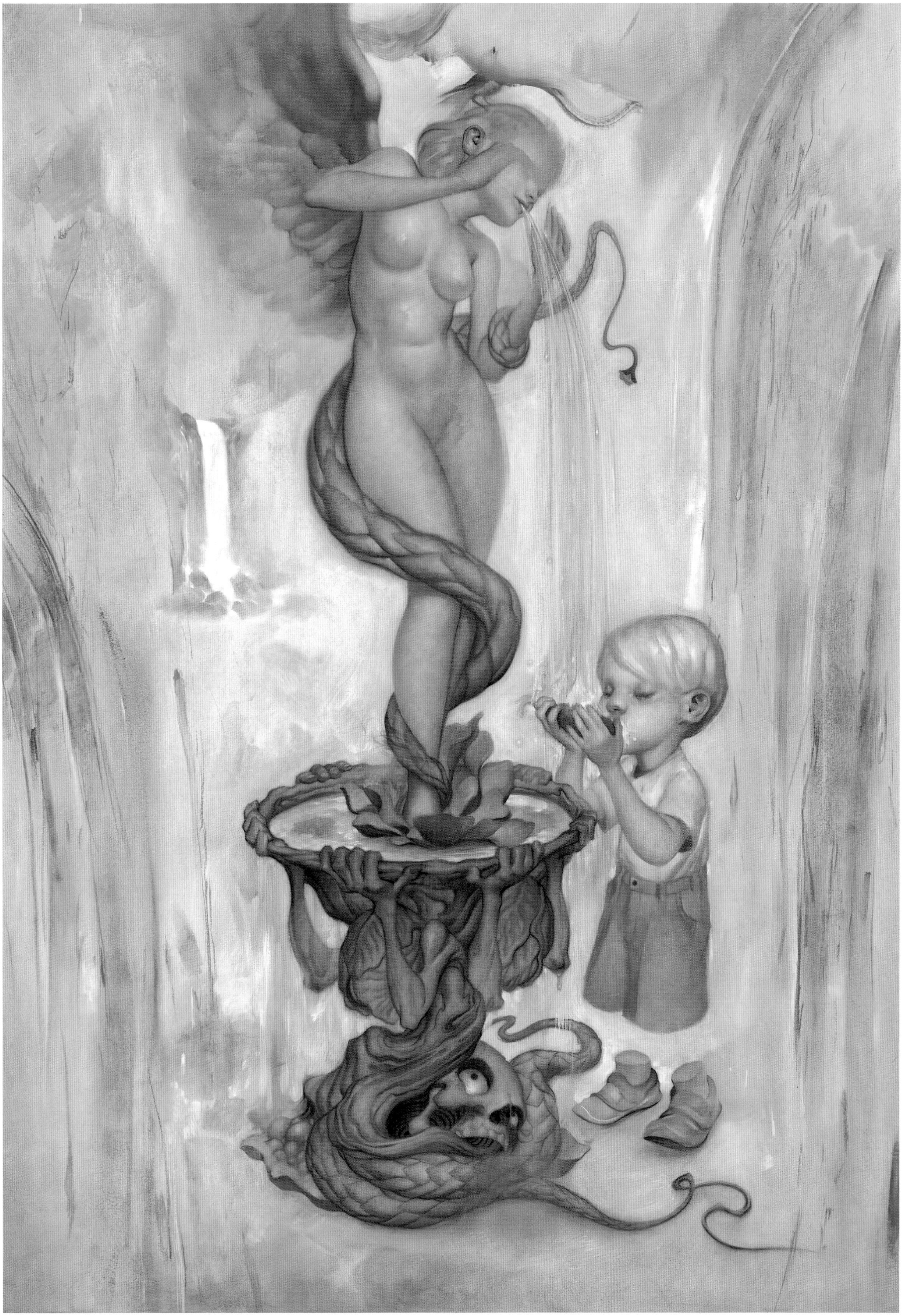

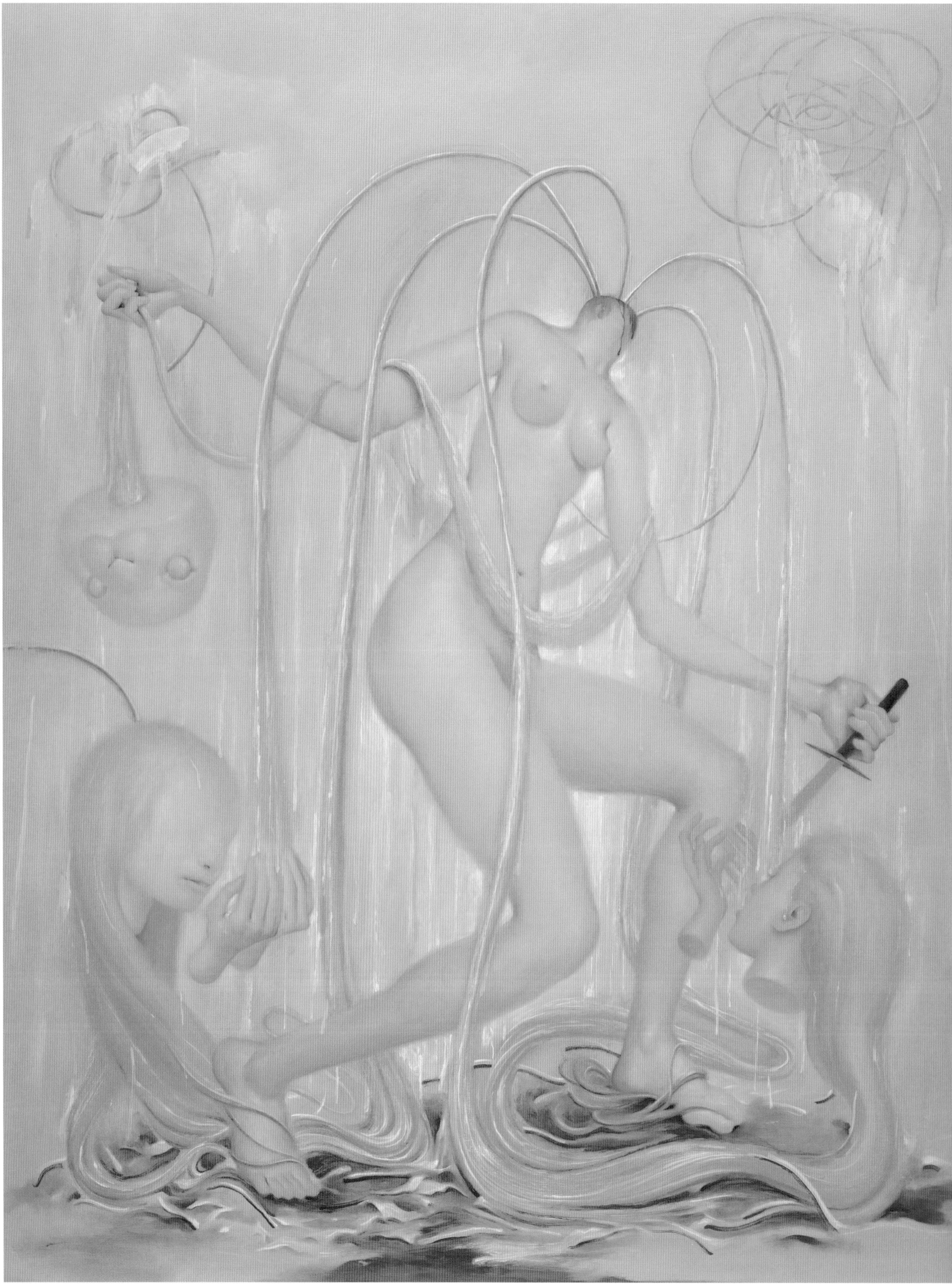

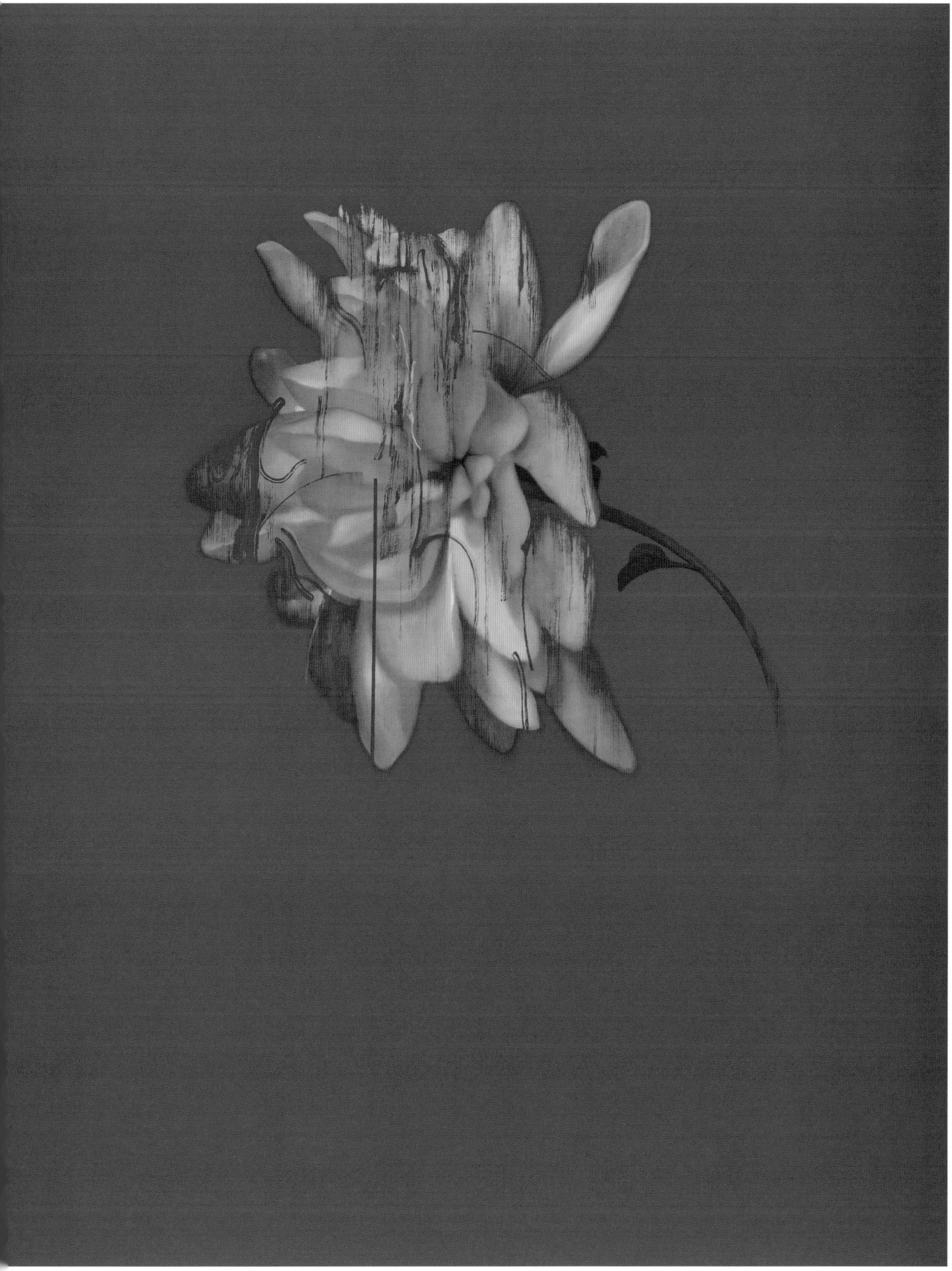

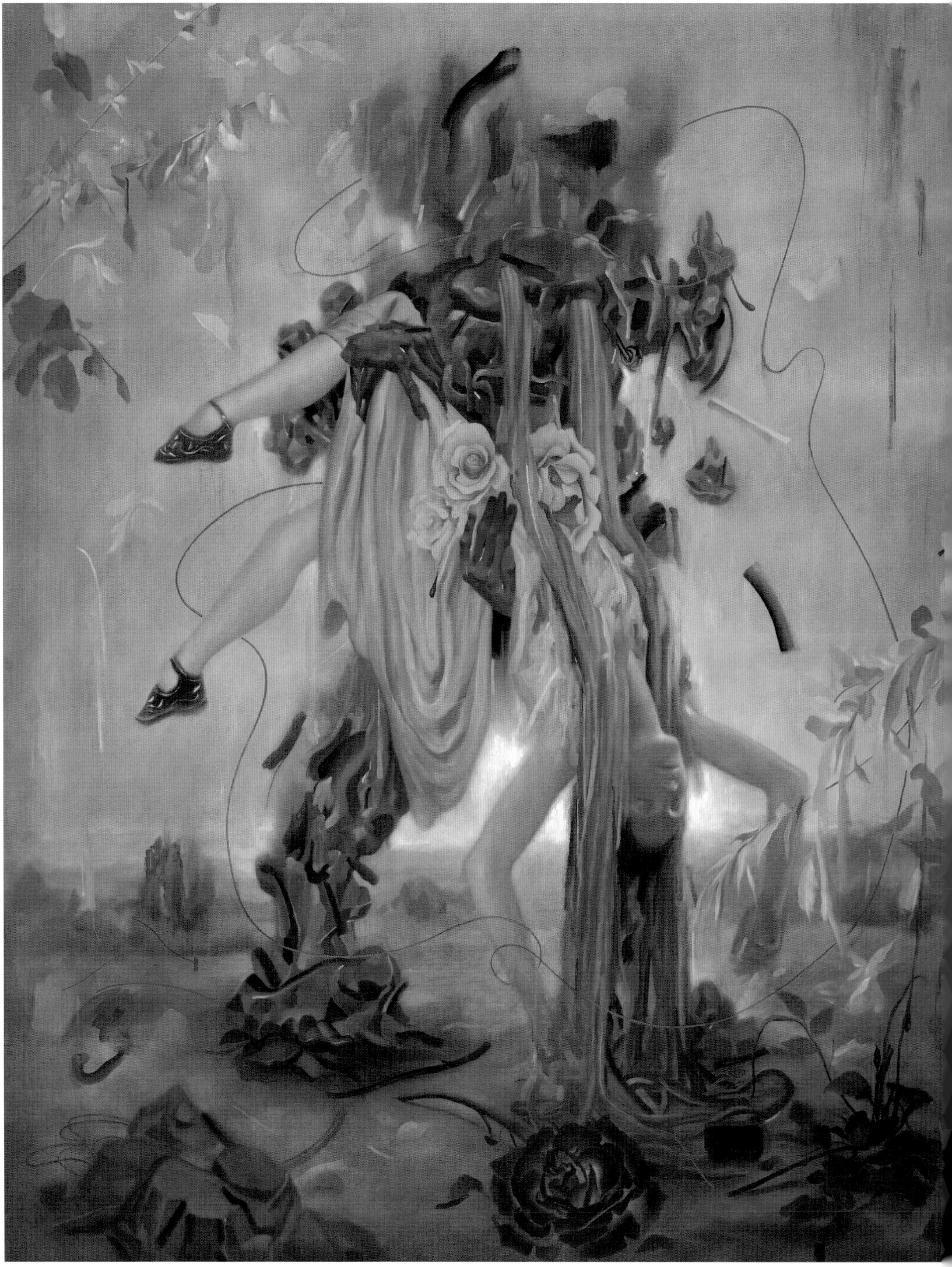

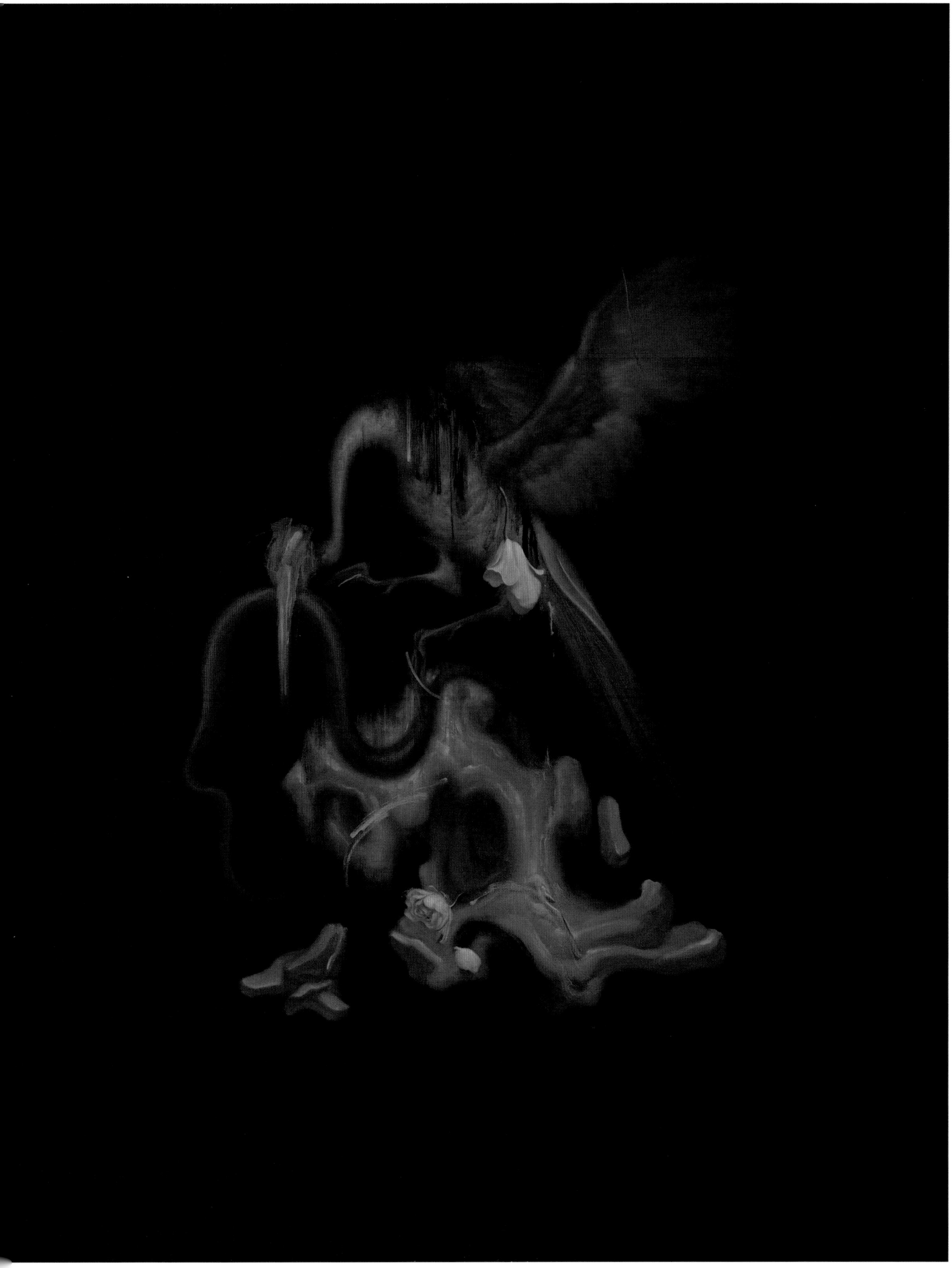

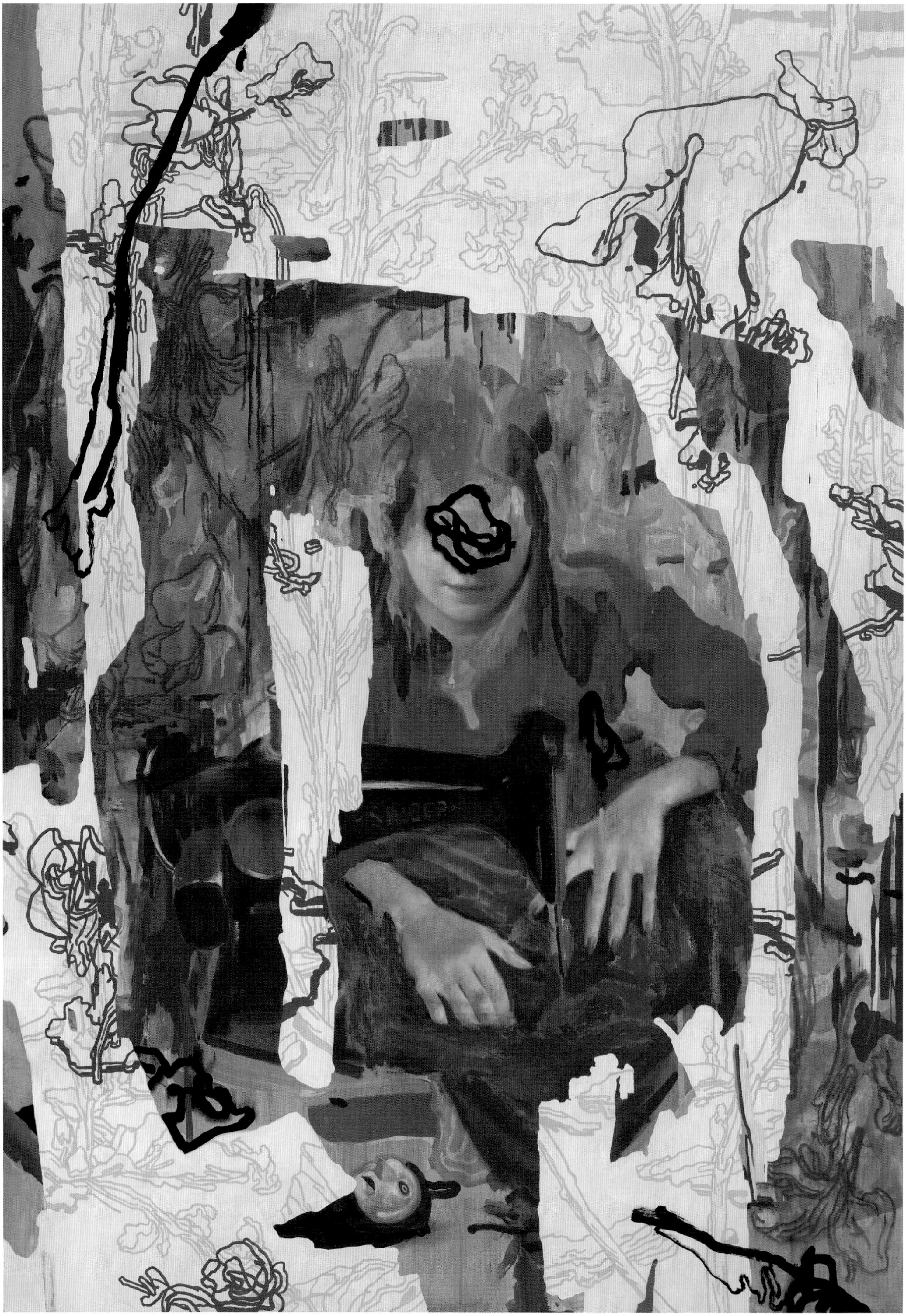

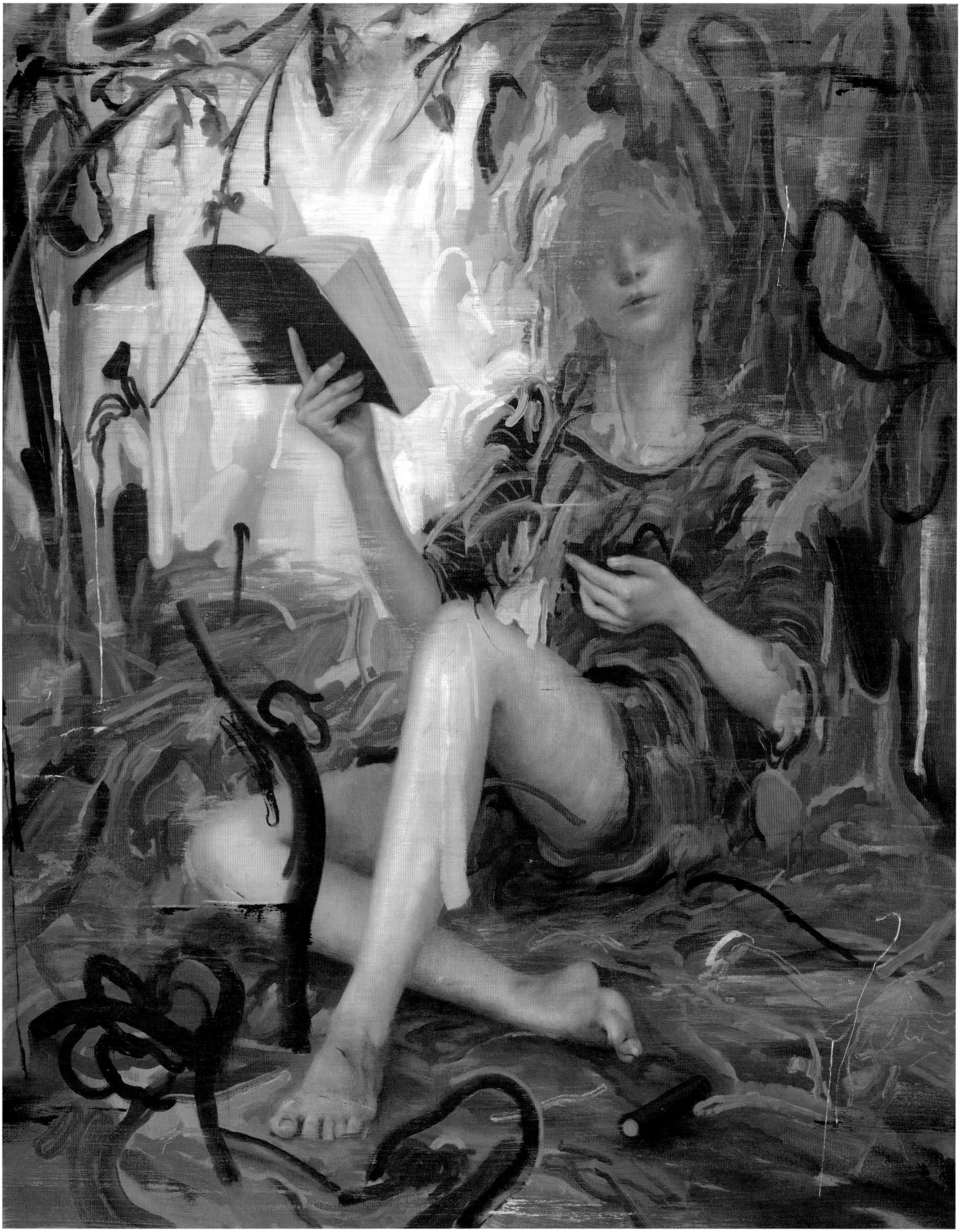

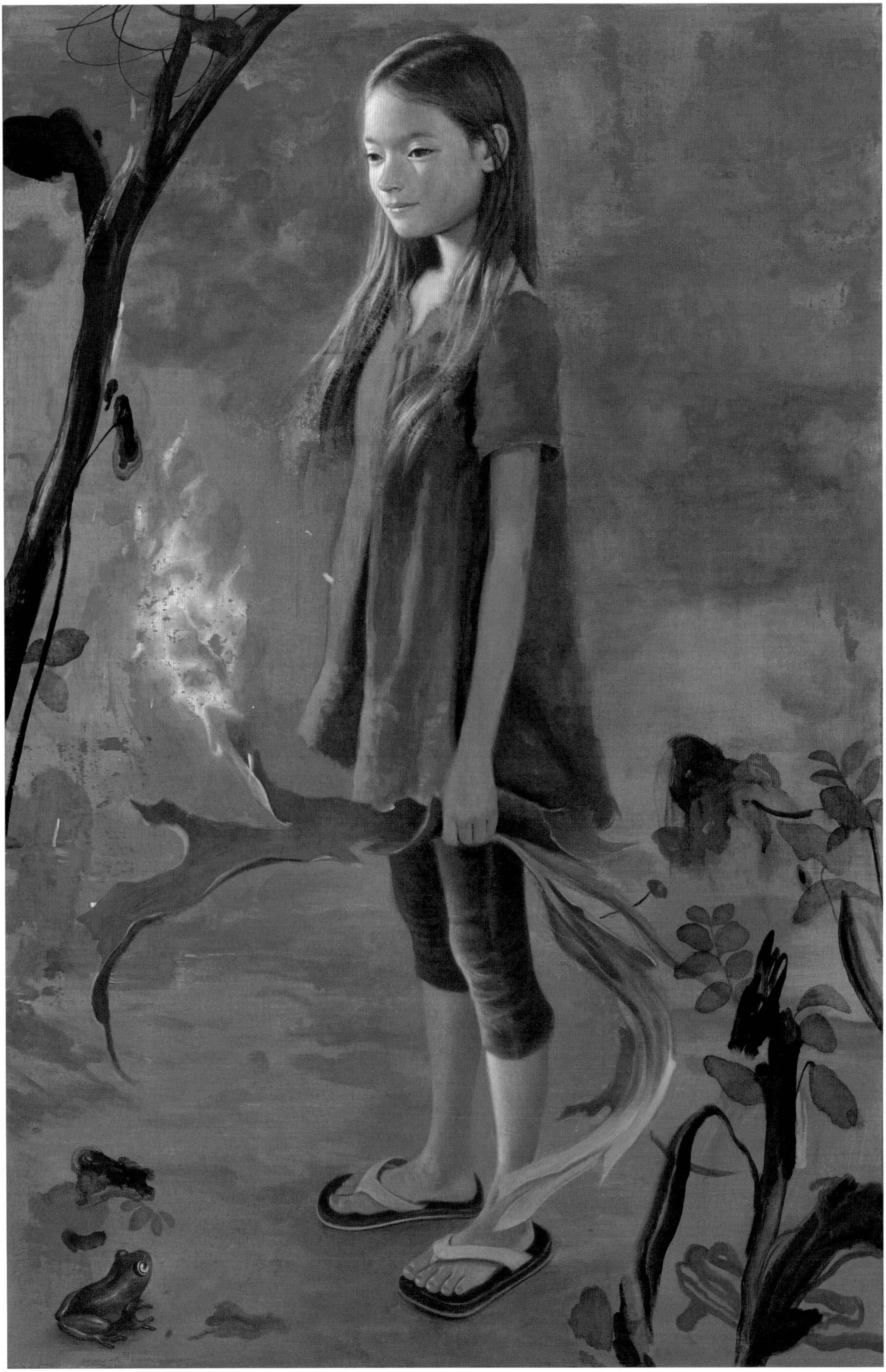

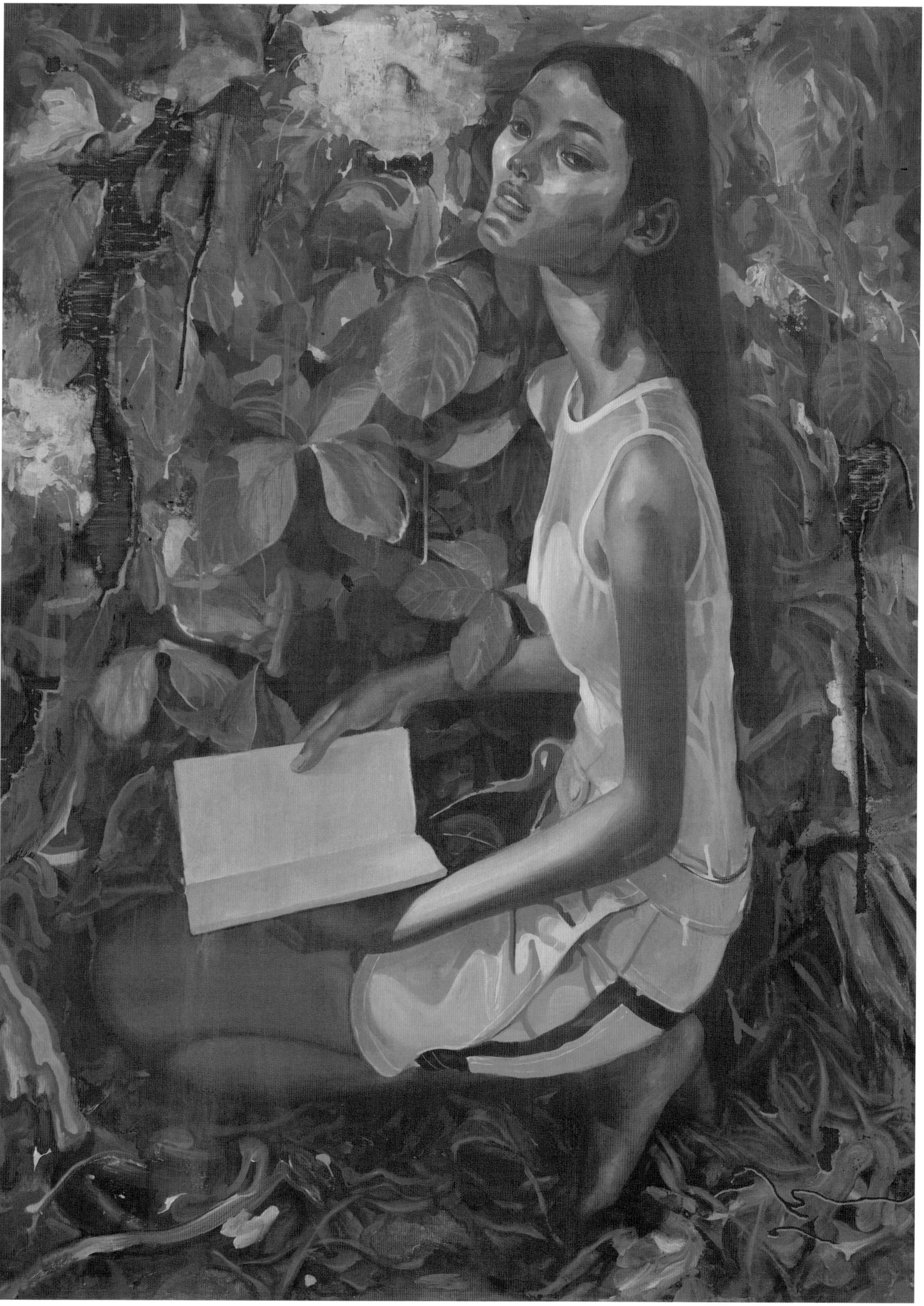

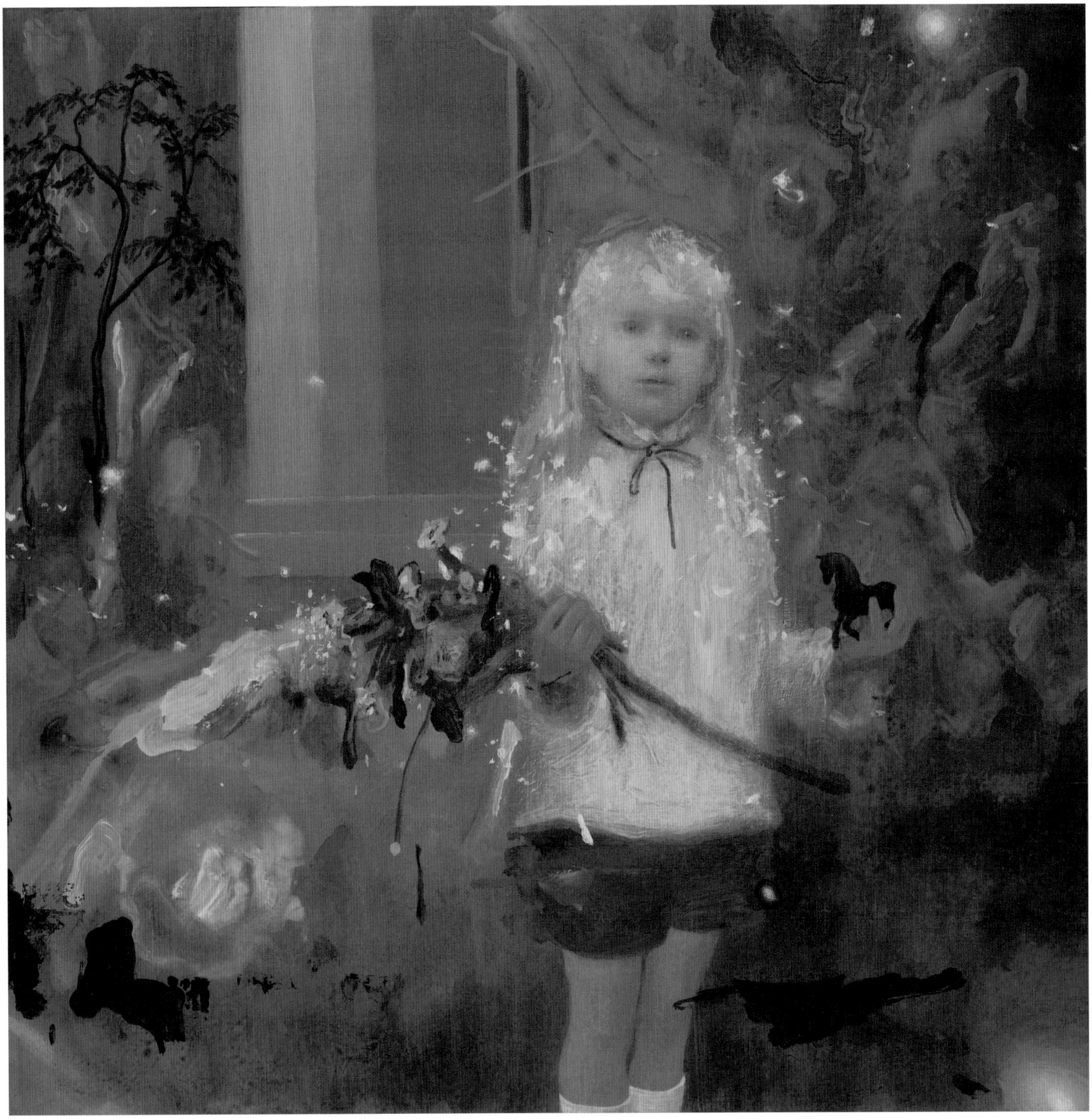

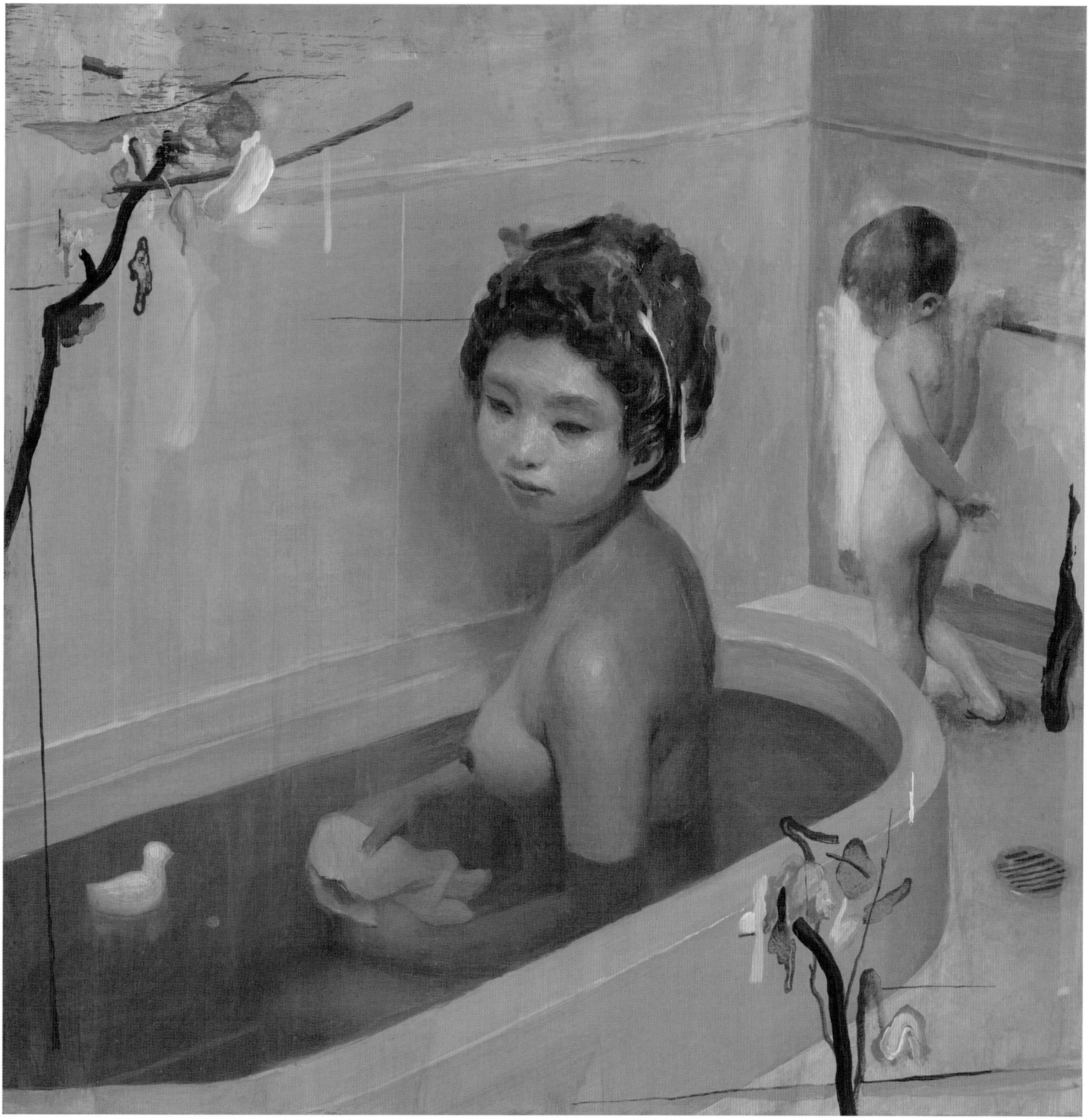

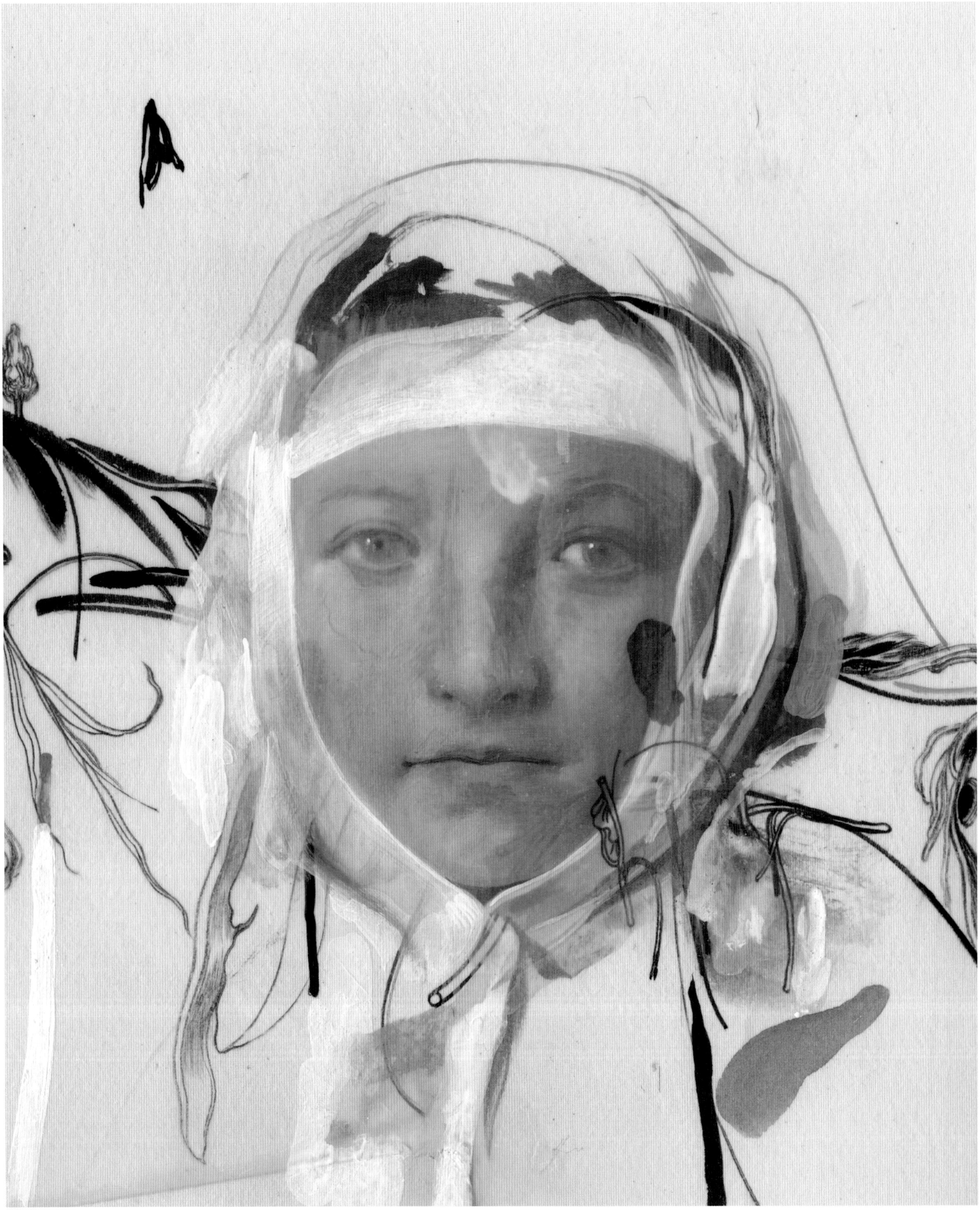

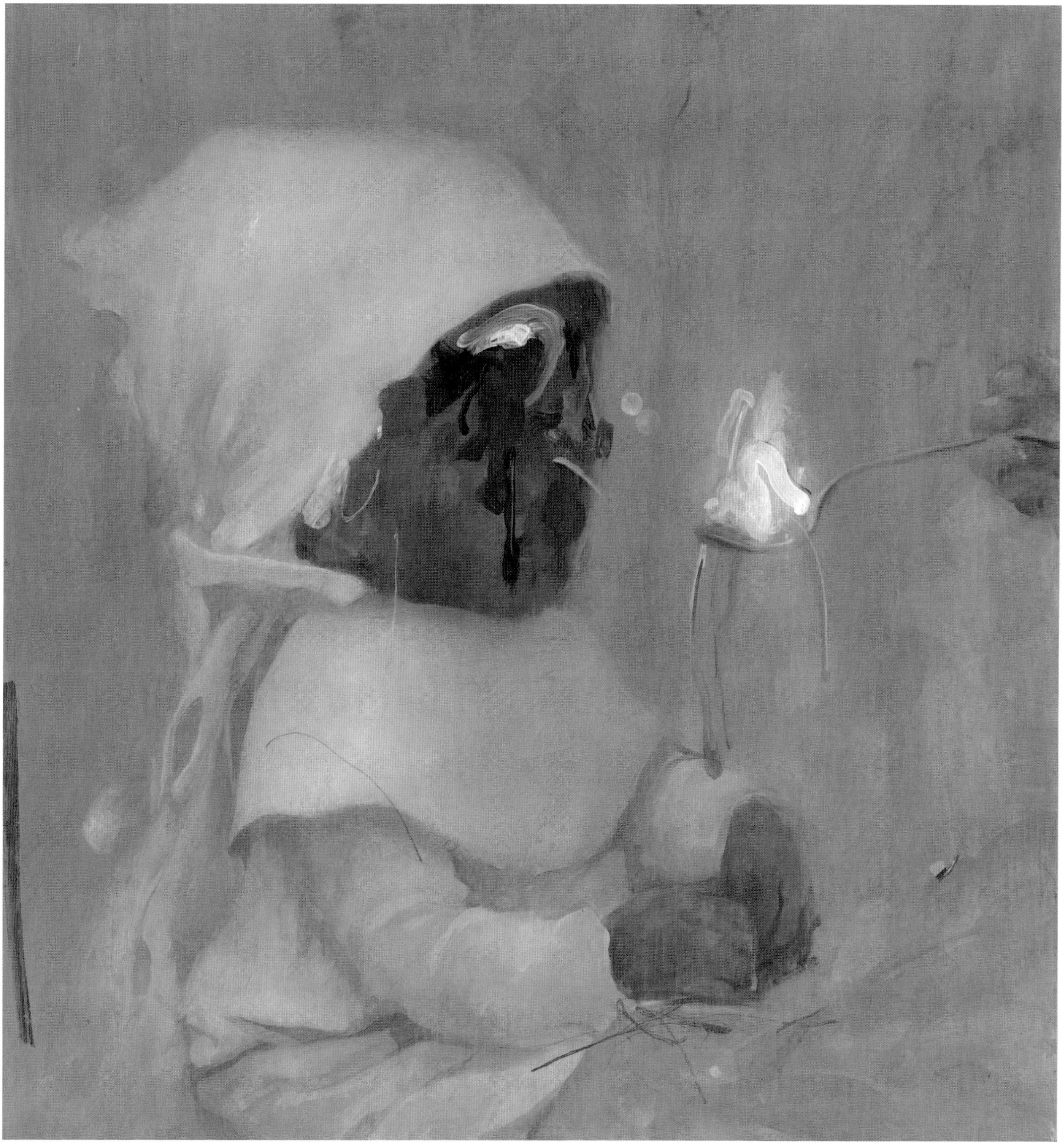

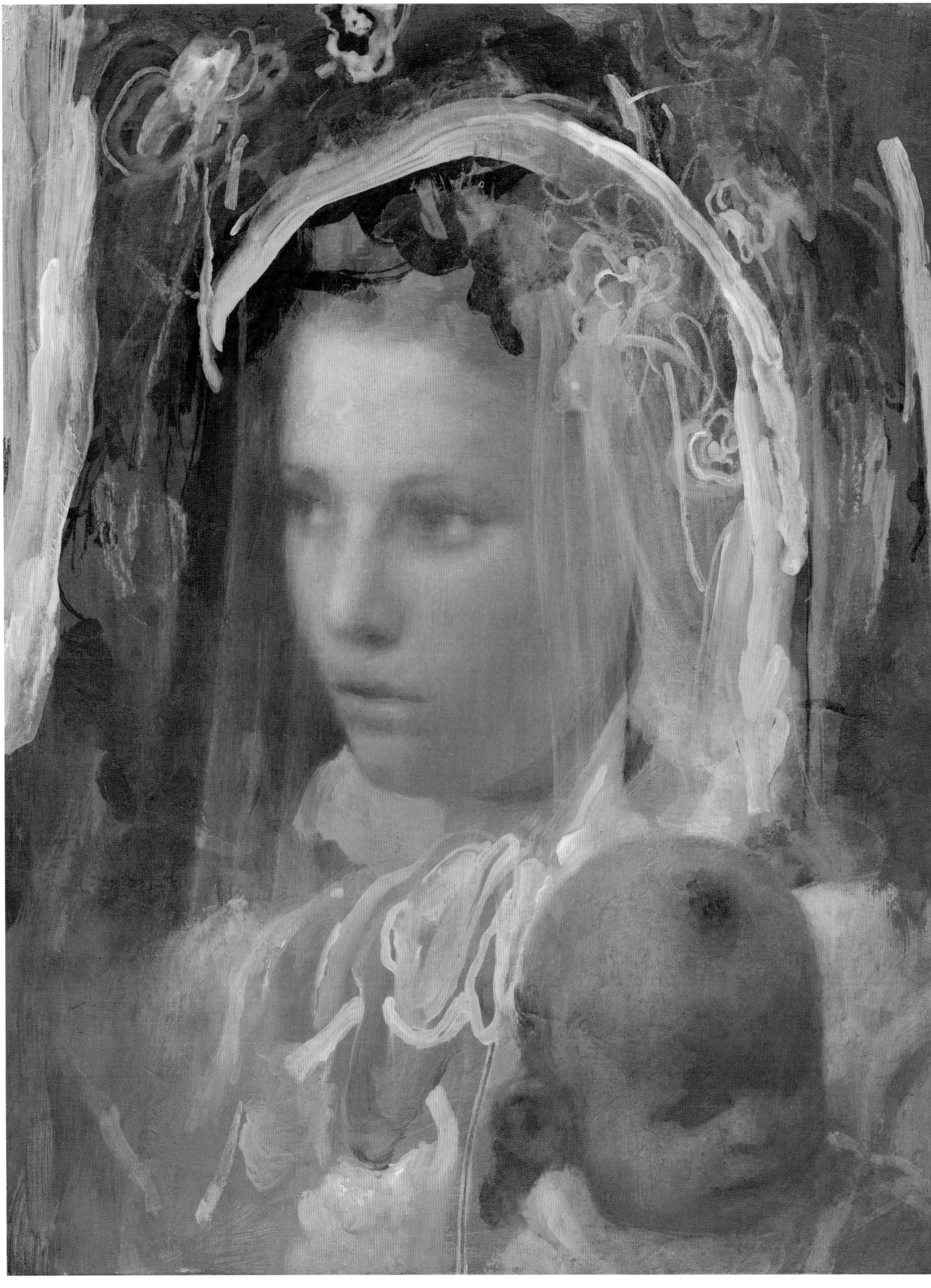

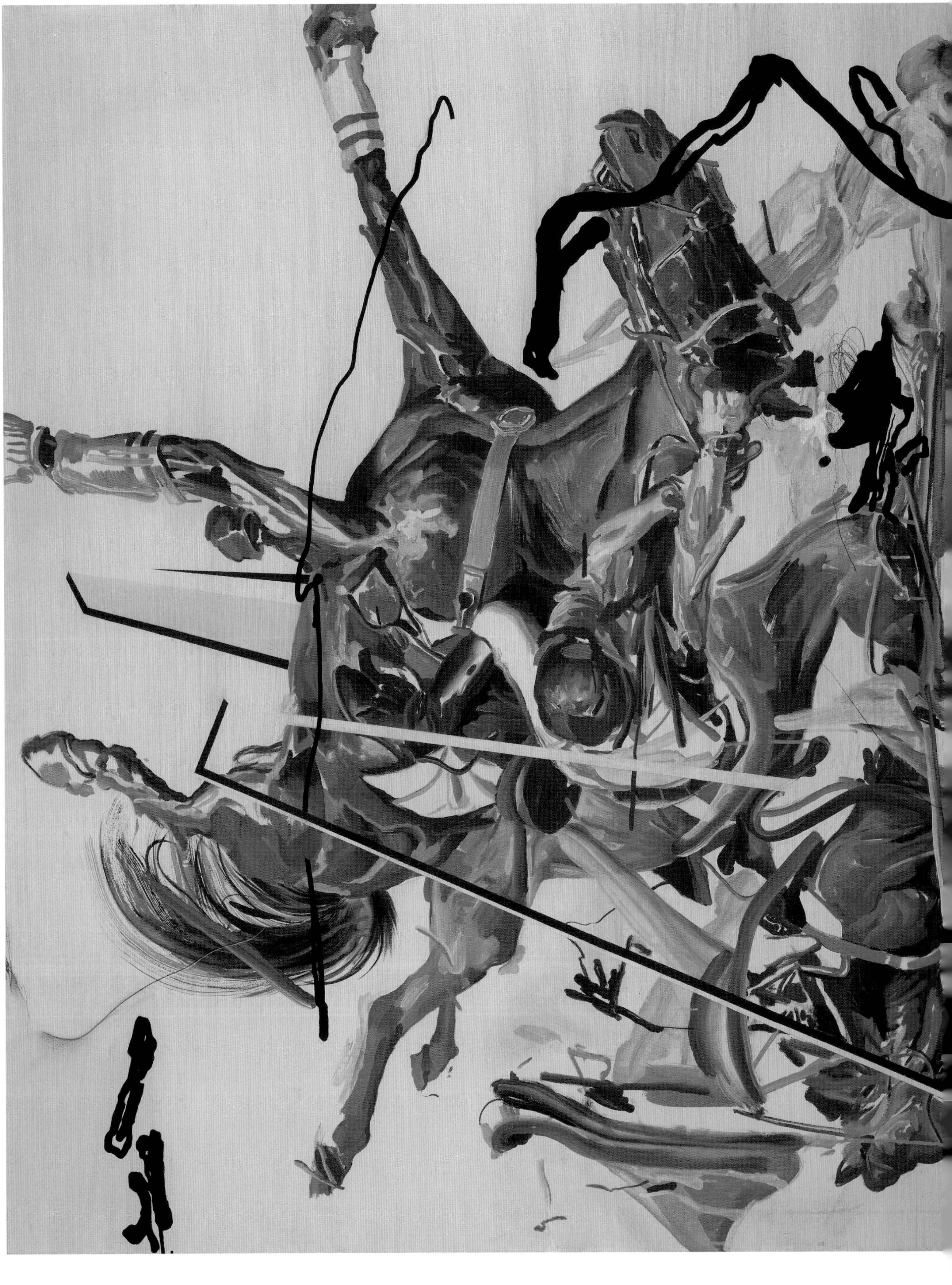

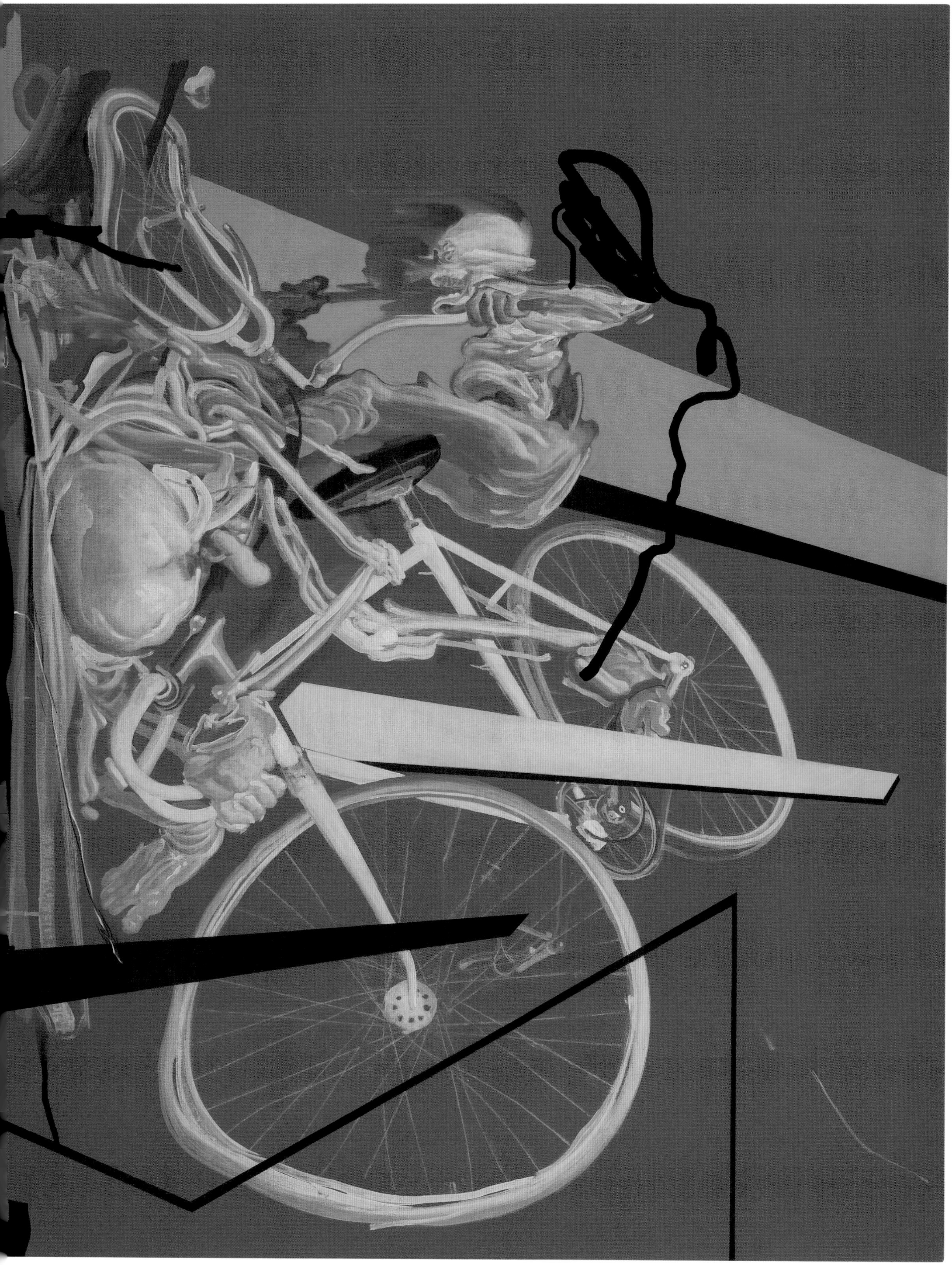

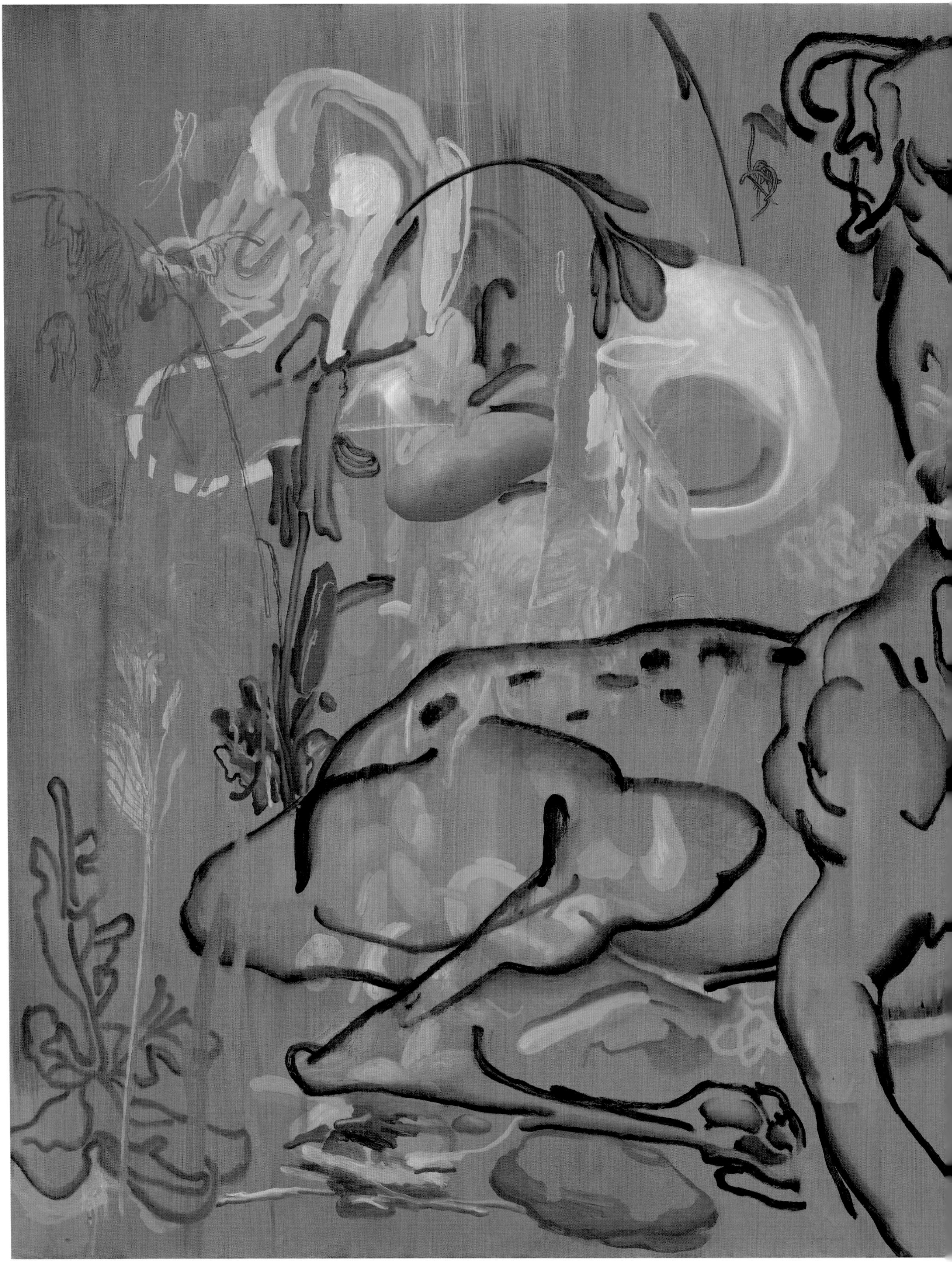

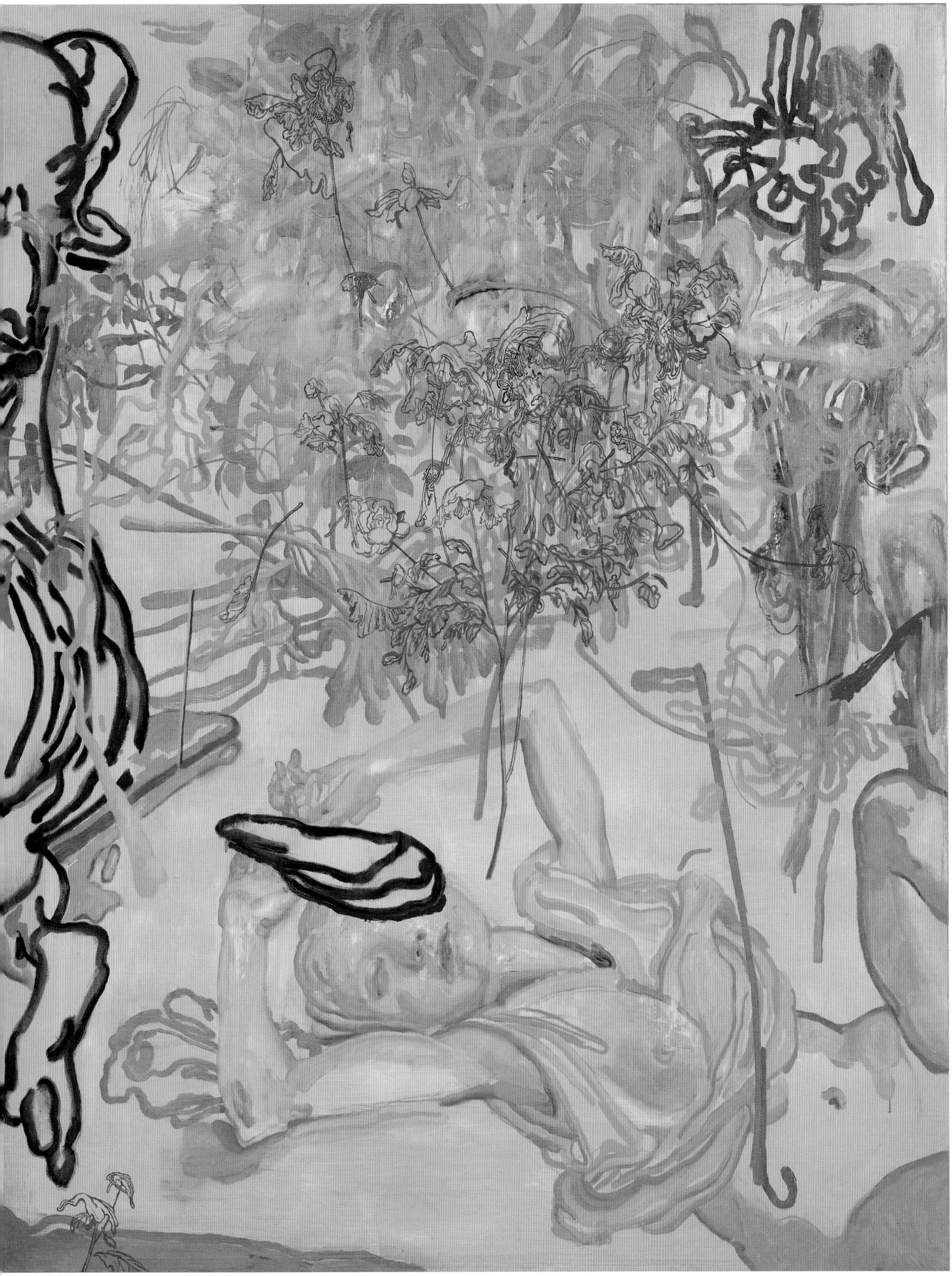

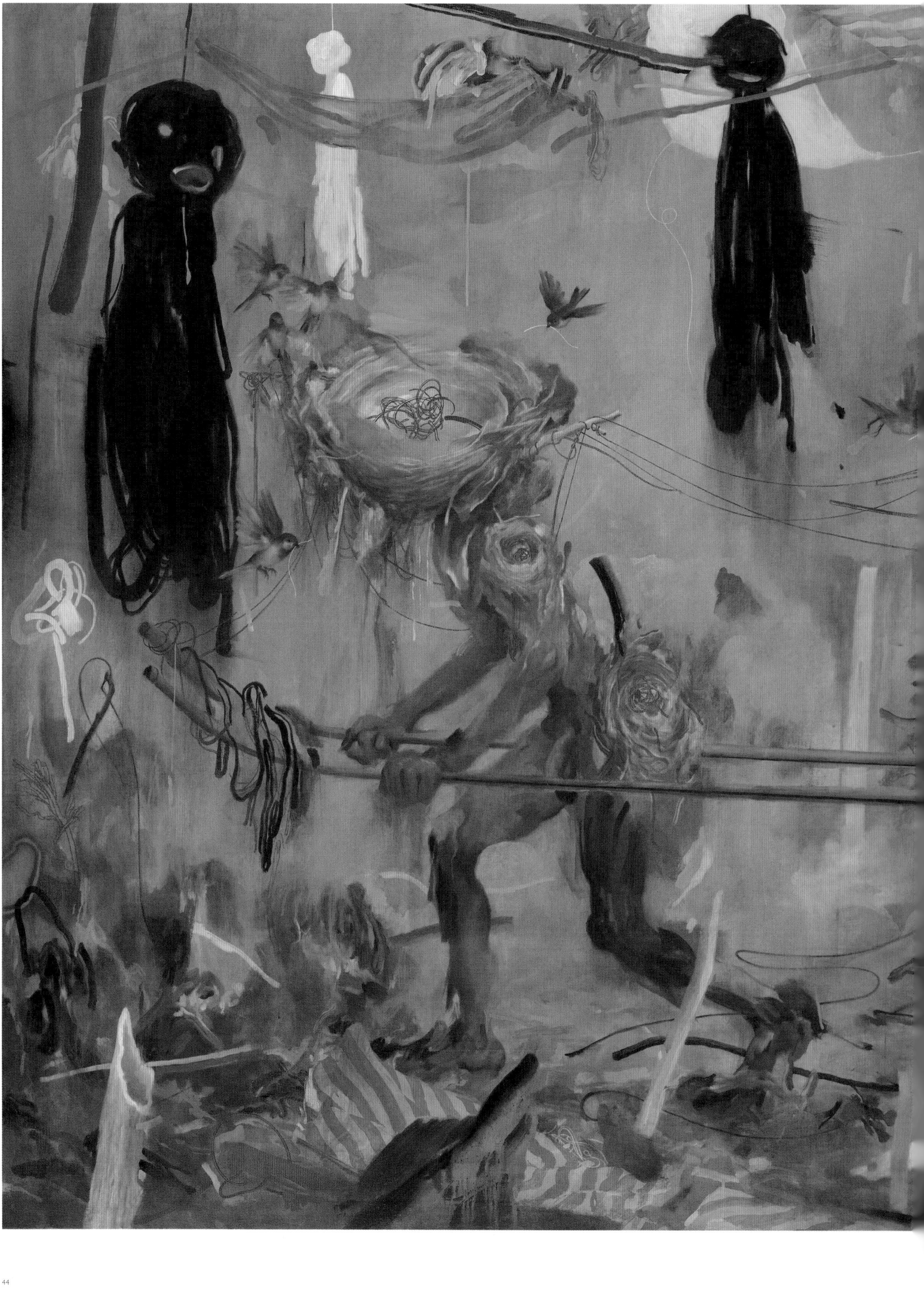

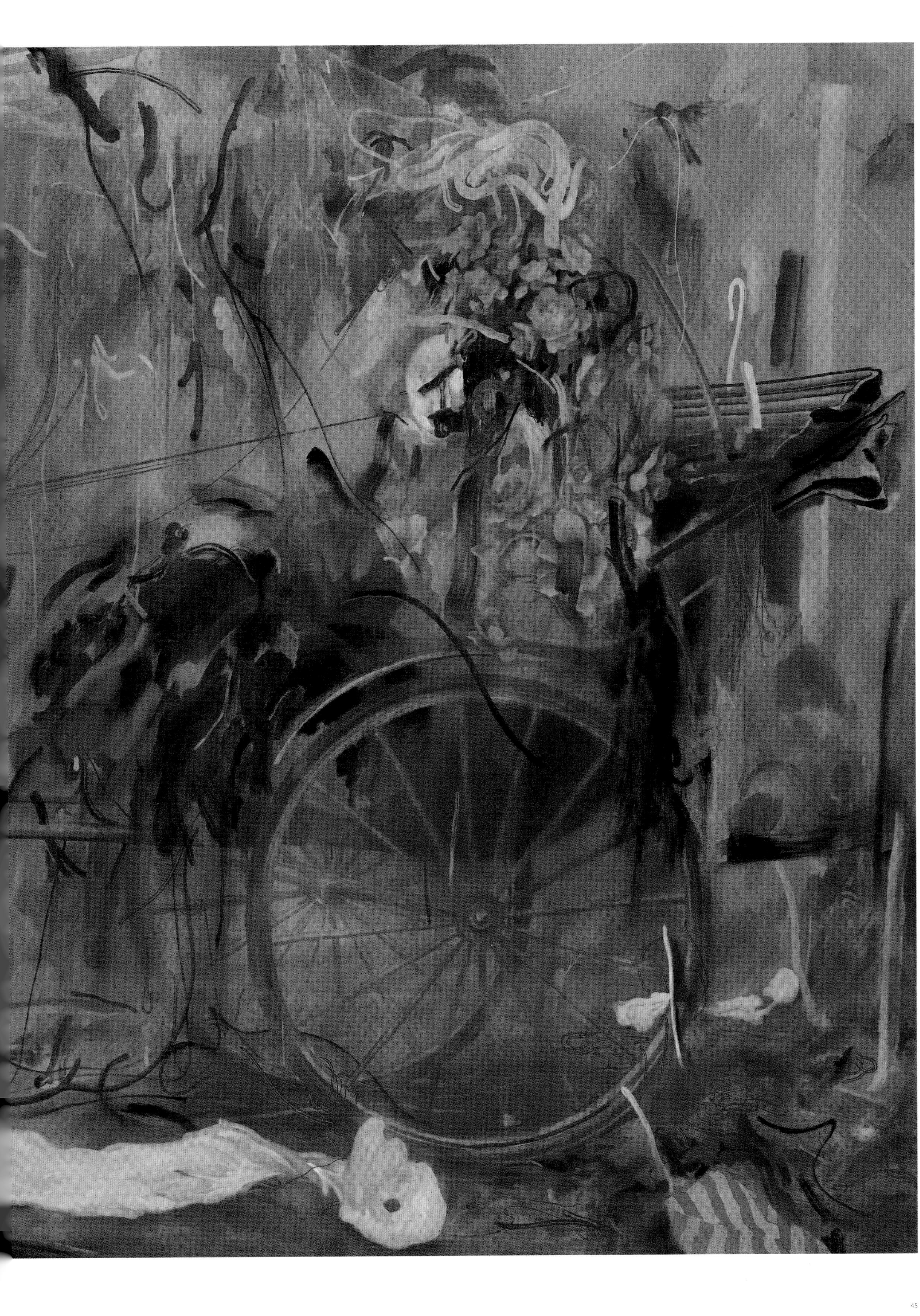

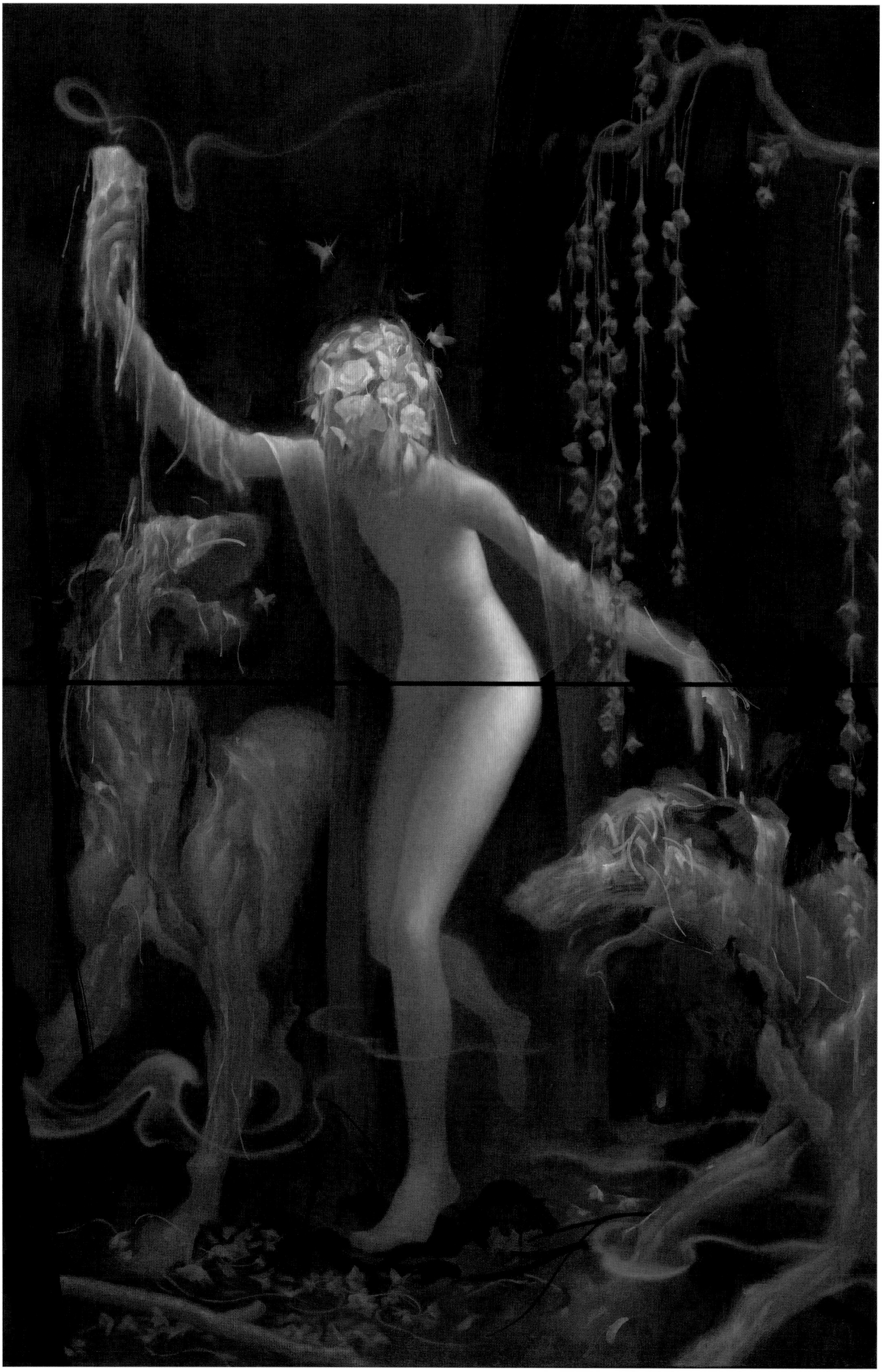

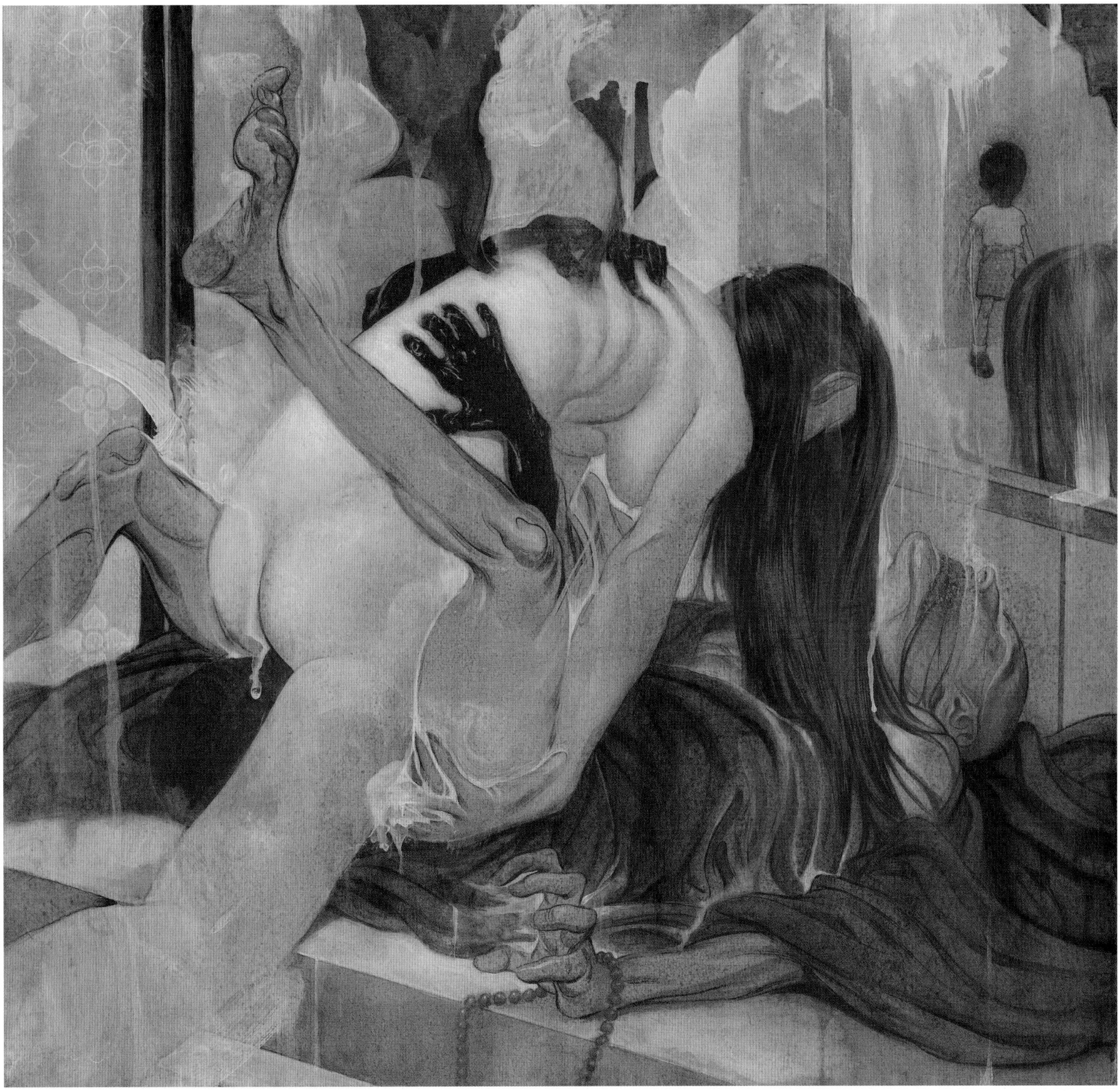

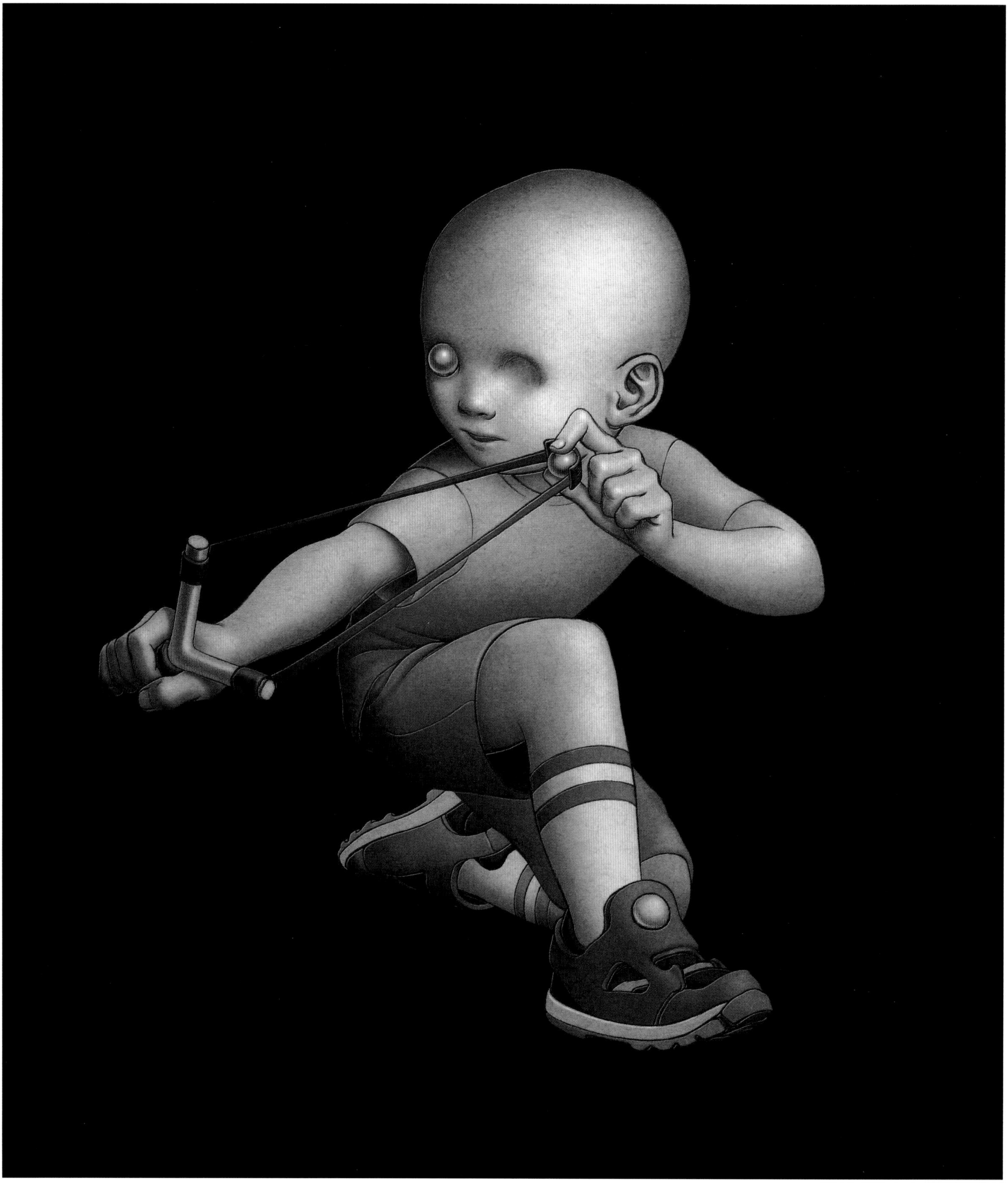

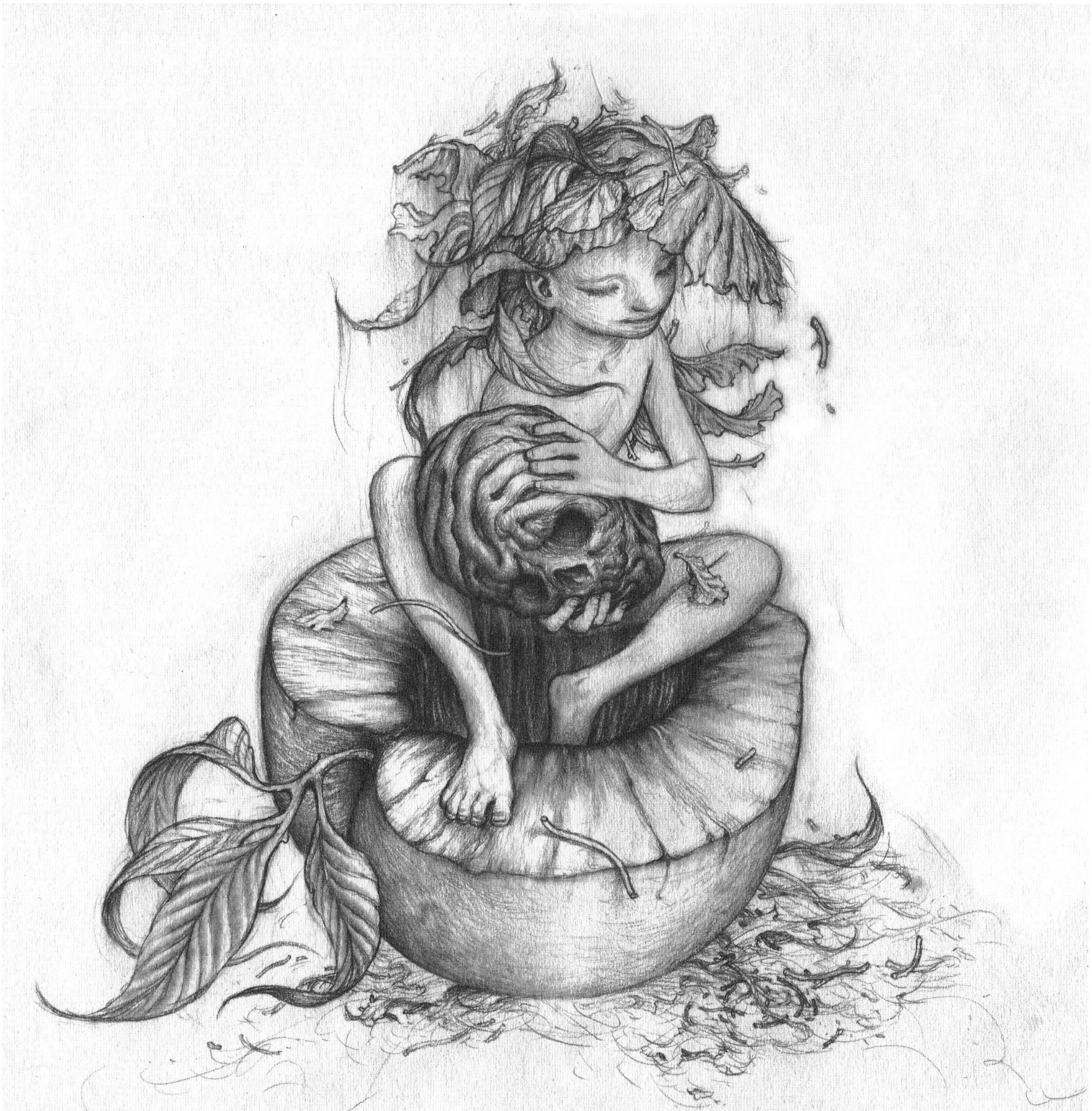

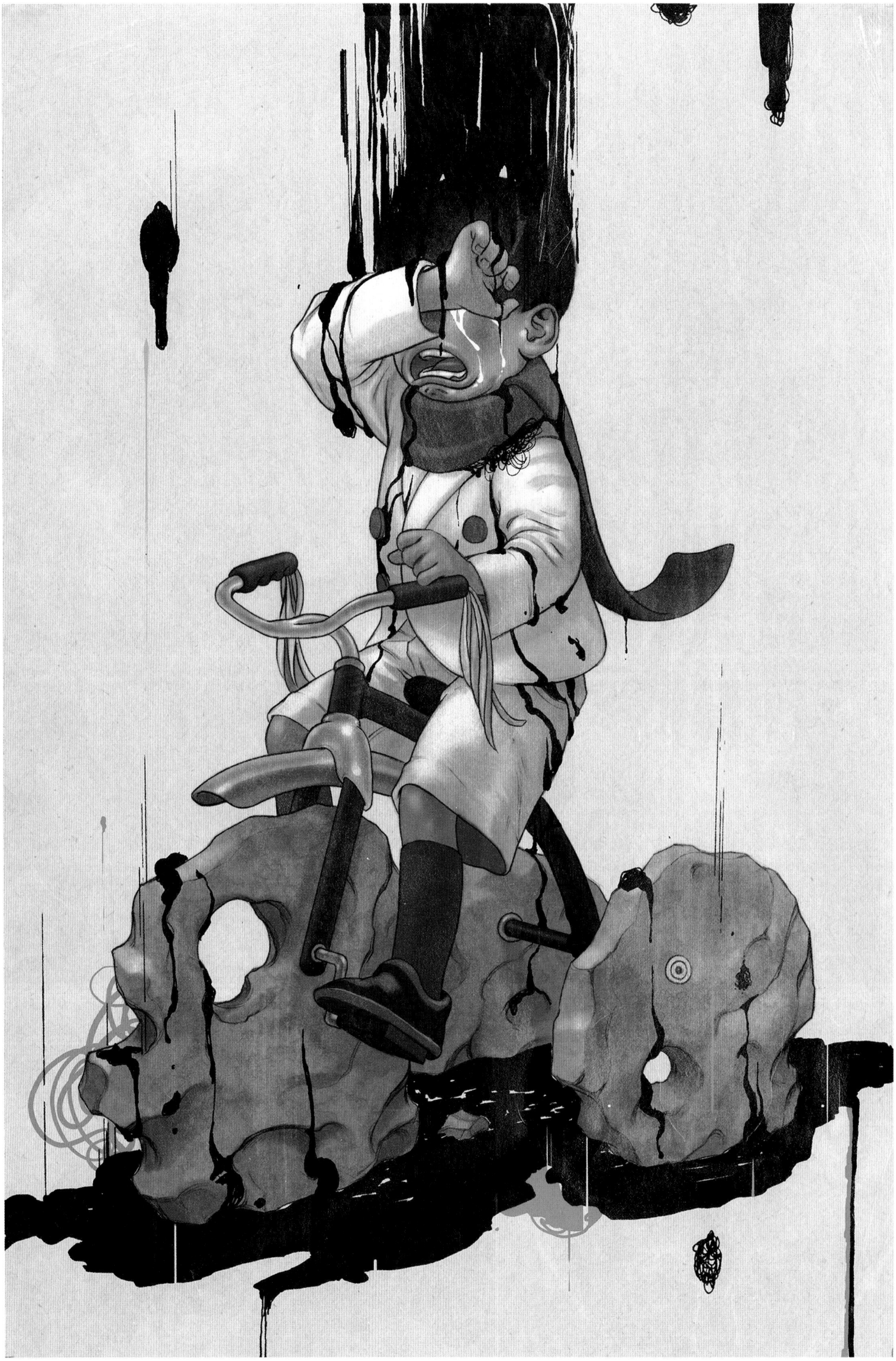

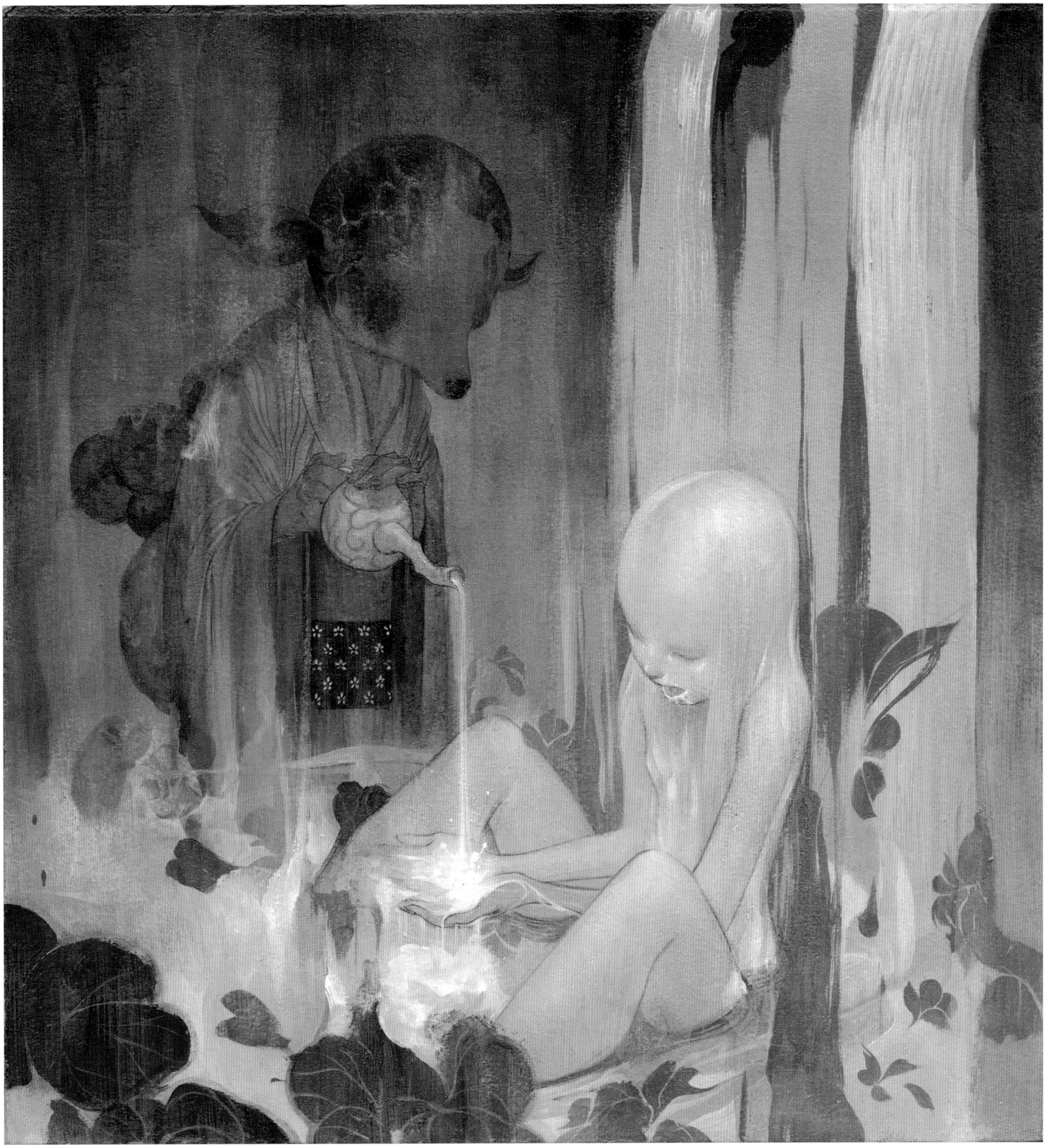

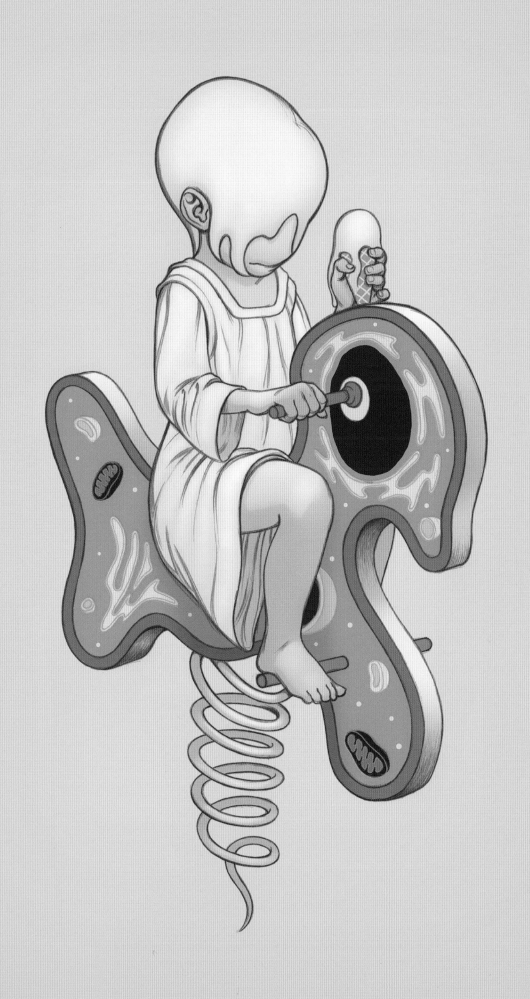

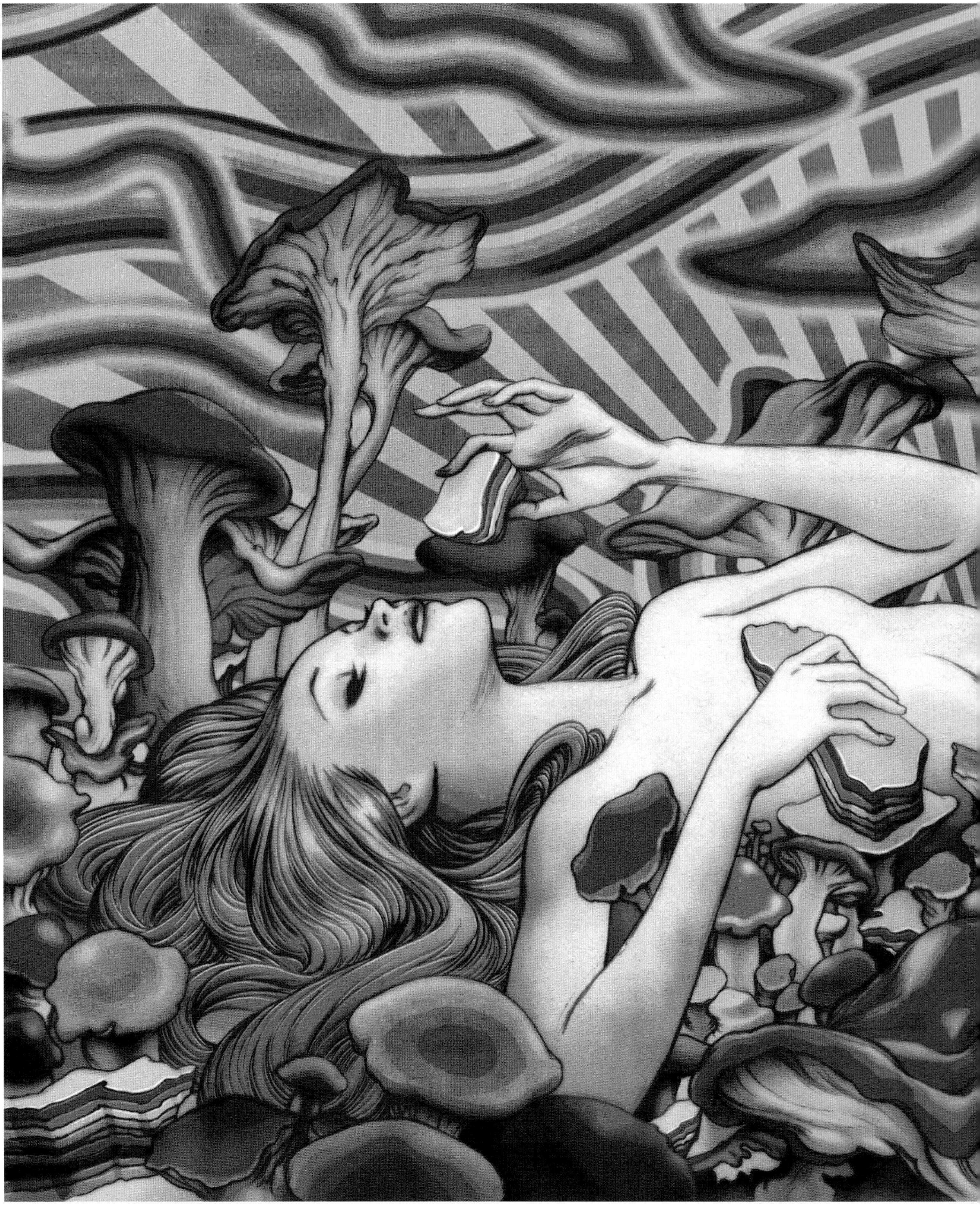

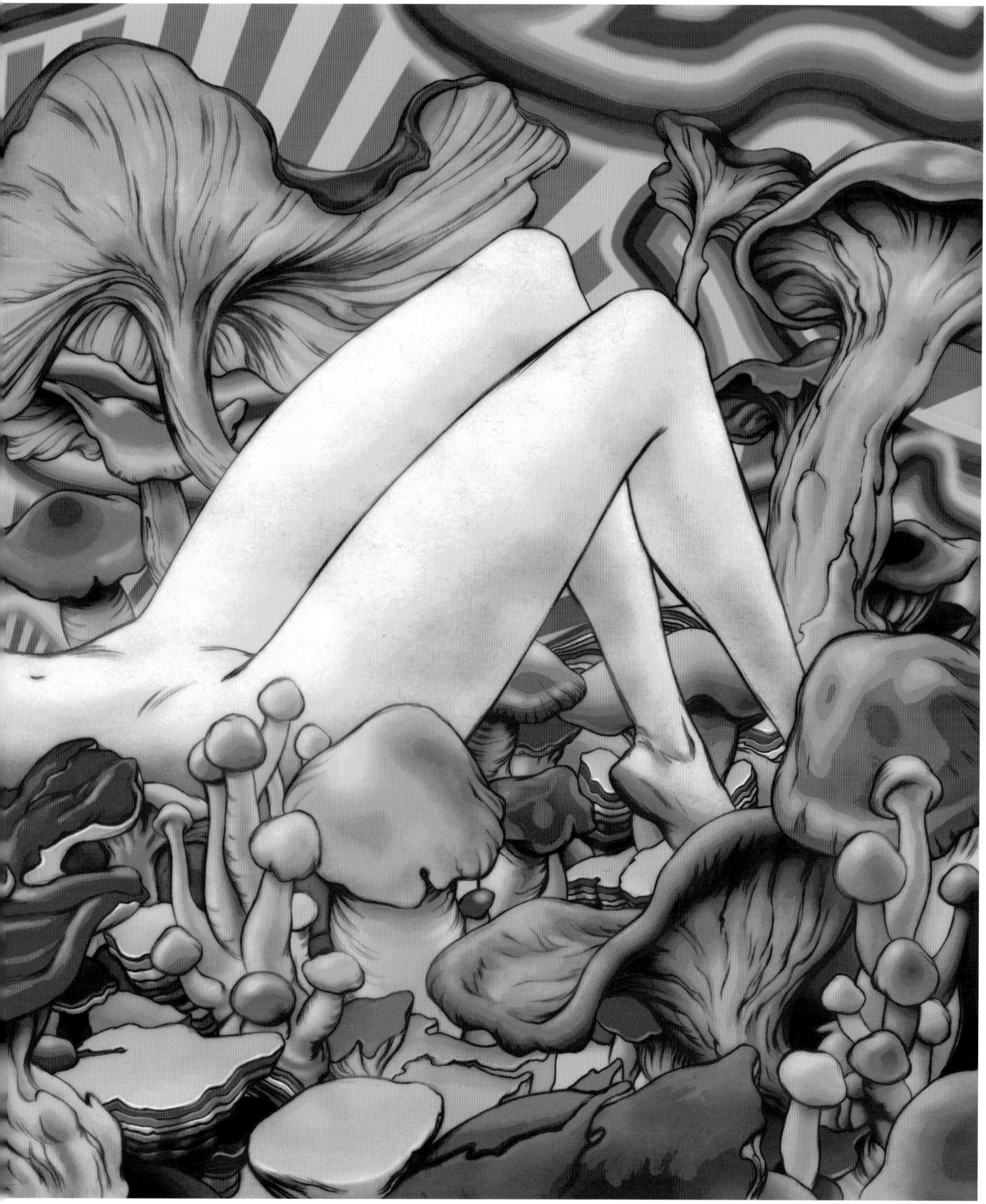

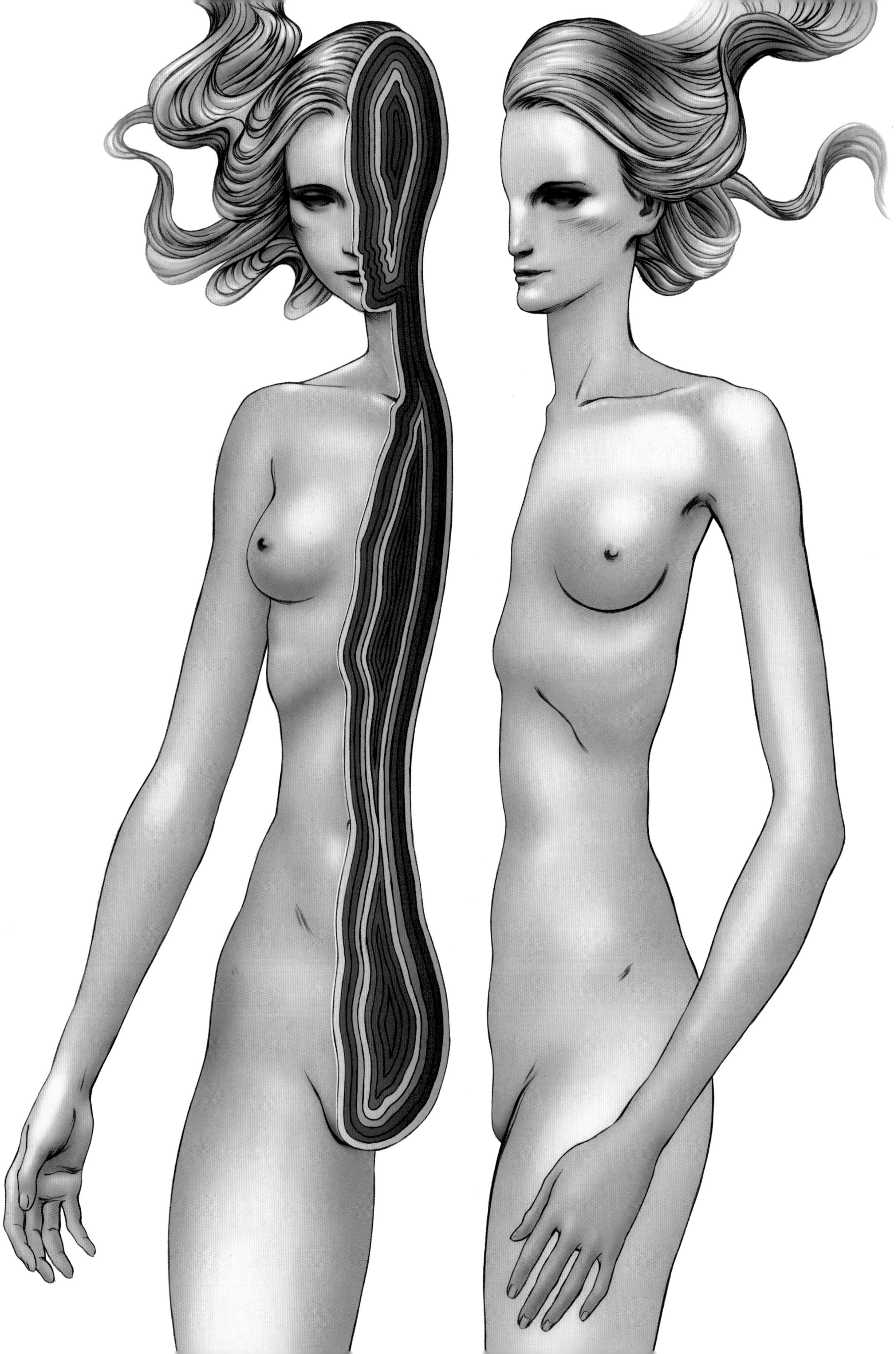

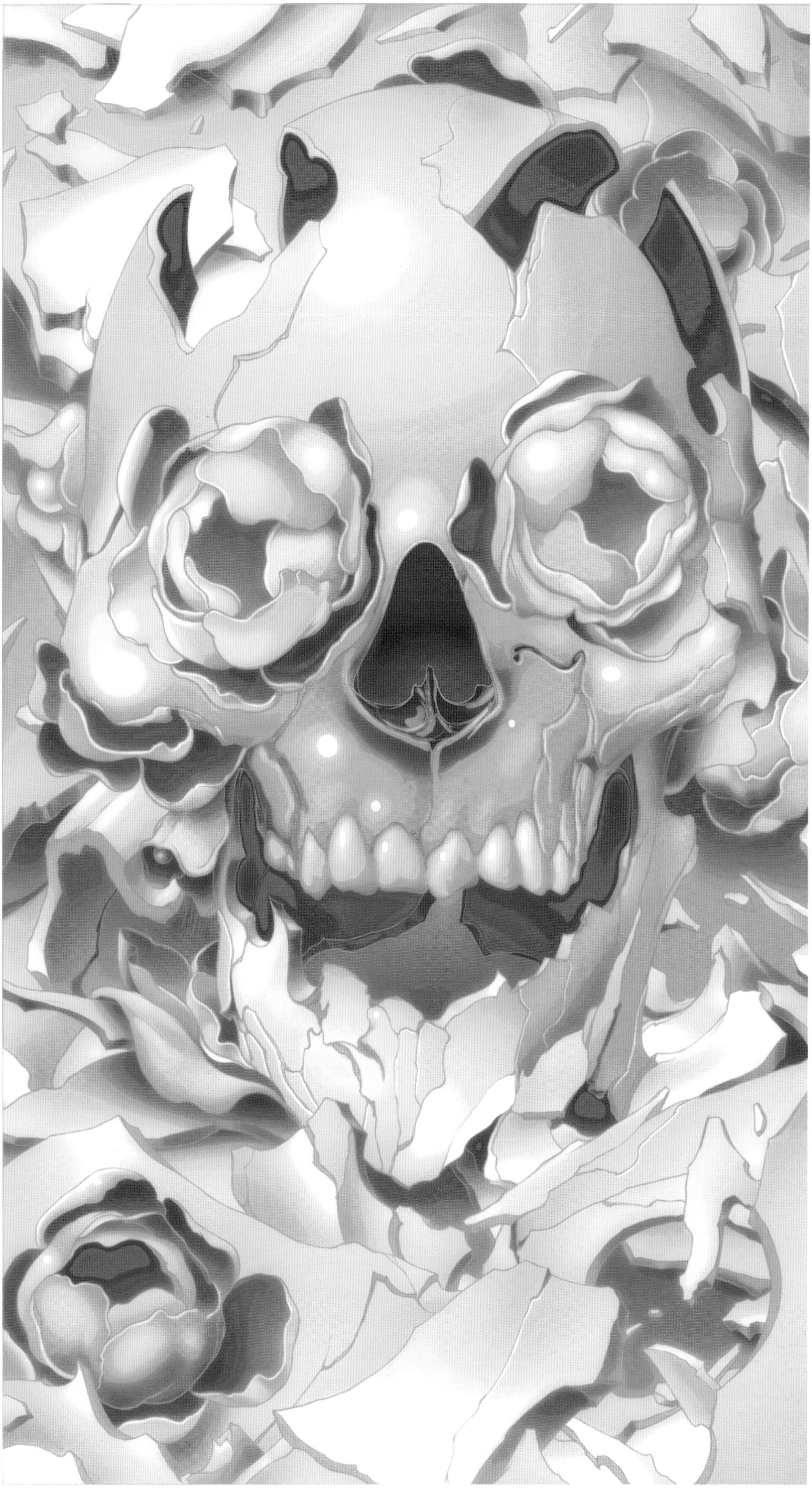

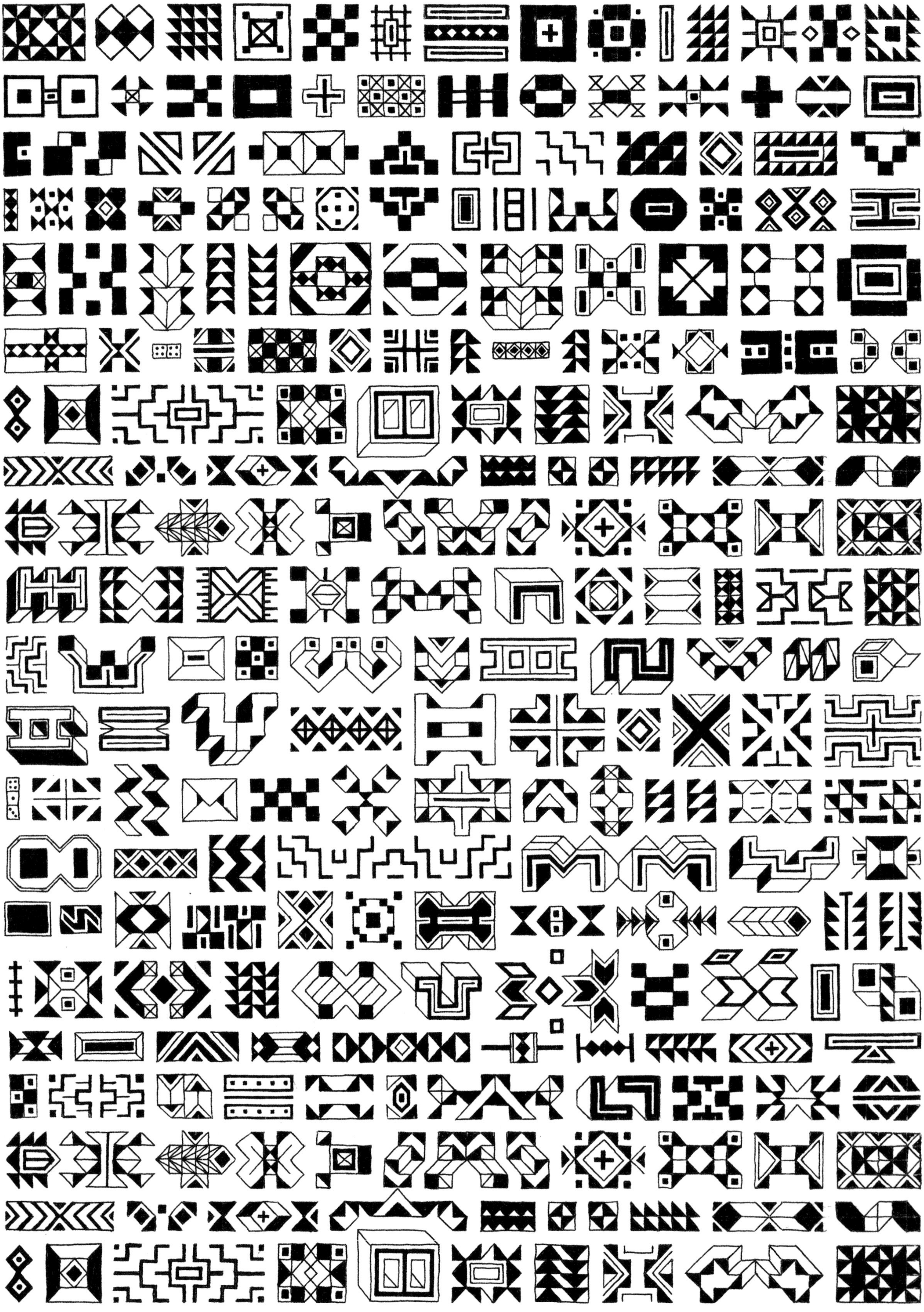

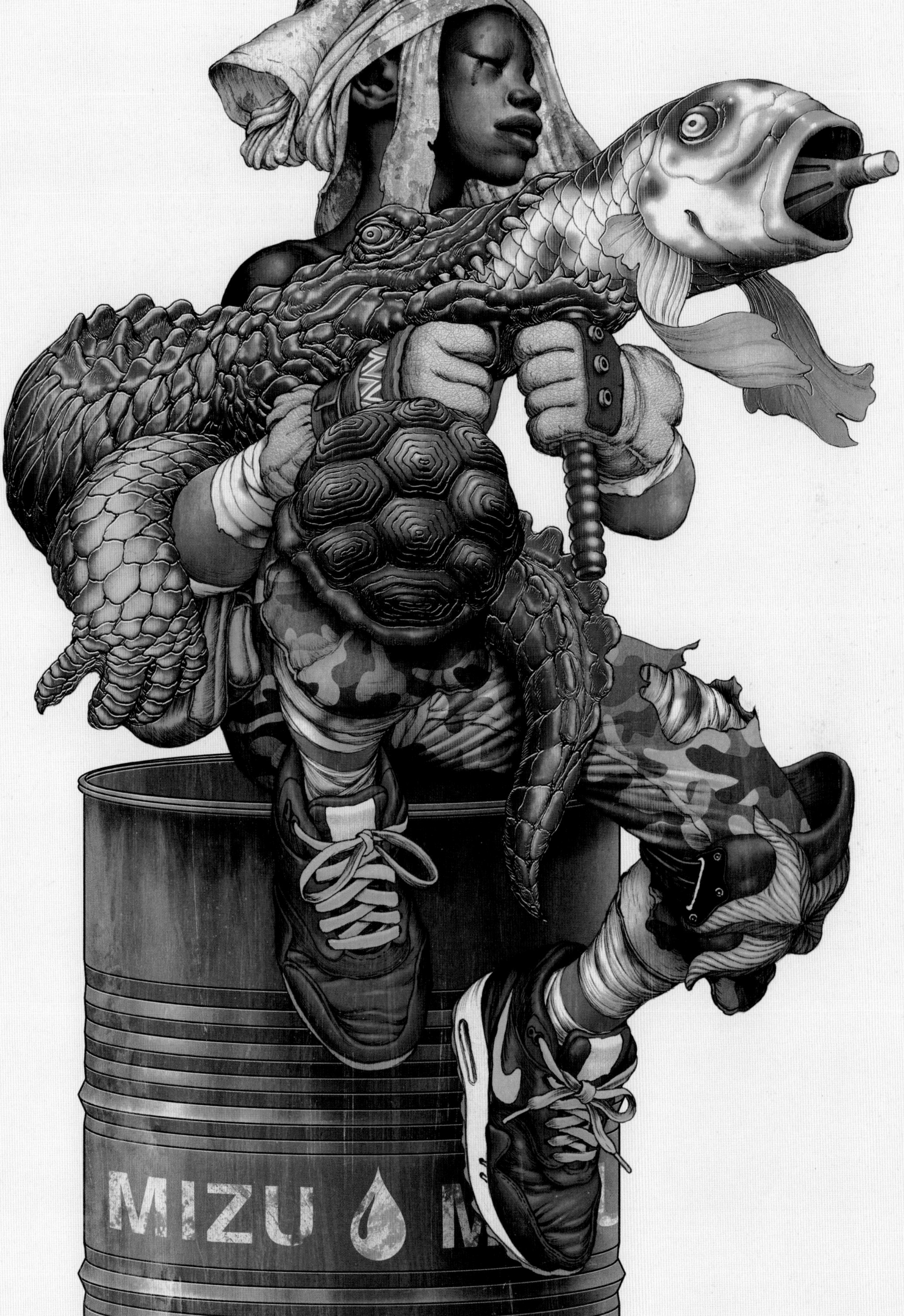
MIZU

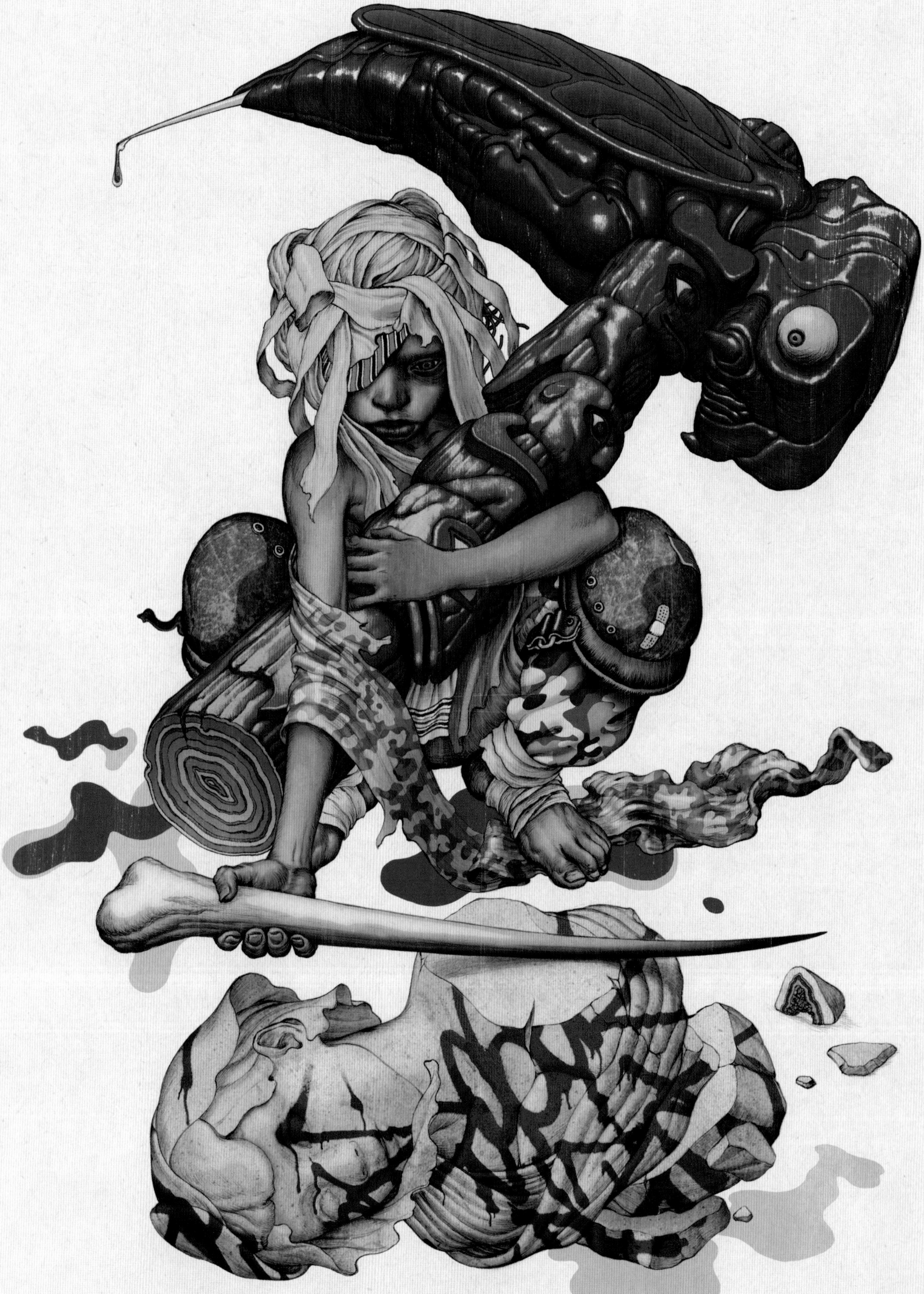

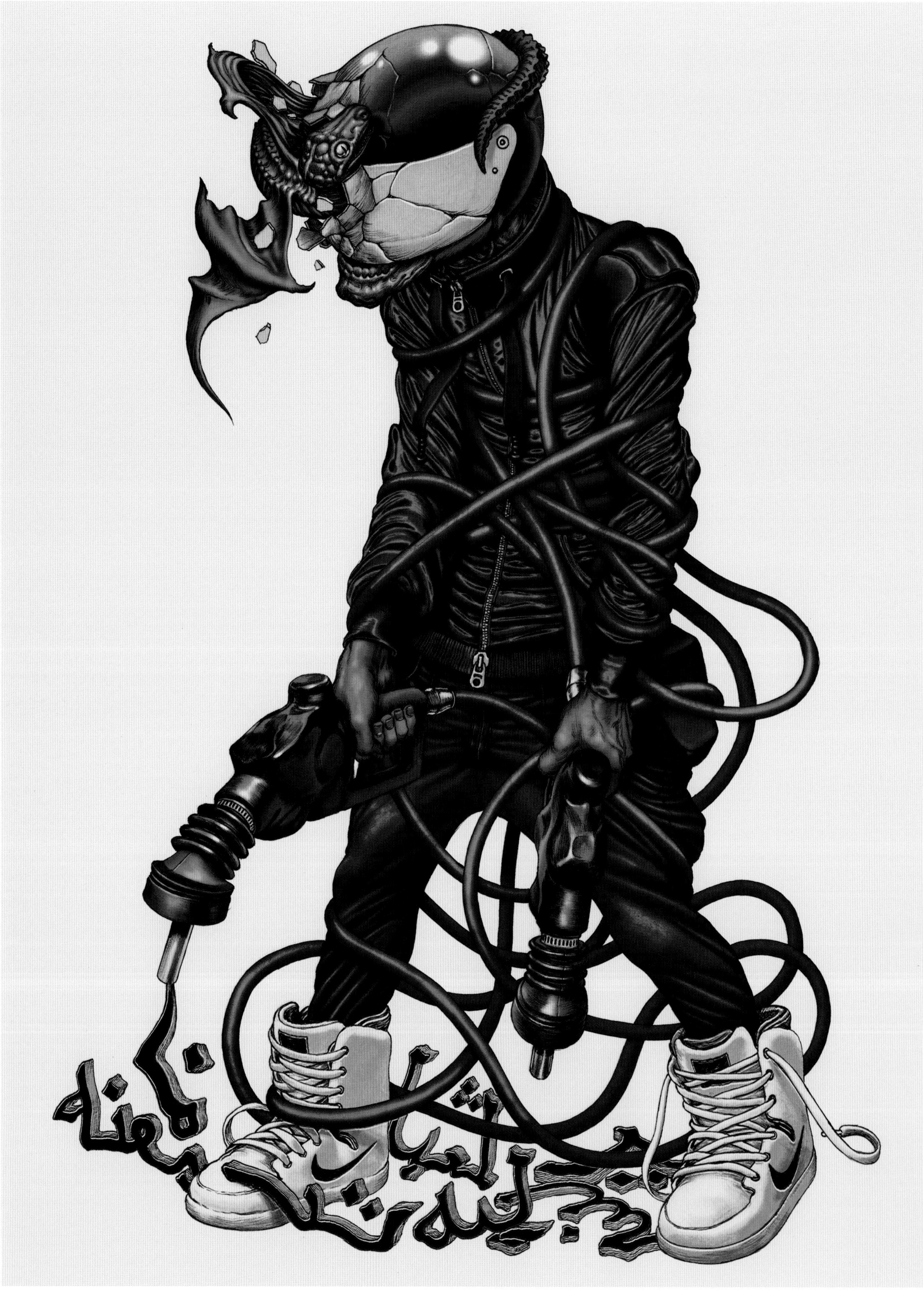

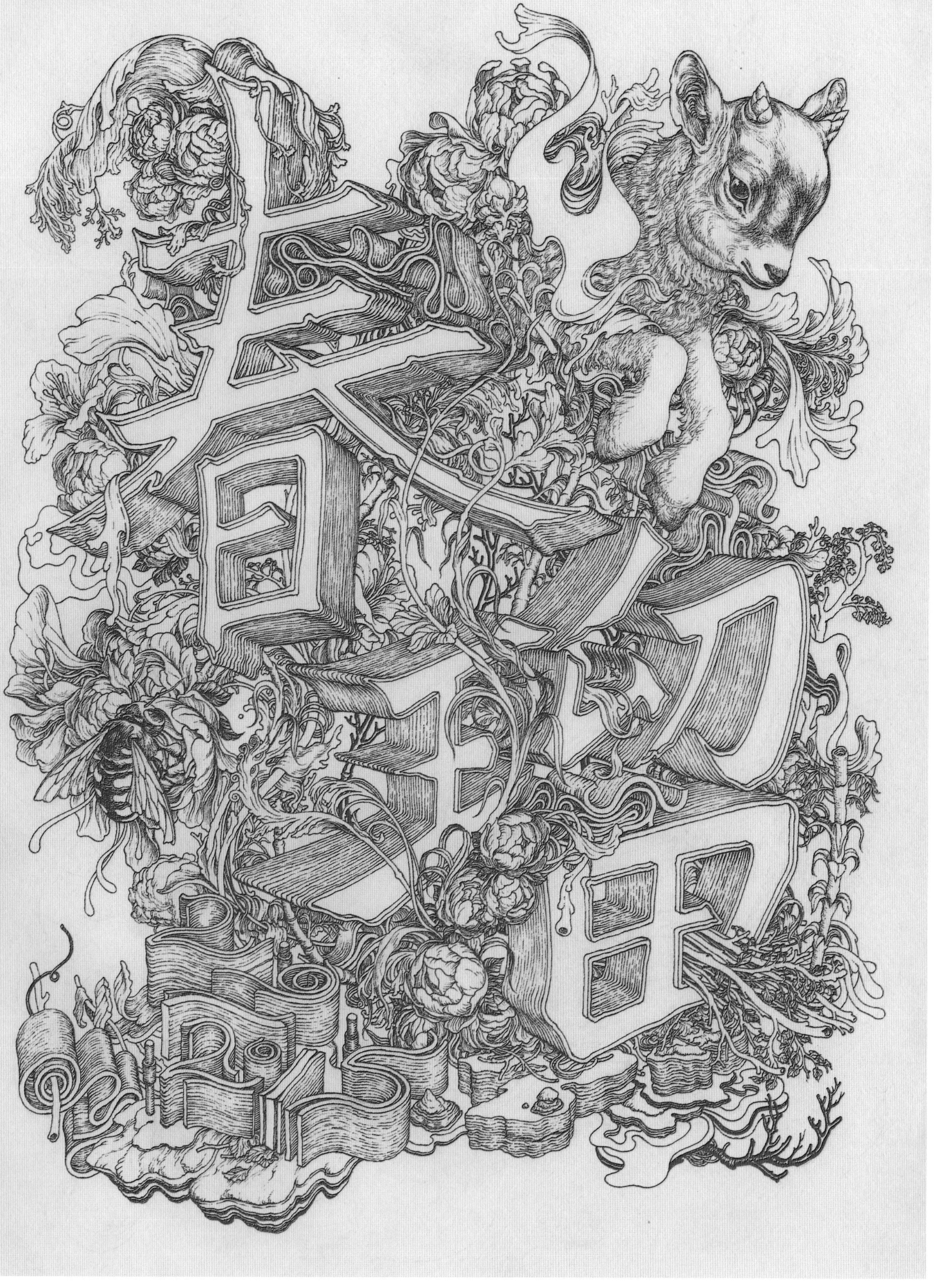

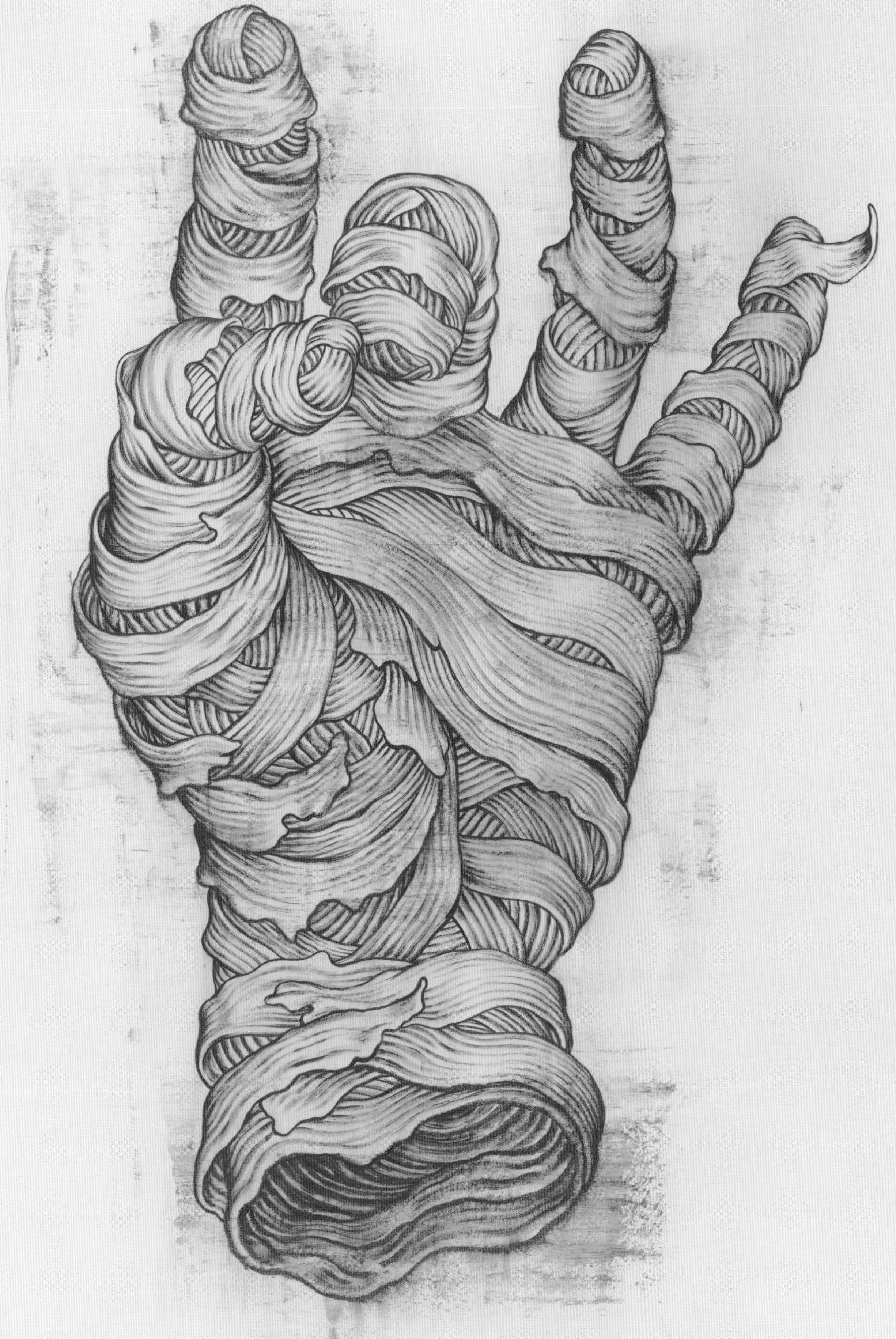

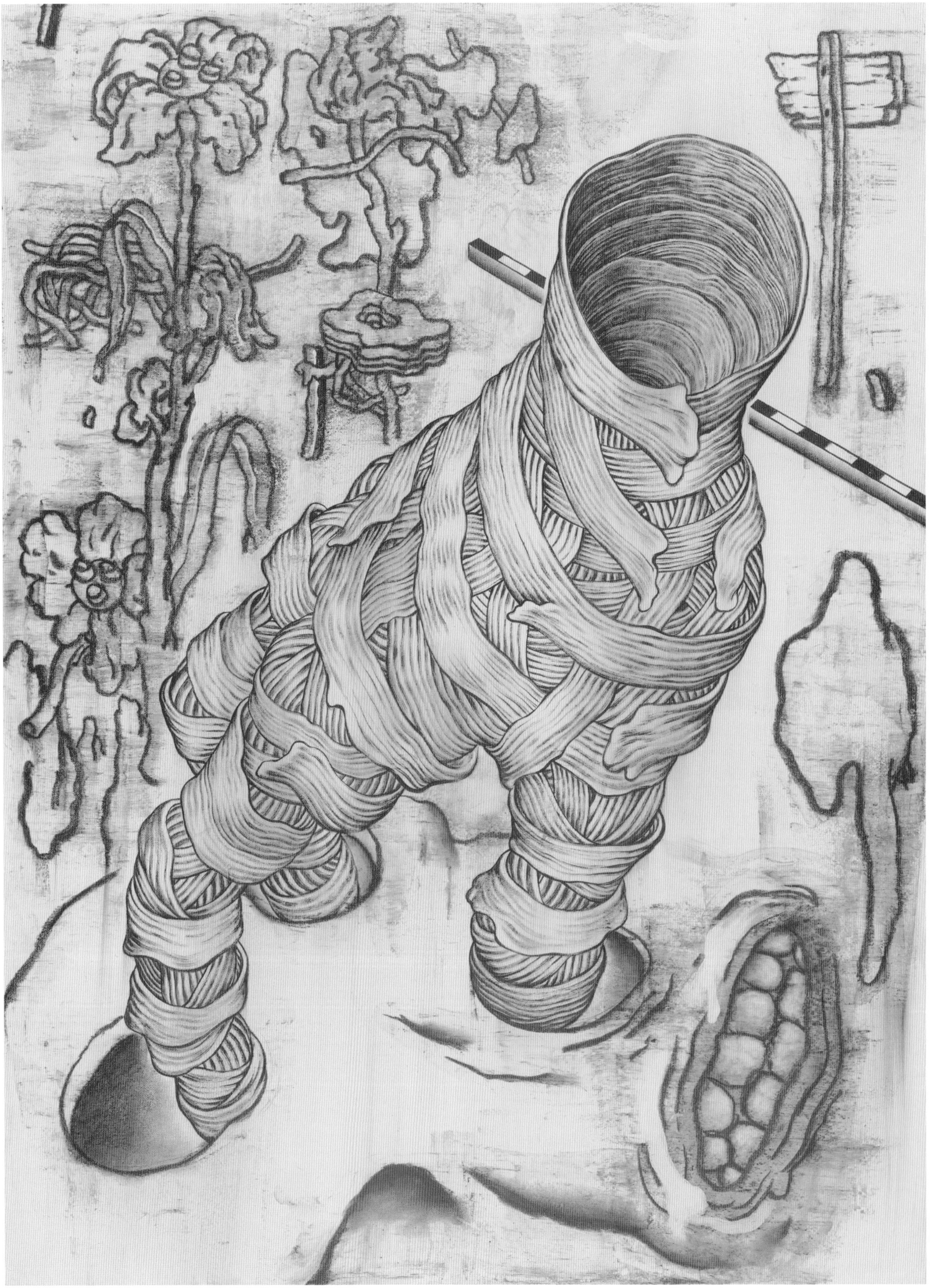

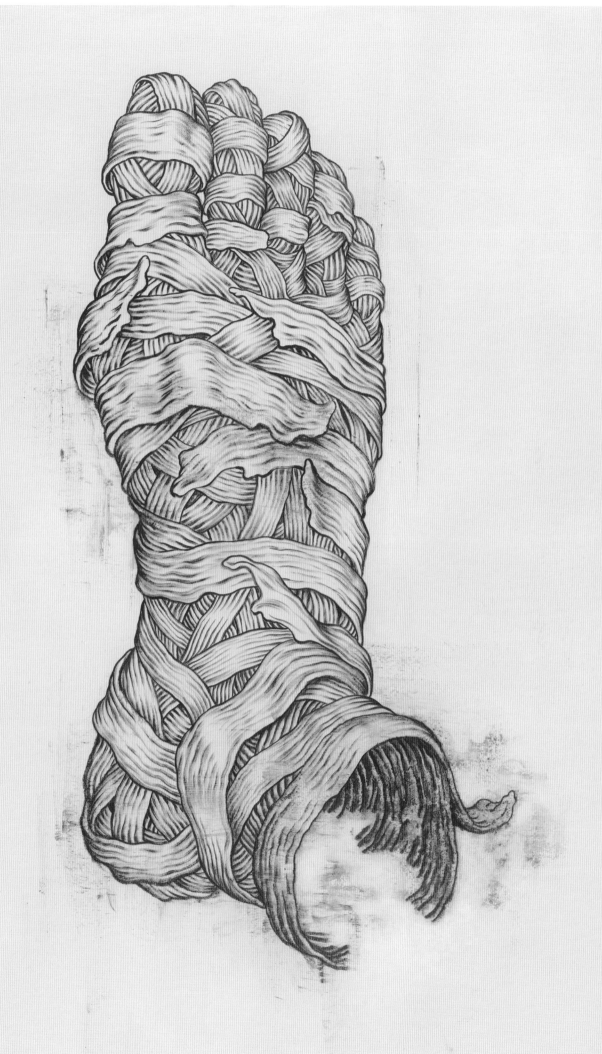

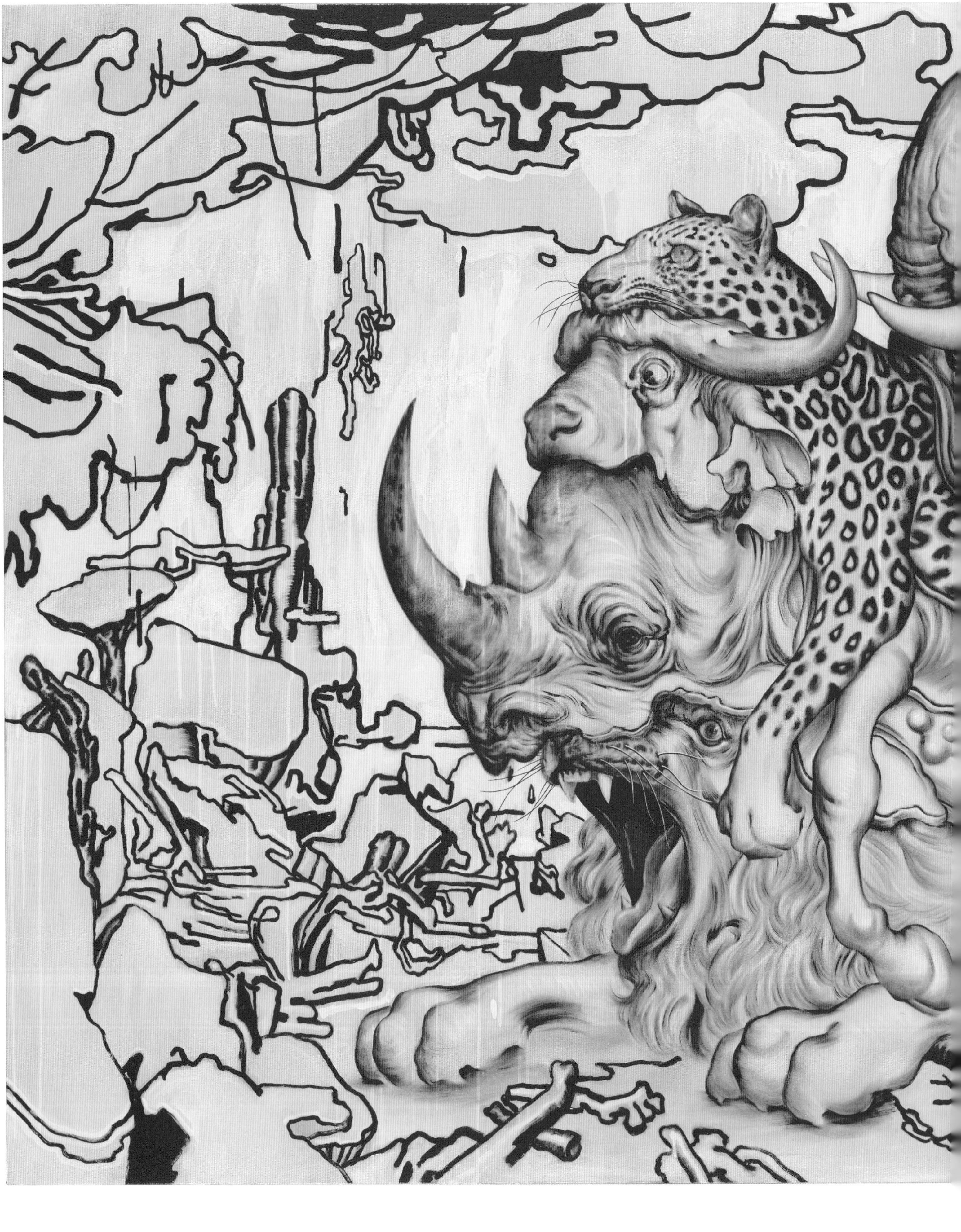

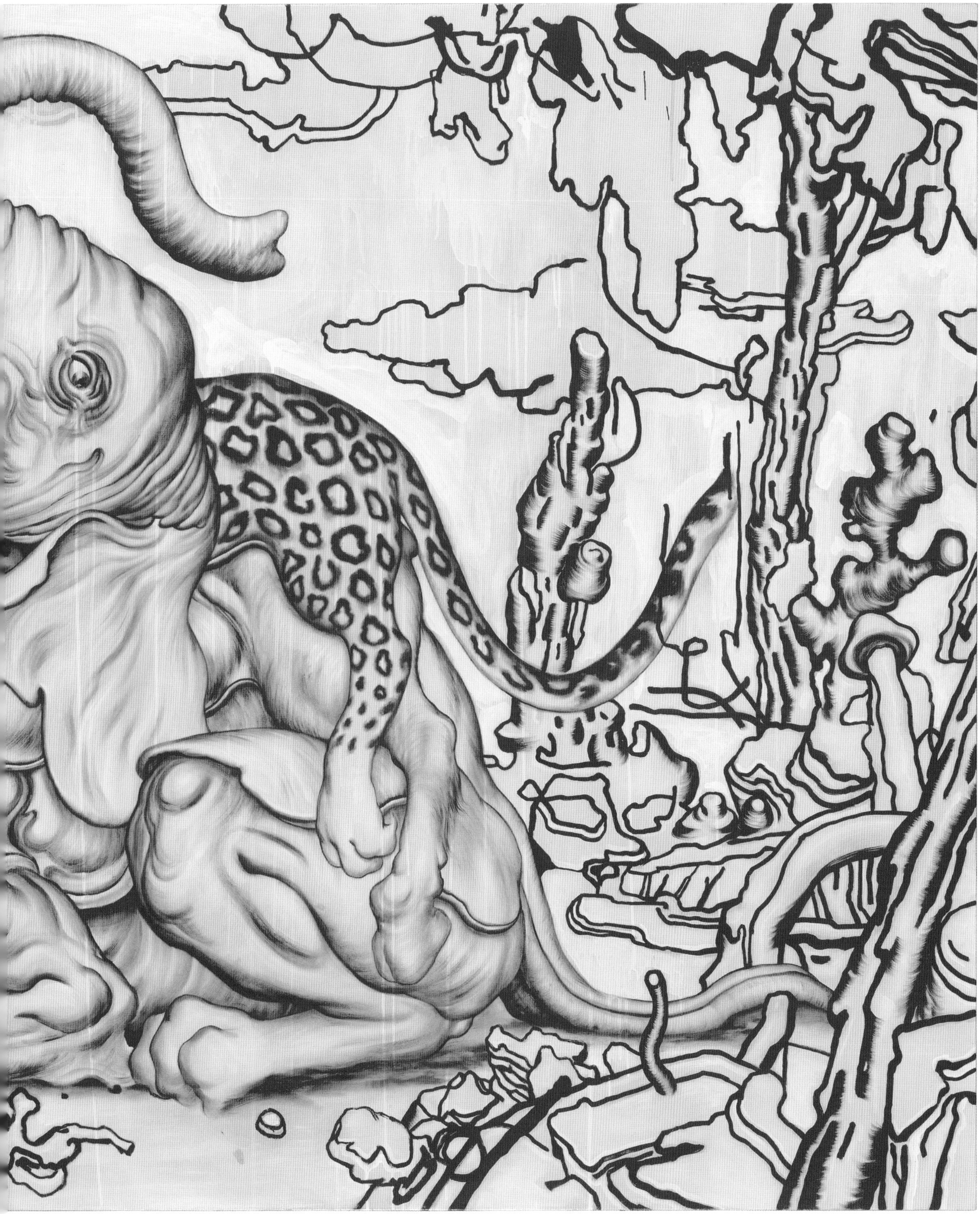

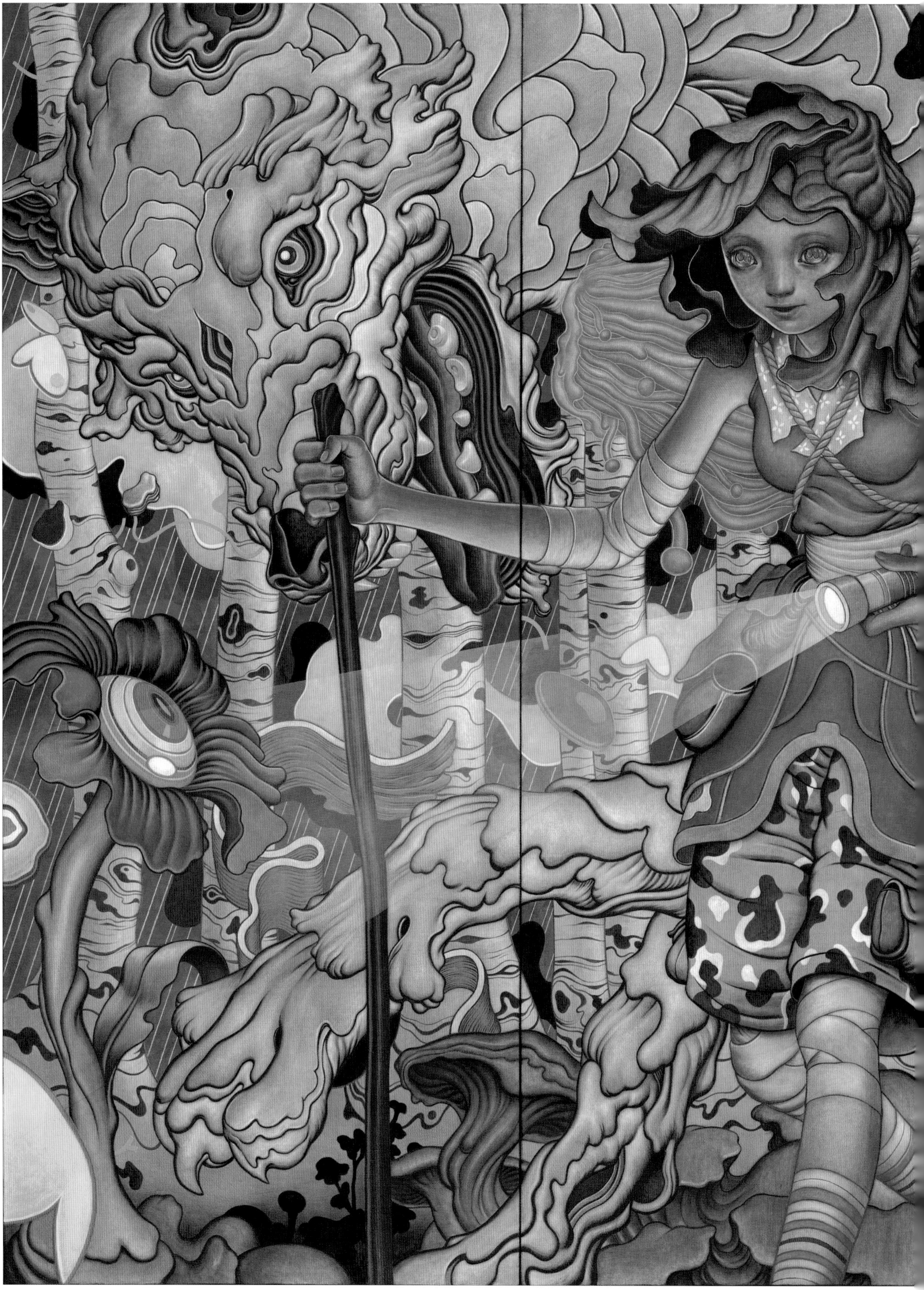

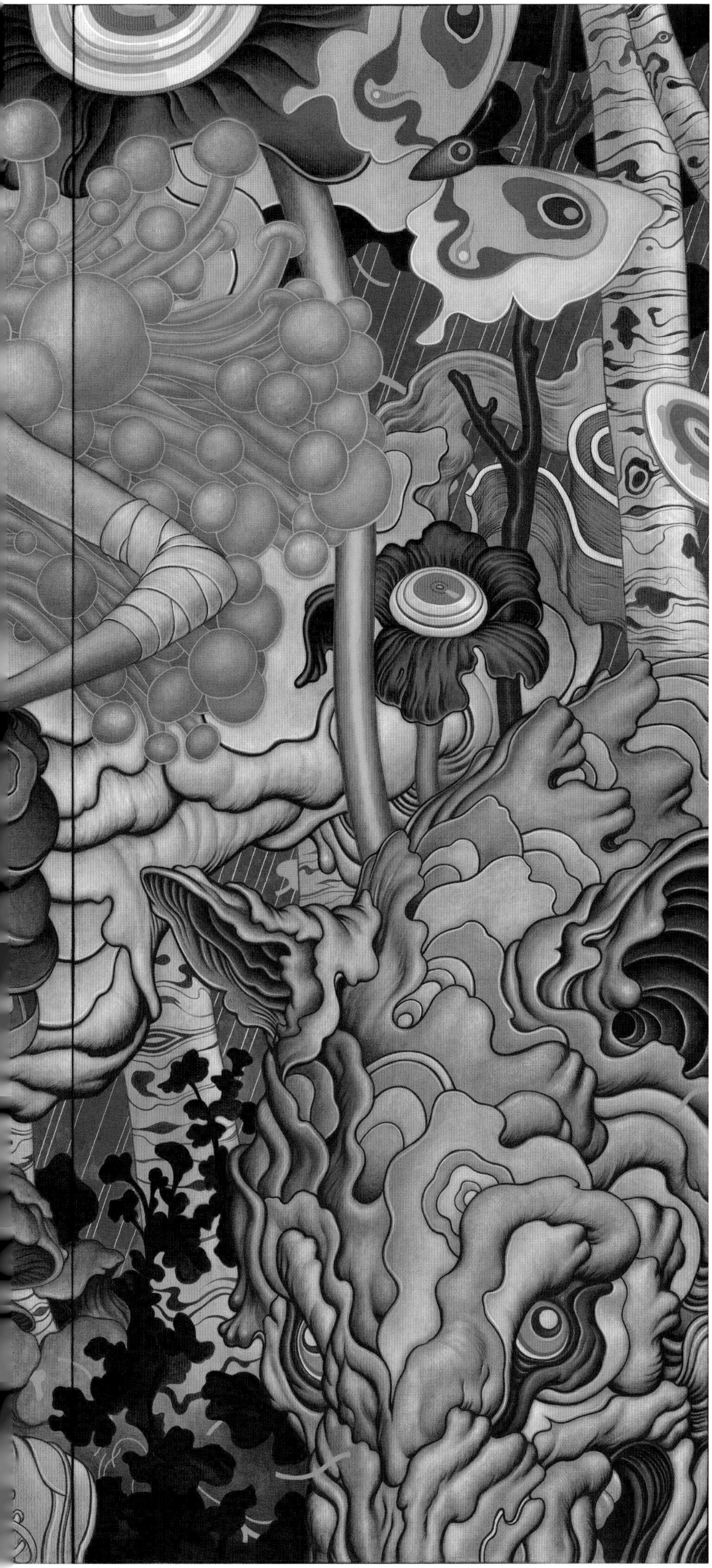

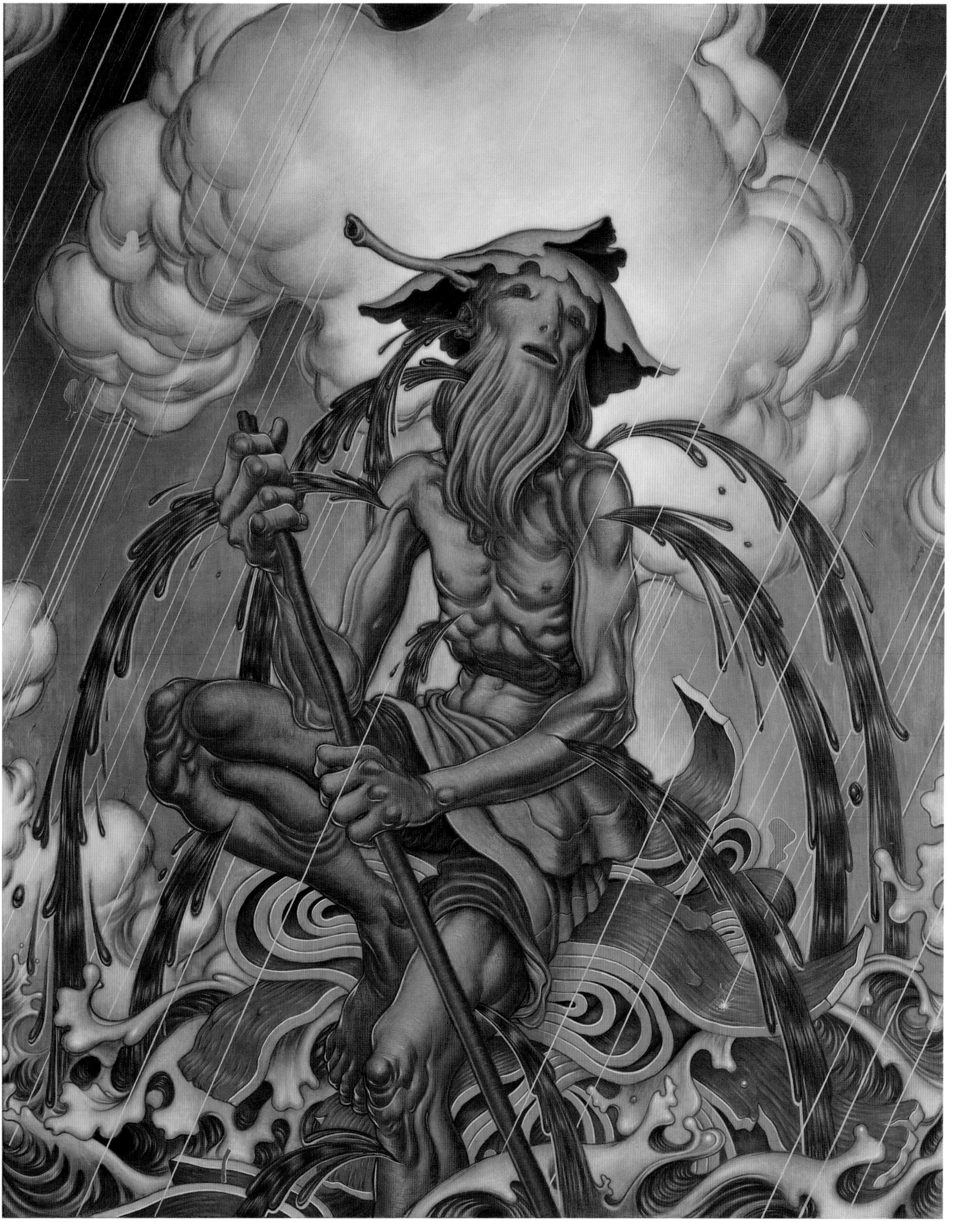

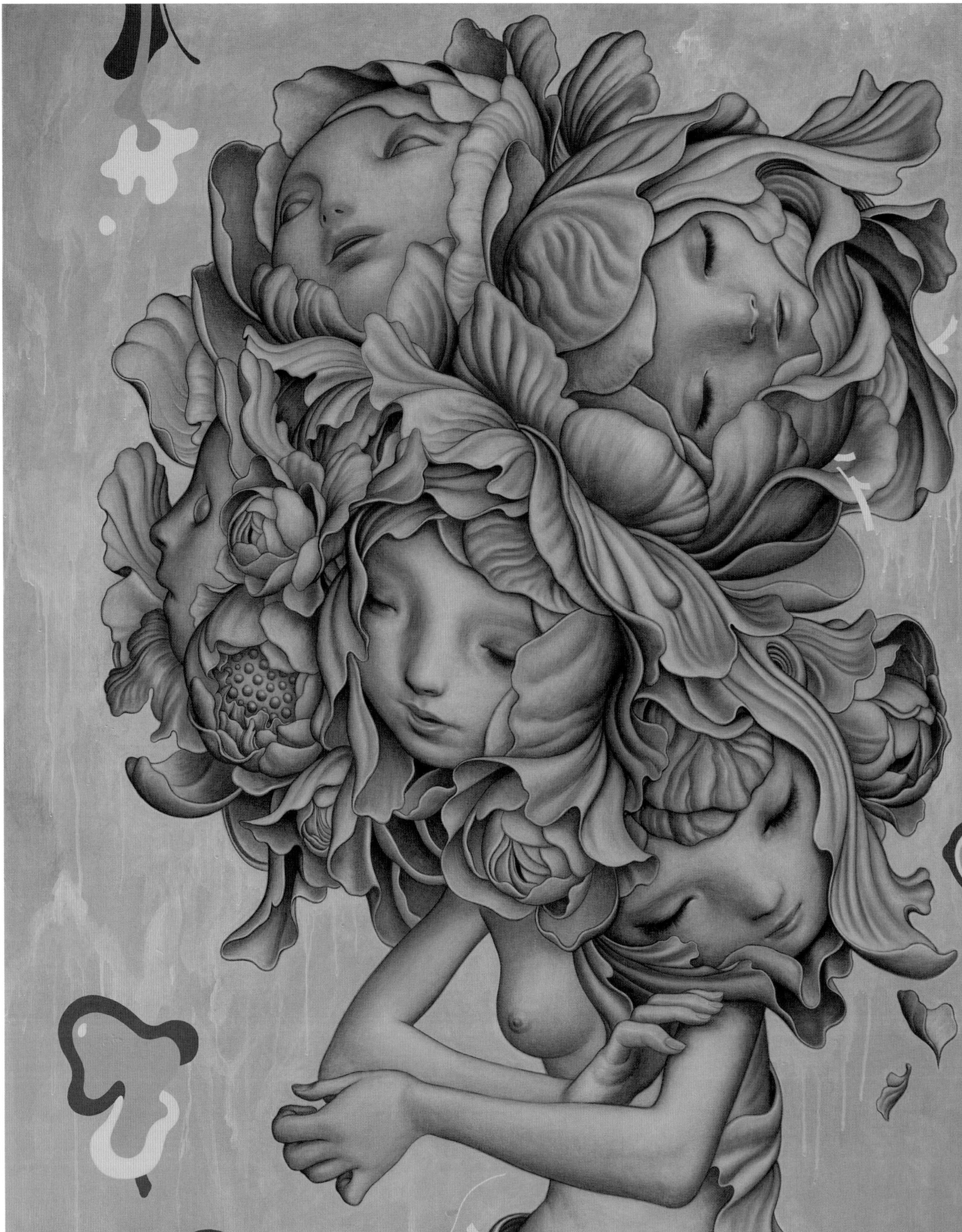

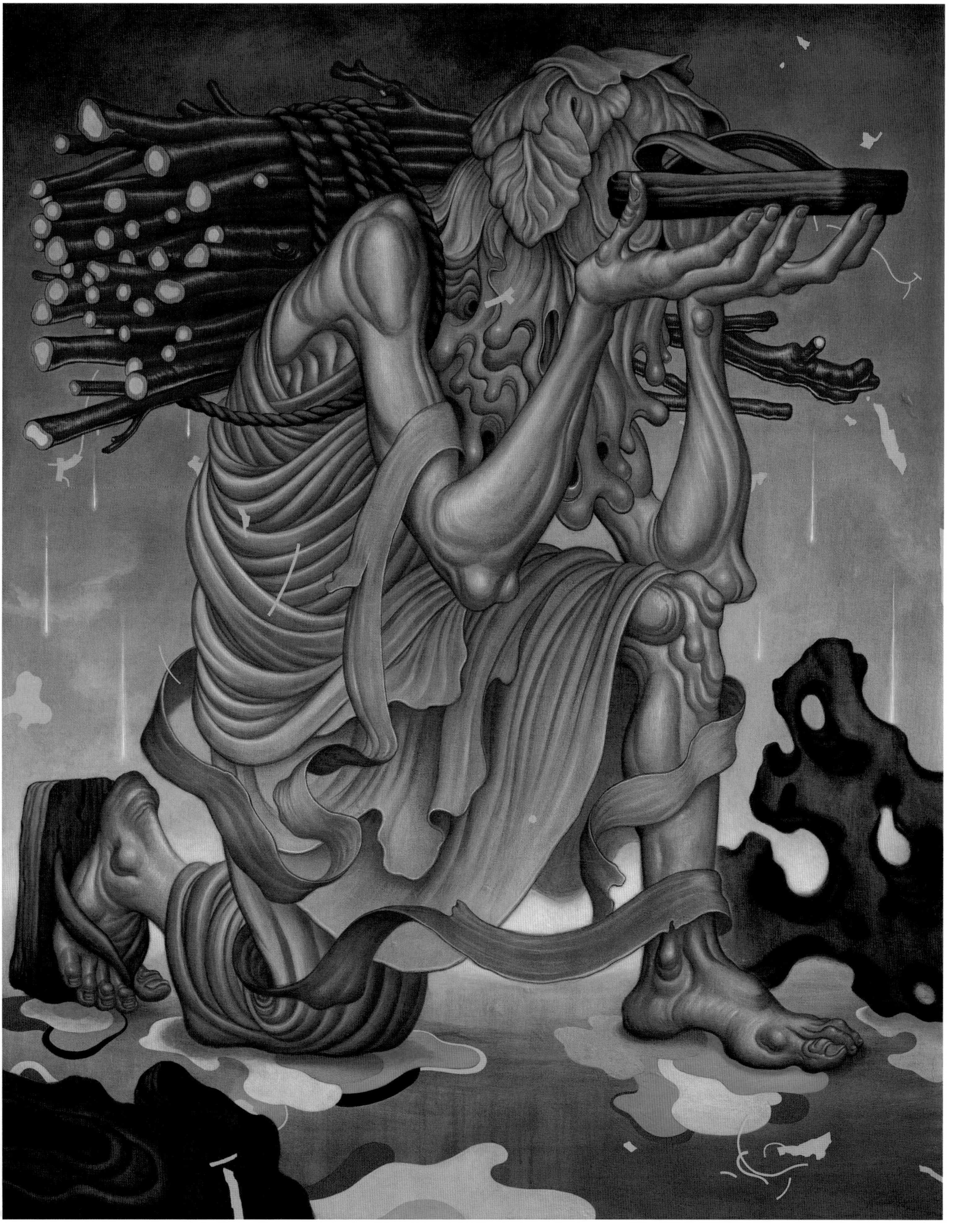

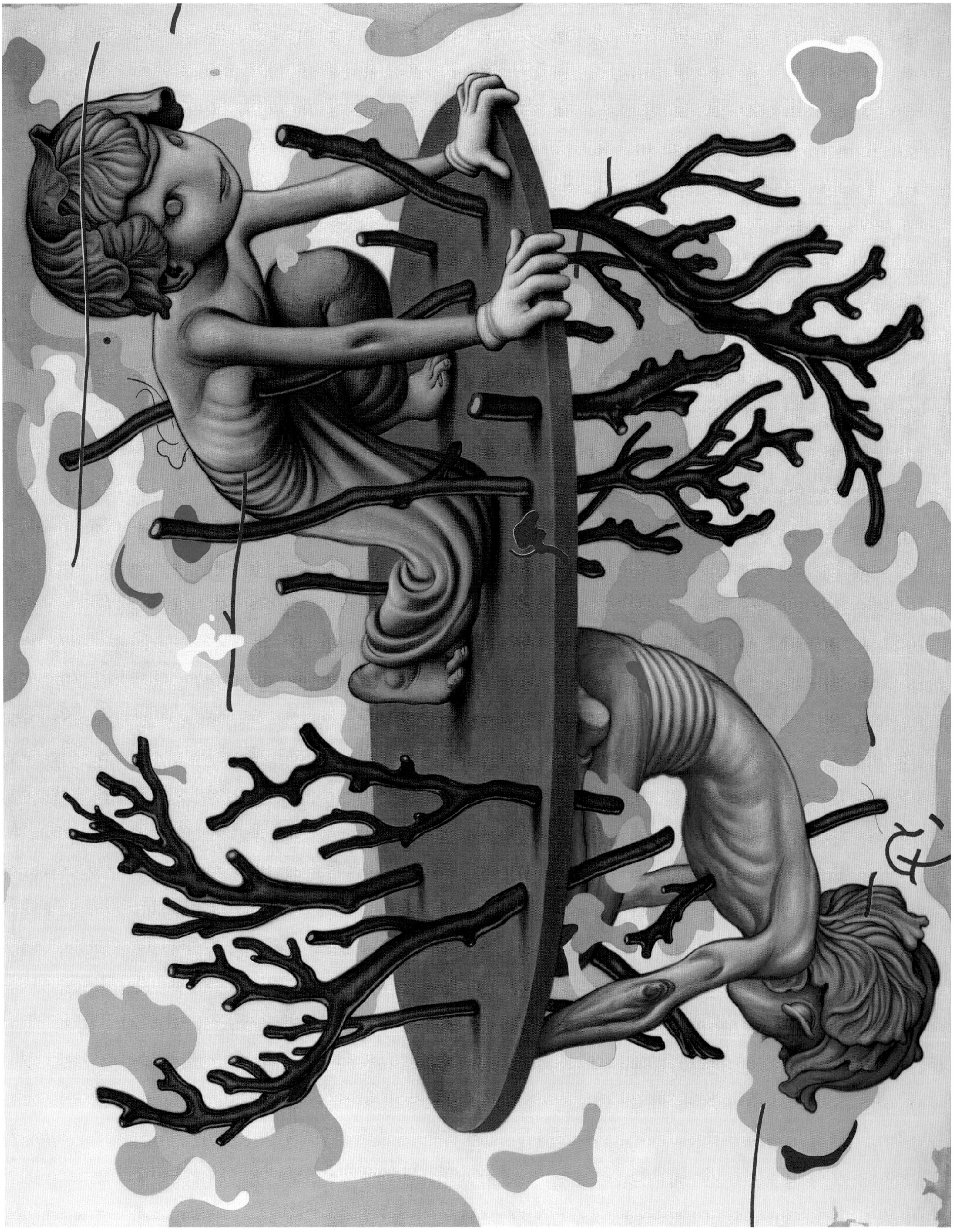

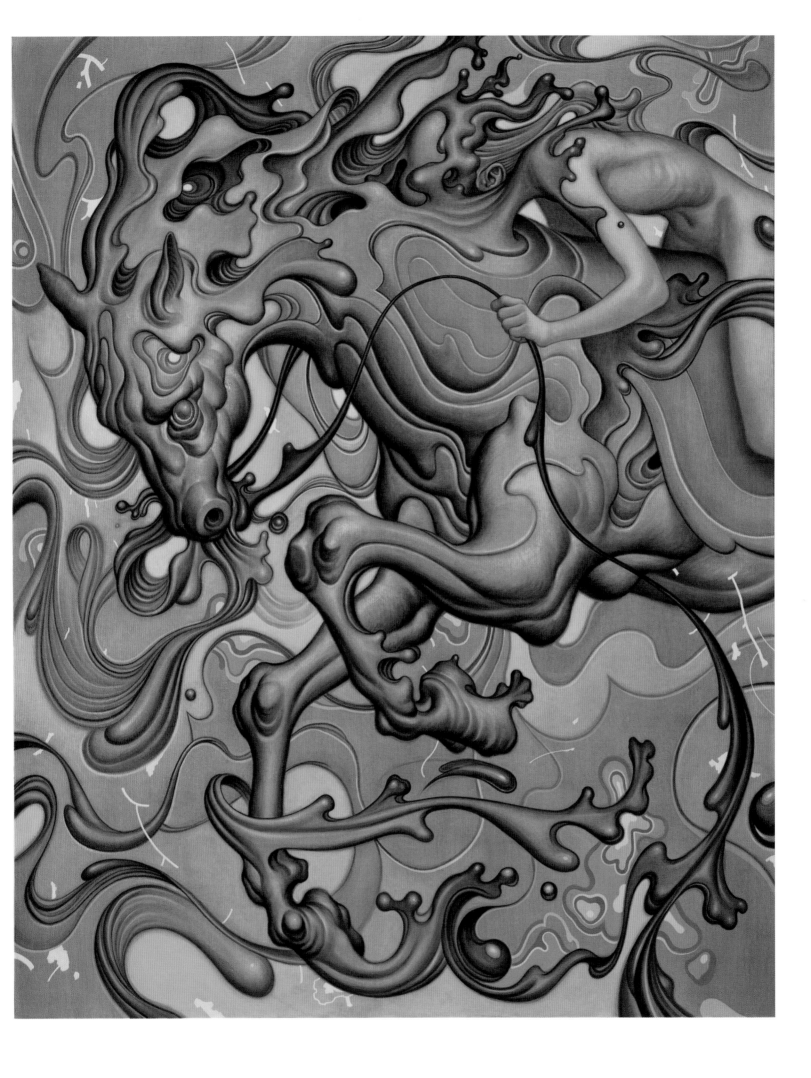

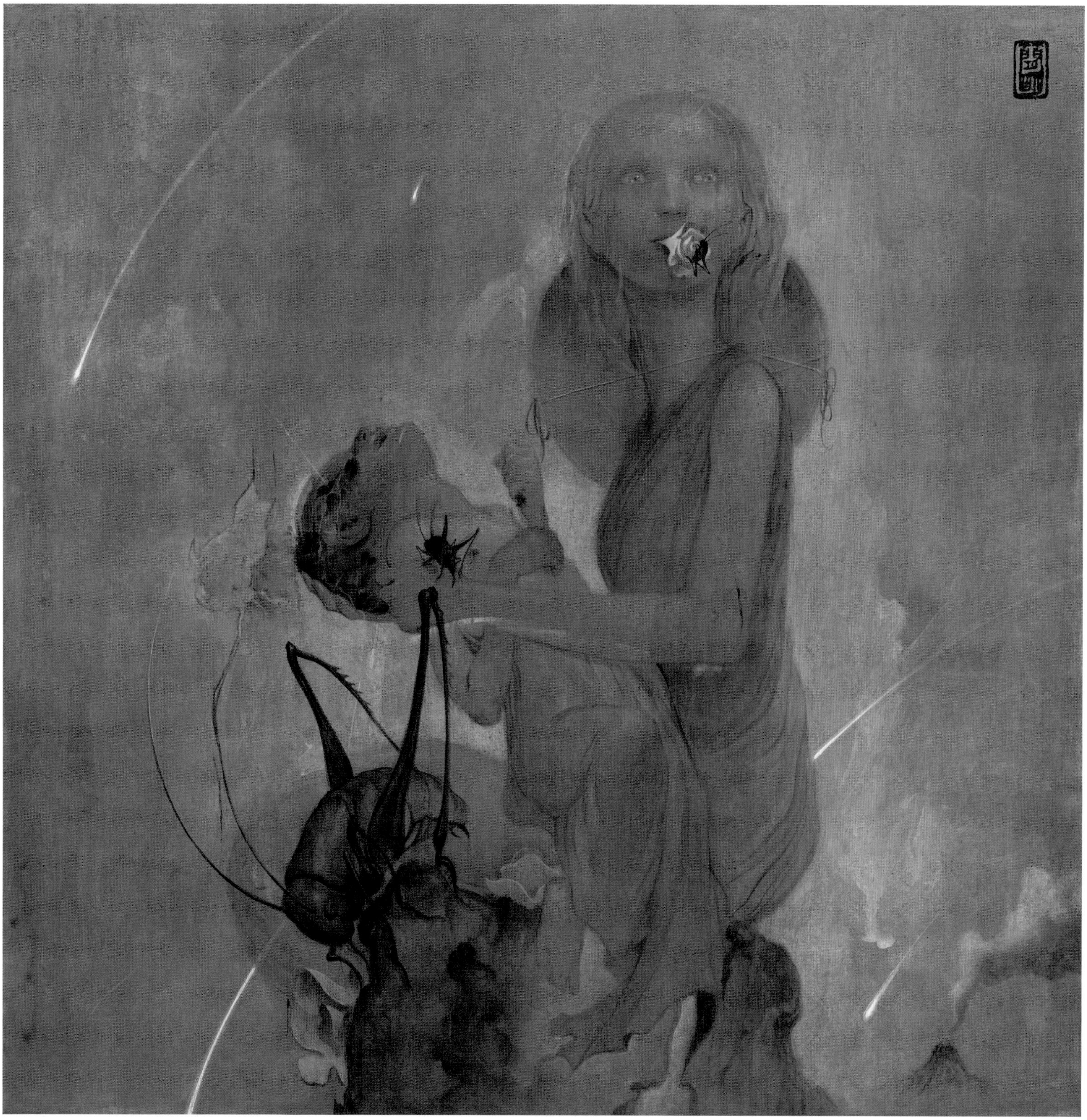

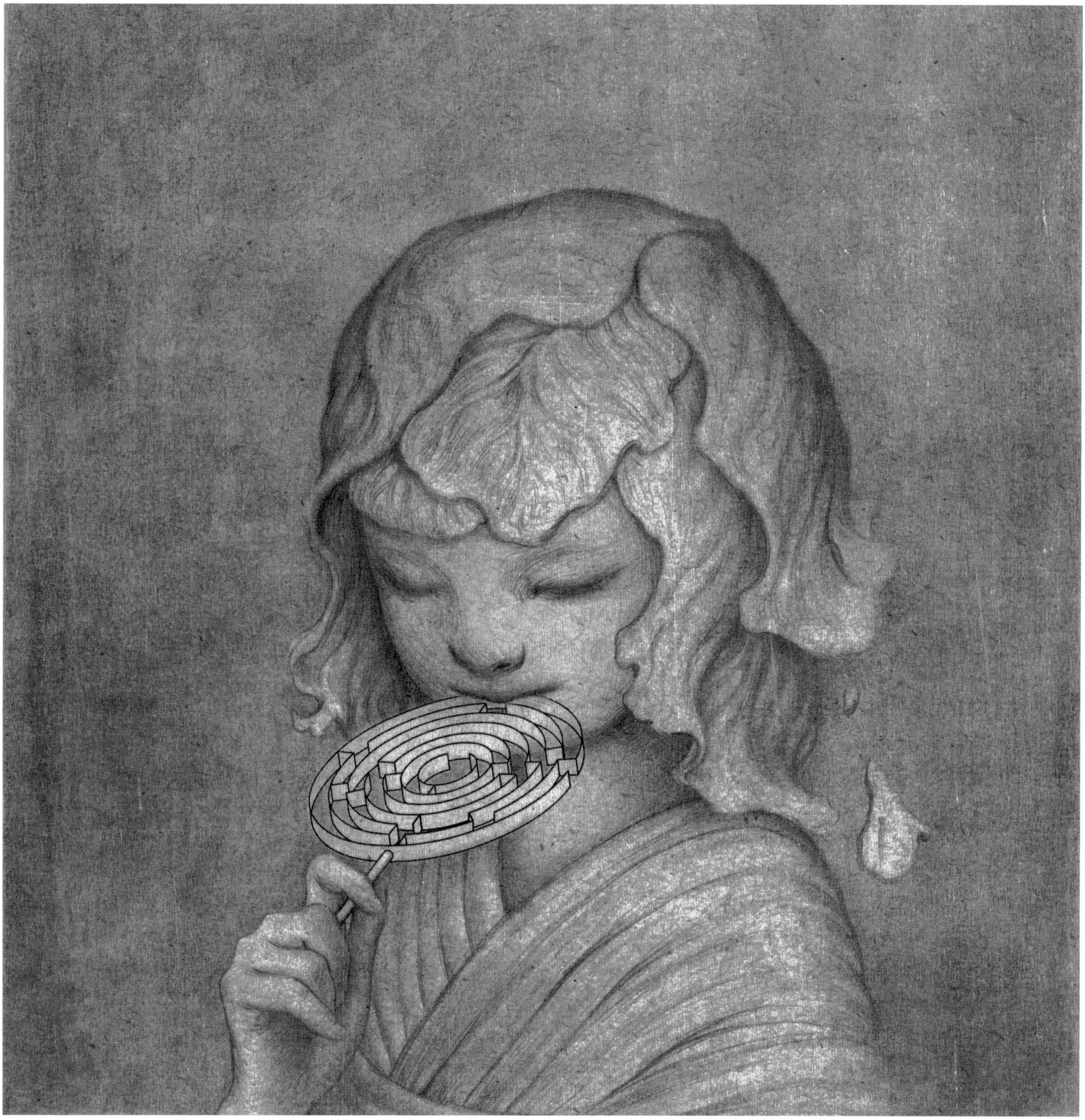

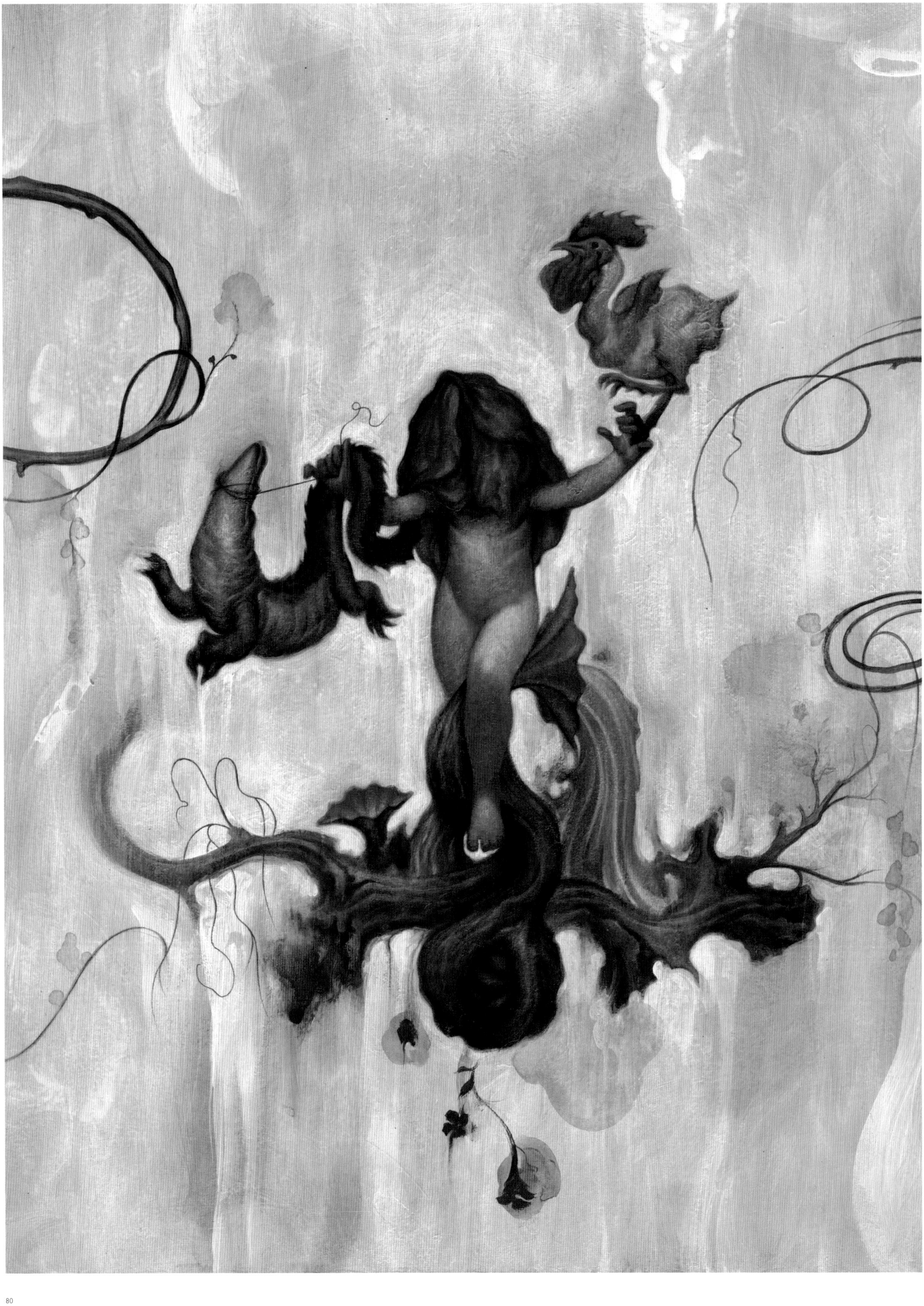

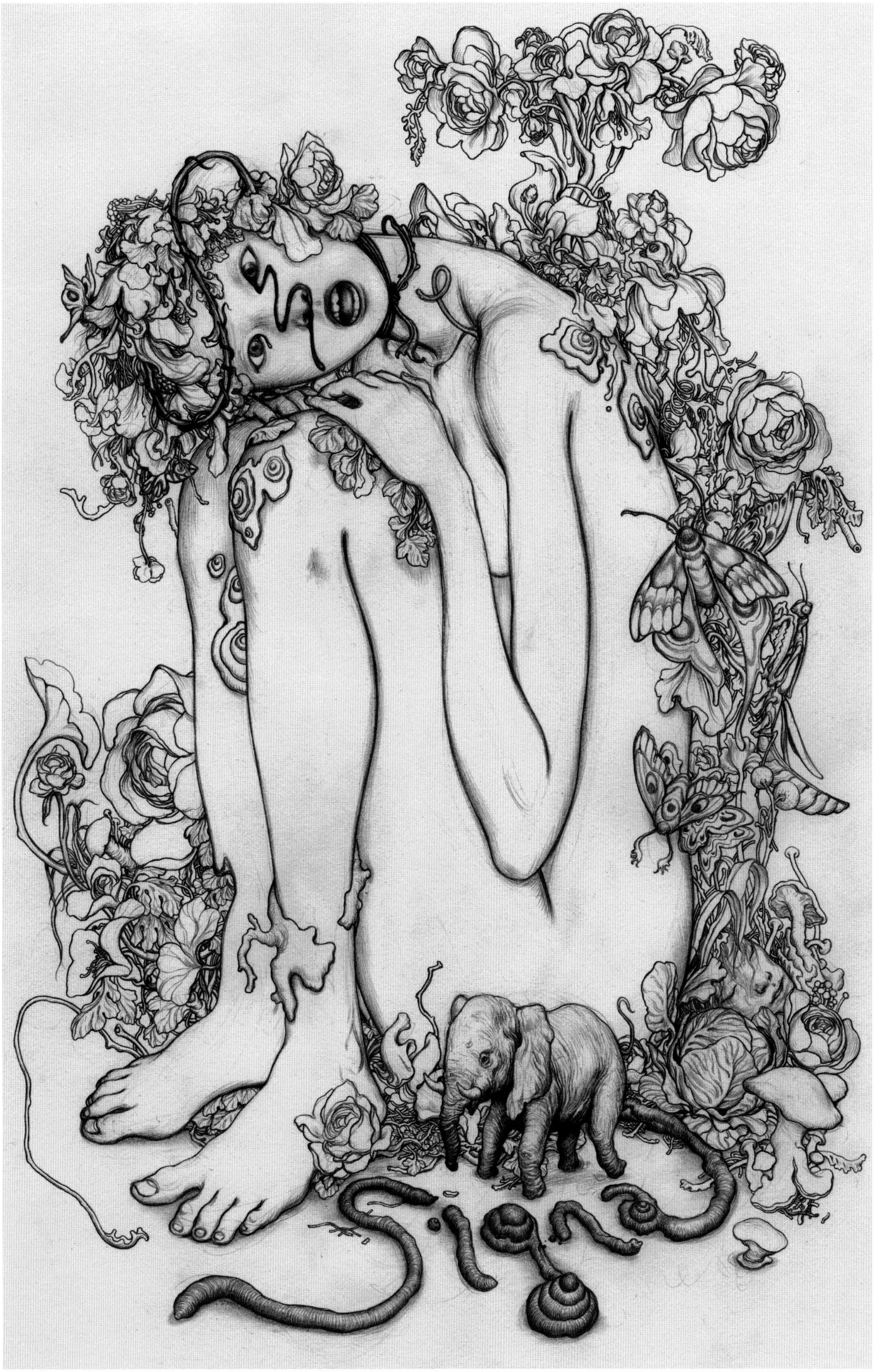

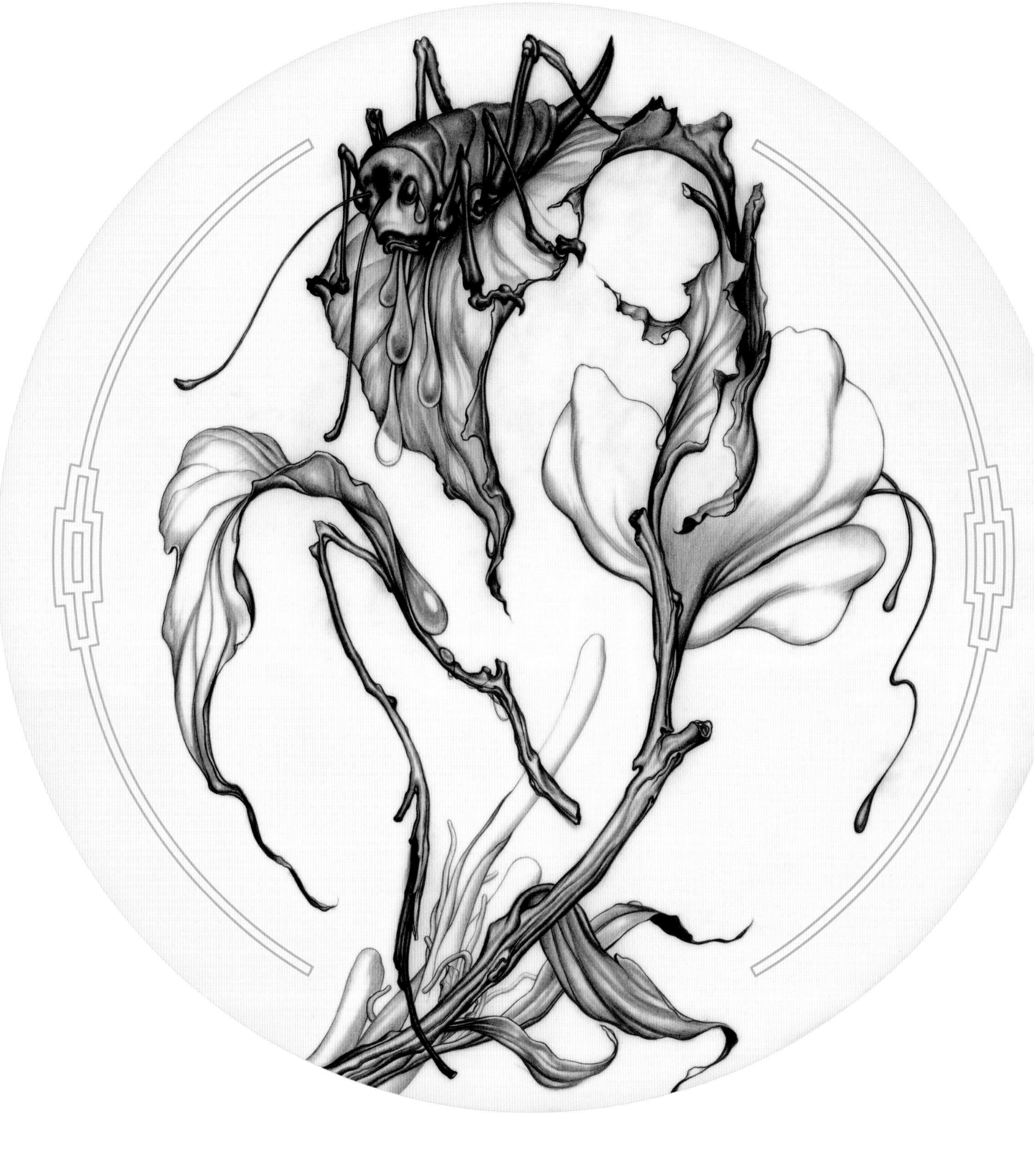

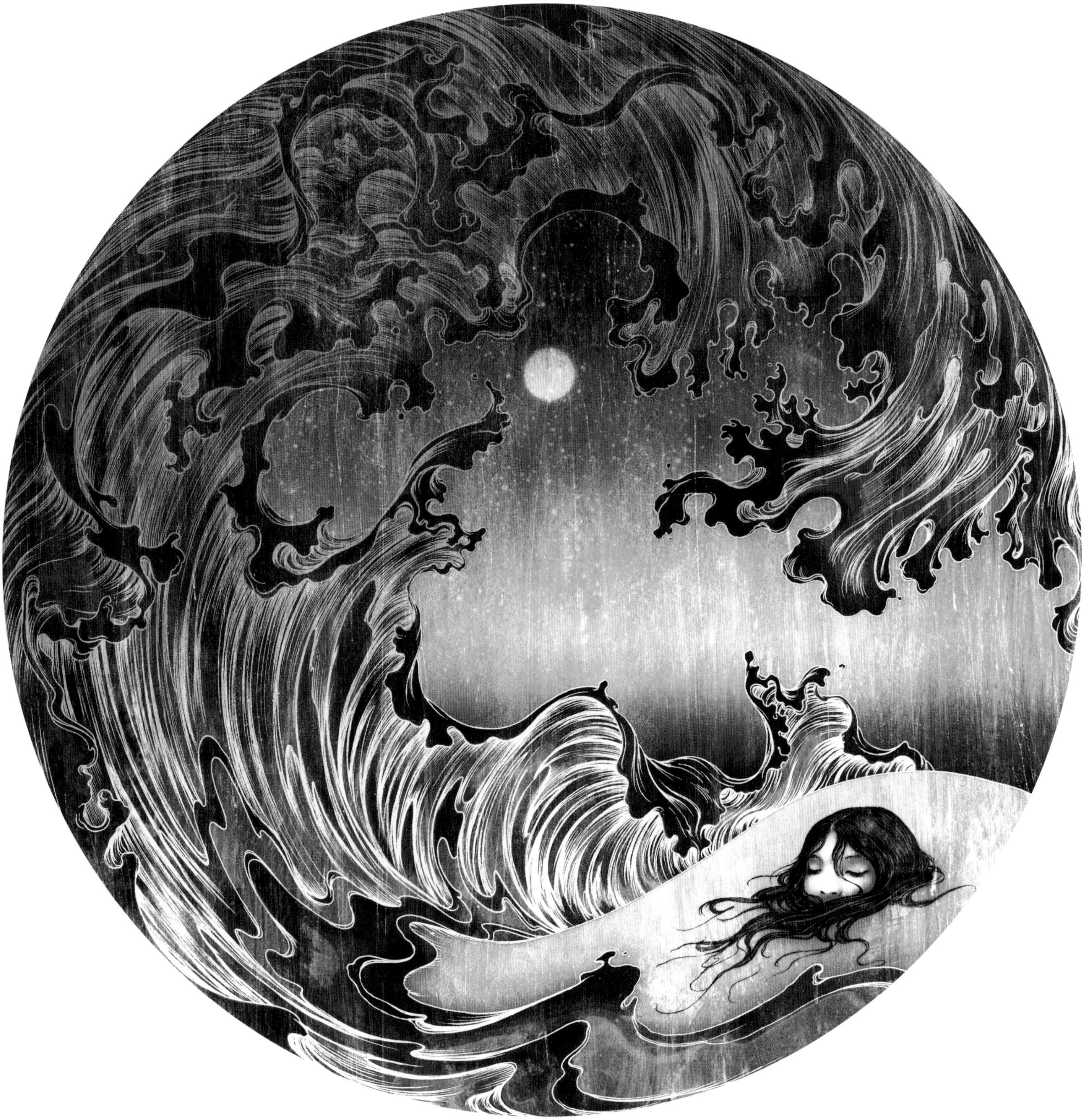

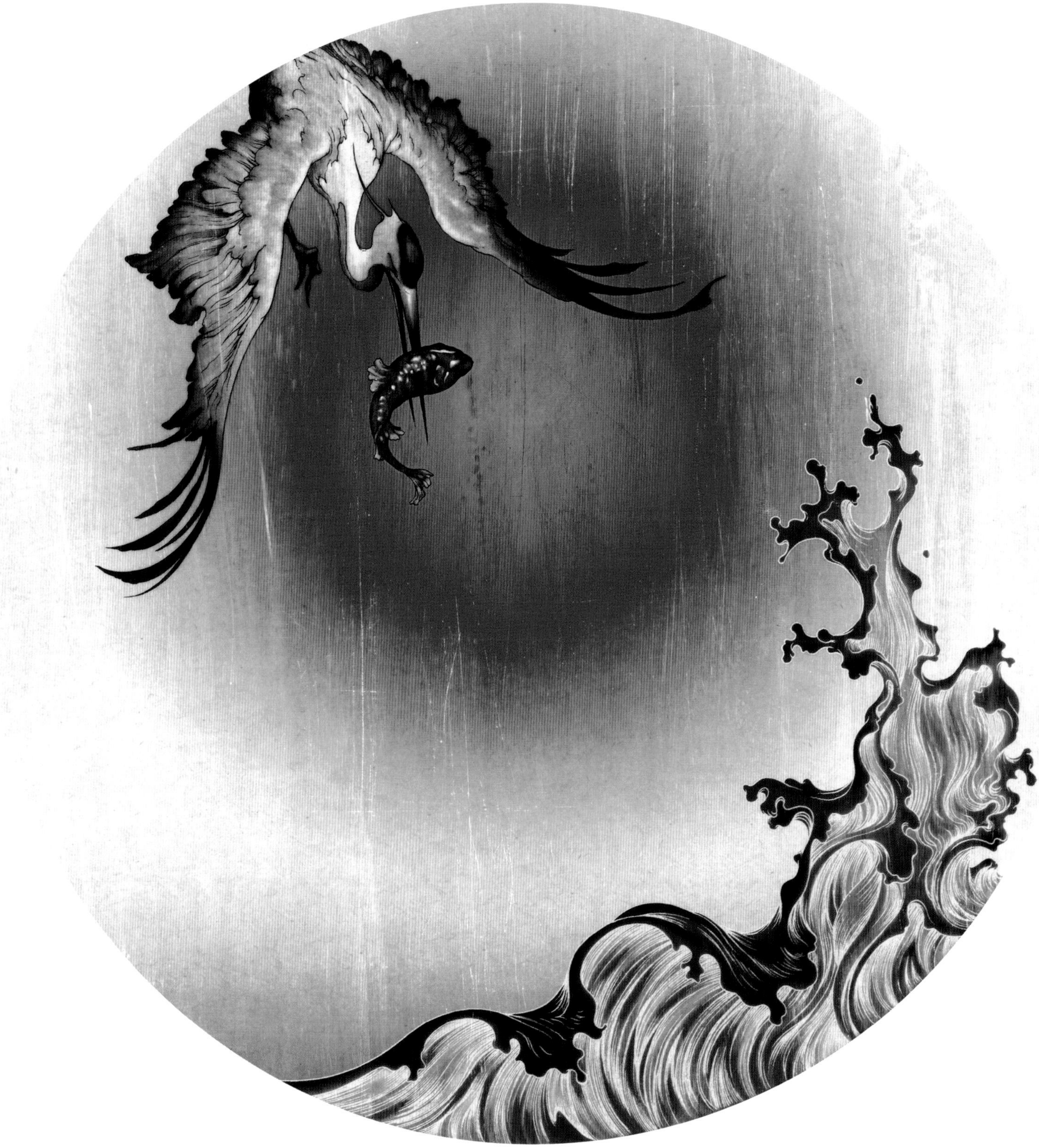

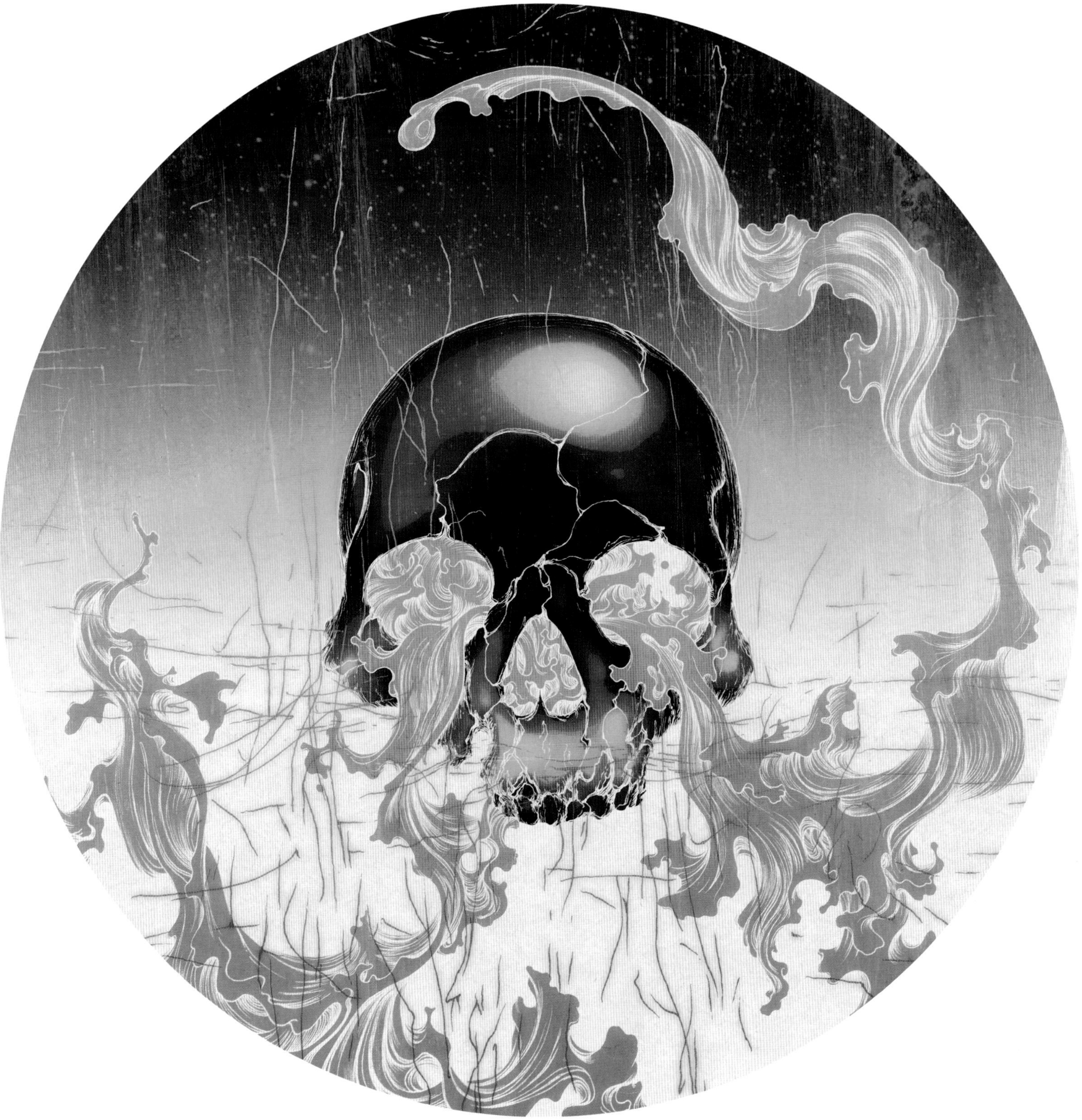

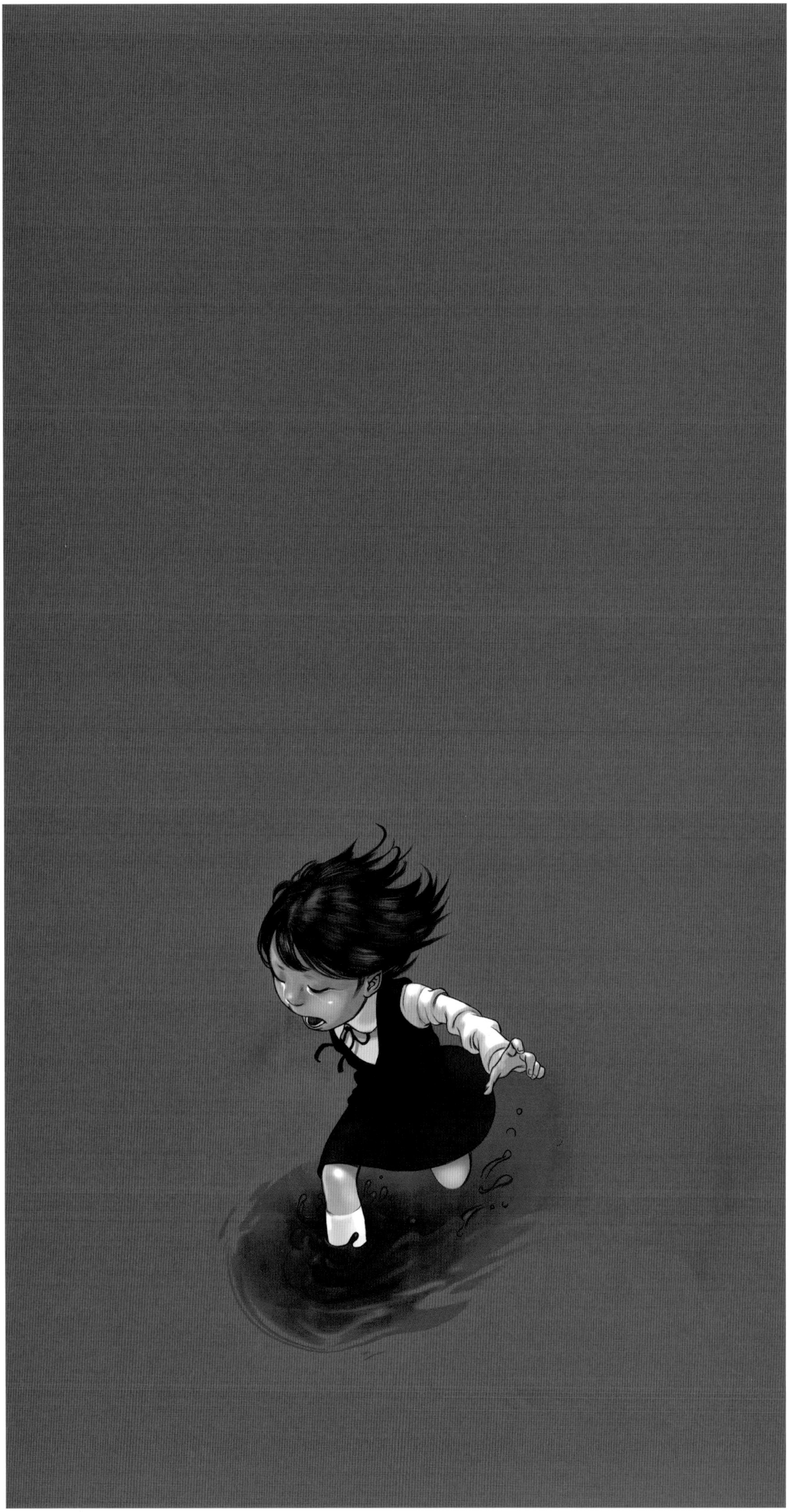

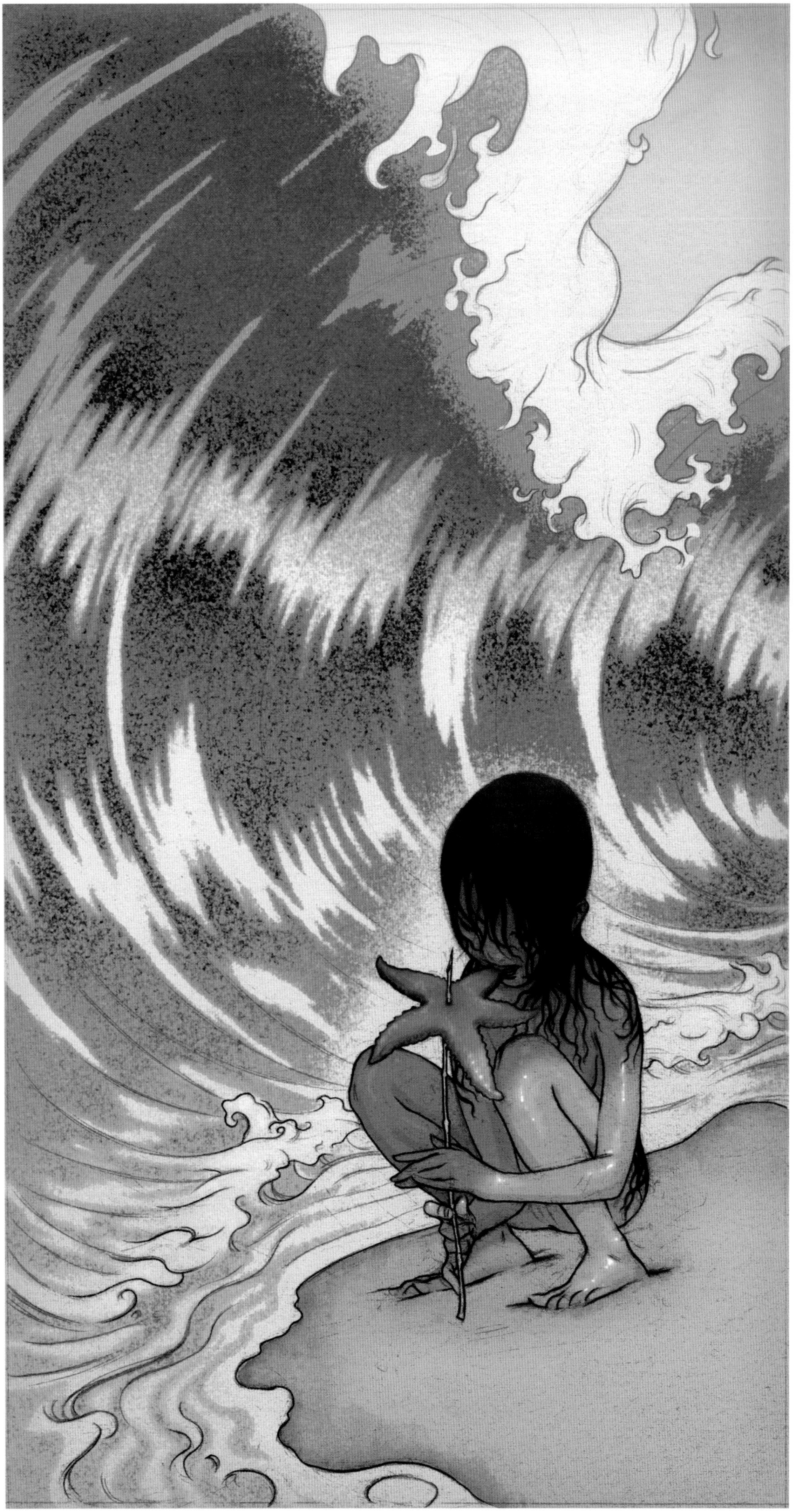

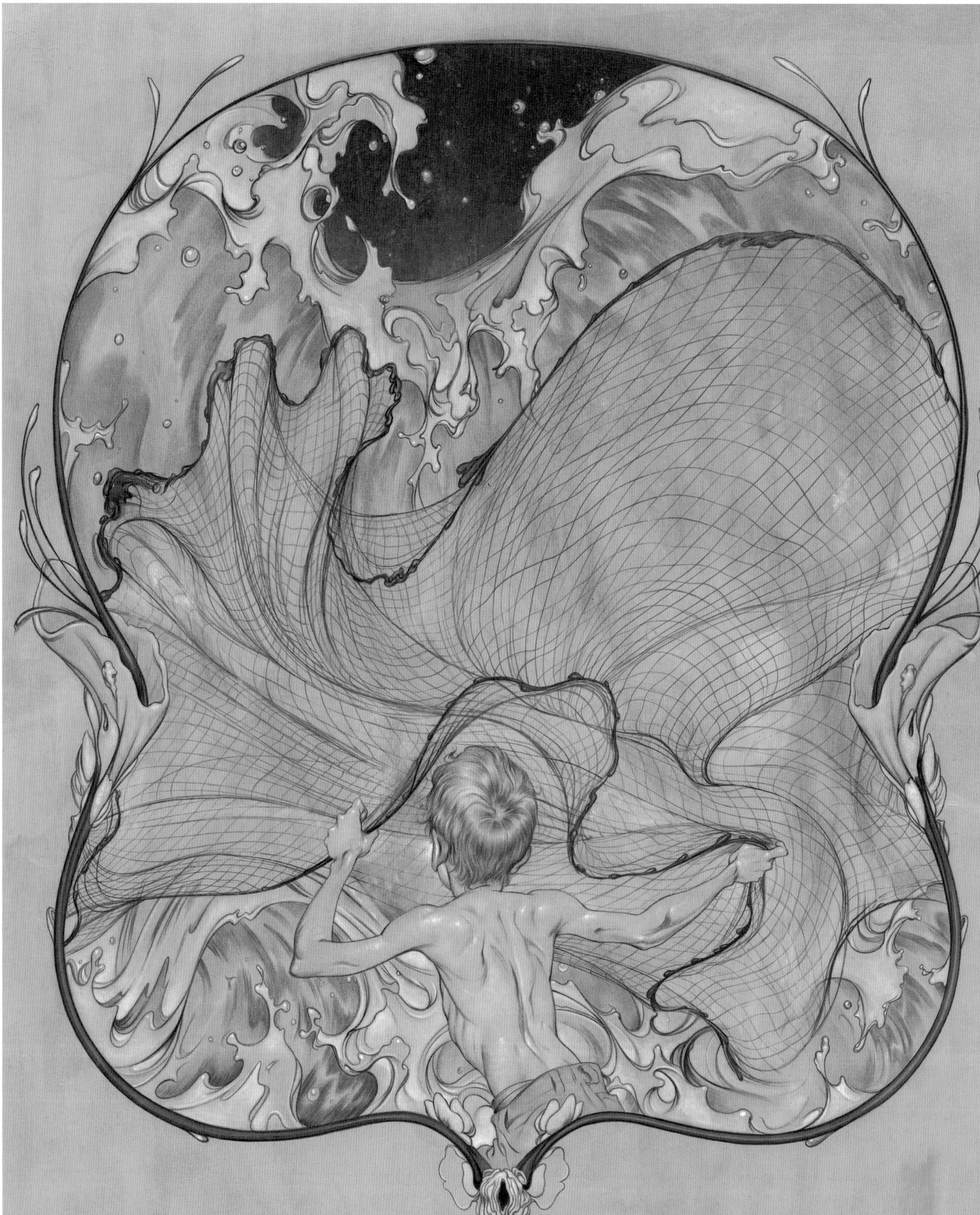

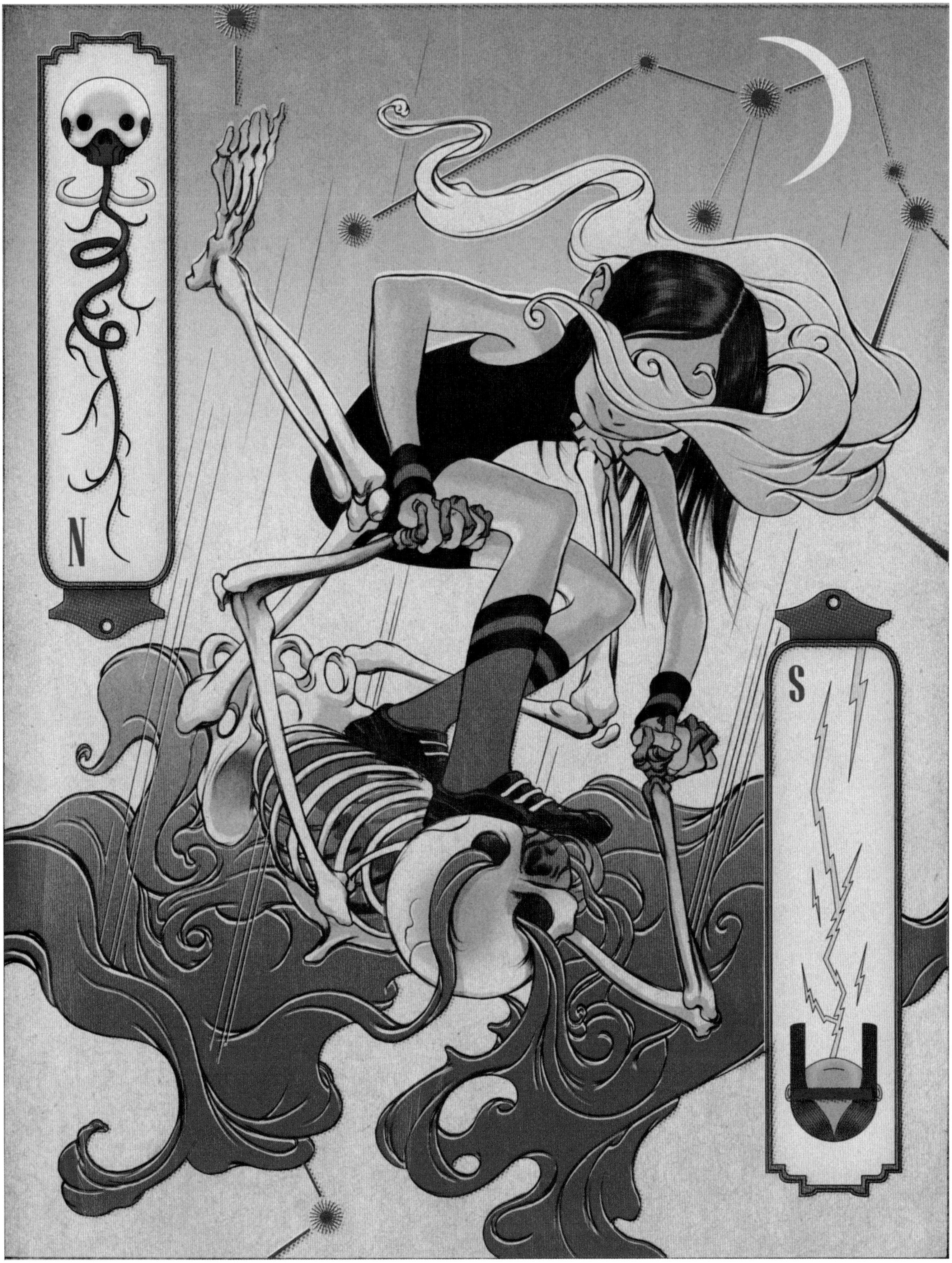
N
S

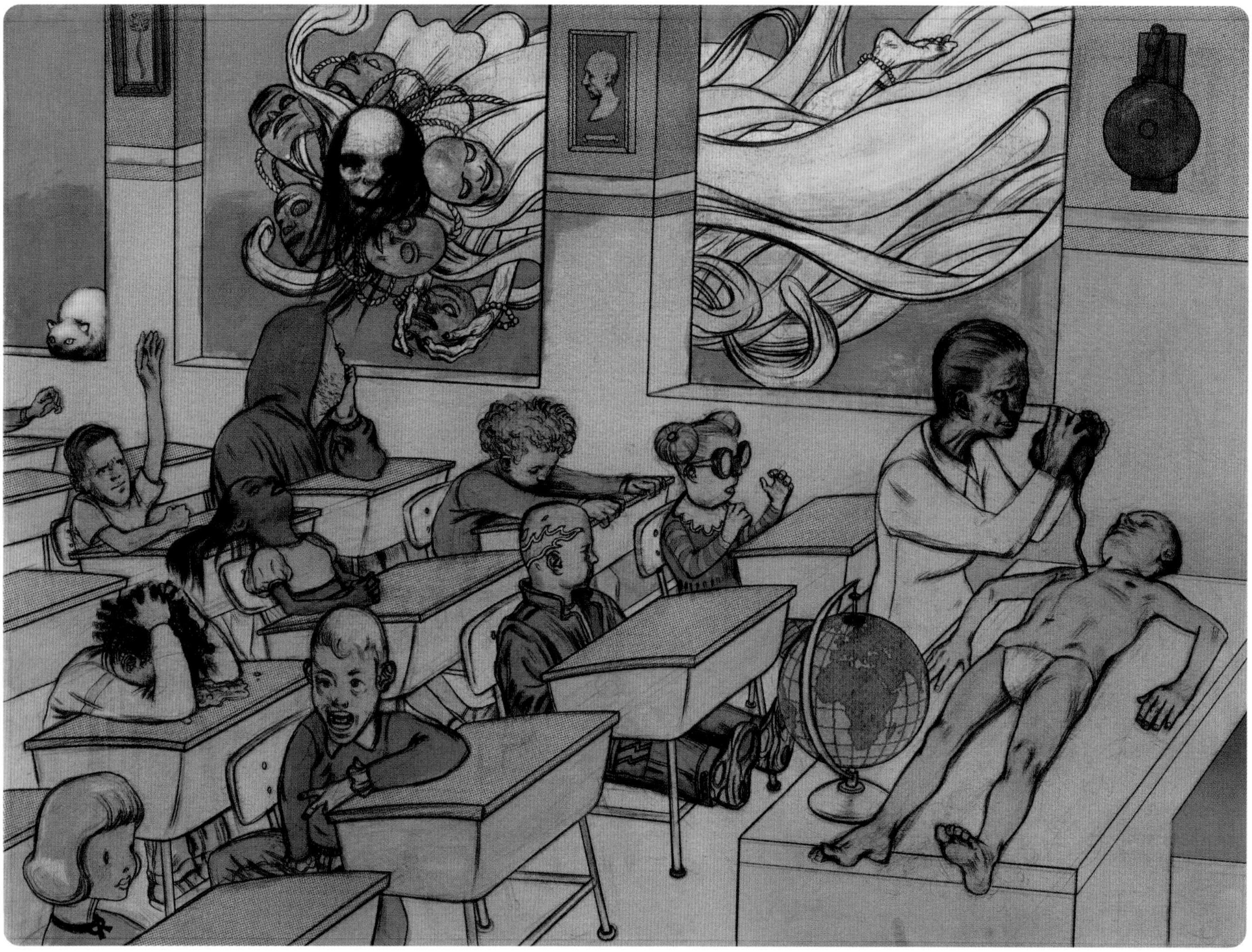

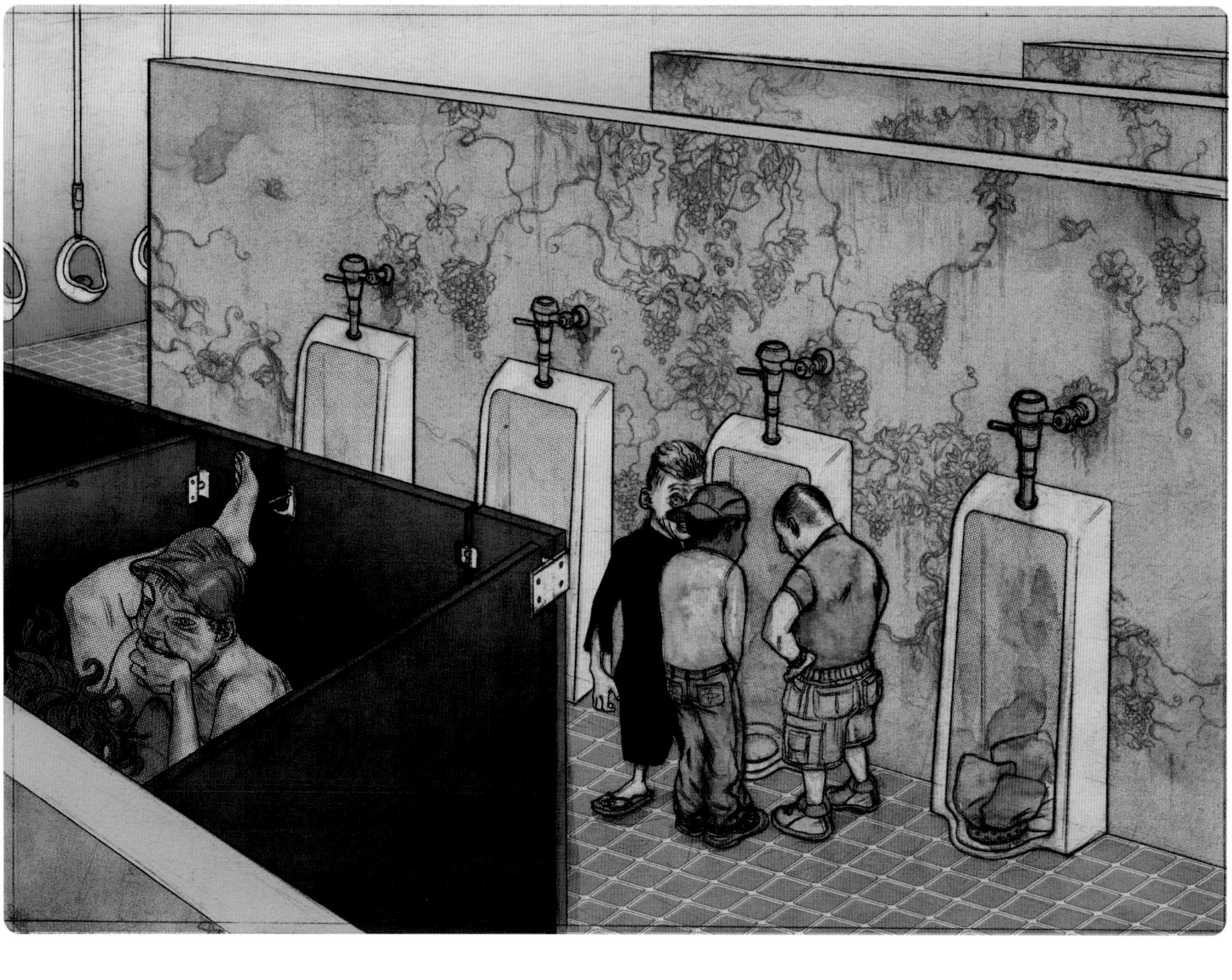

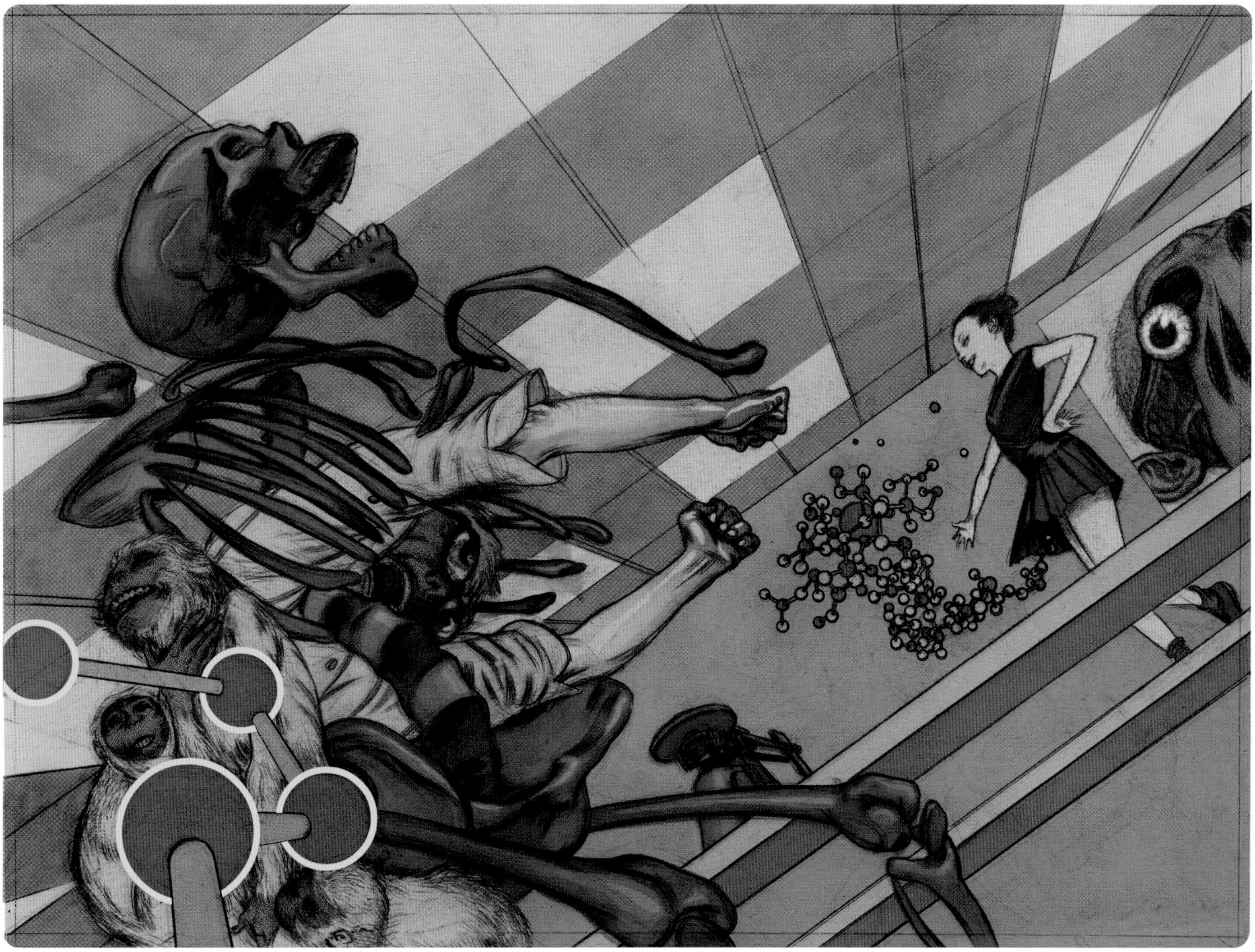

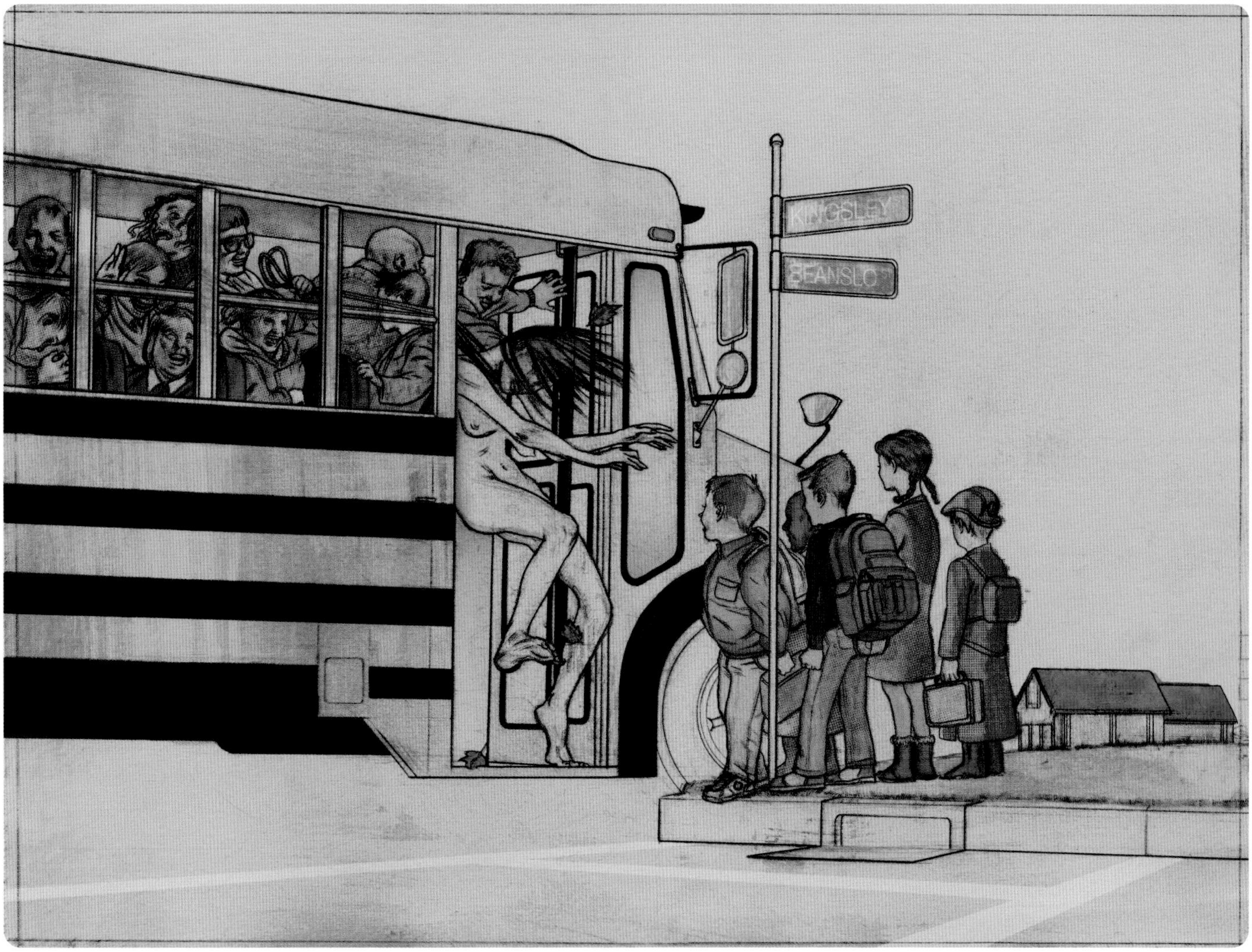

KINGSLEY
BEANSLO

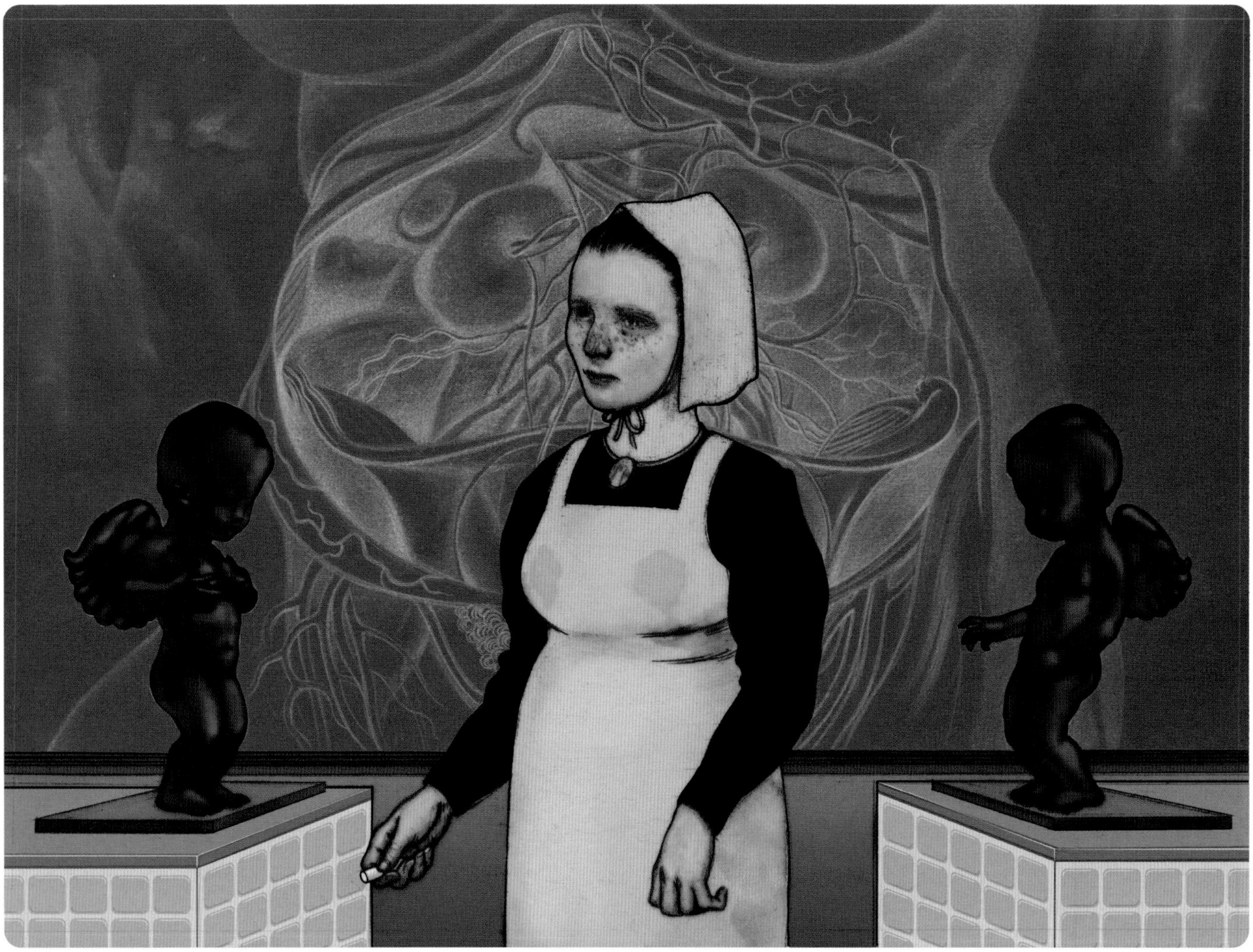

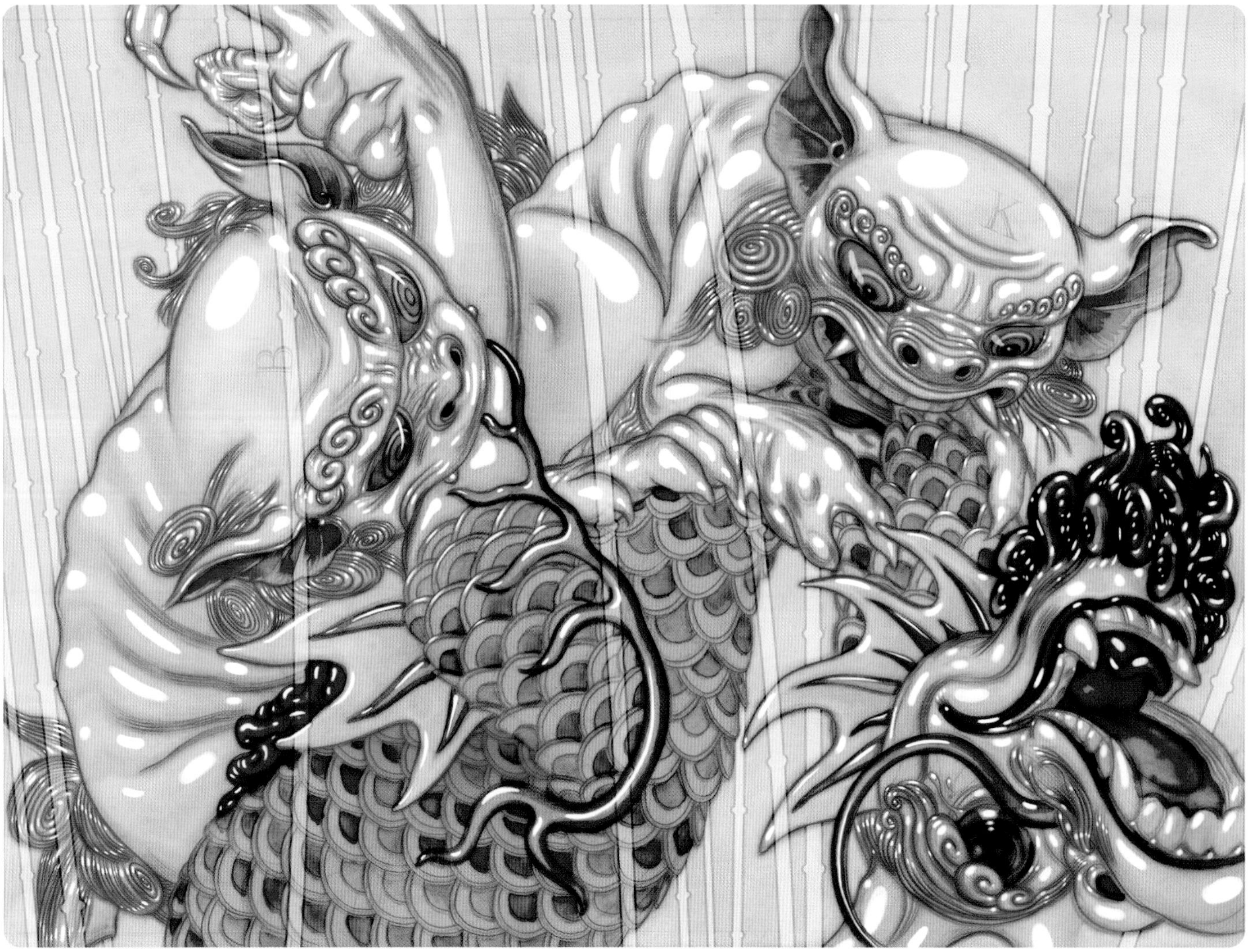

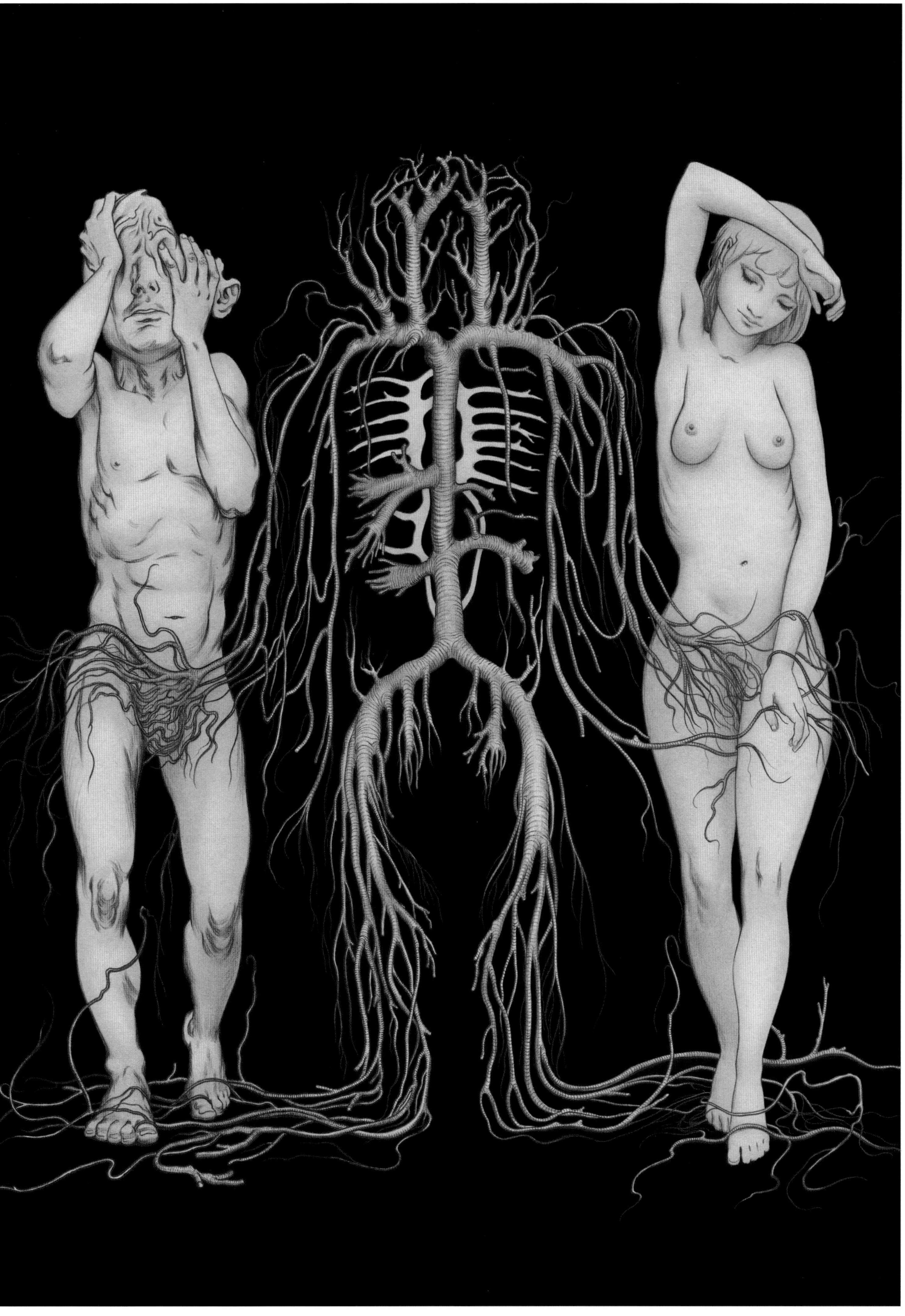

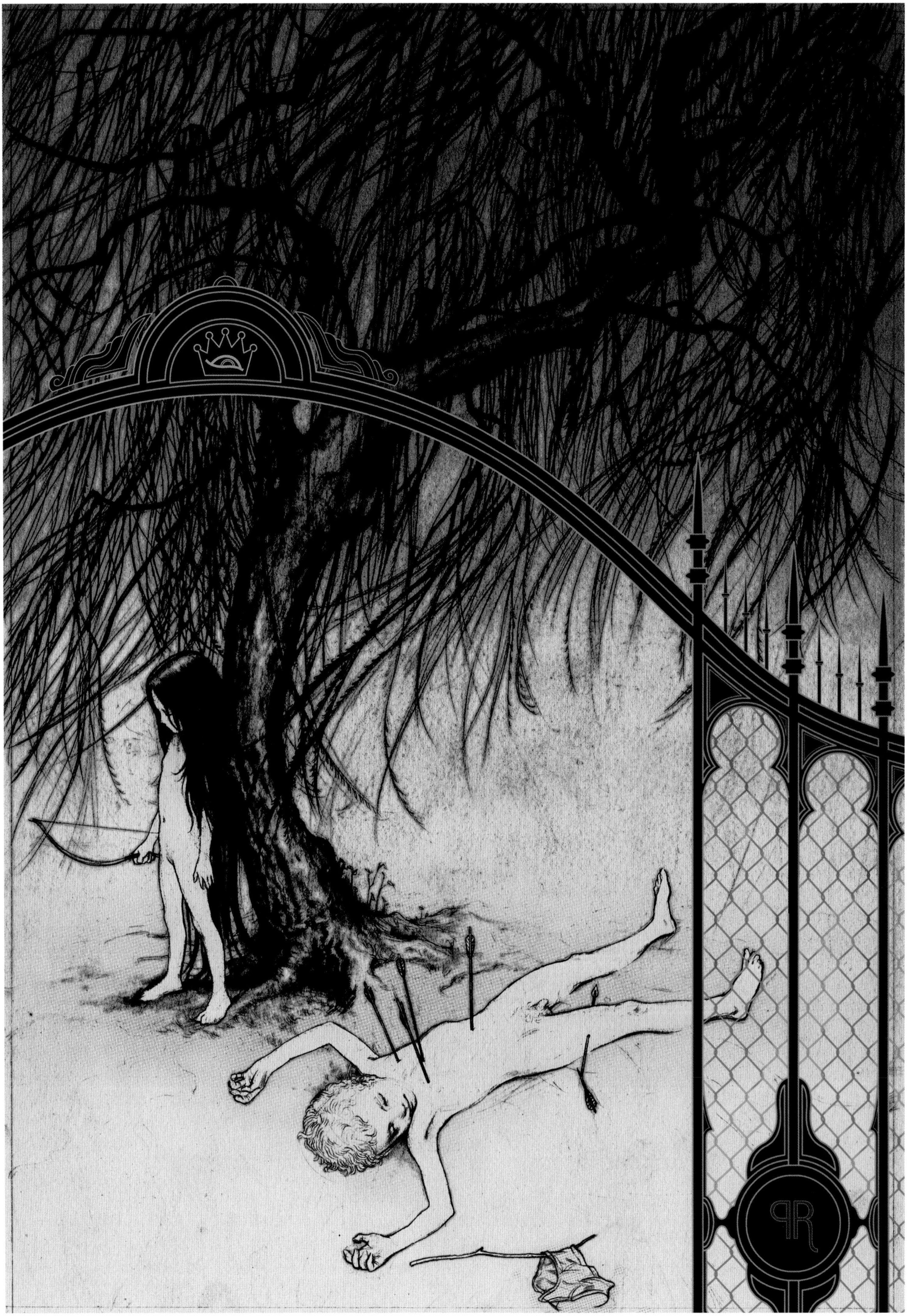

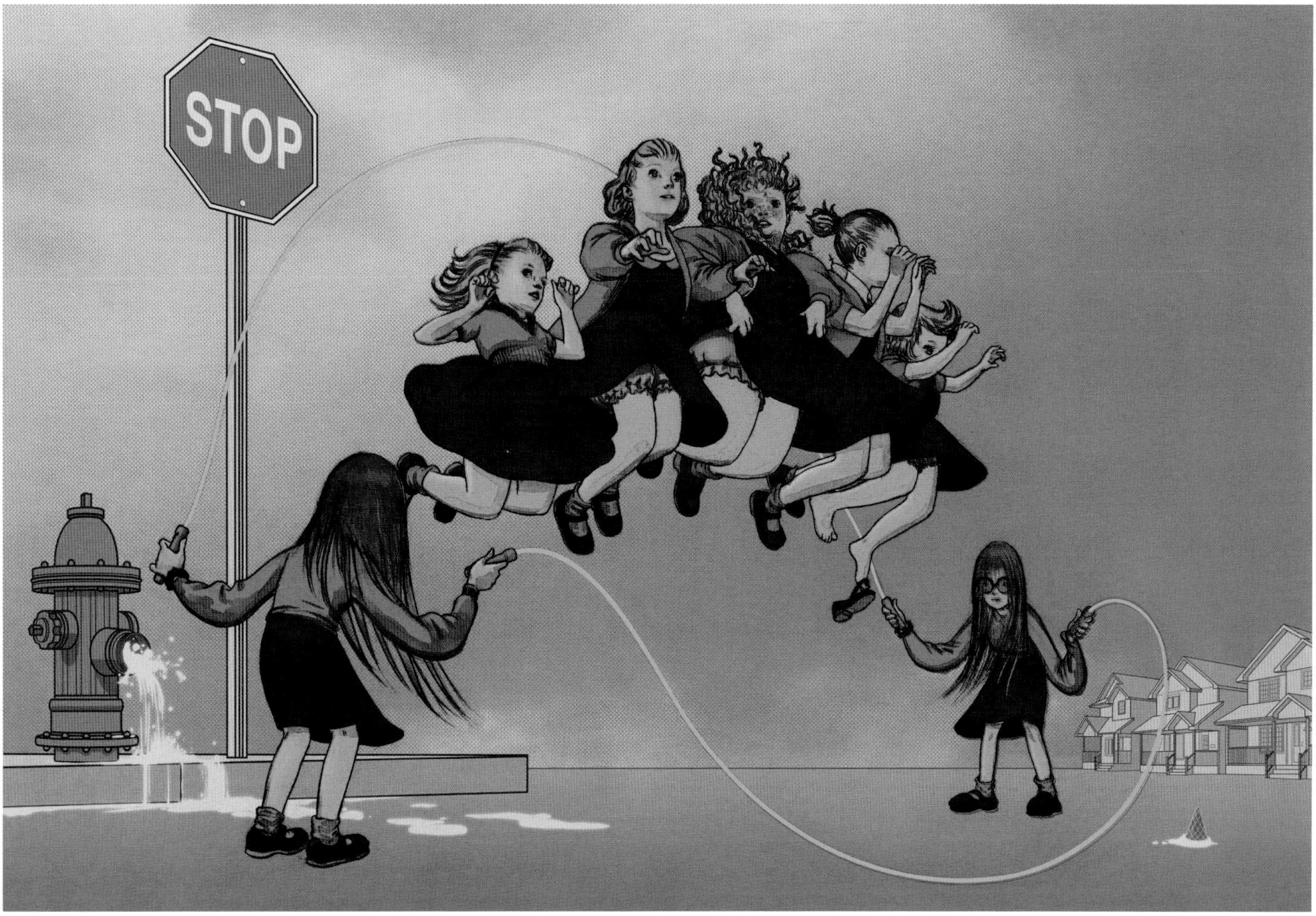
STOP

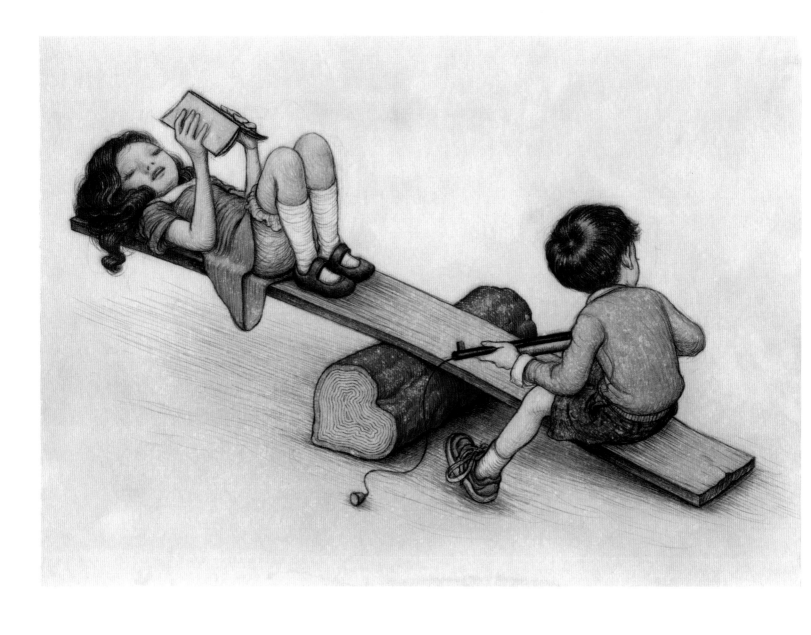

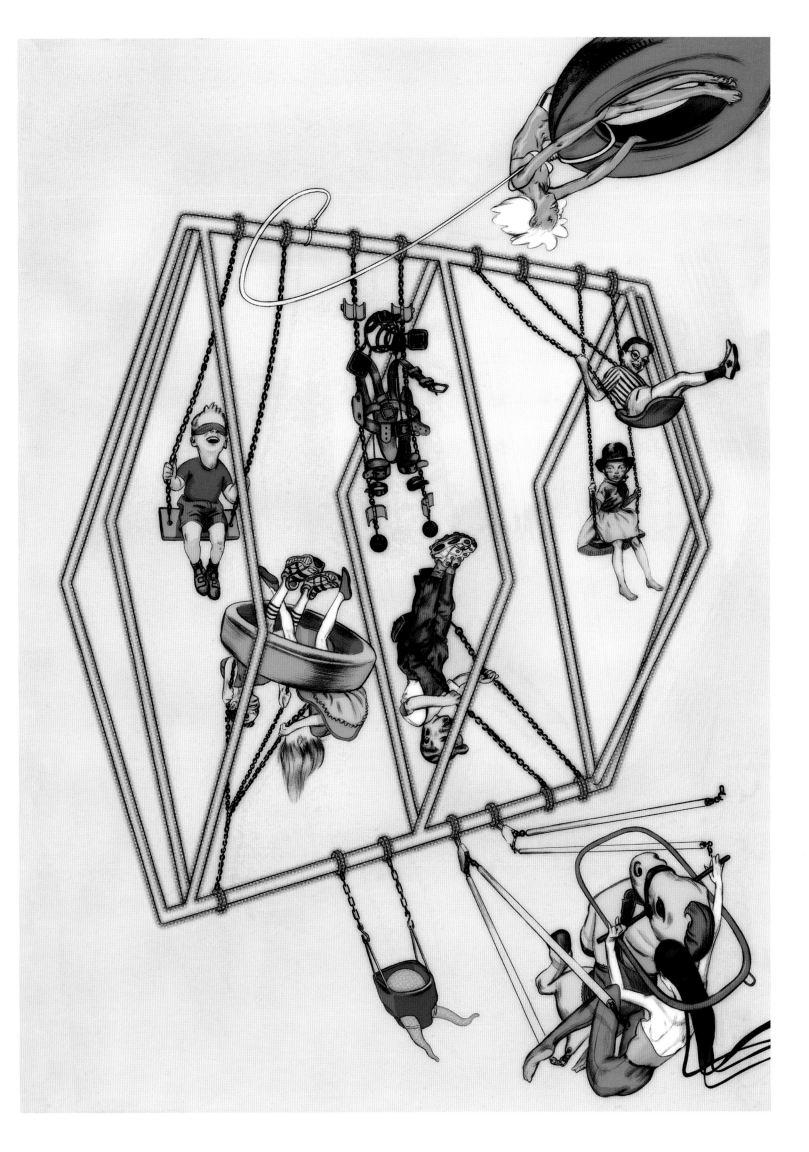

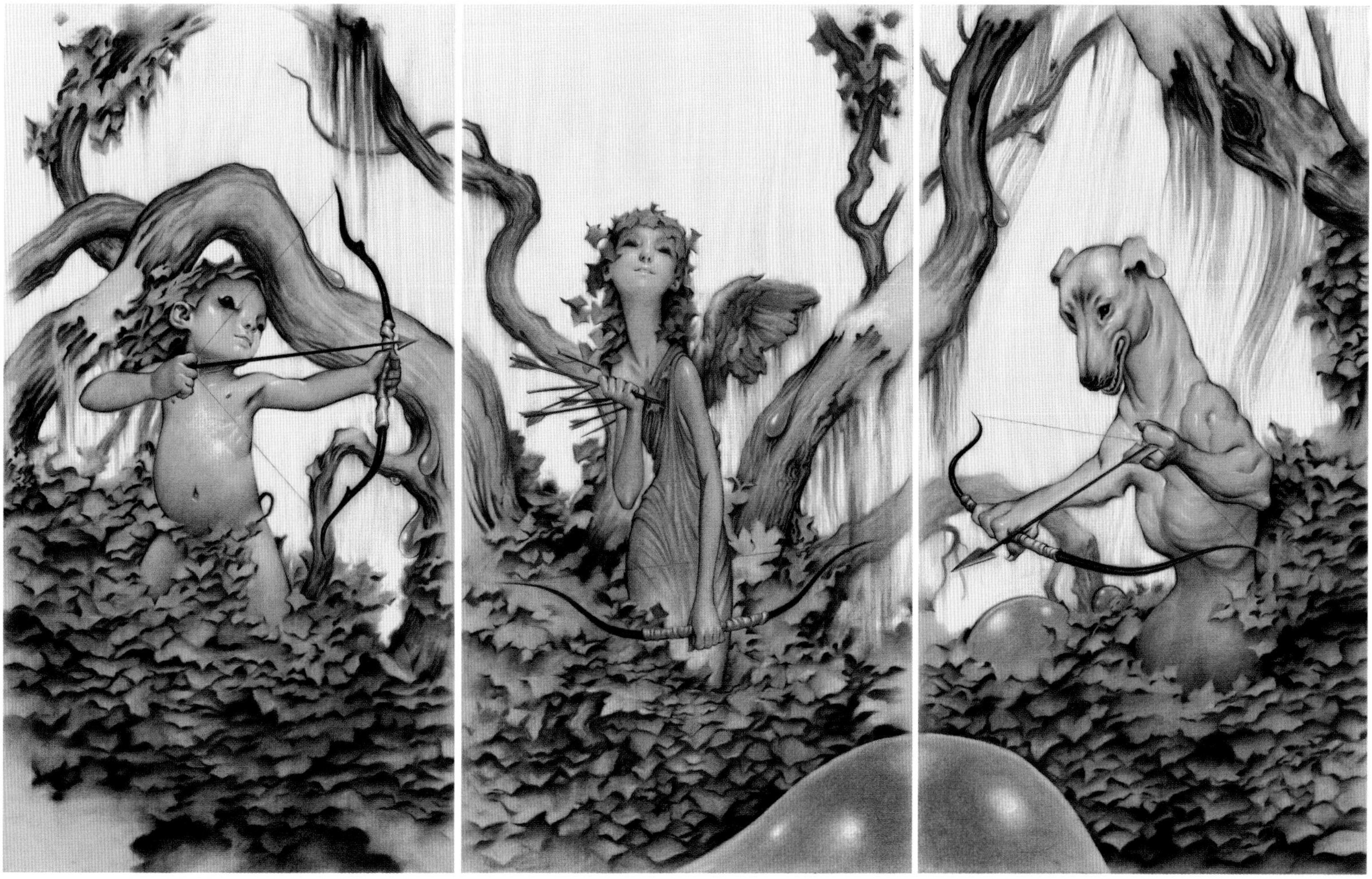

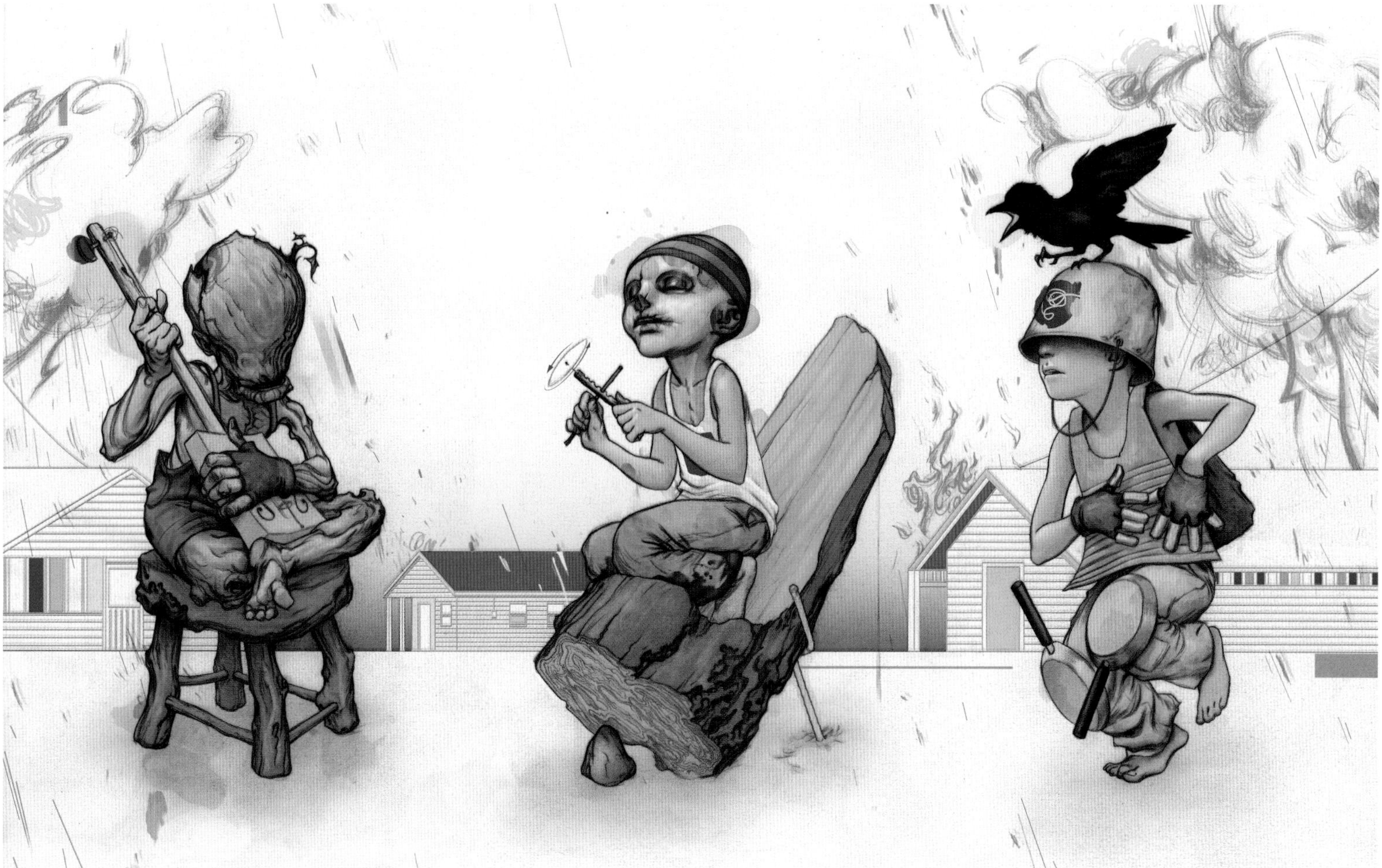

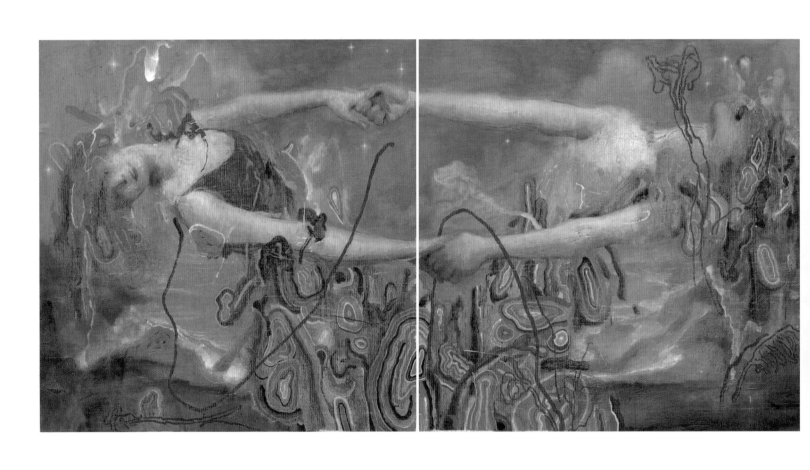

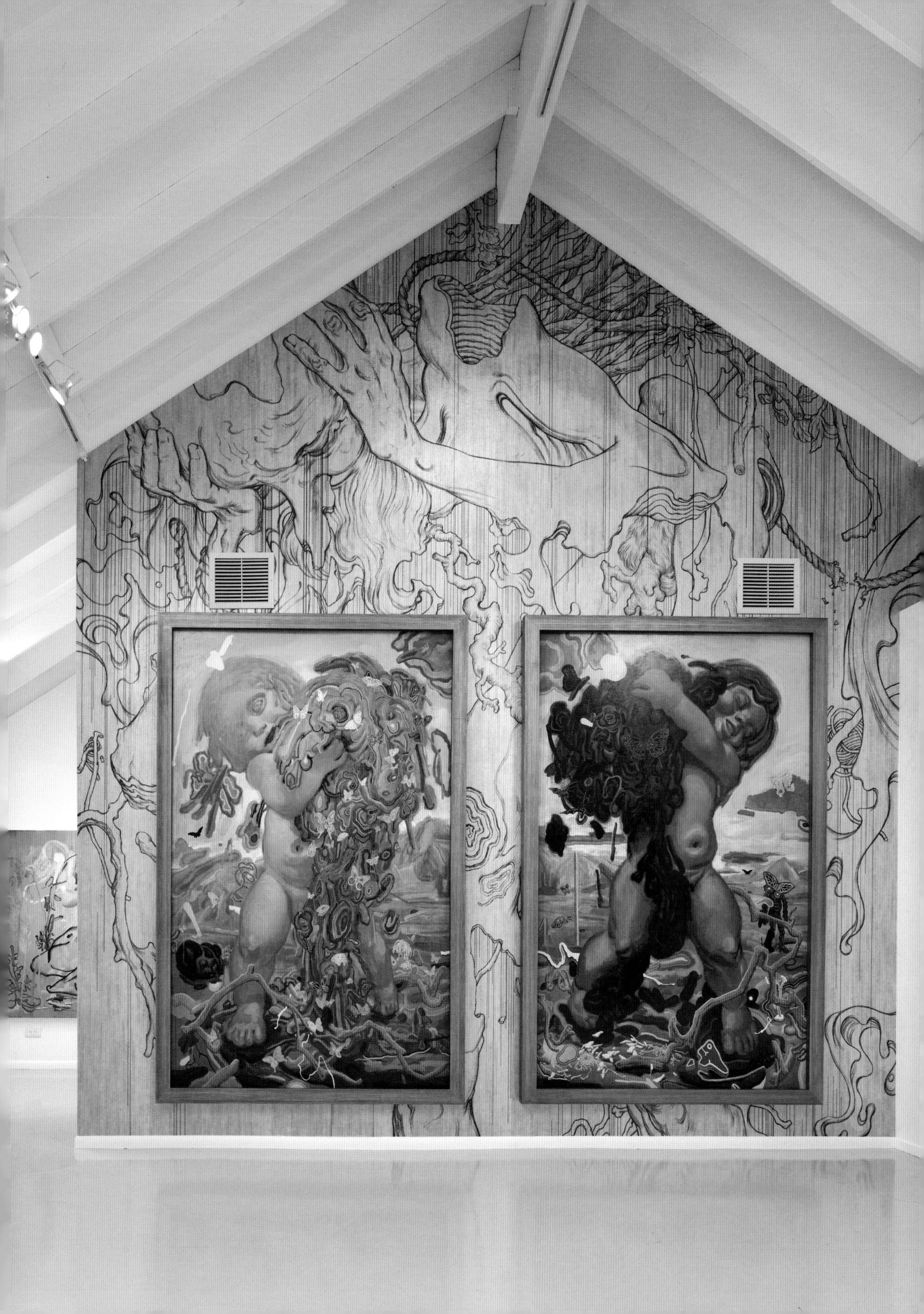

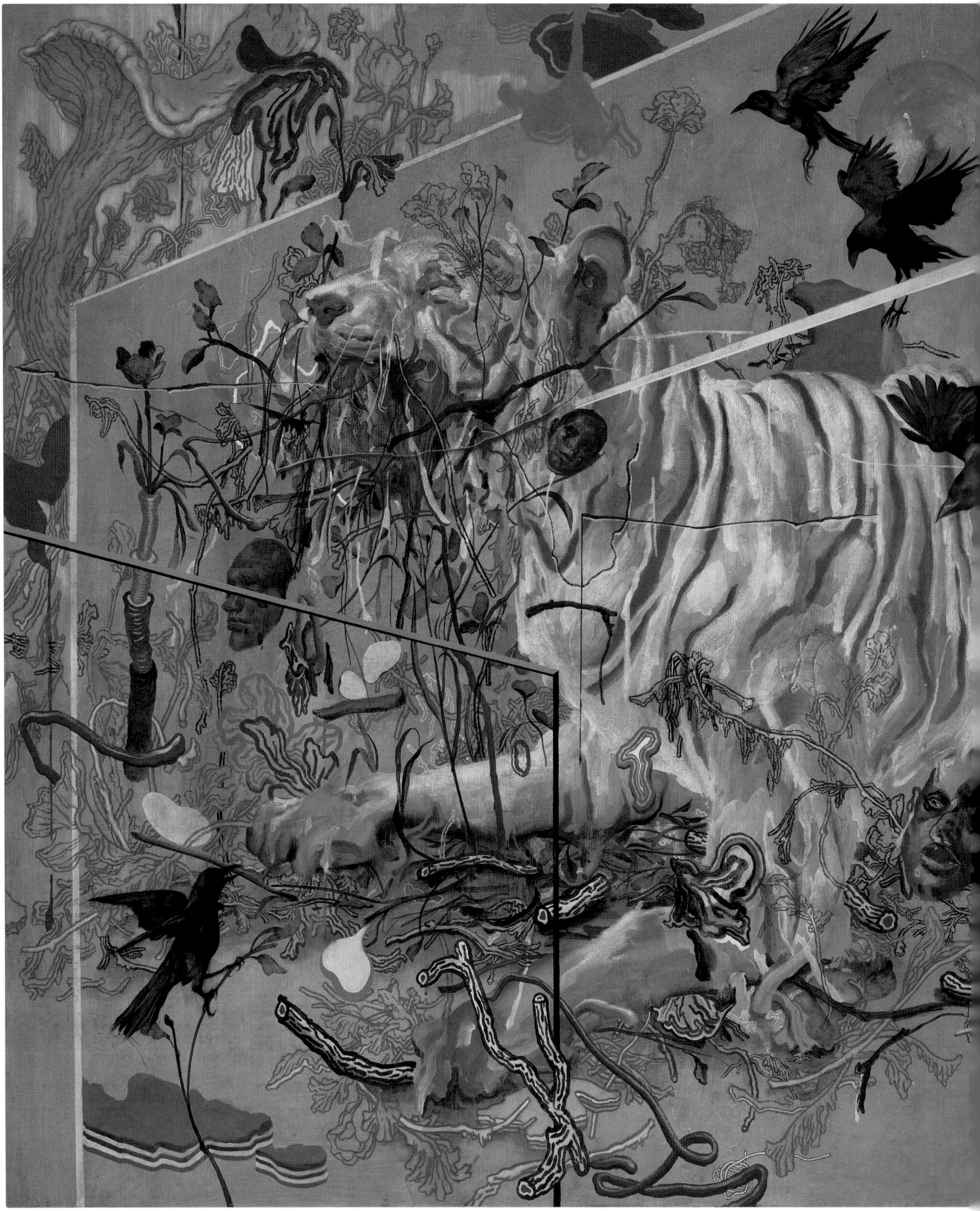

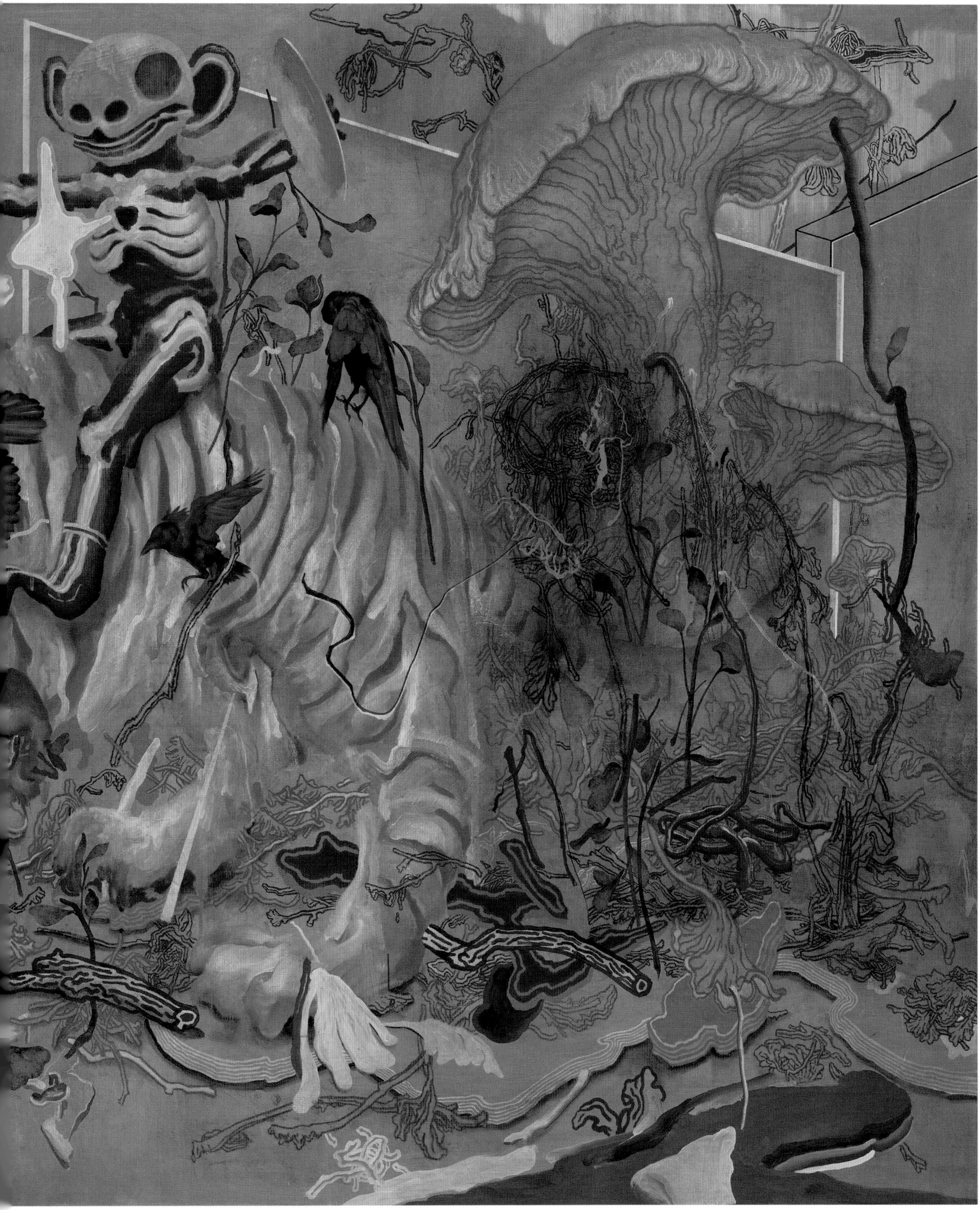

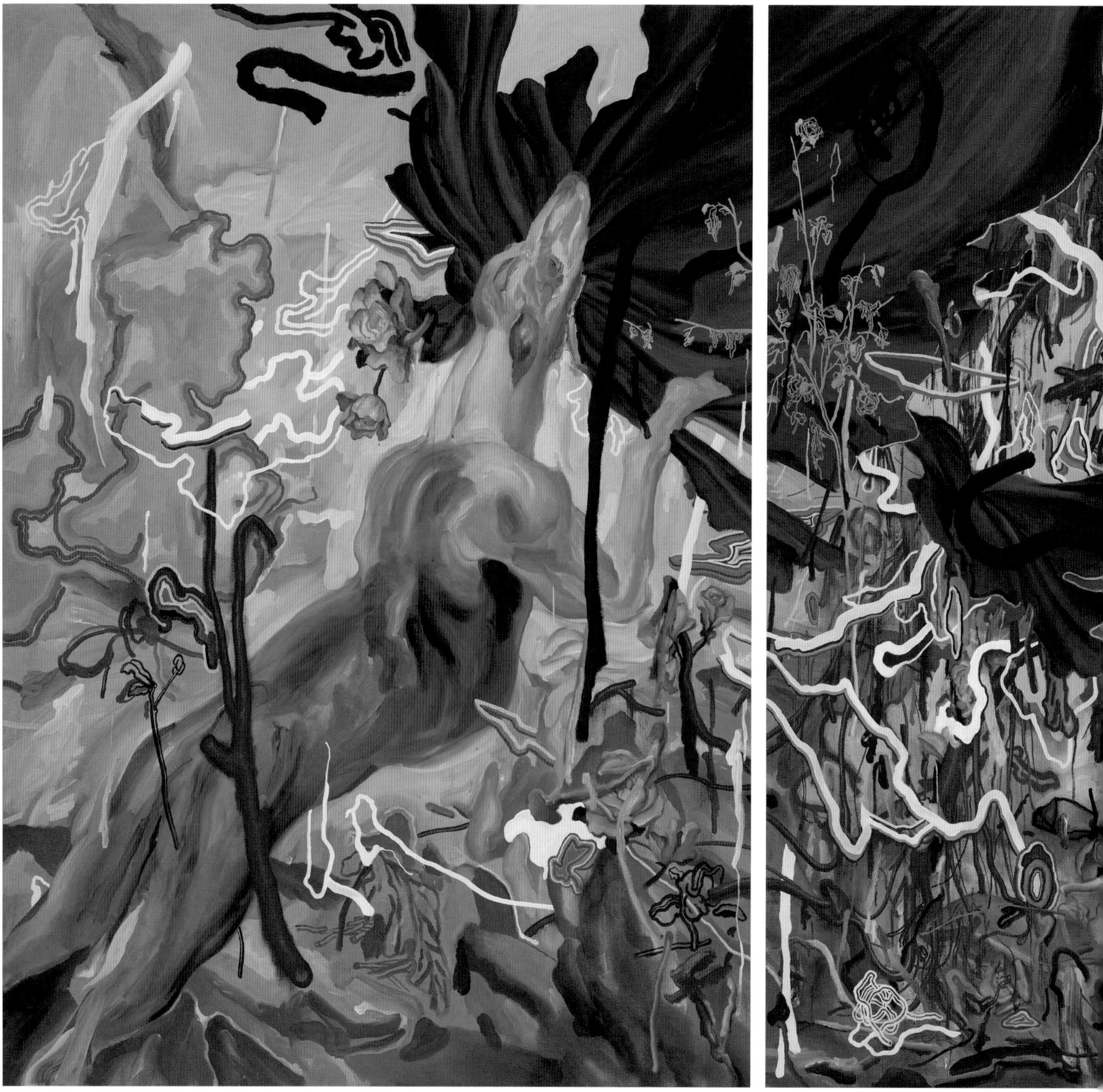

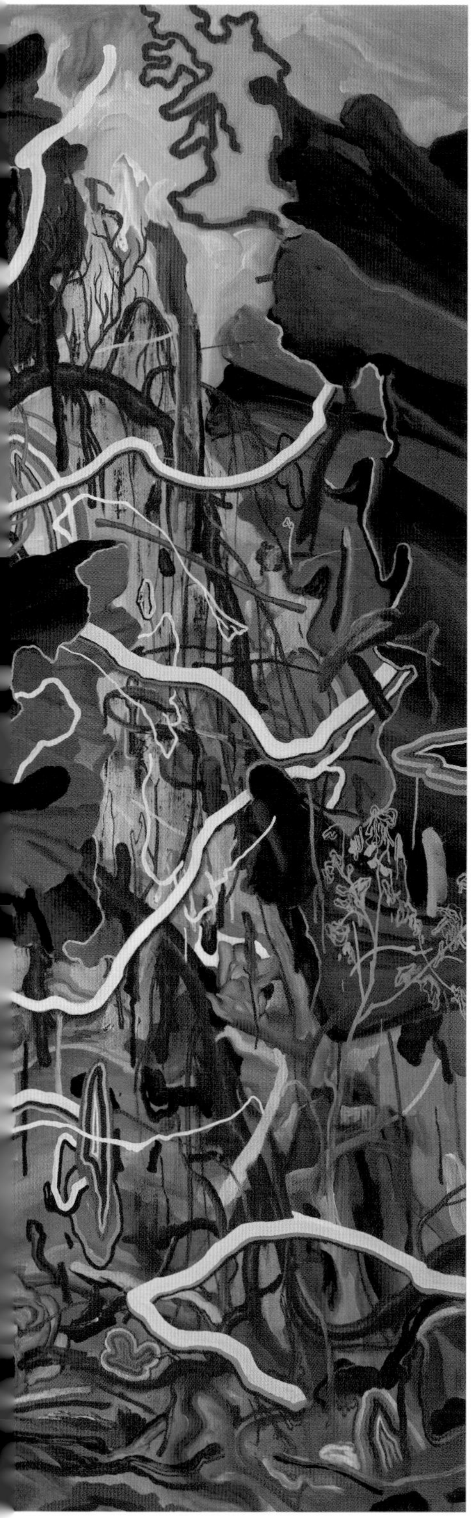

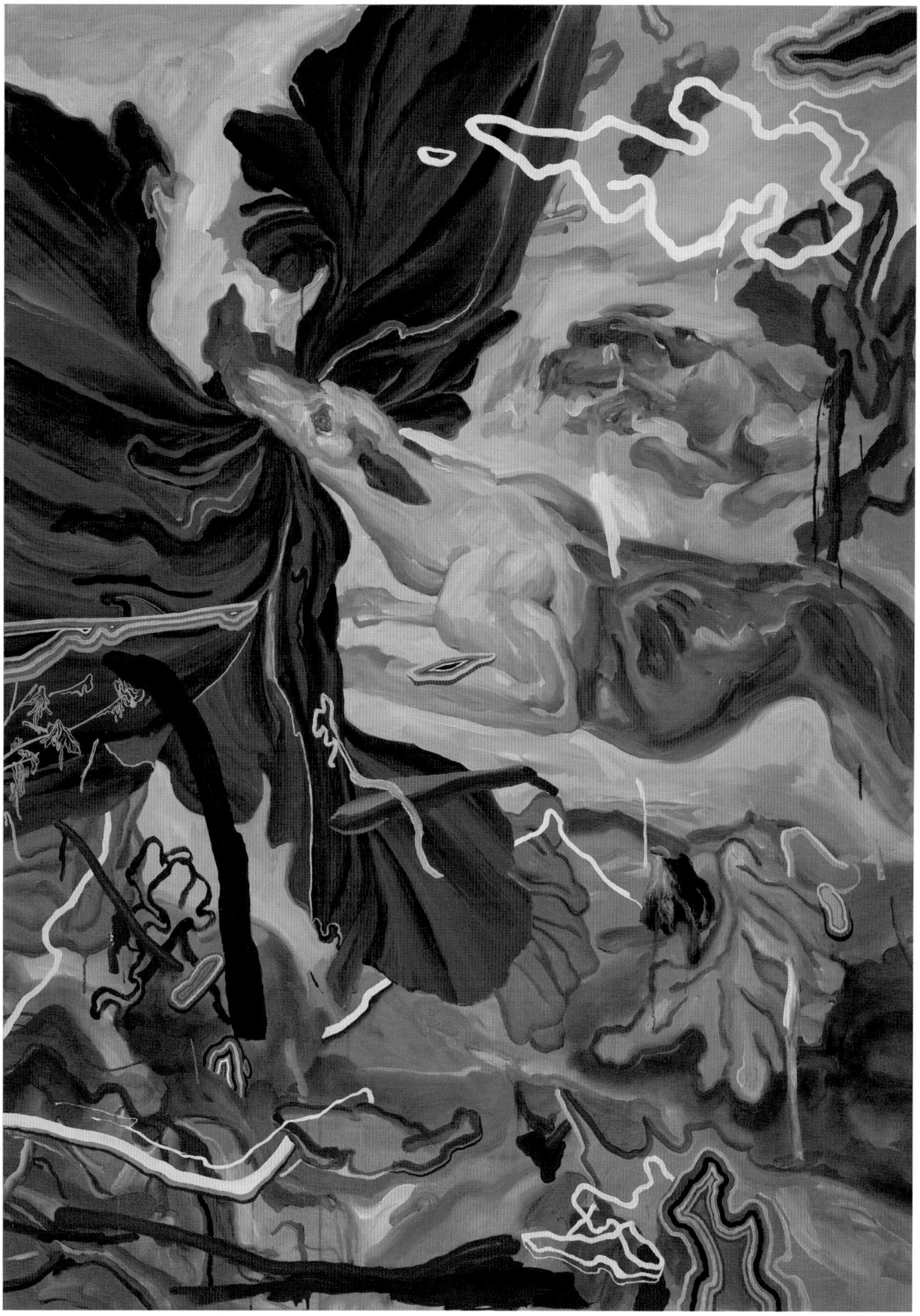

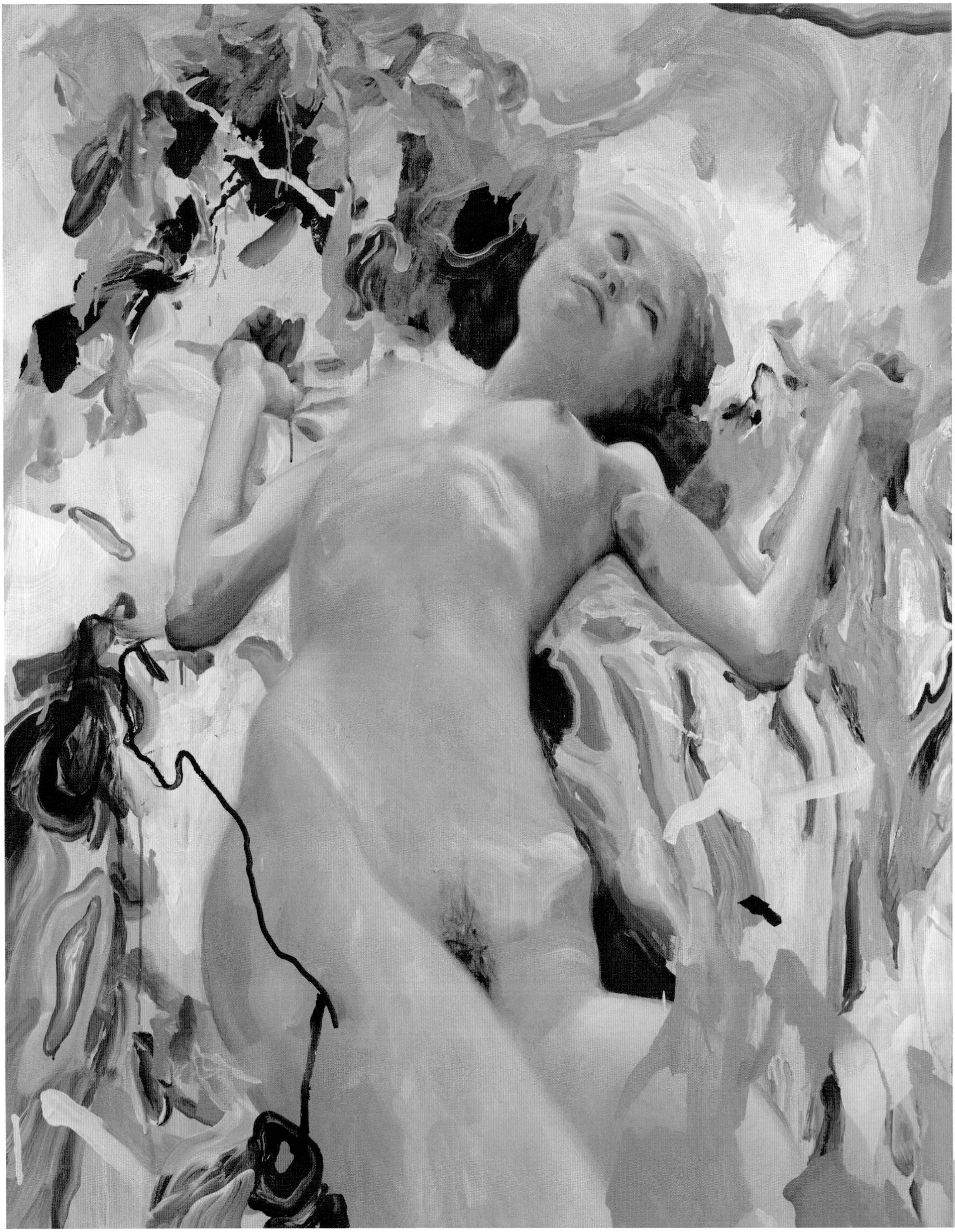

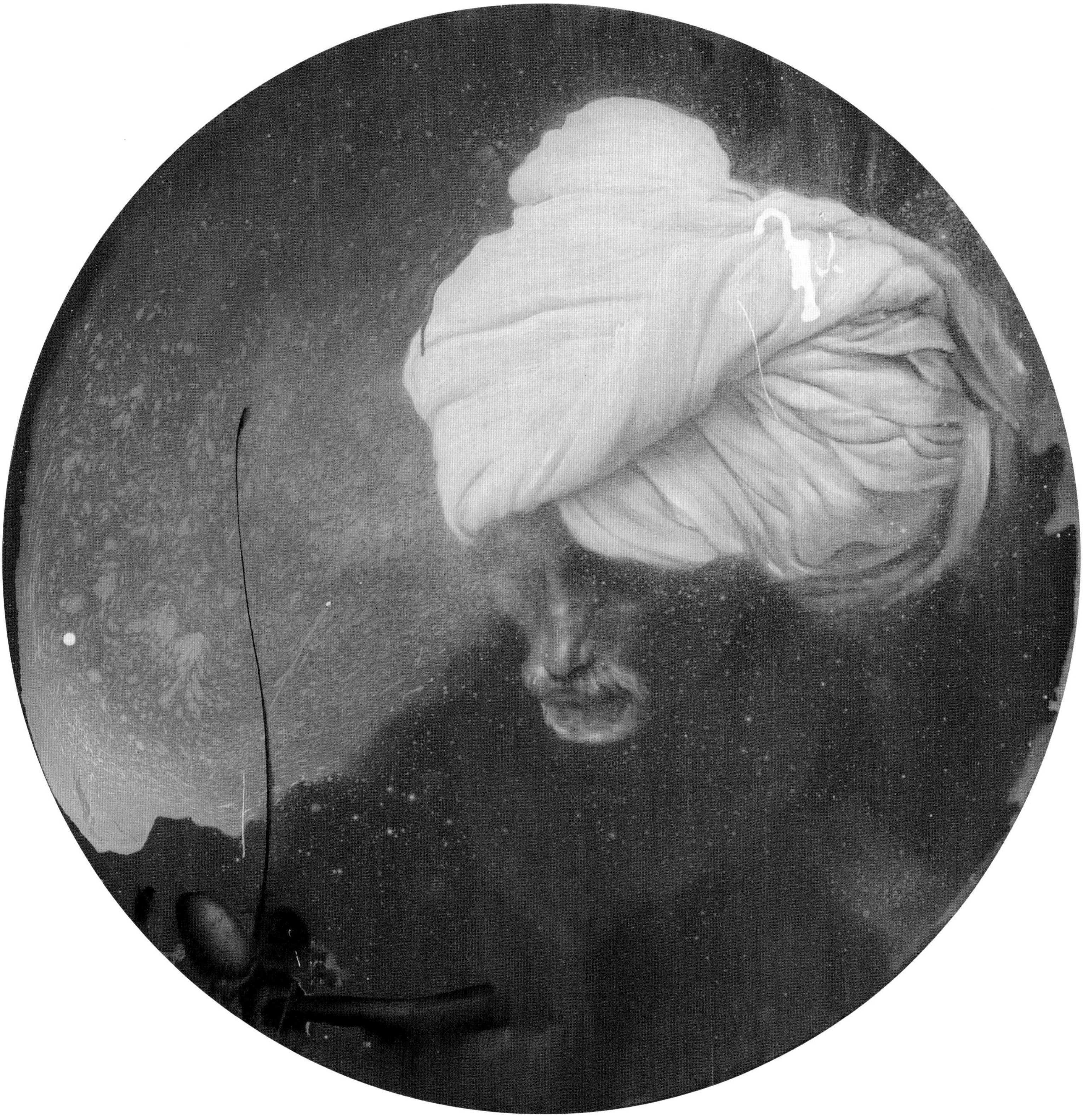

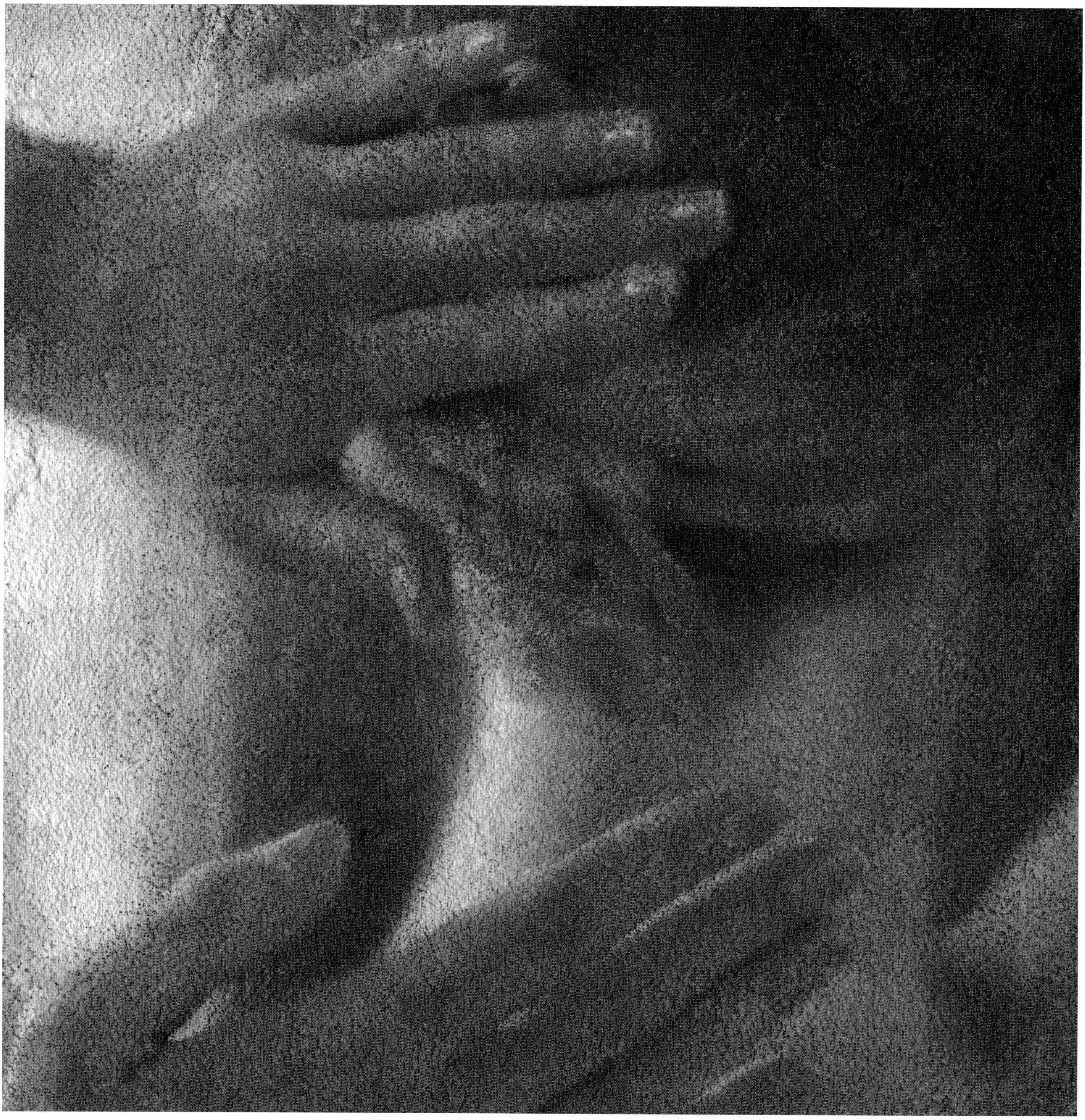

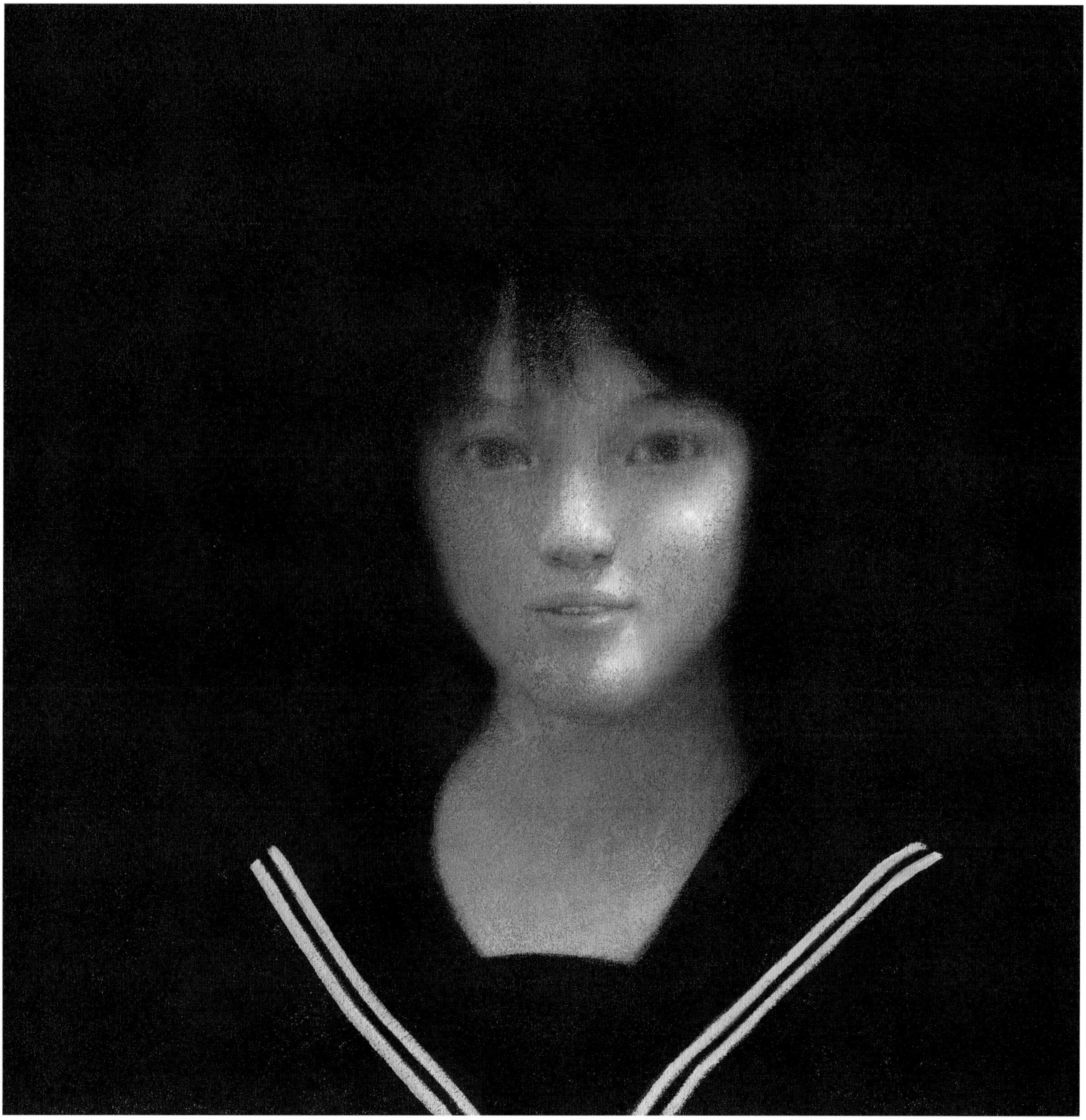

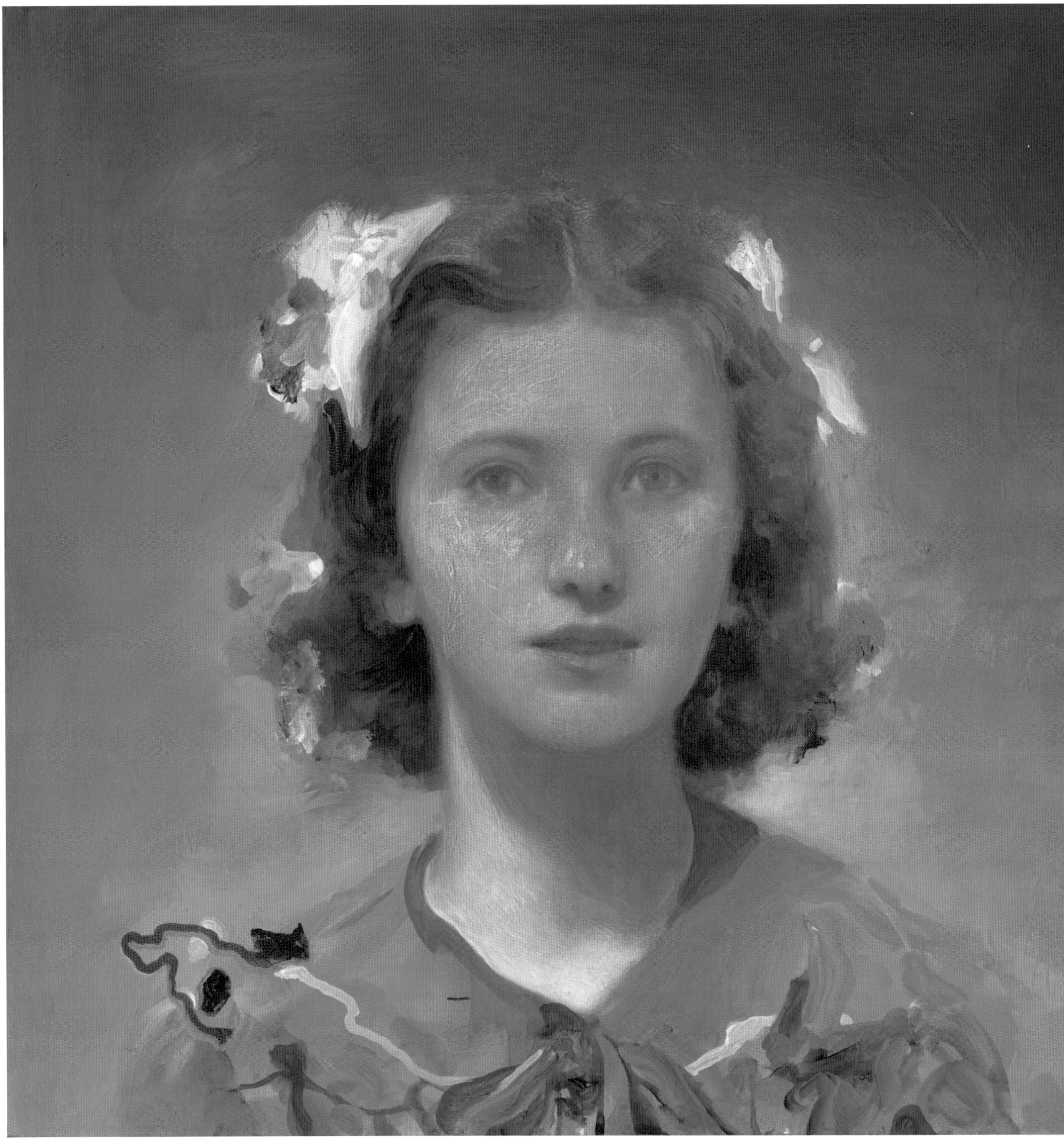

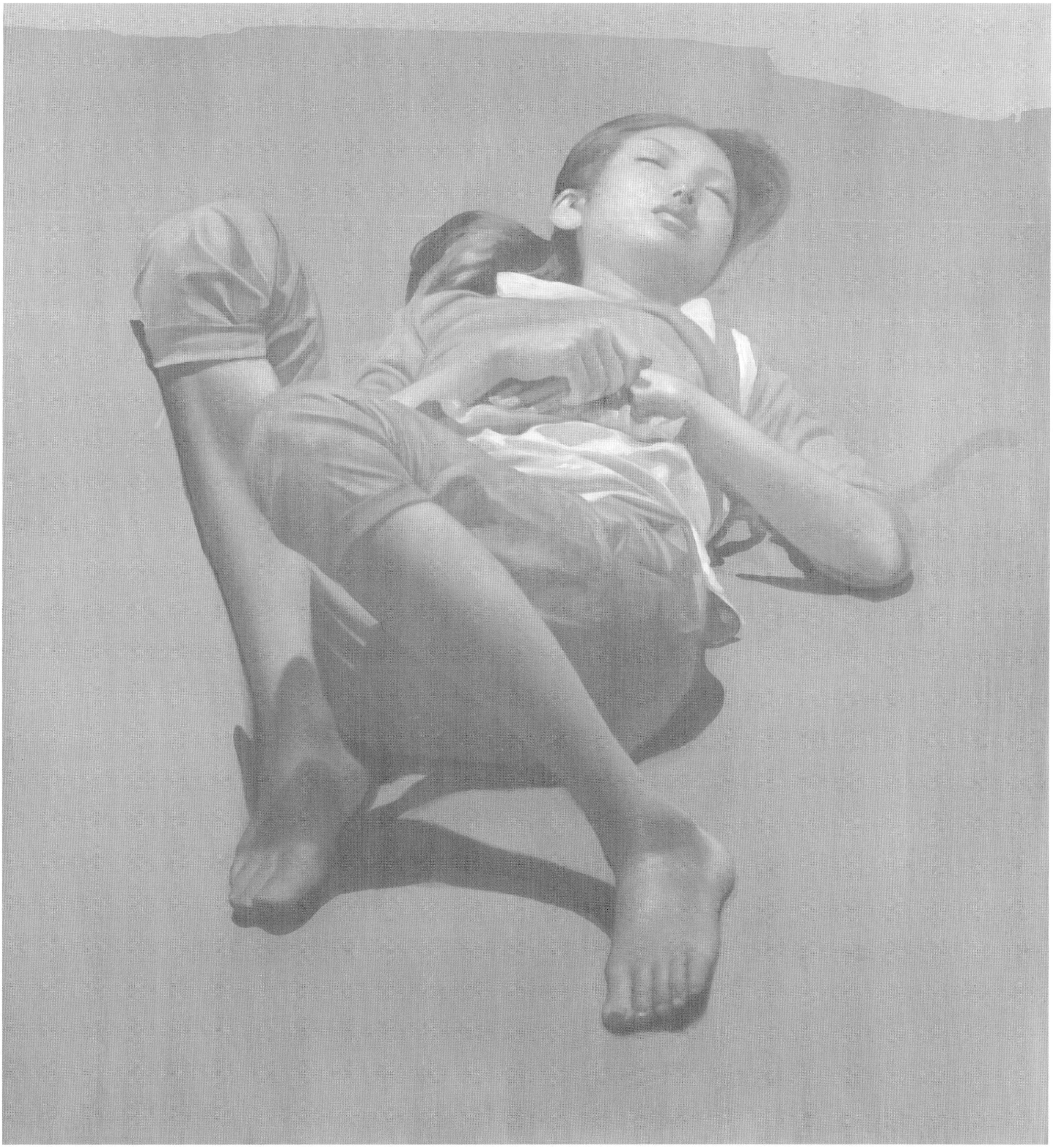

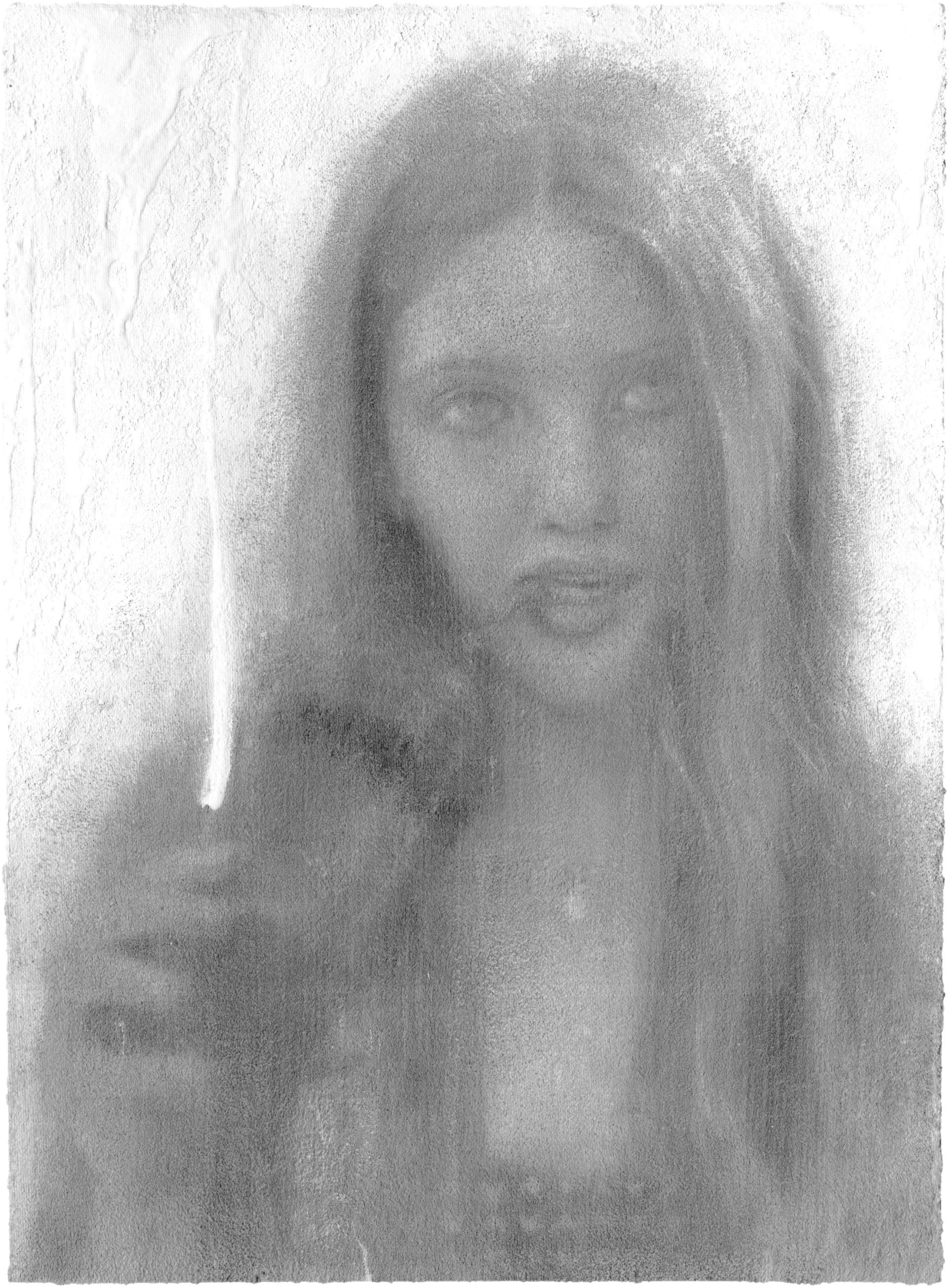

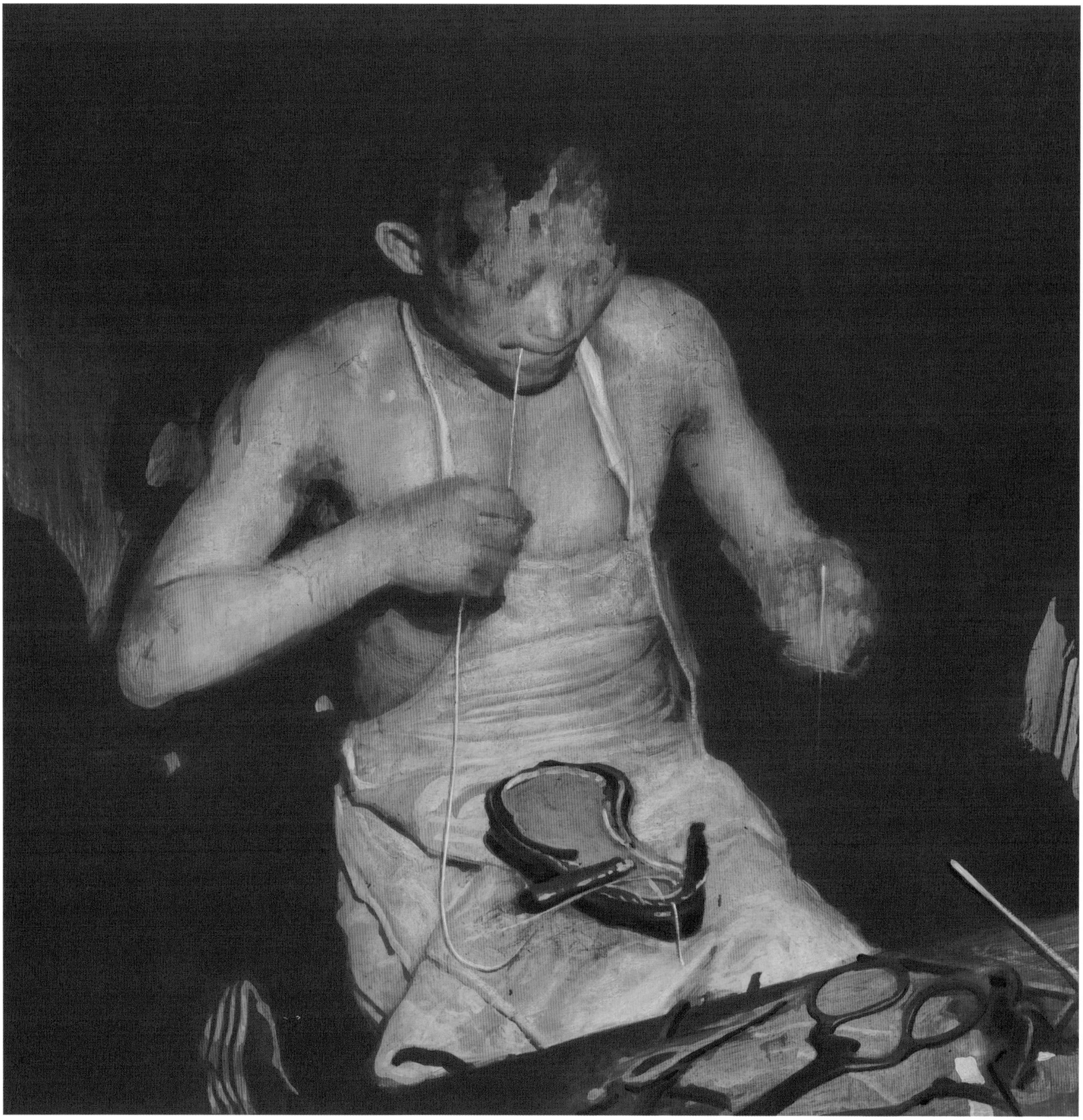

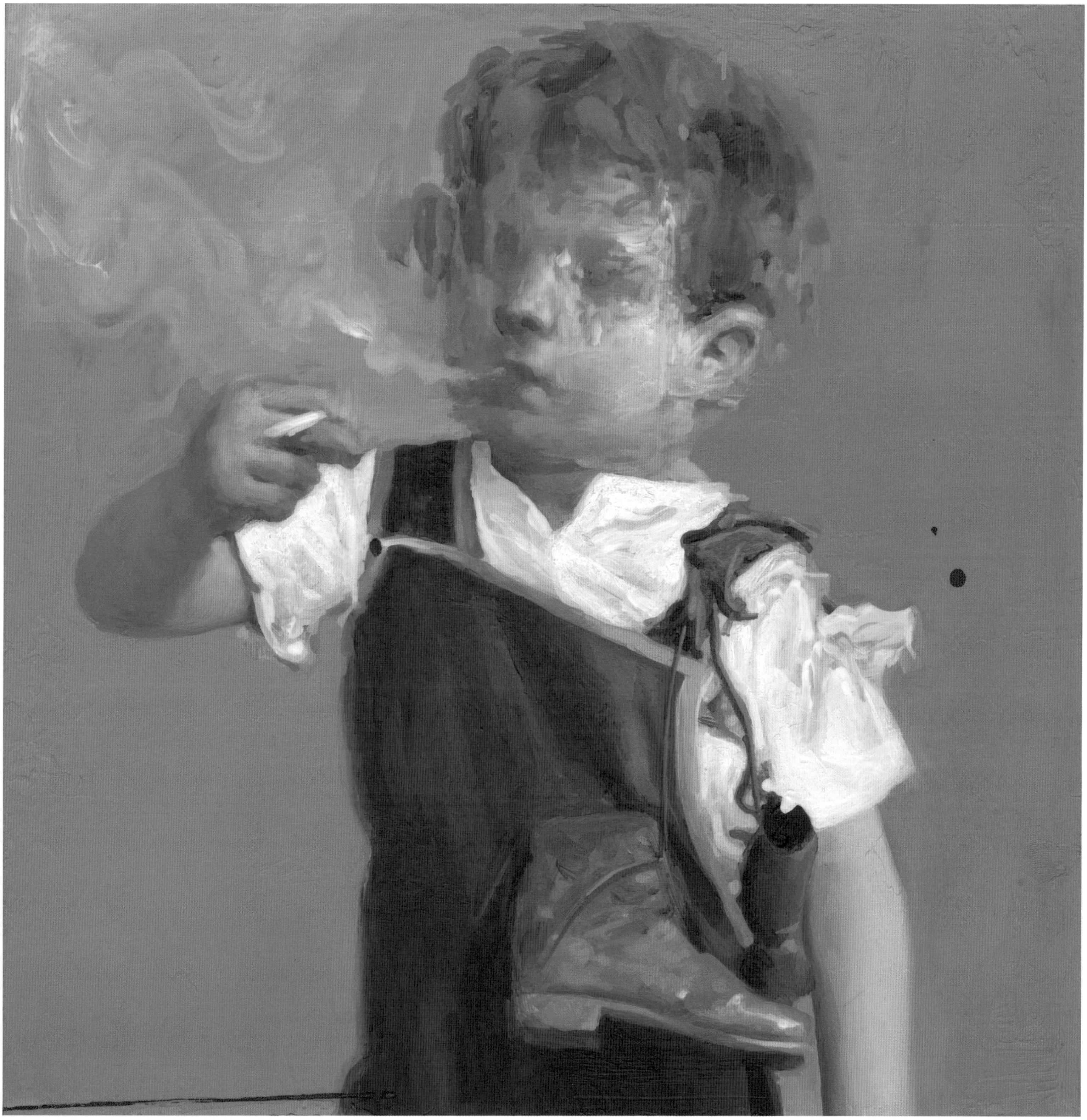

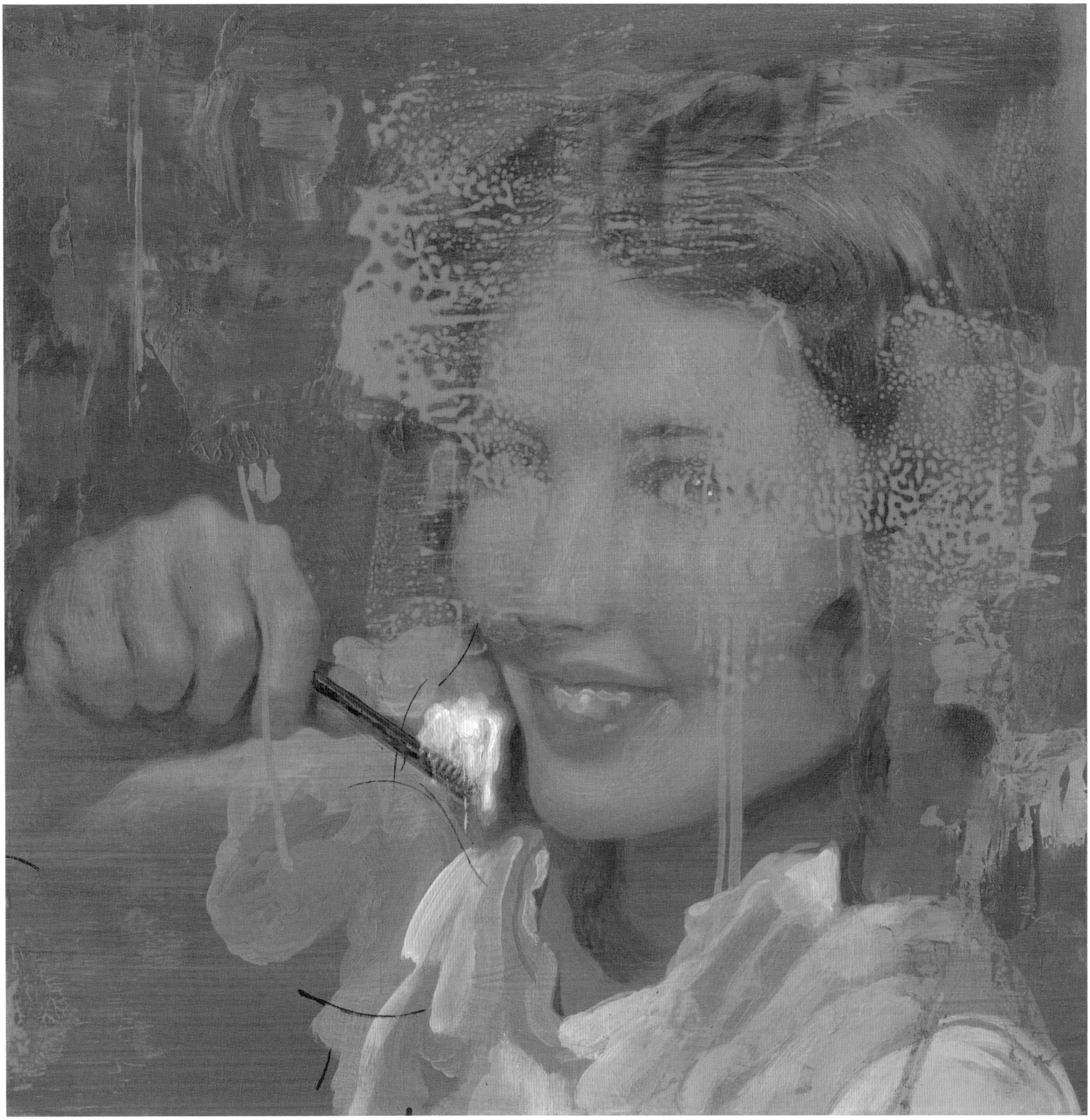

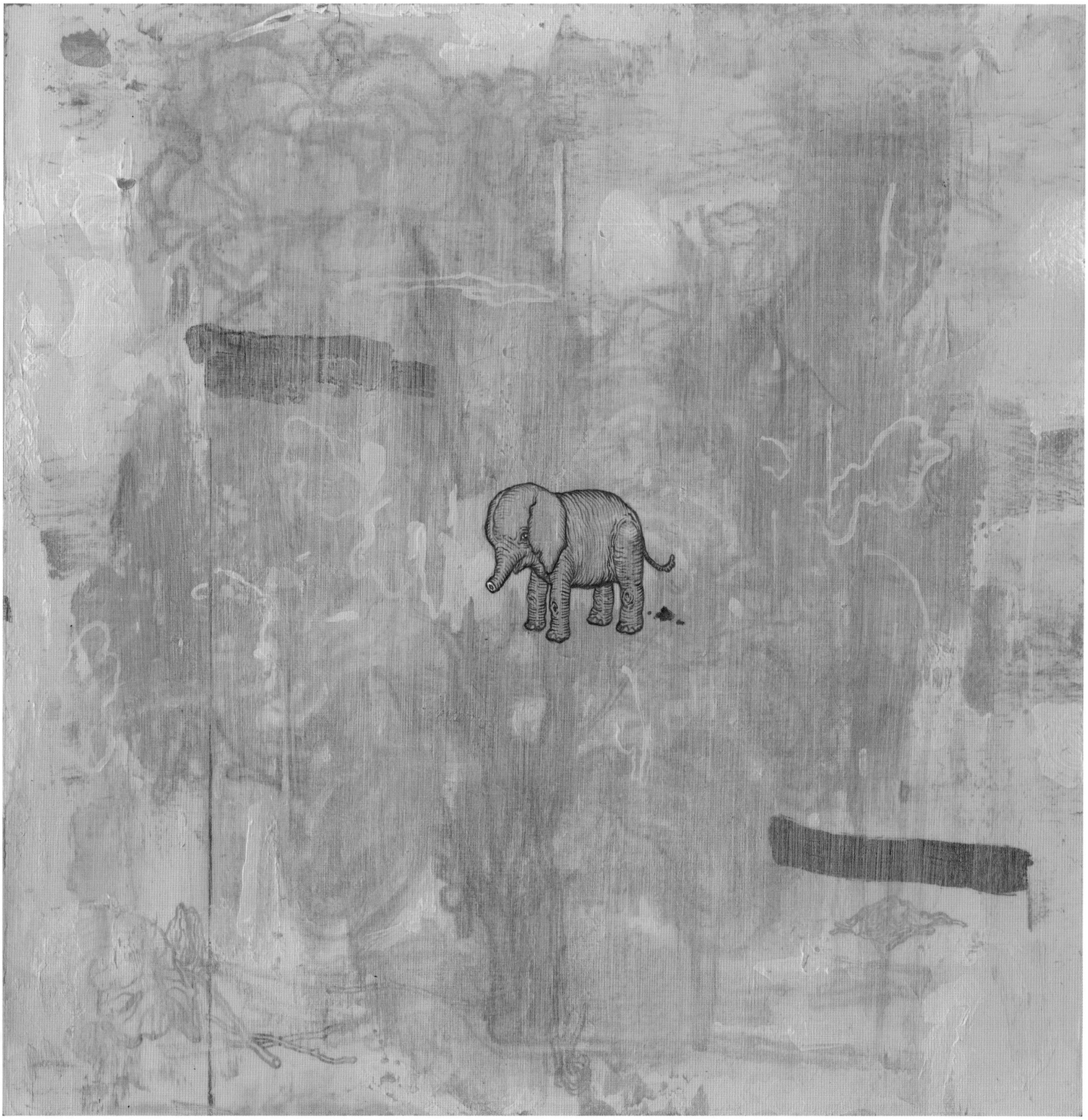

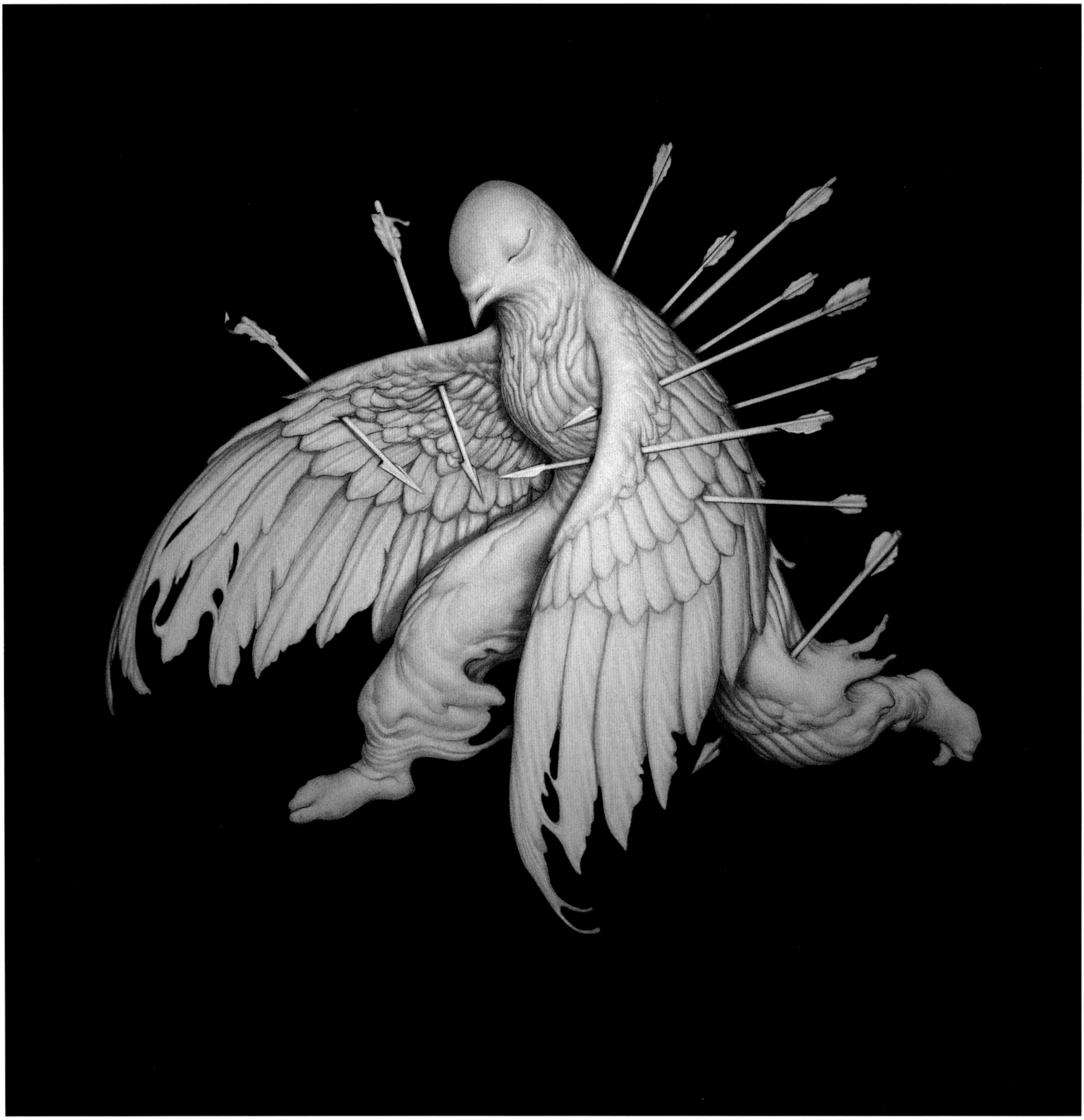

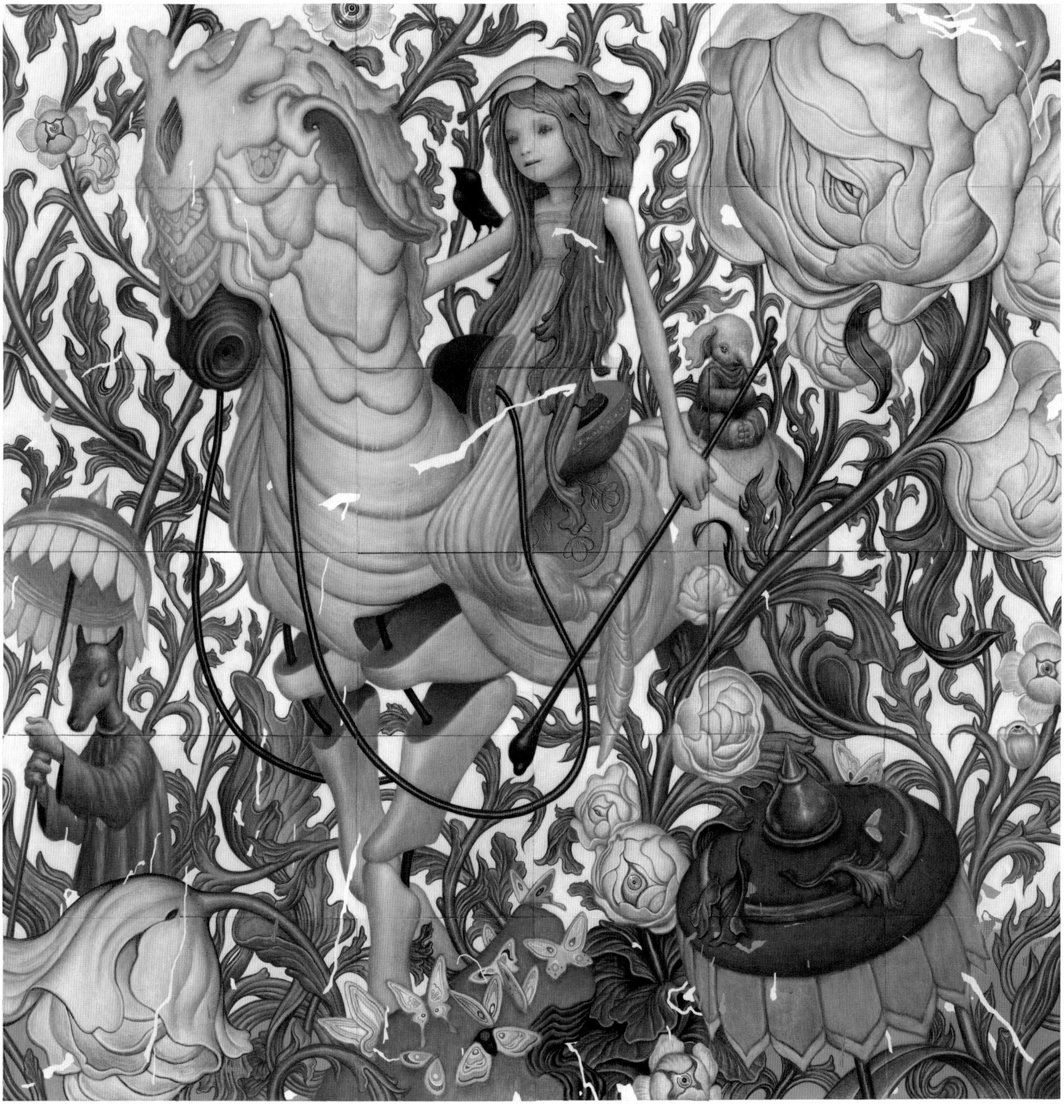

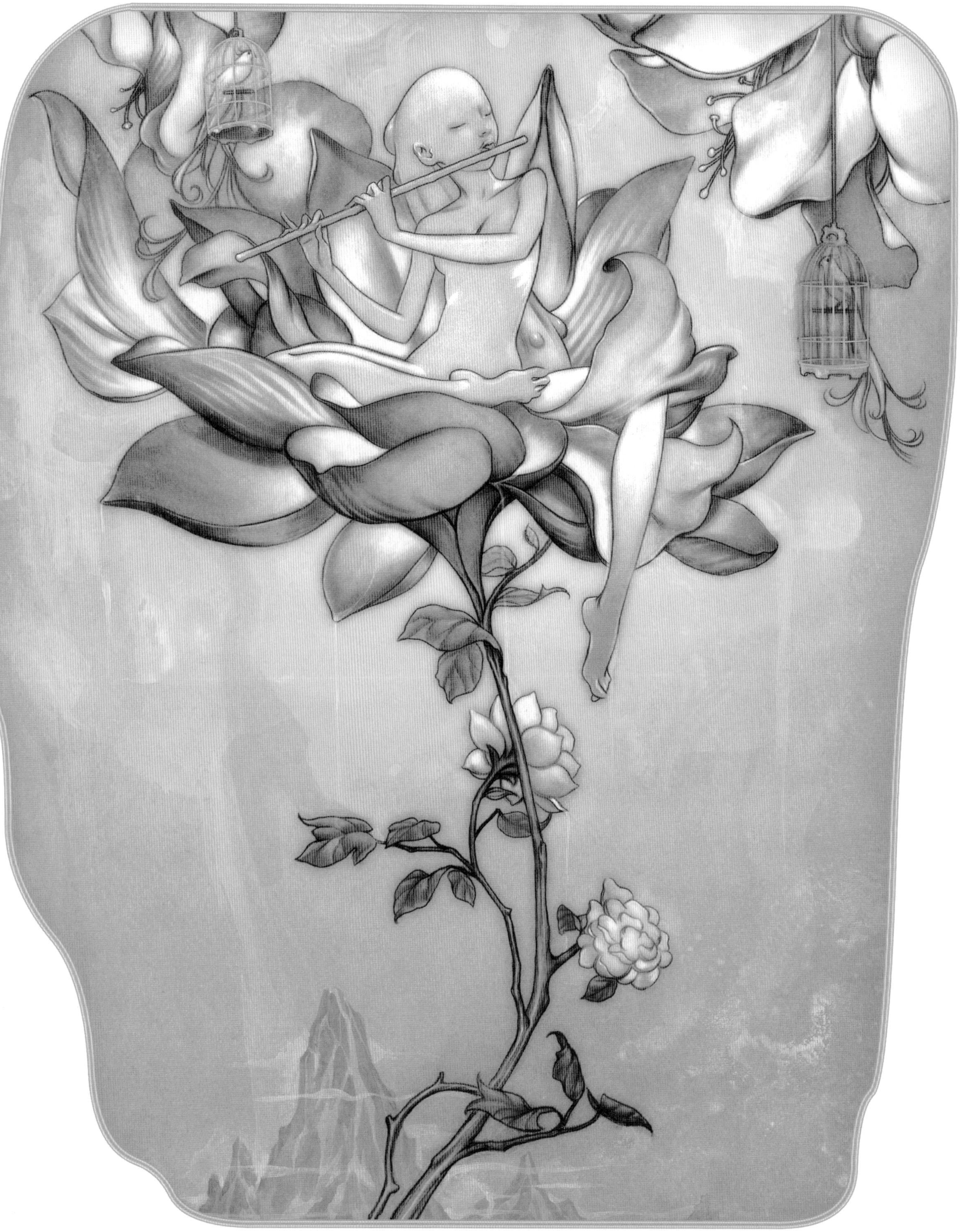

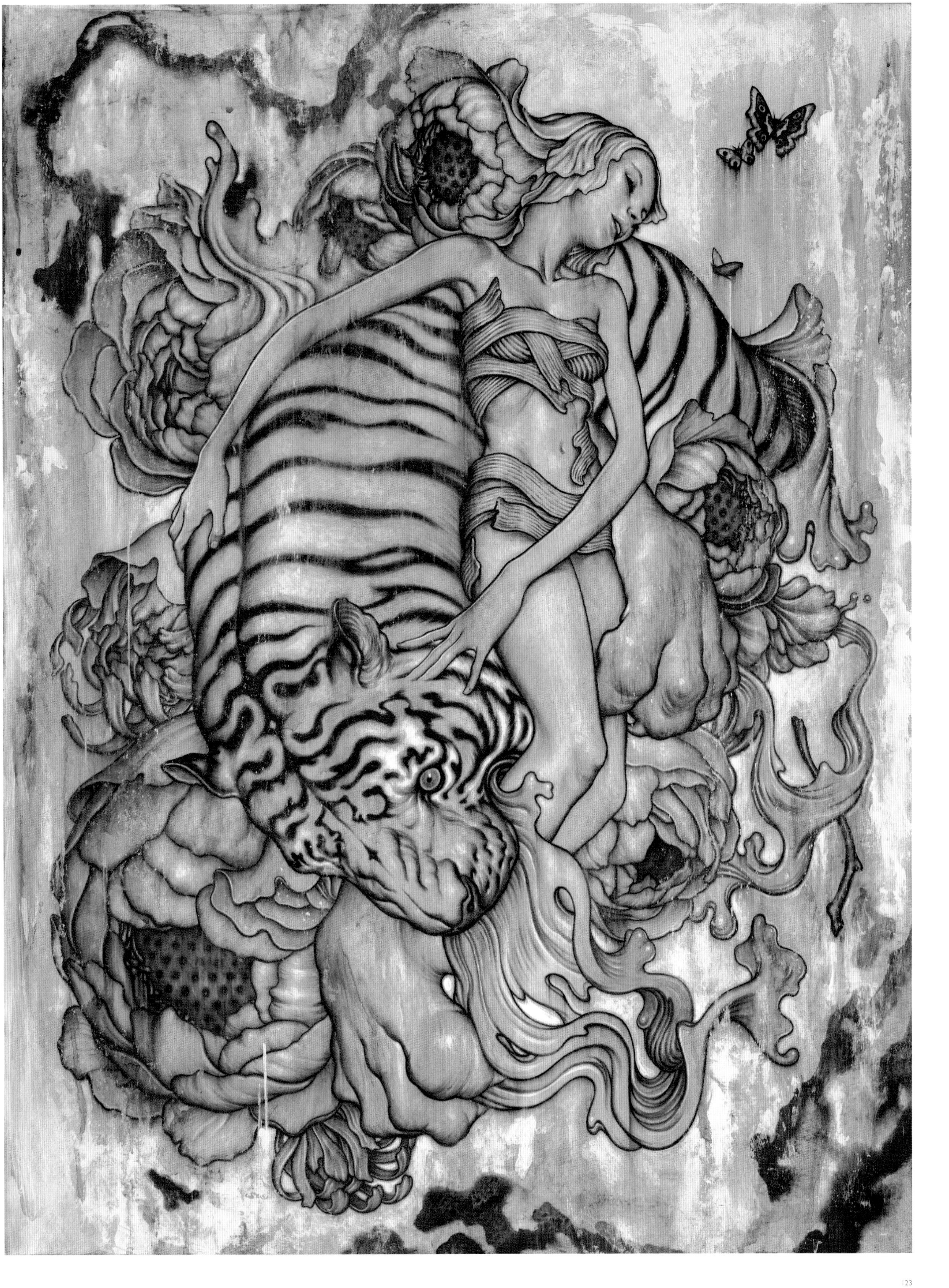

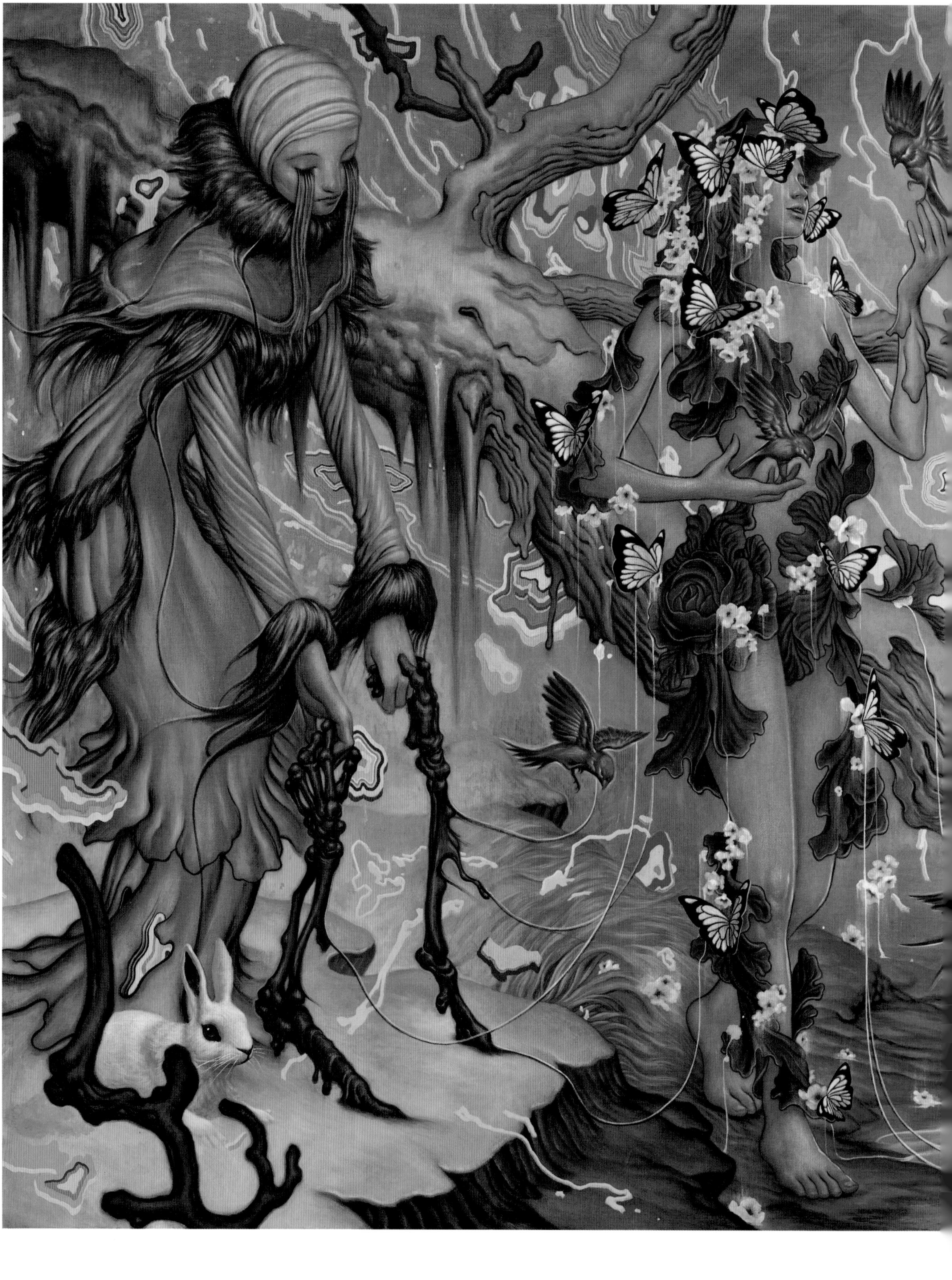

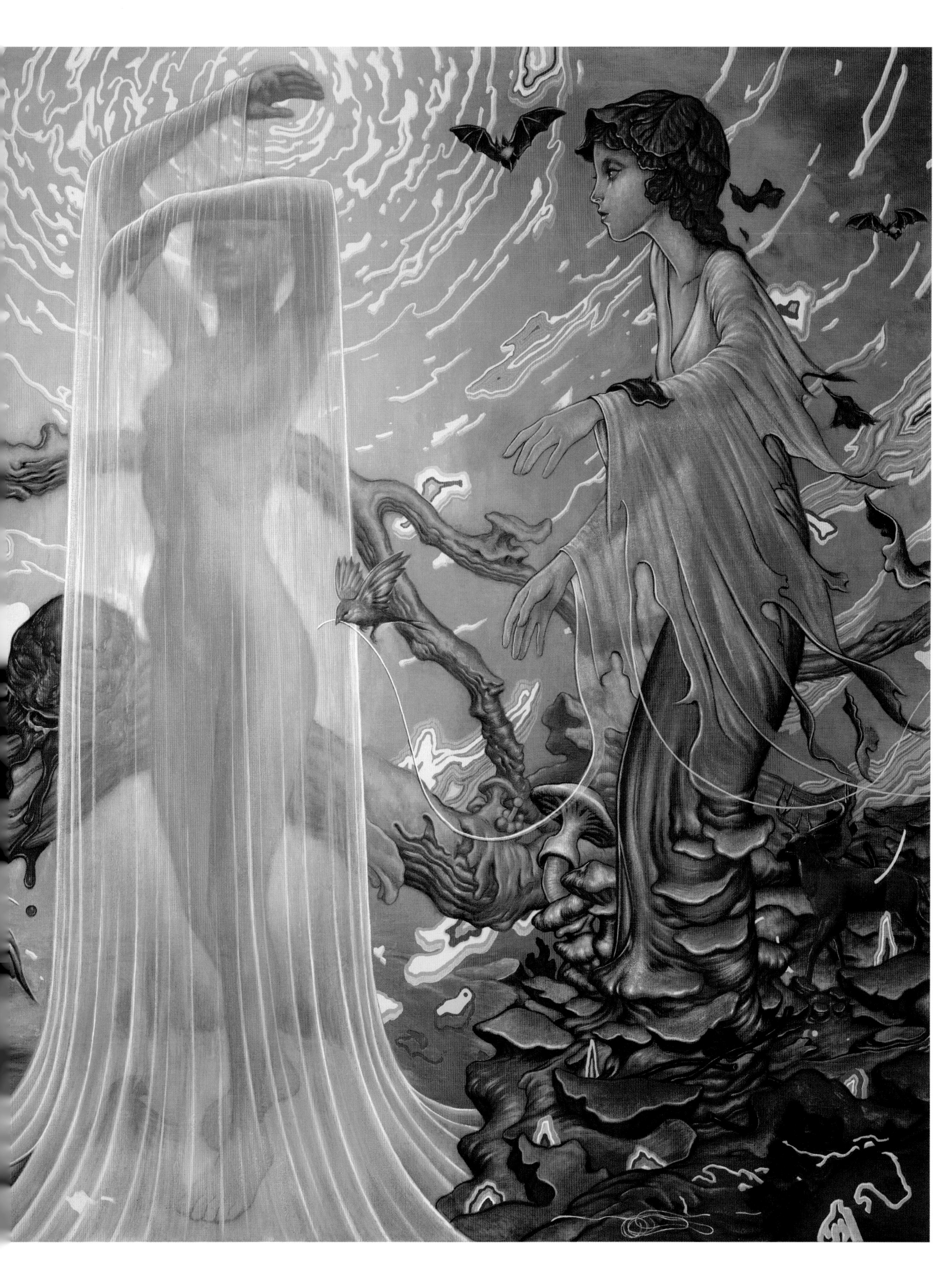

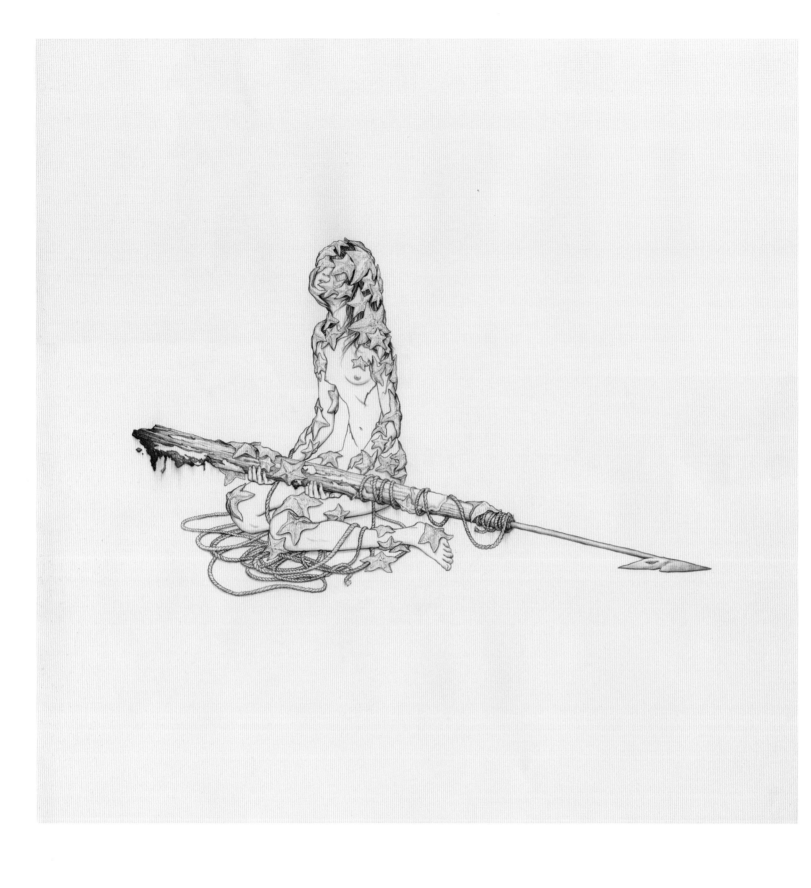

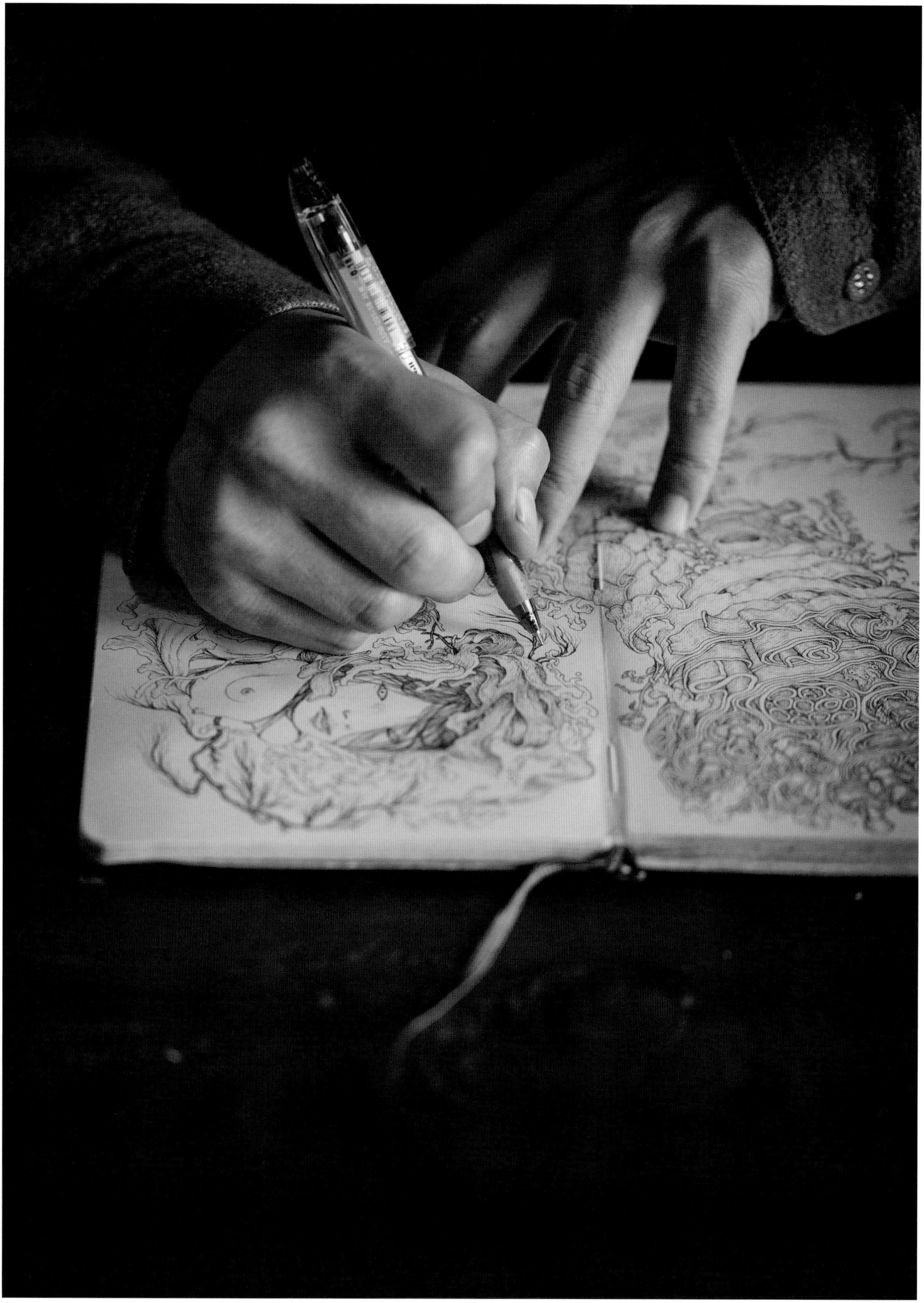

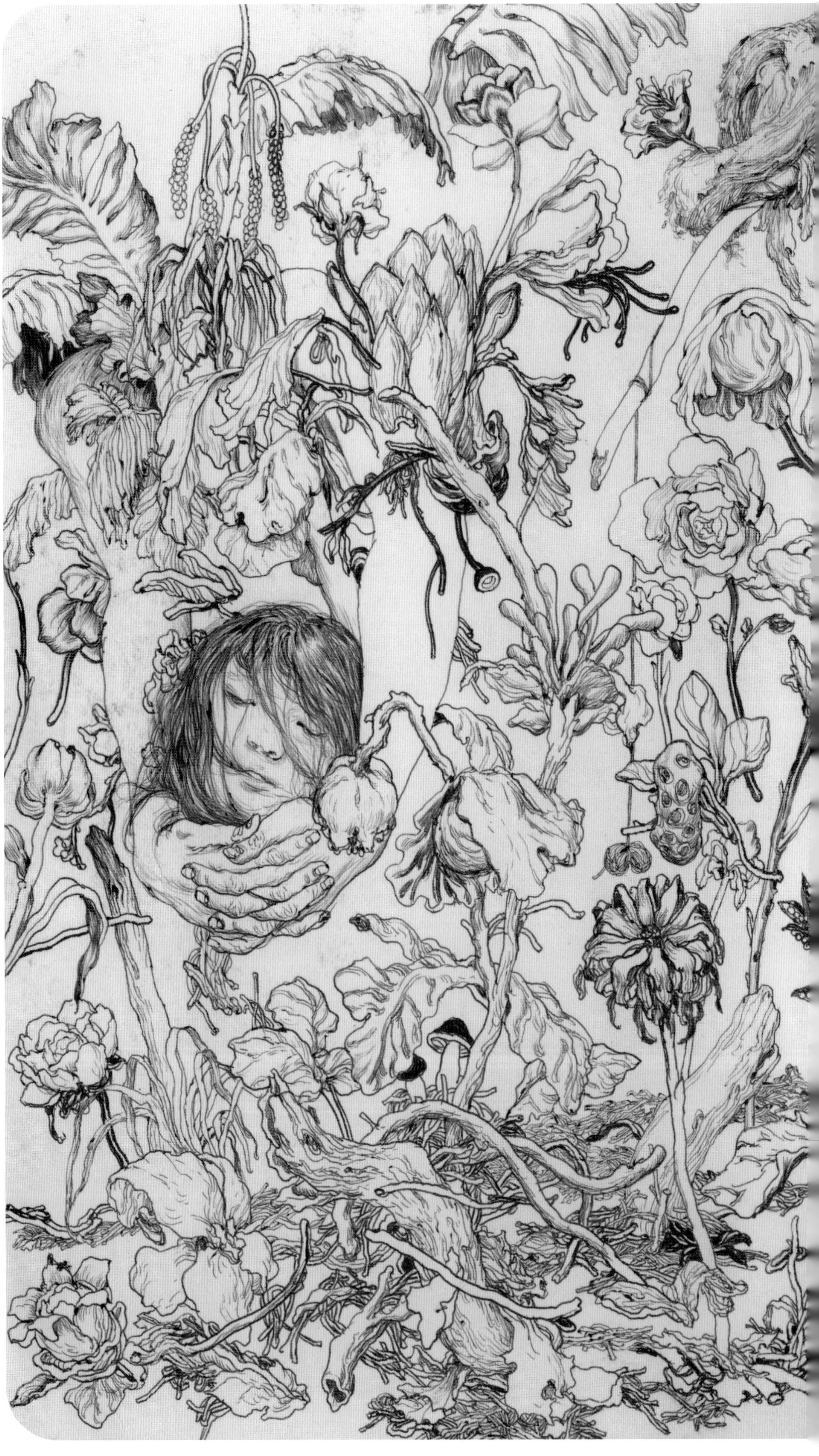

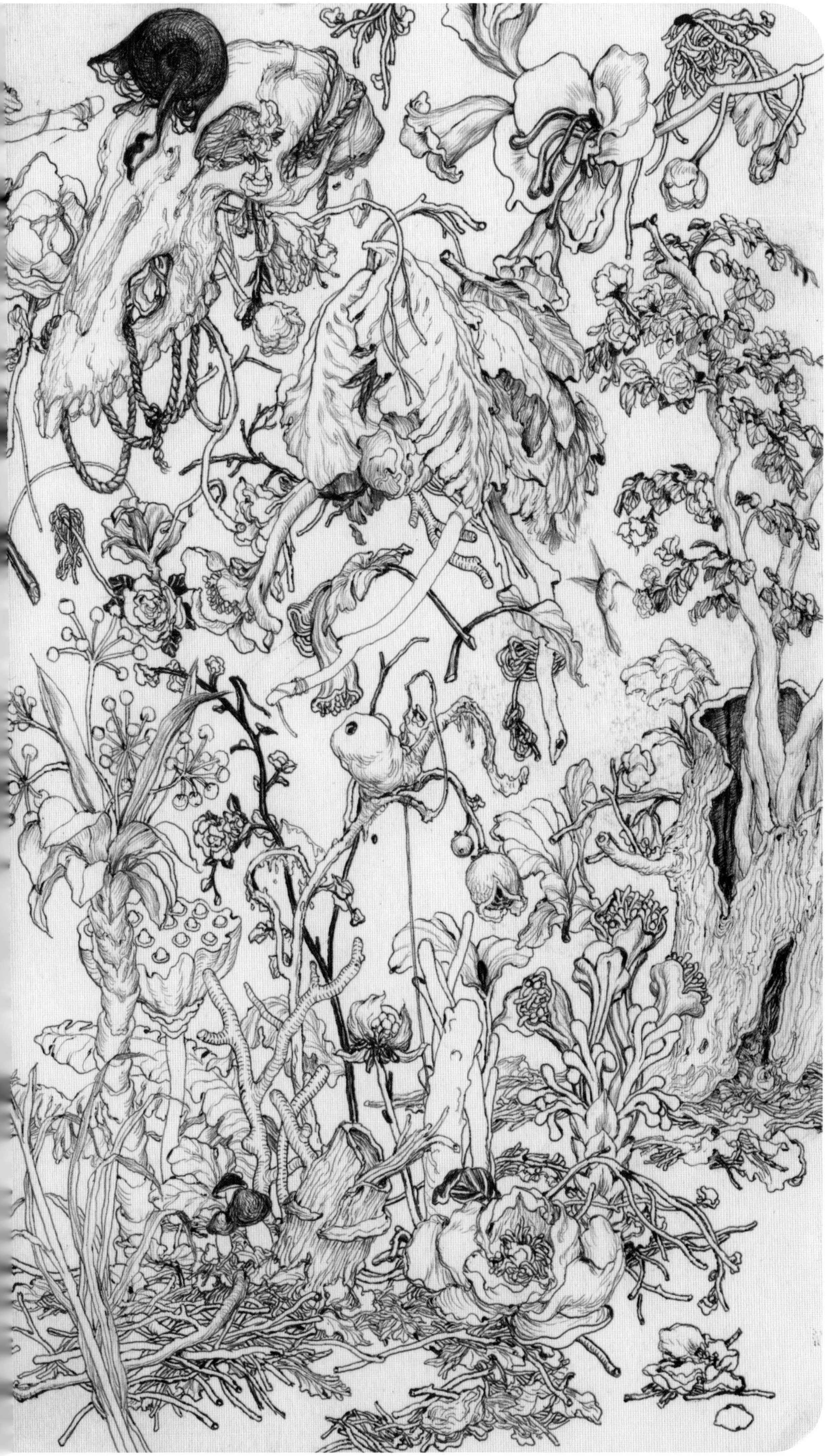

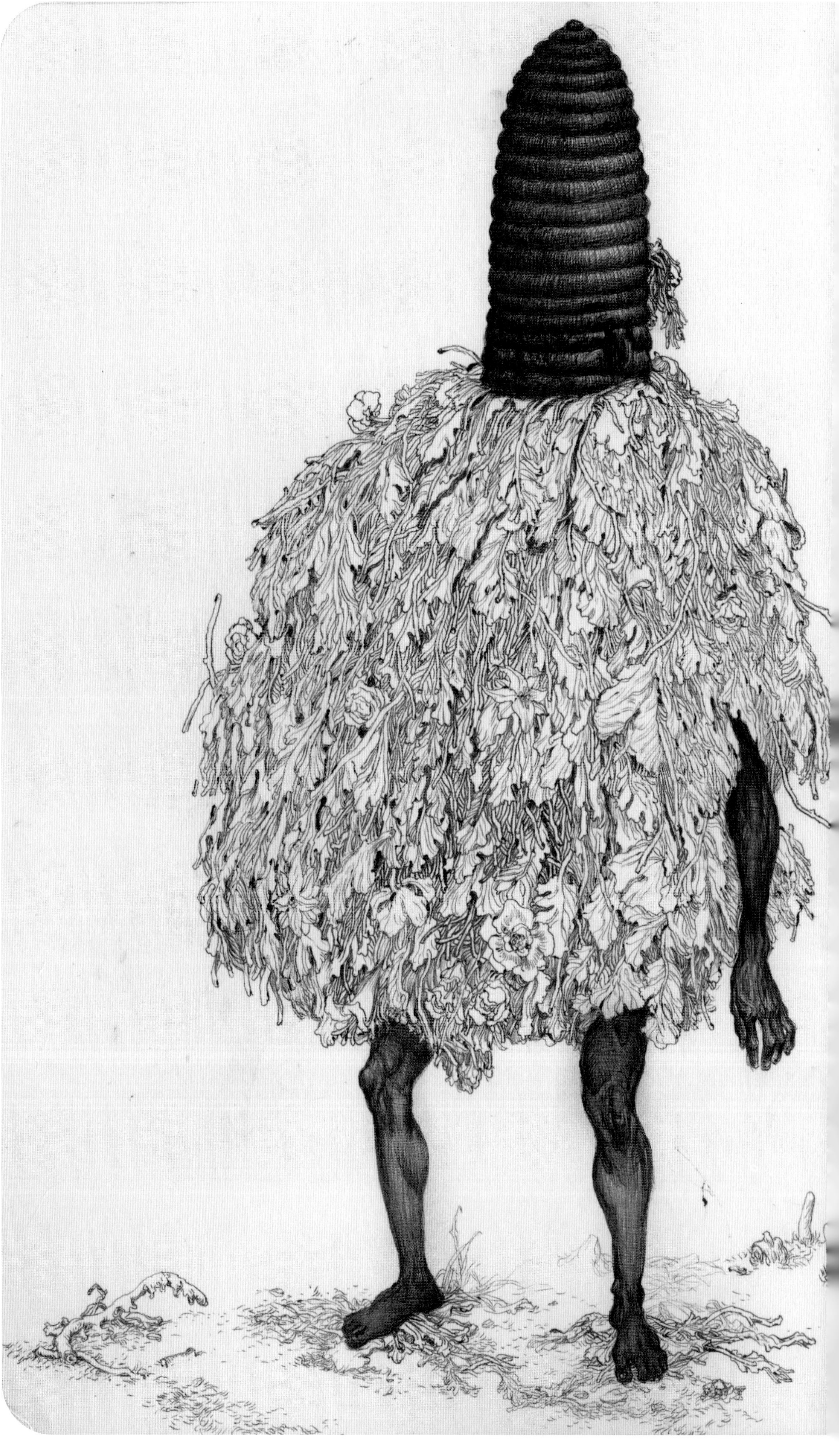

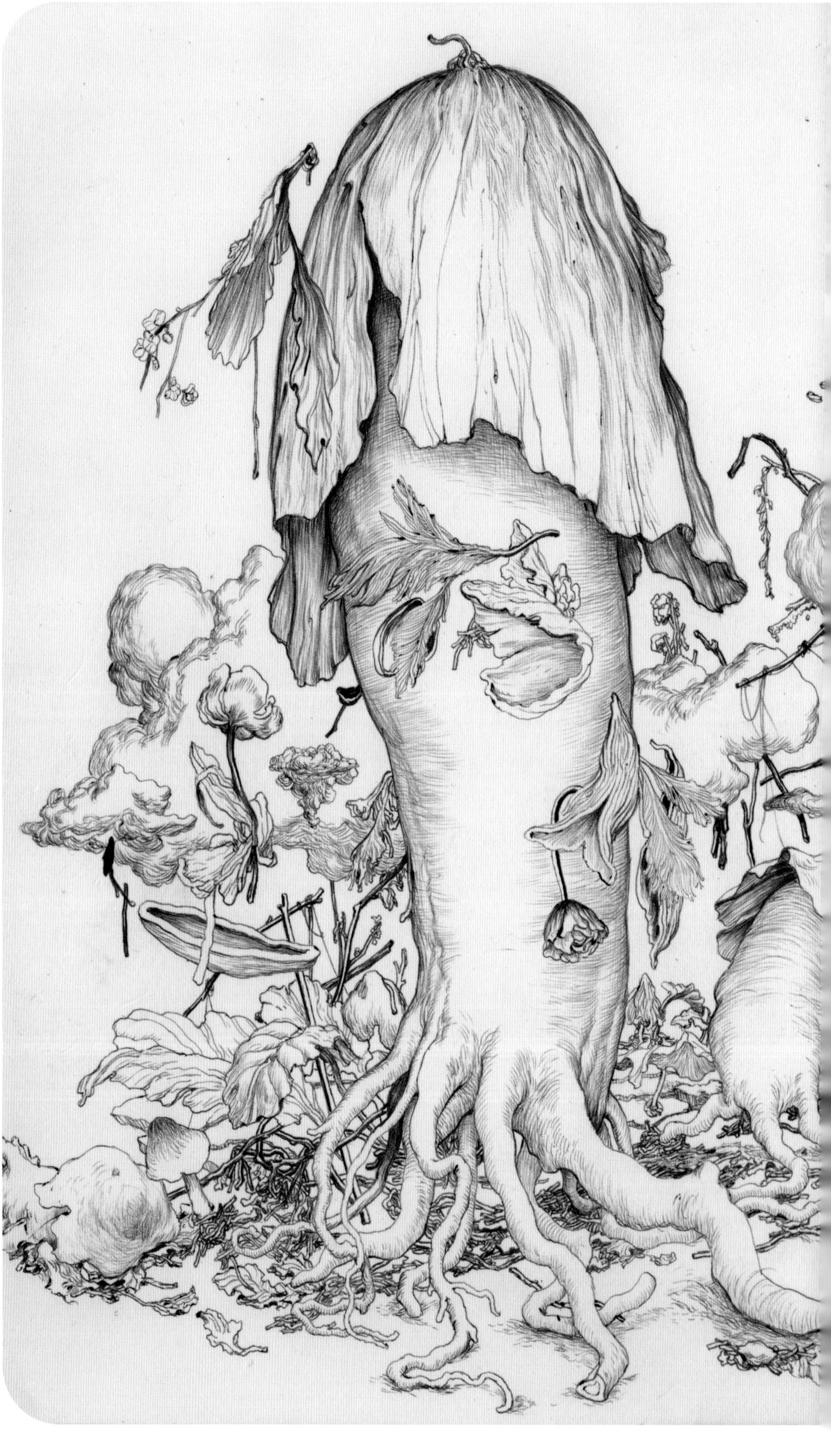

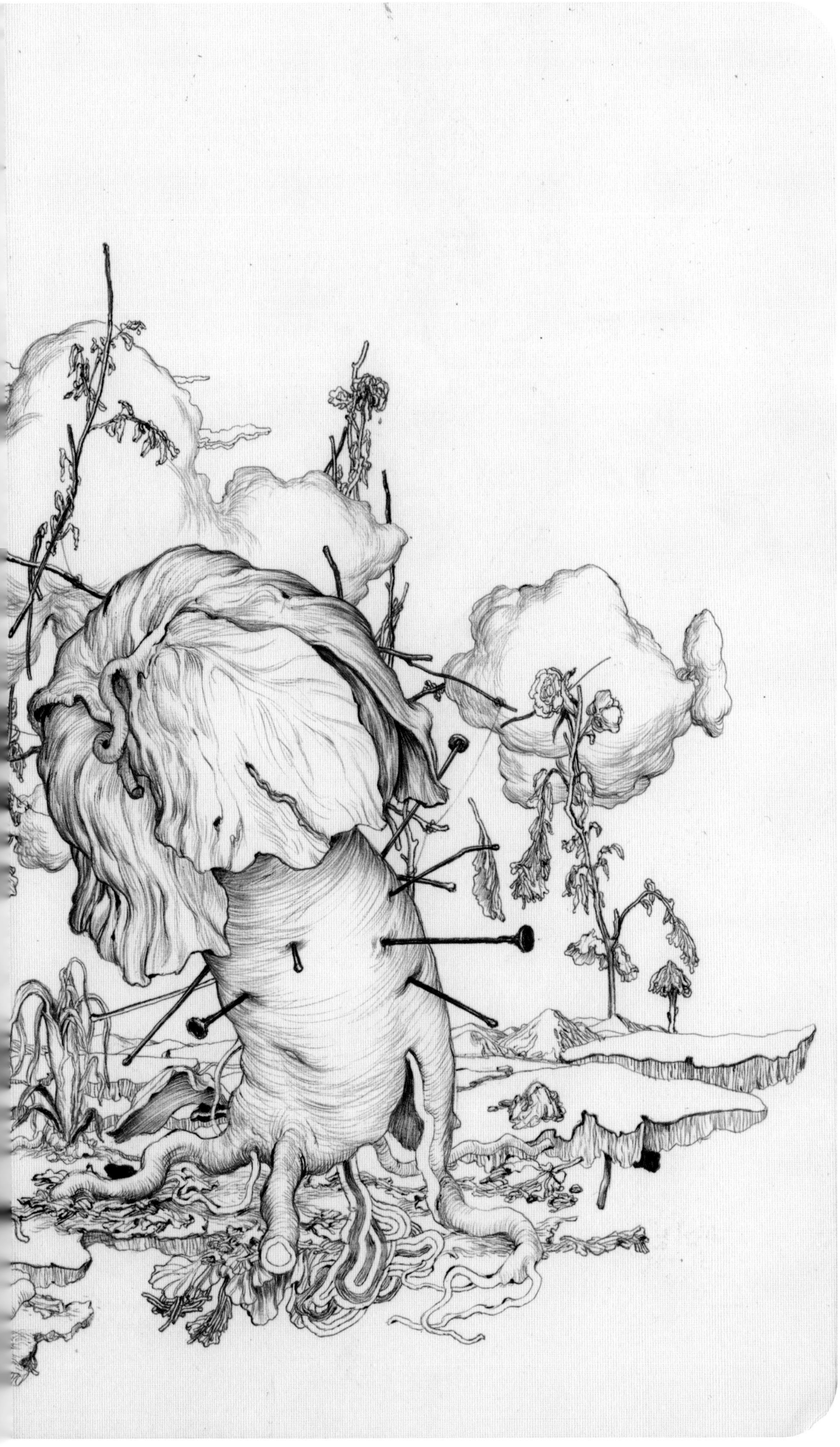

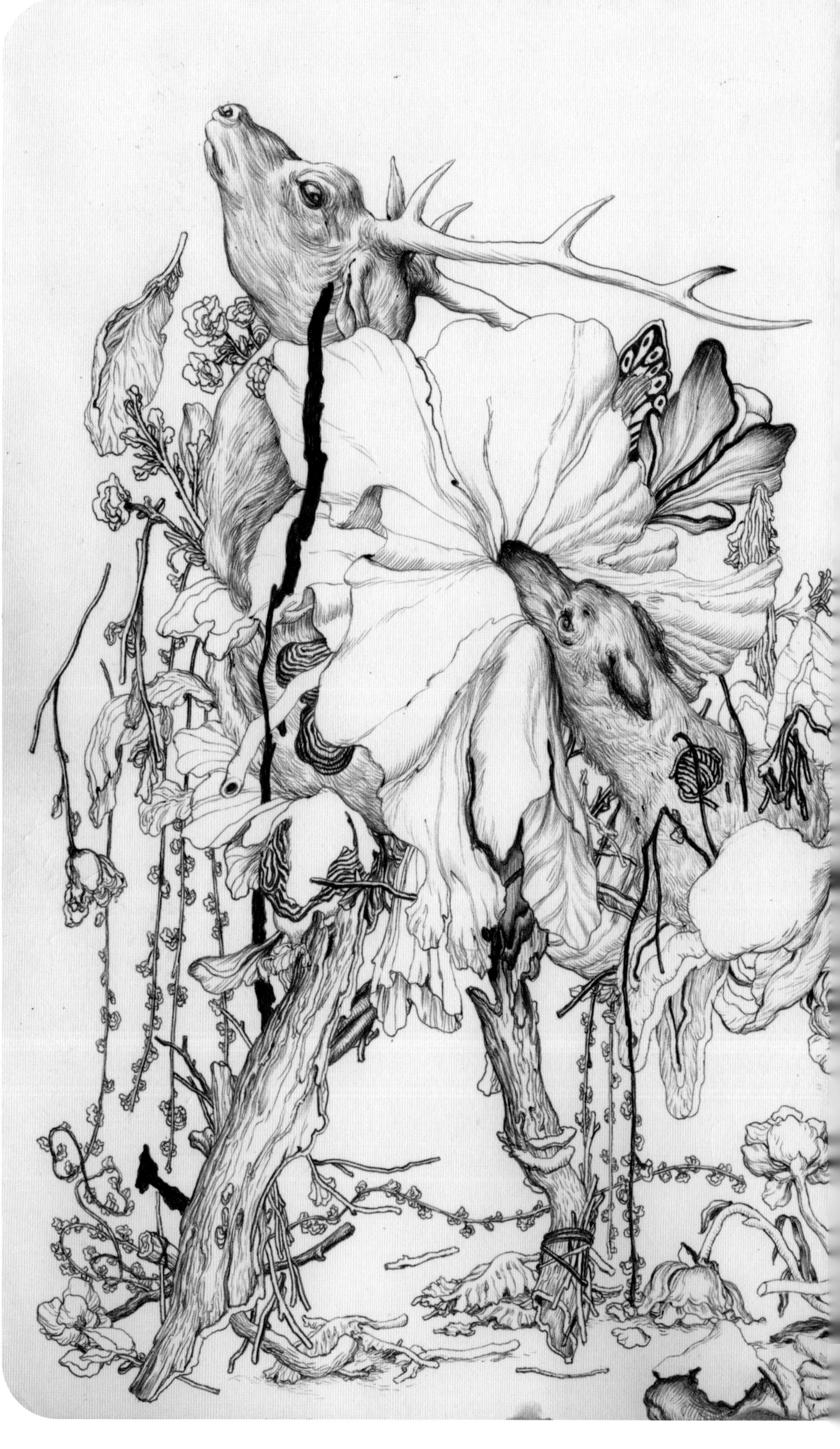

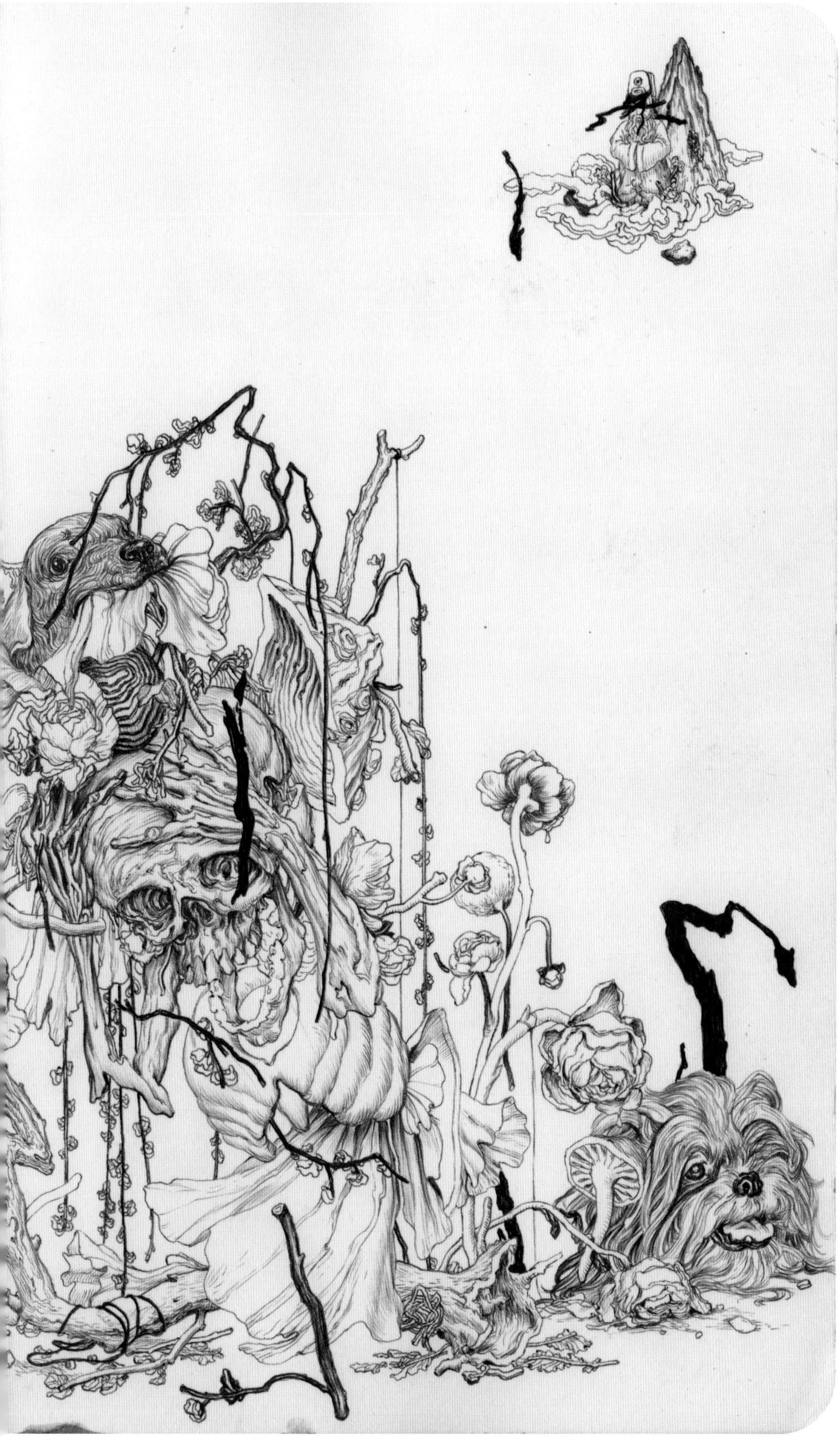

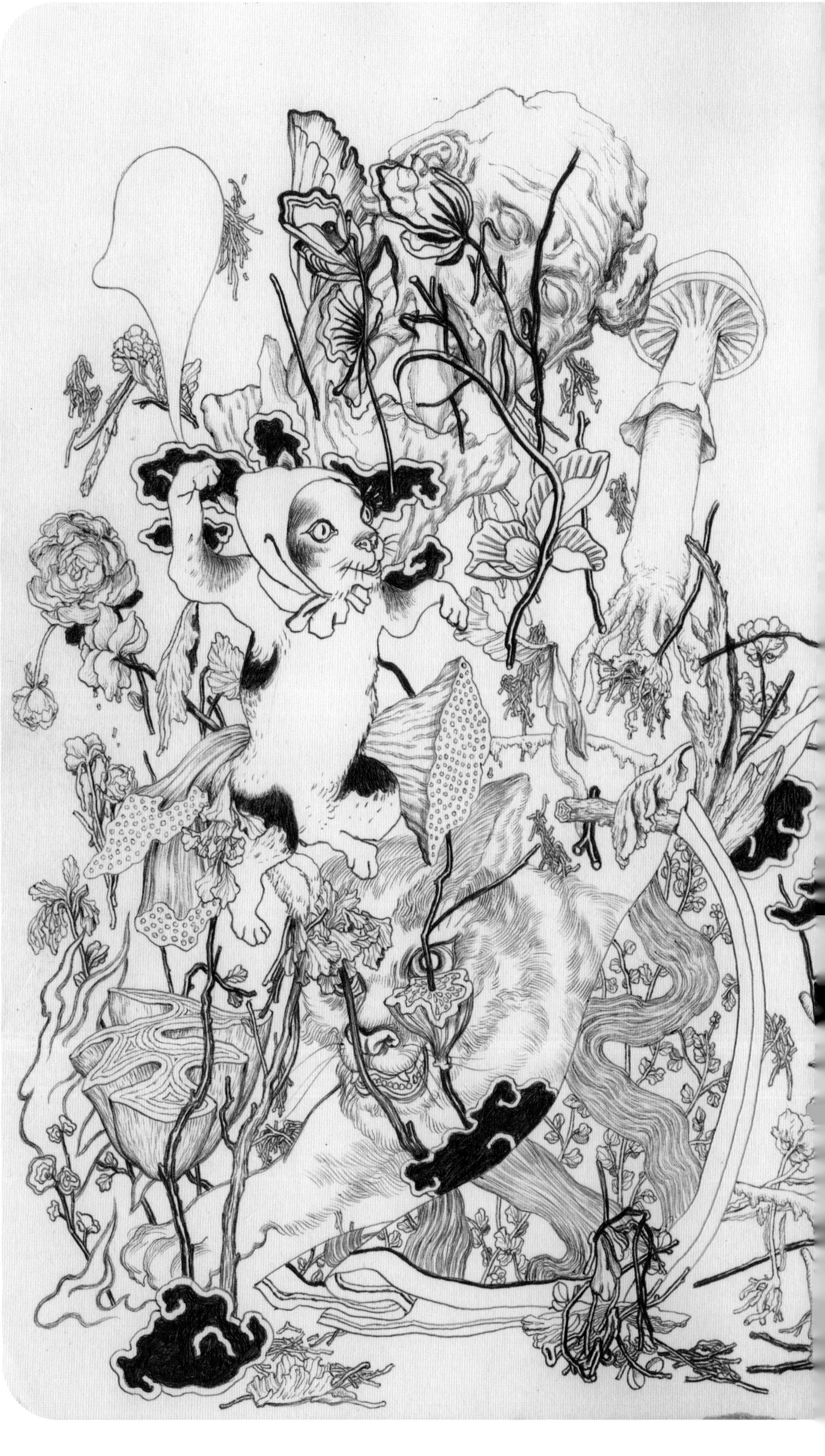

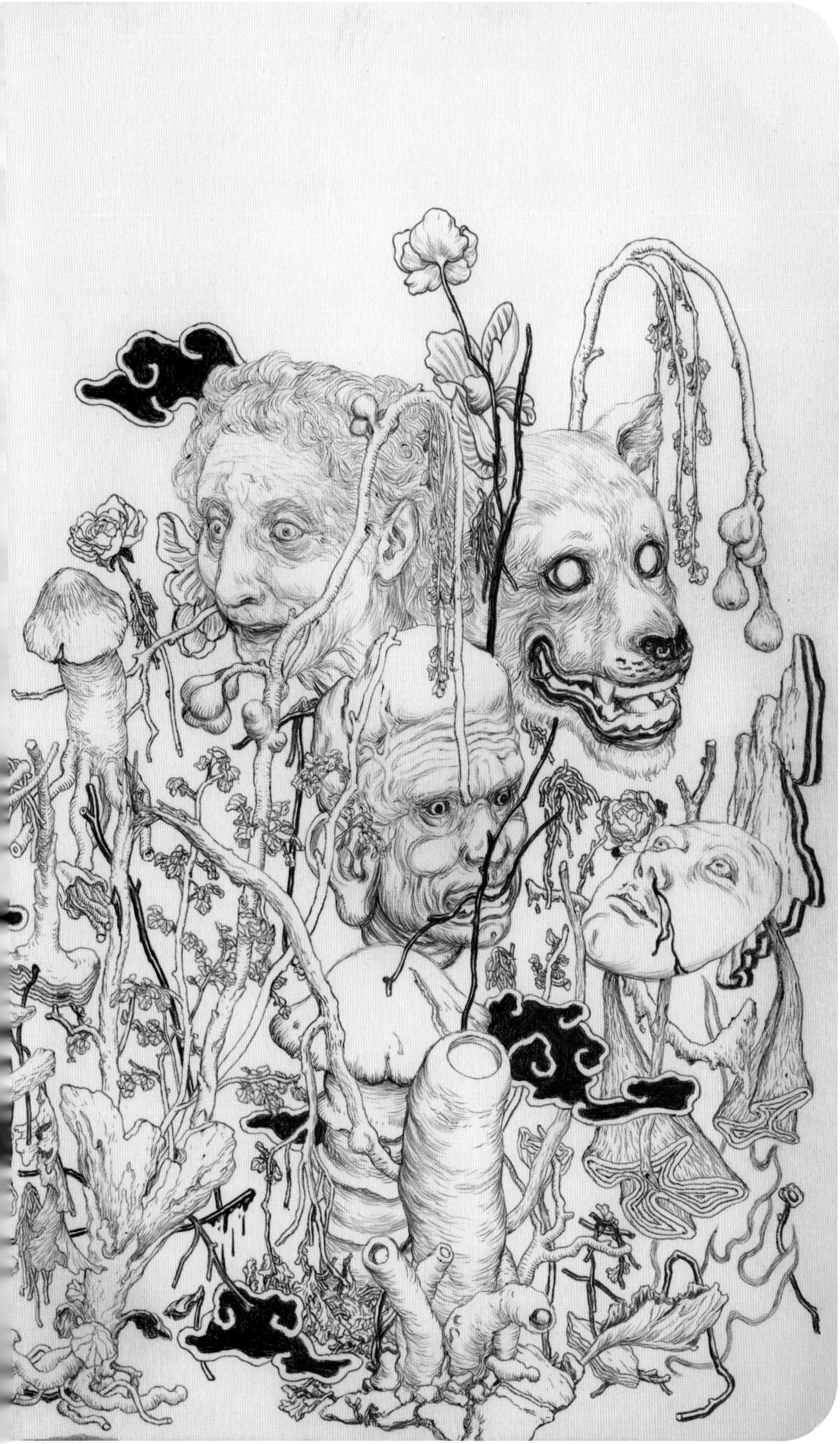

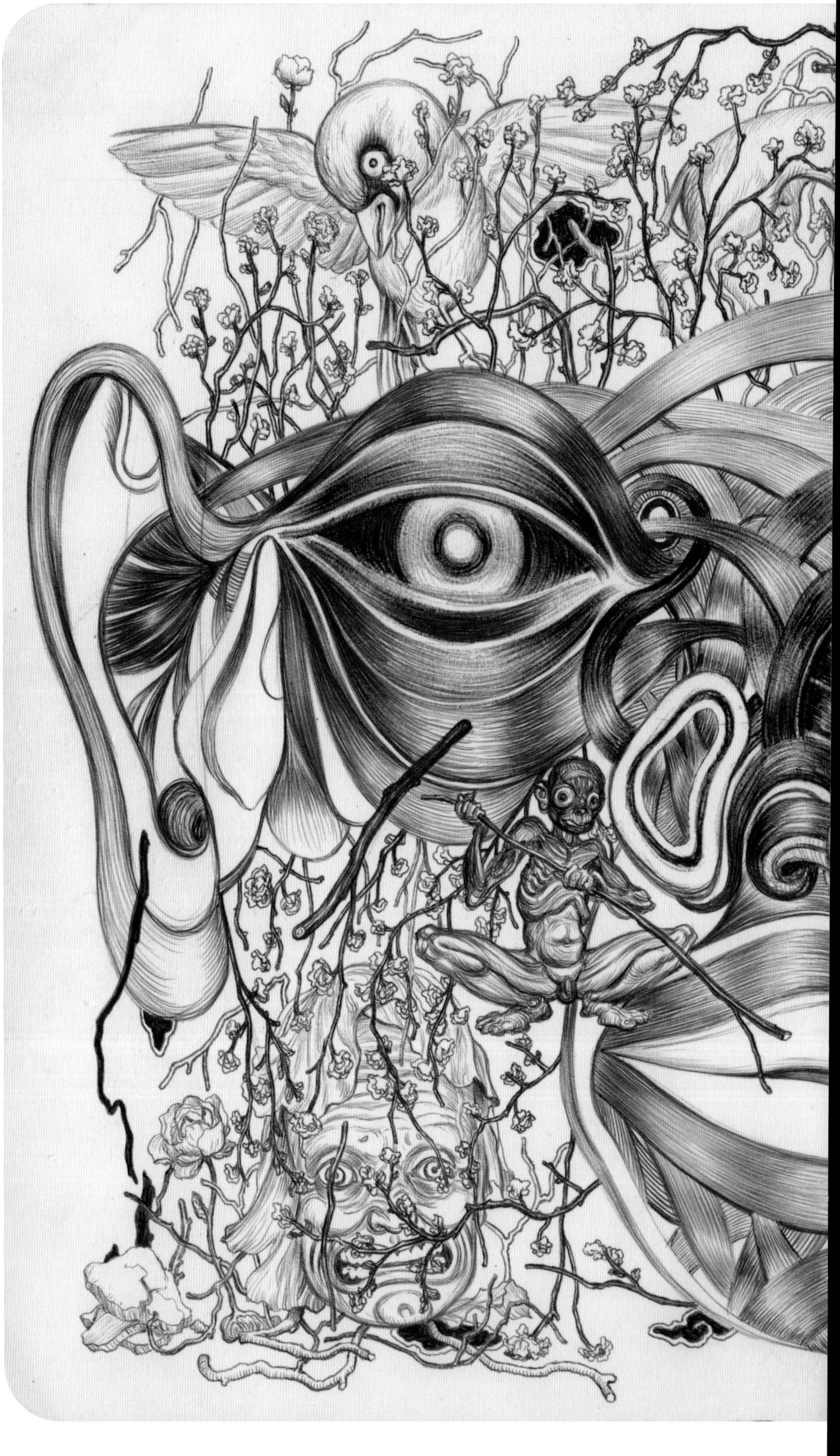

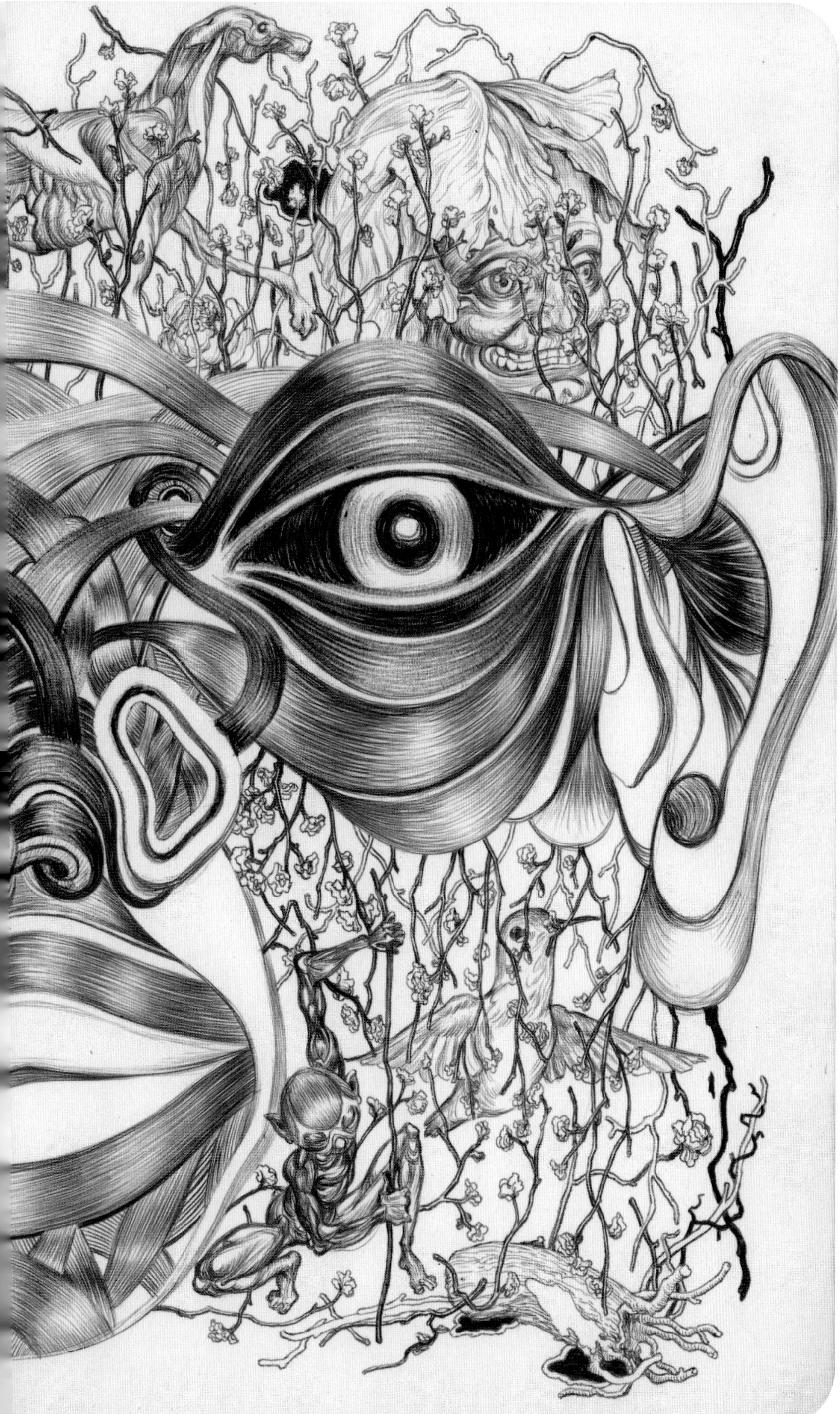

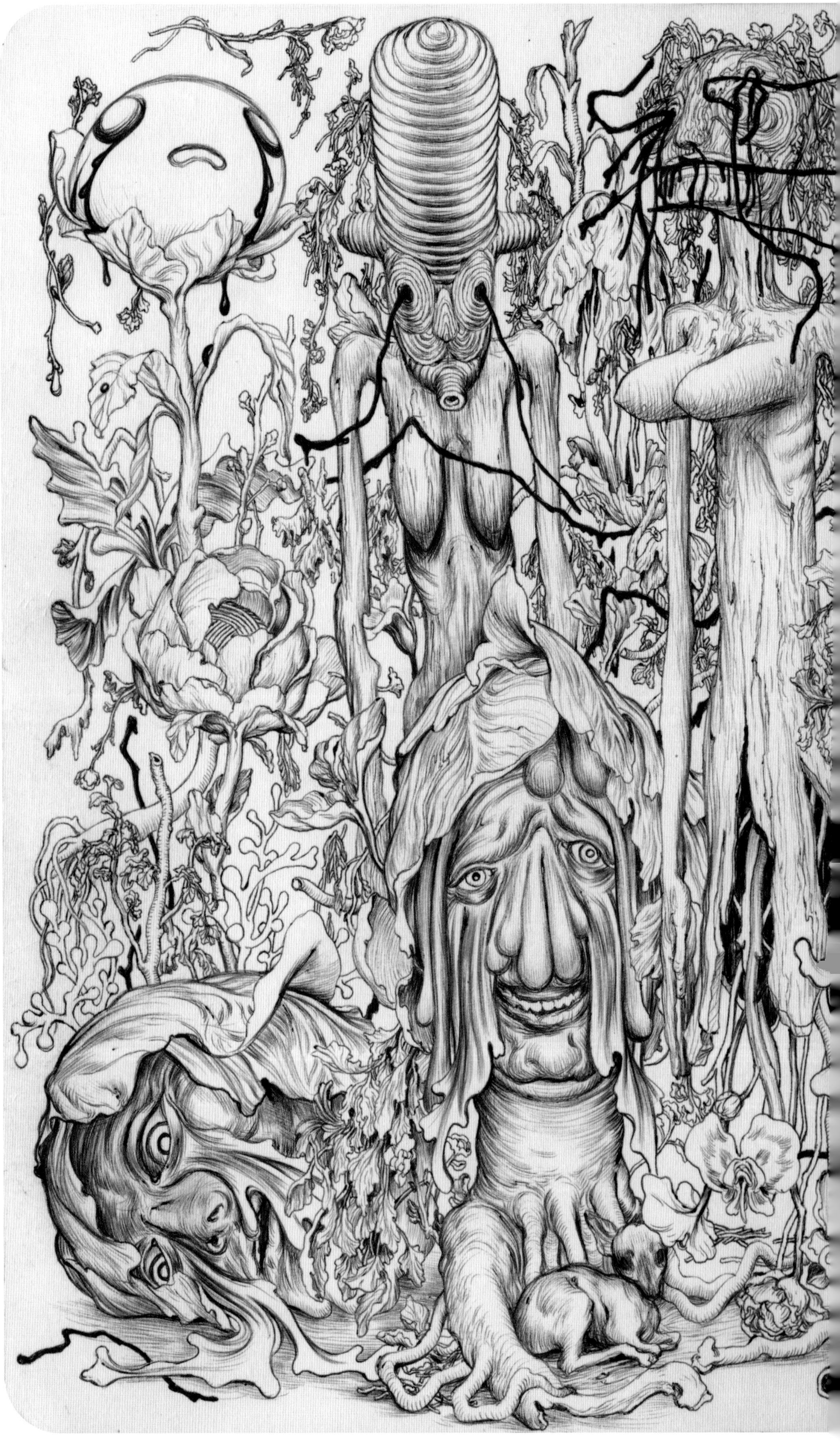

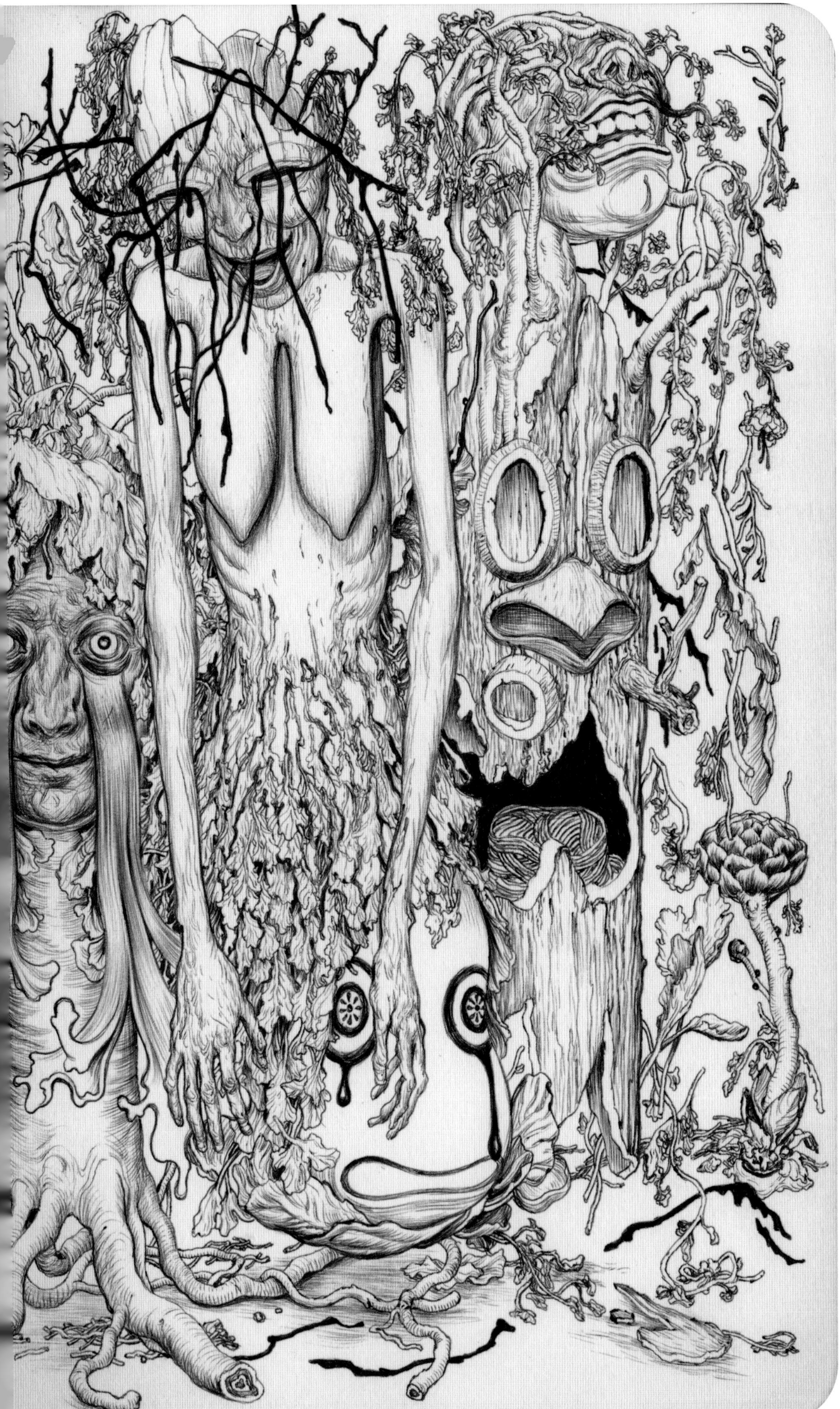

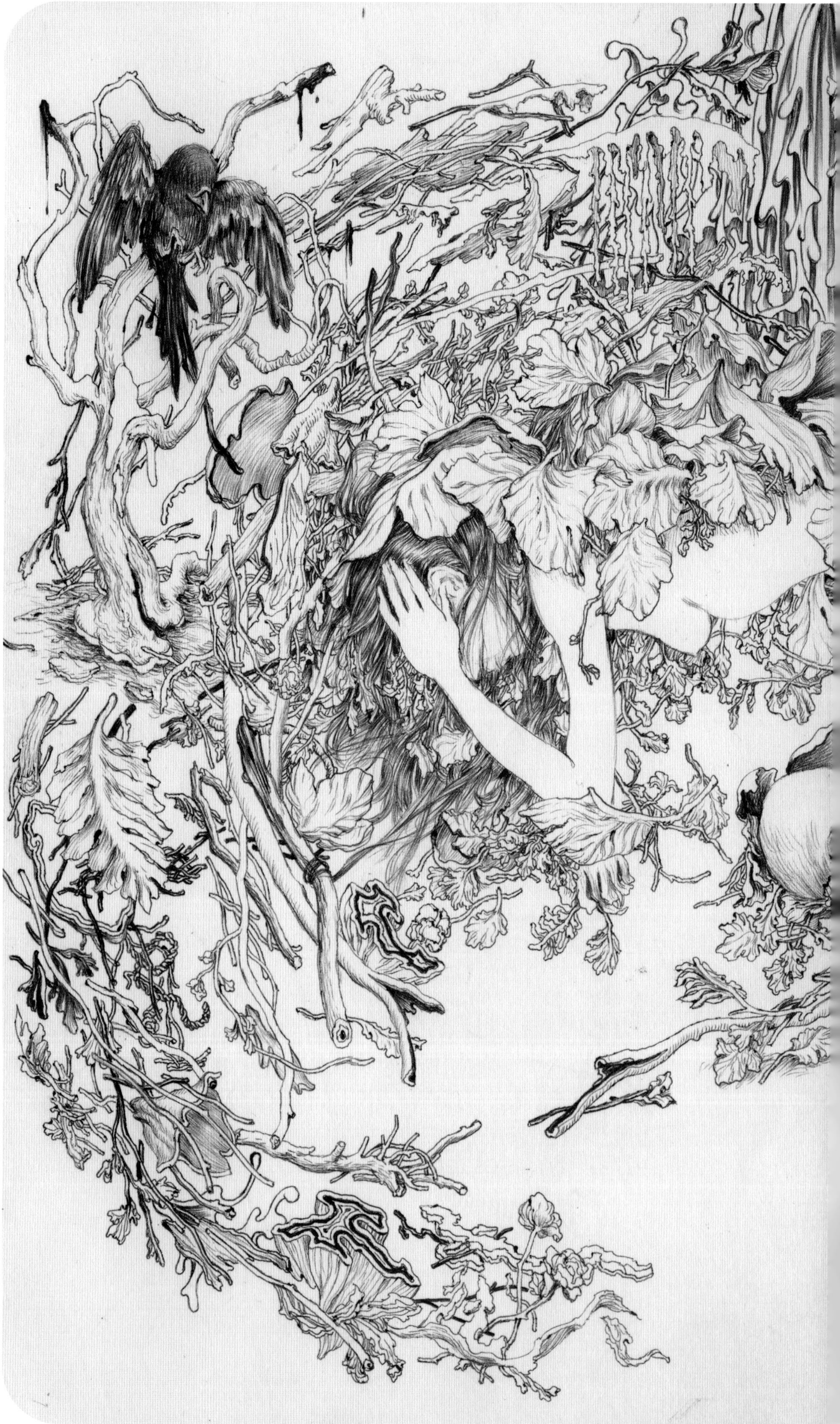

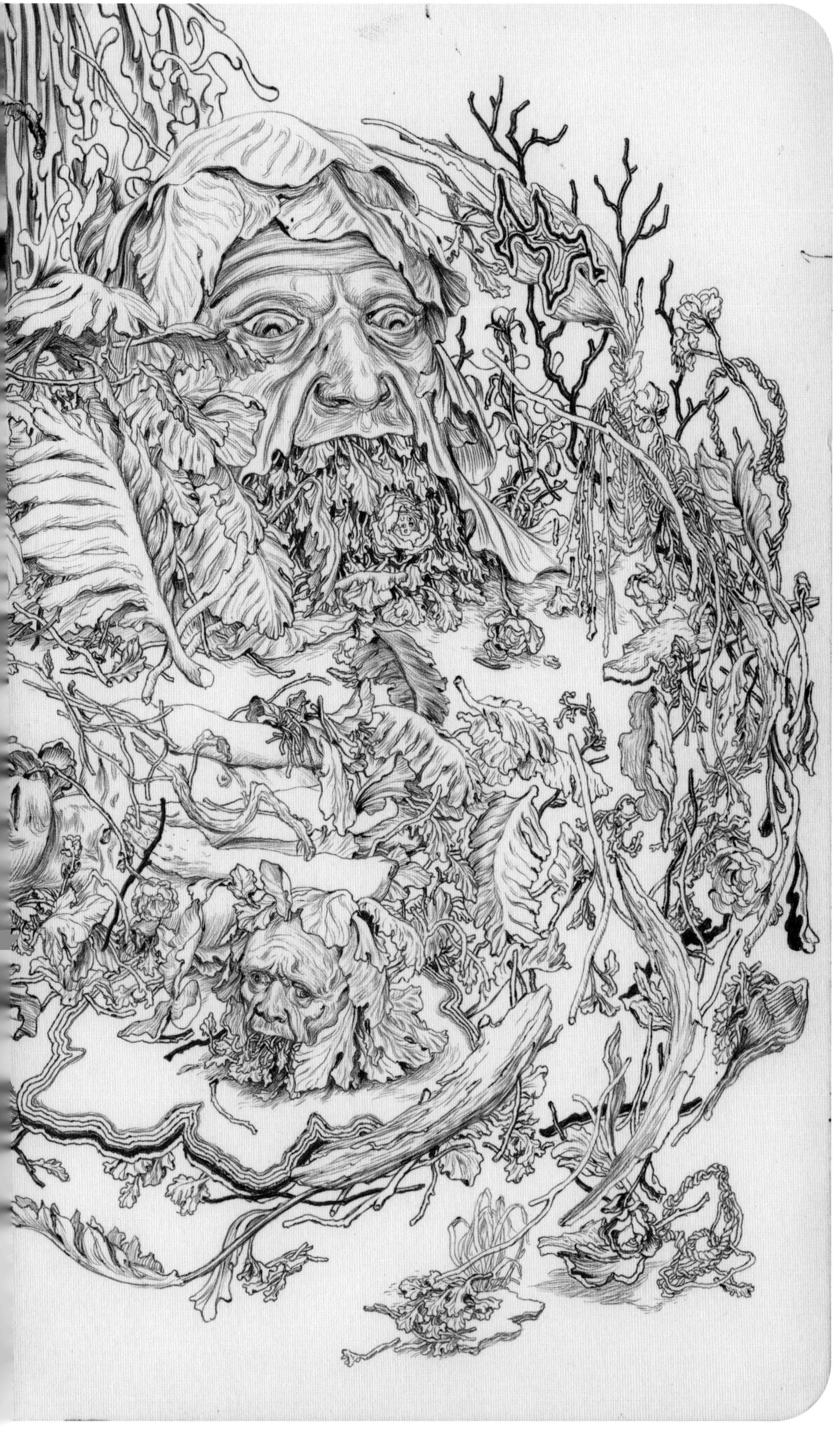

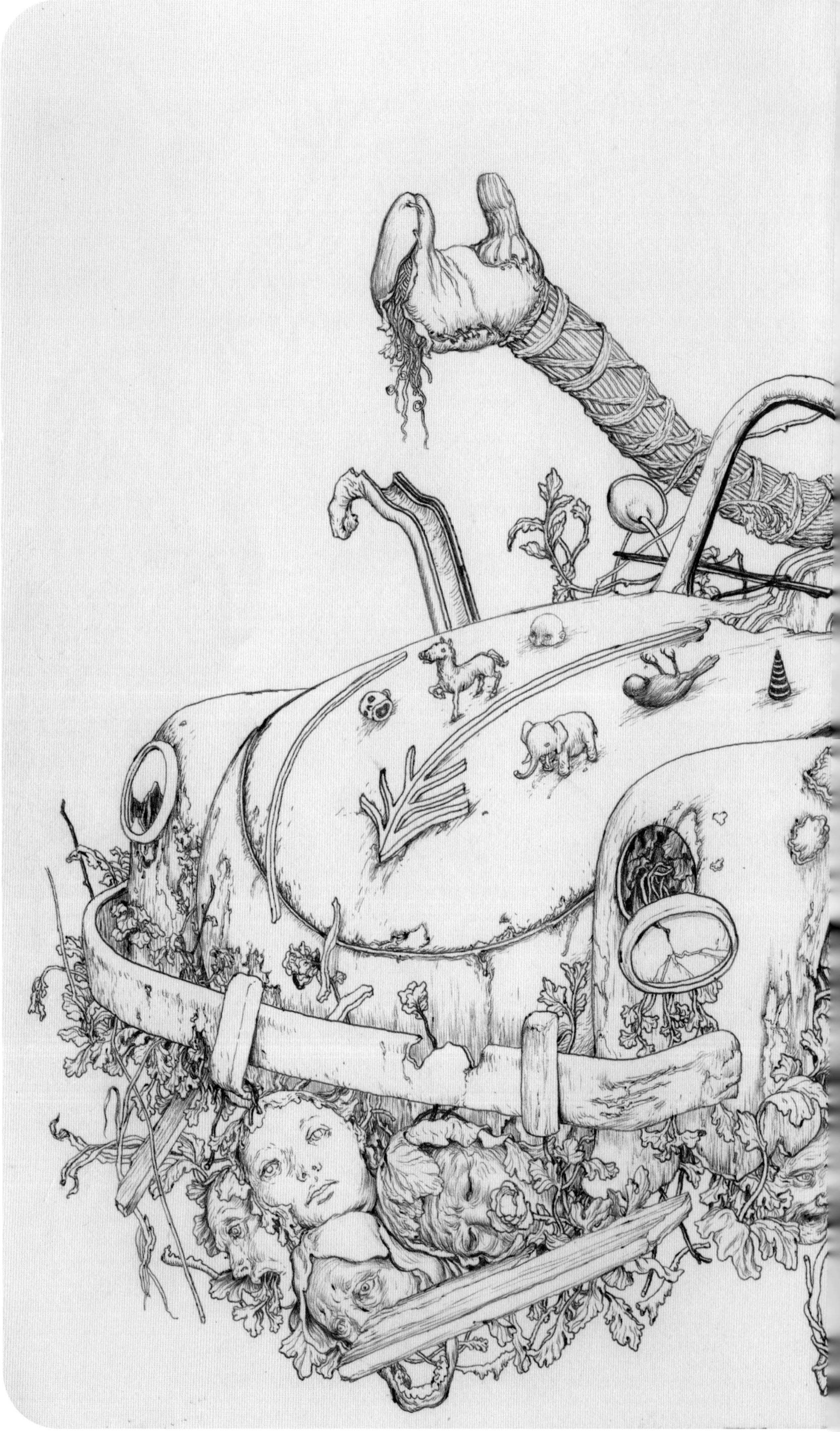

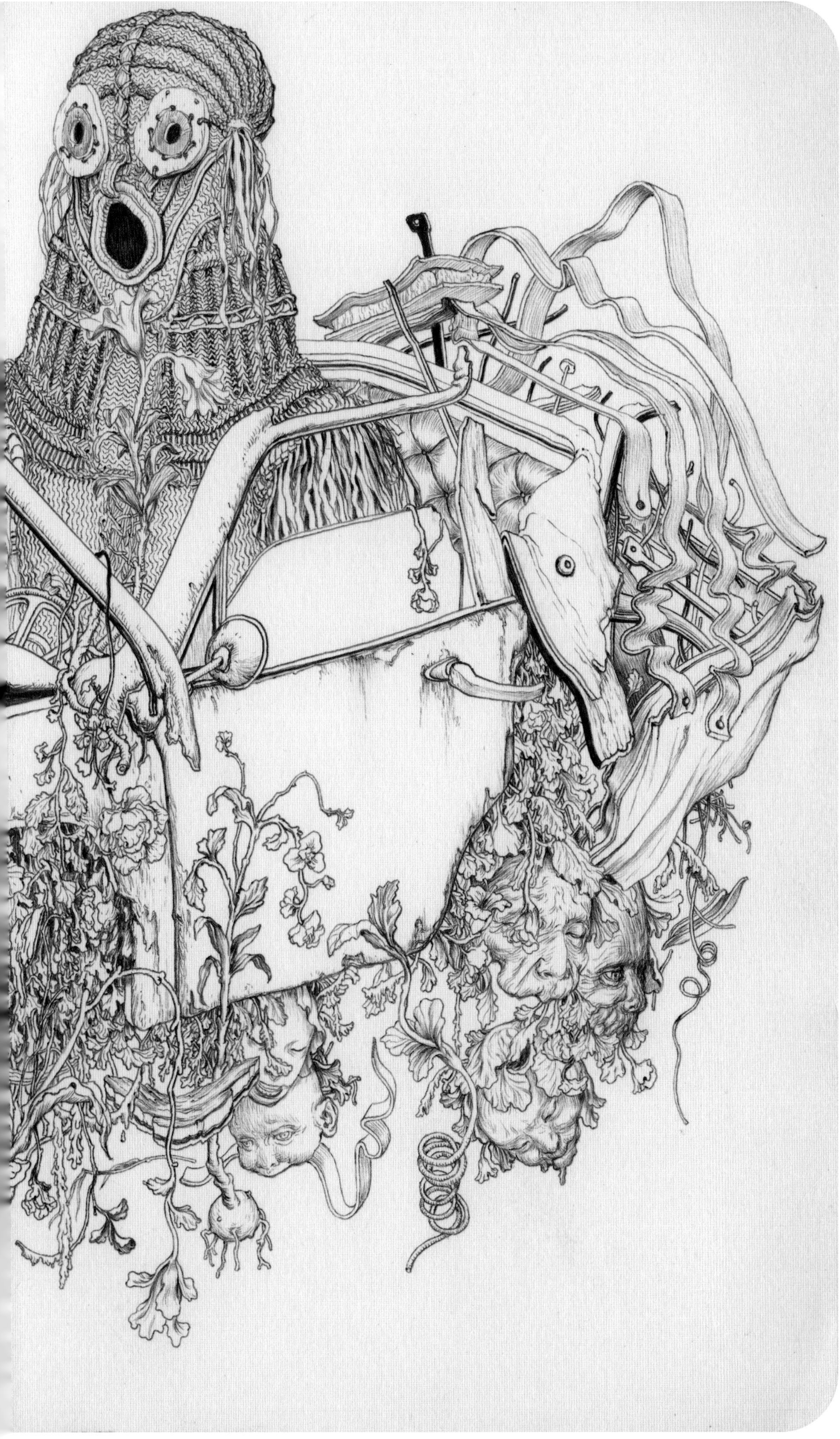

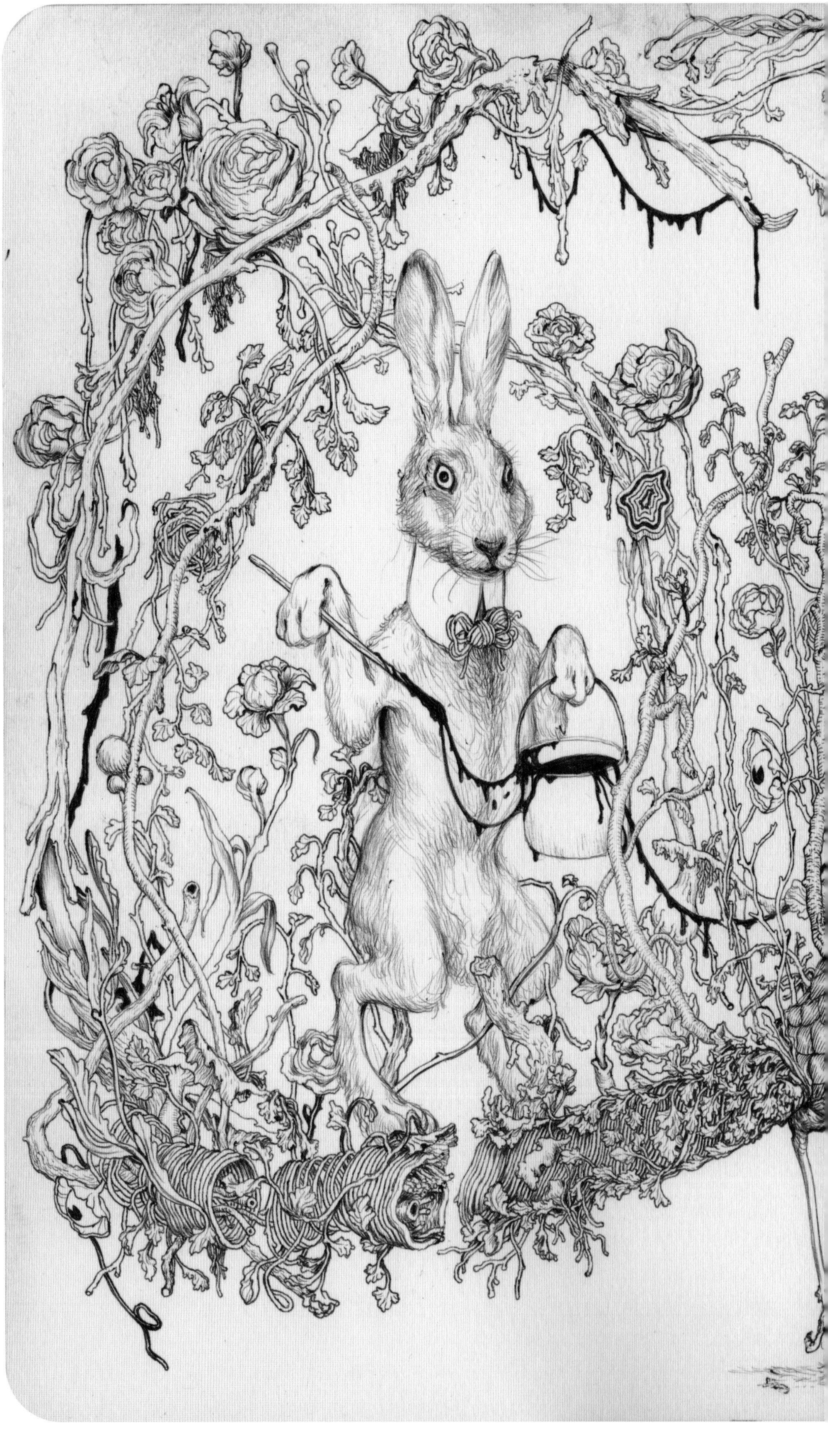

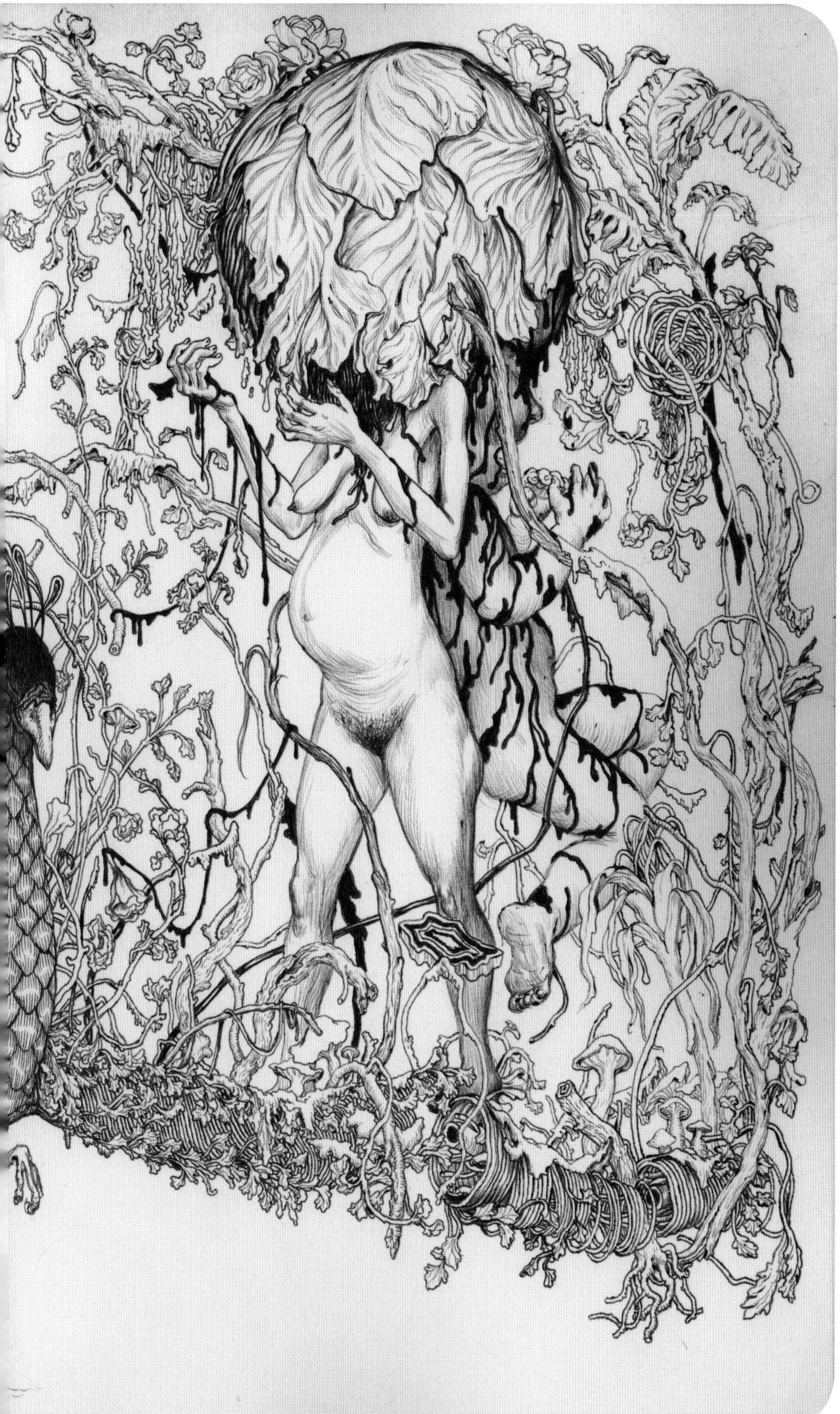

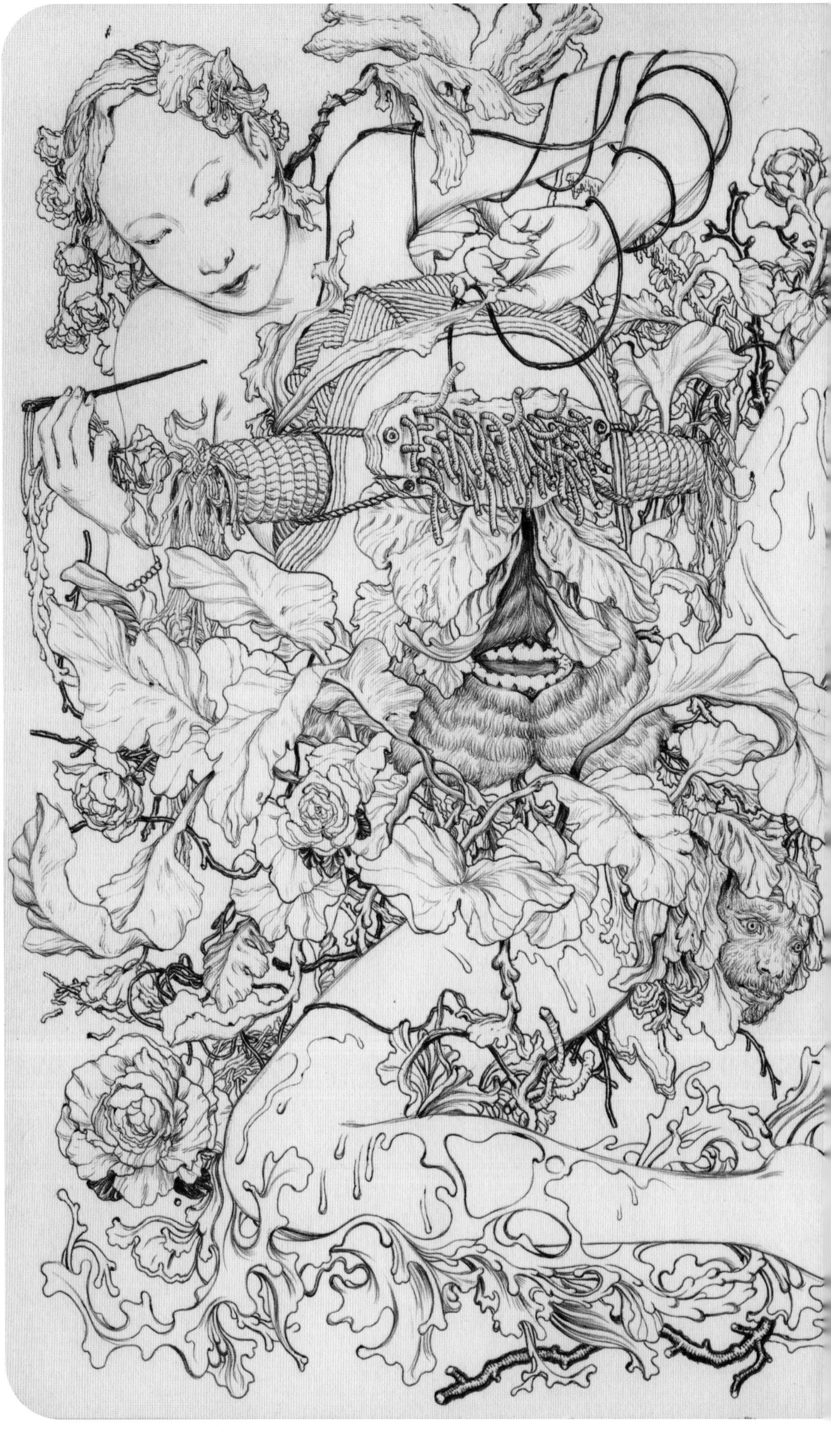

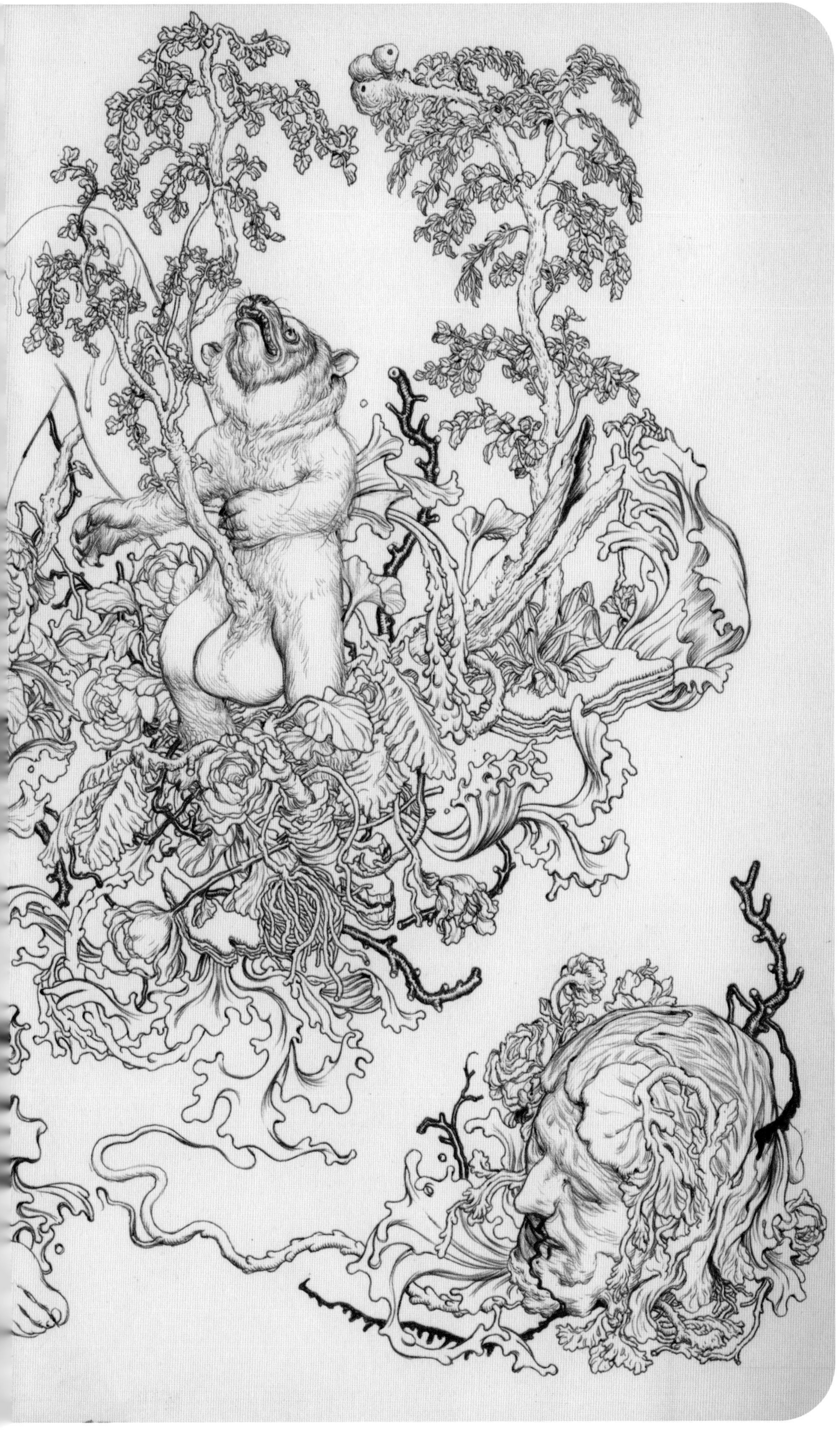

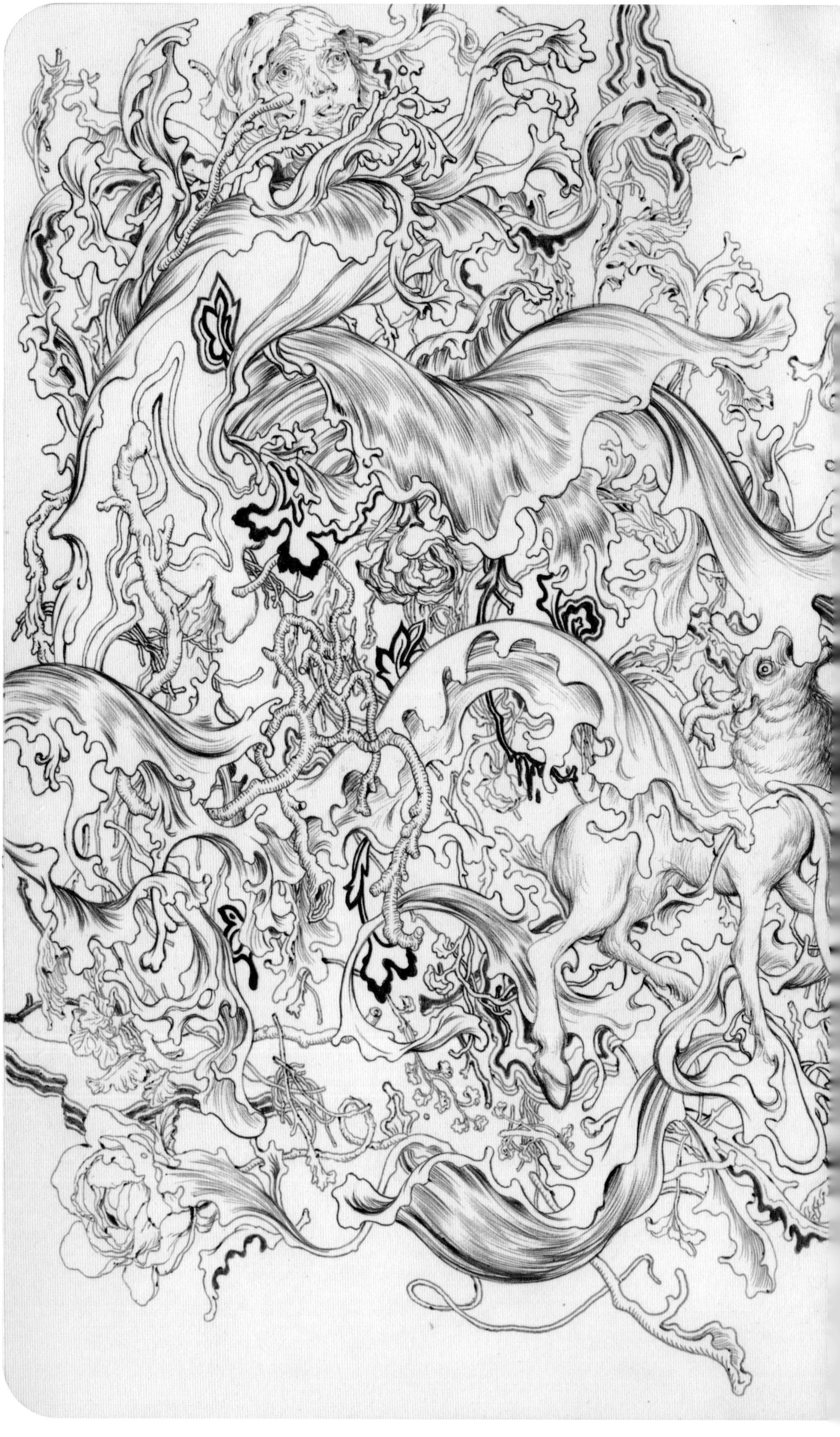

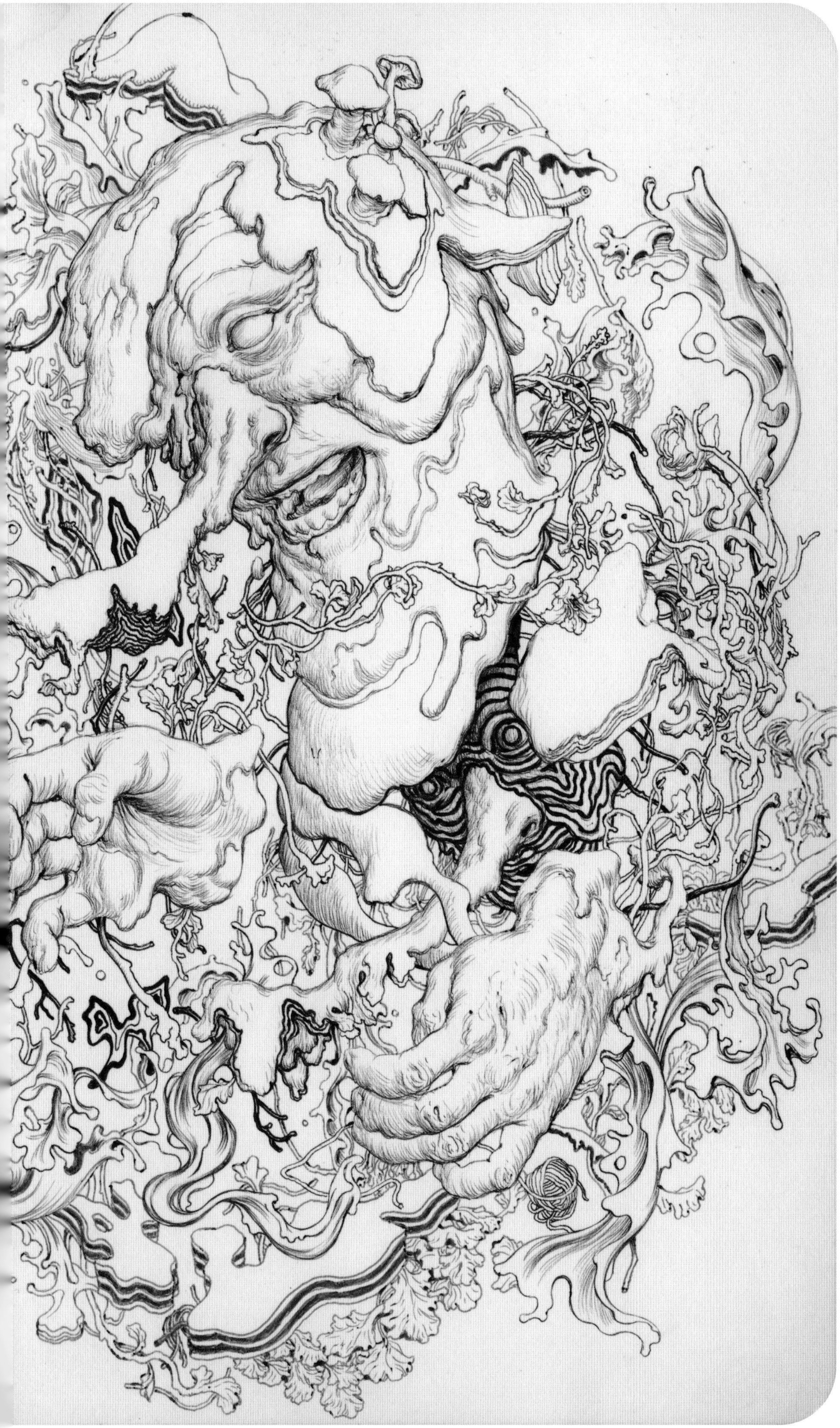

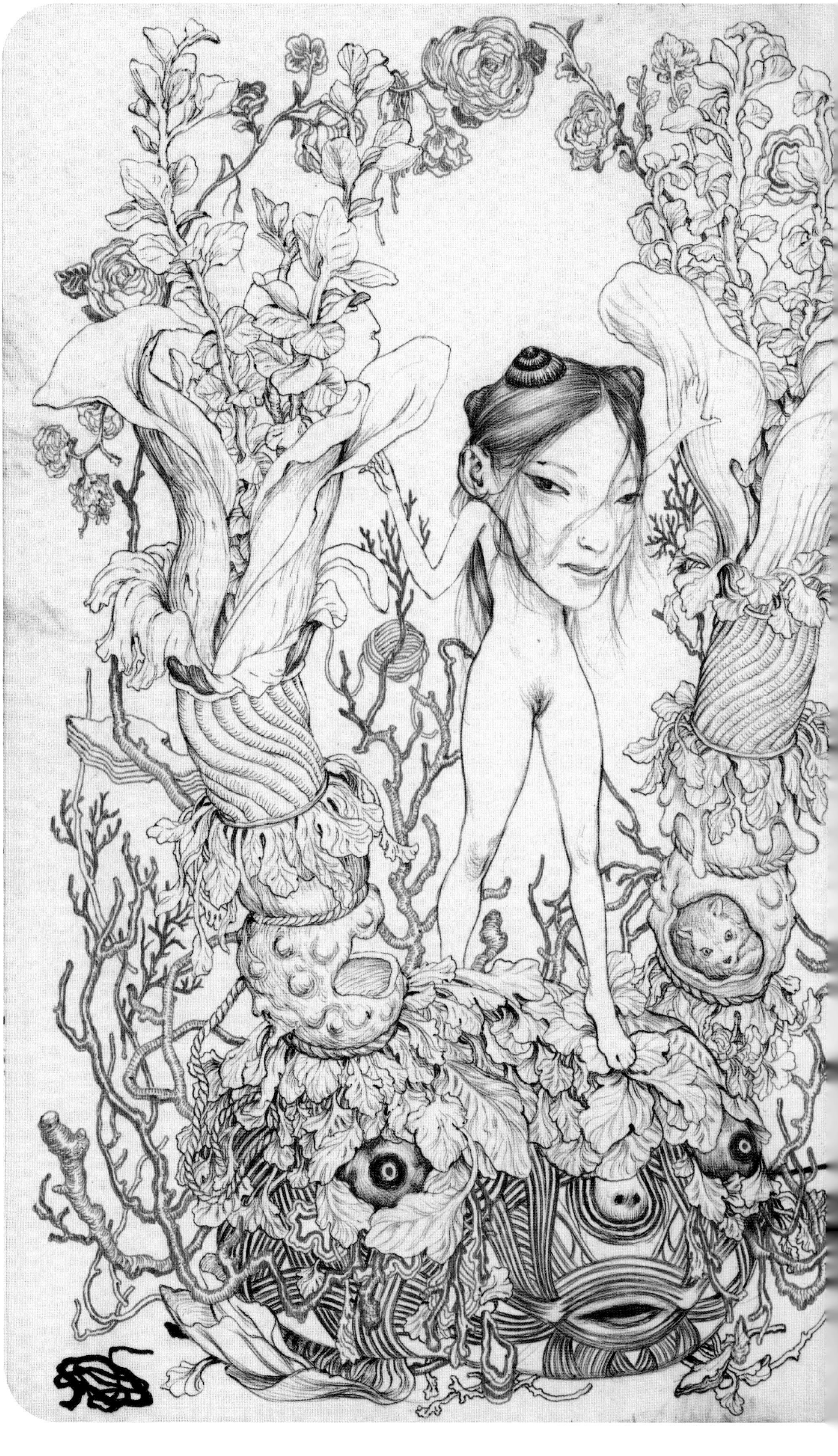

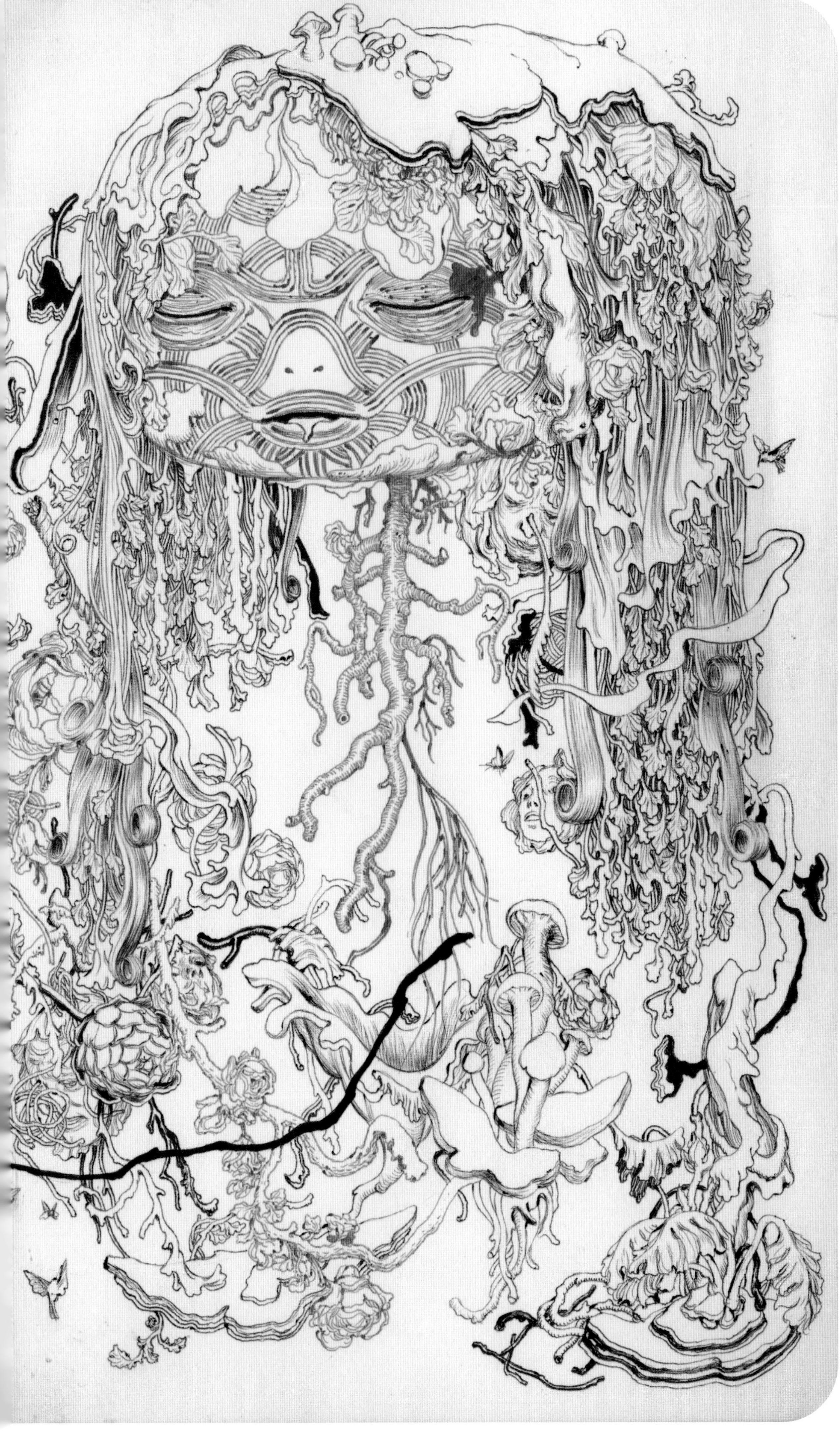

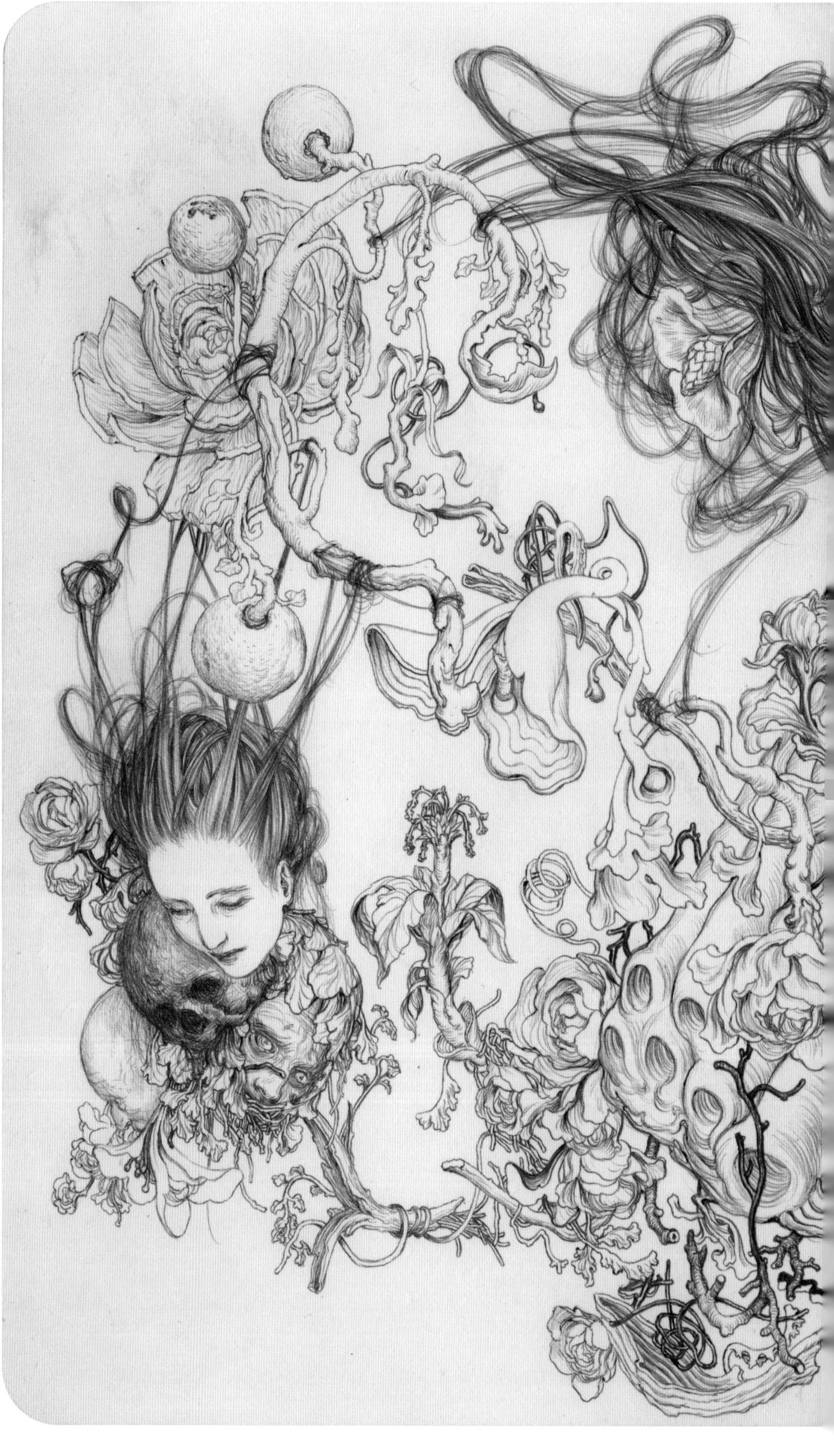

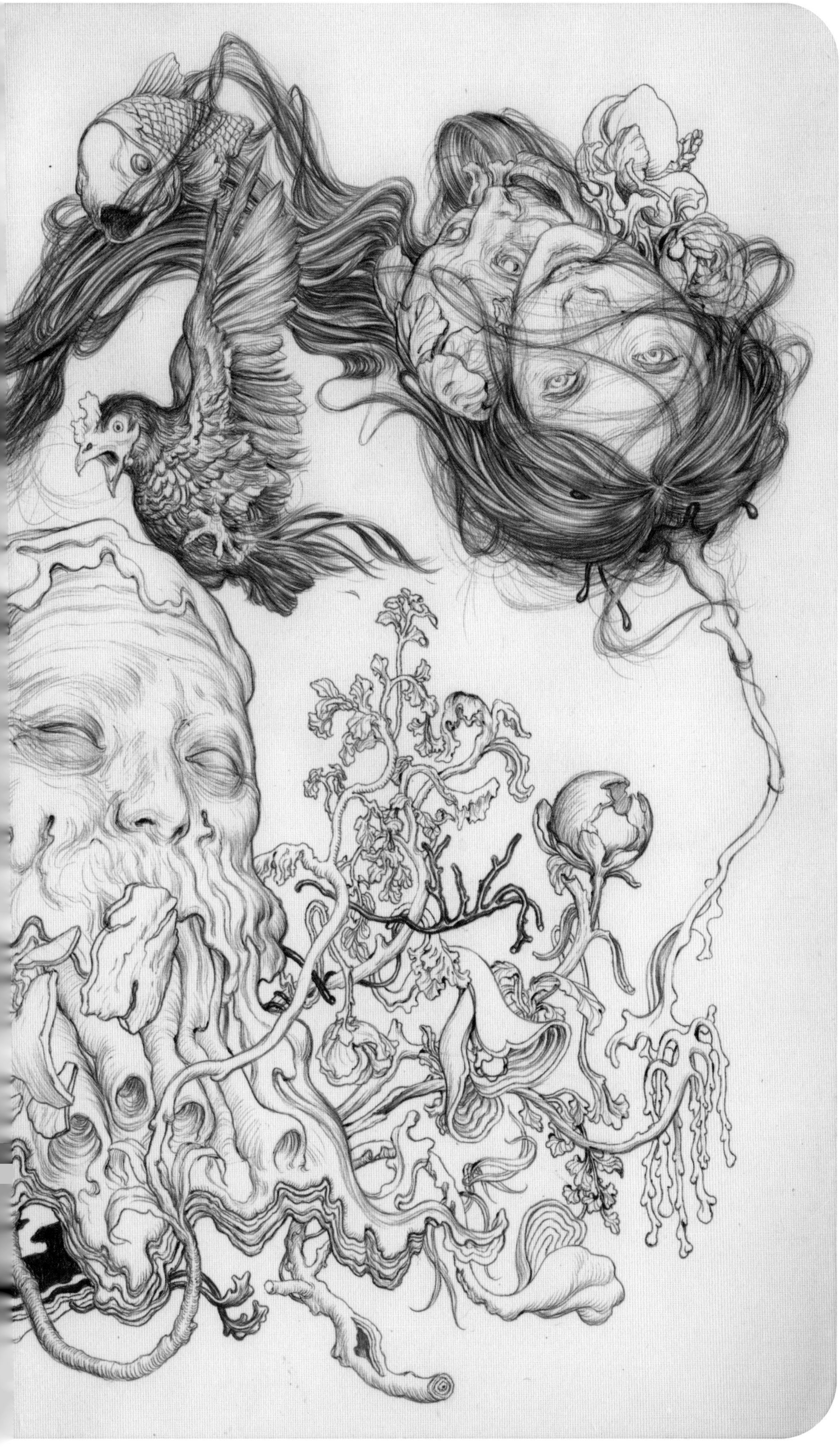

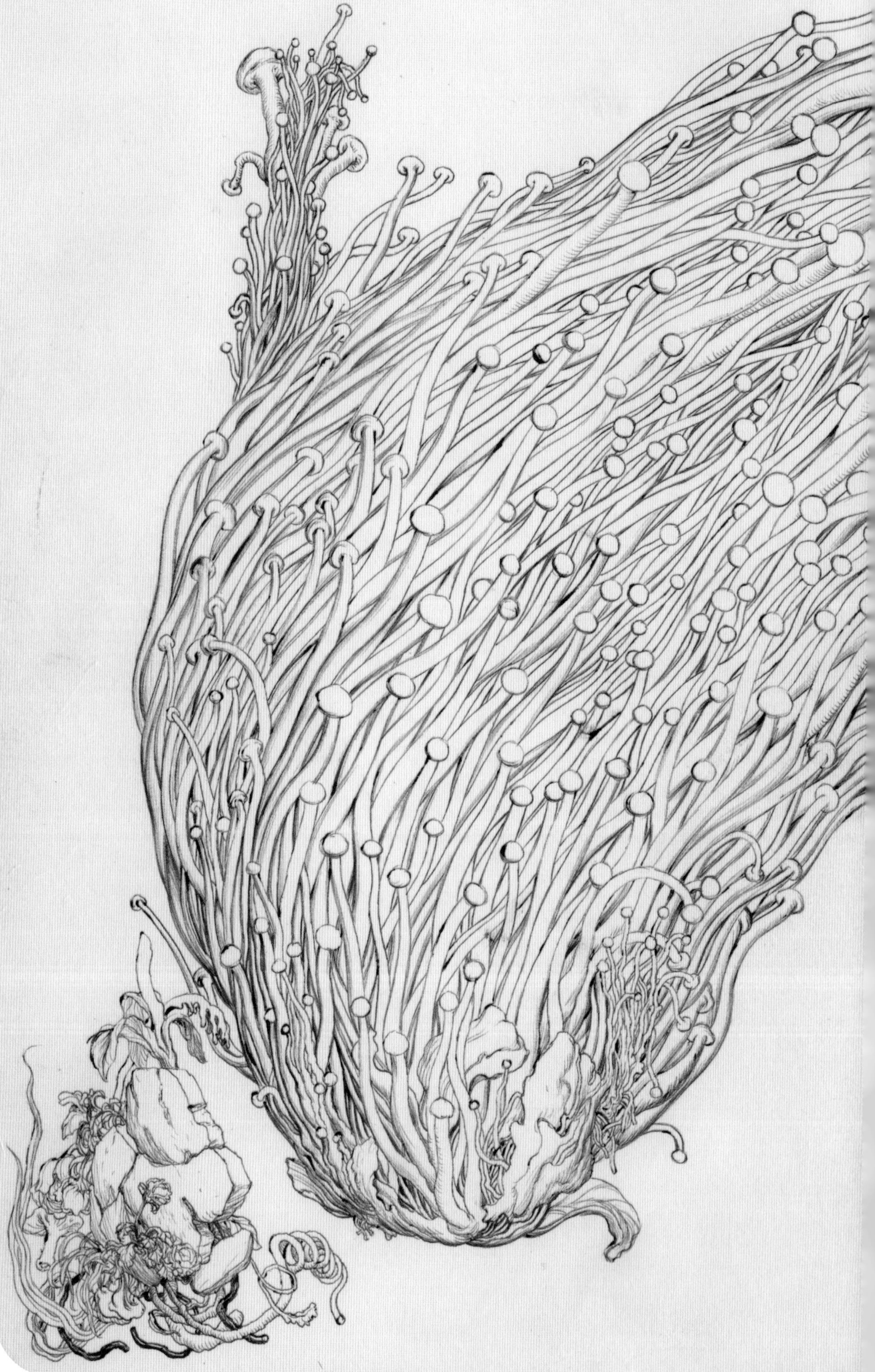

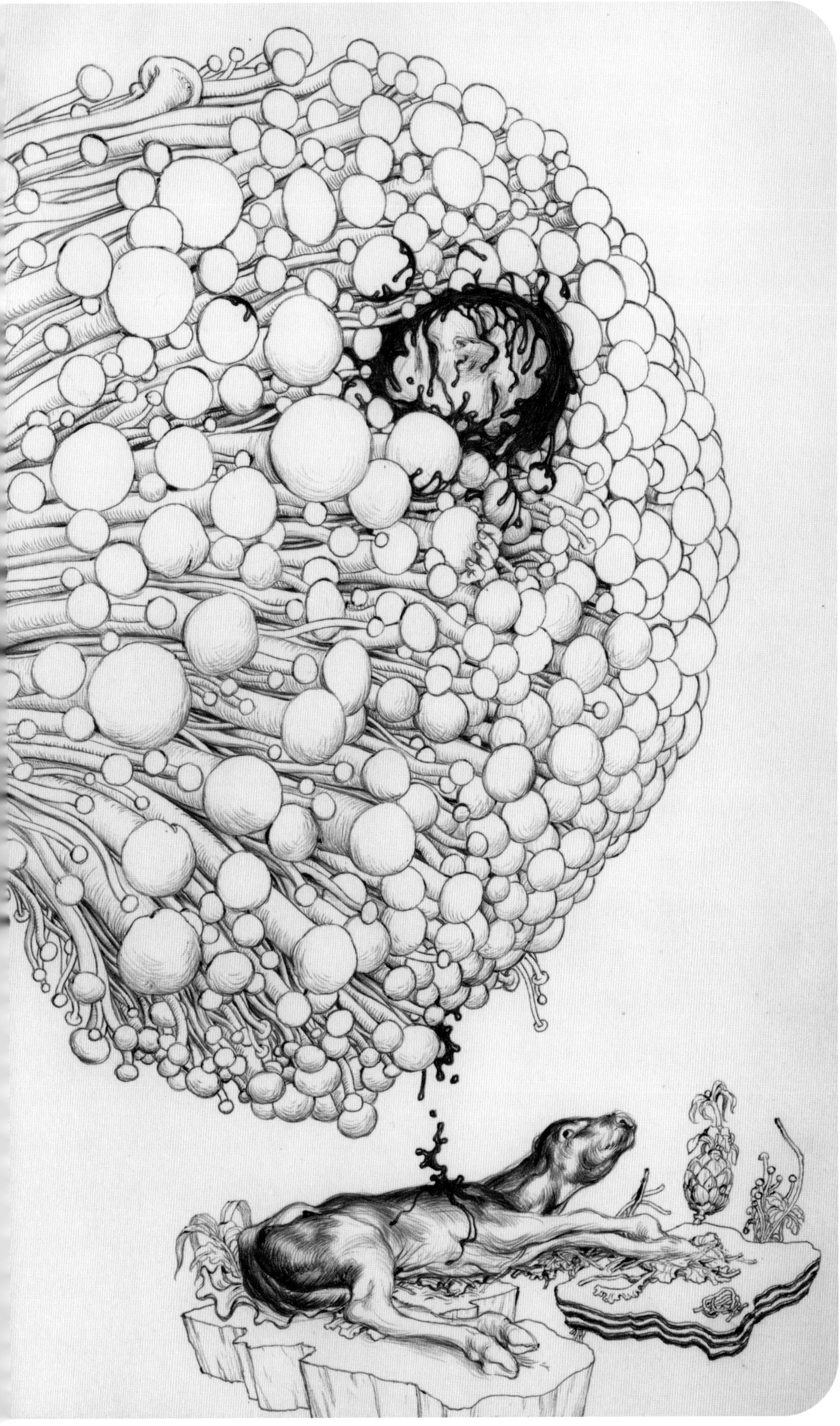

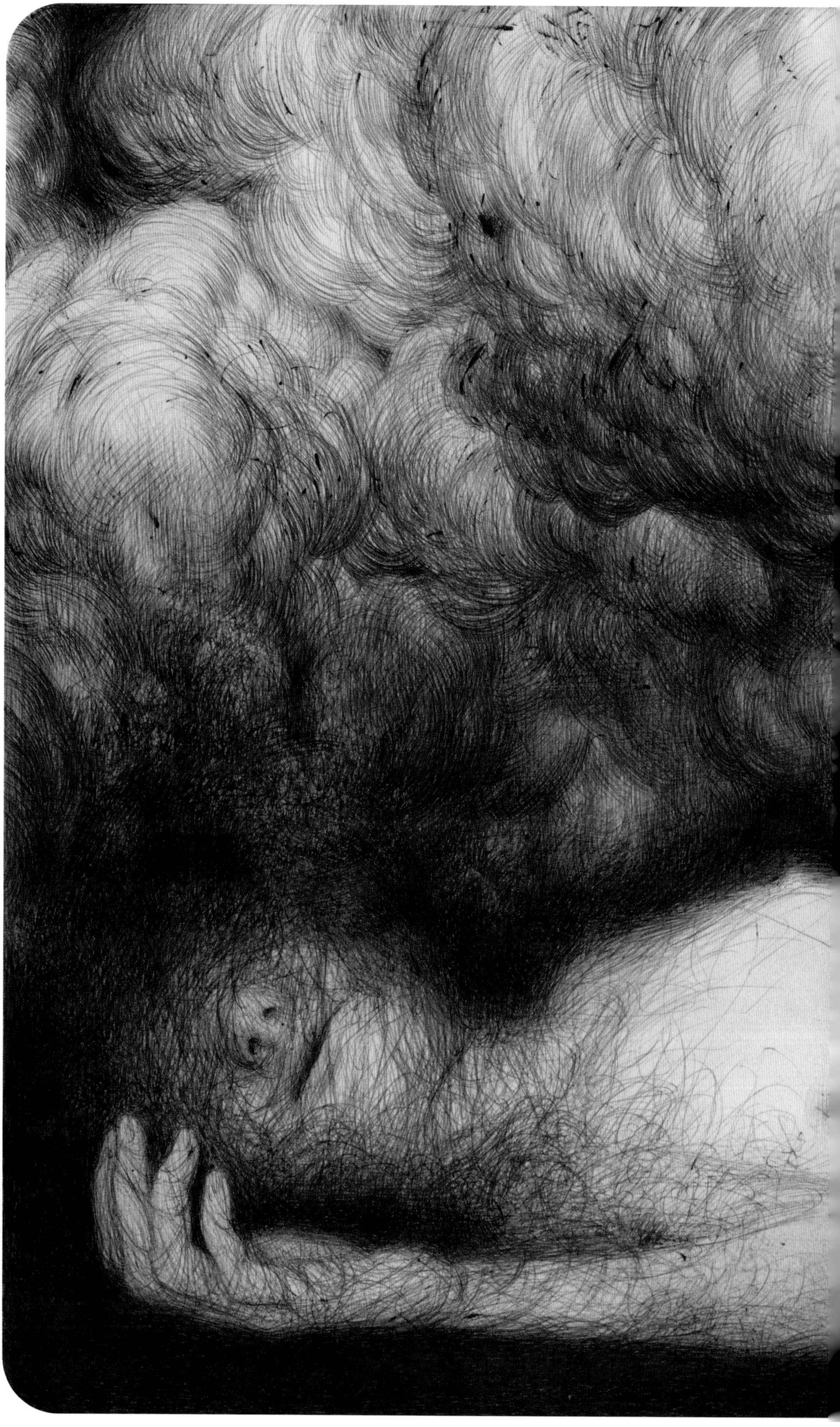

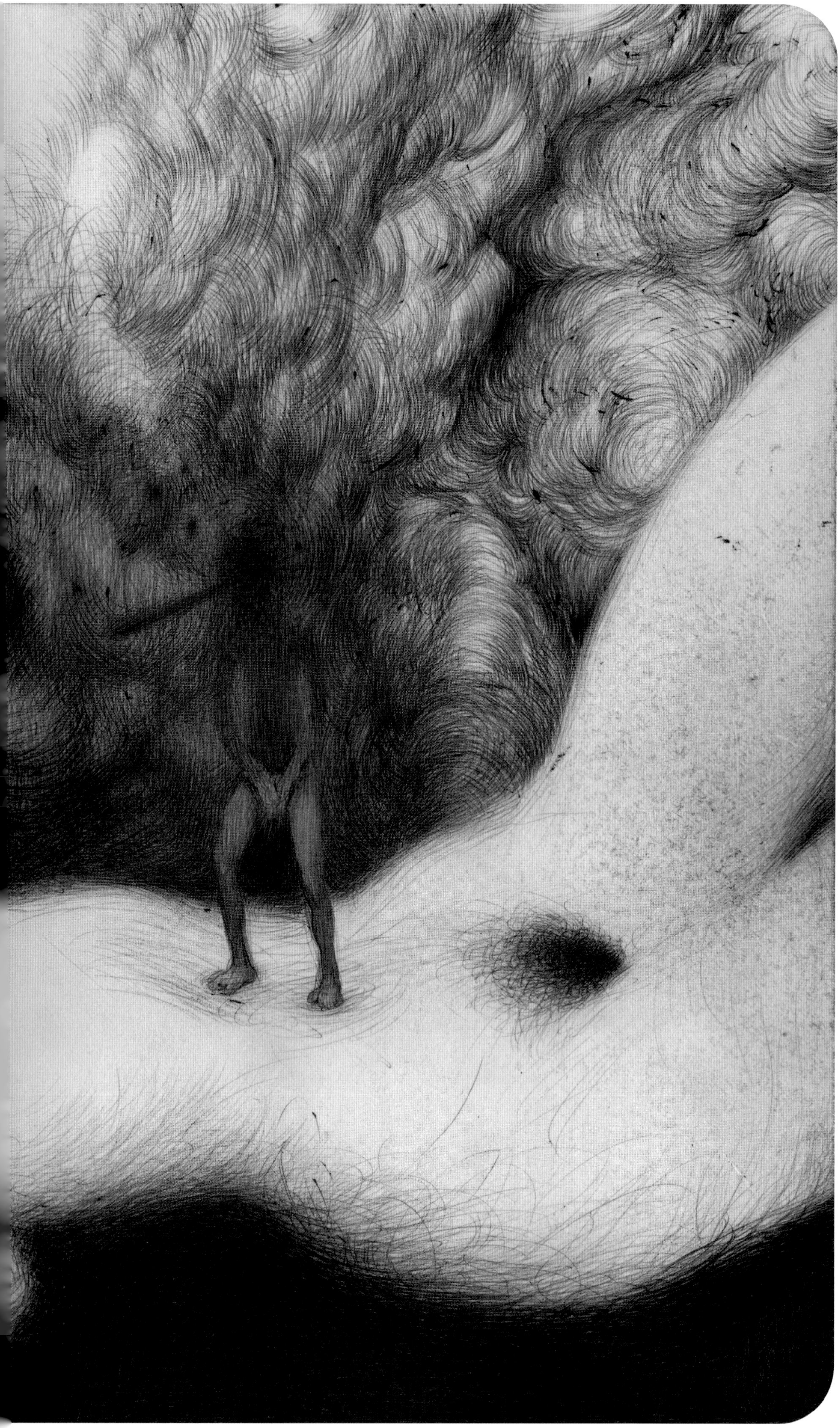

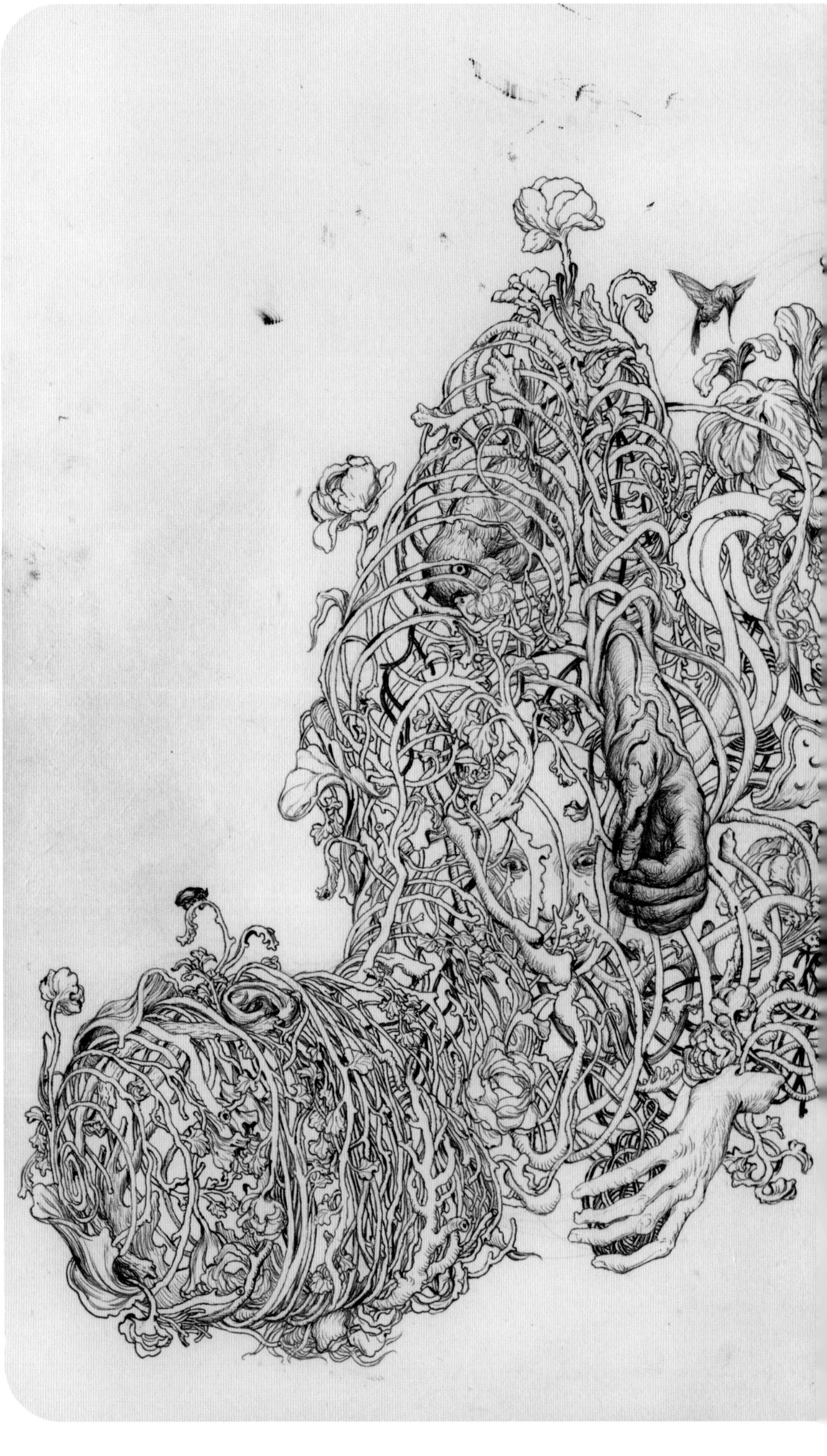

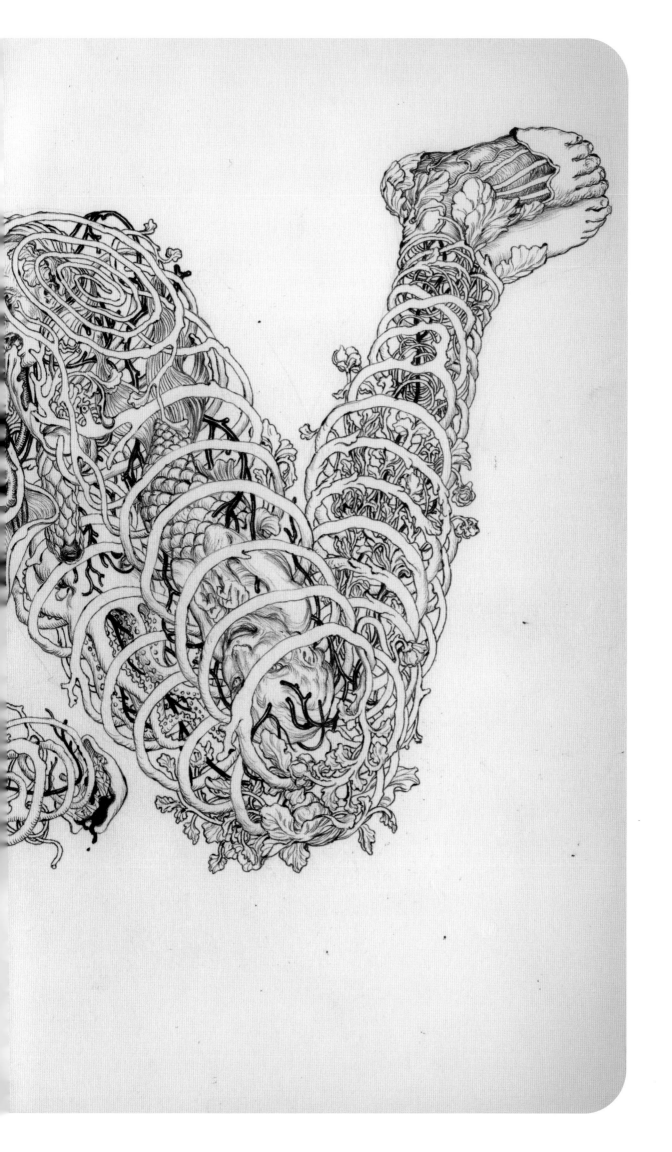

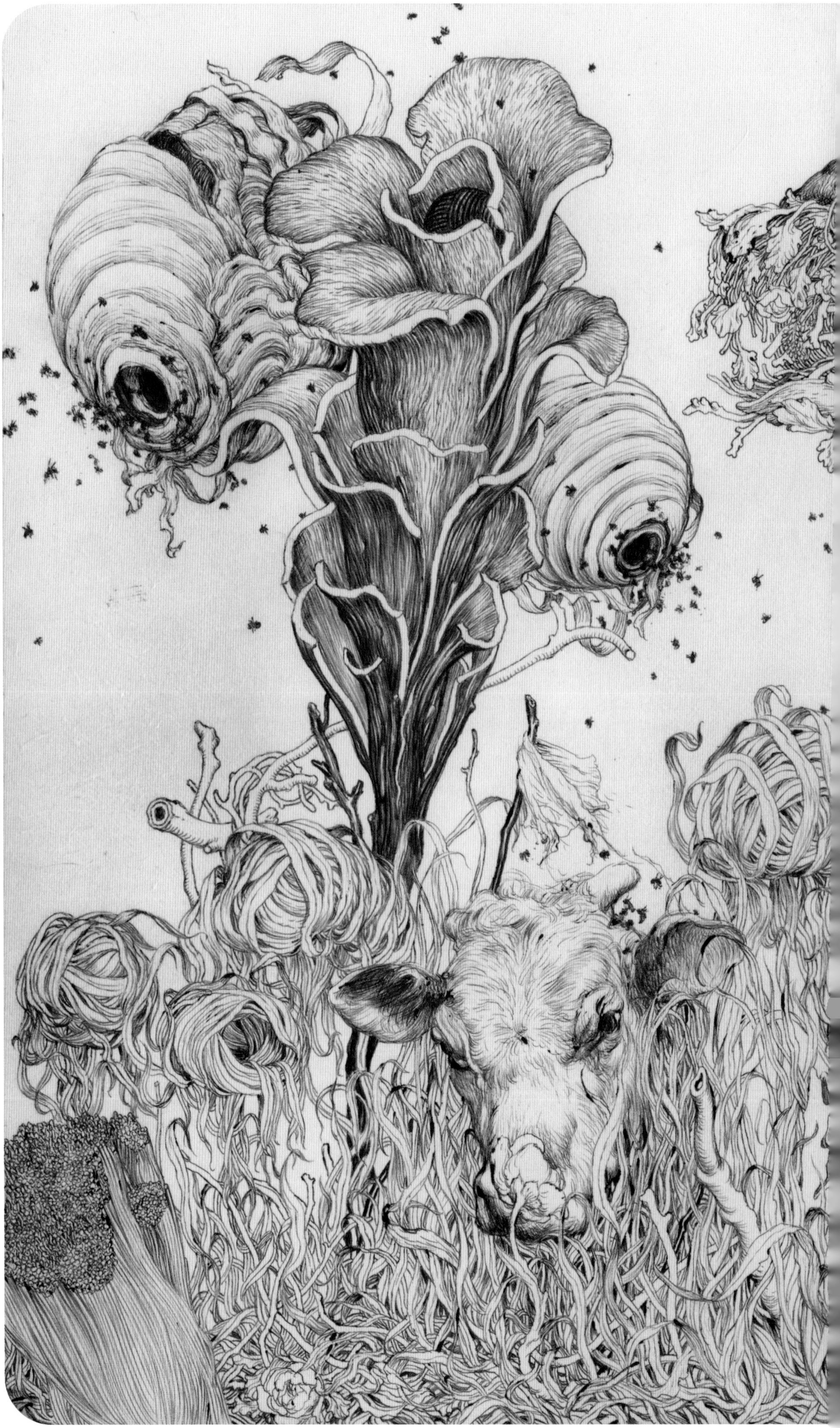

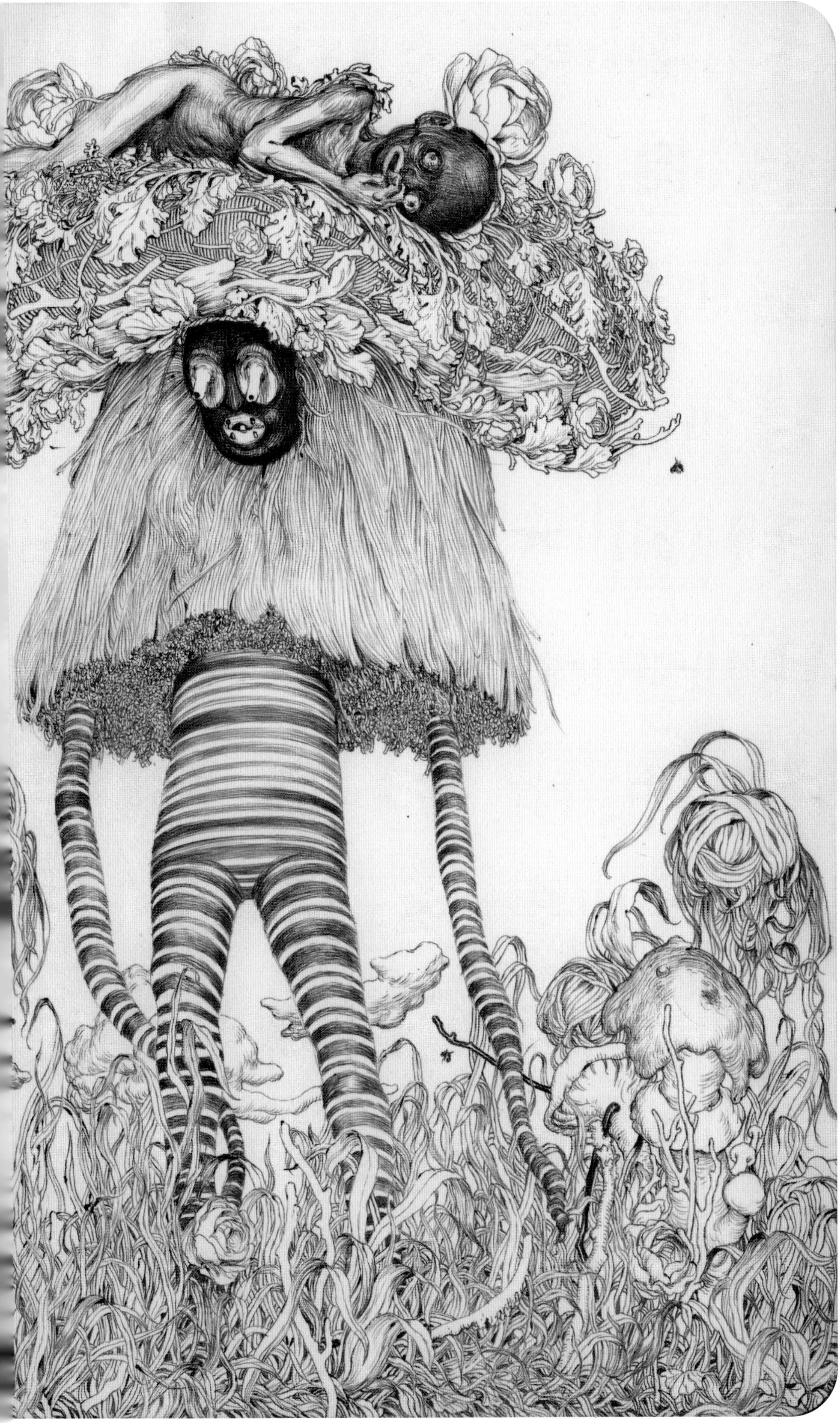

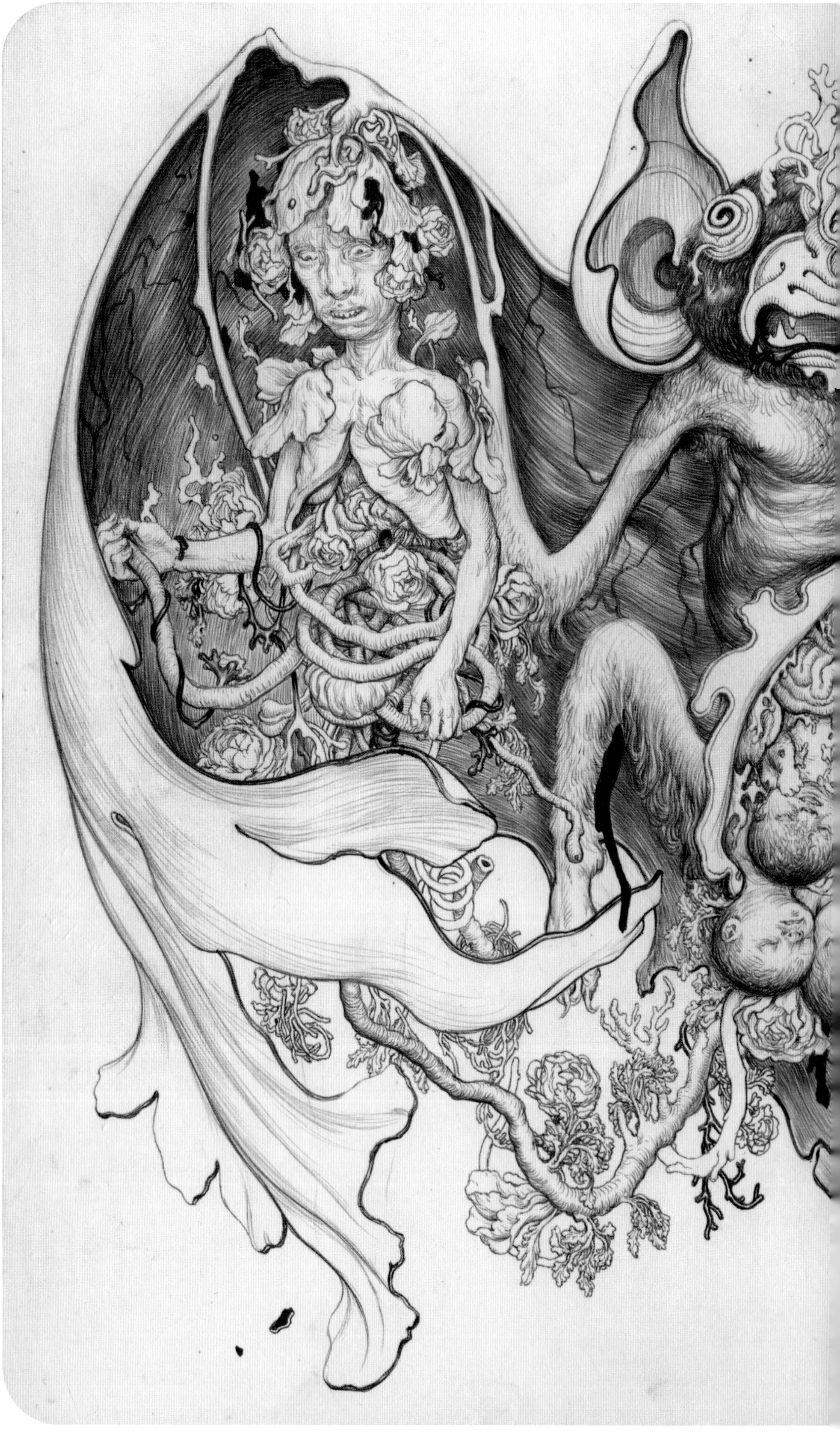

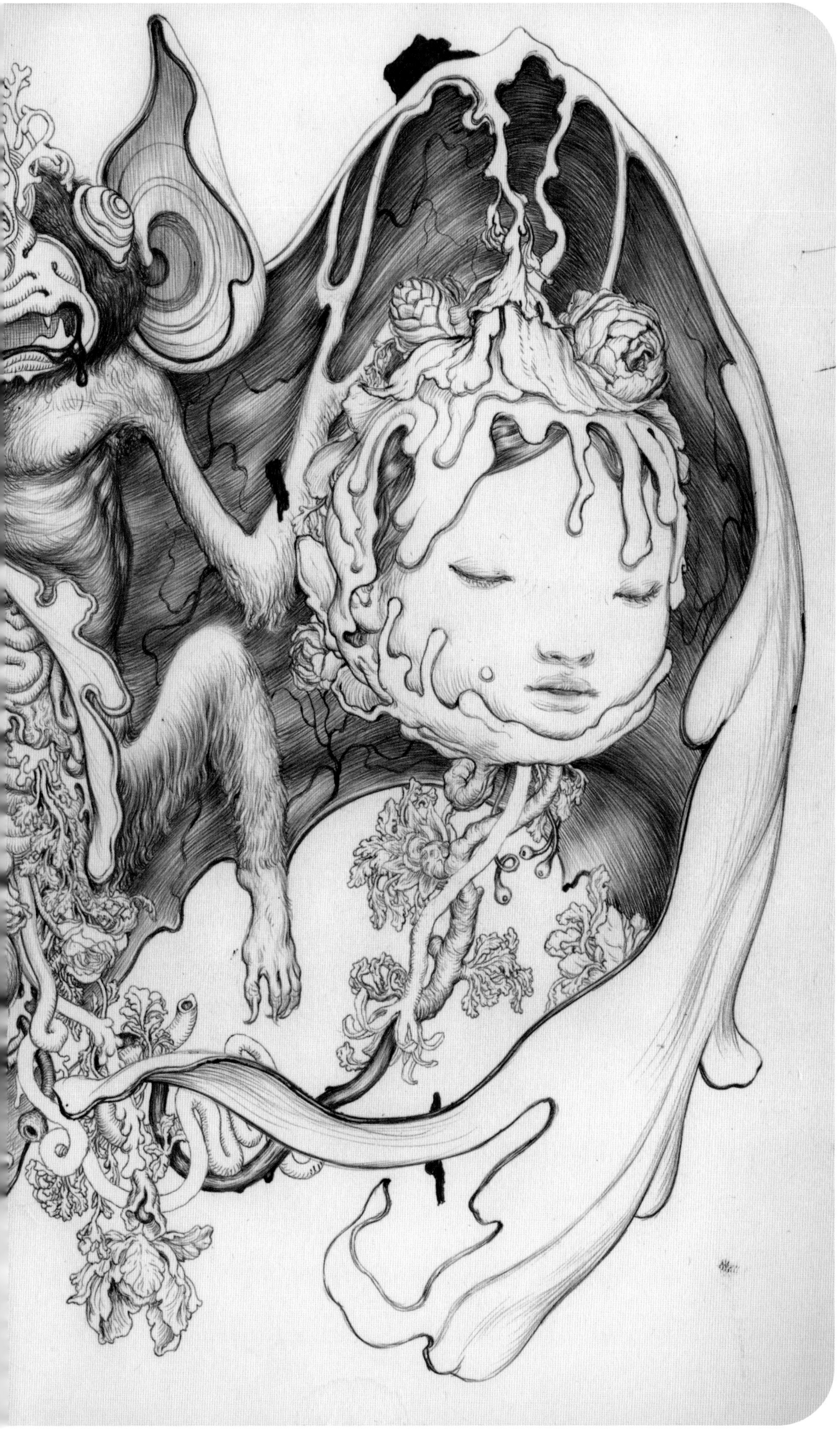

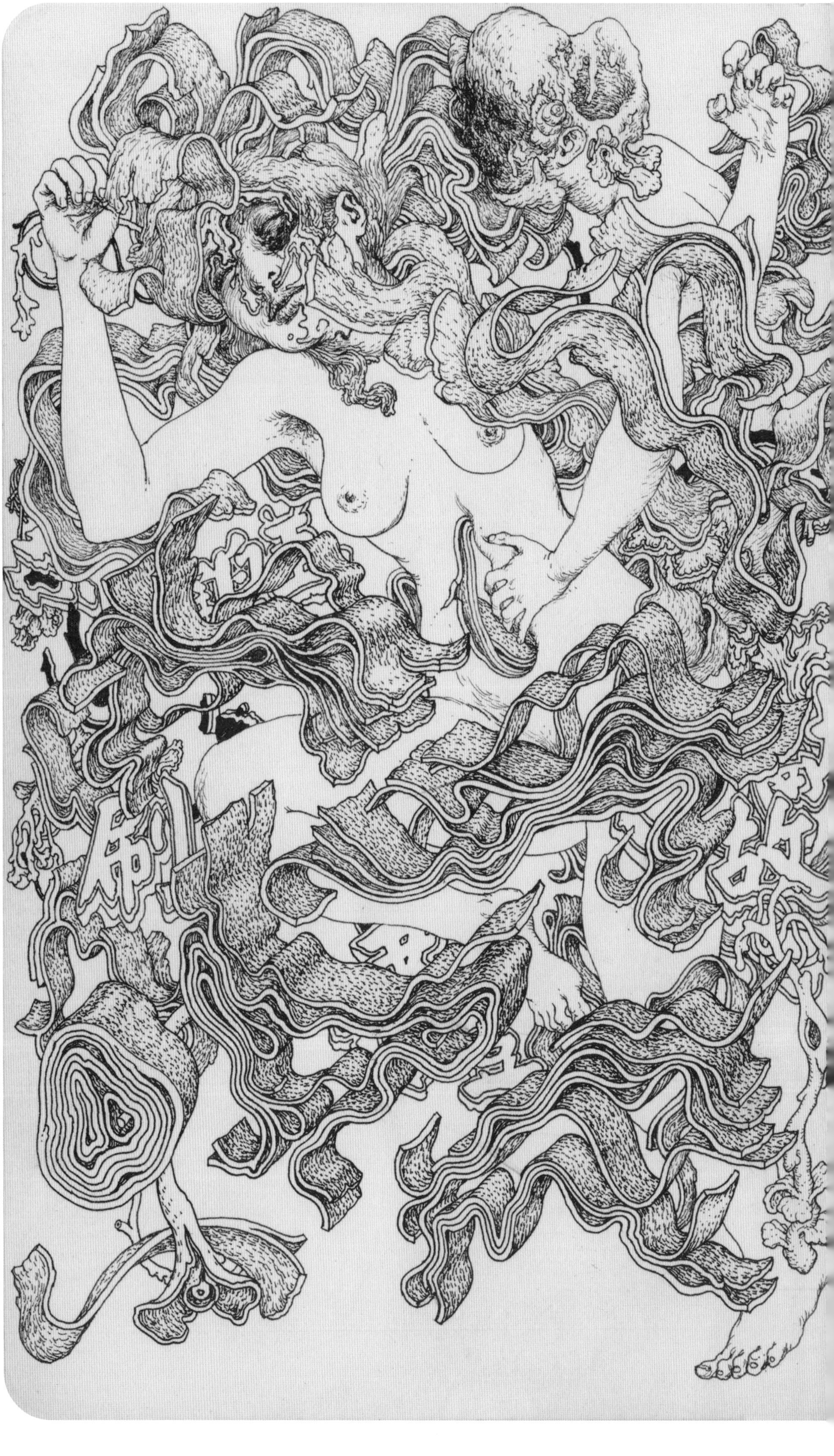

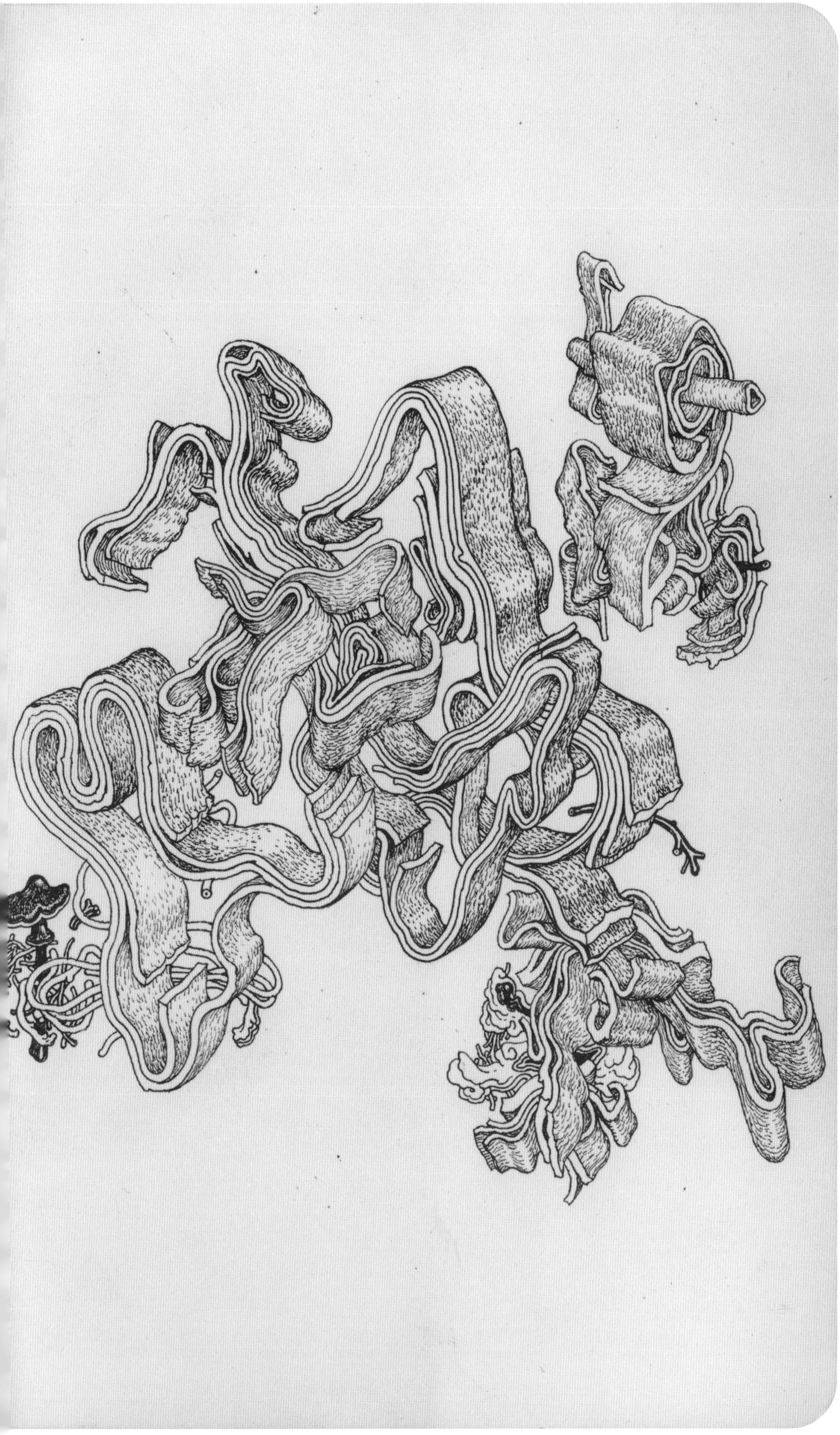

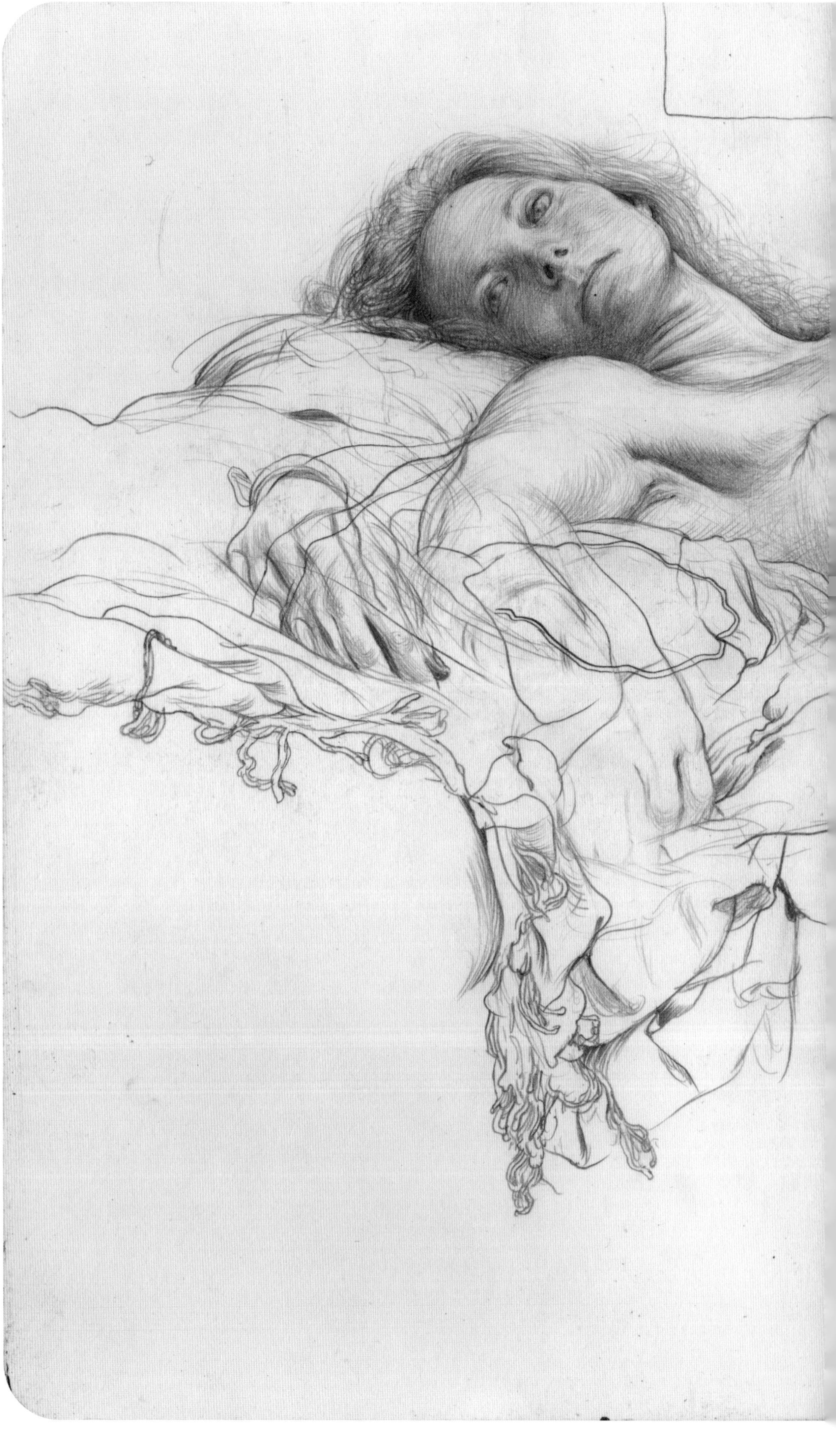

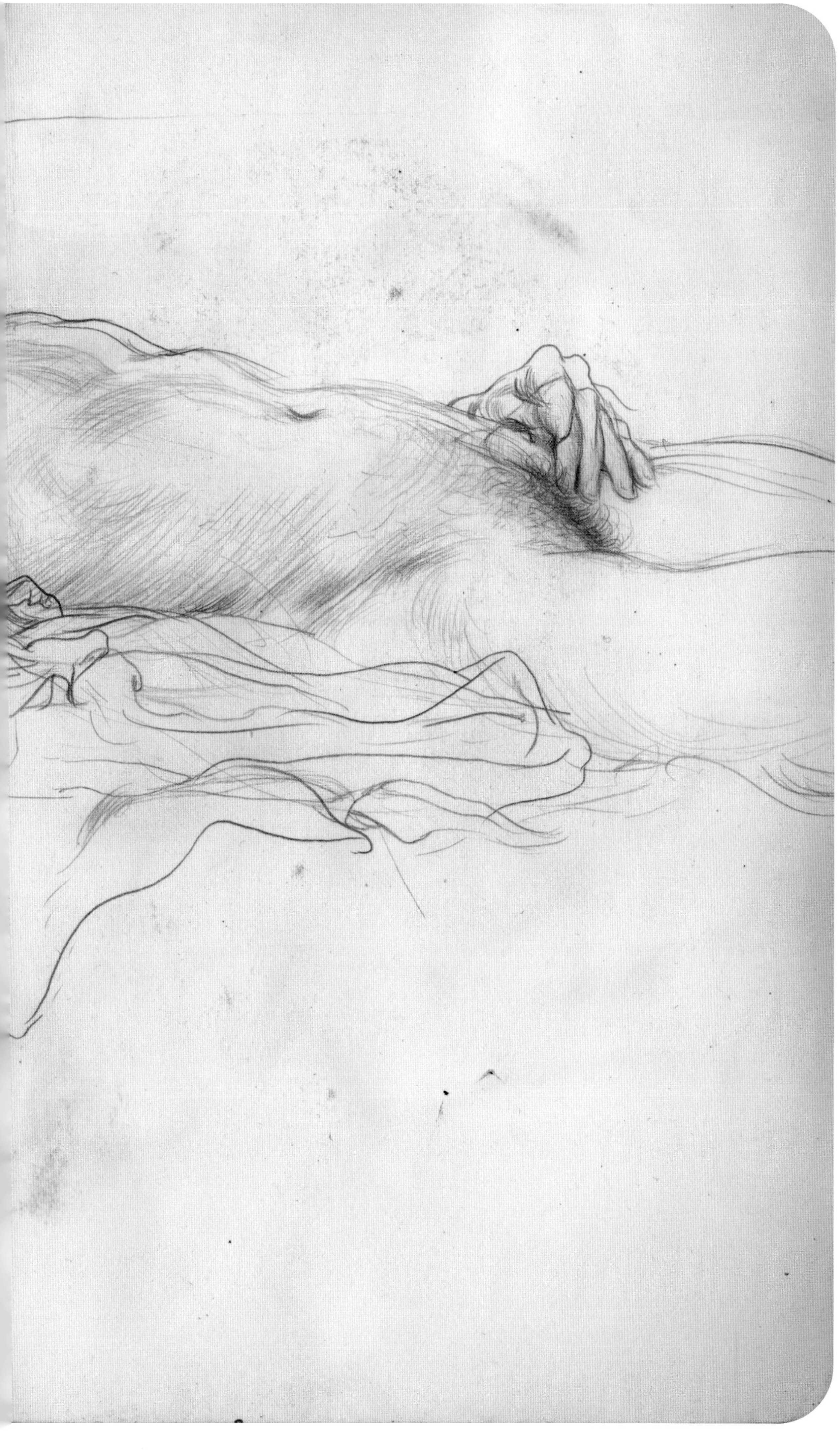

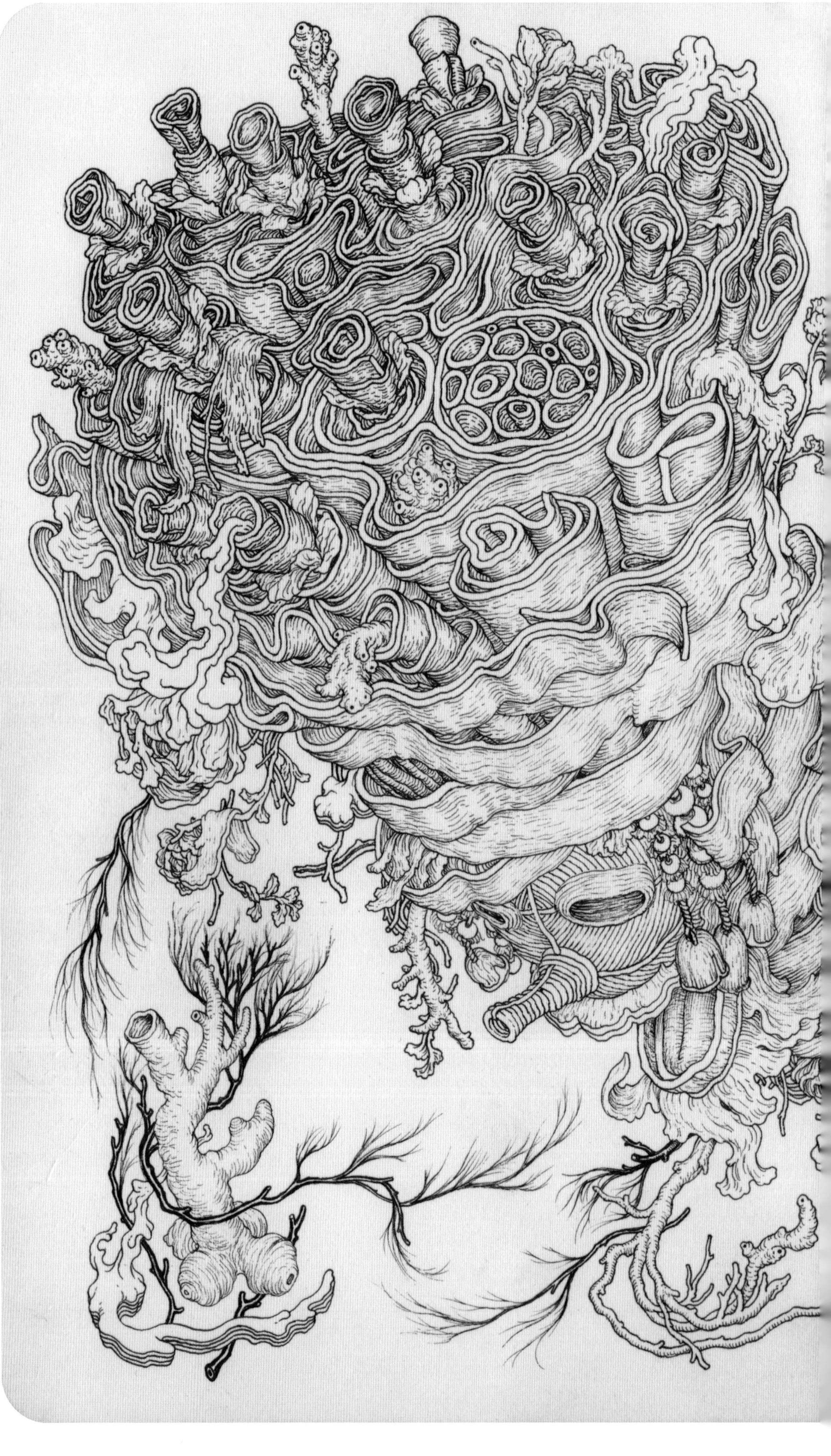

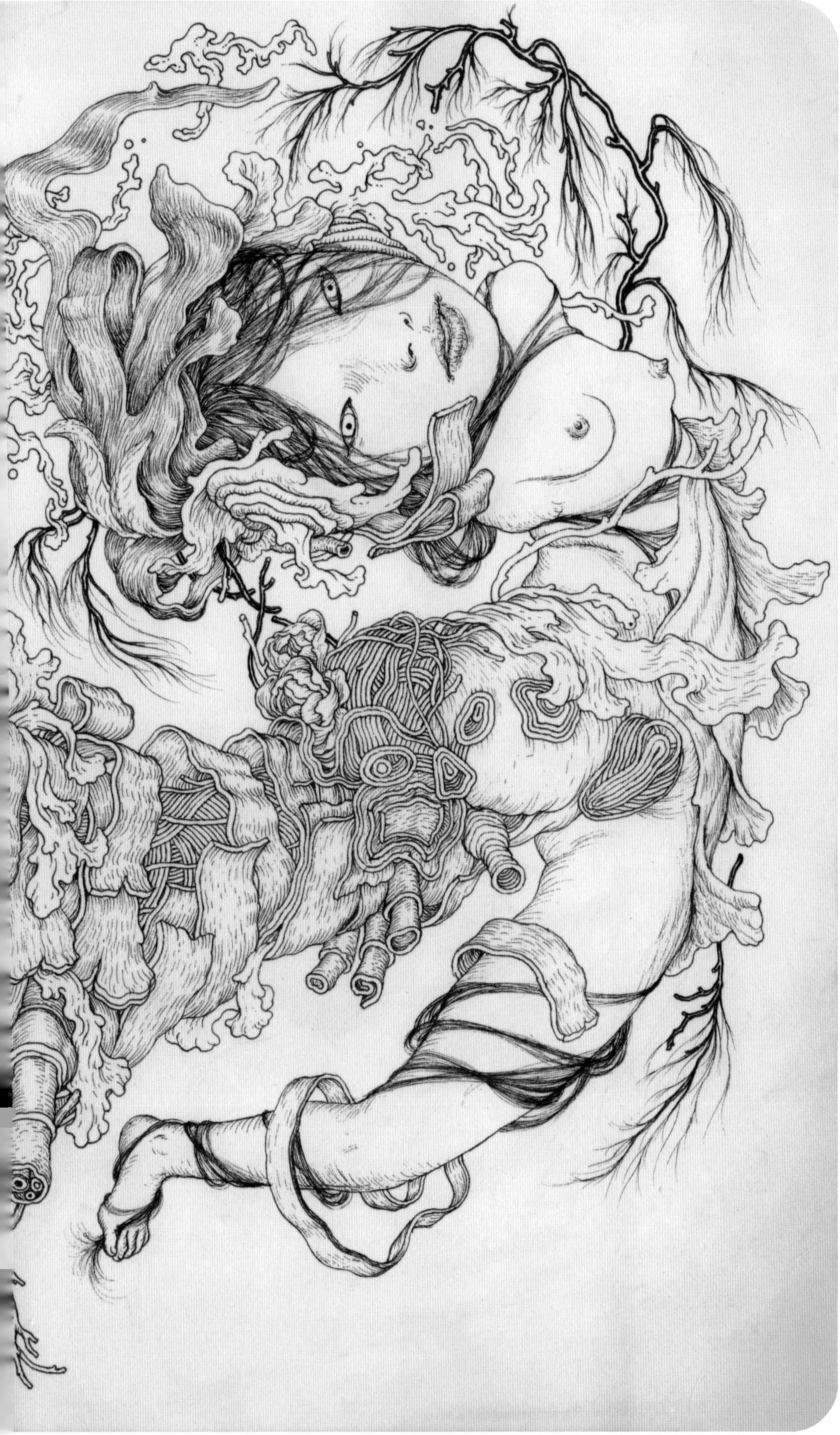

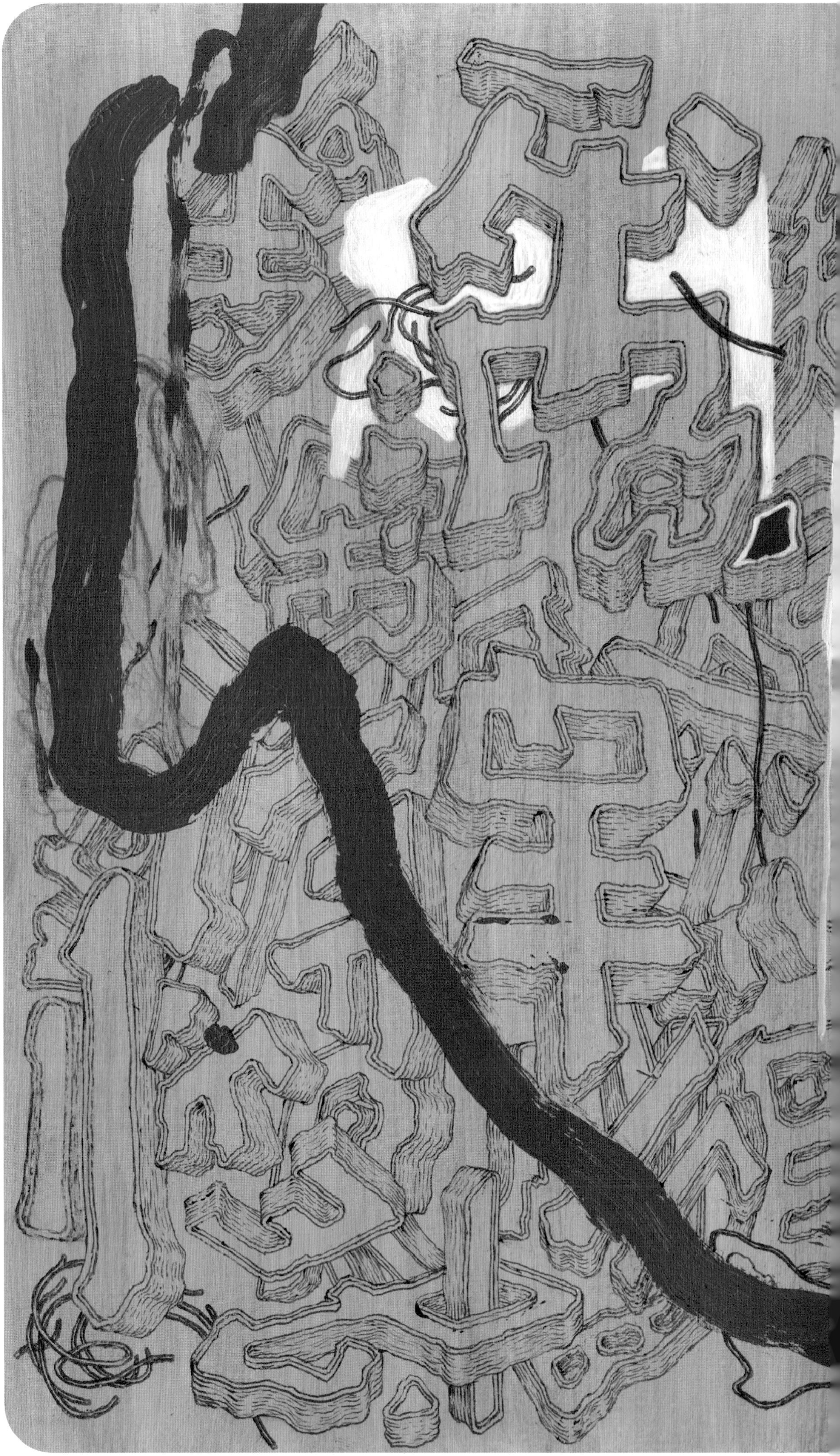

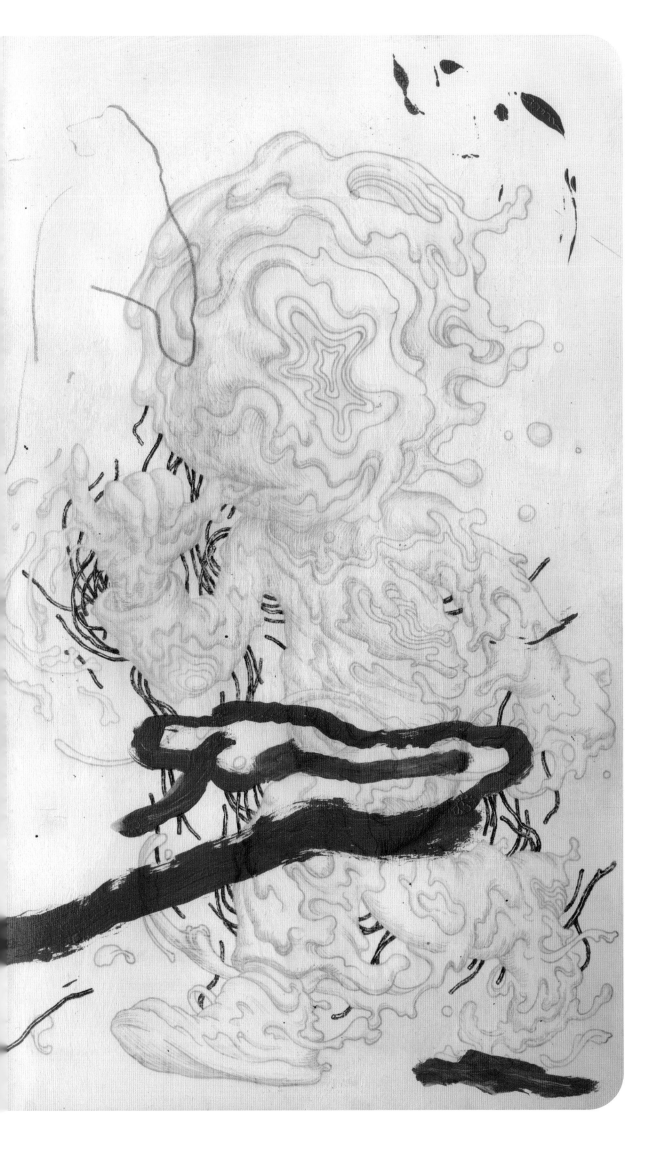

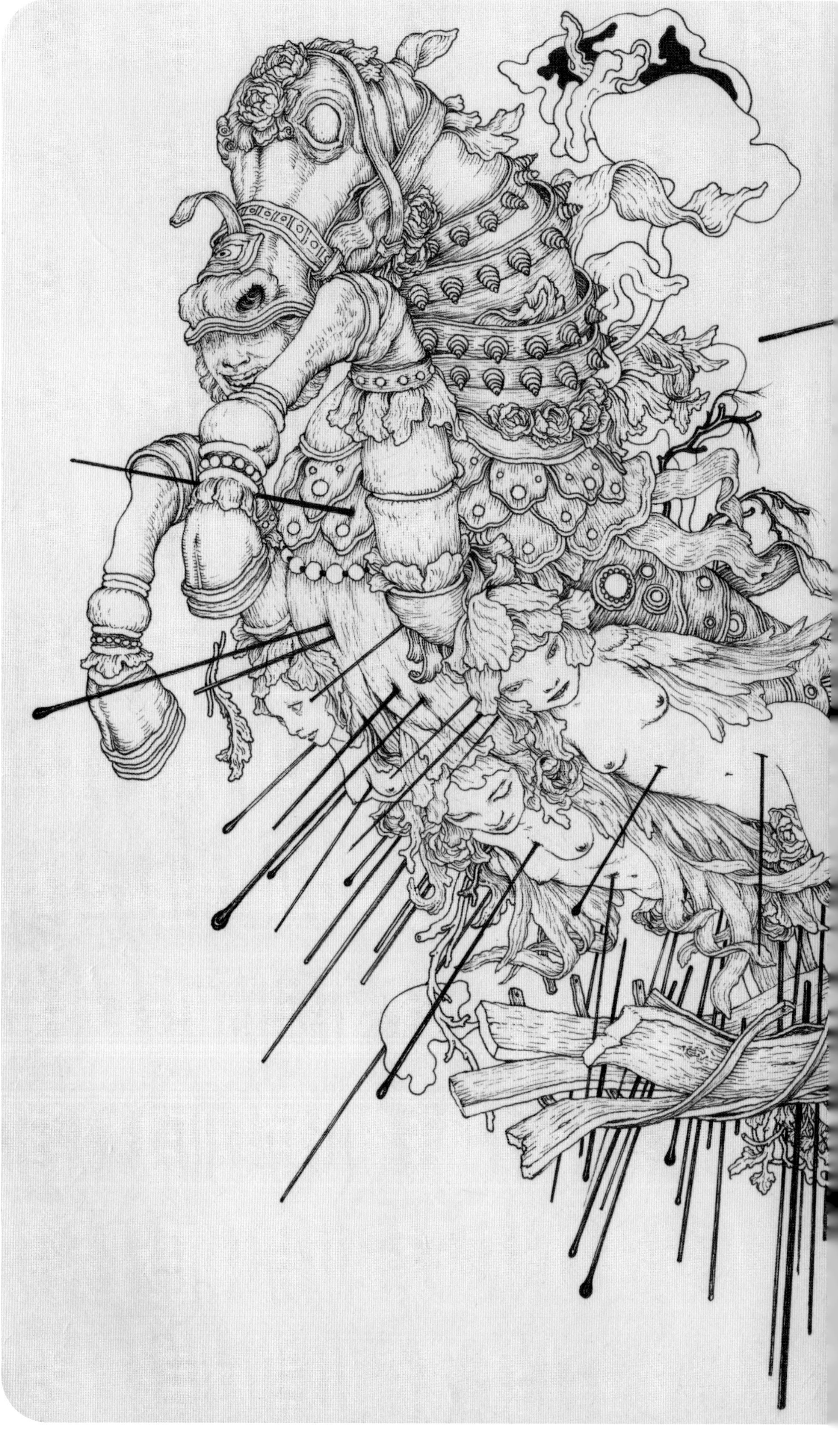

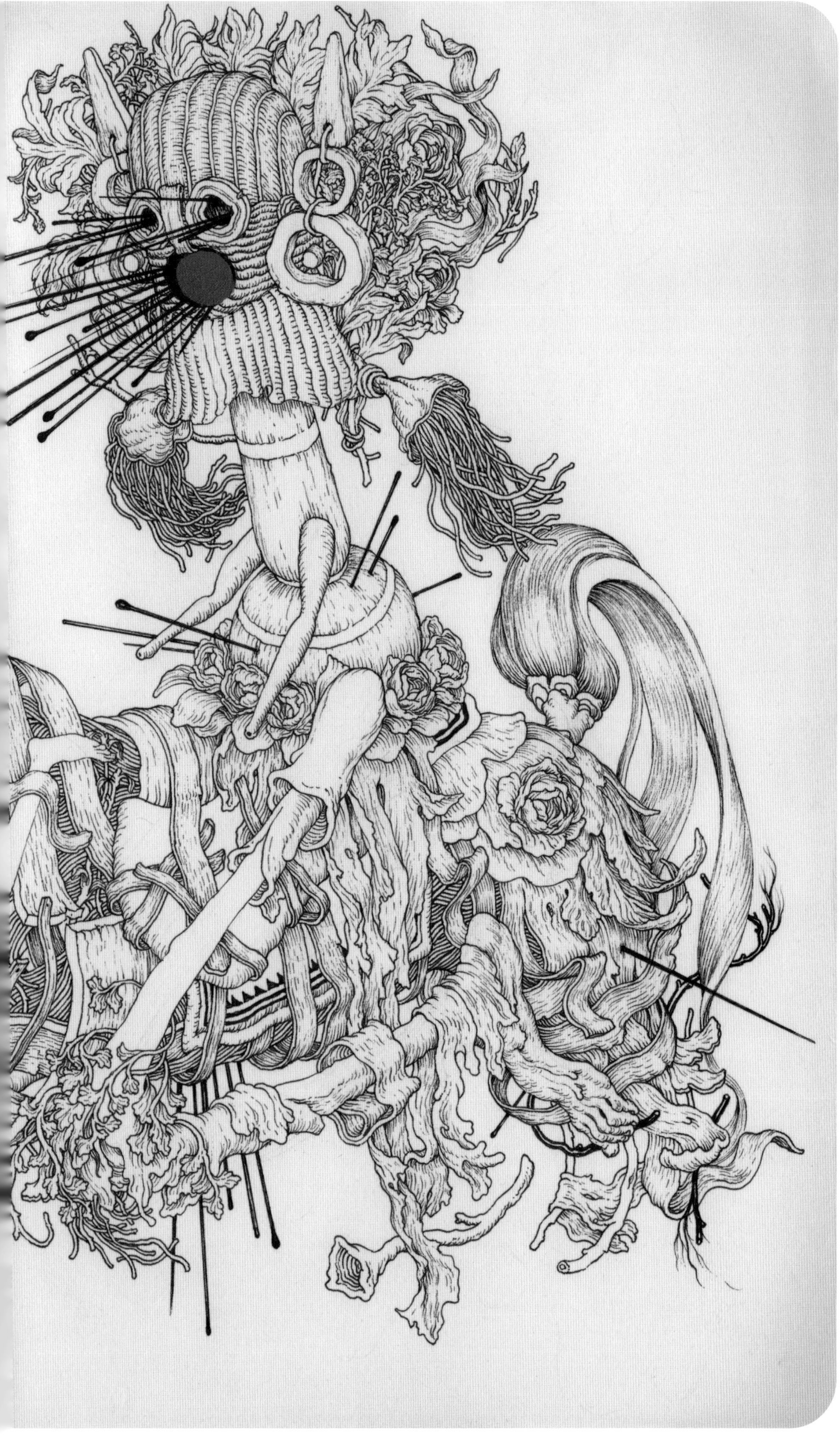

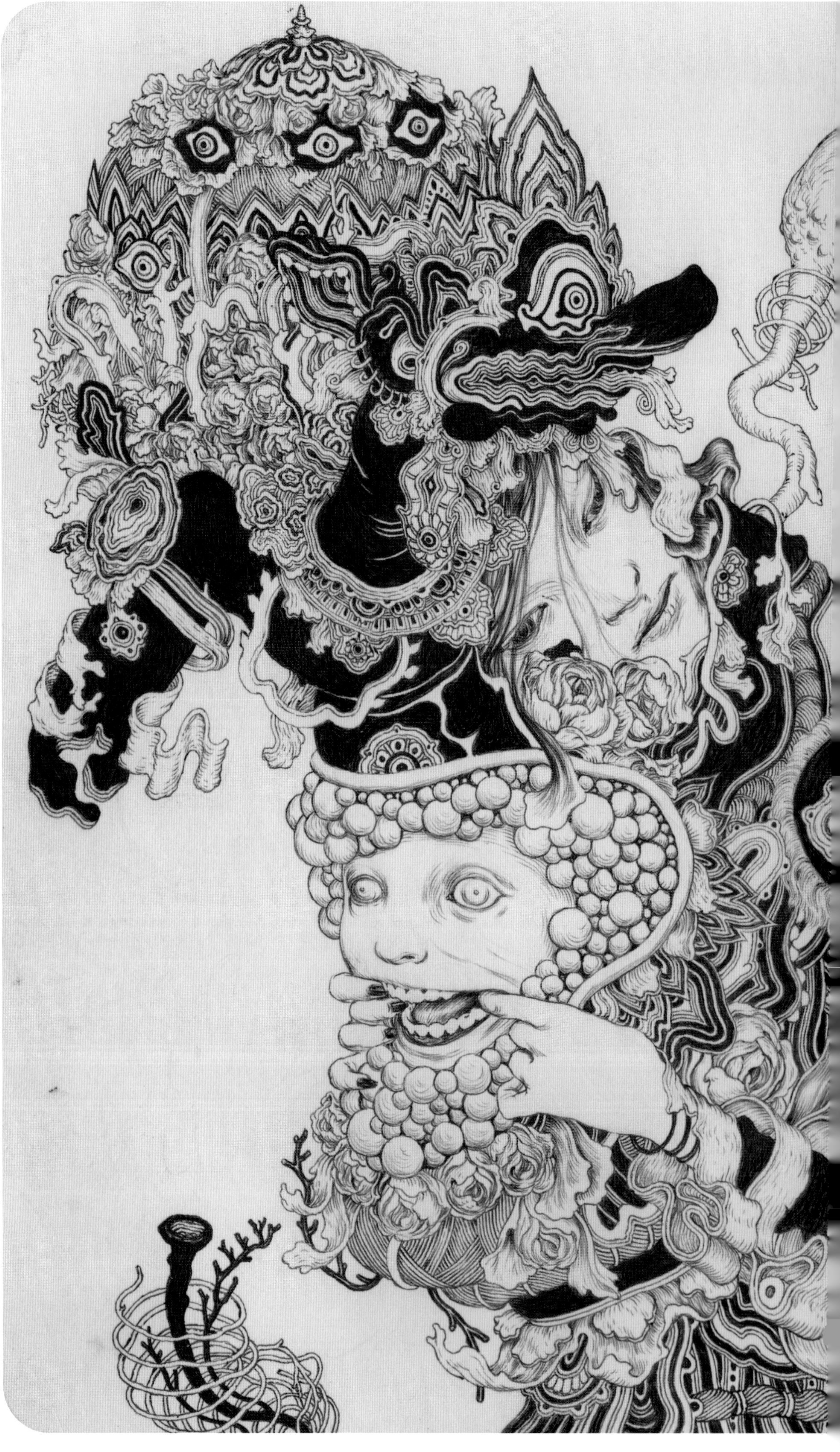

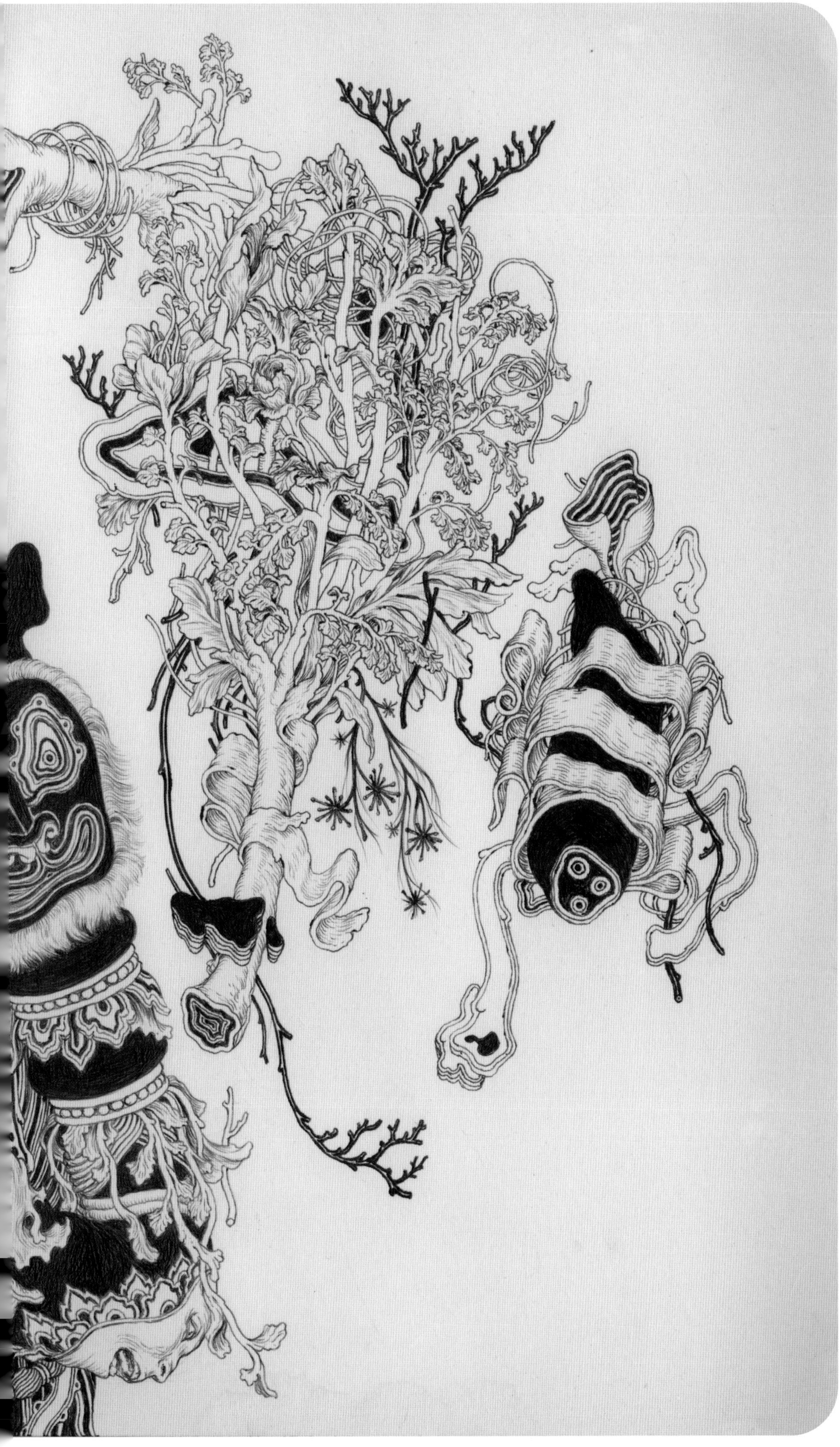

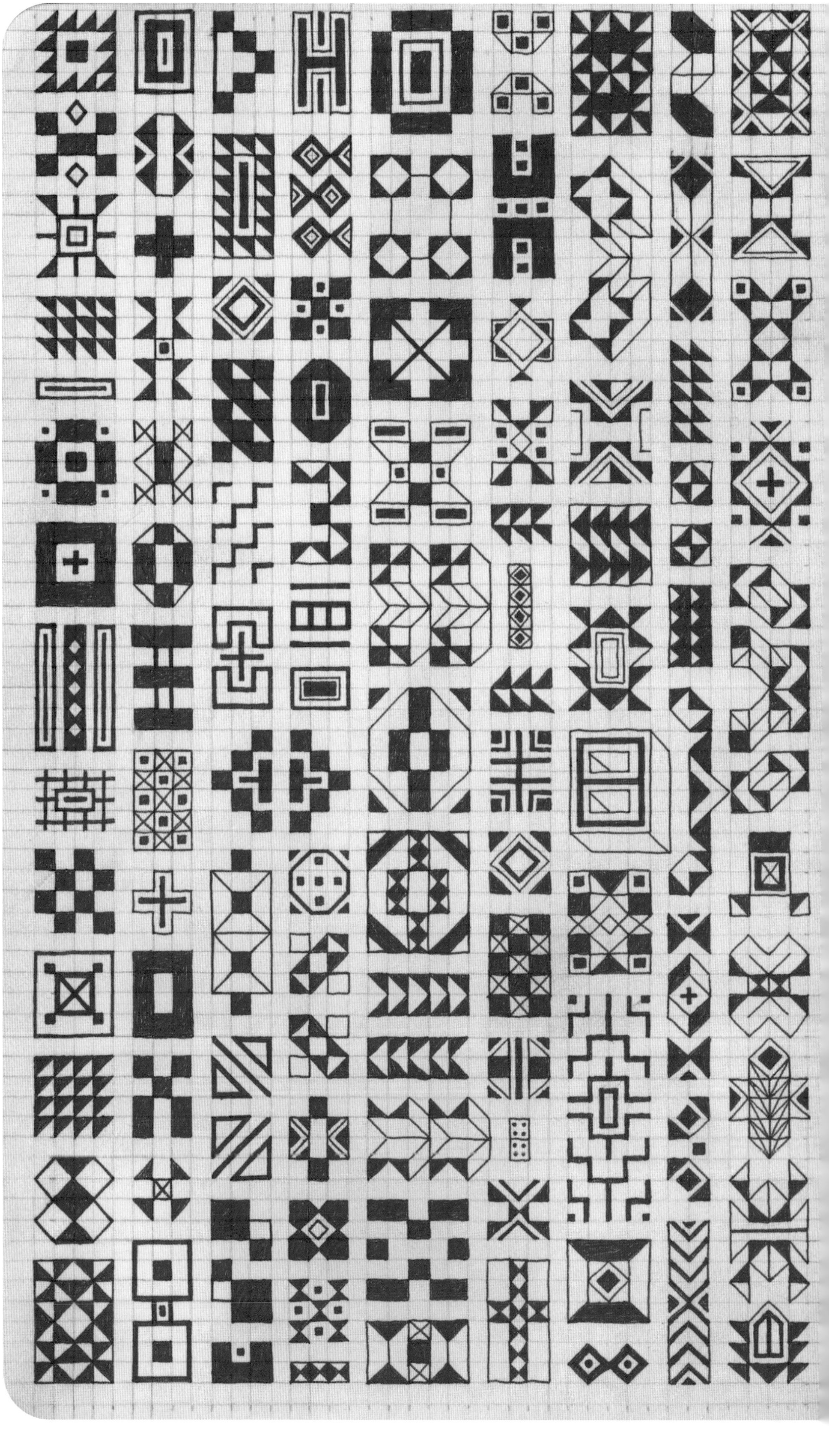

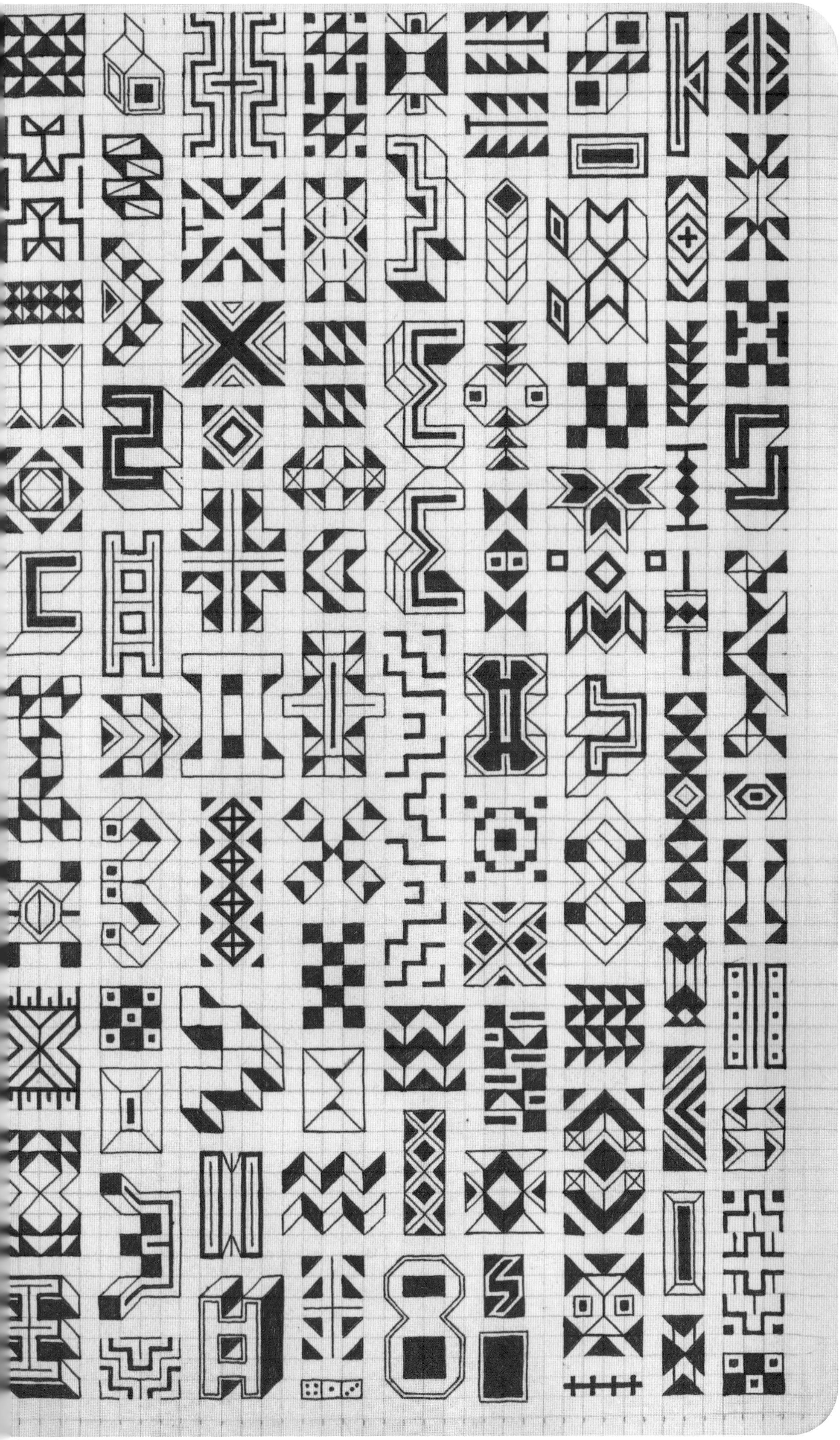

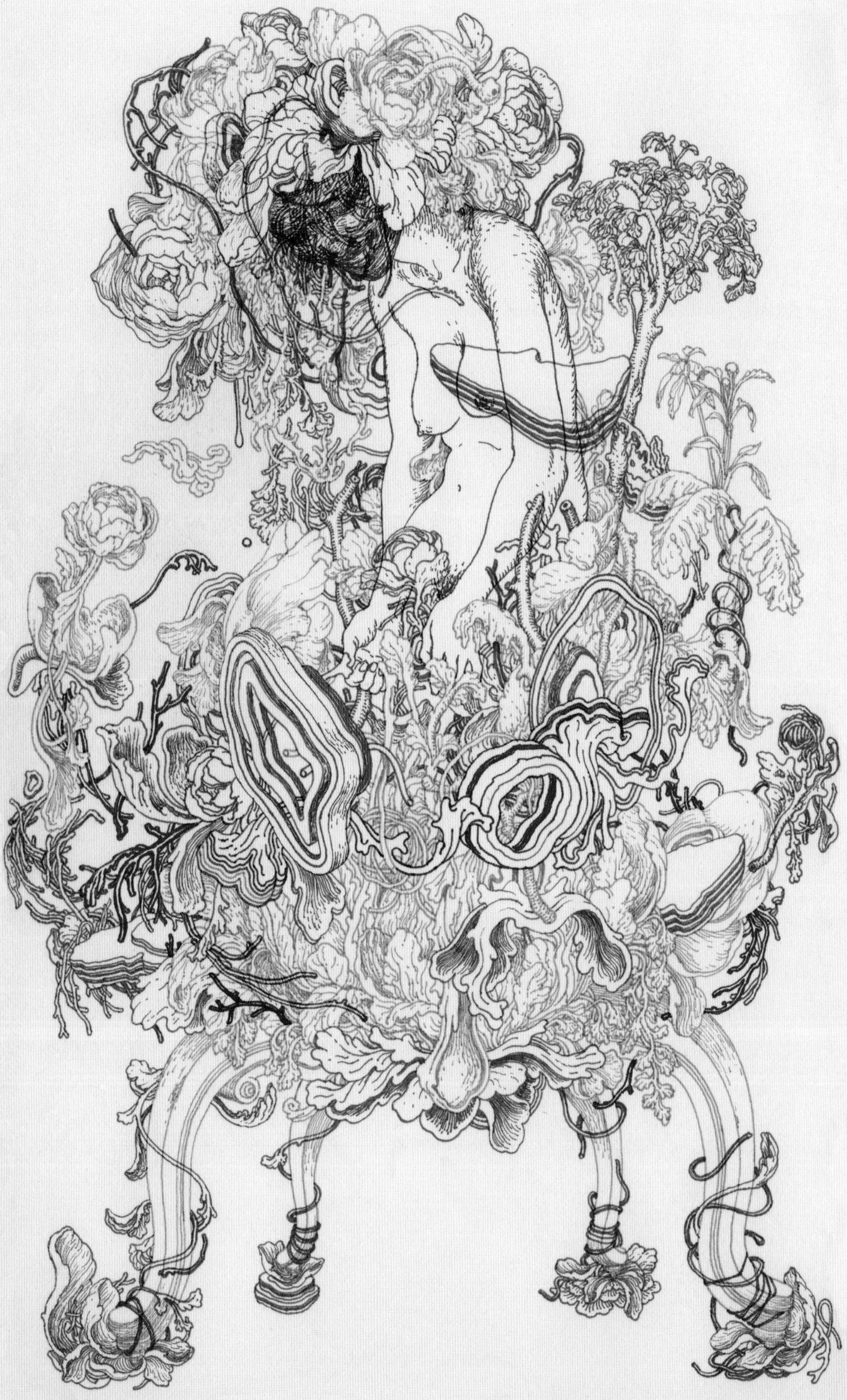

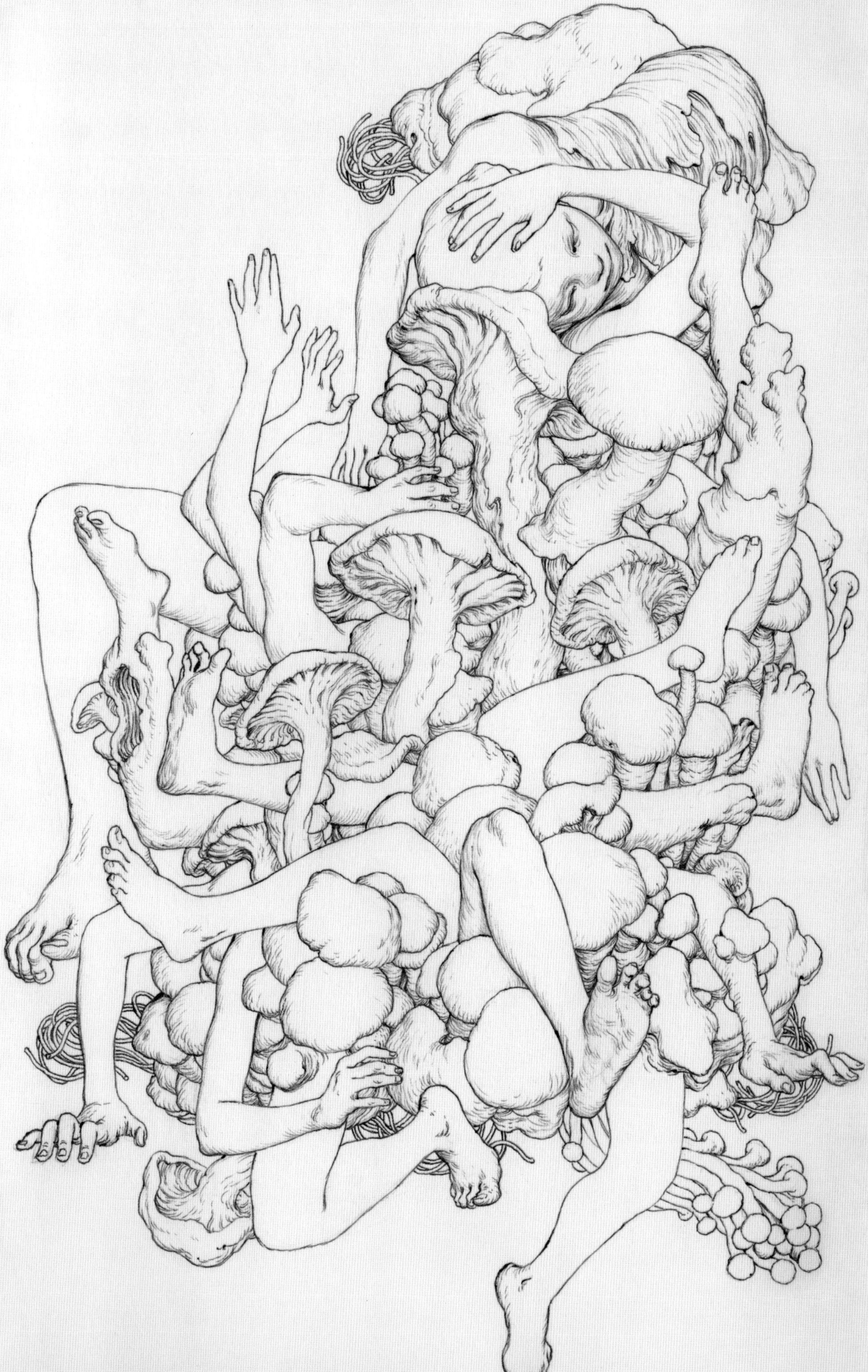

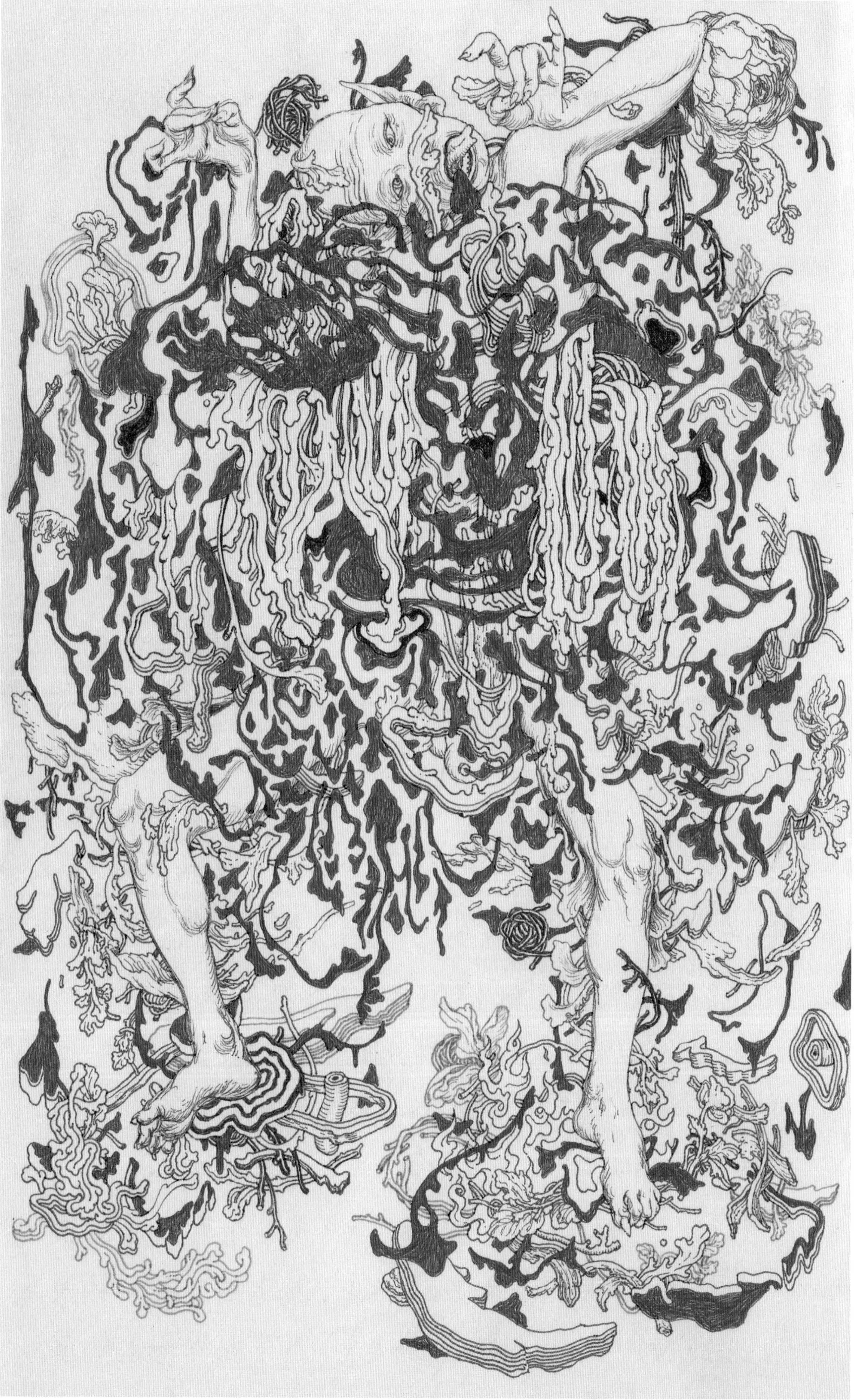

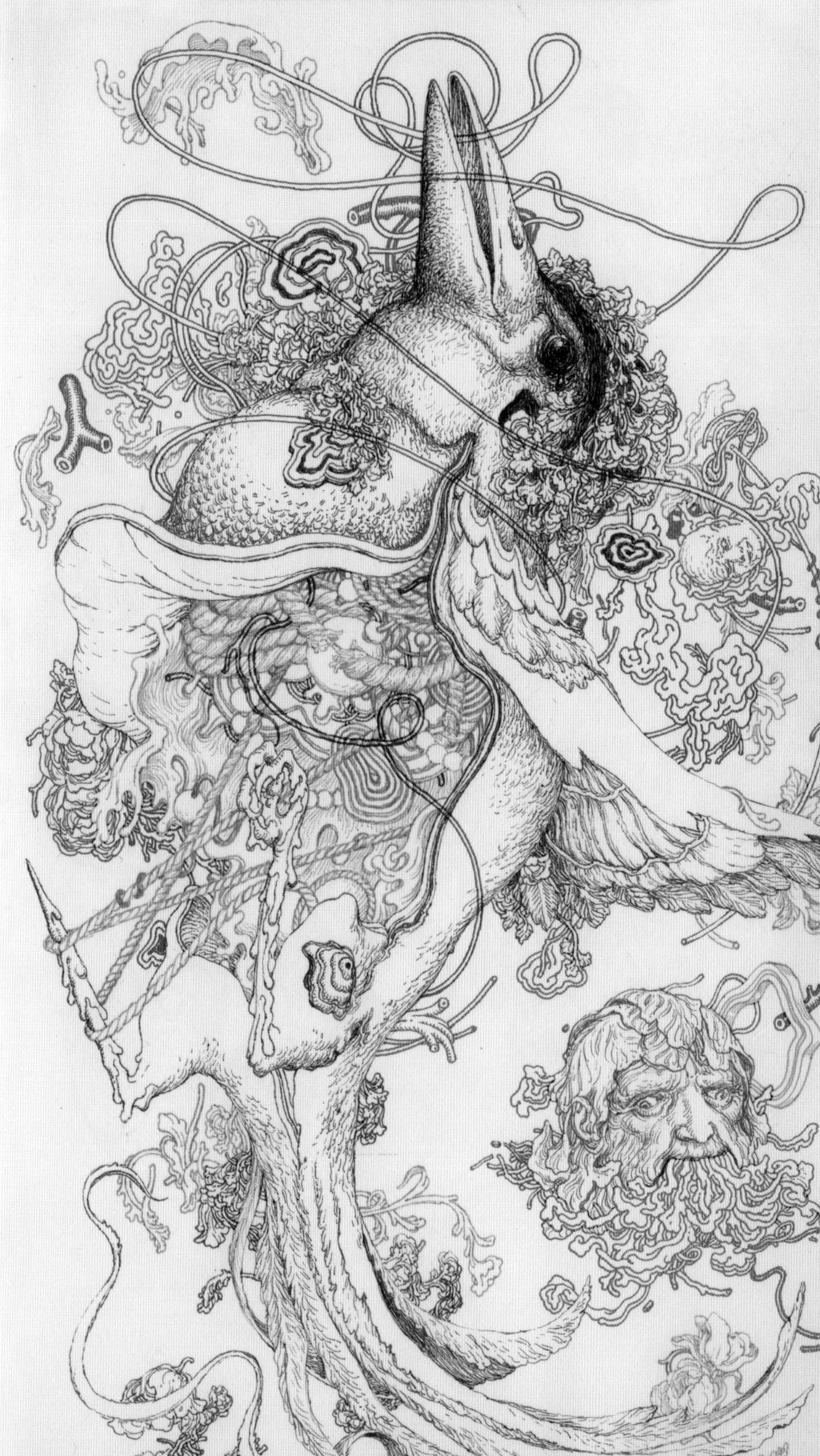

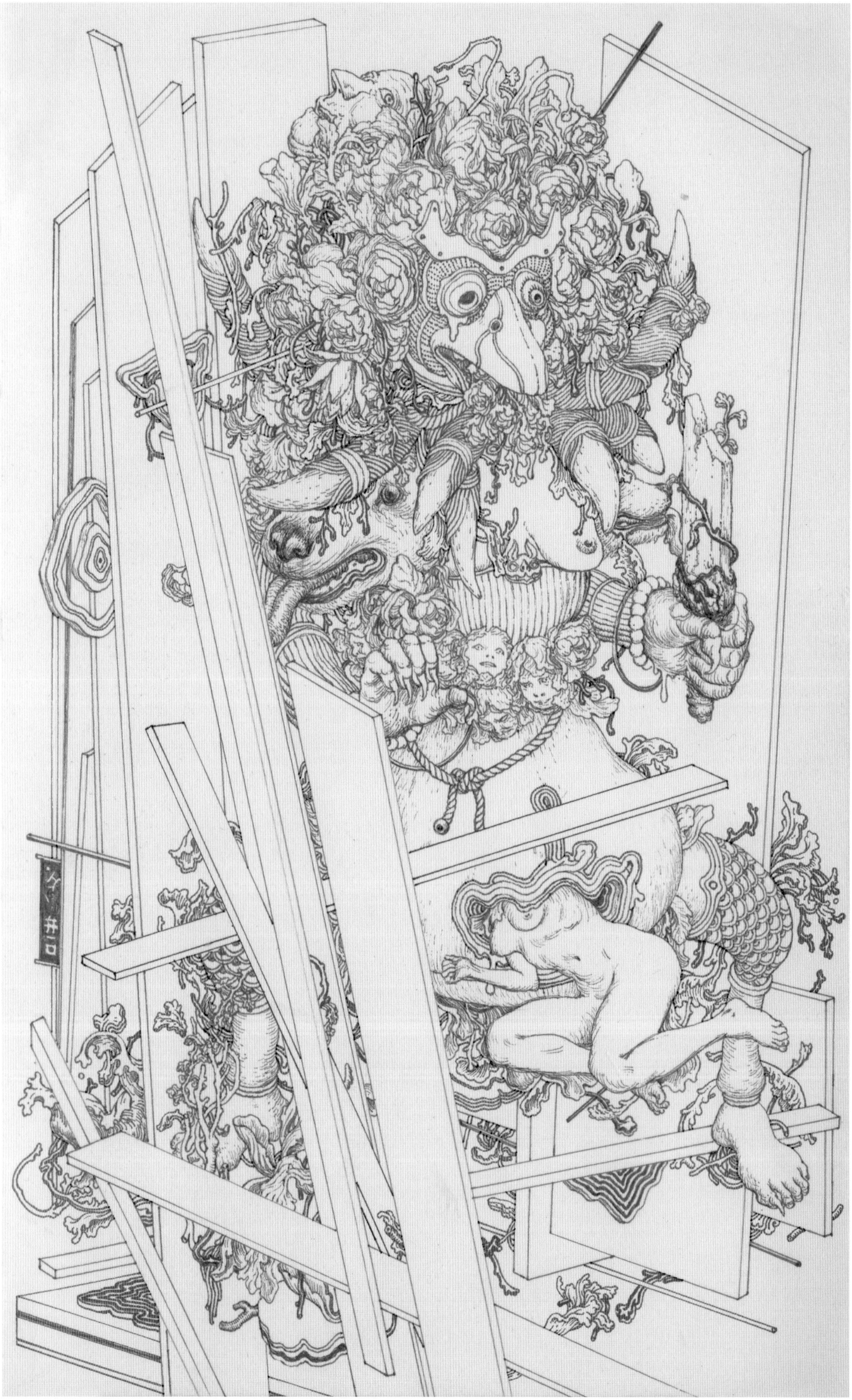
井口

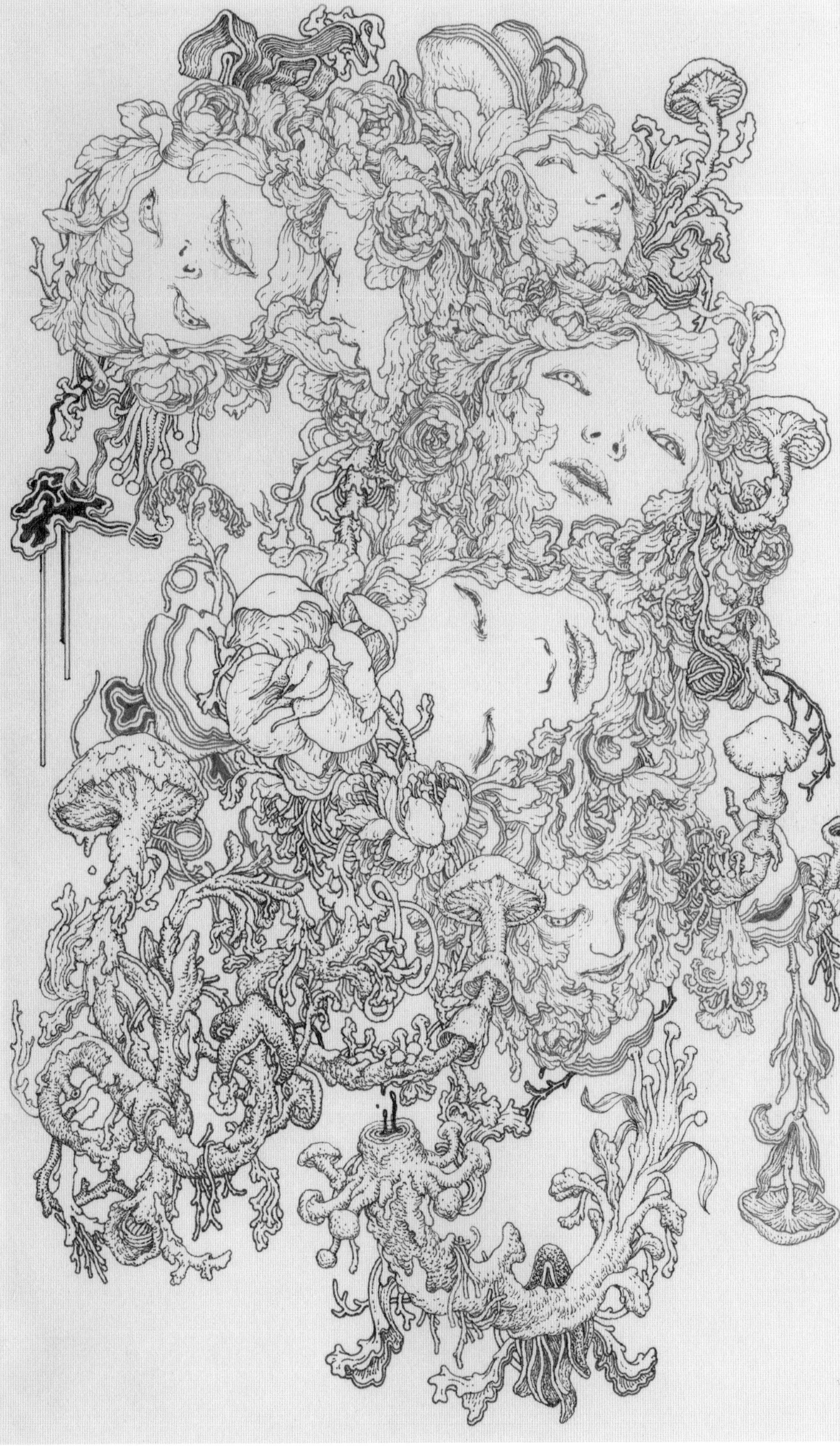

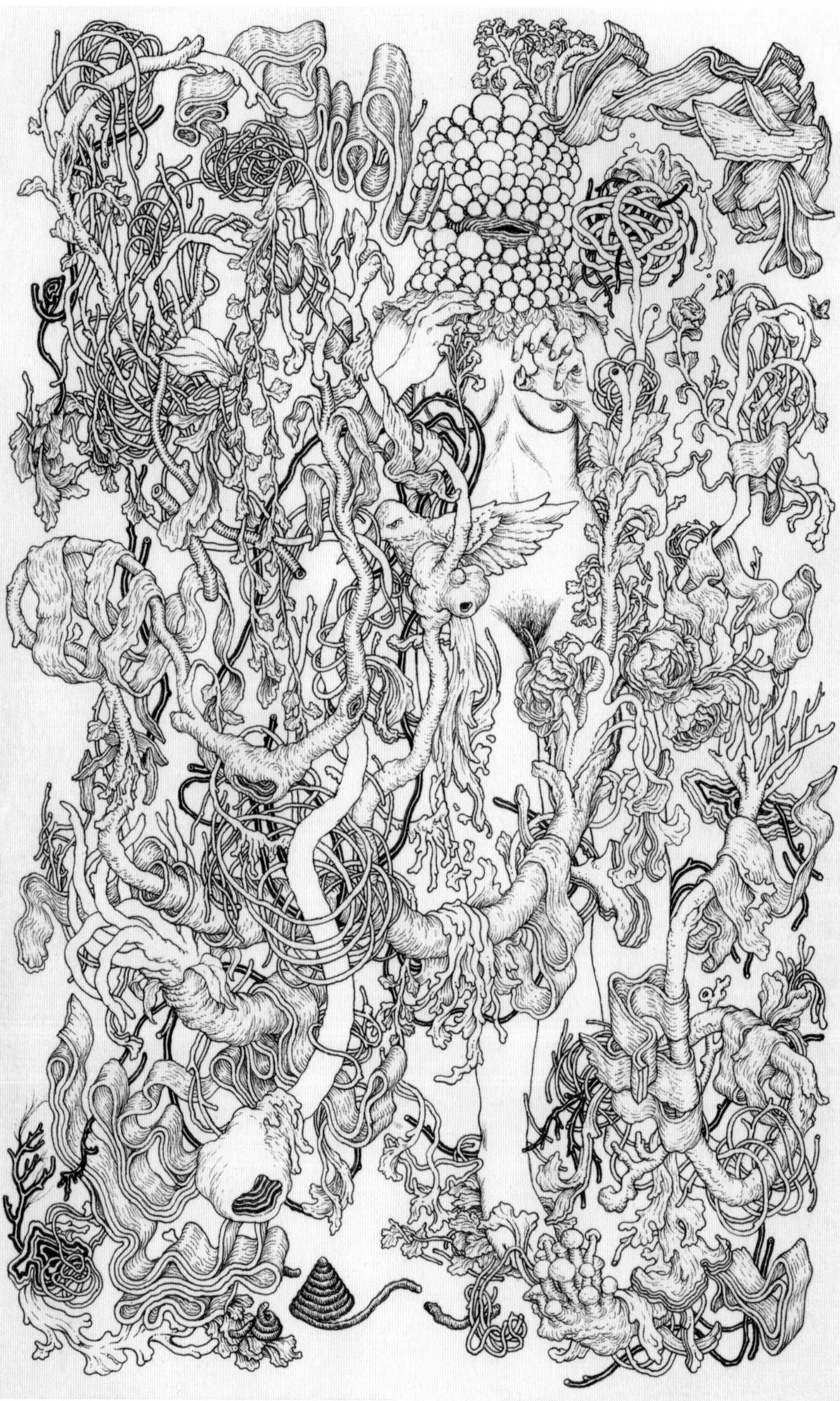

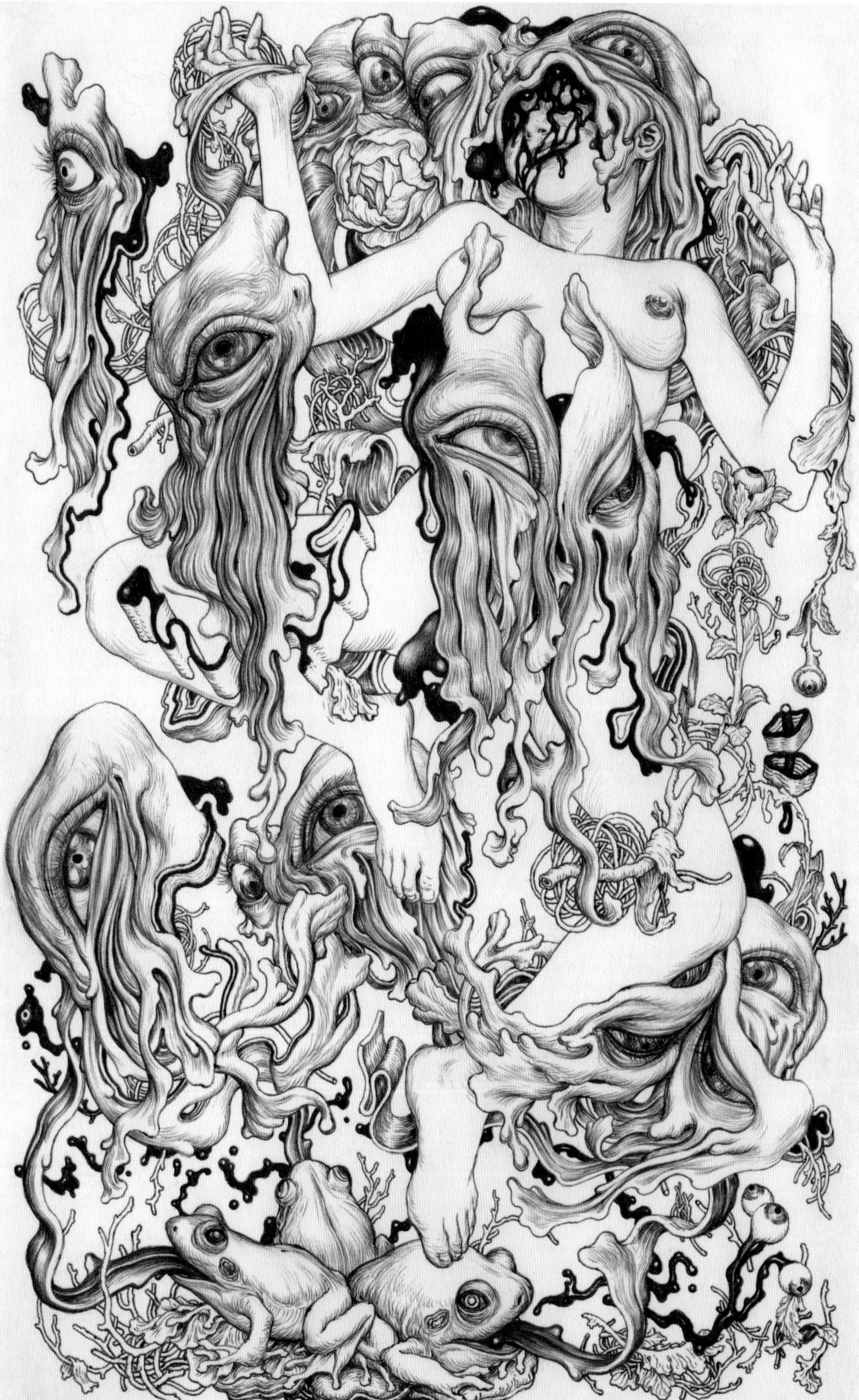

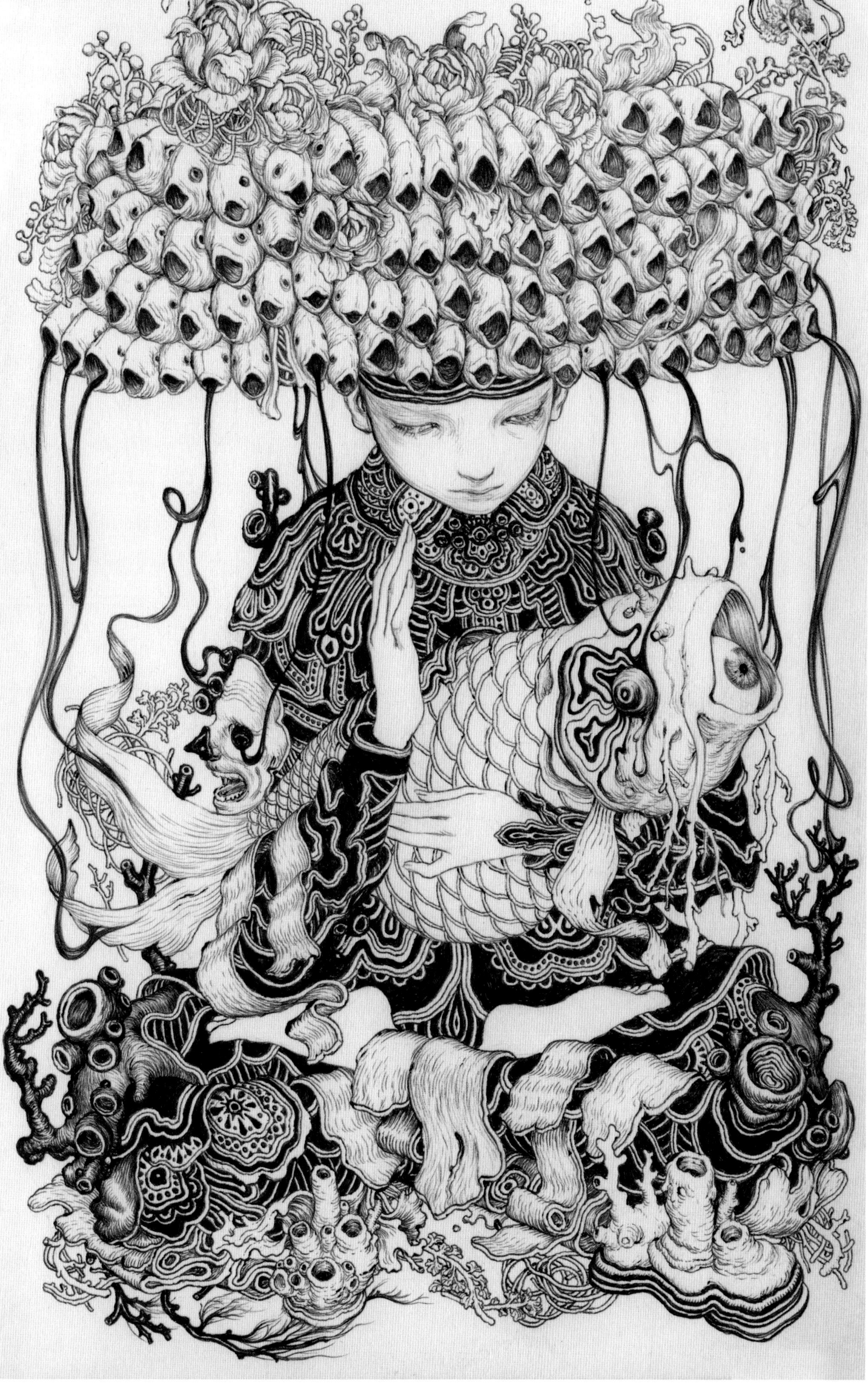

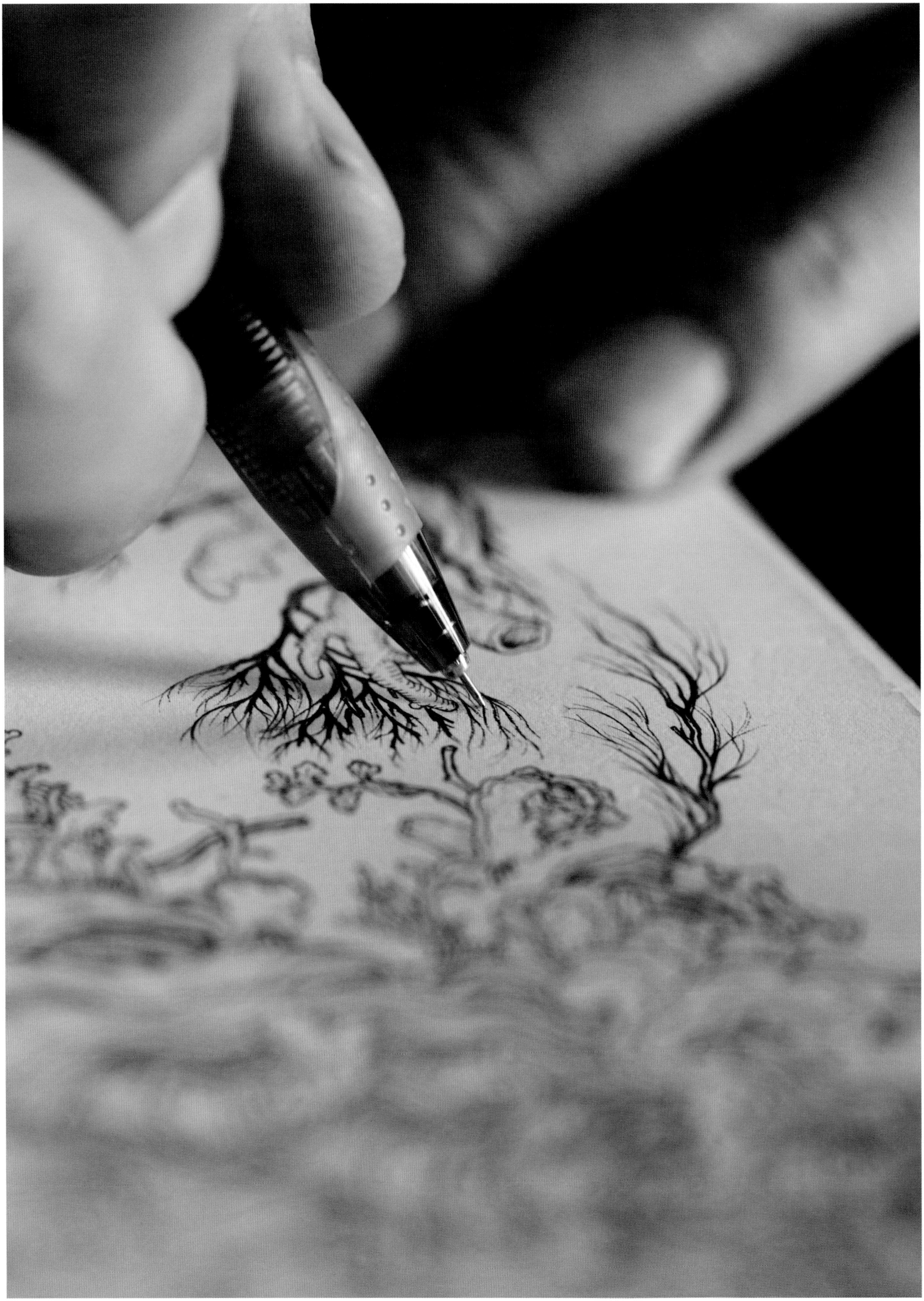

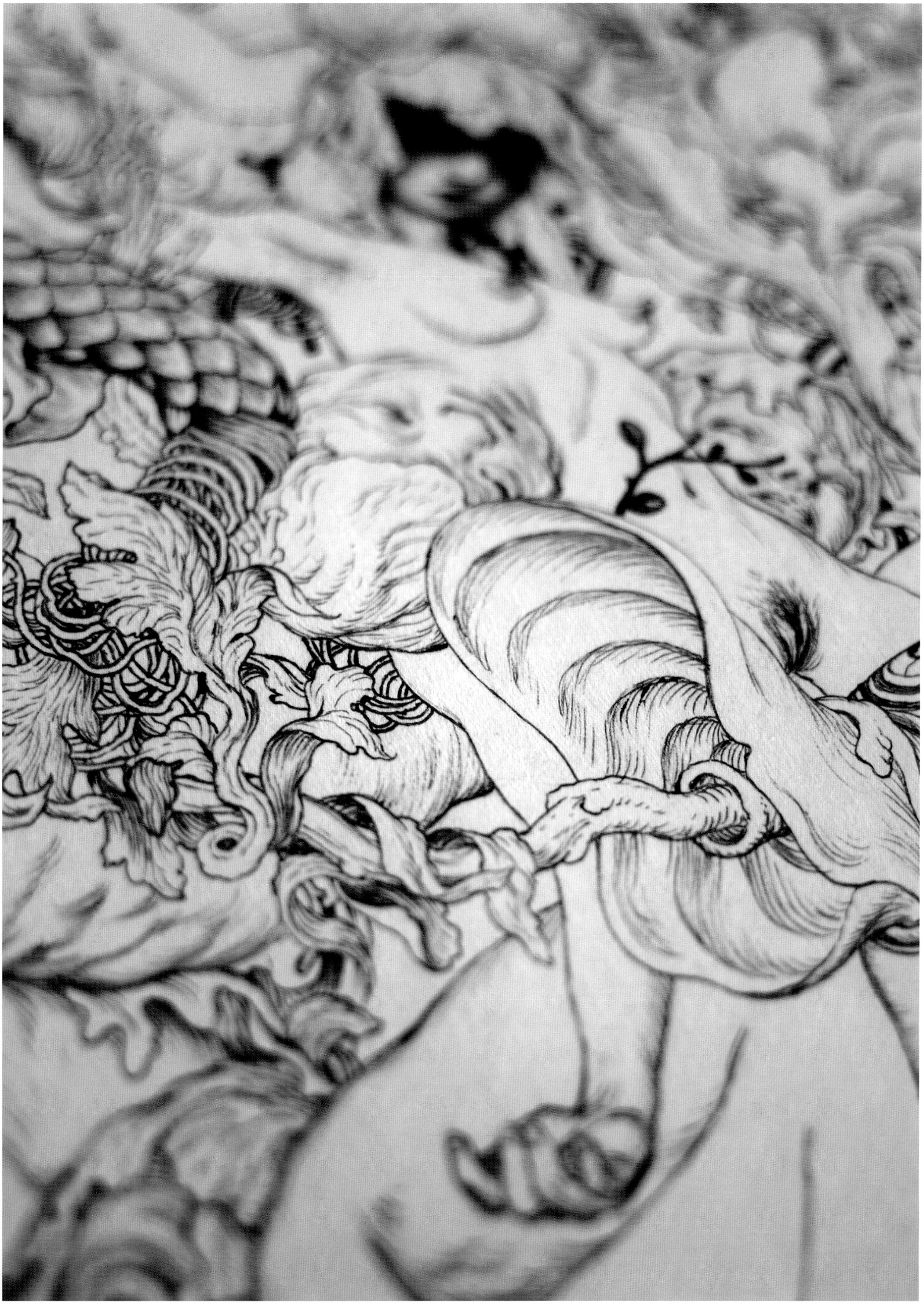

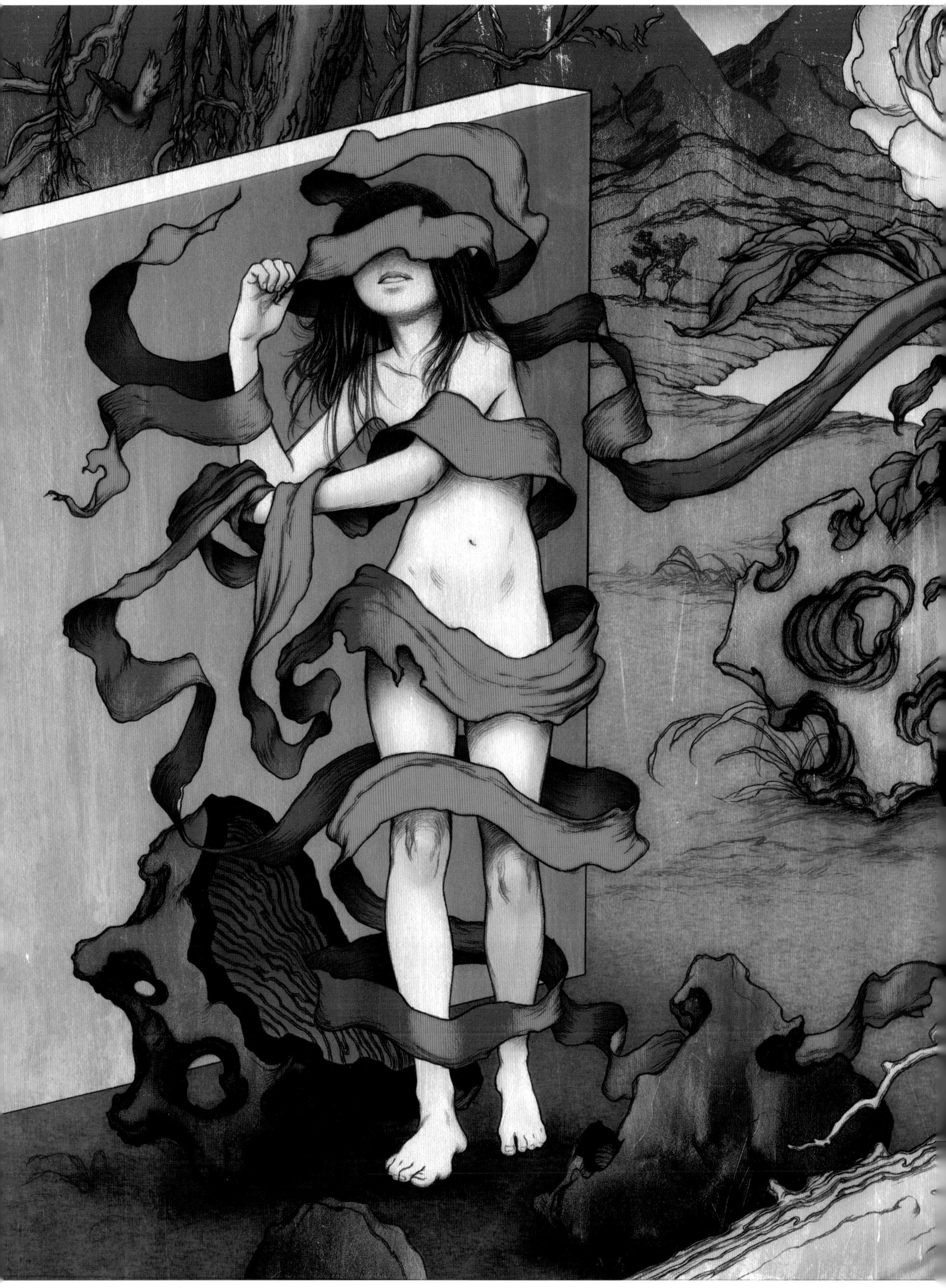

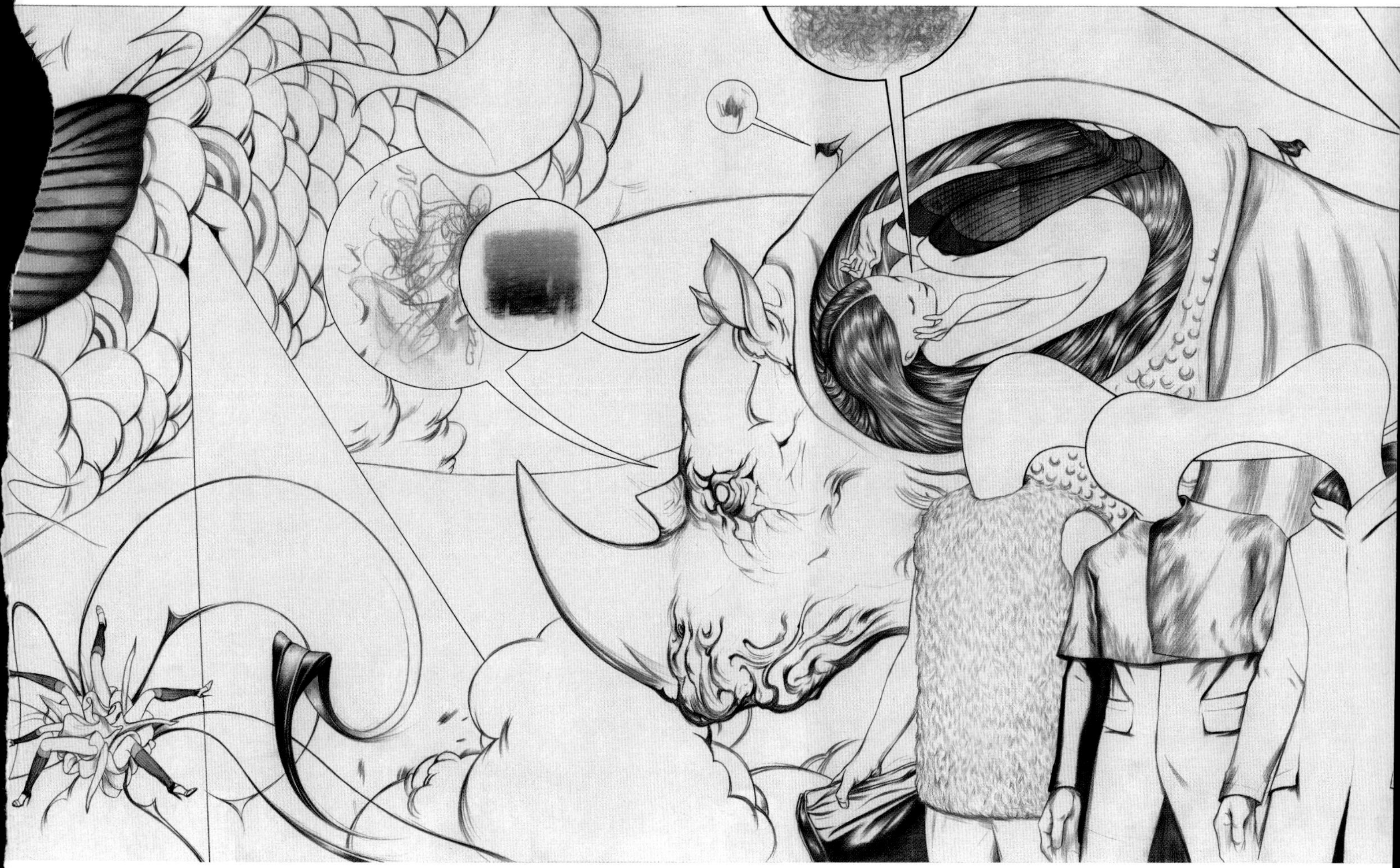

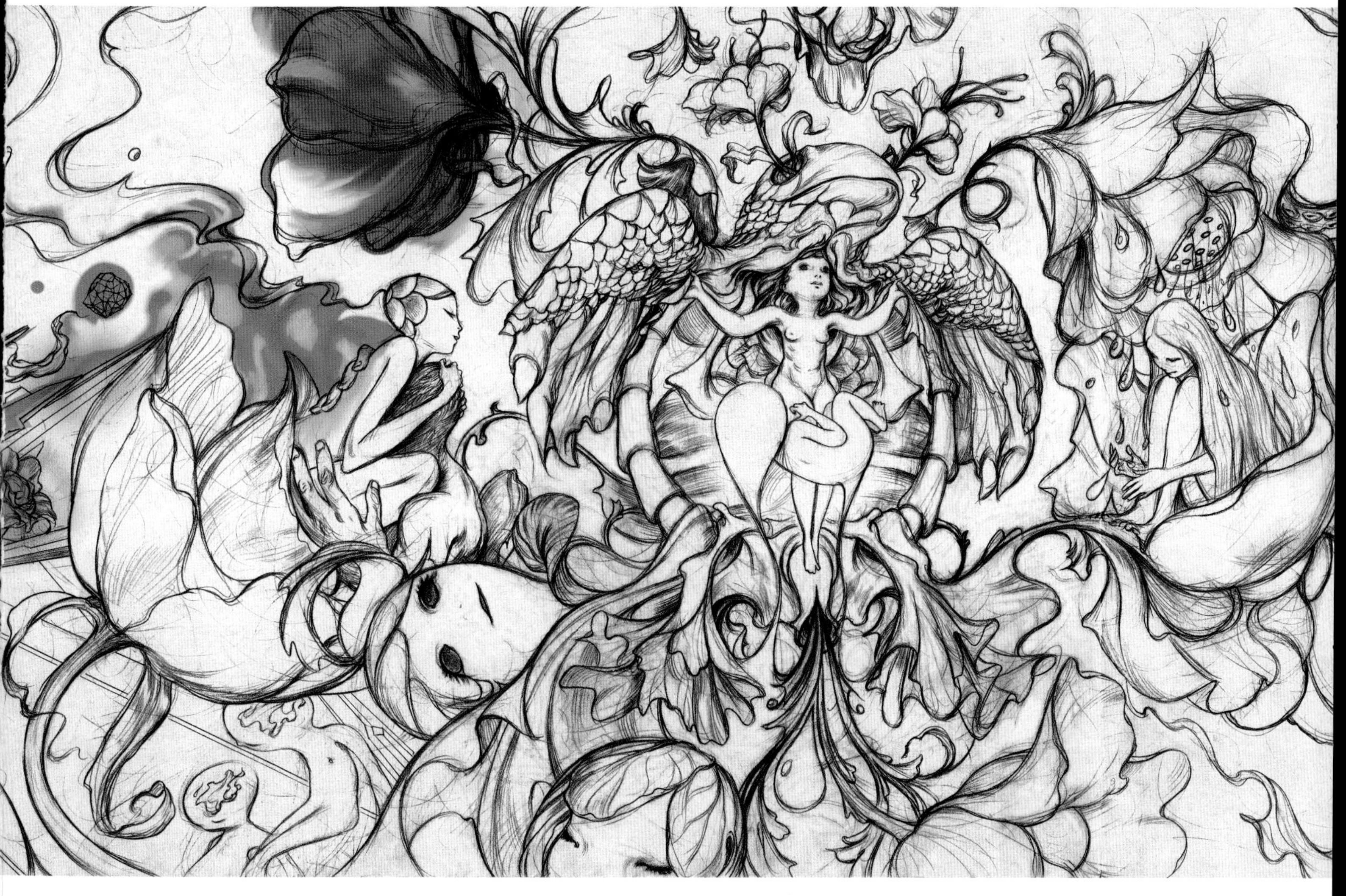

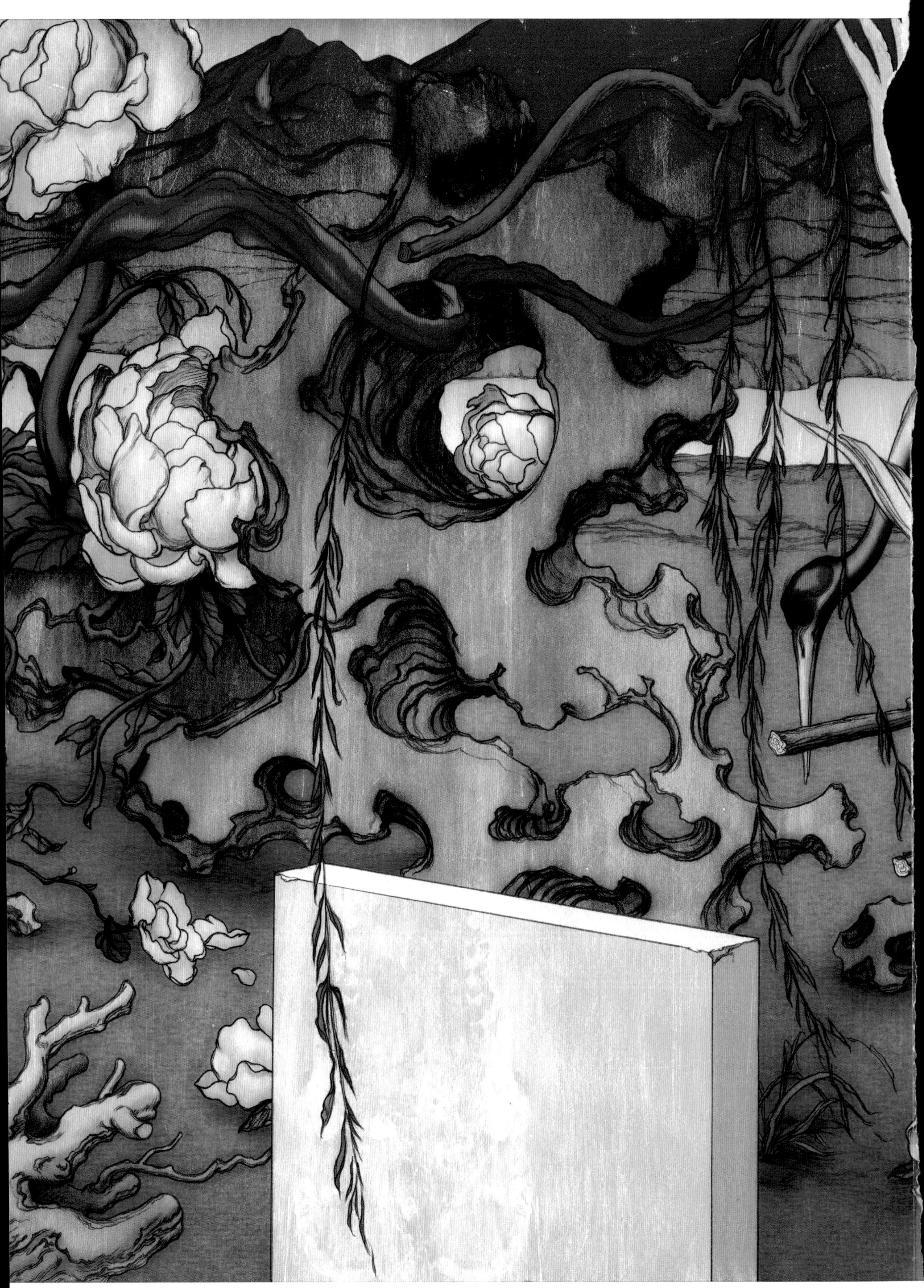

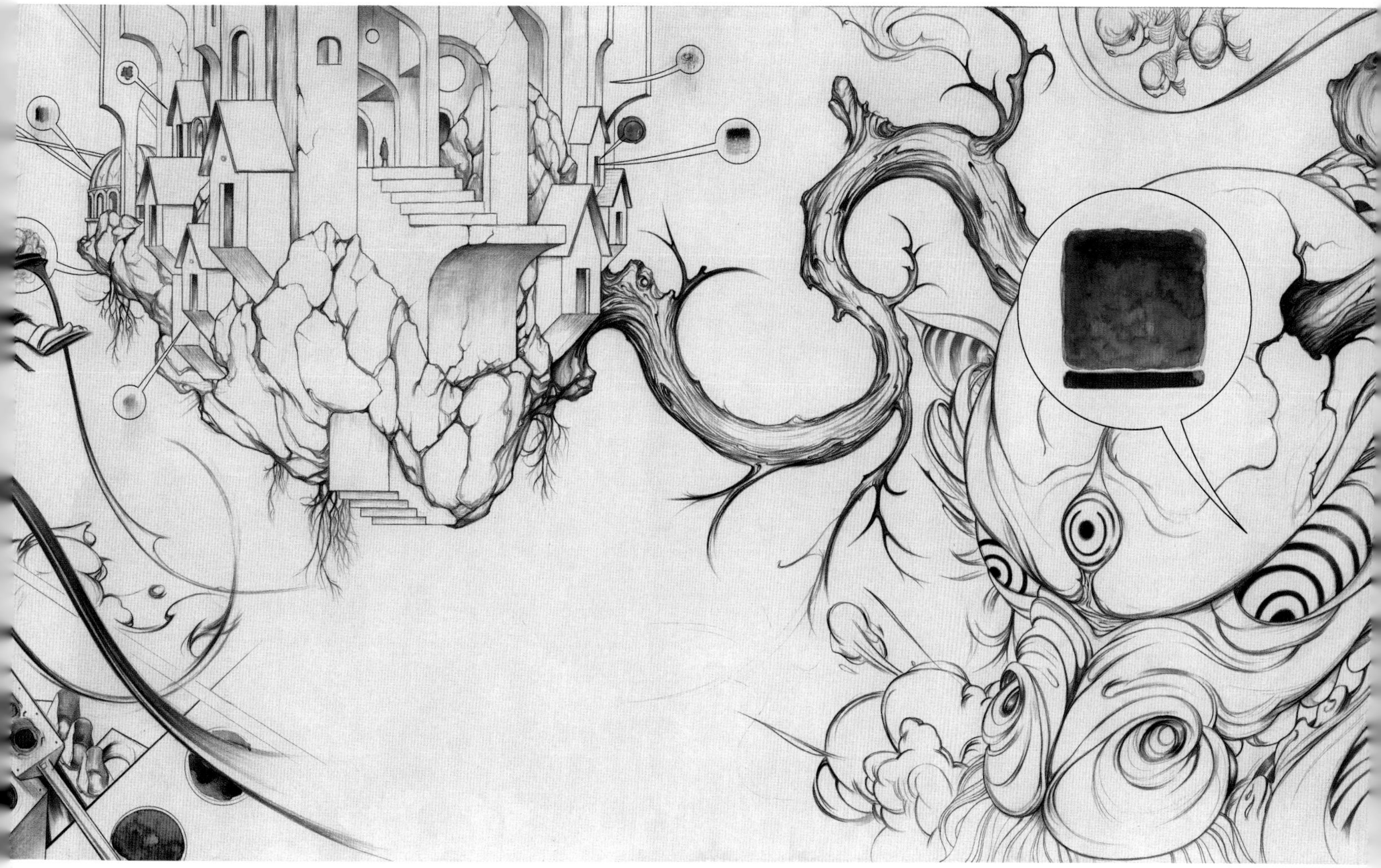

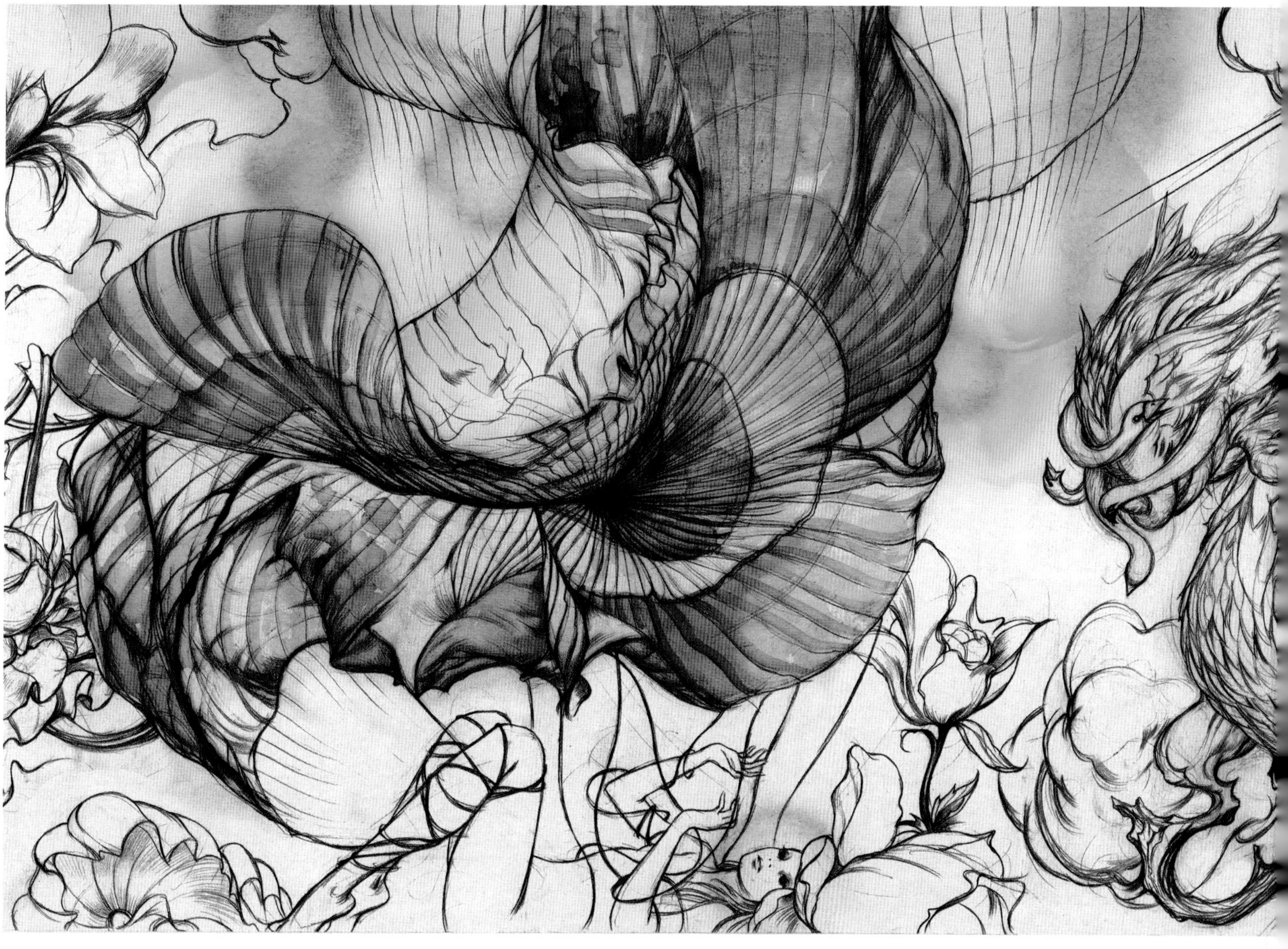

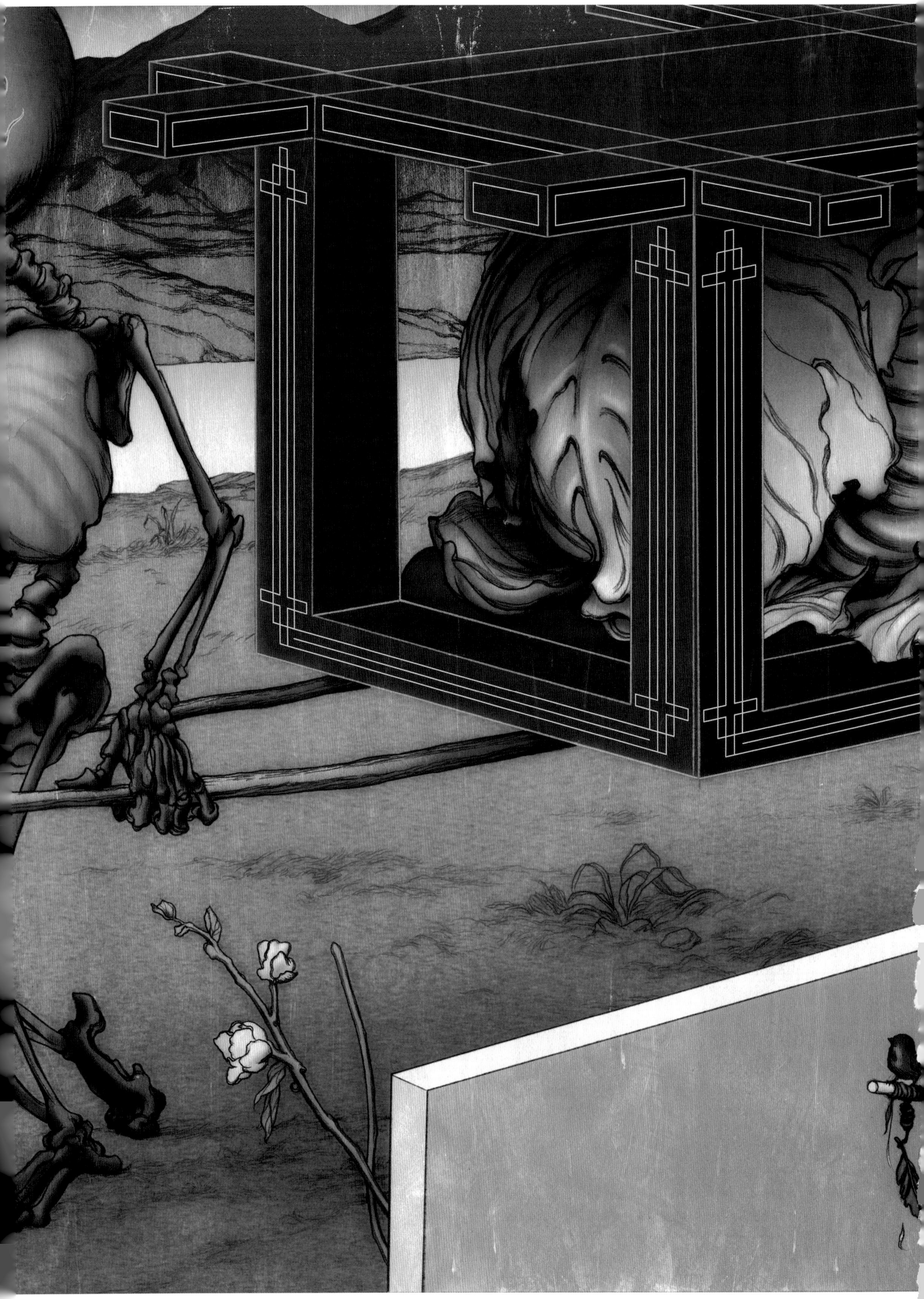

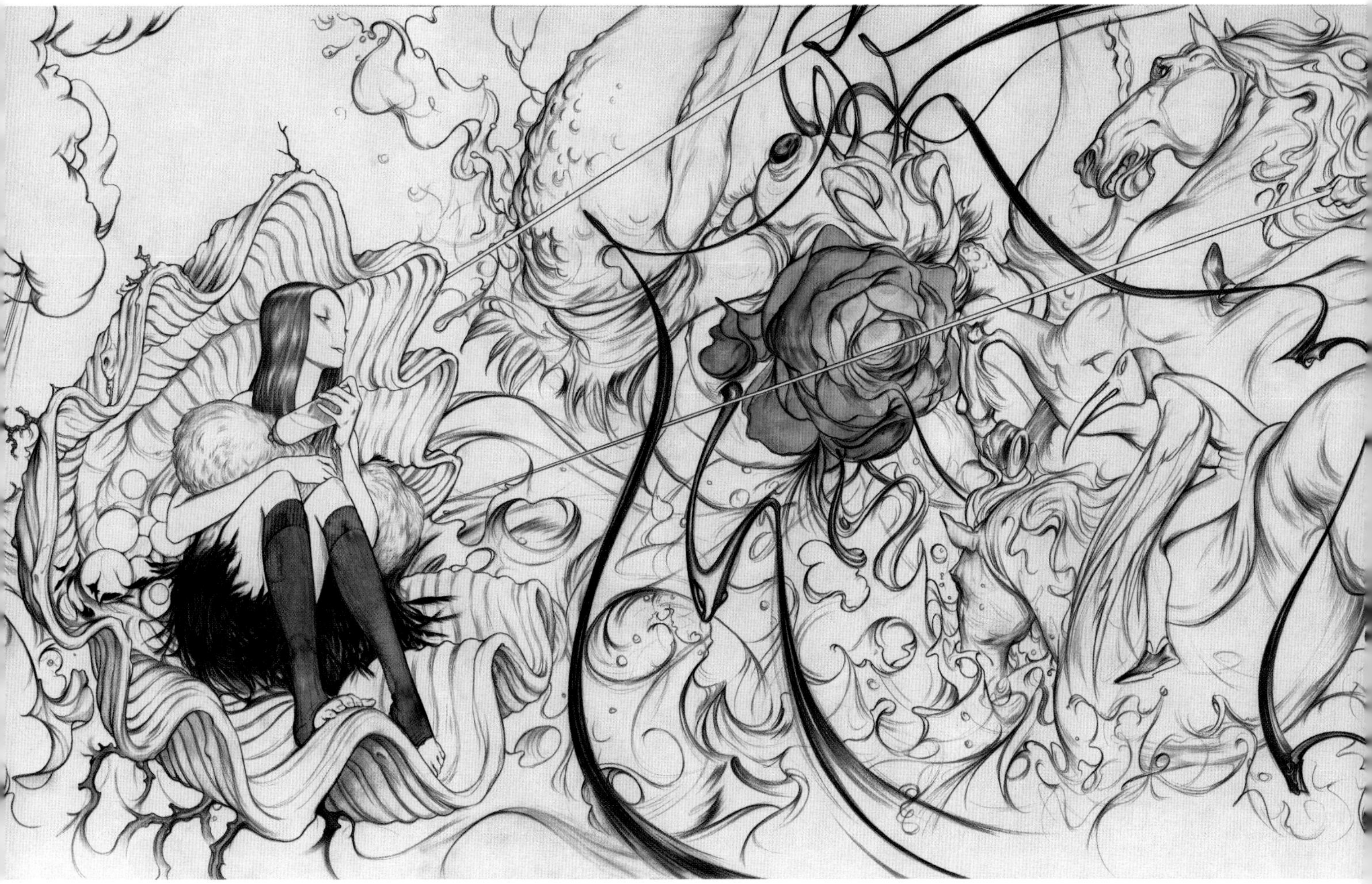

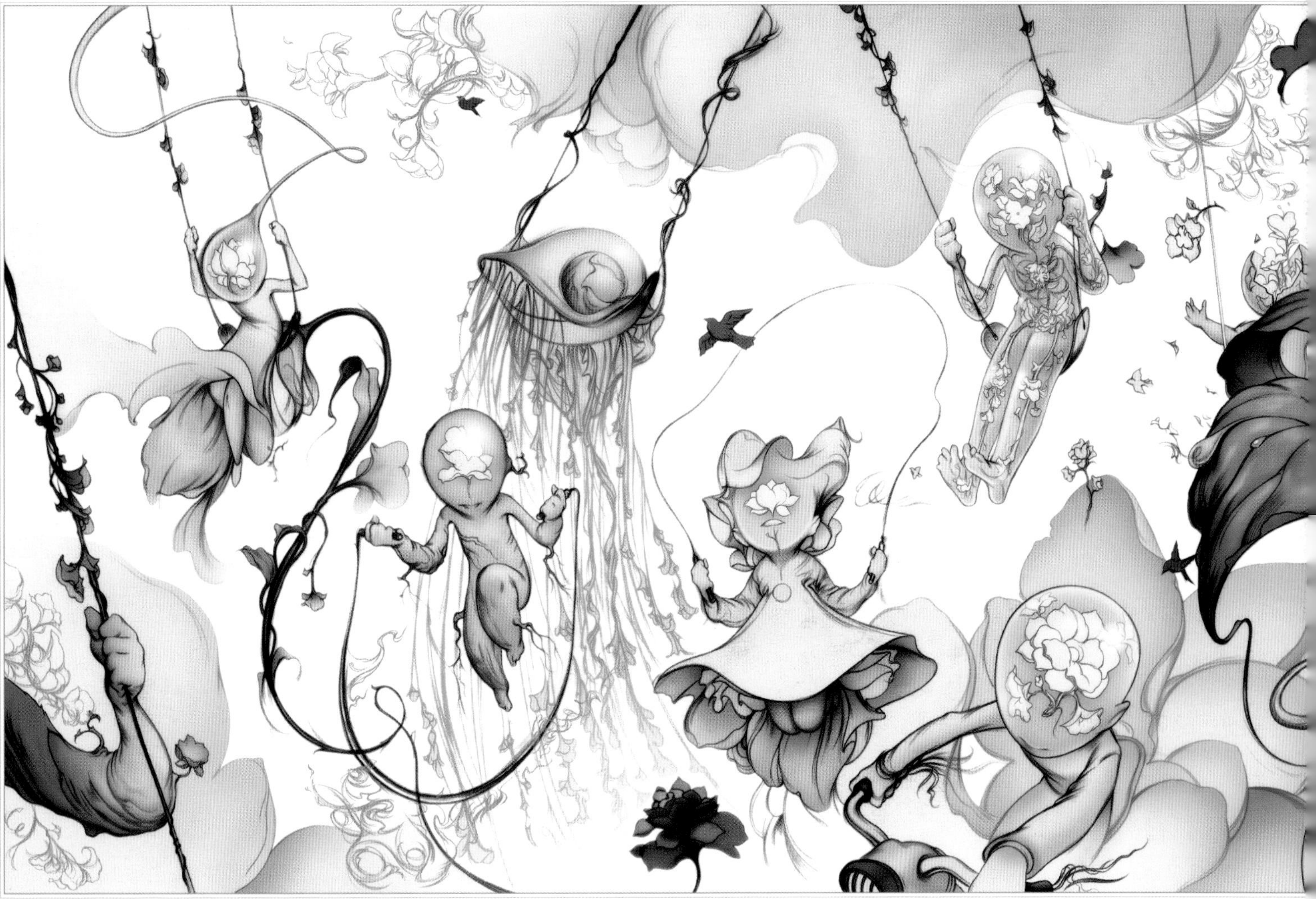

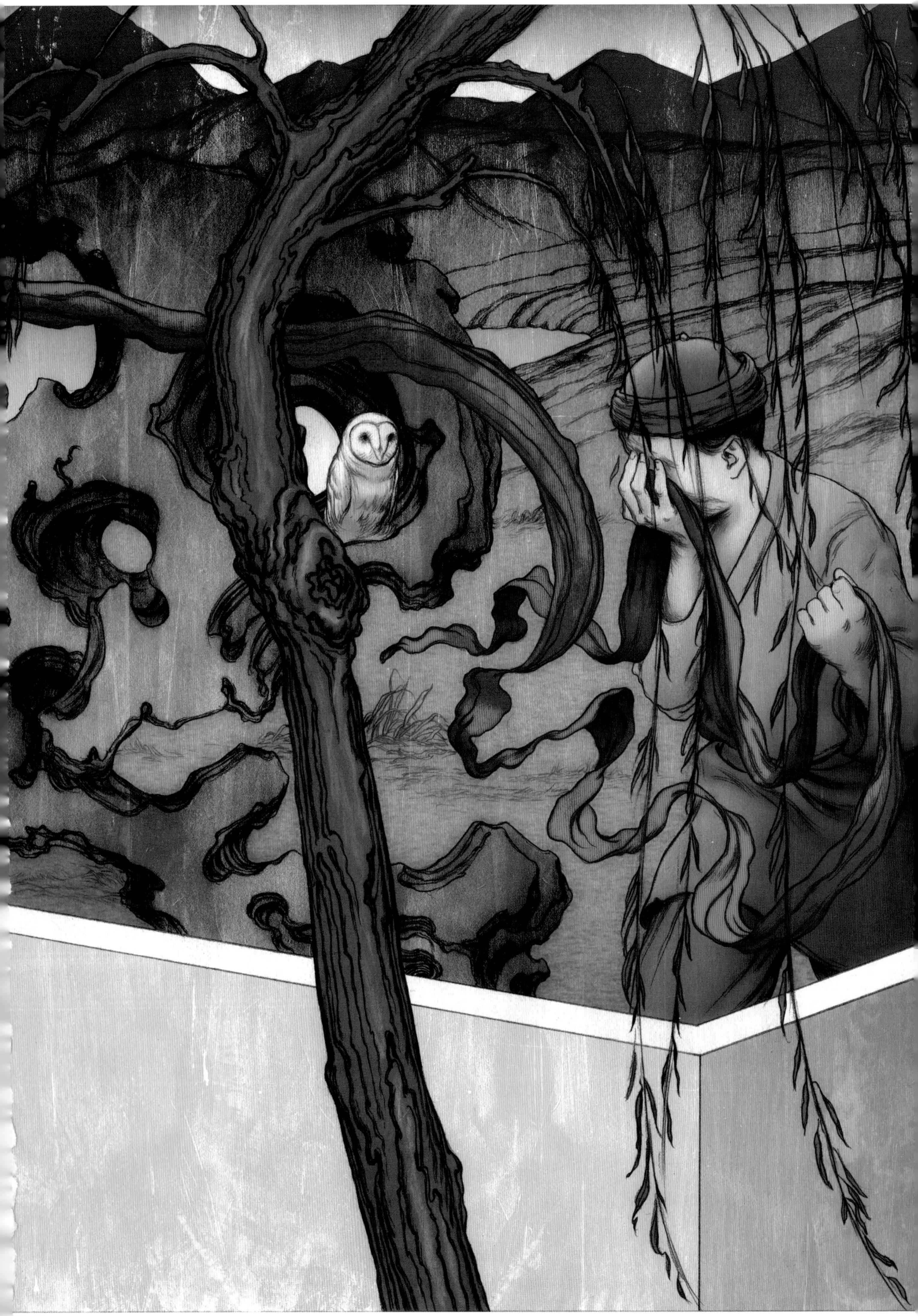

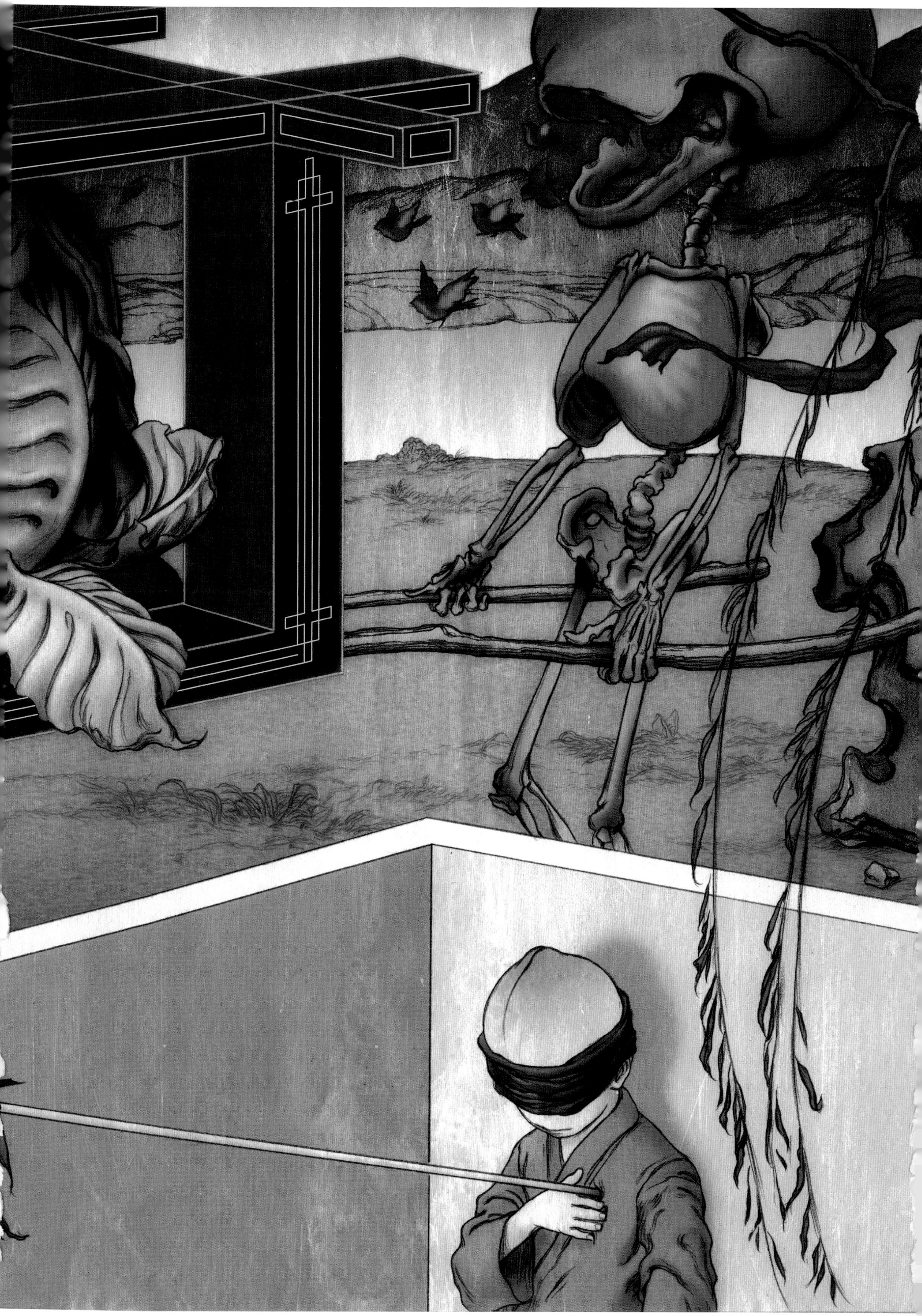

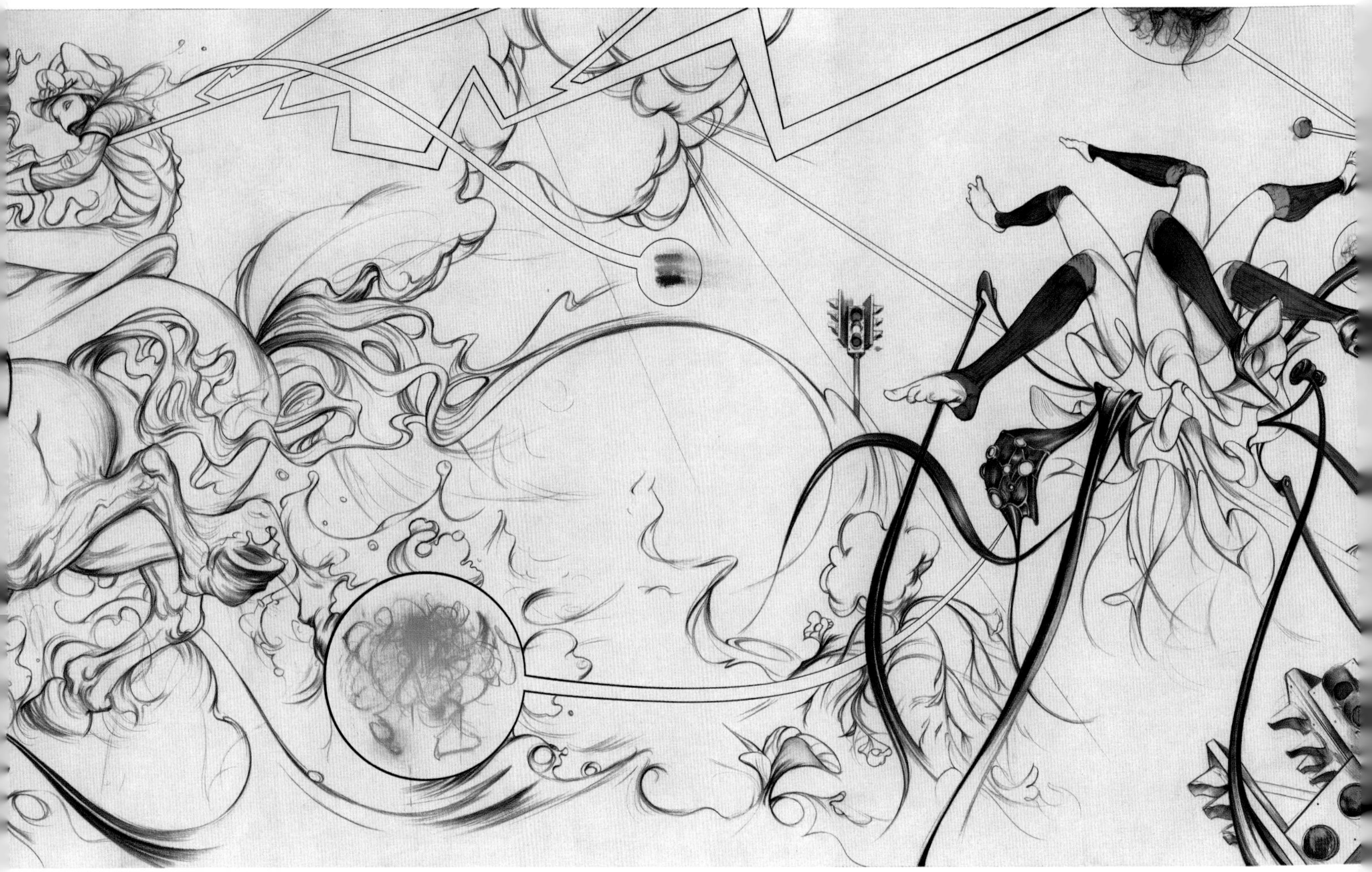

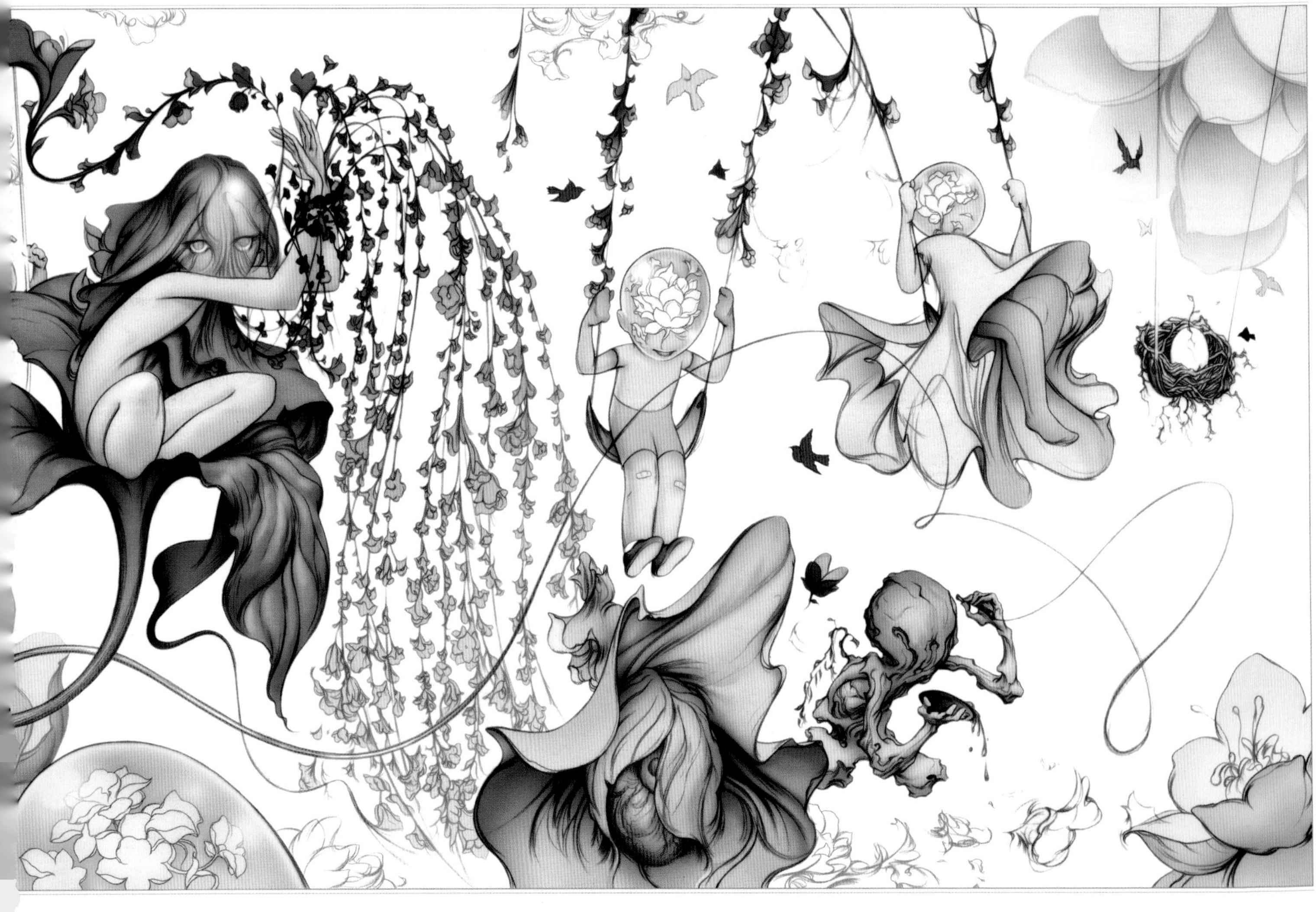

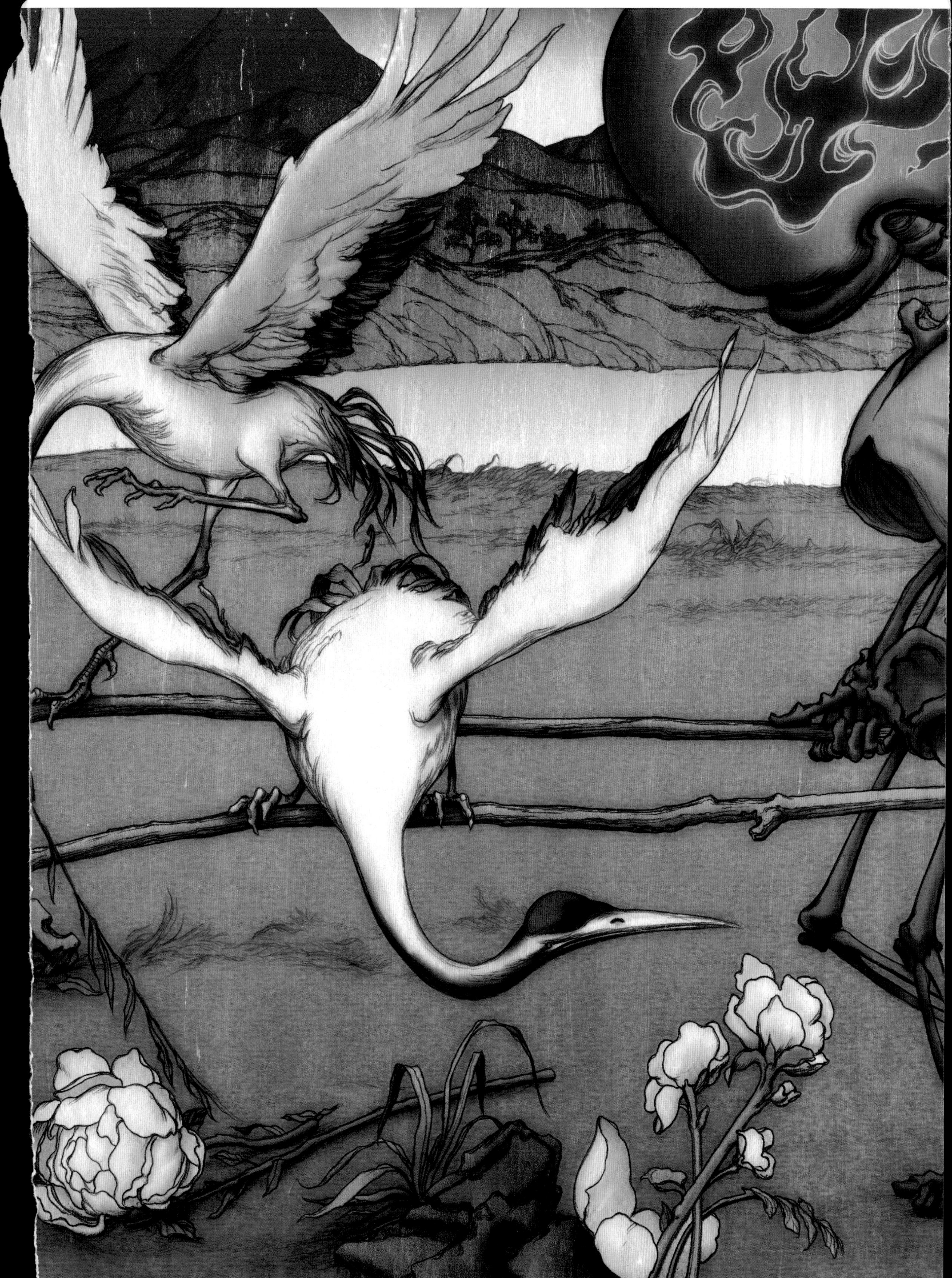

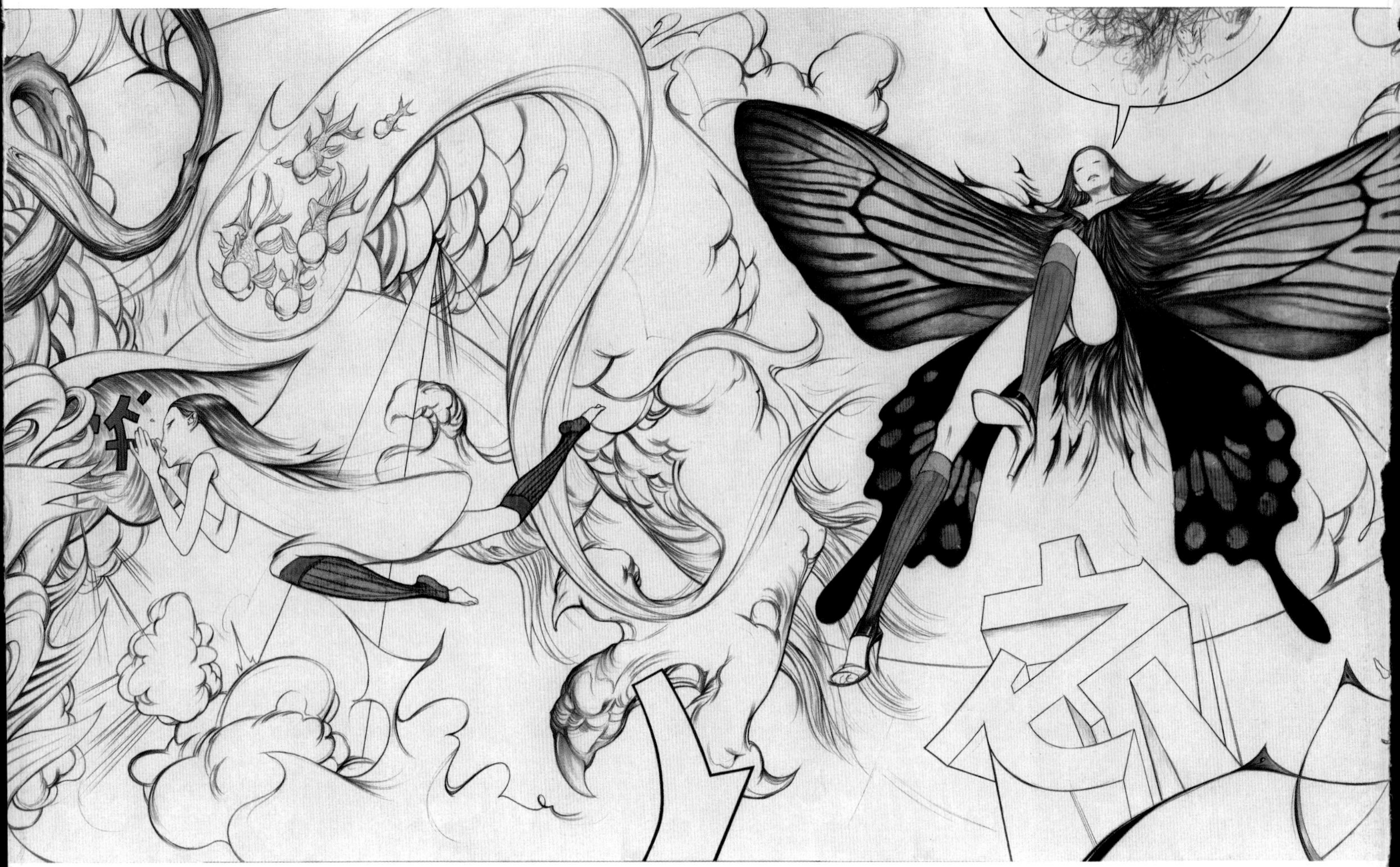

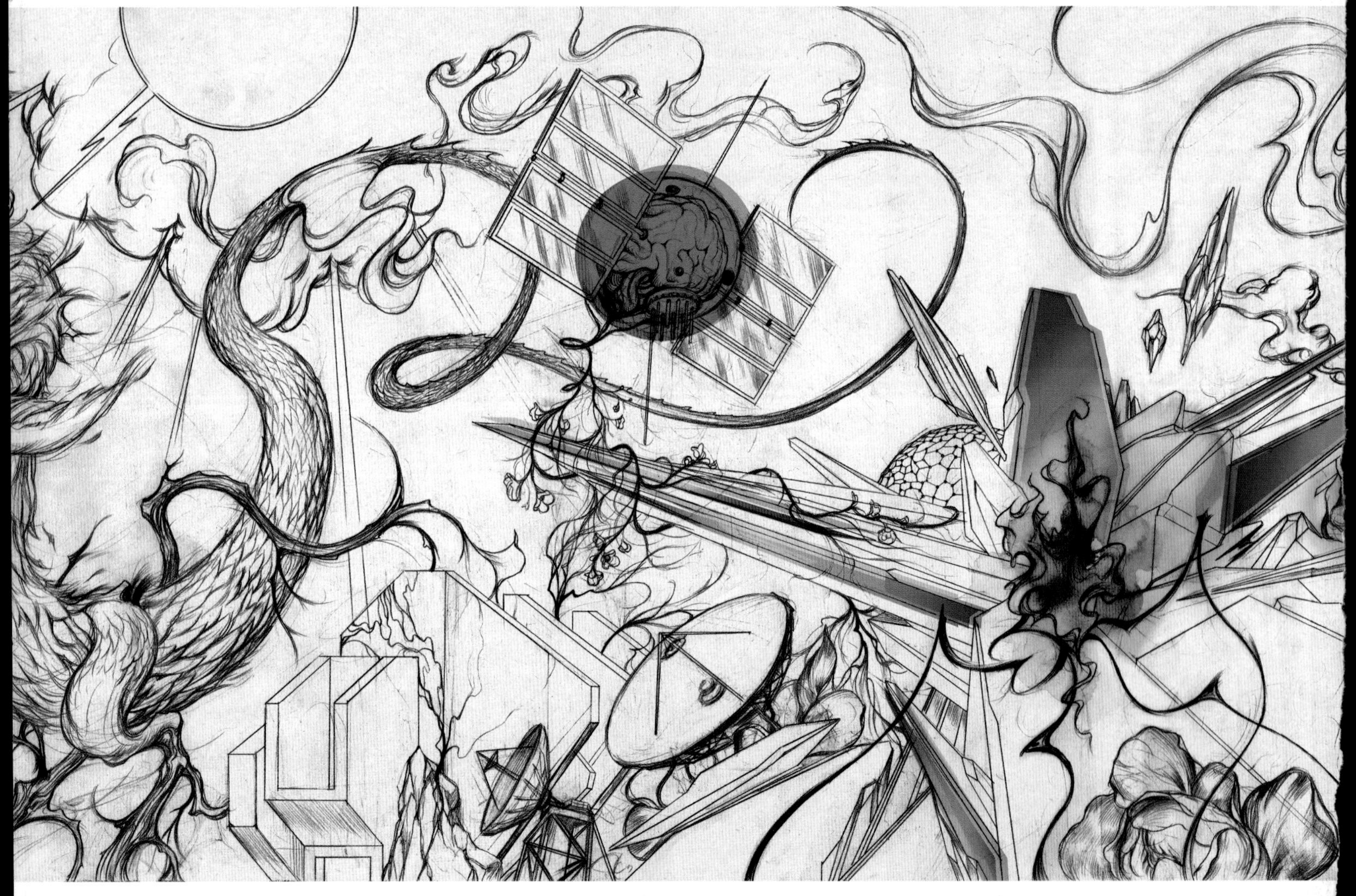

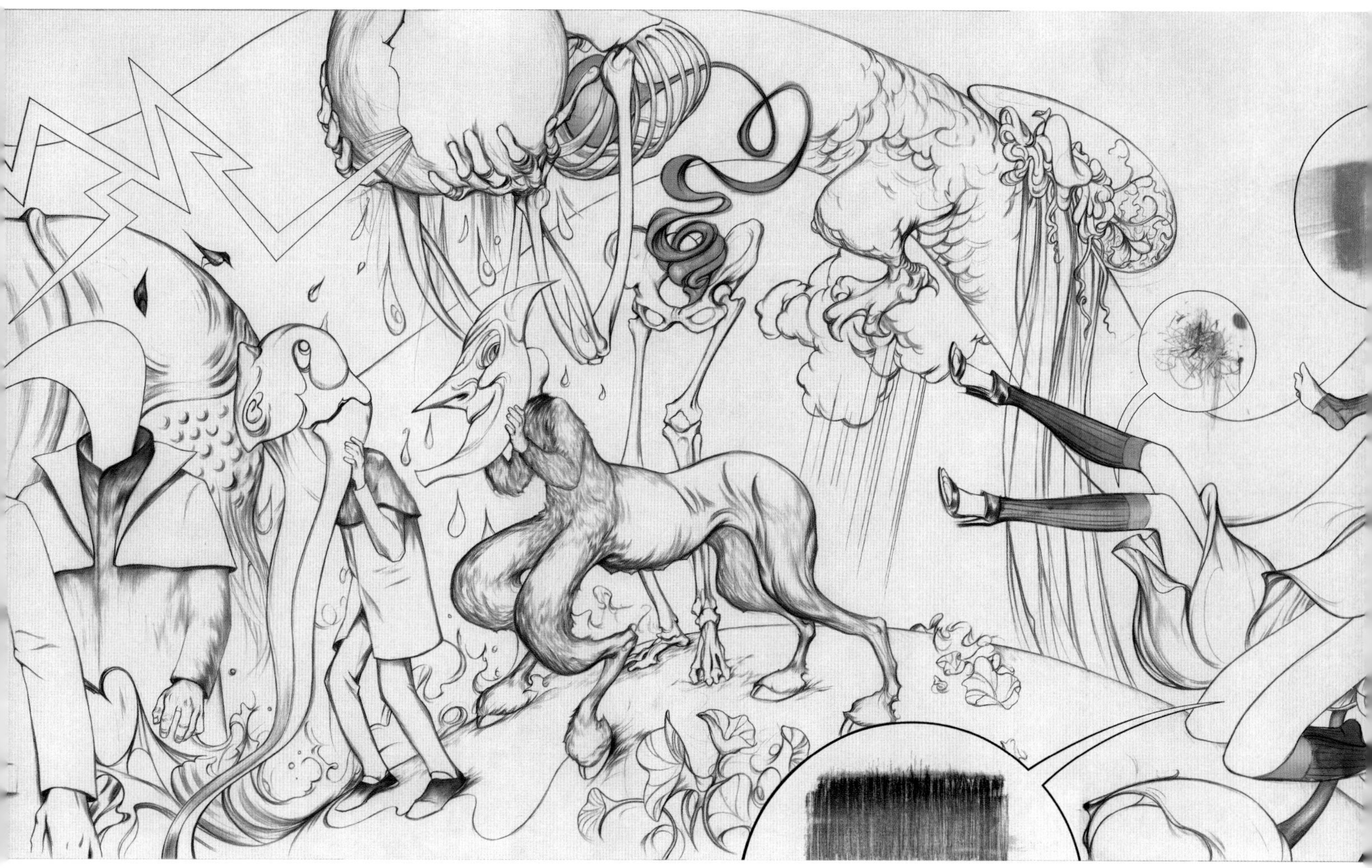

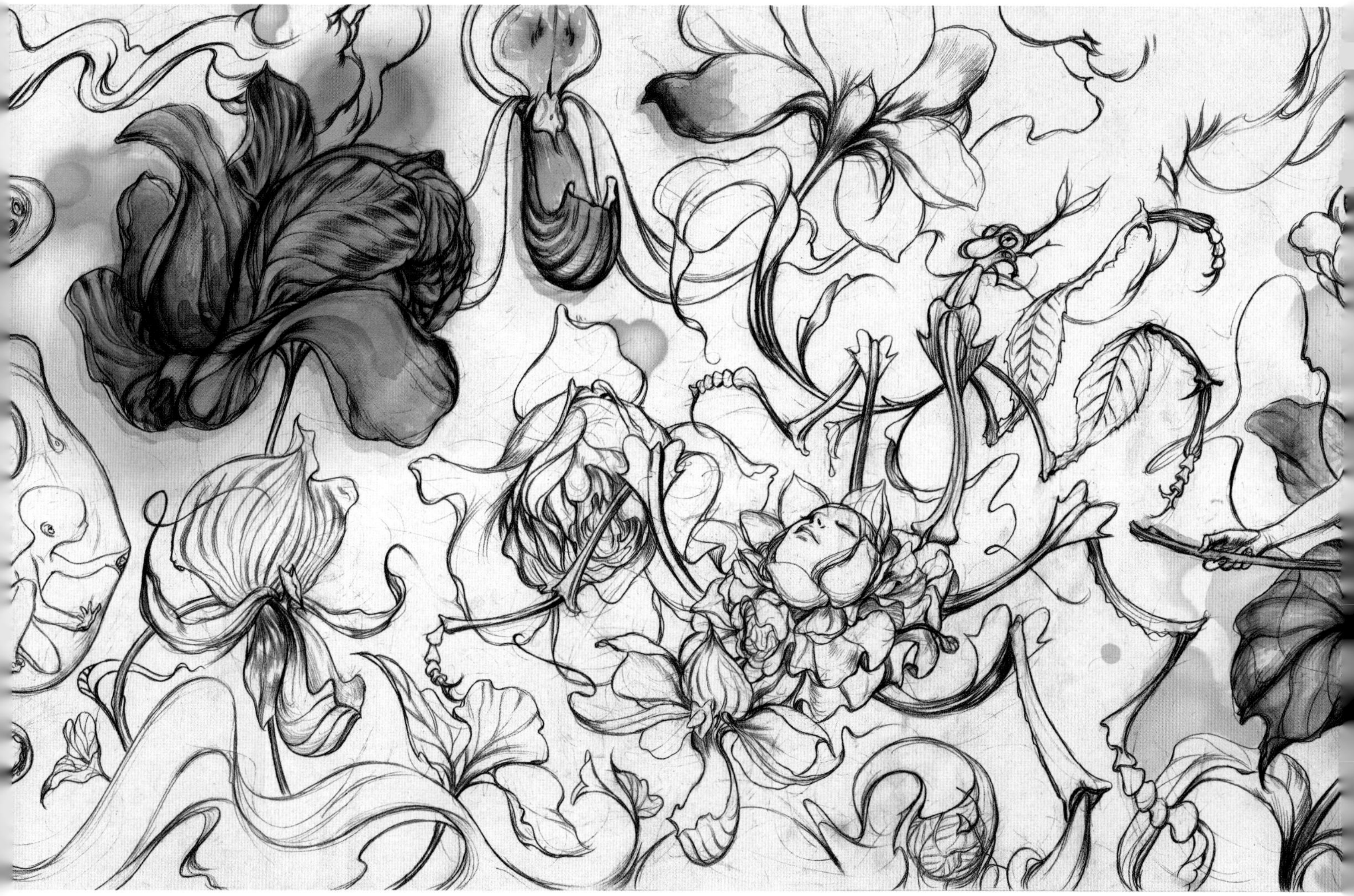

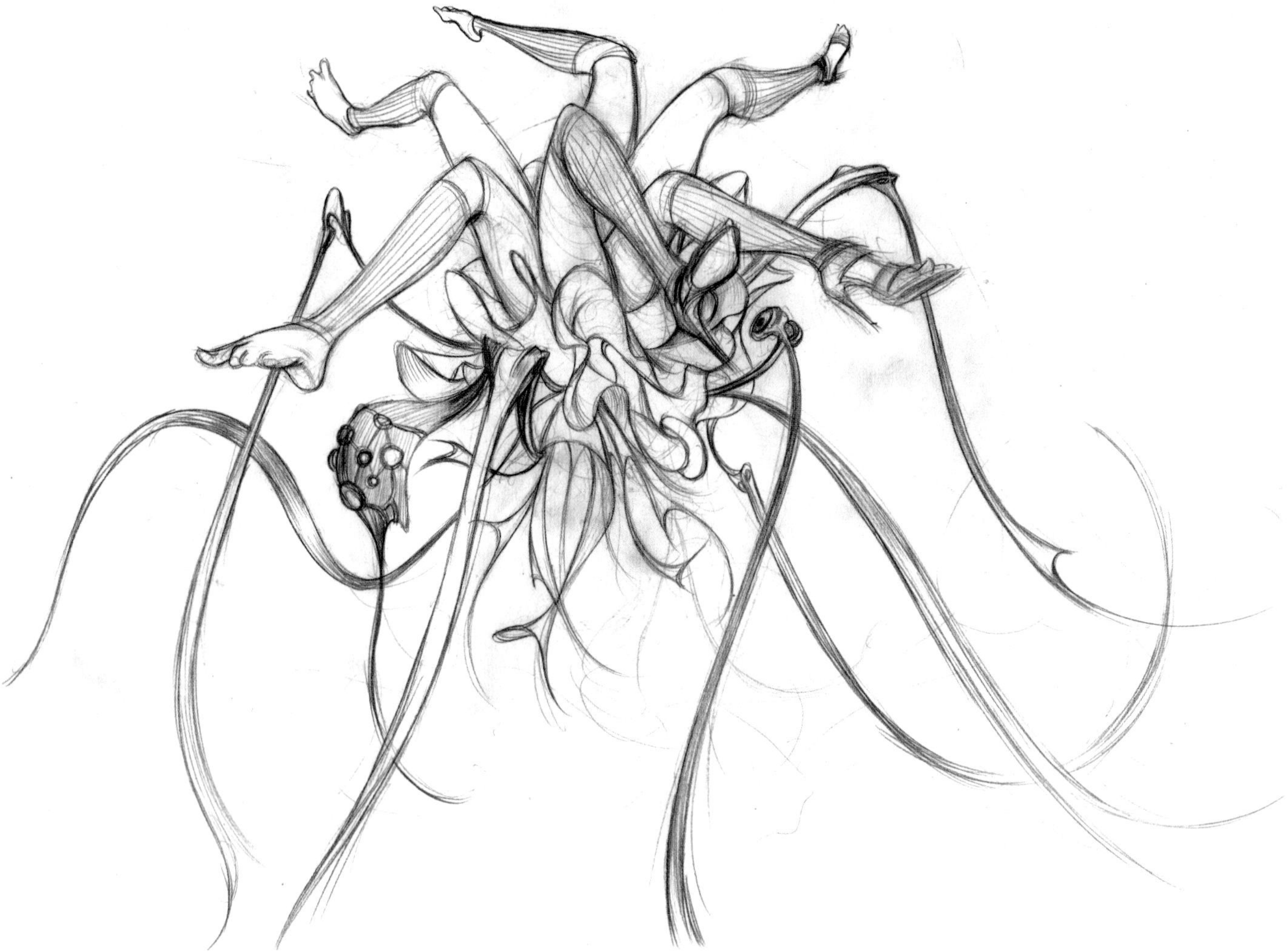

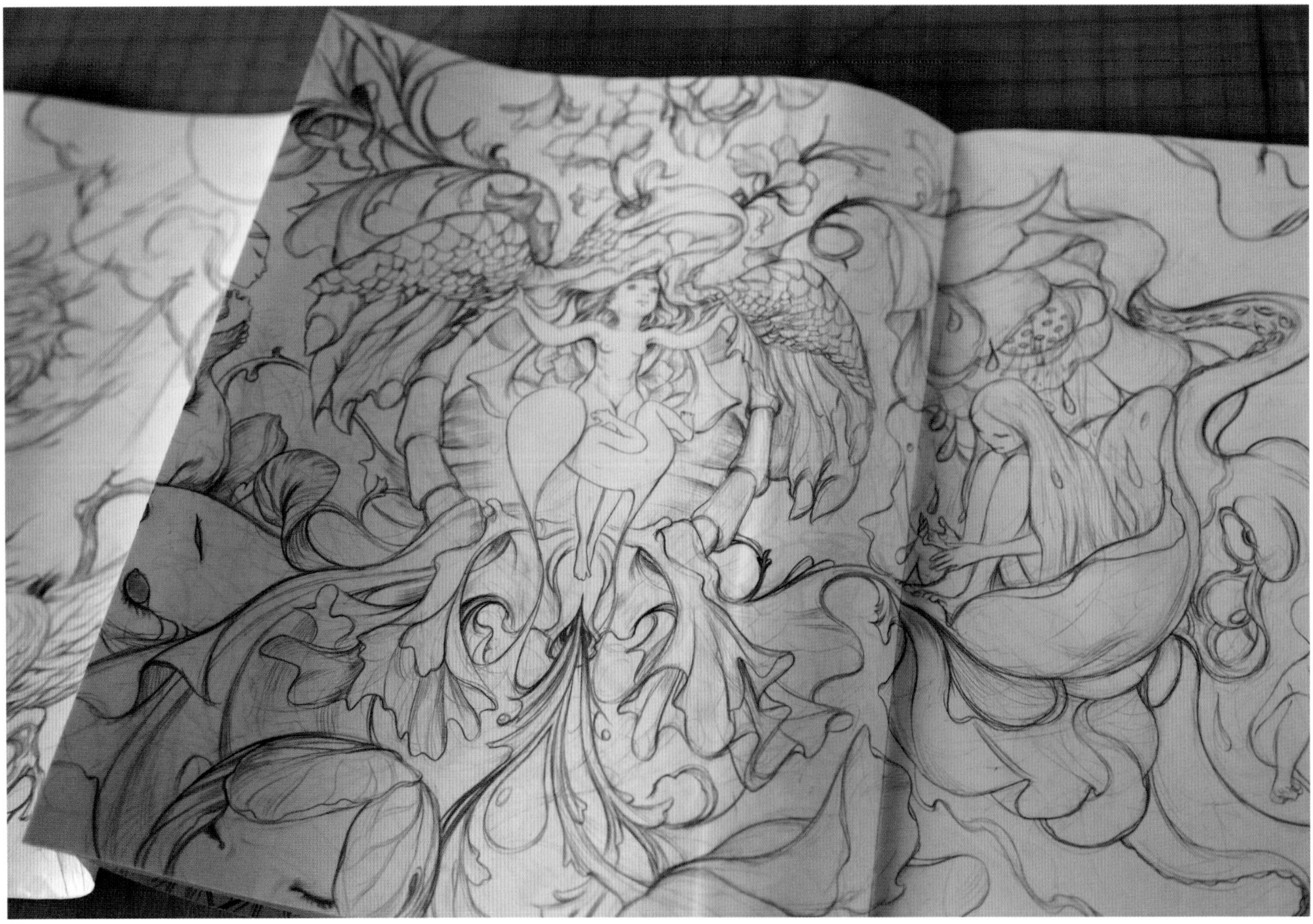

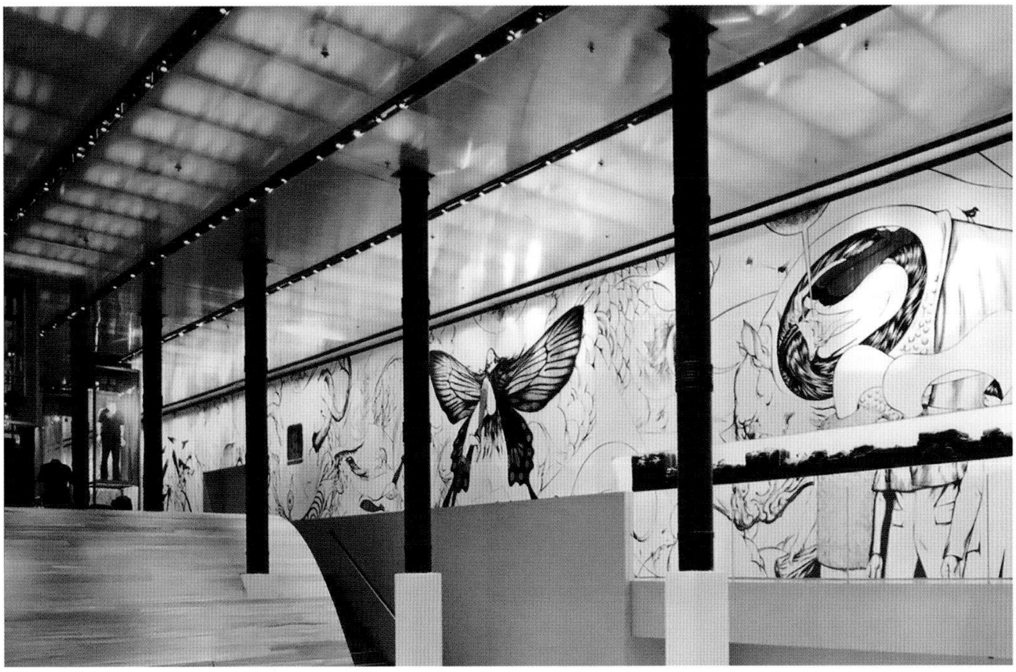

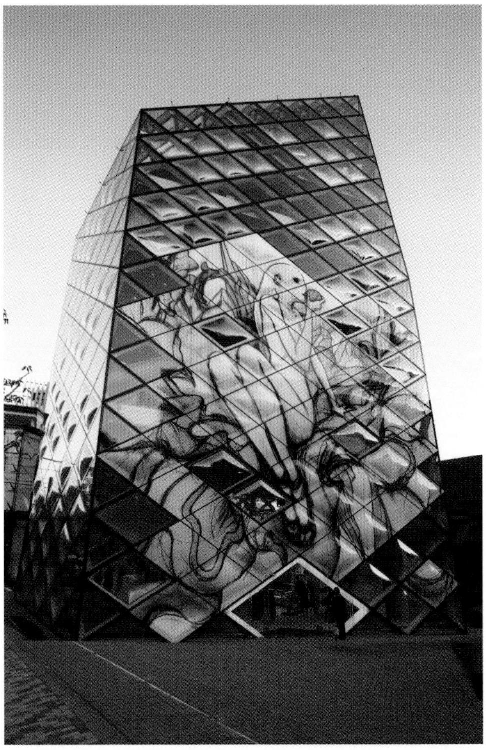

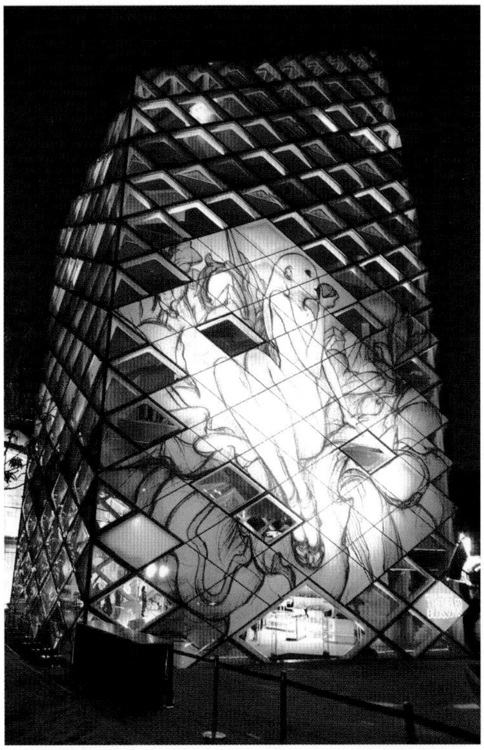

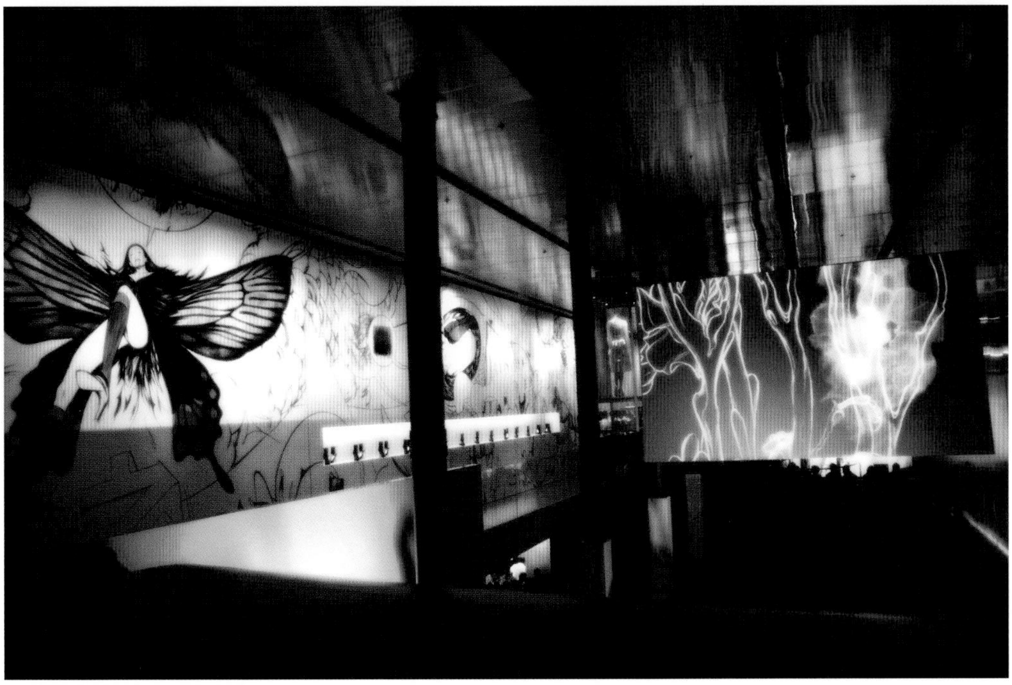

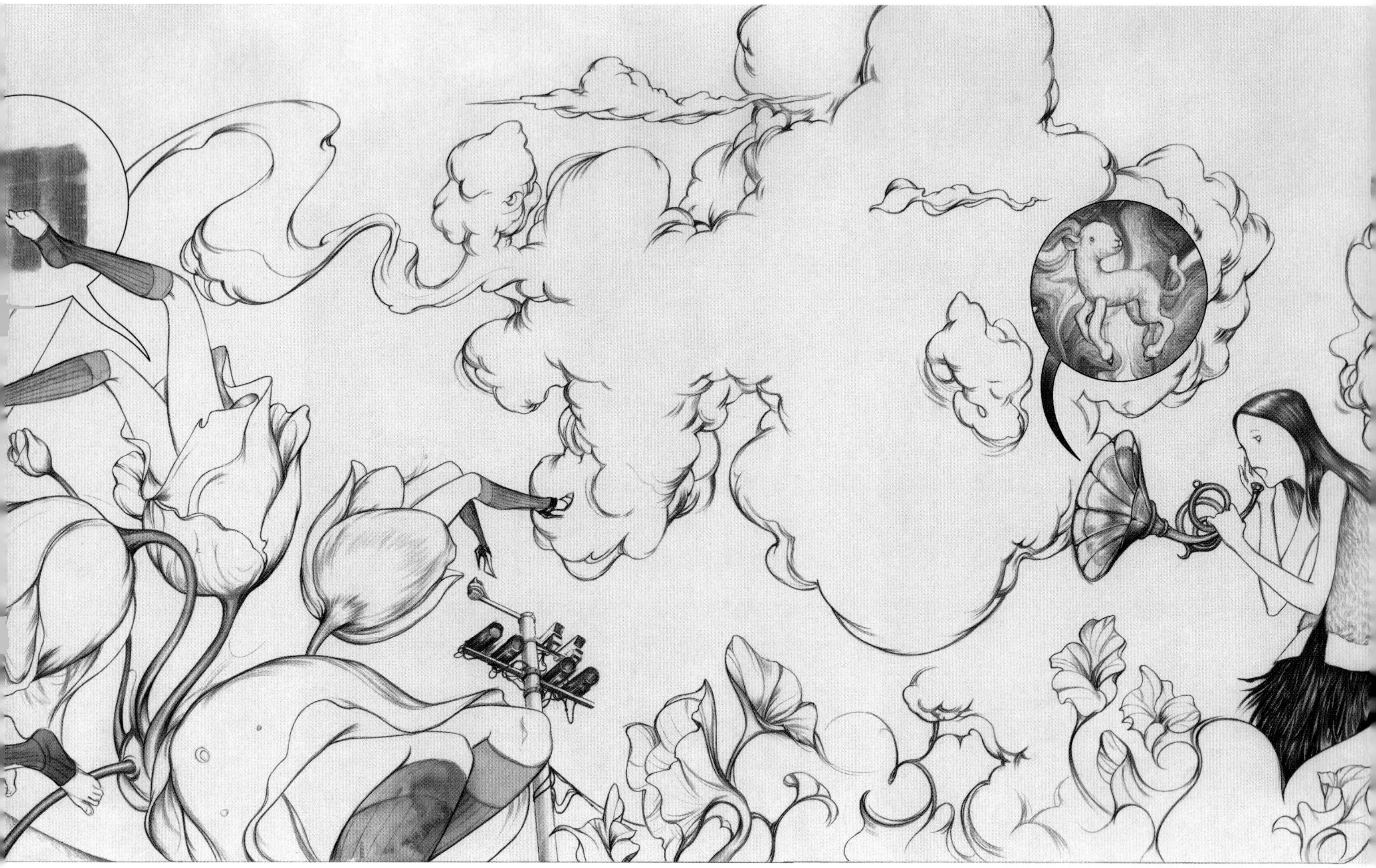

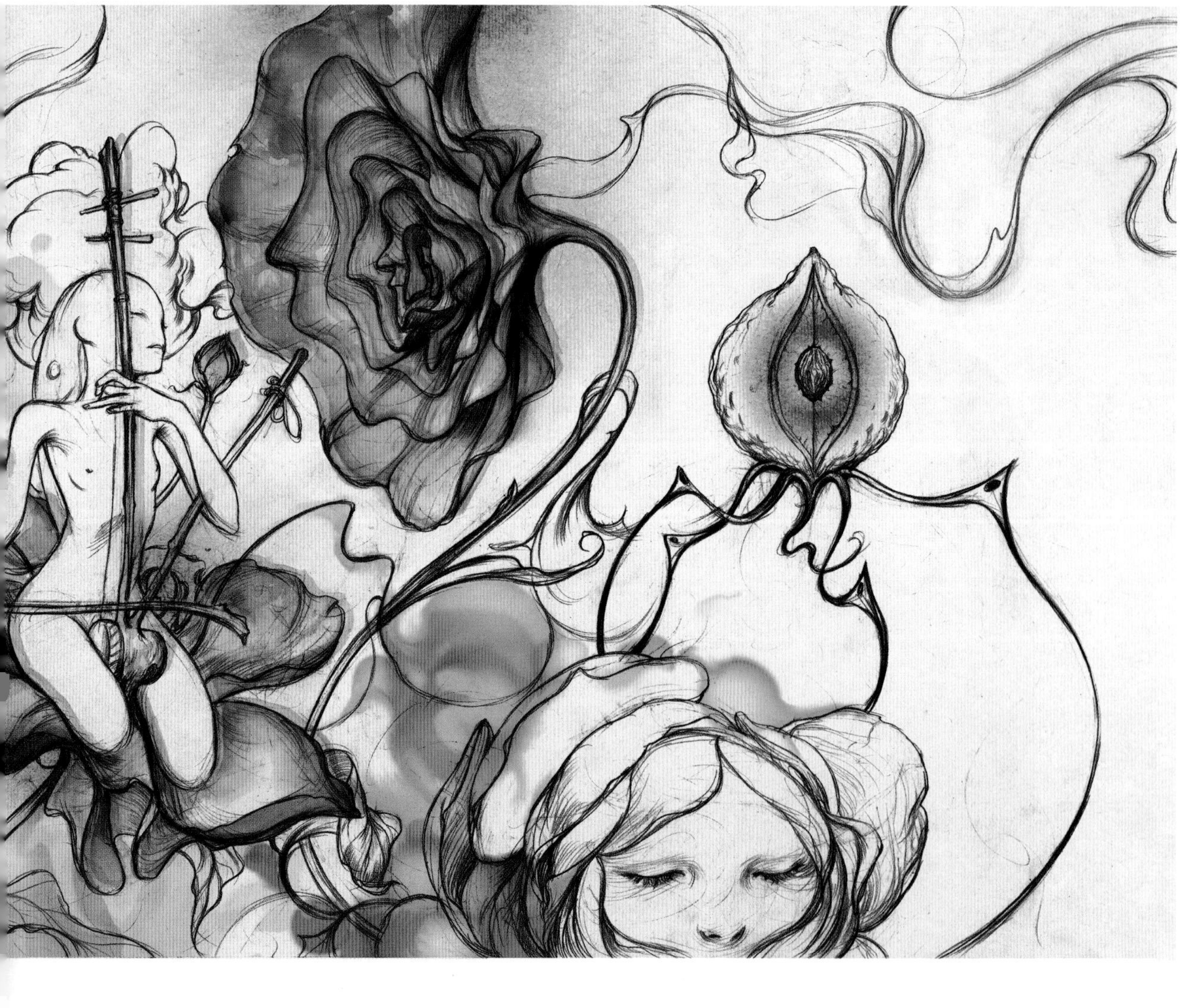

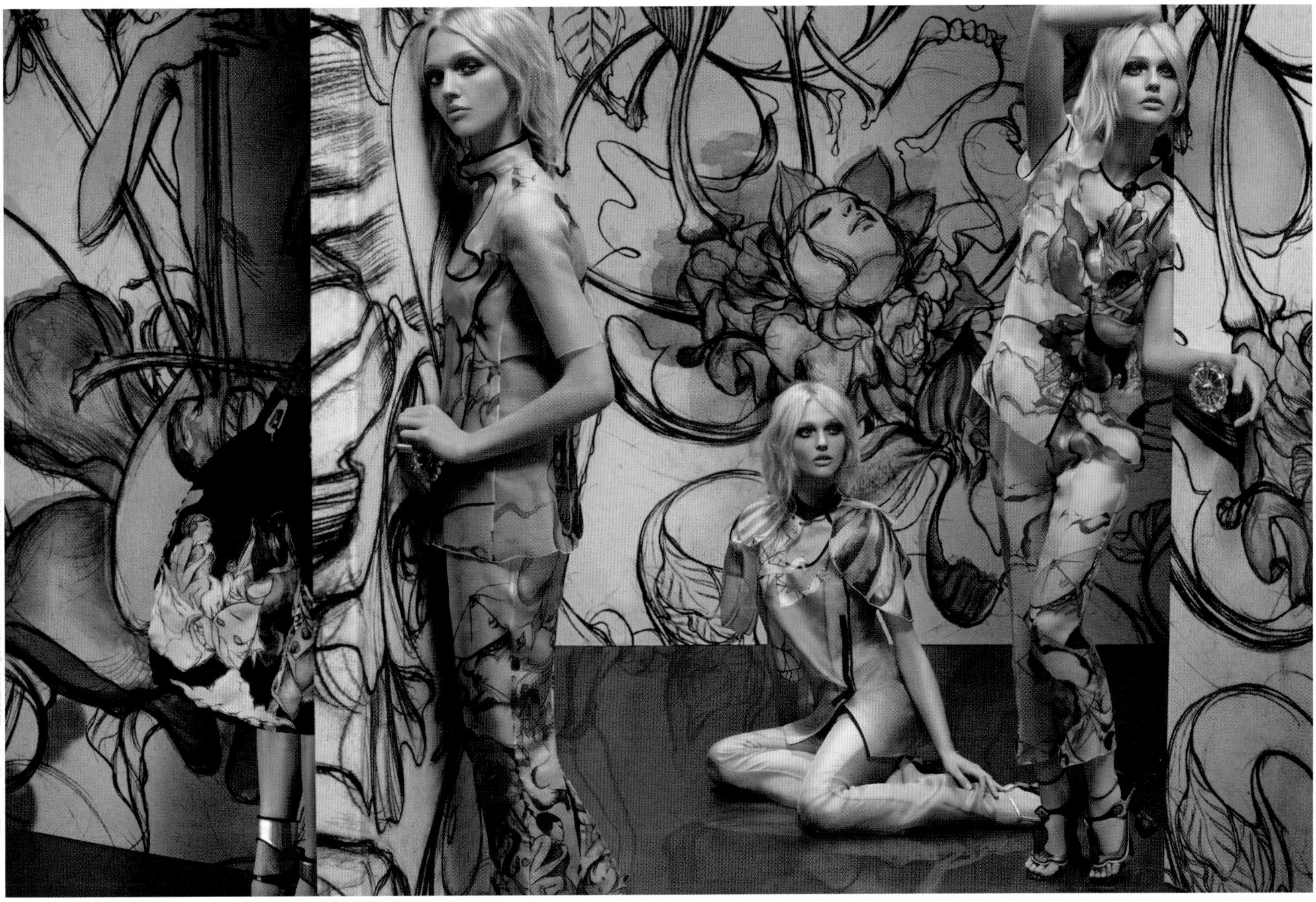

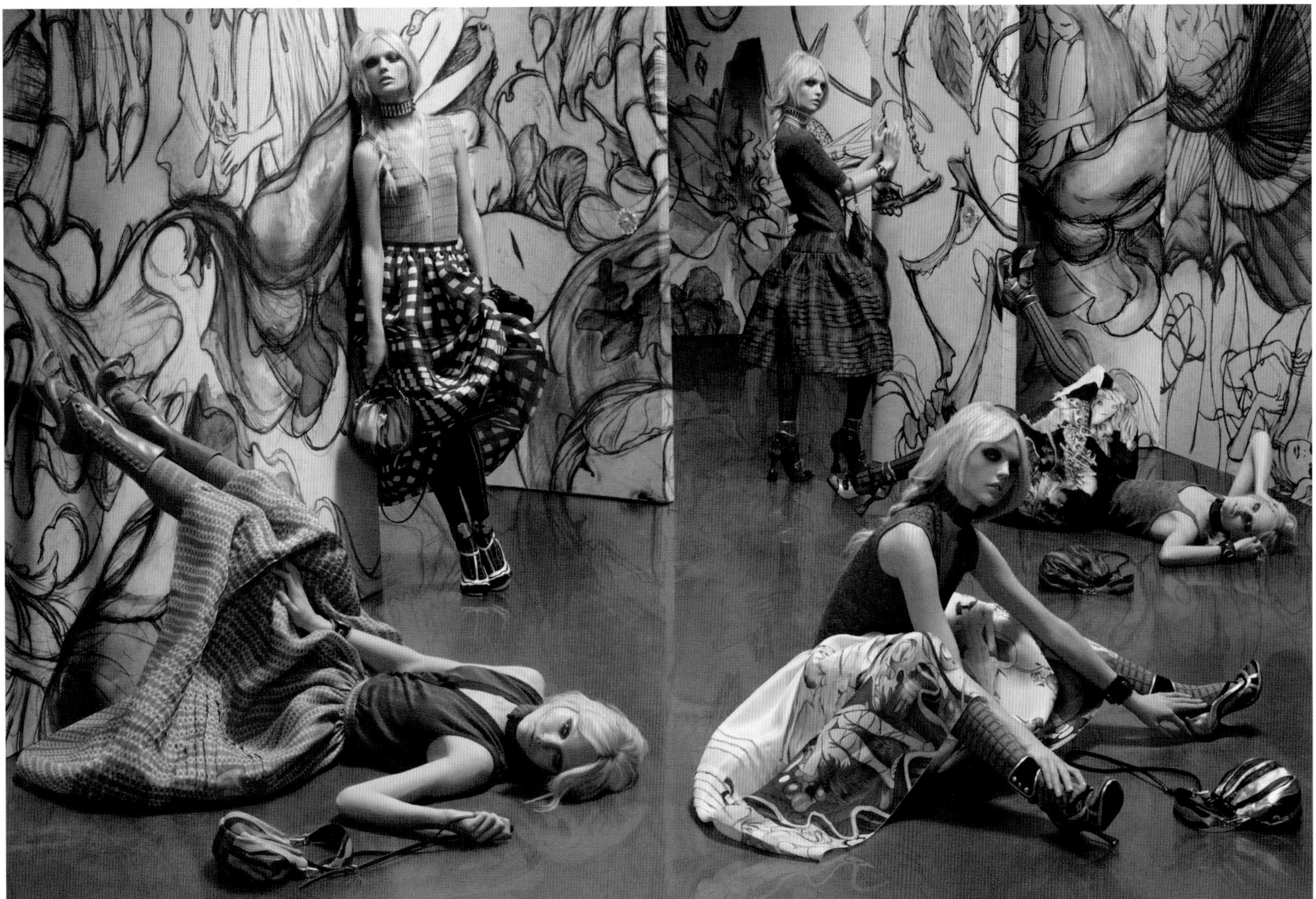

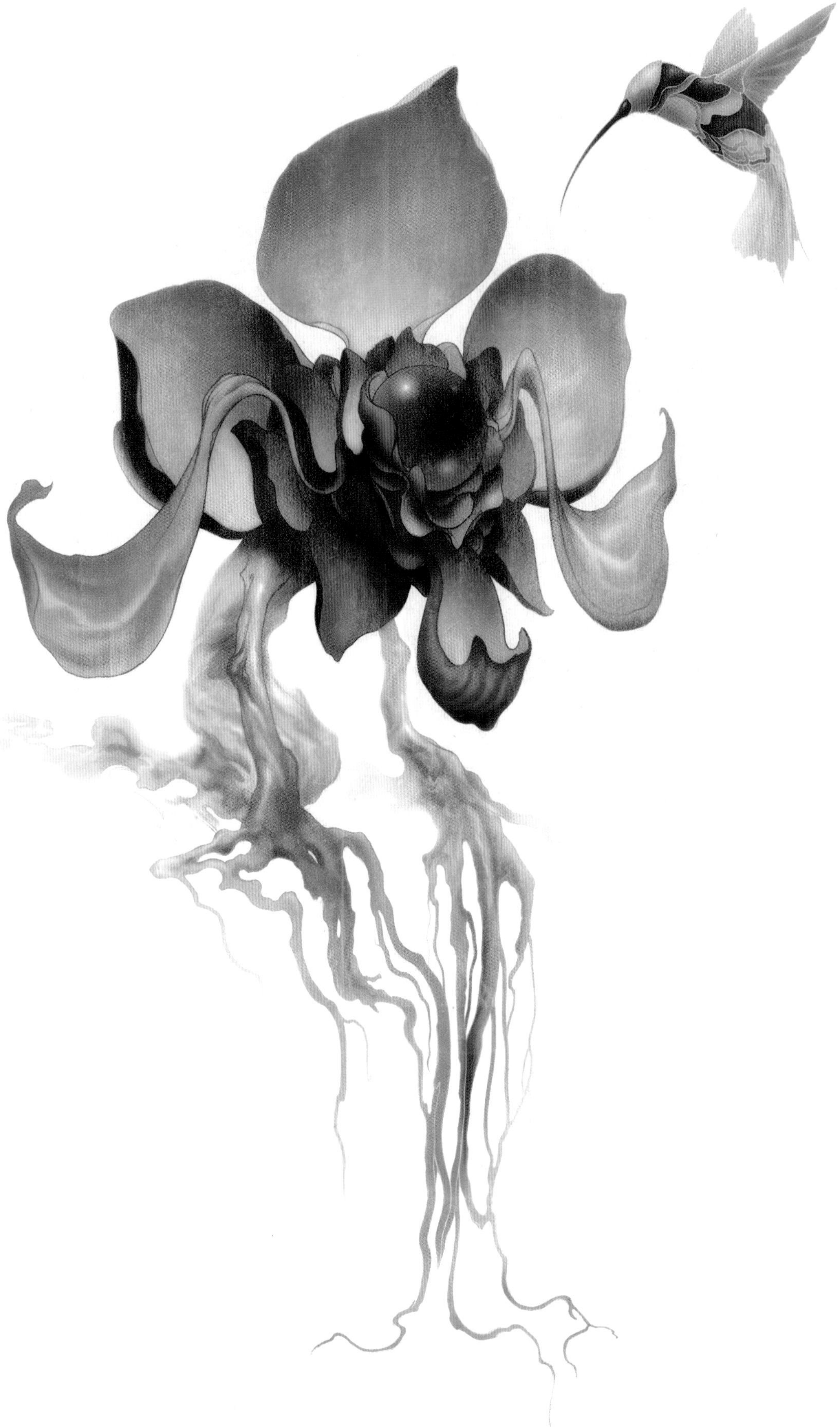

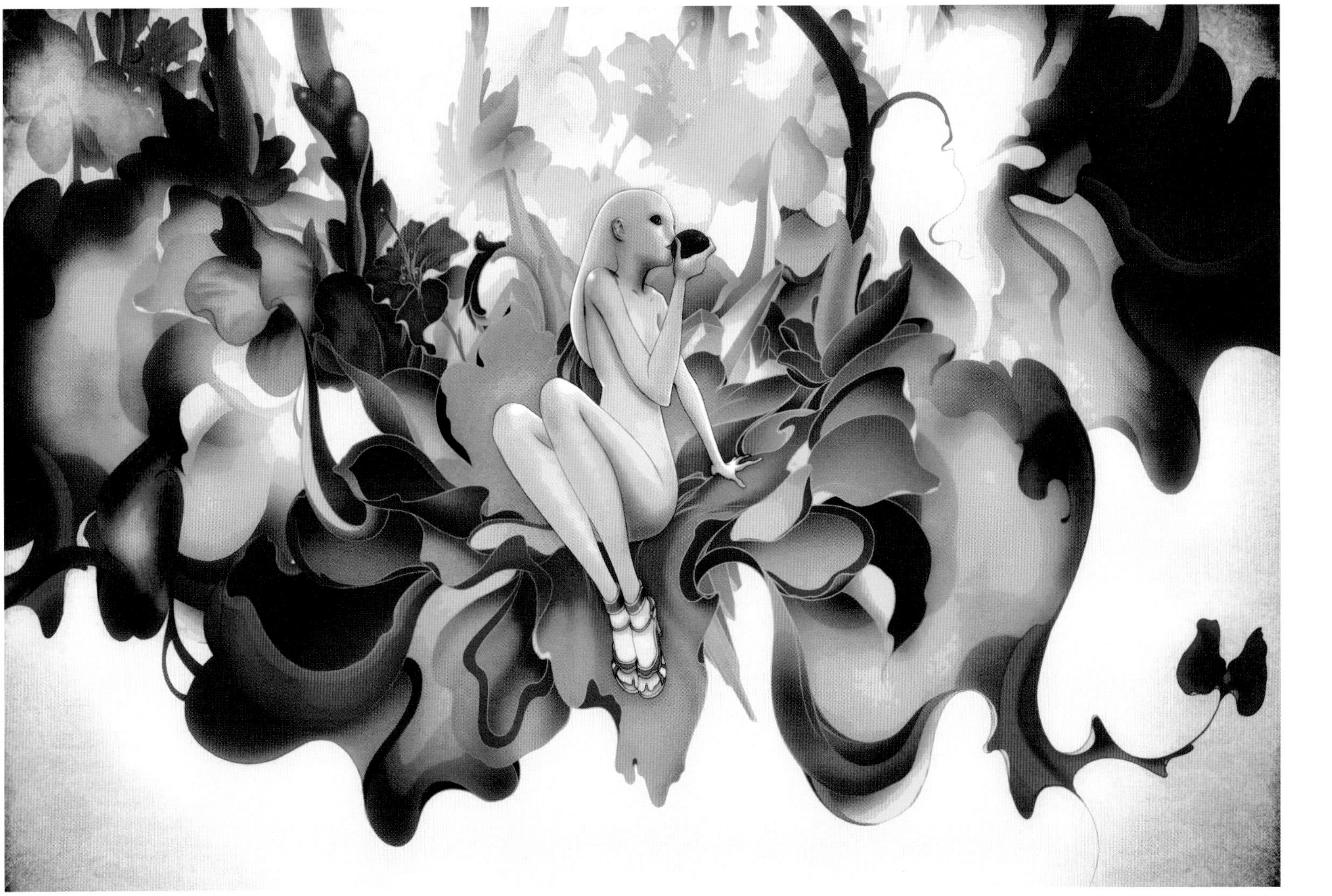

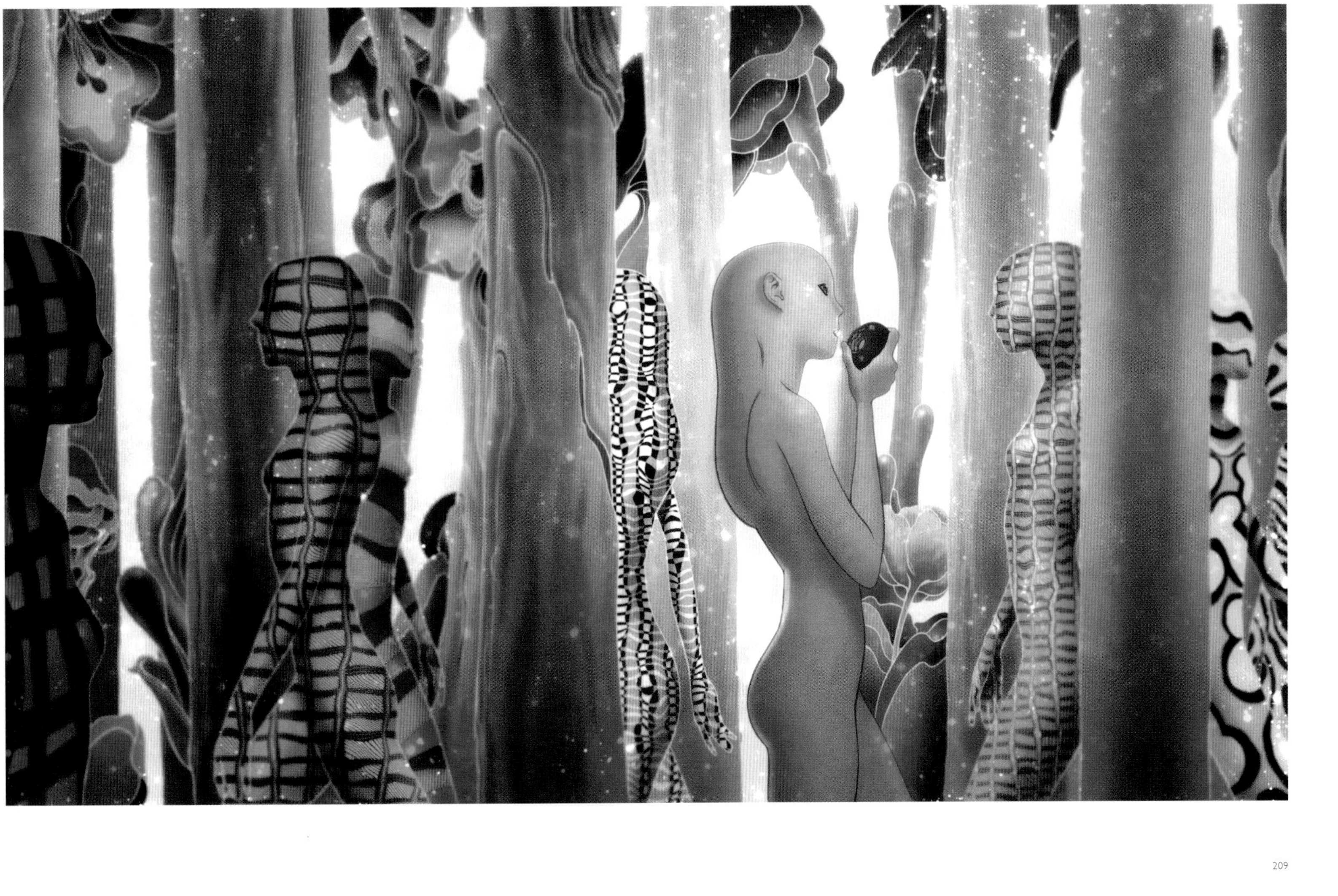

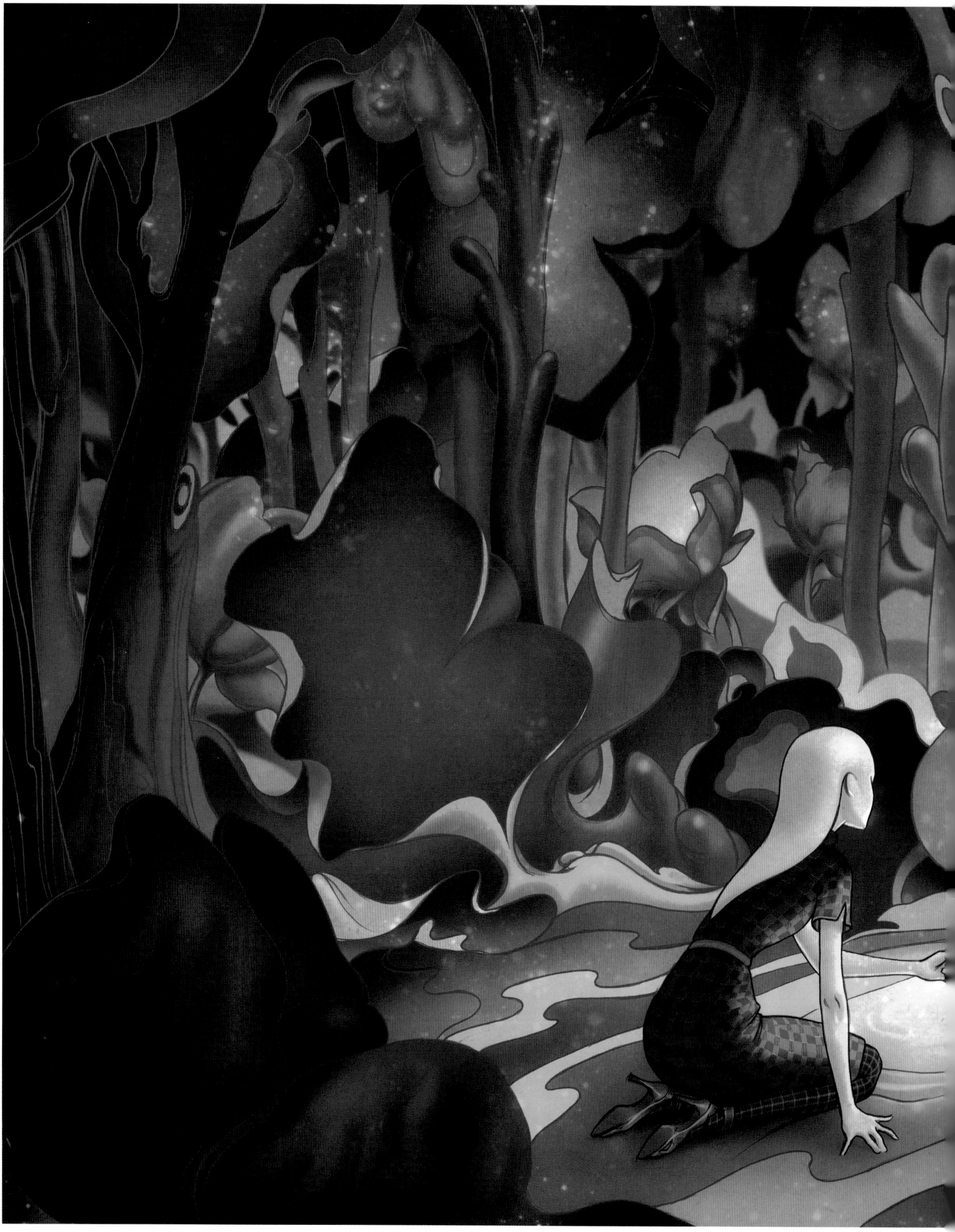

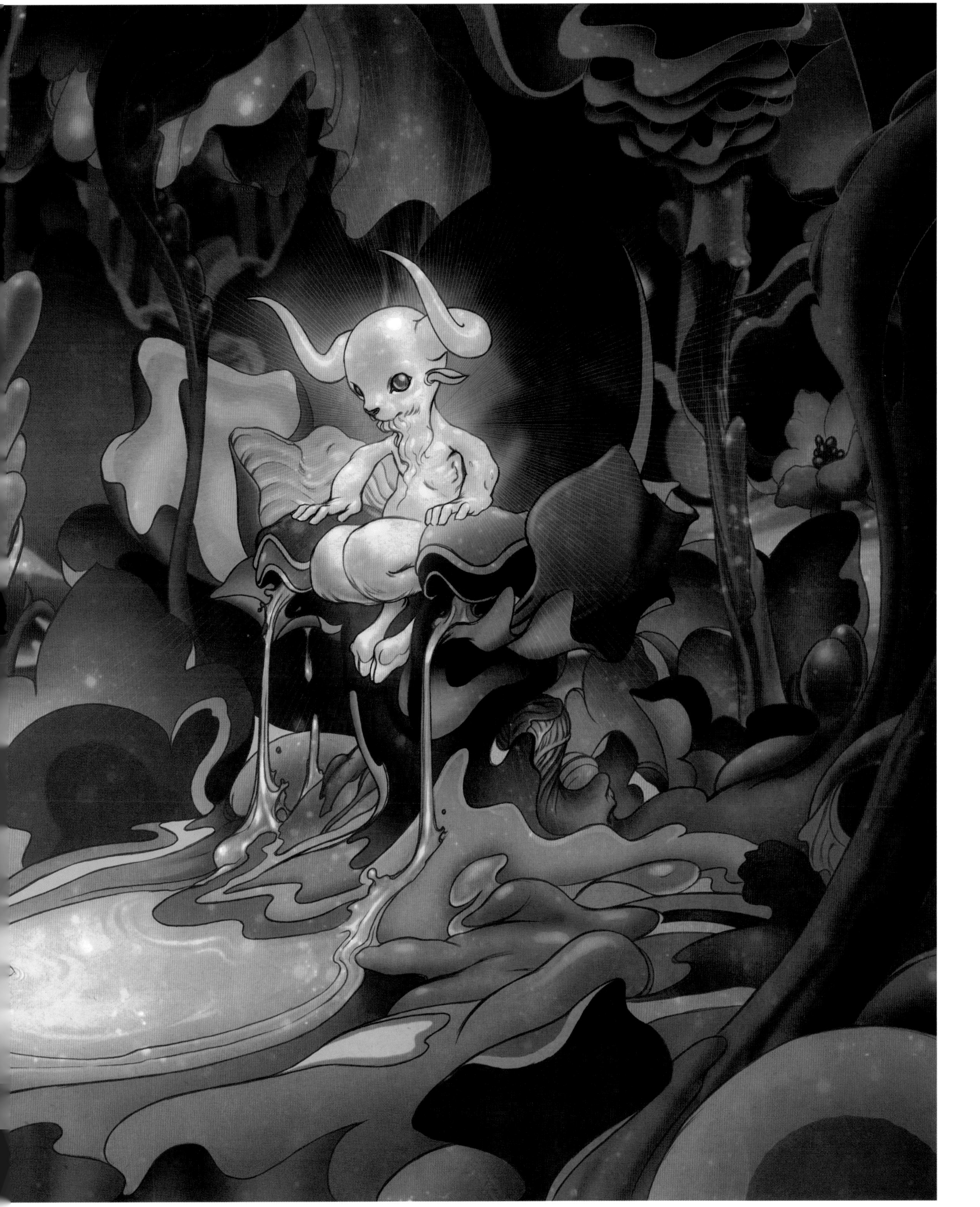

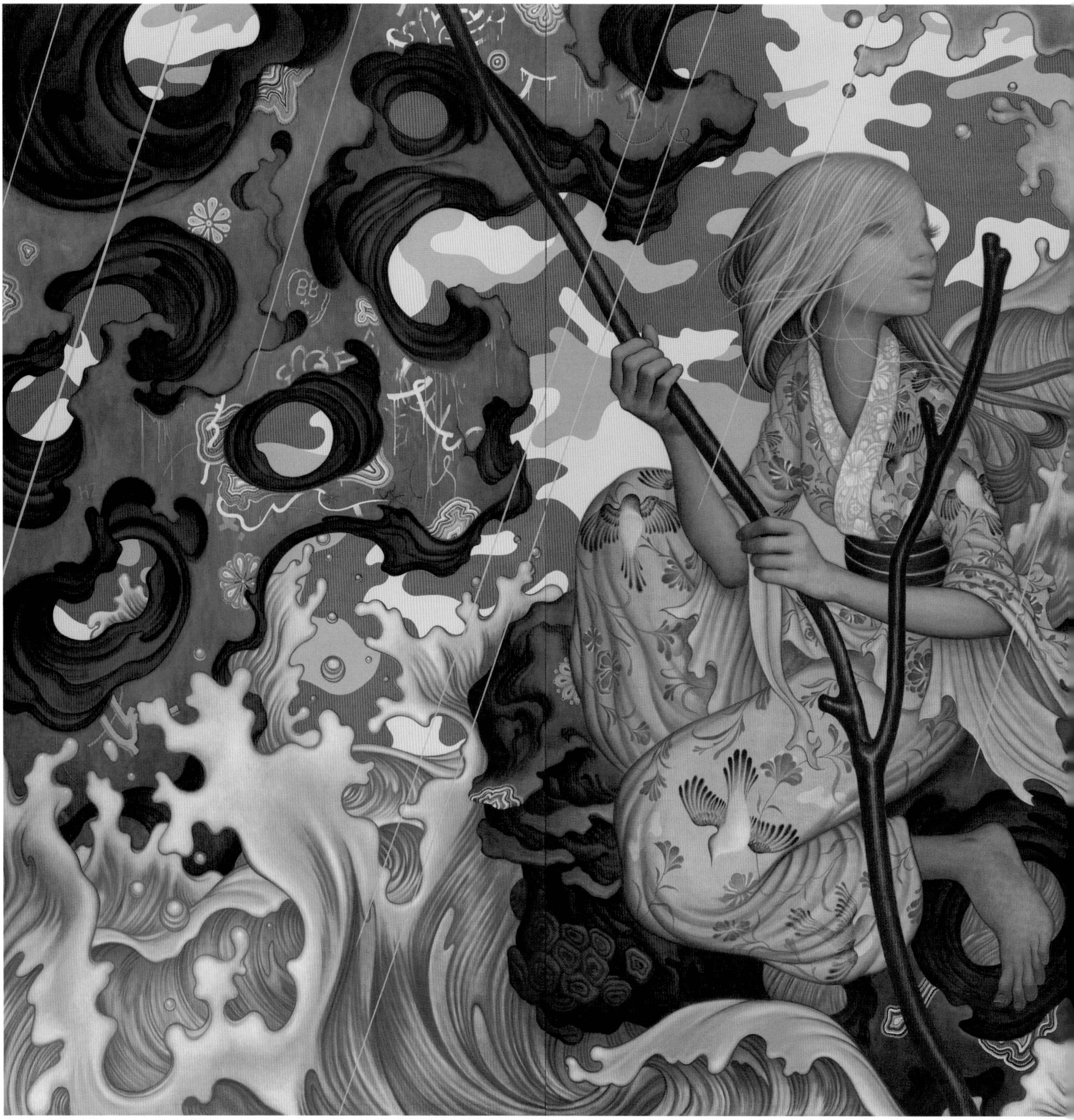

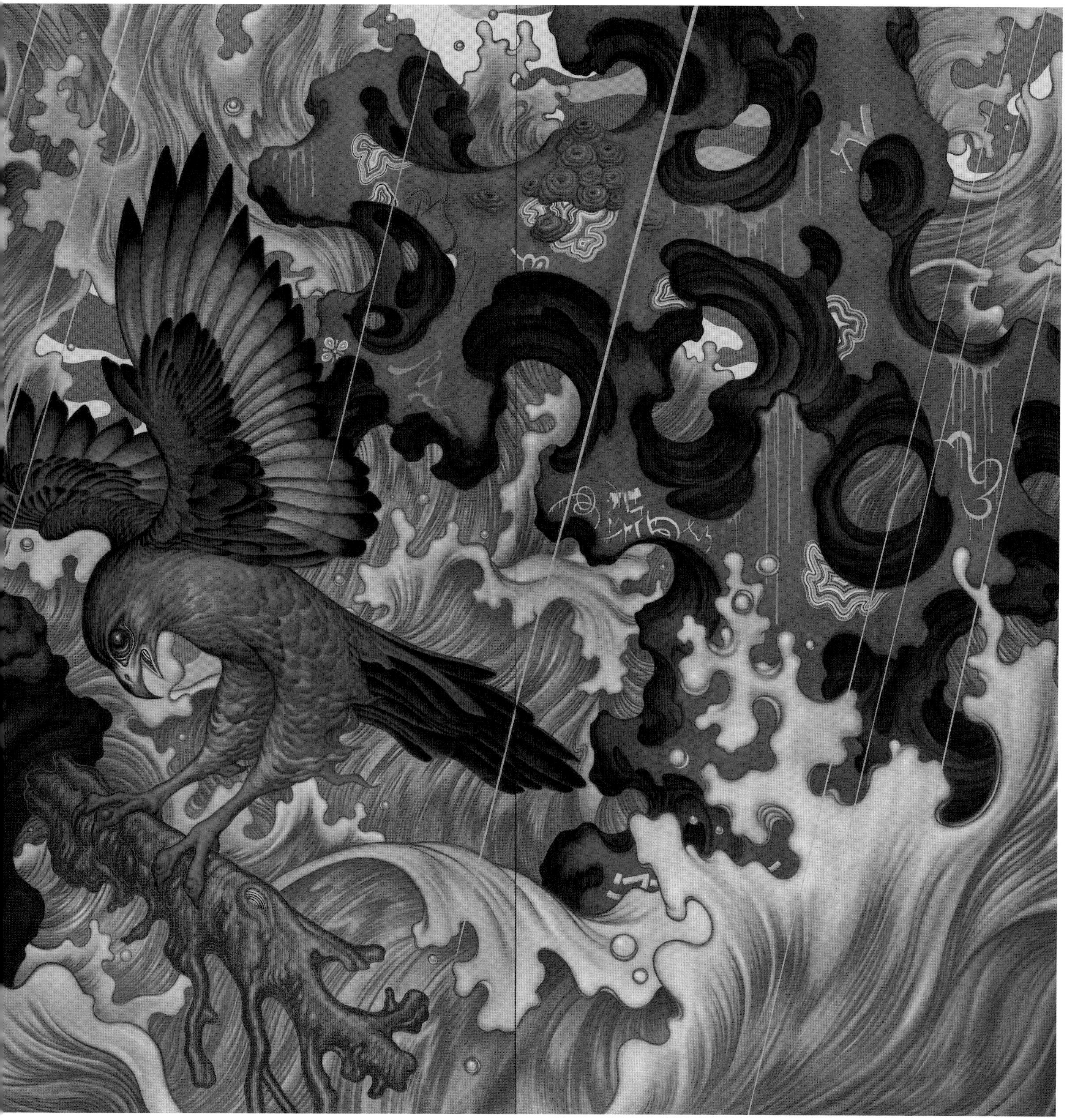

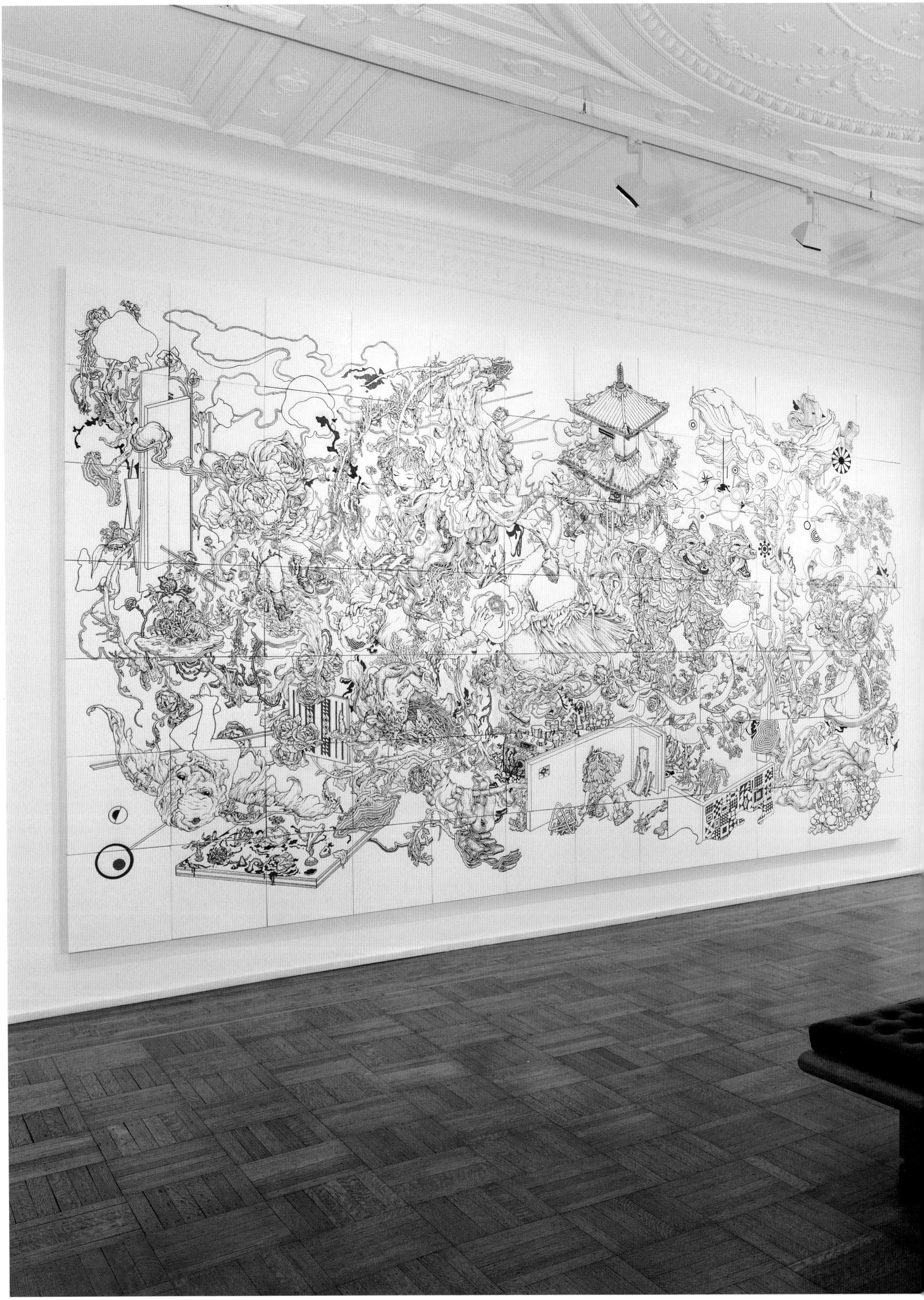

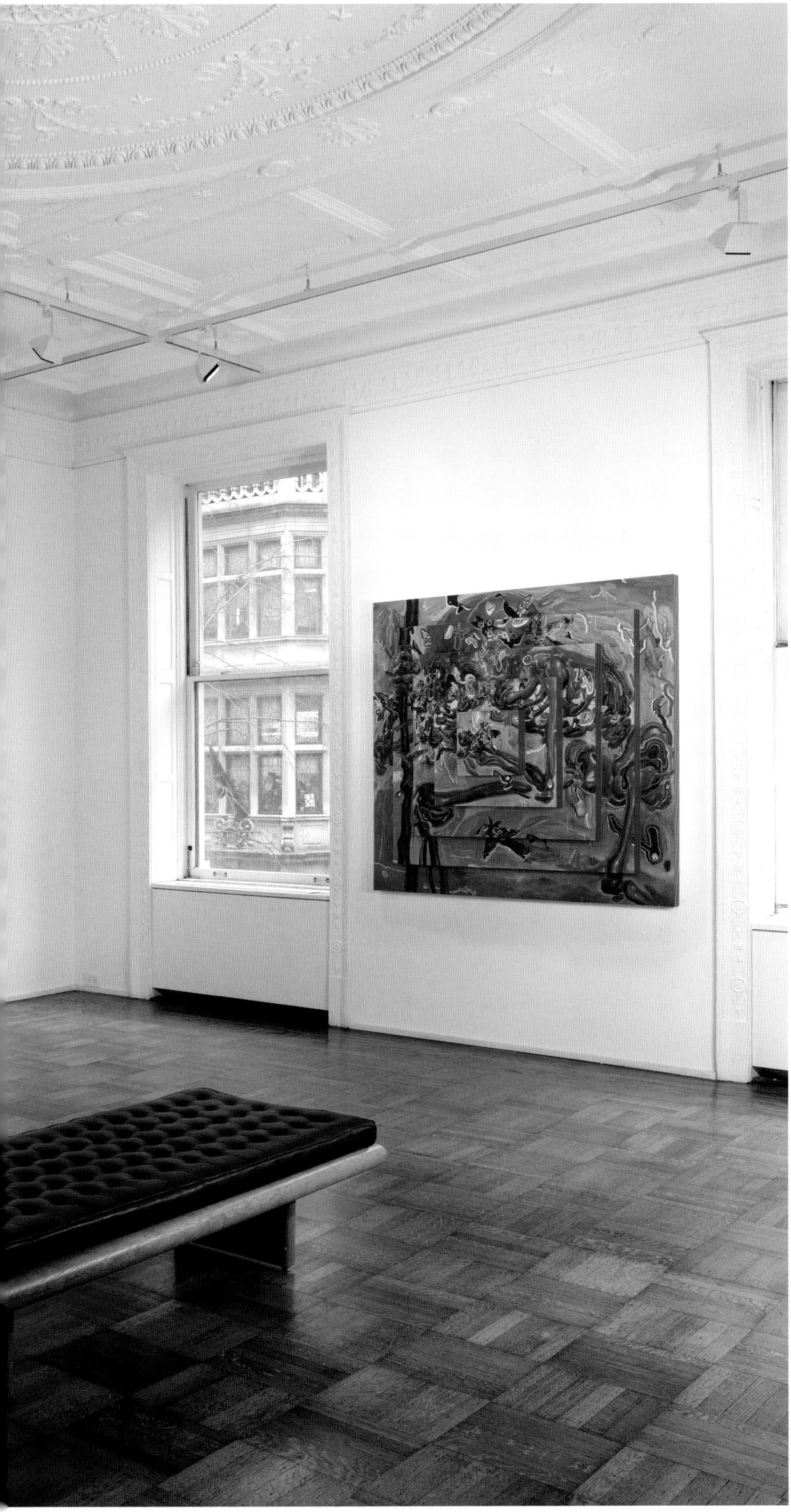

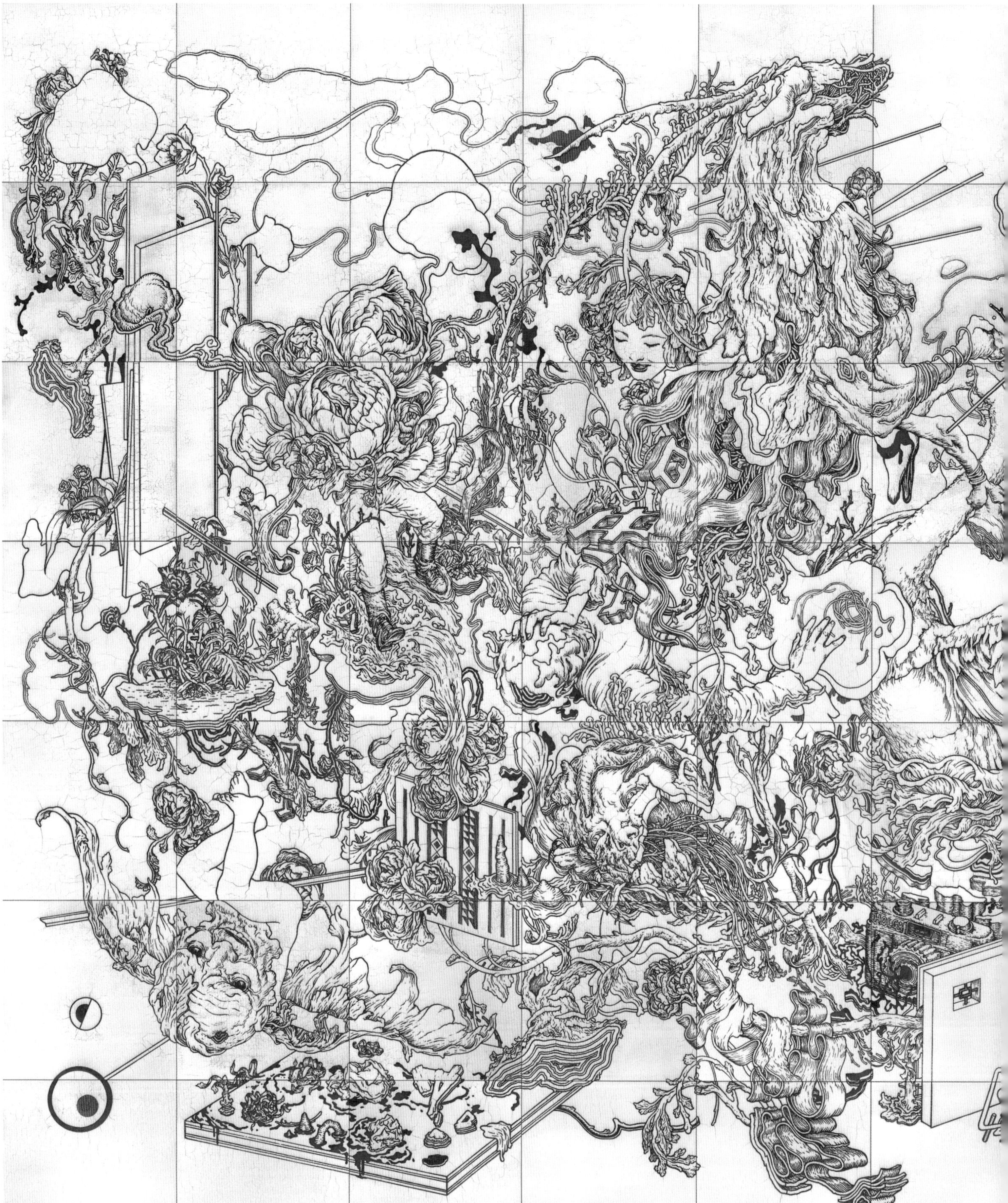

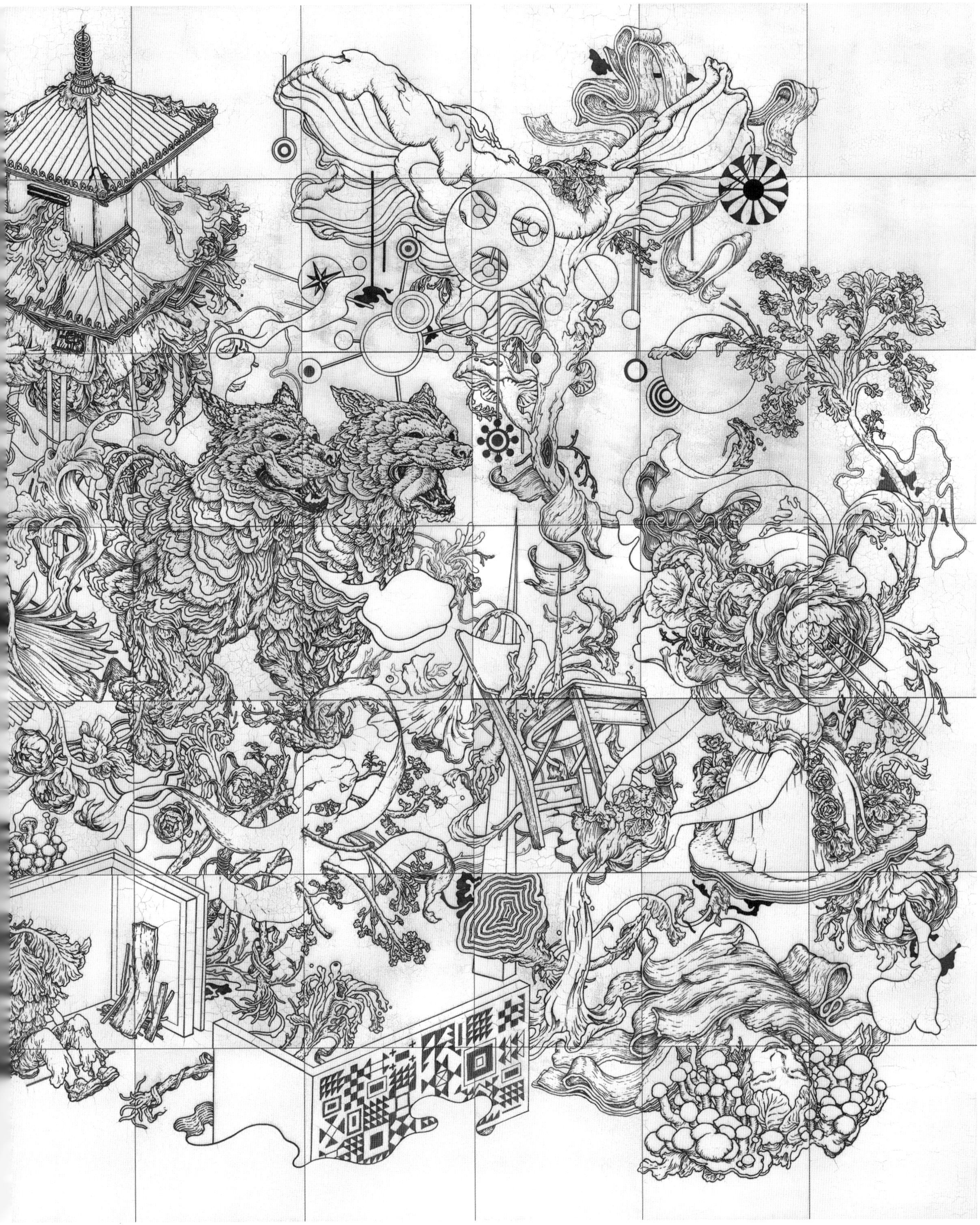

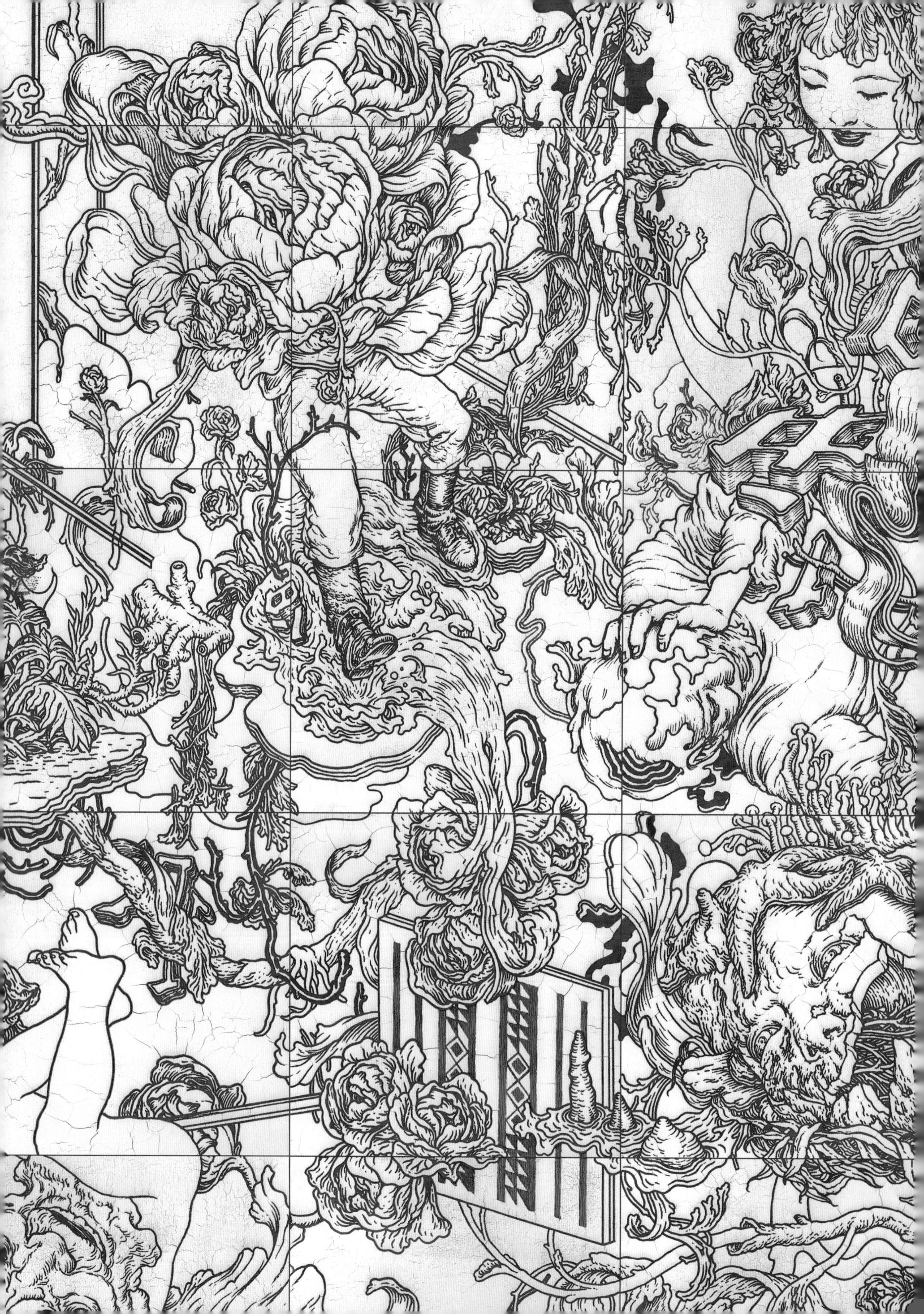

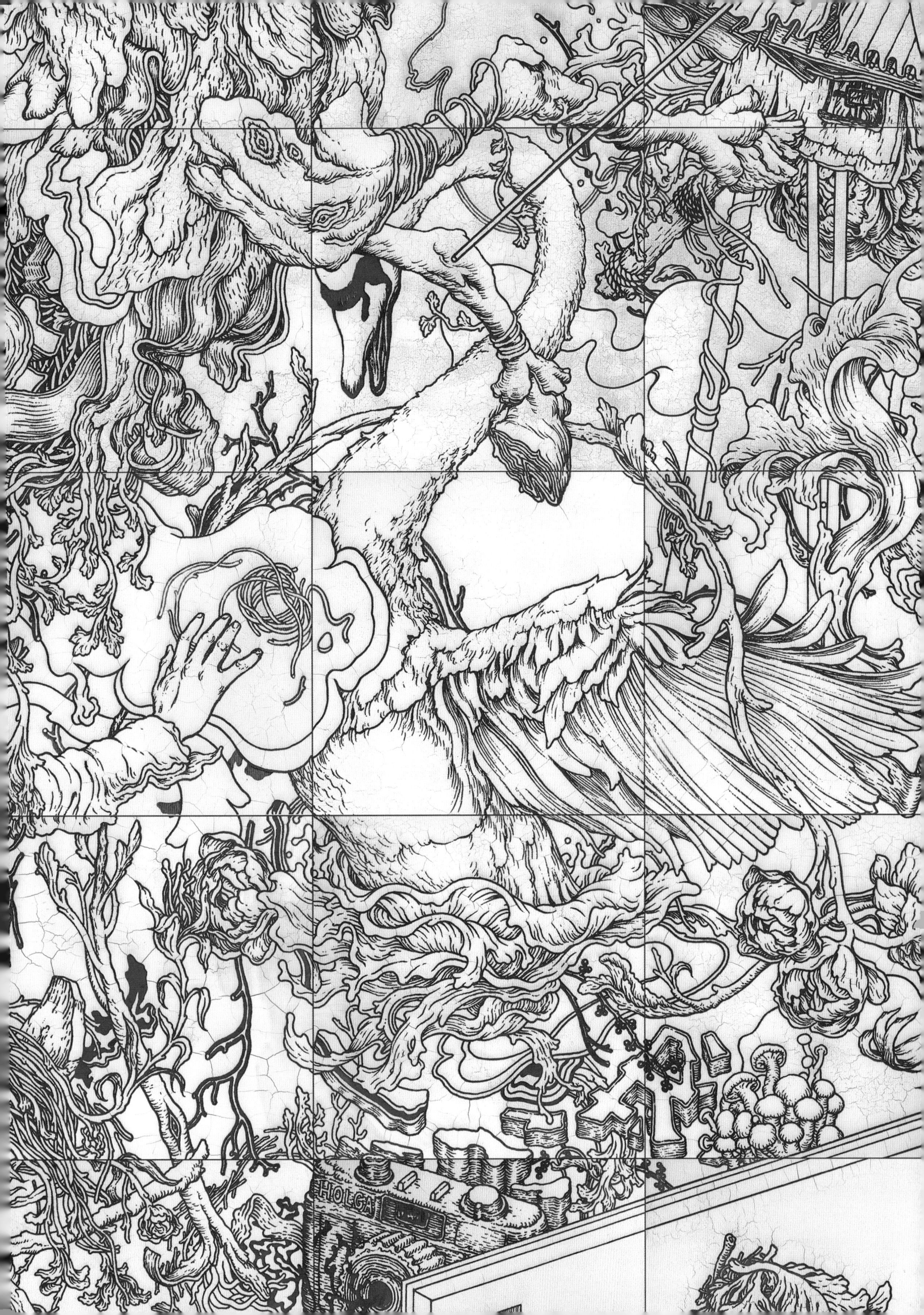
HOLGA

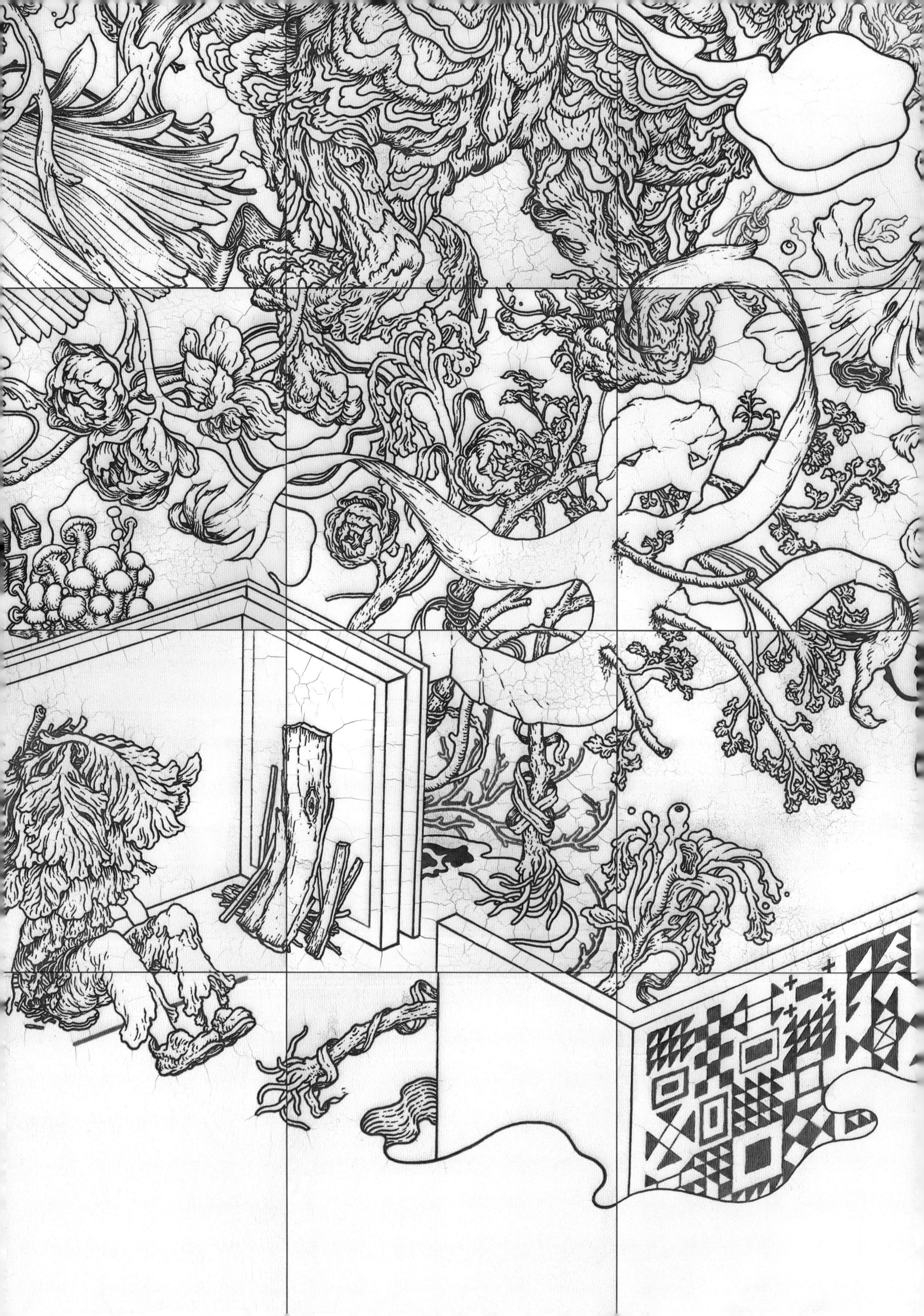

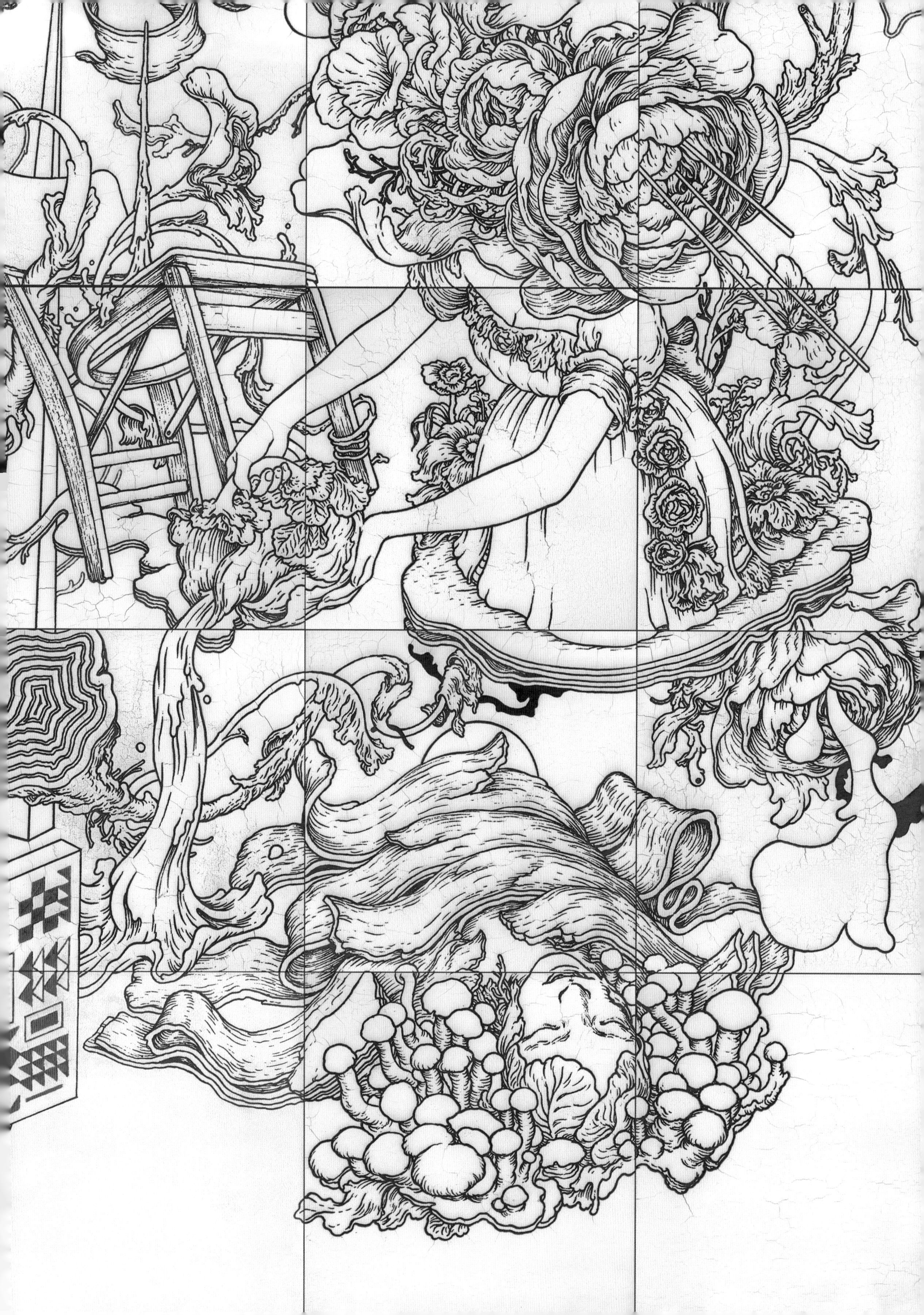

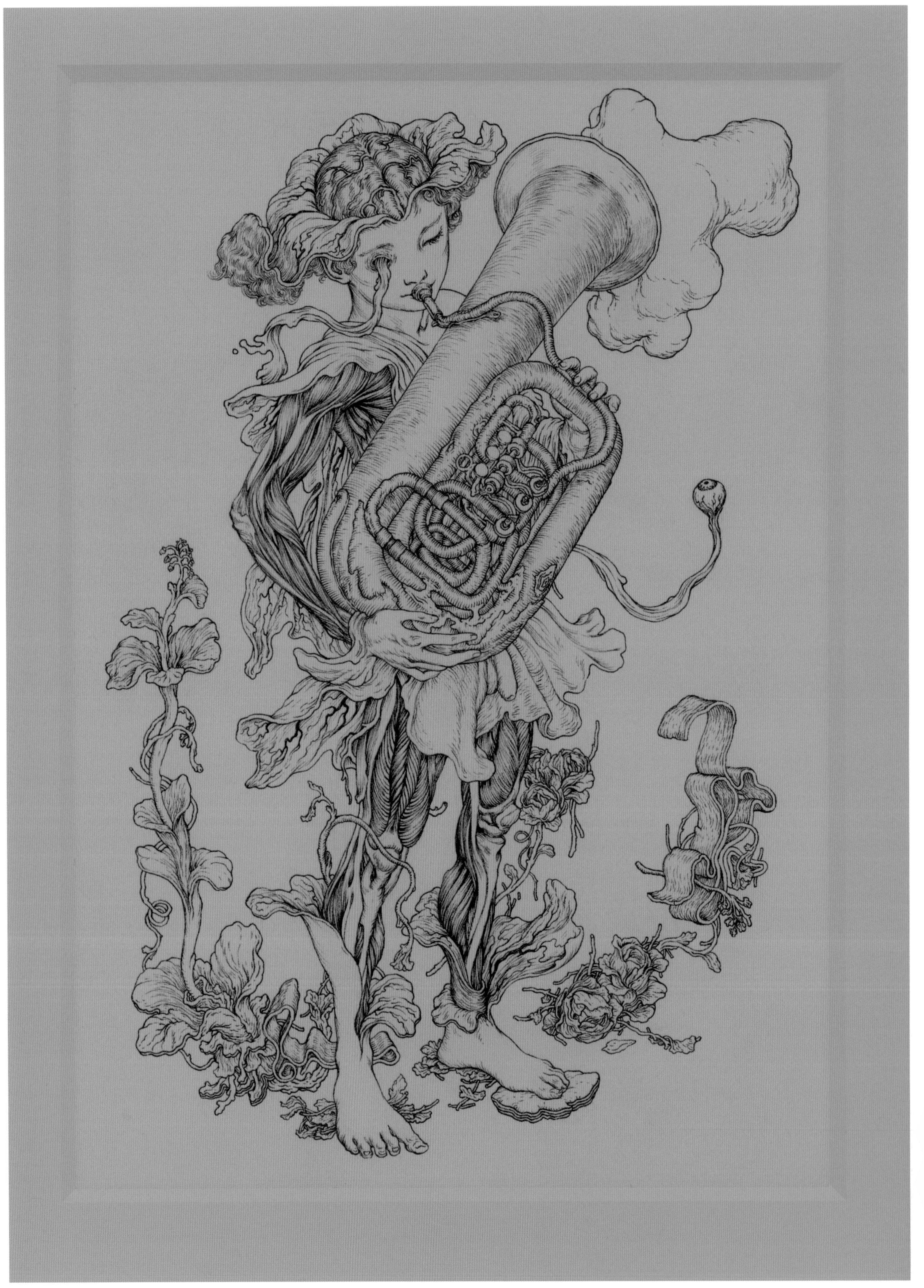

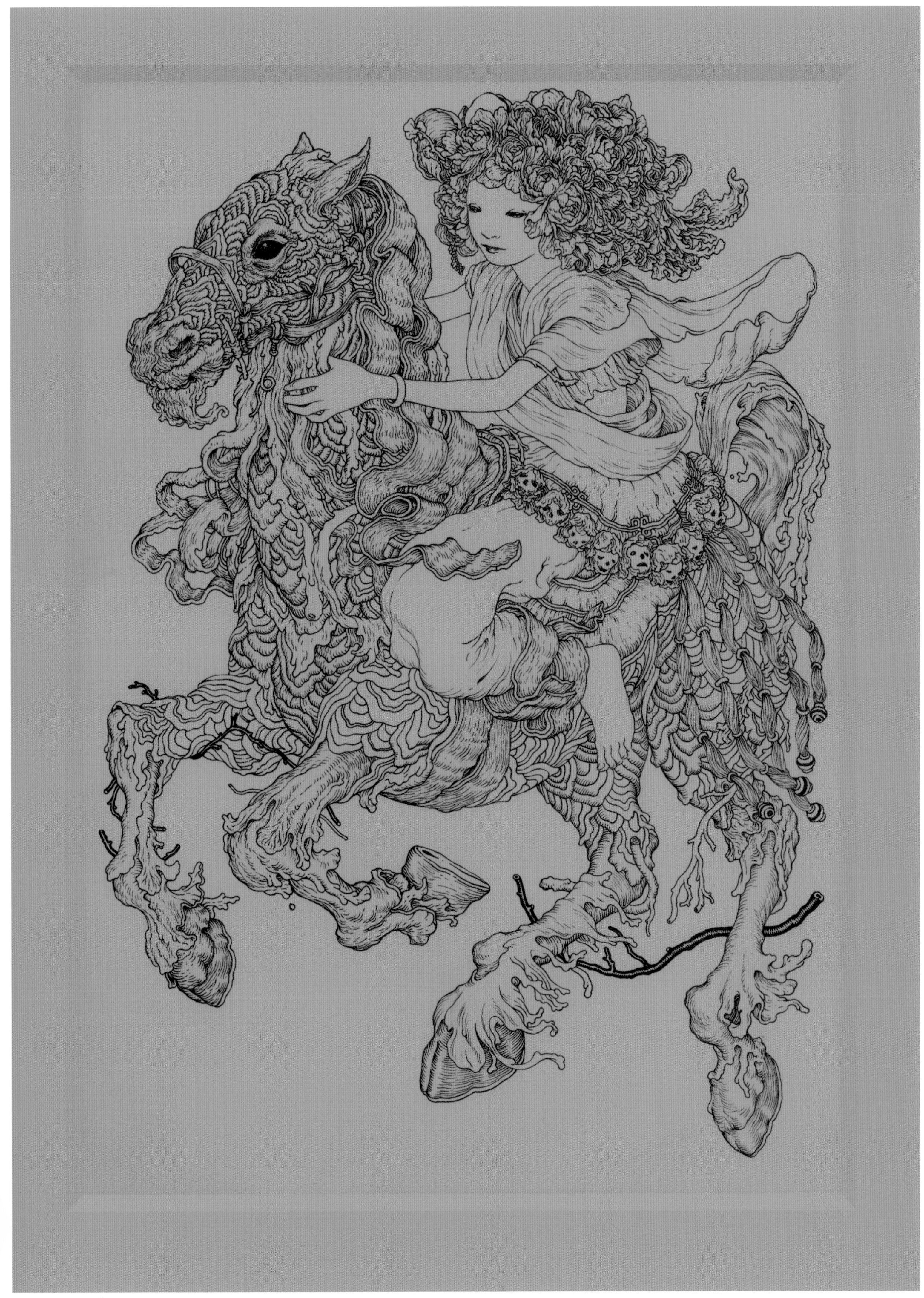

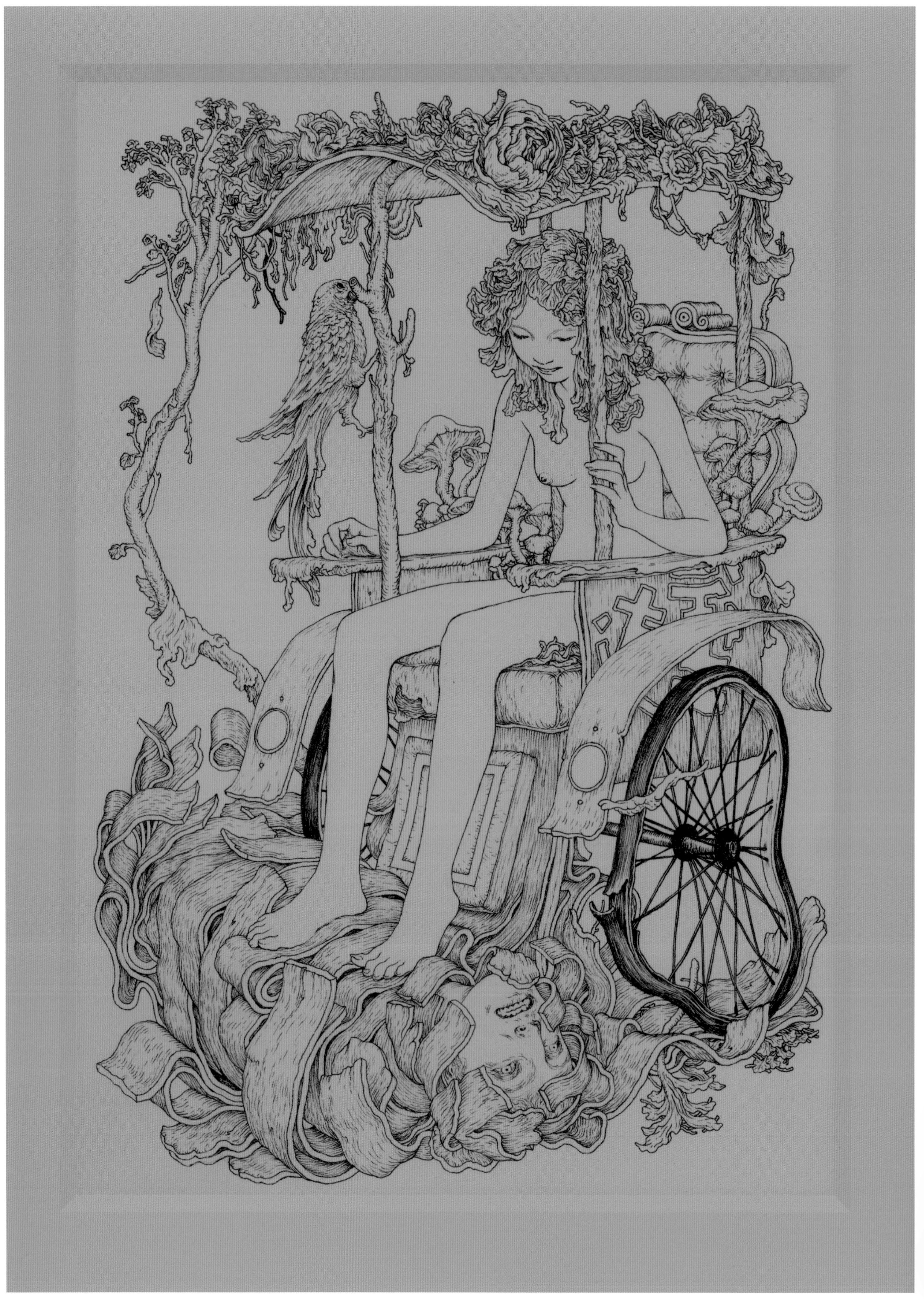

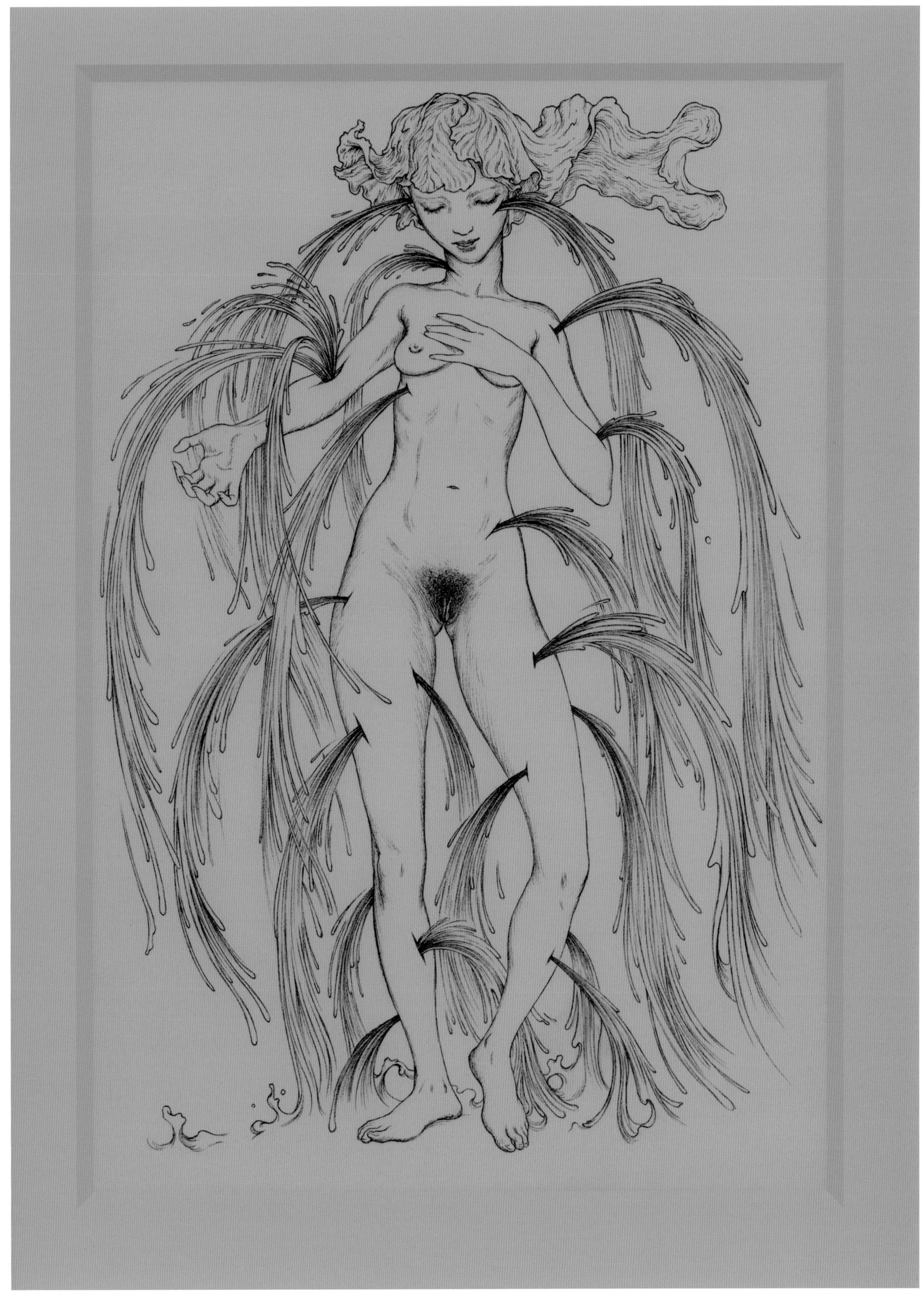

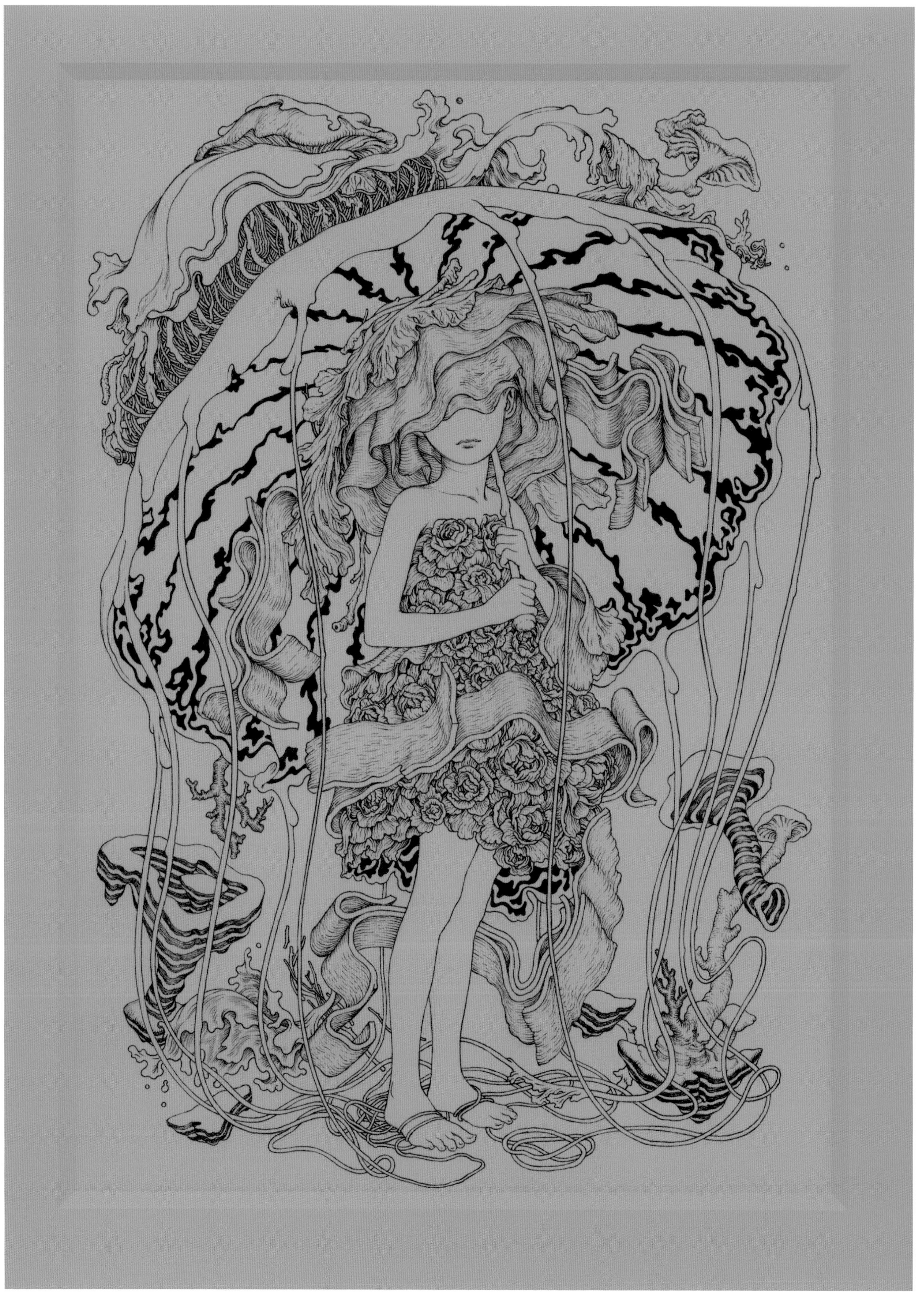

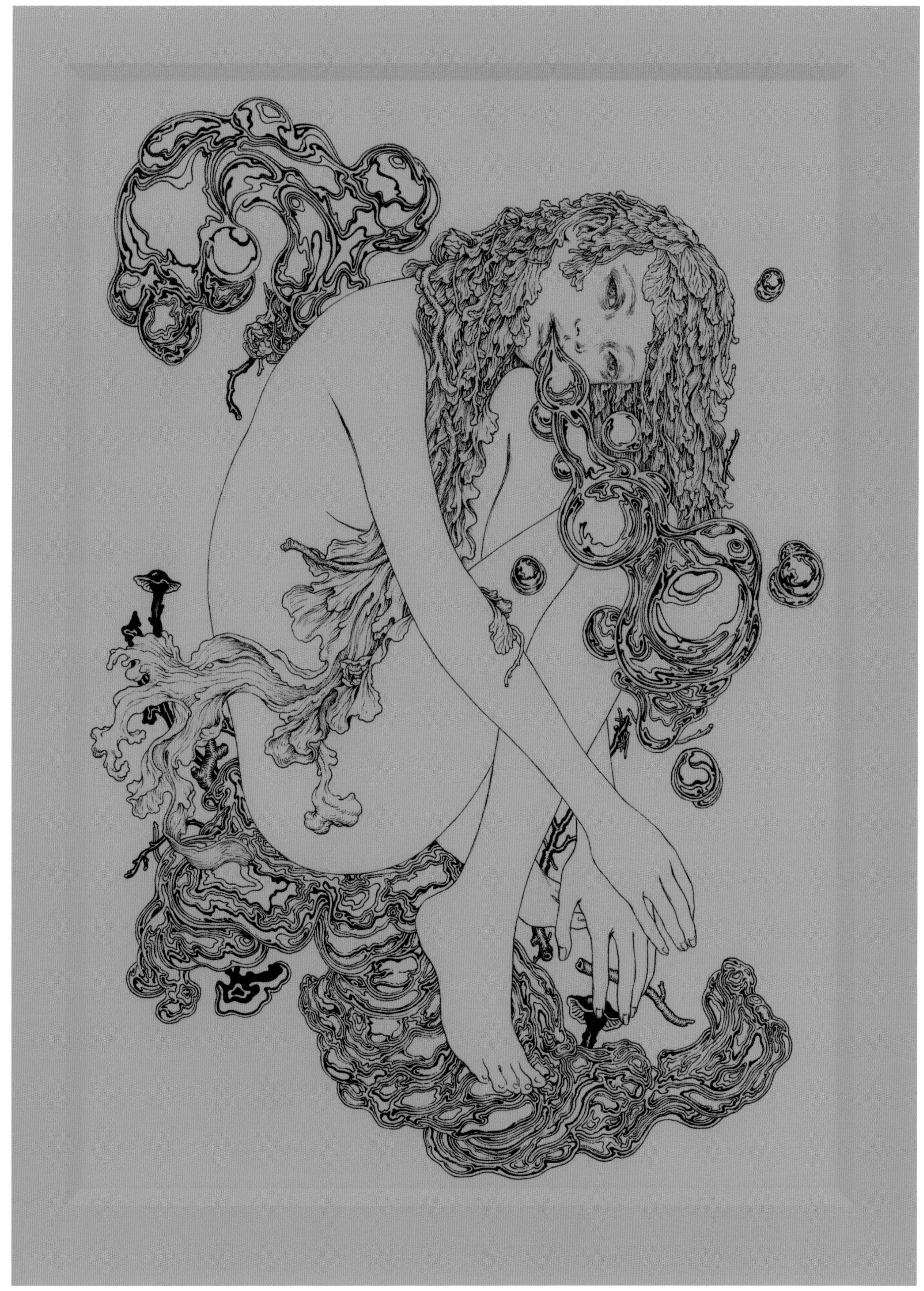

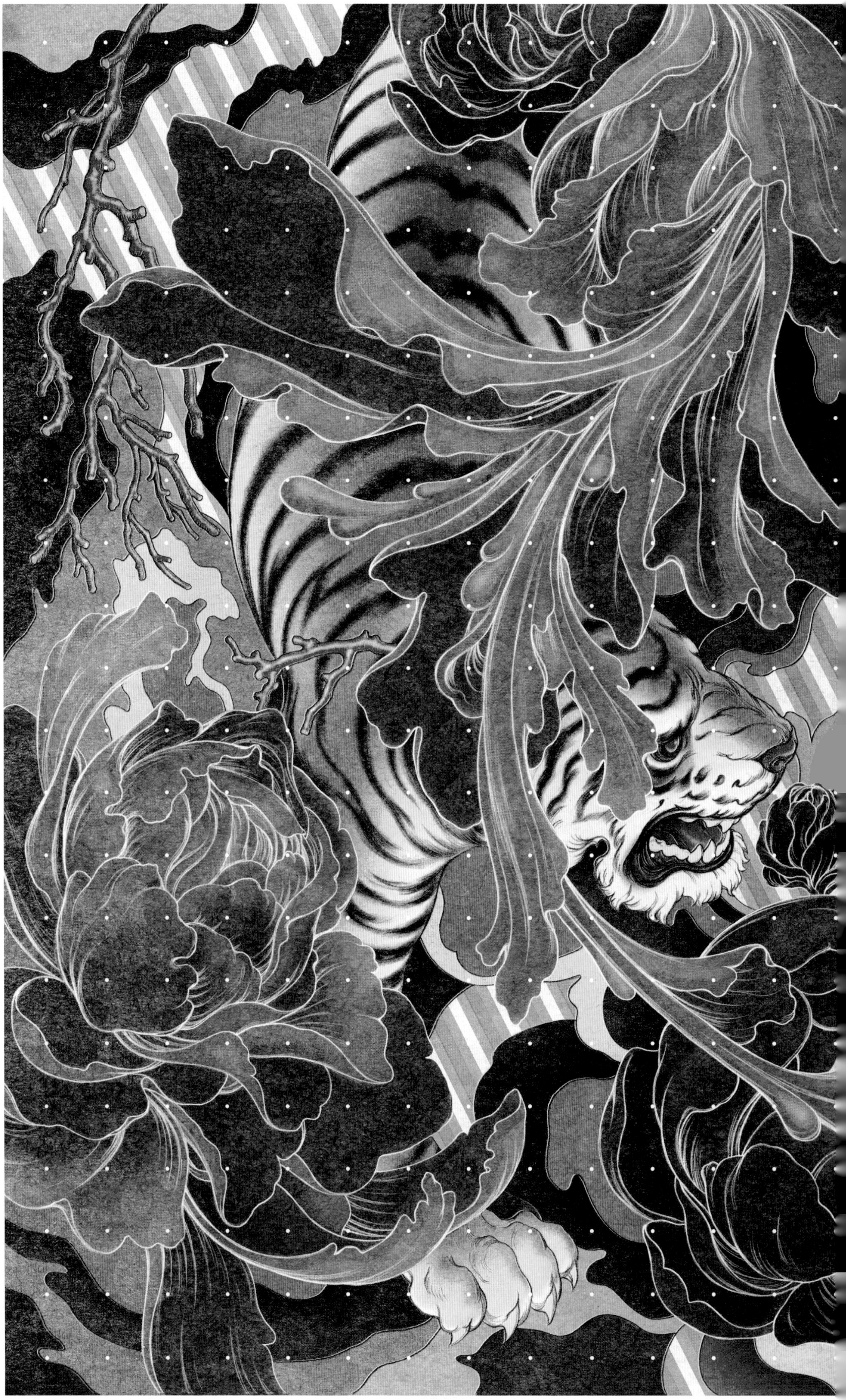

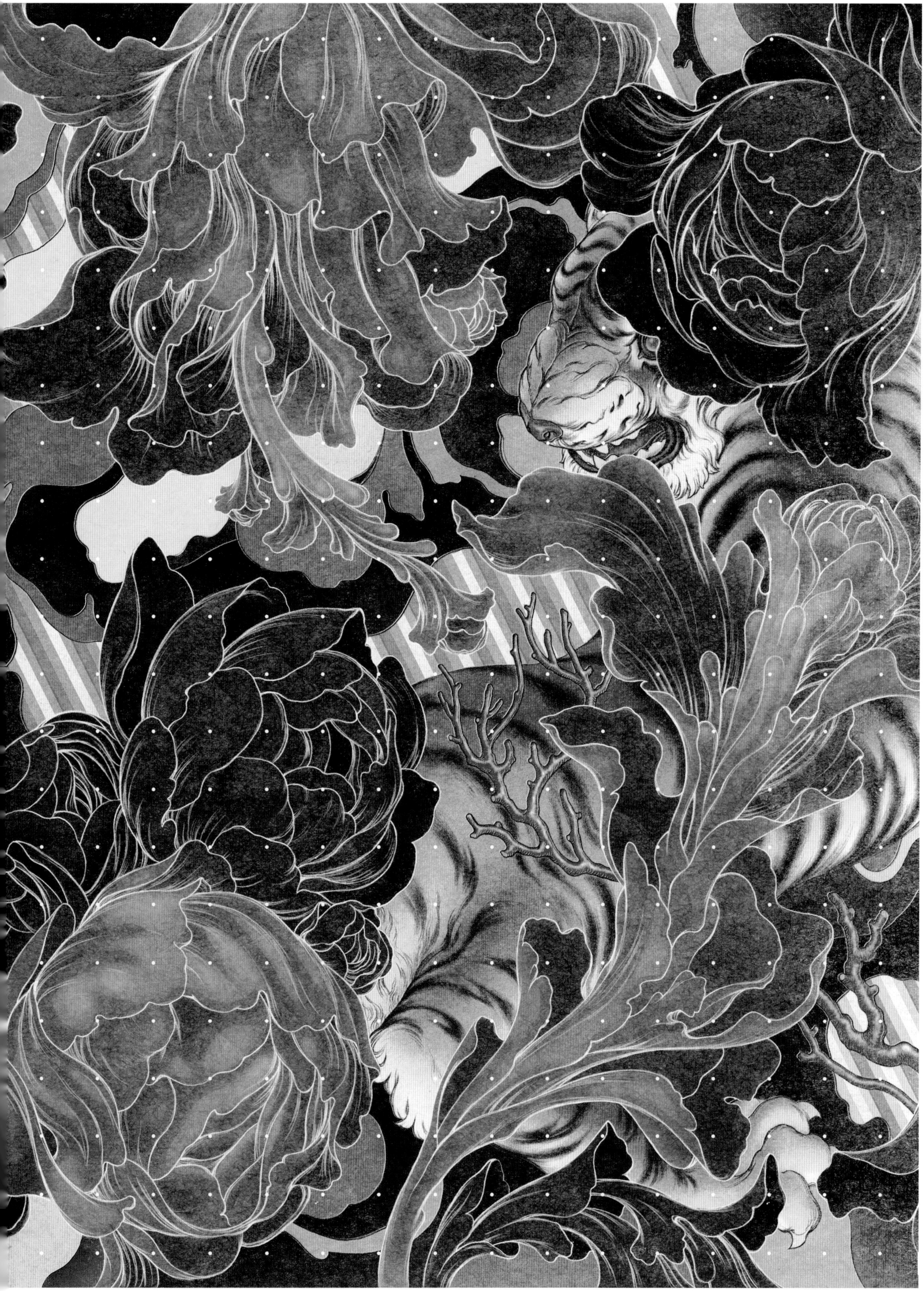

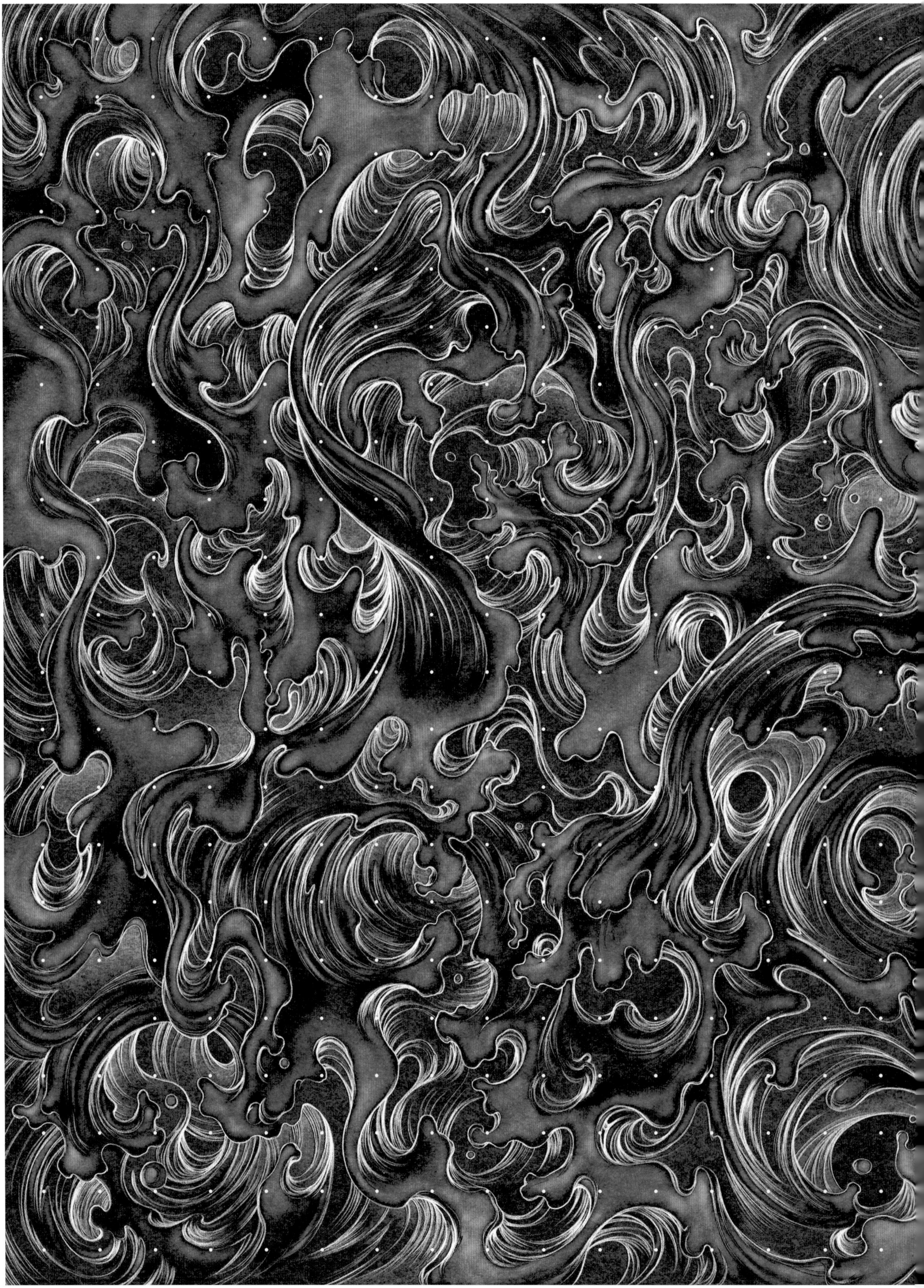

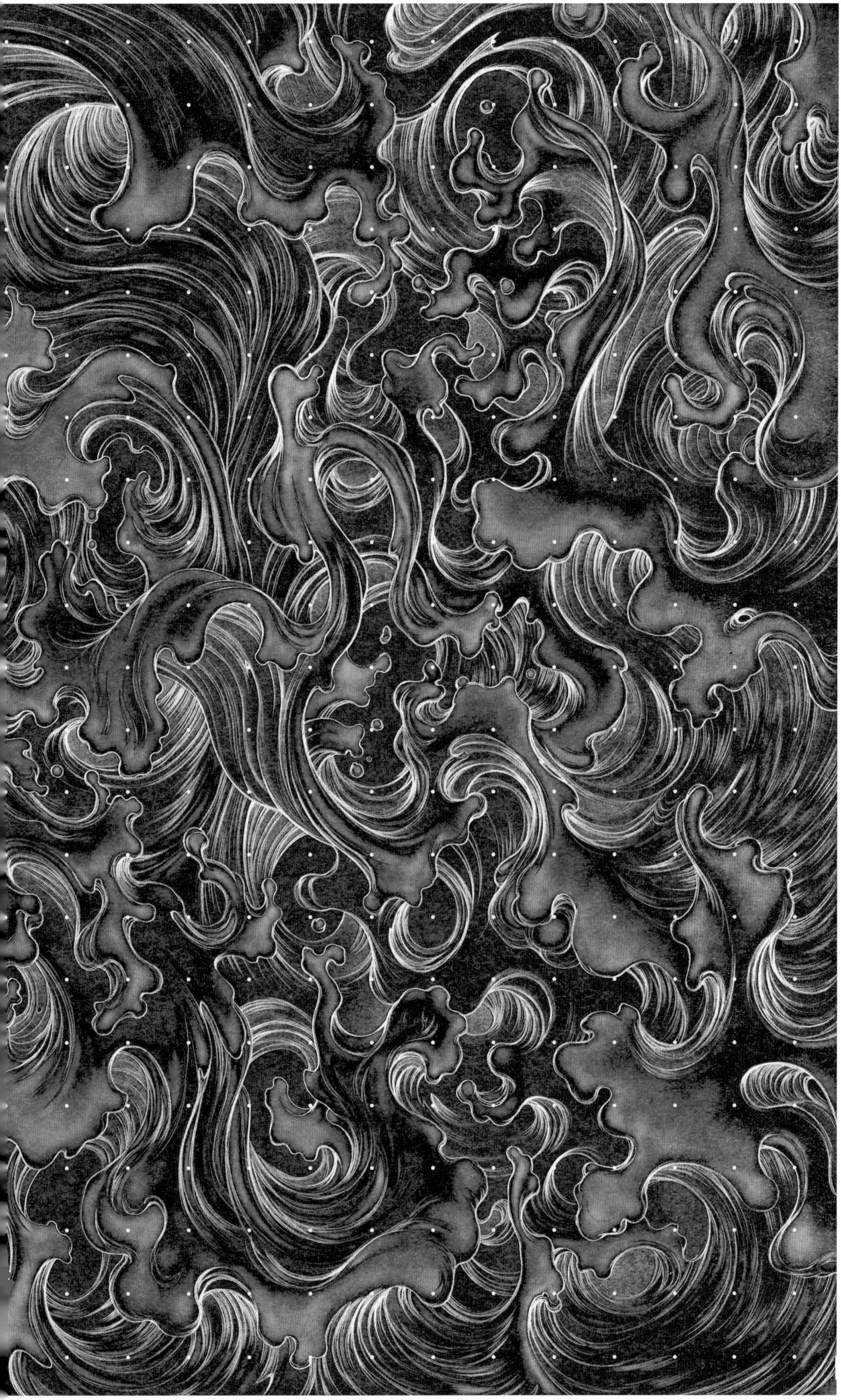

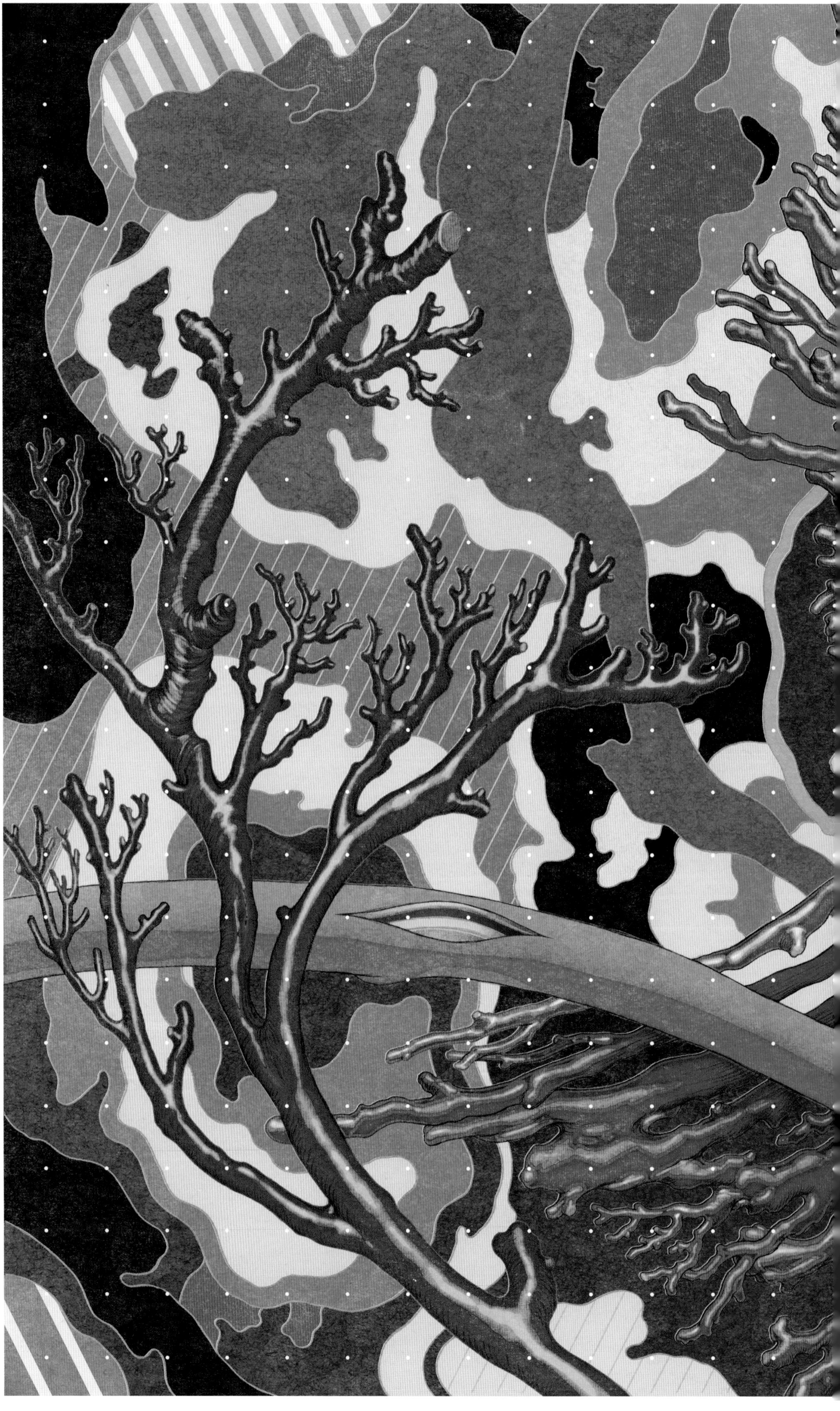

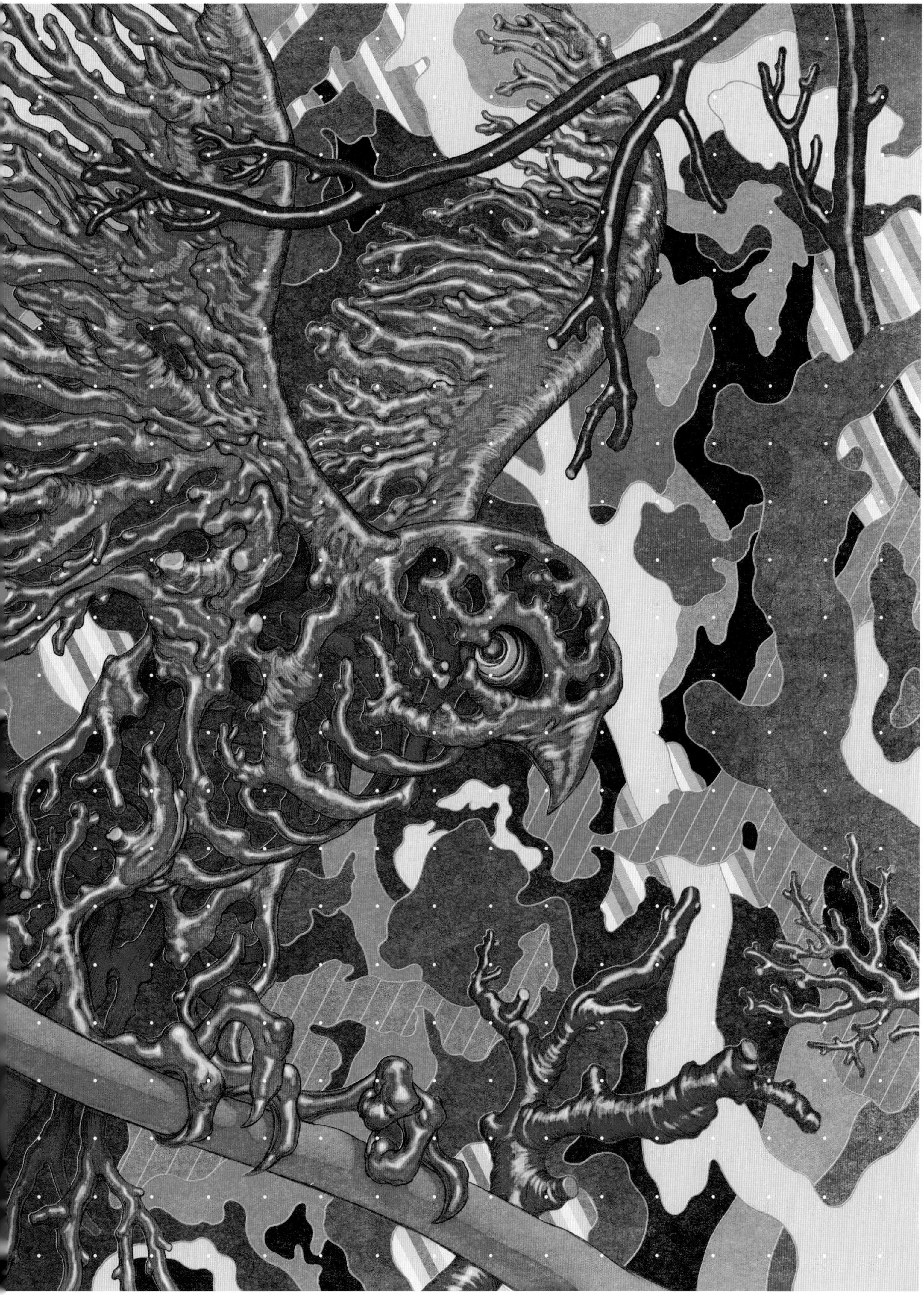

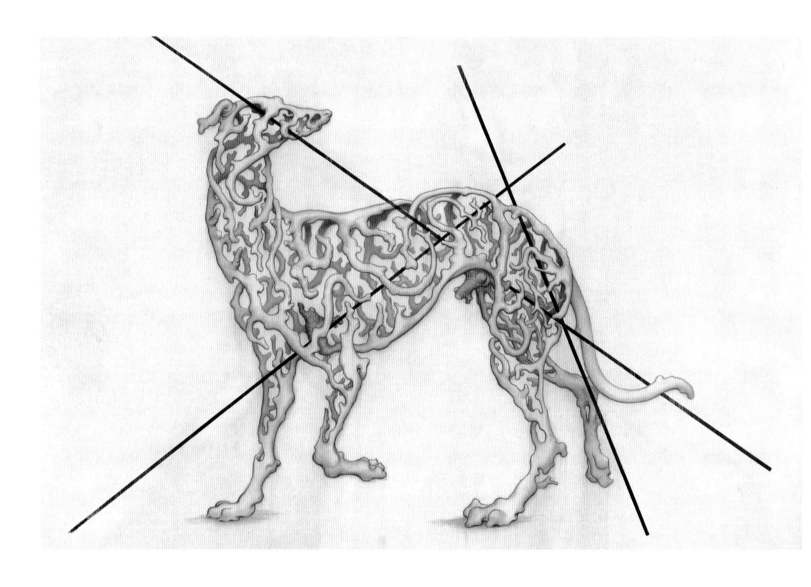

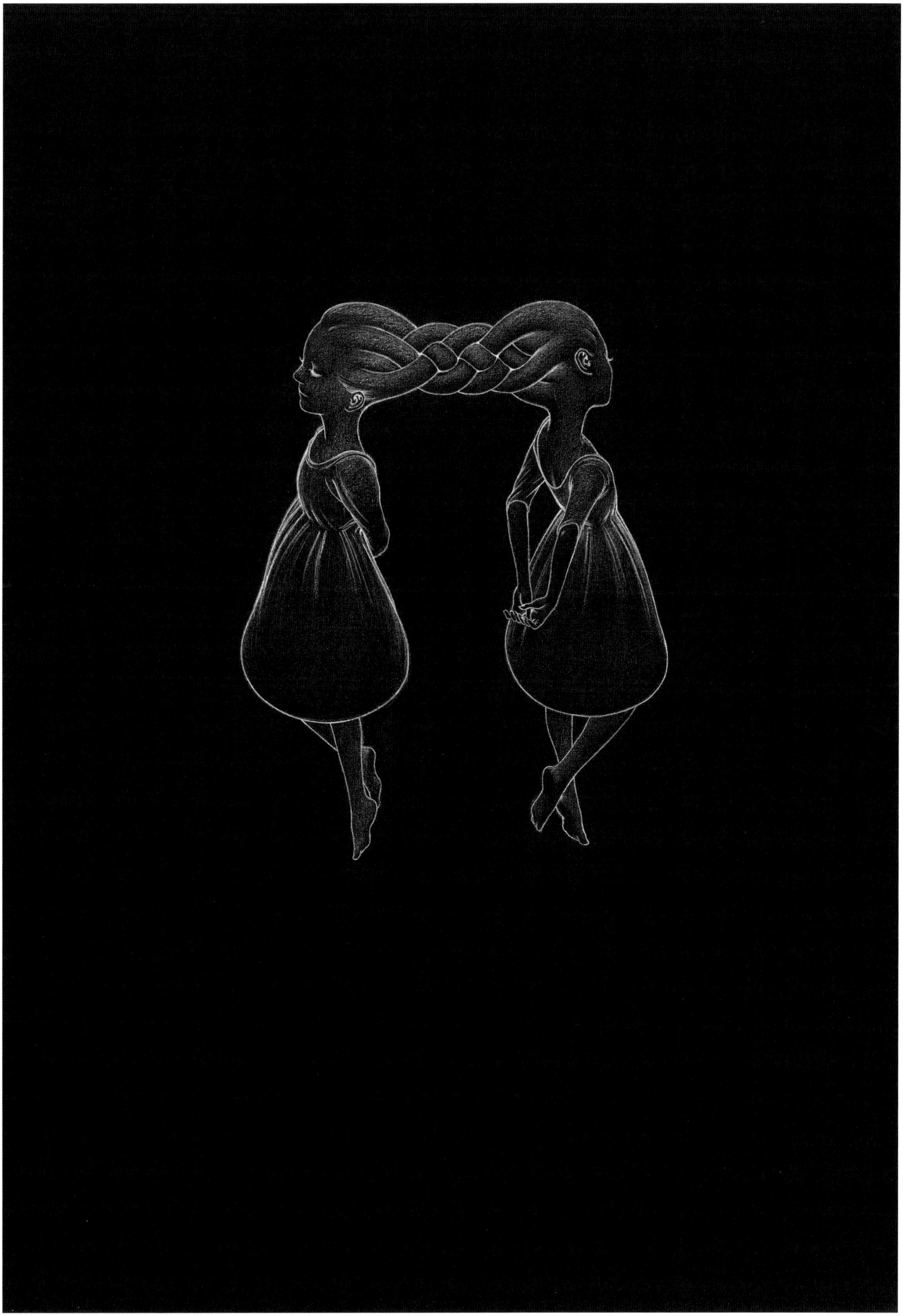

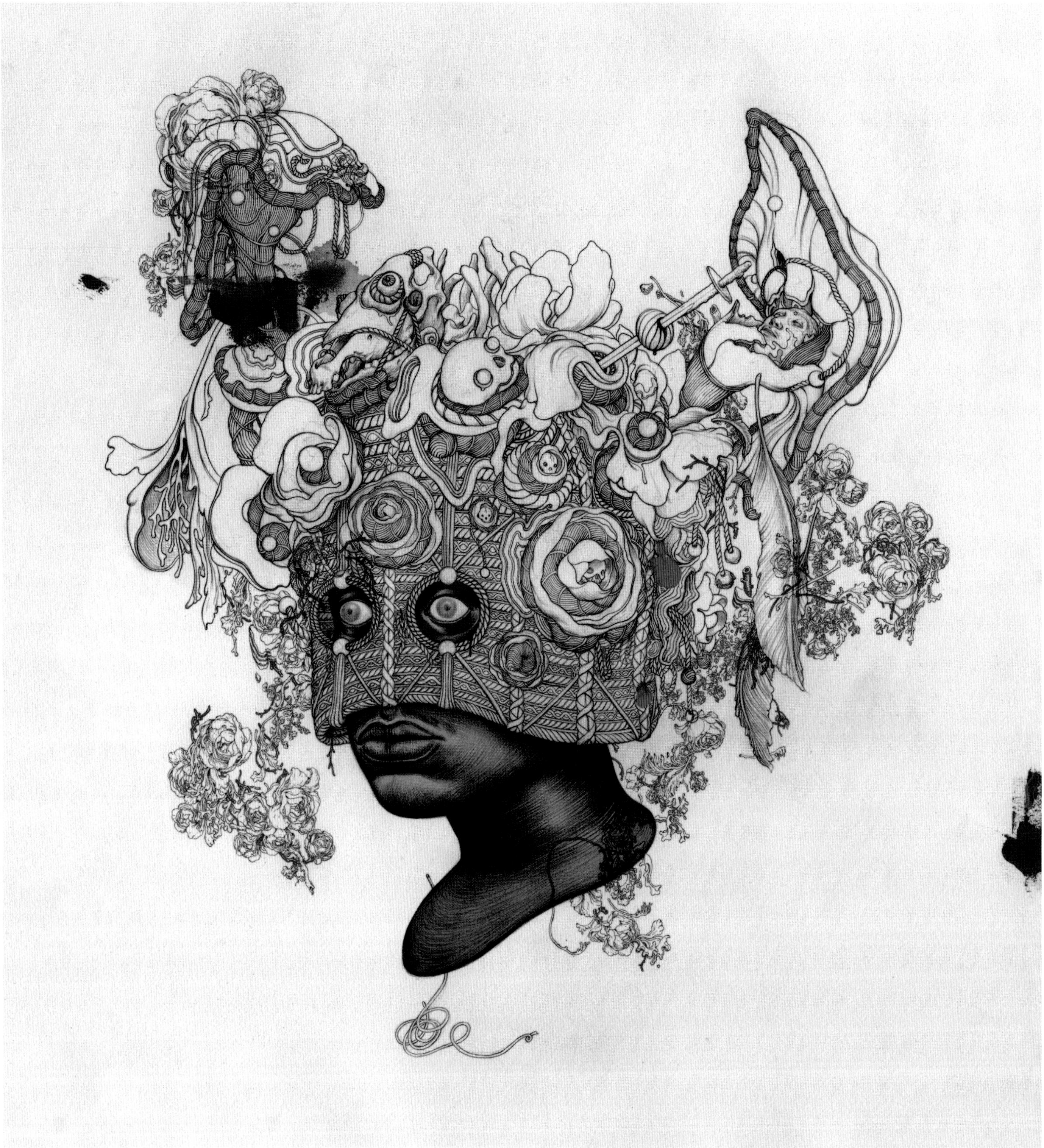

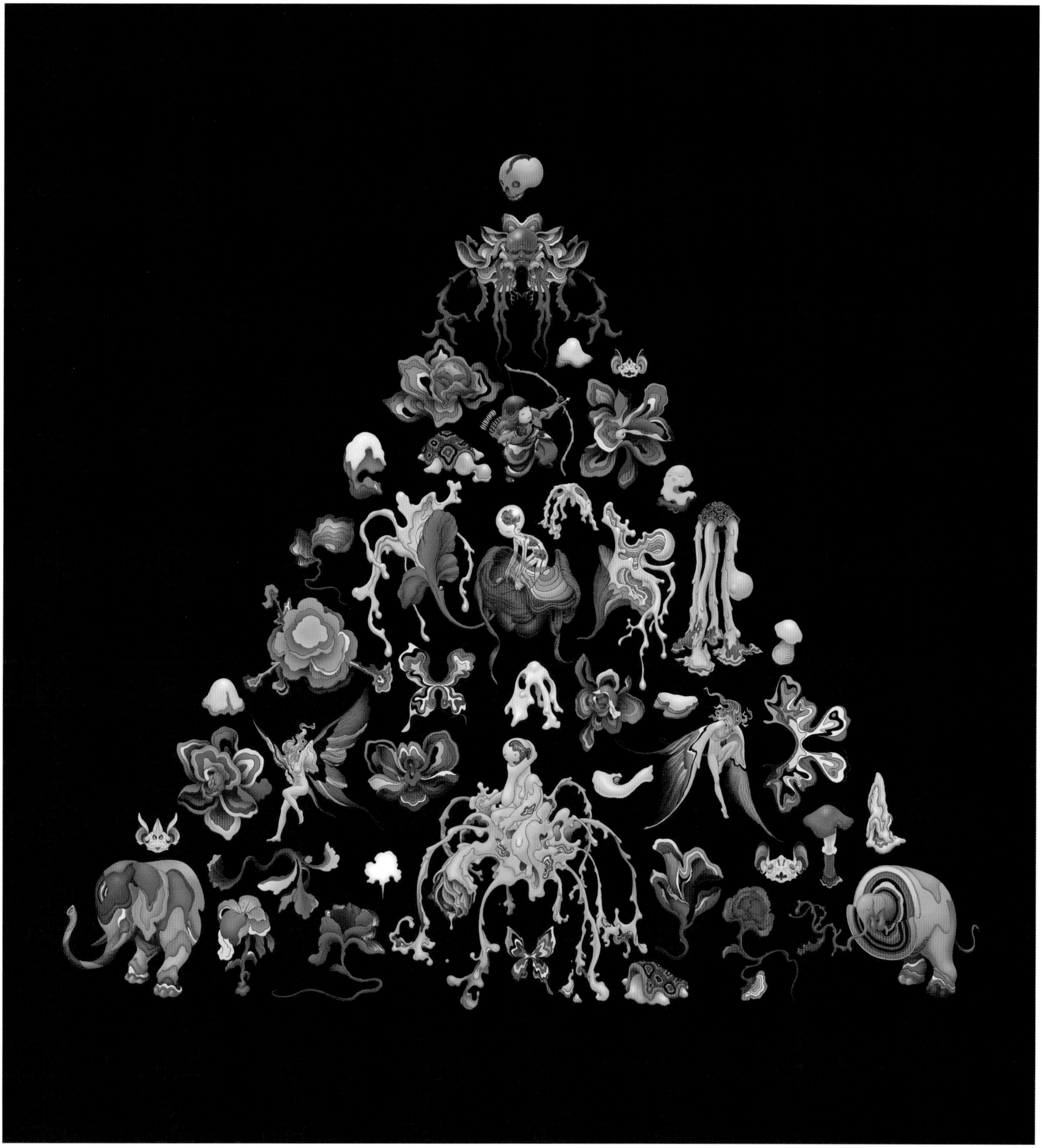

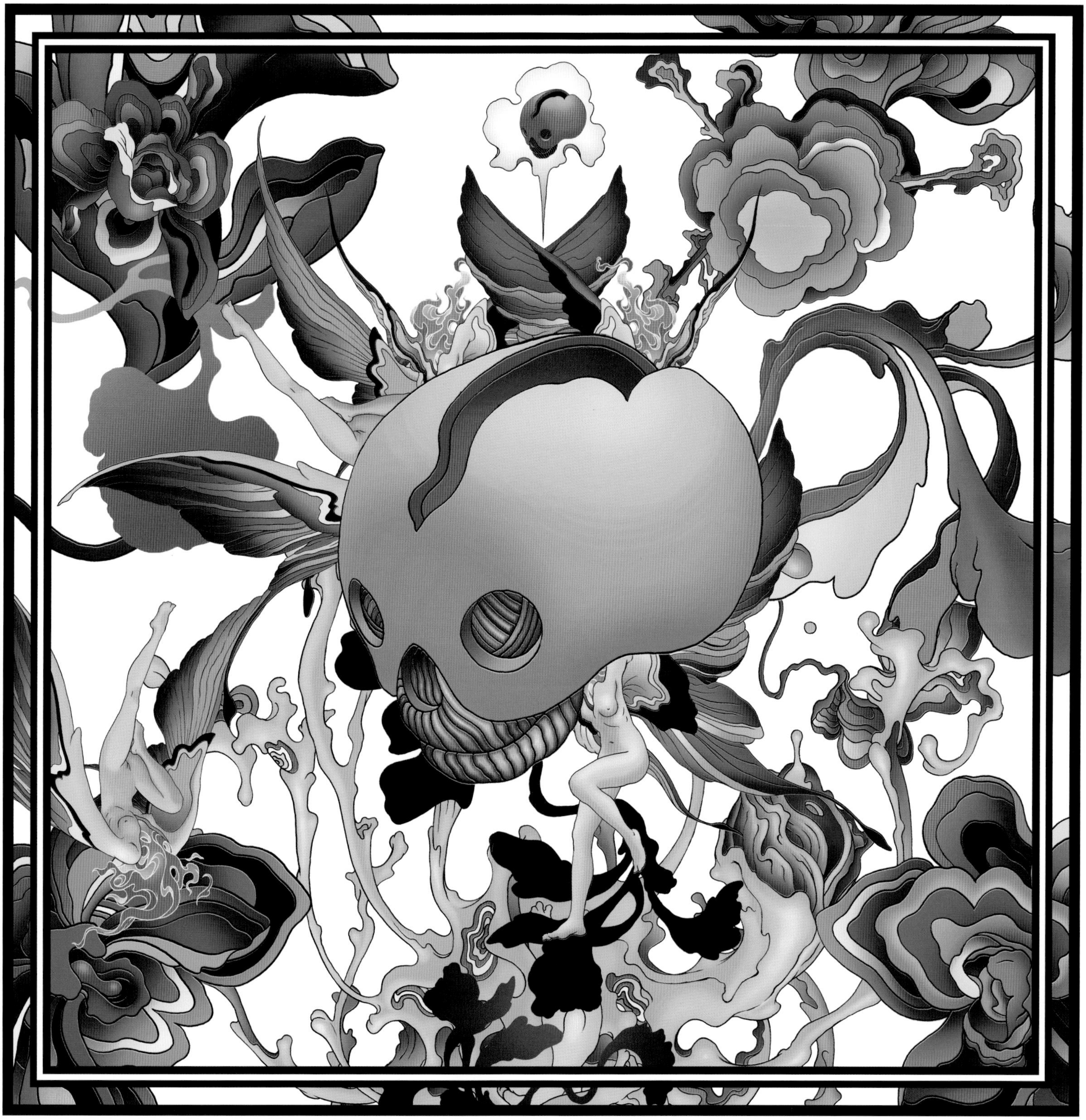

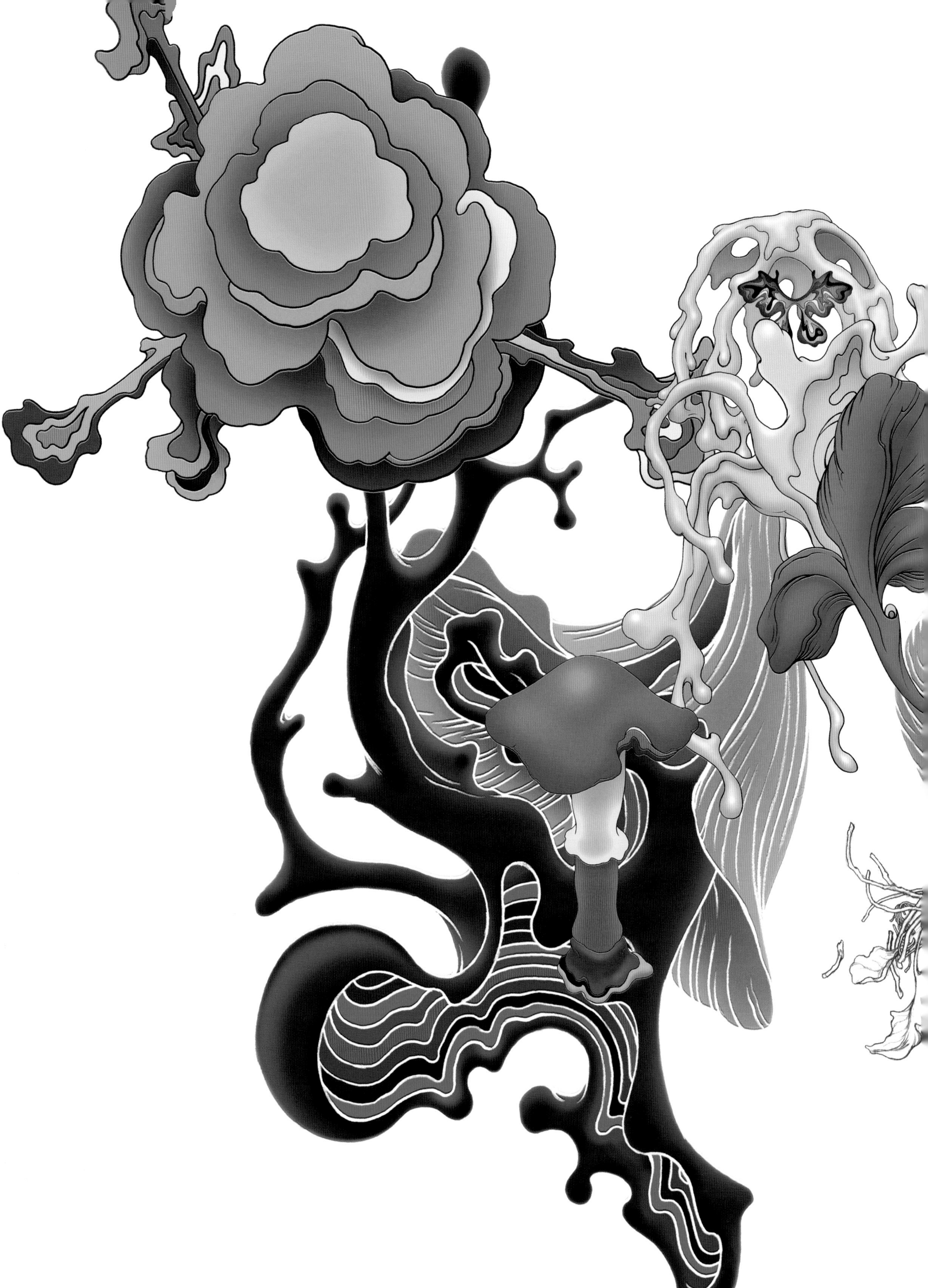

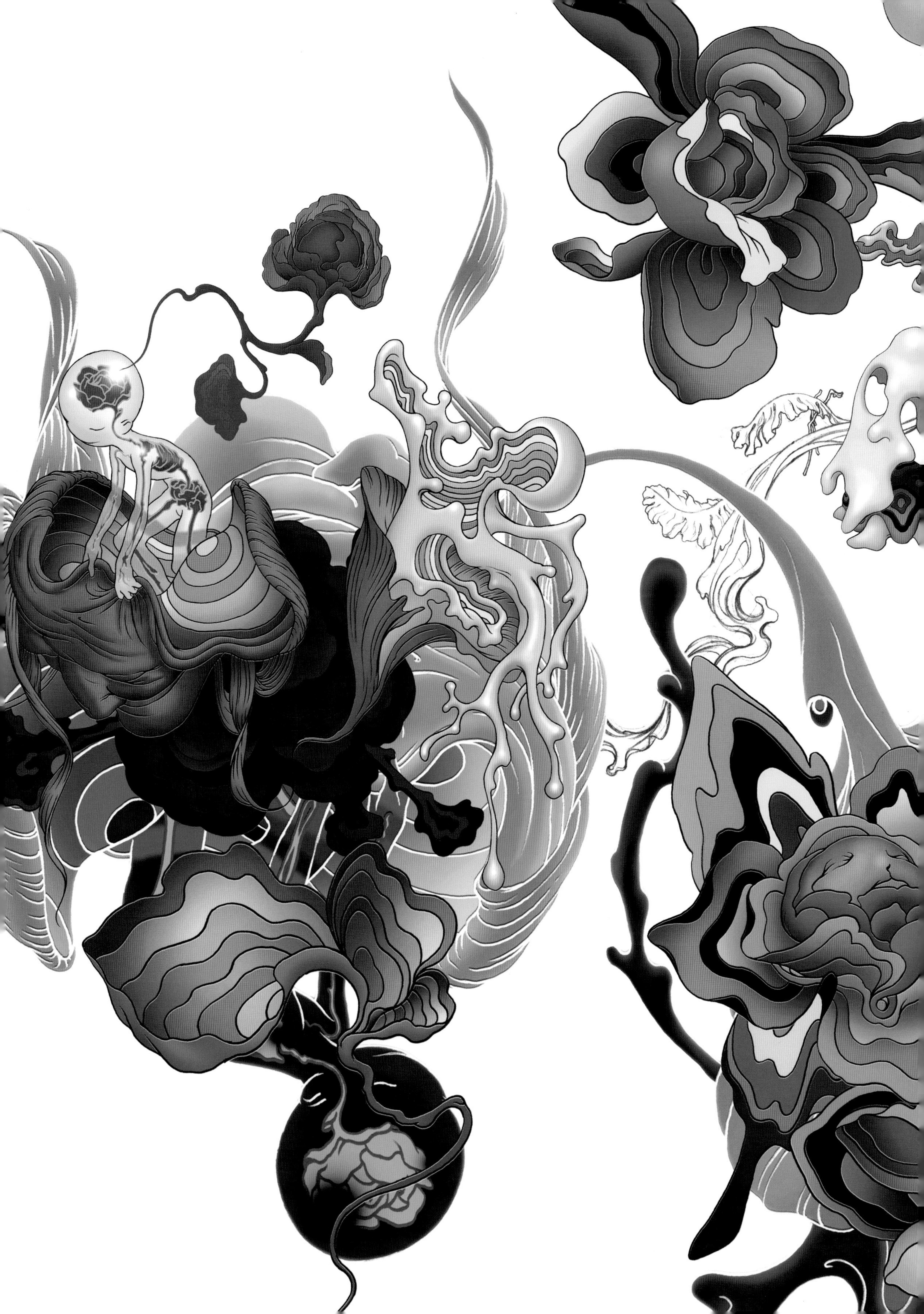

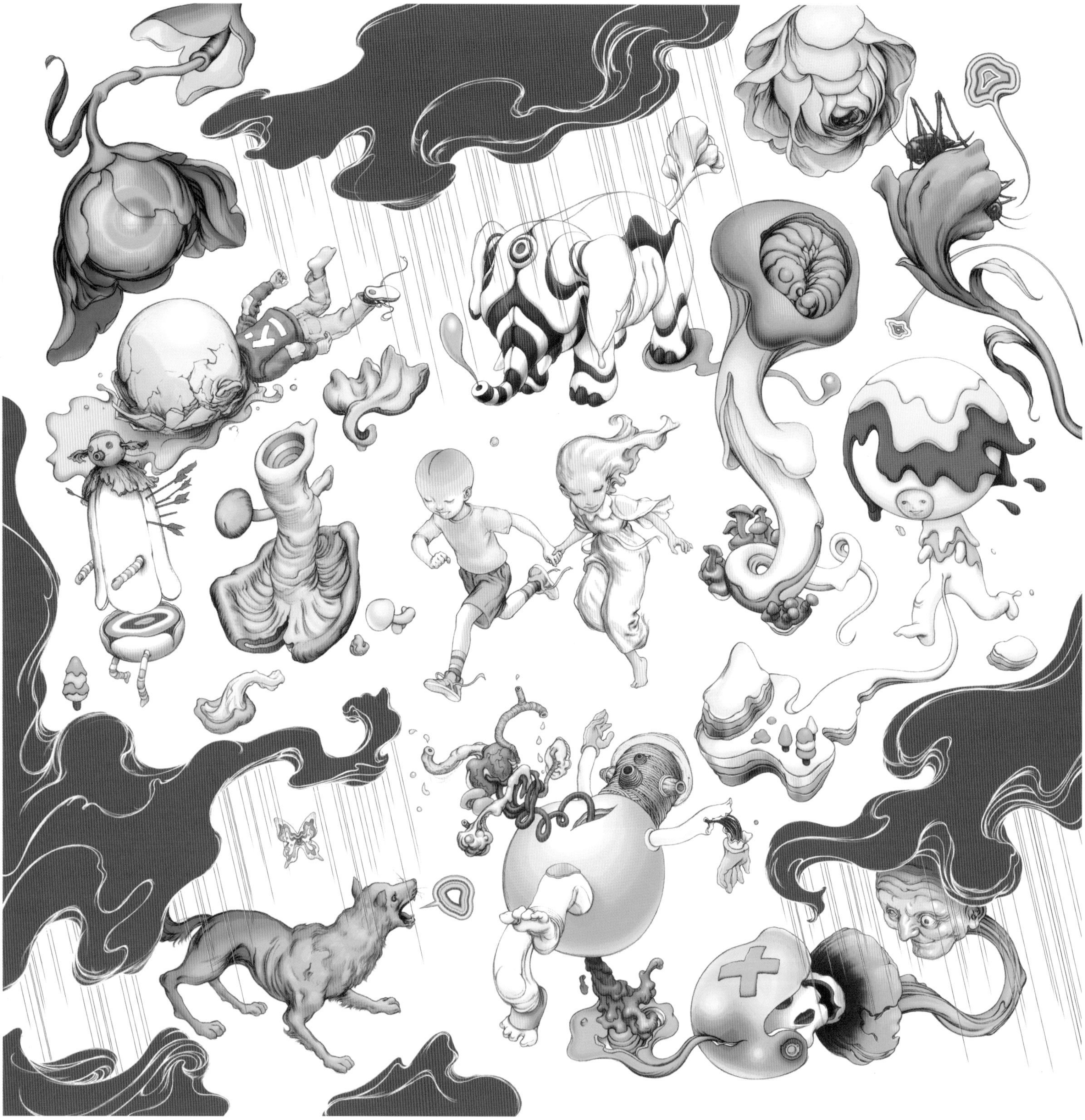

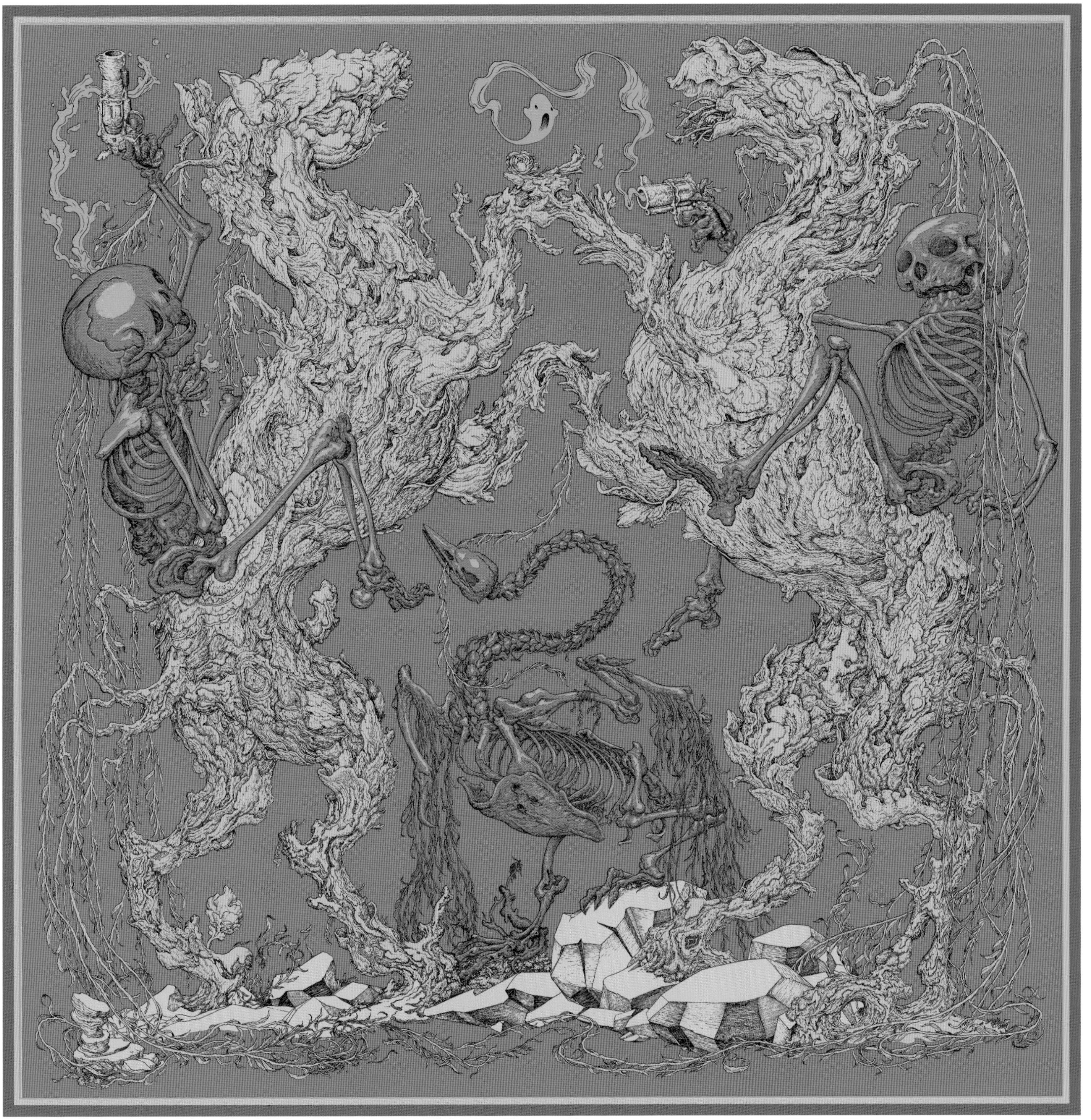

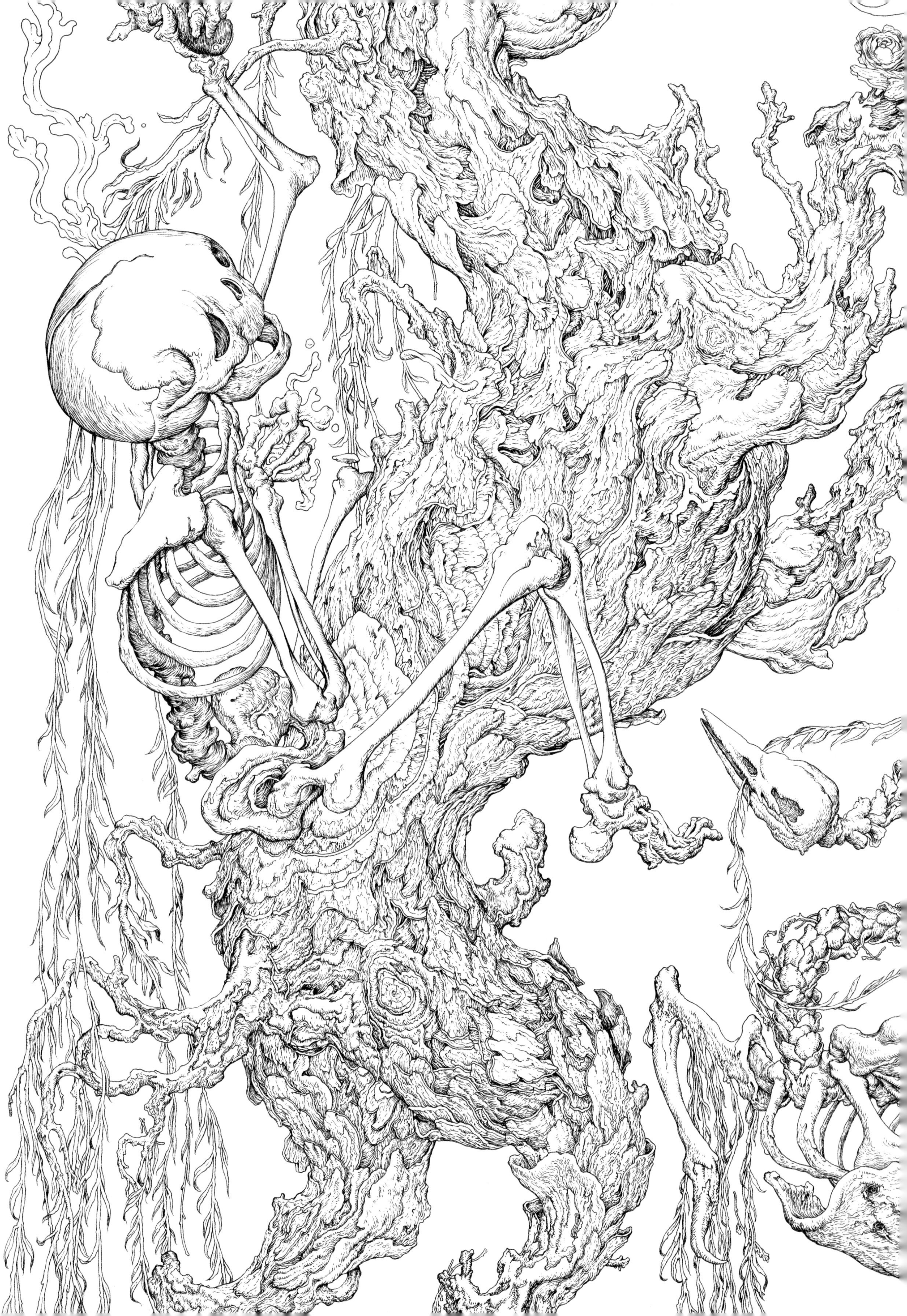

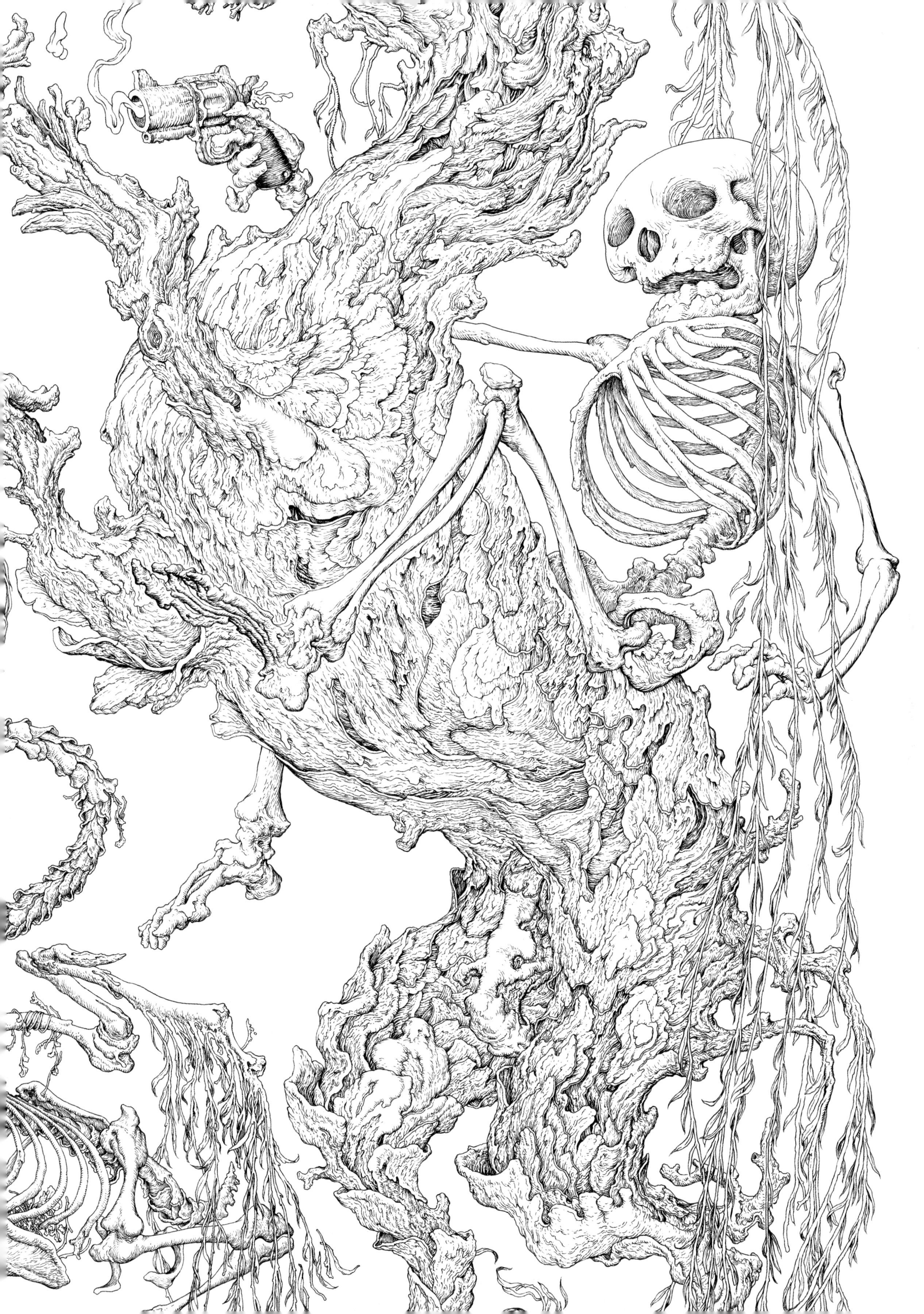

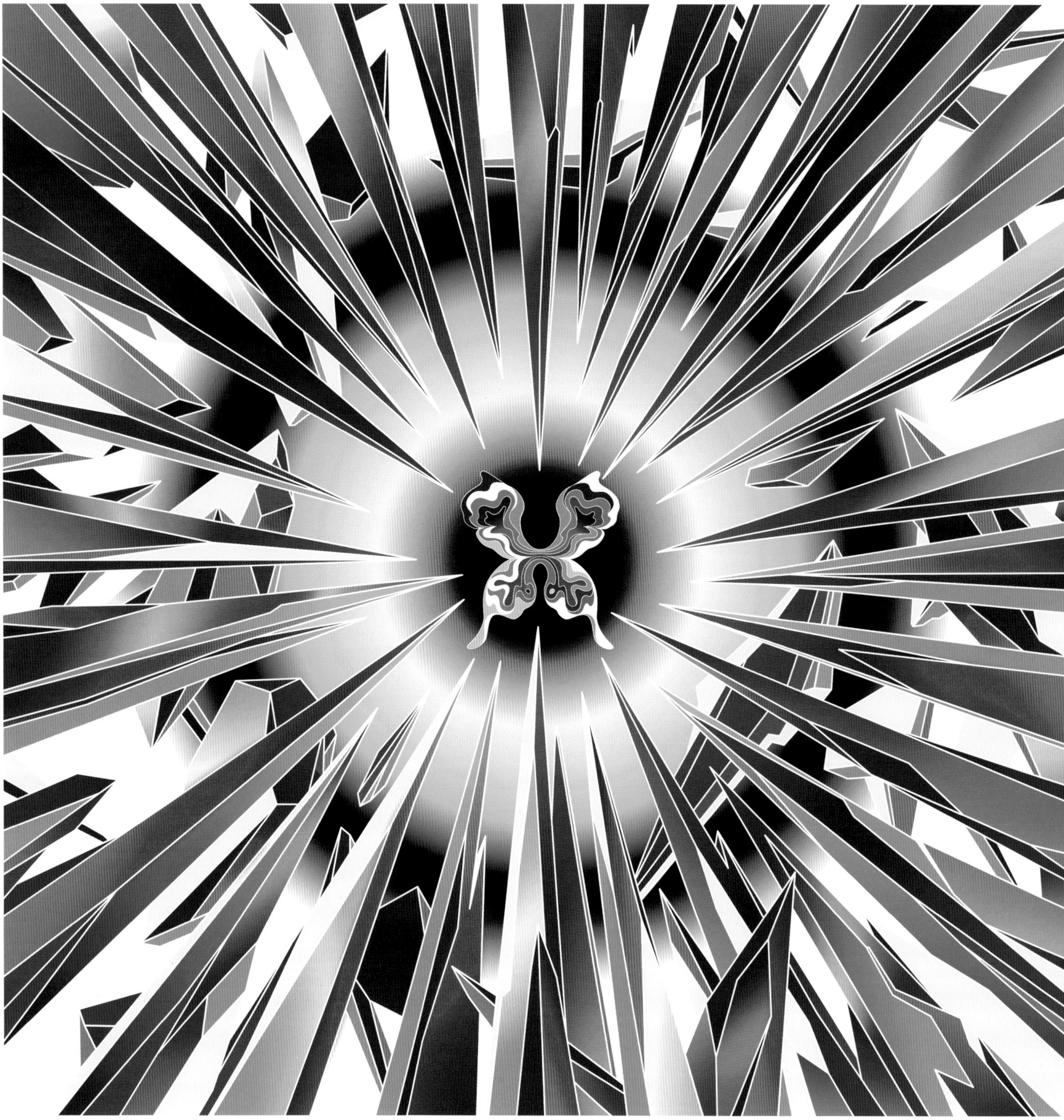

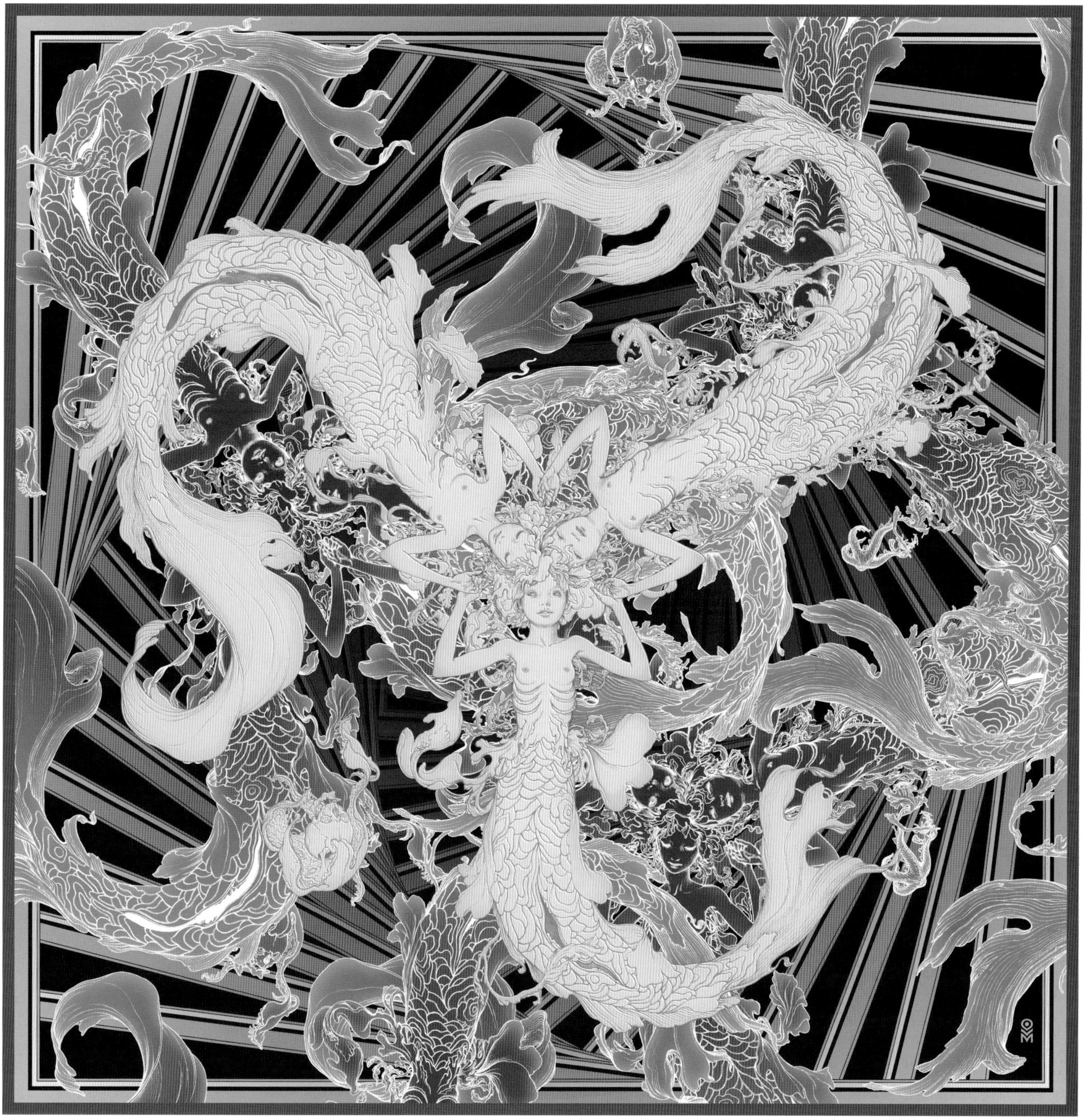

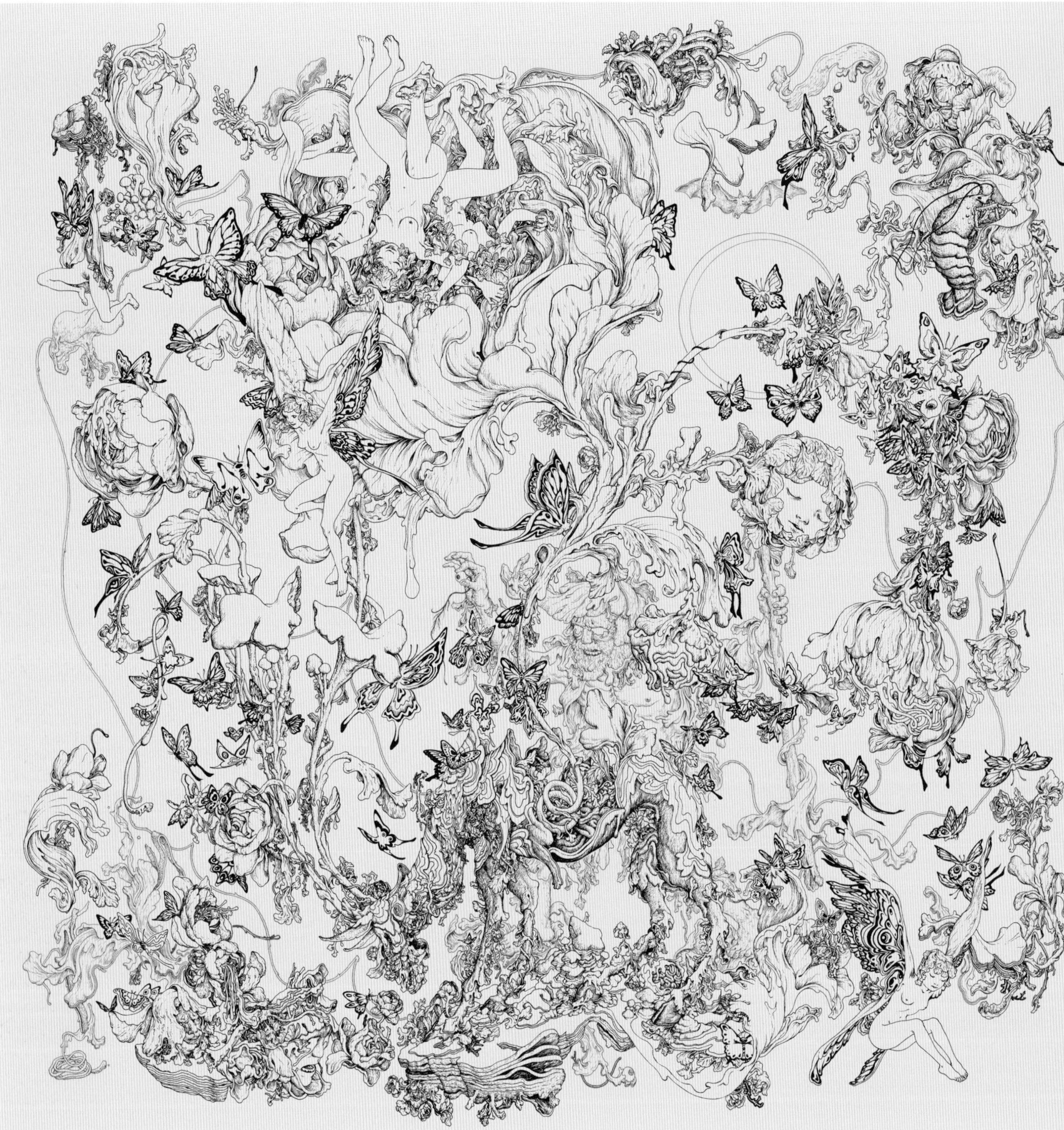

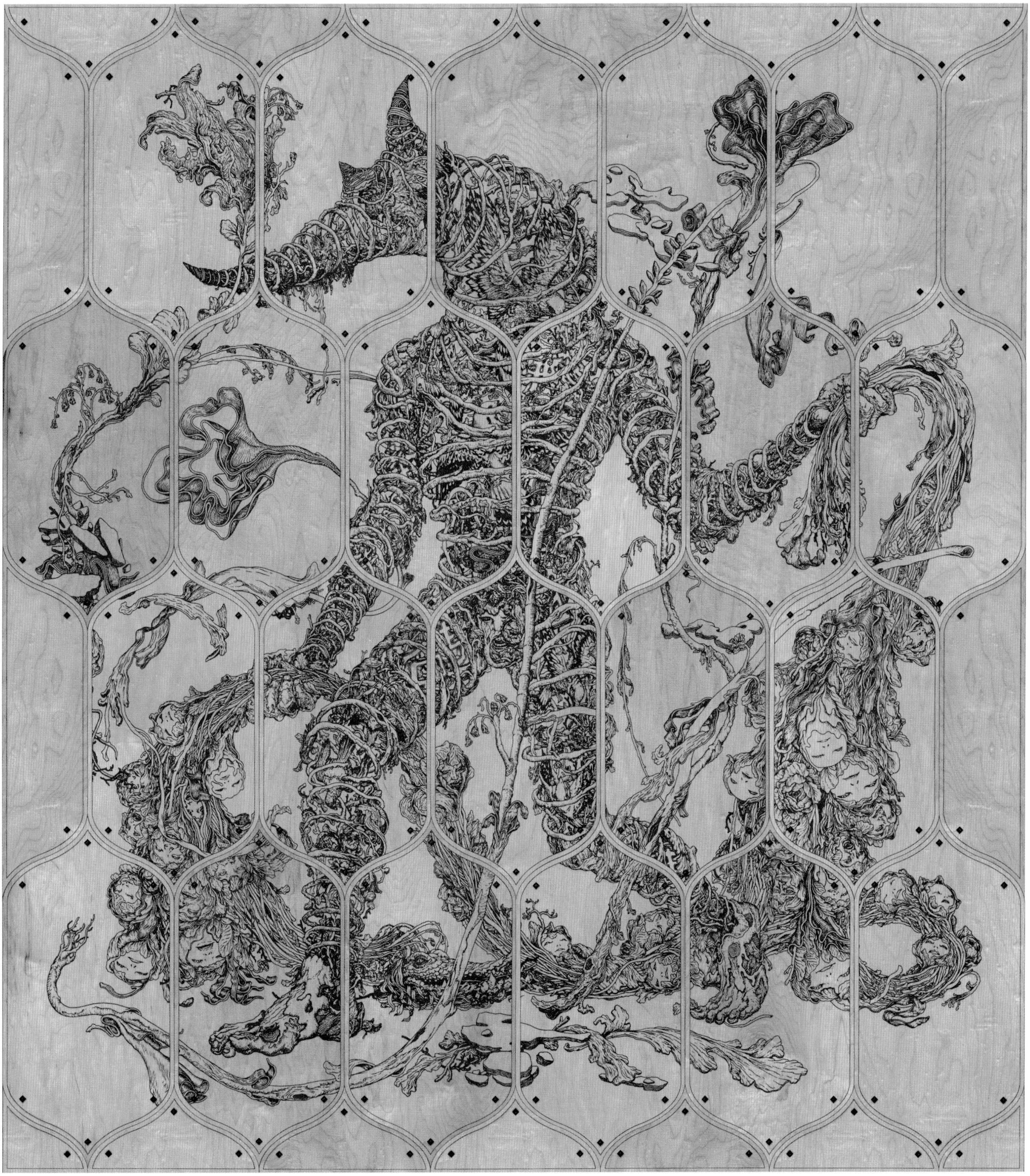

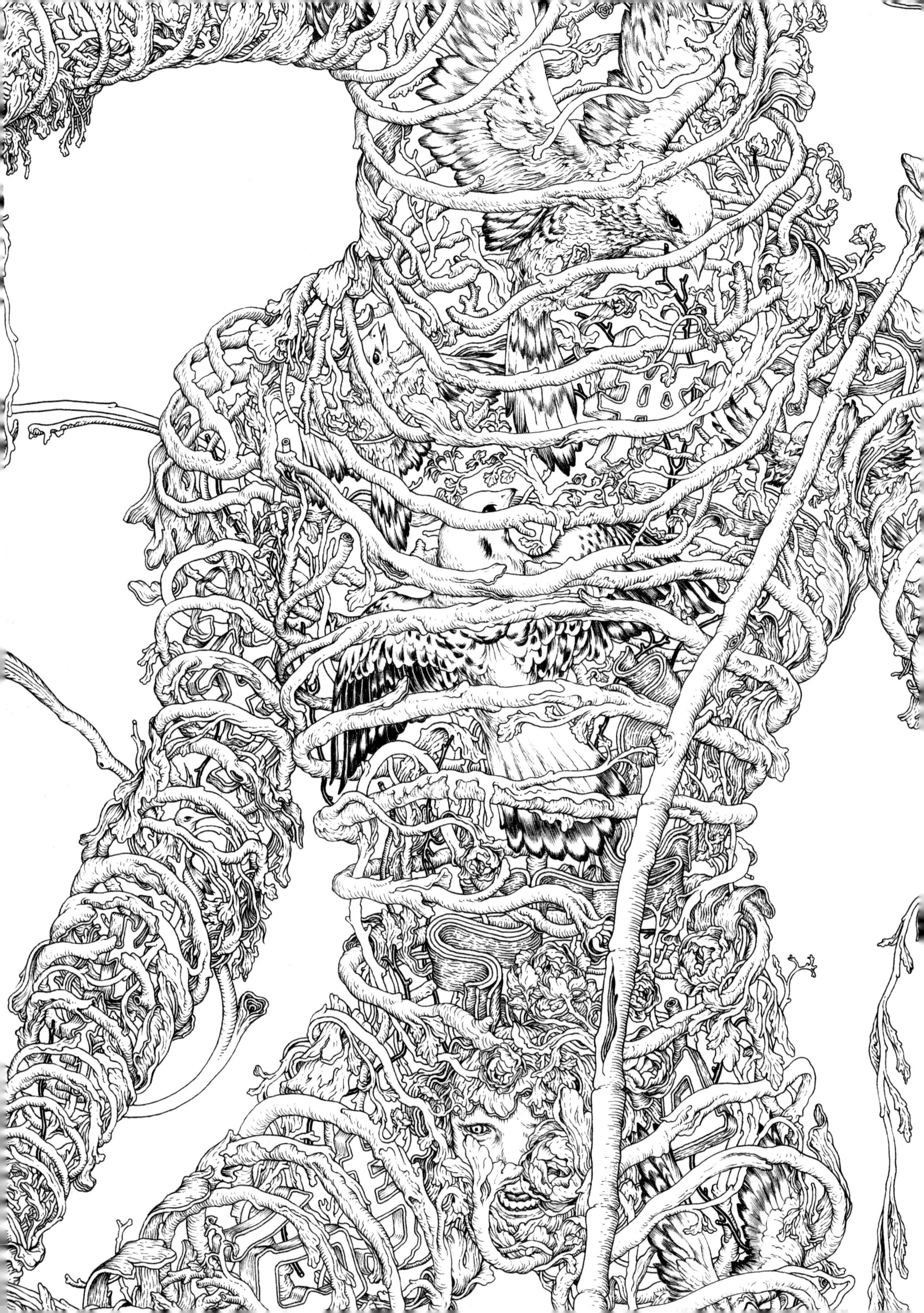

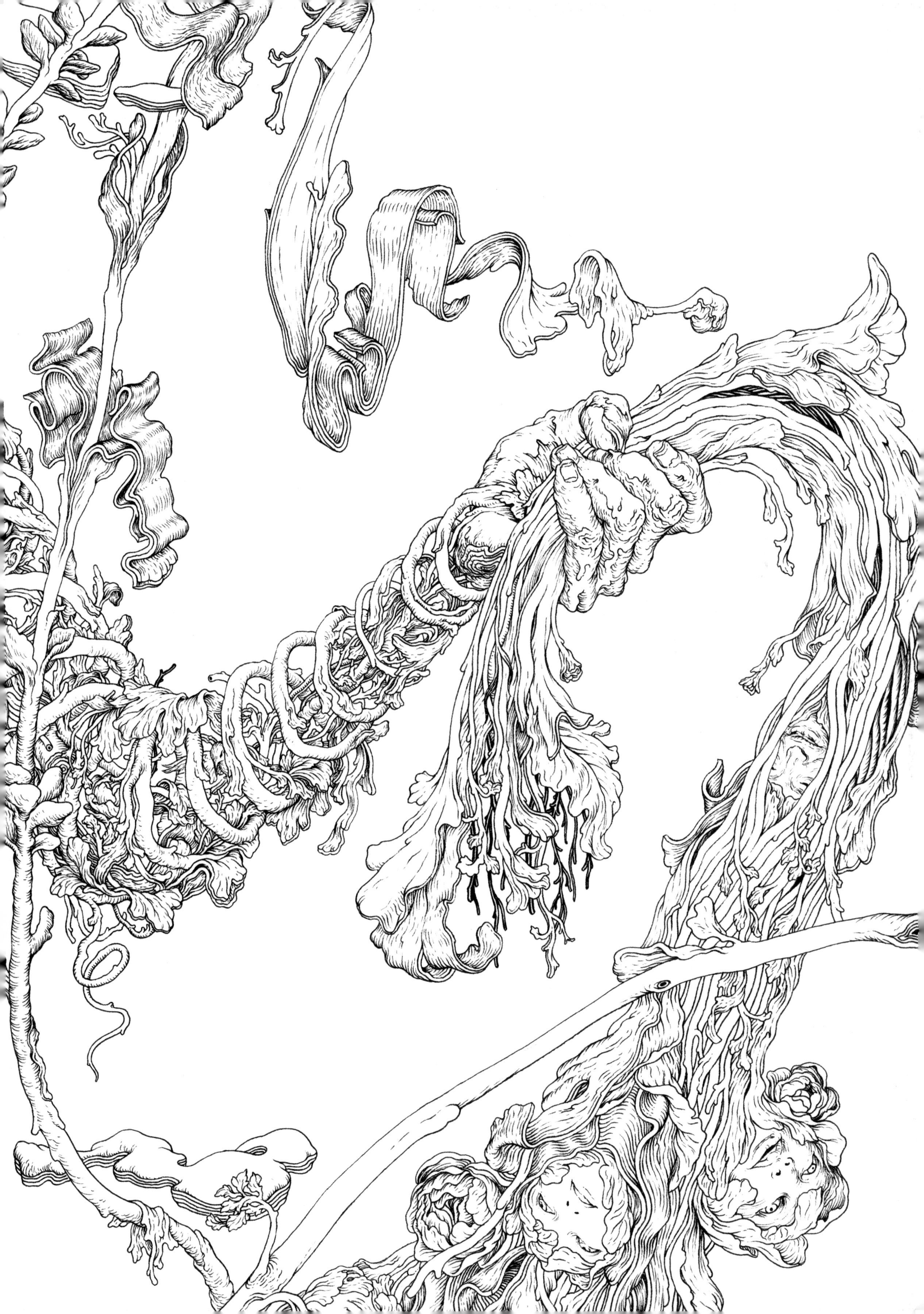

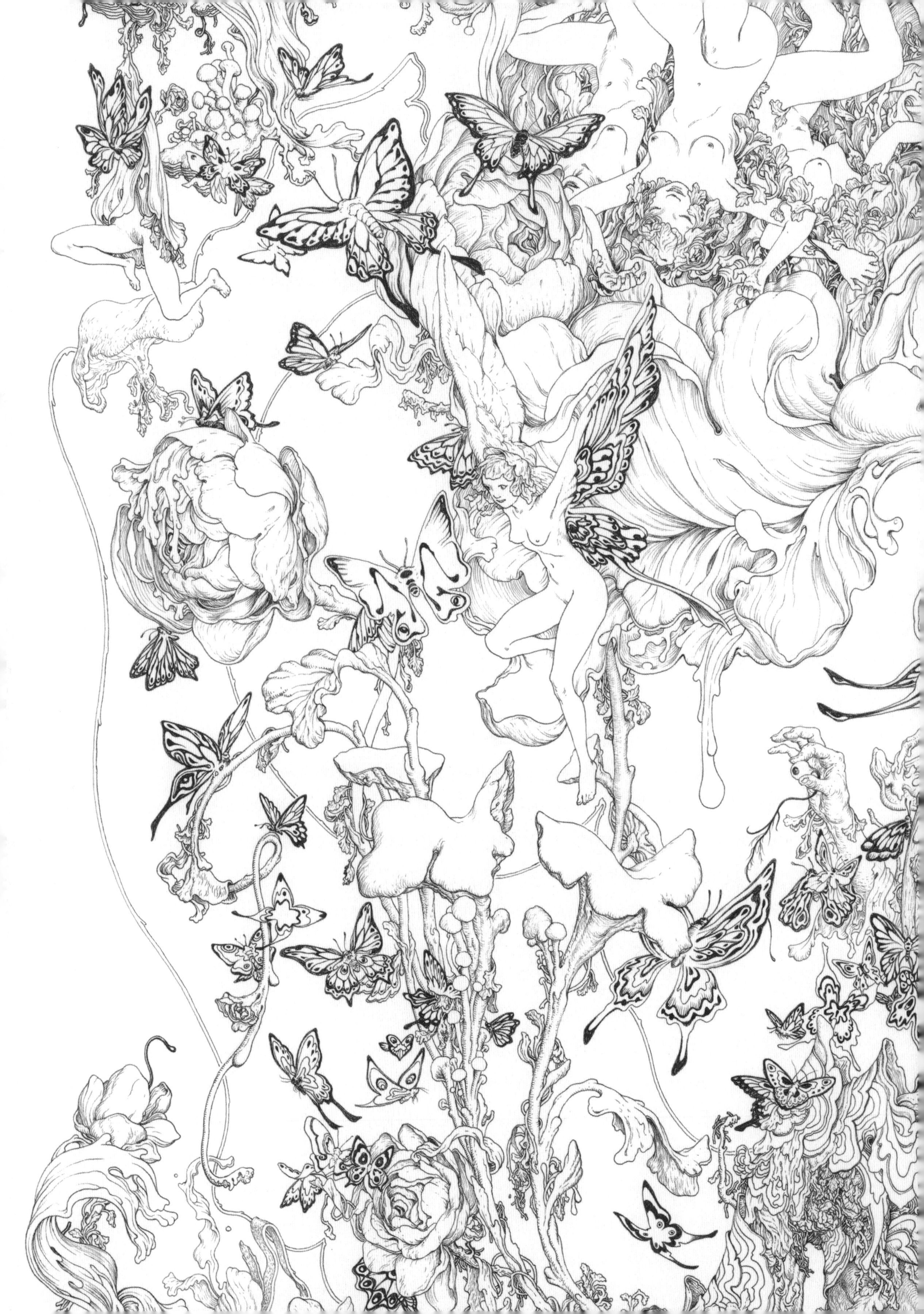

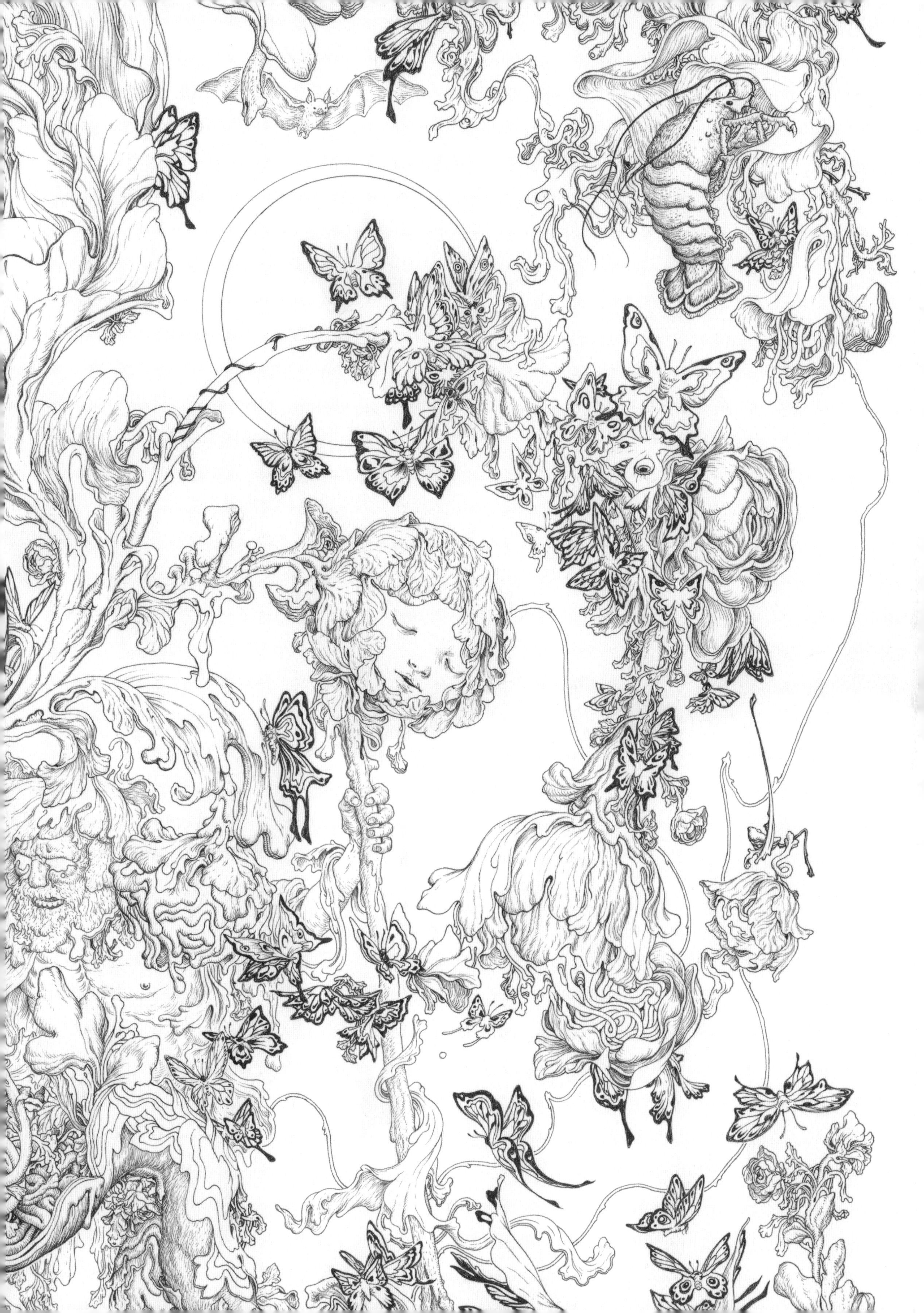

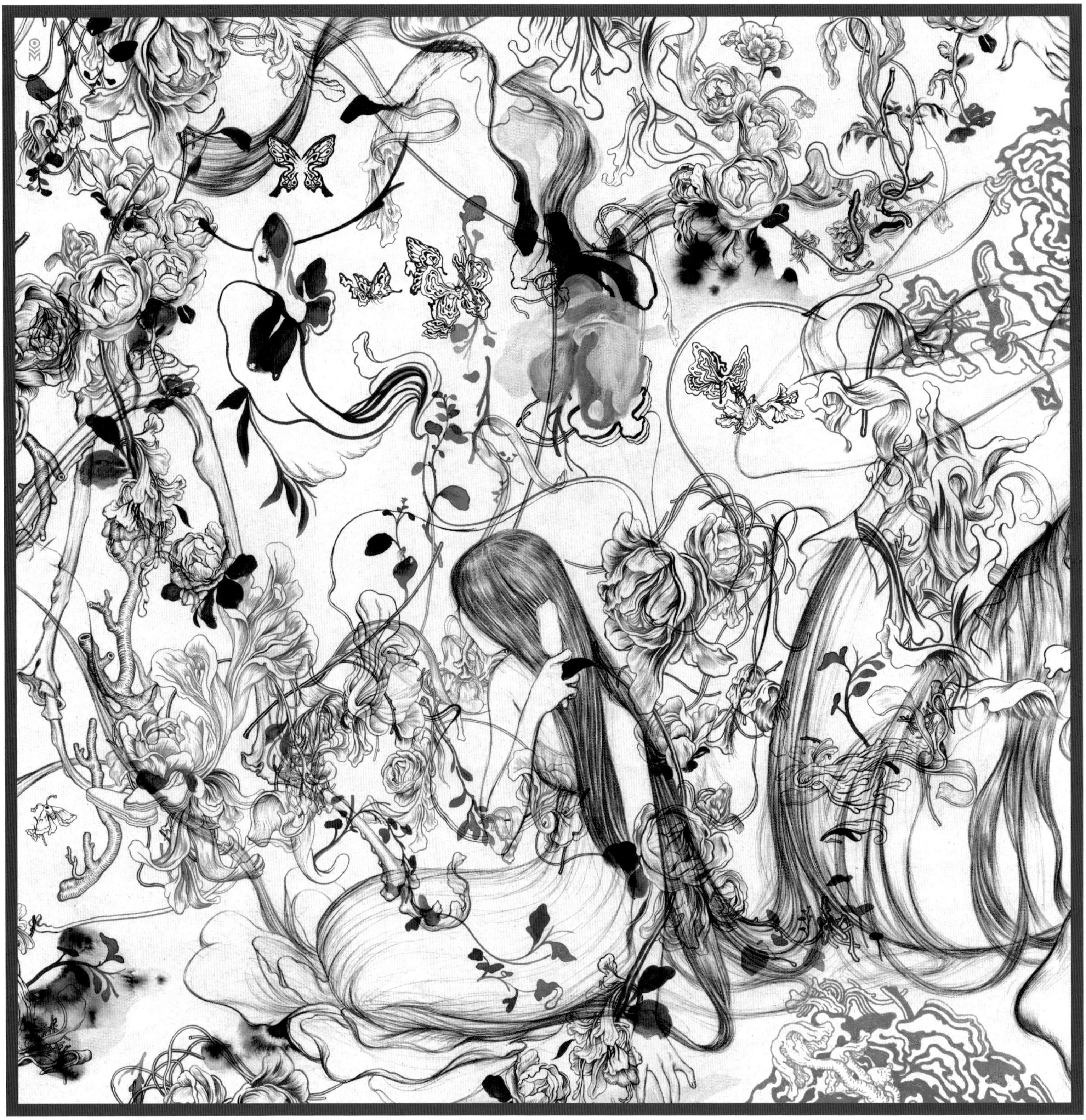

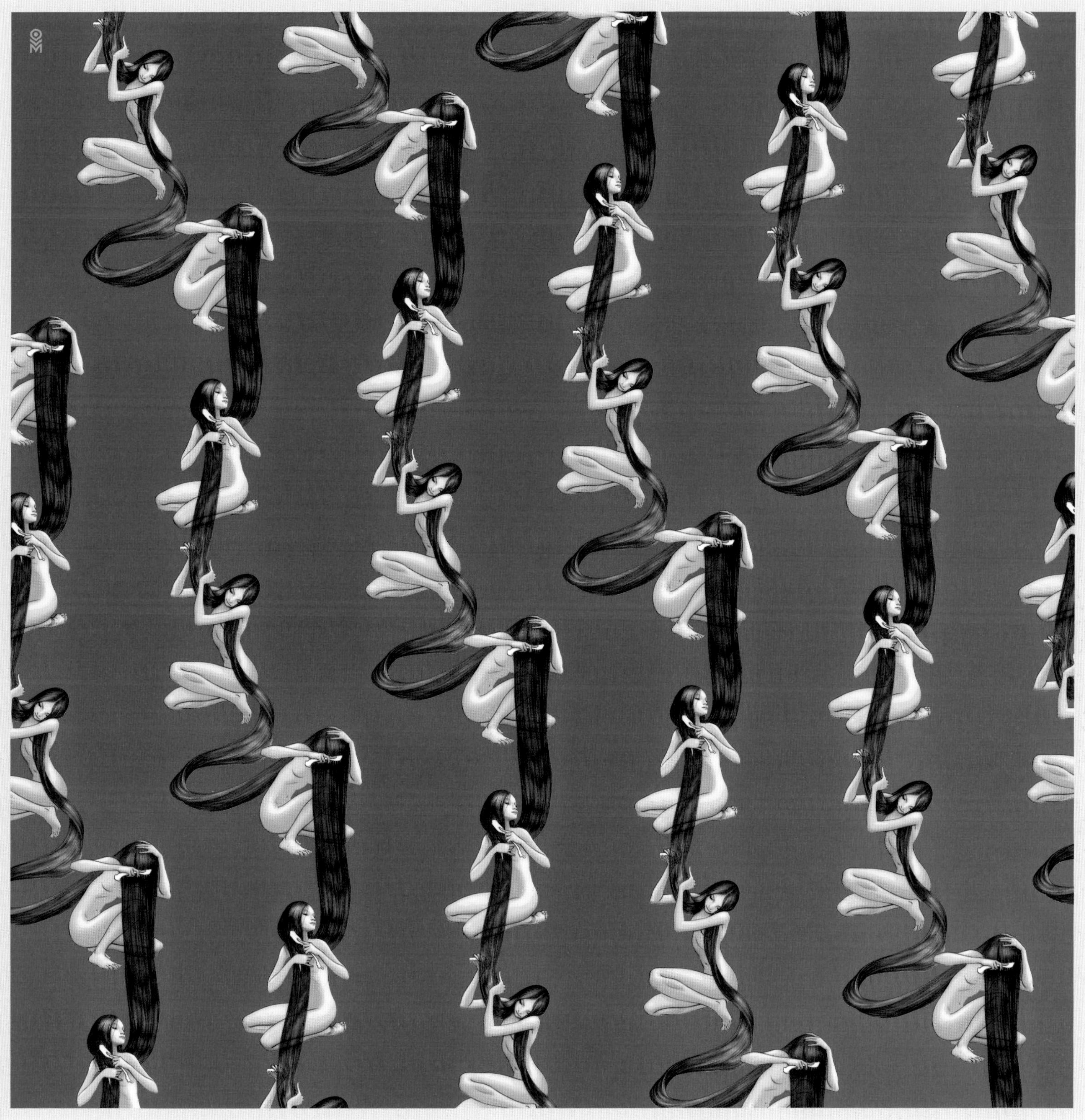

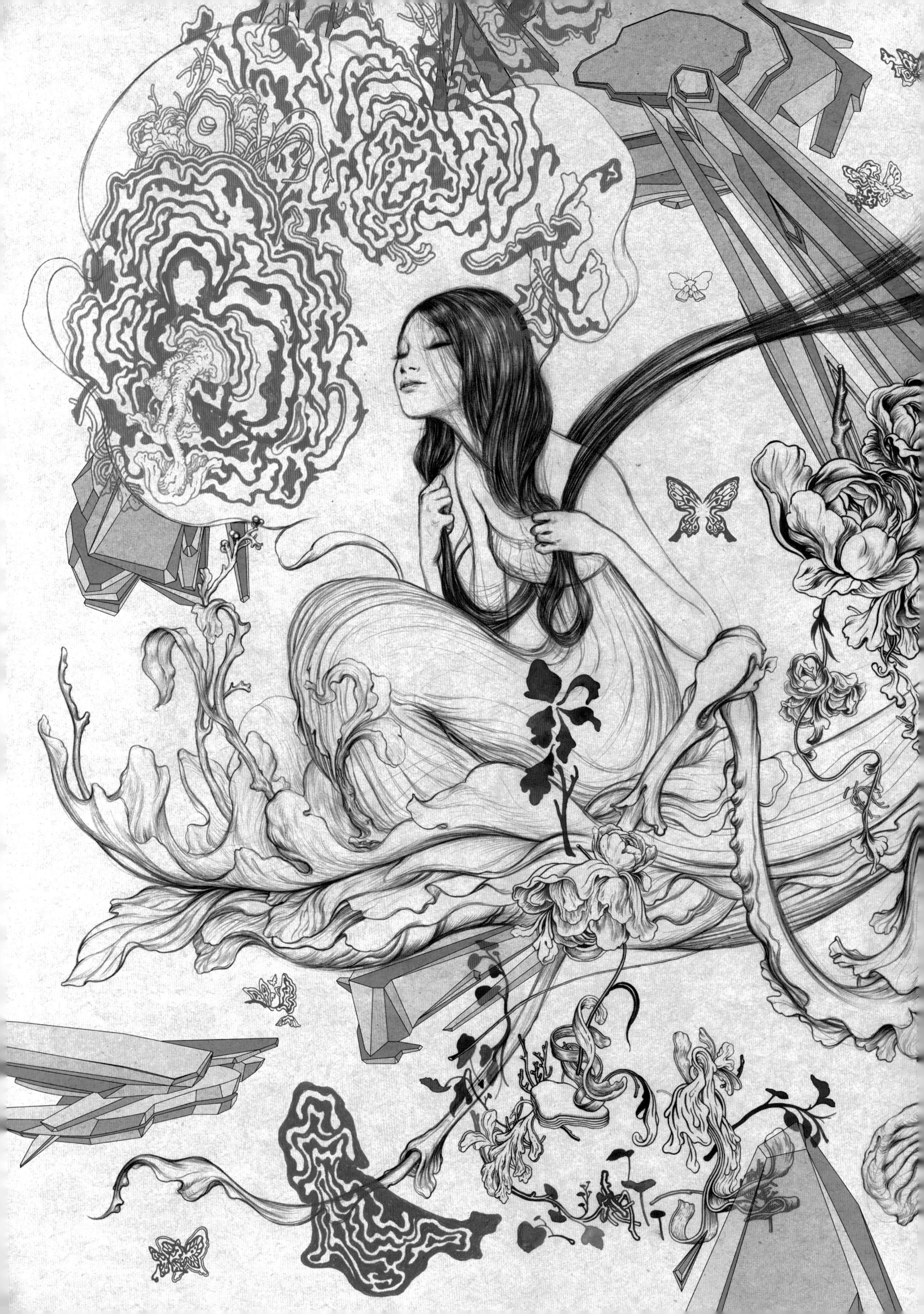

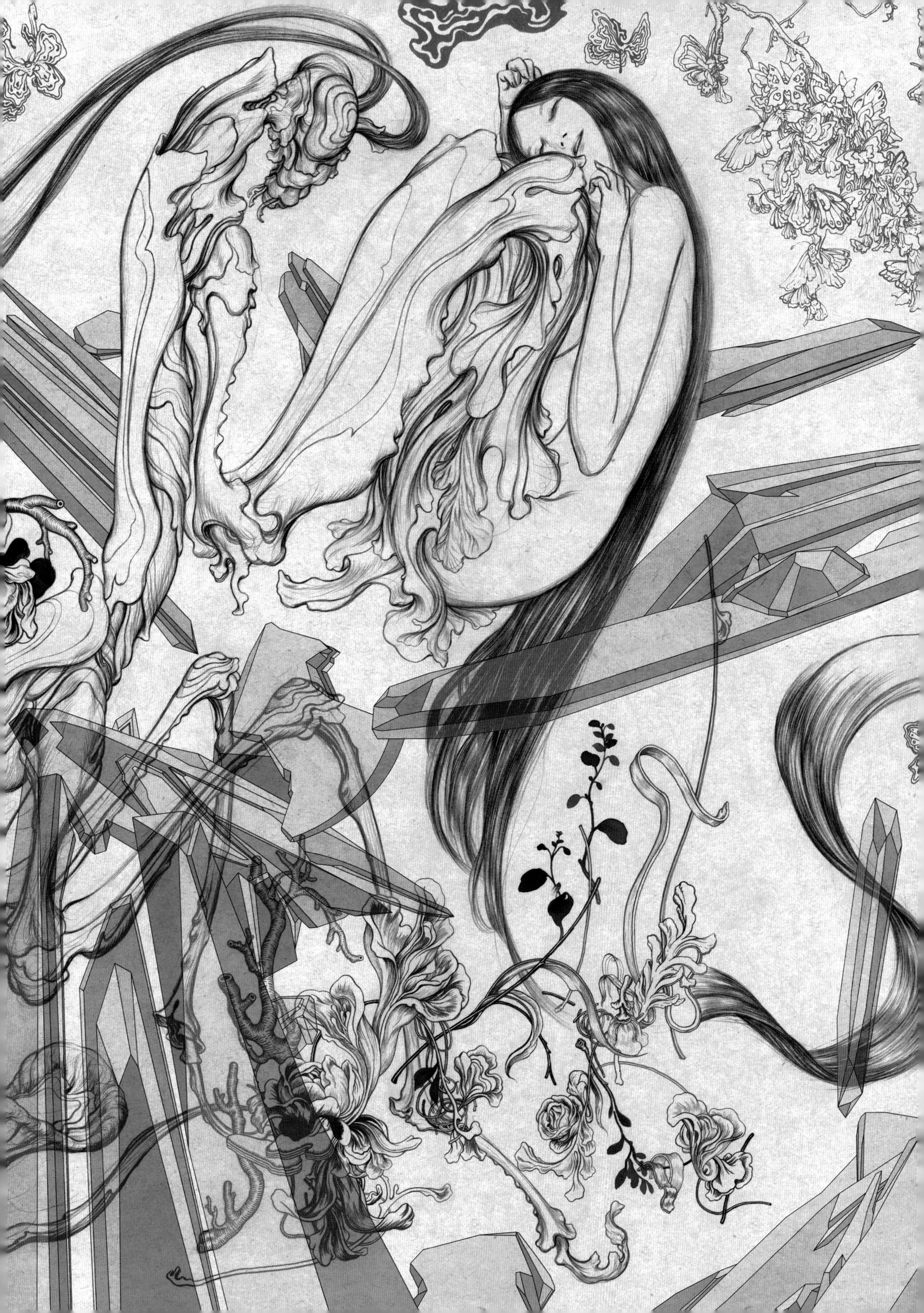

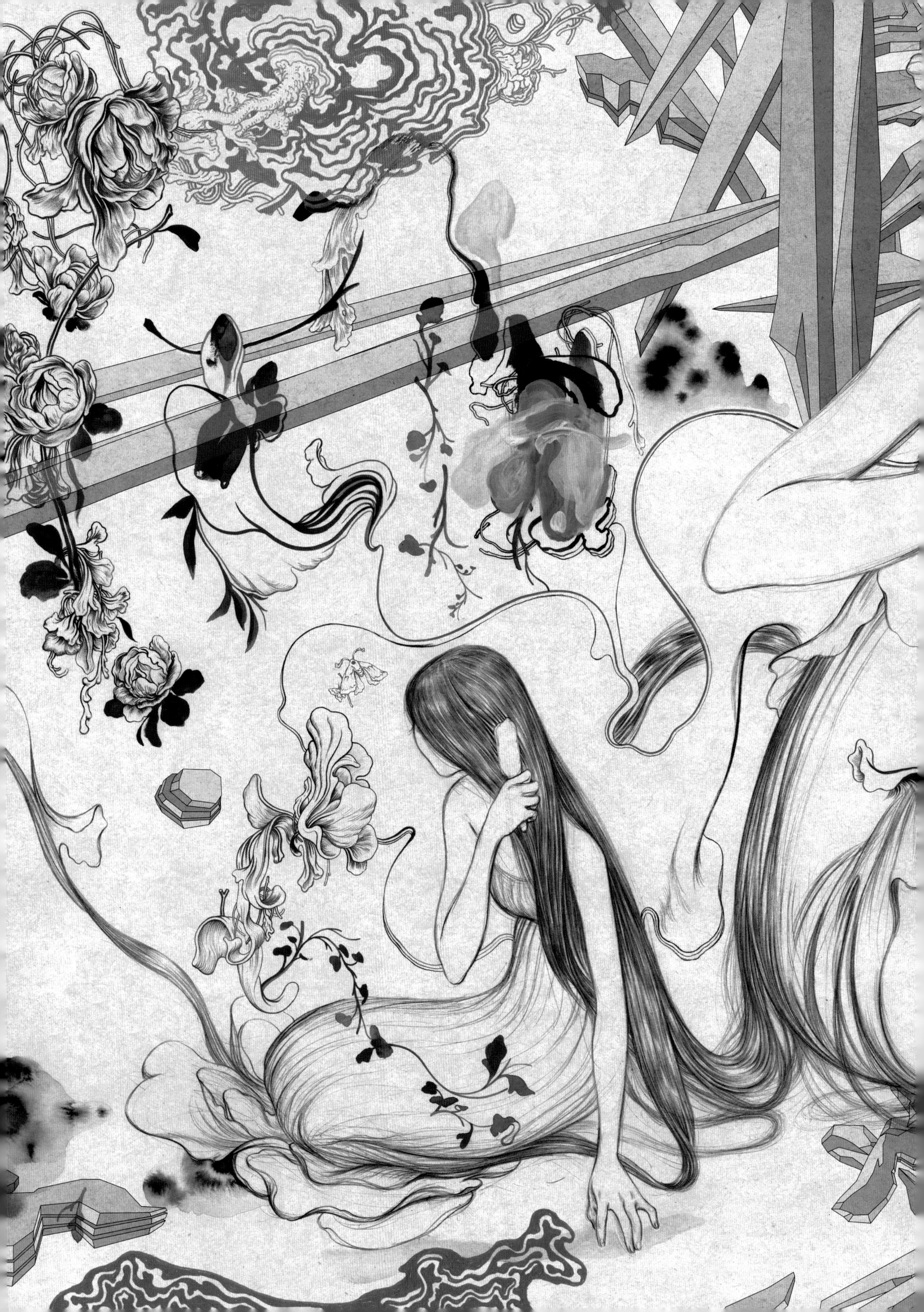

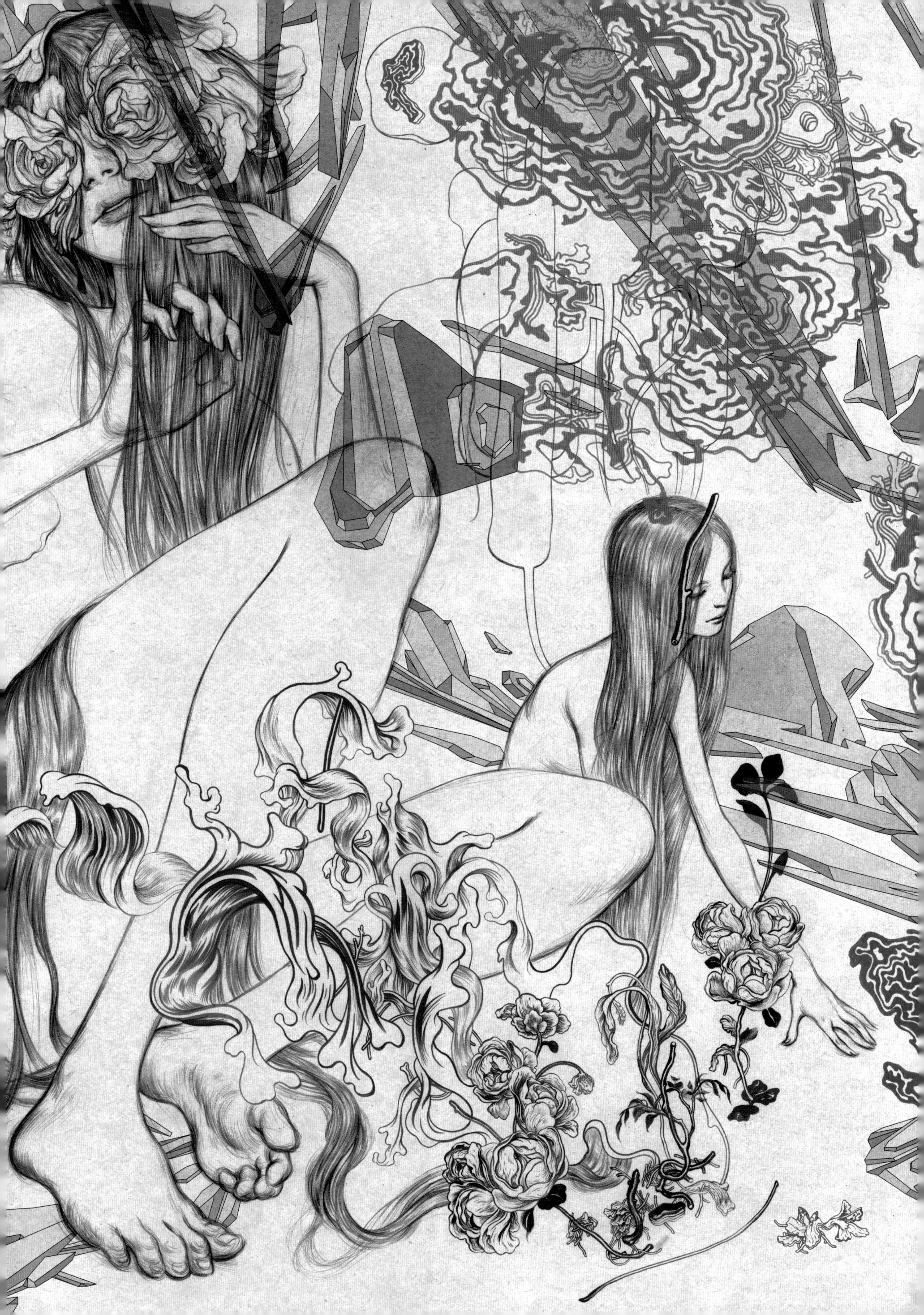

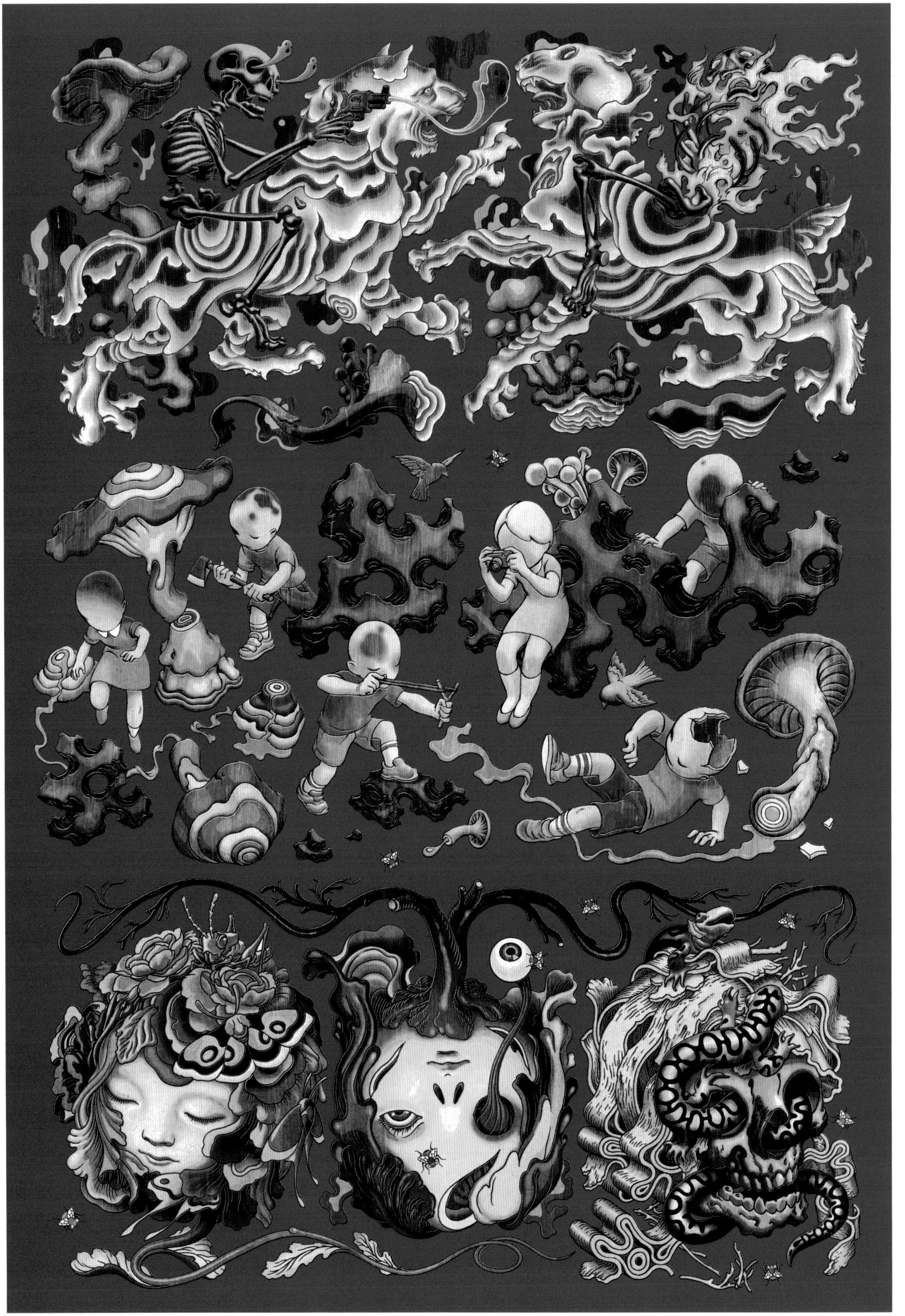

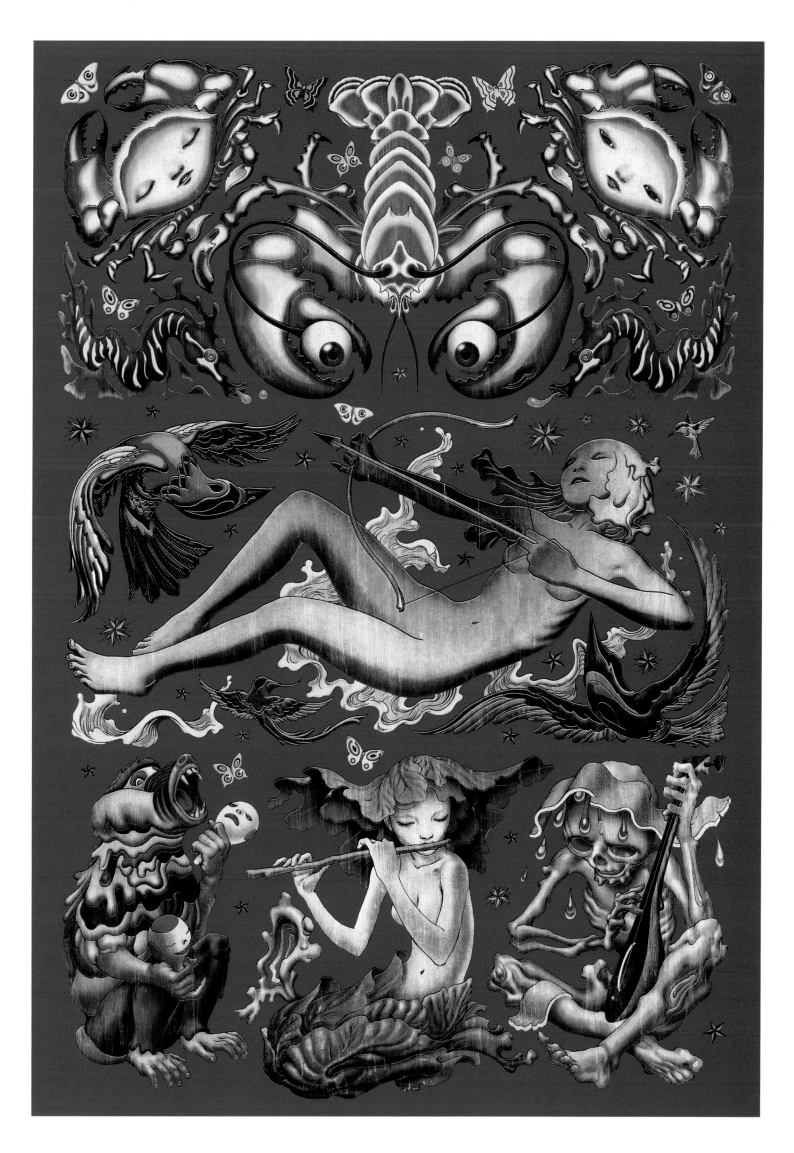

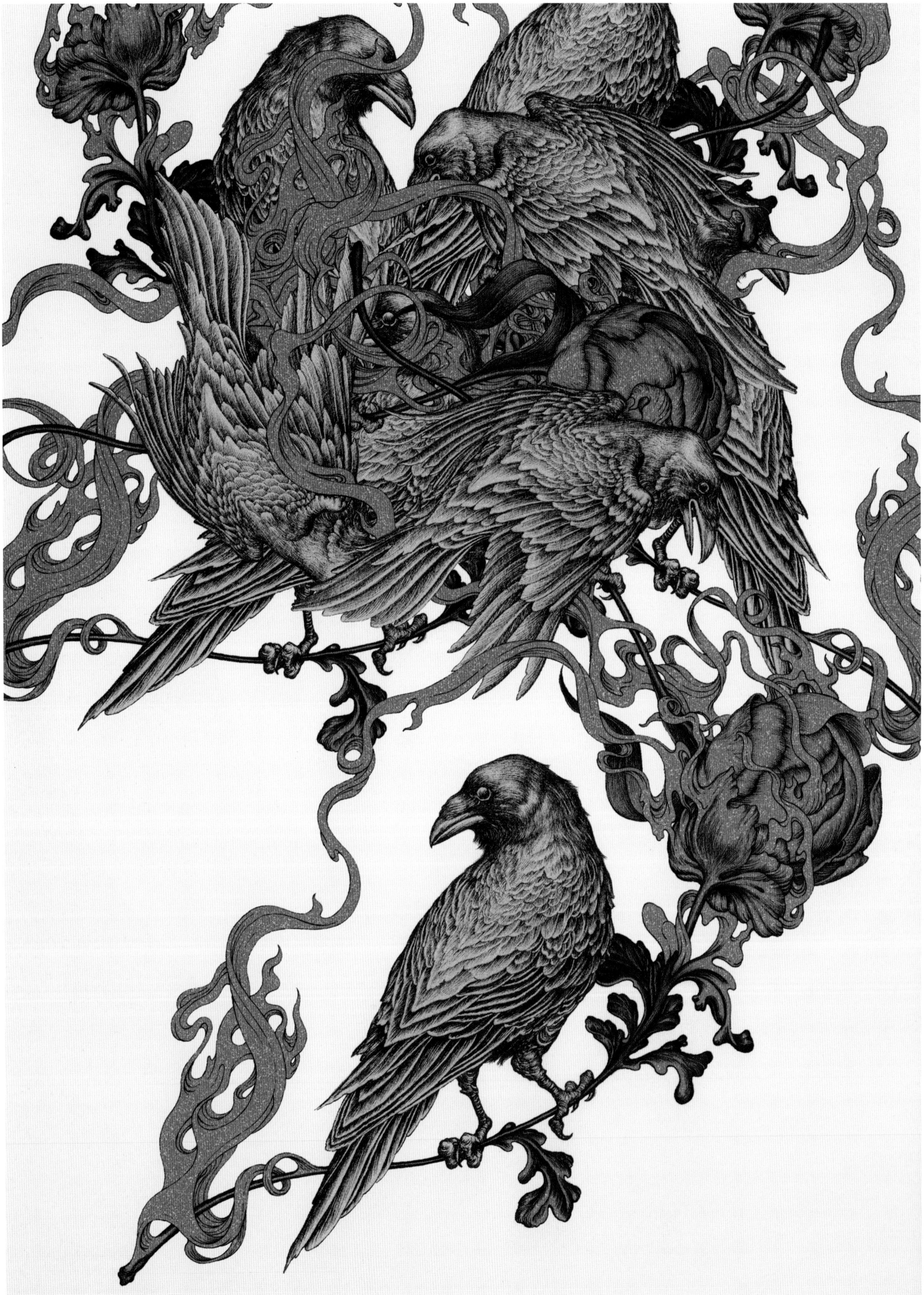

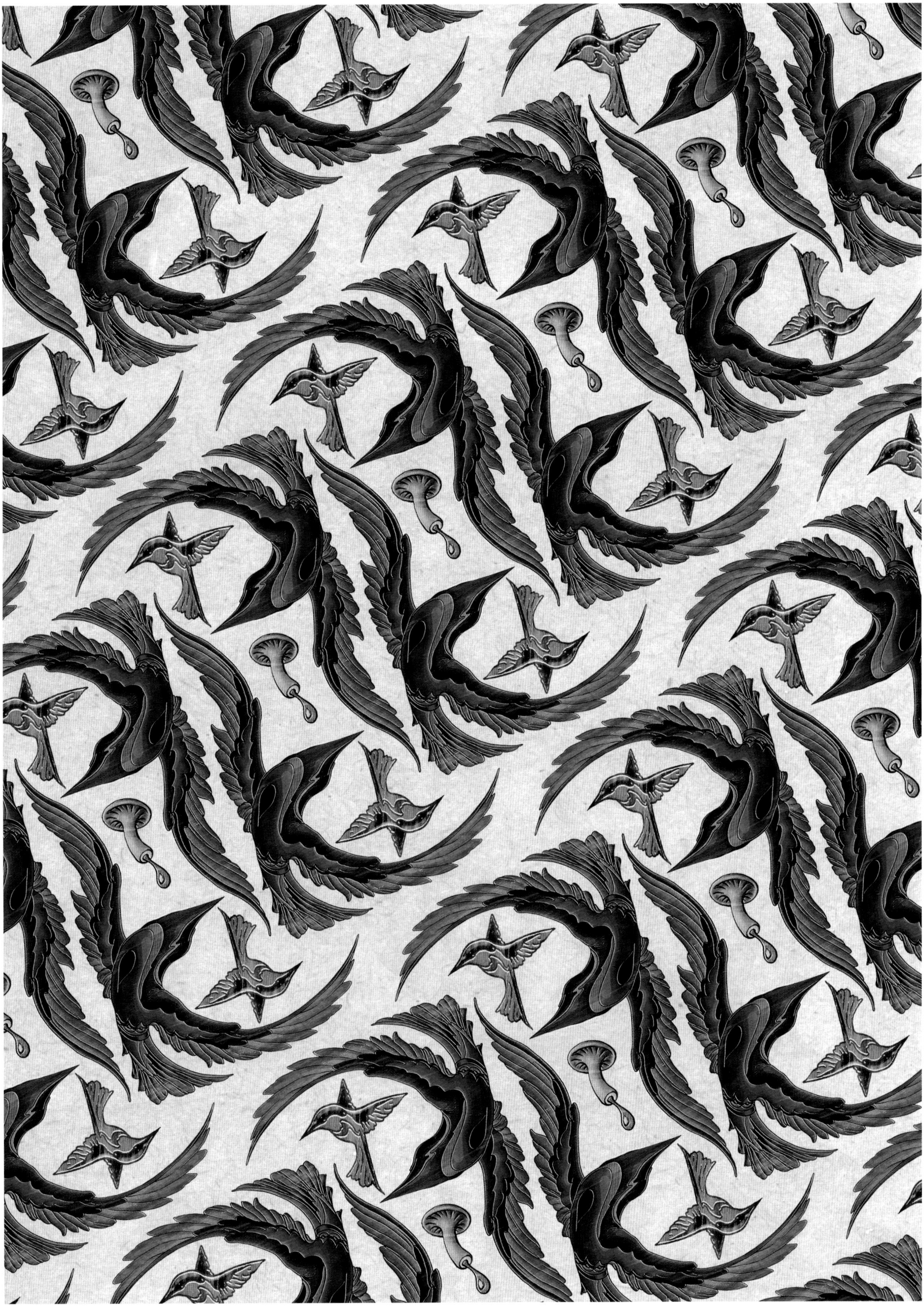

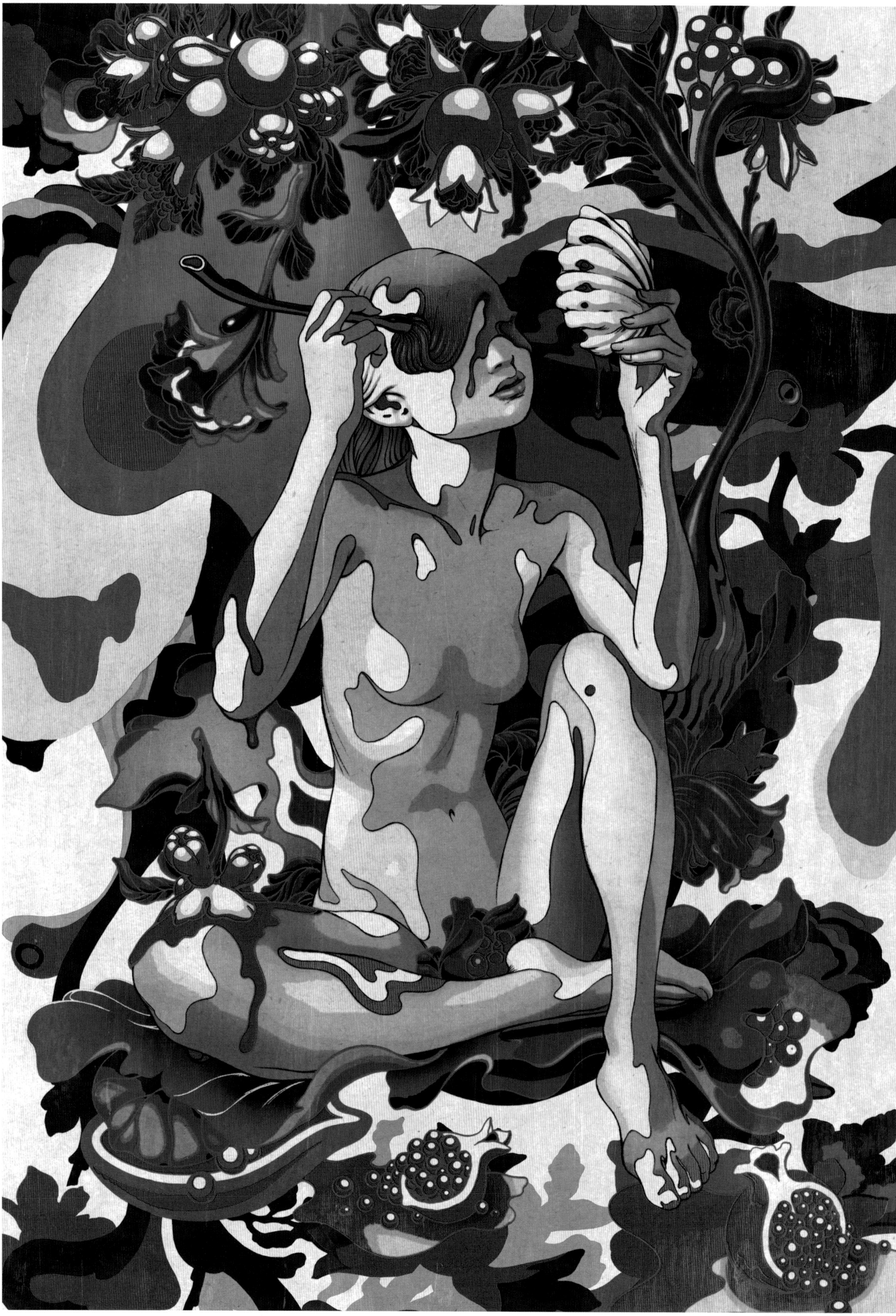

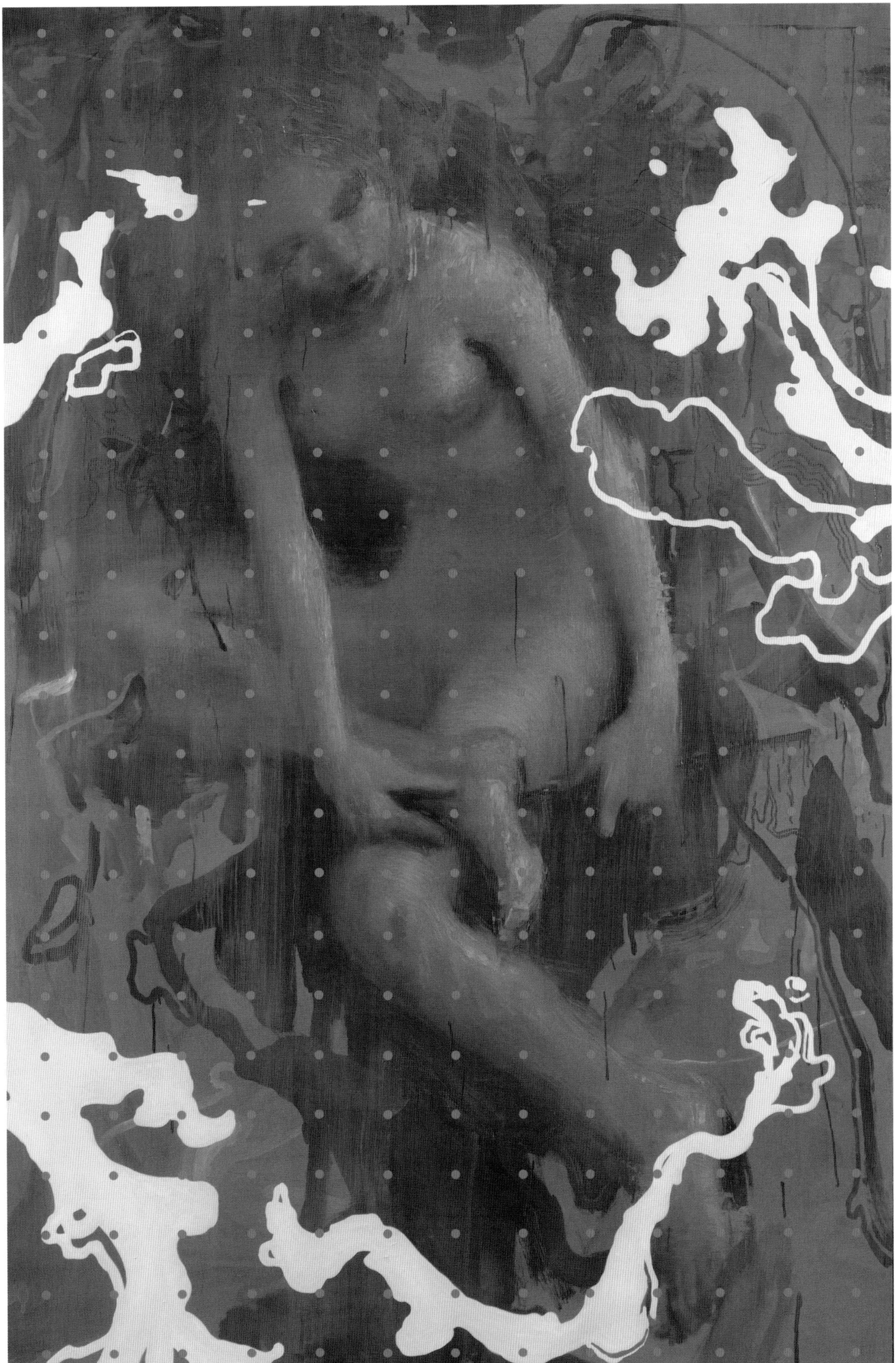

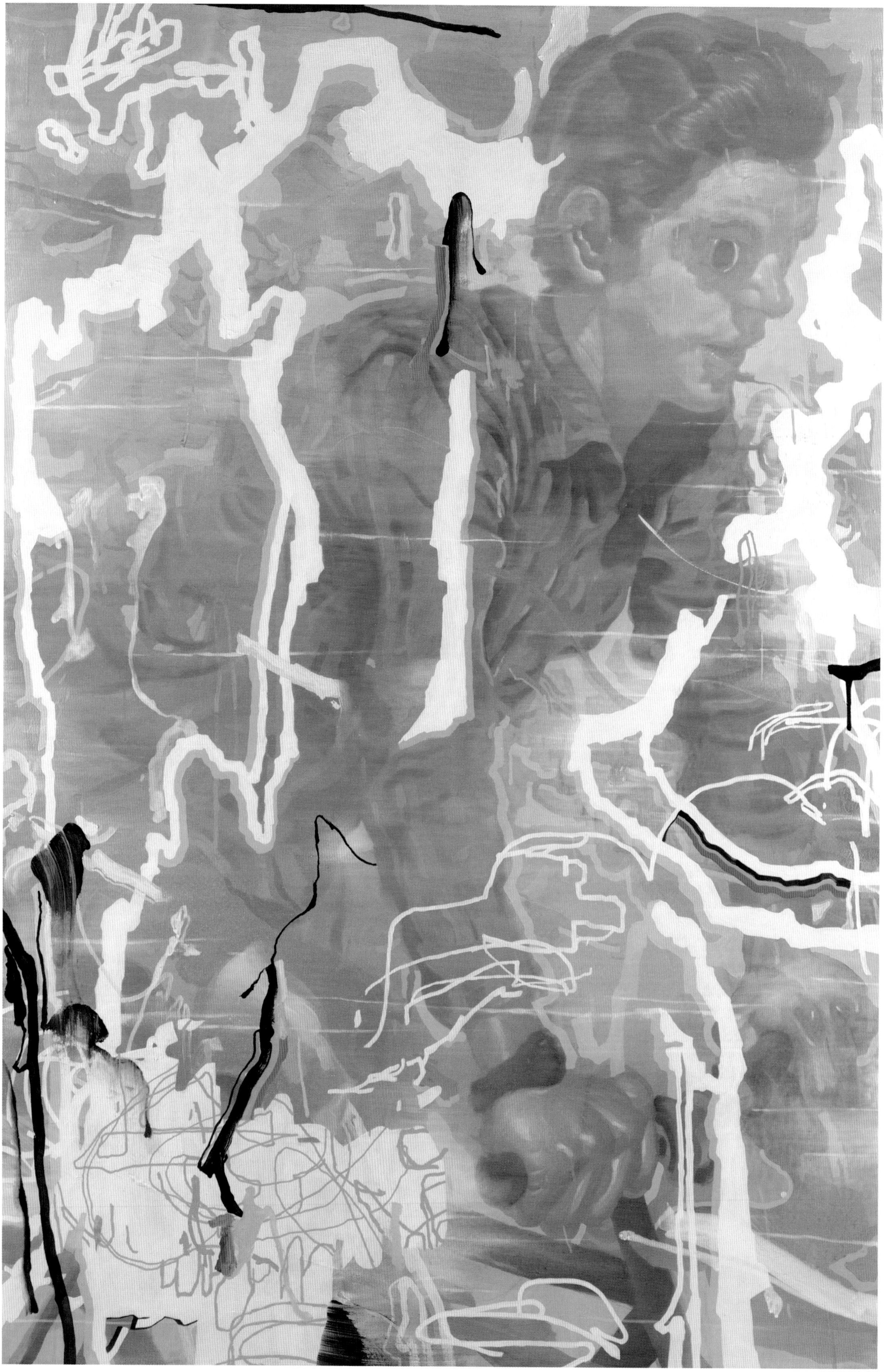

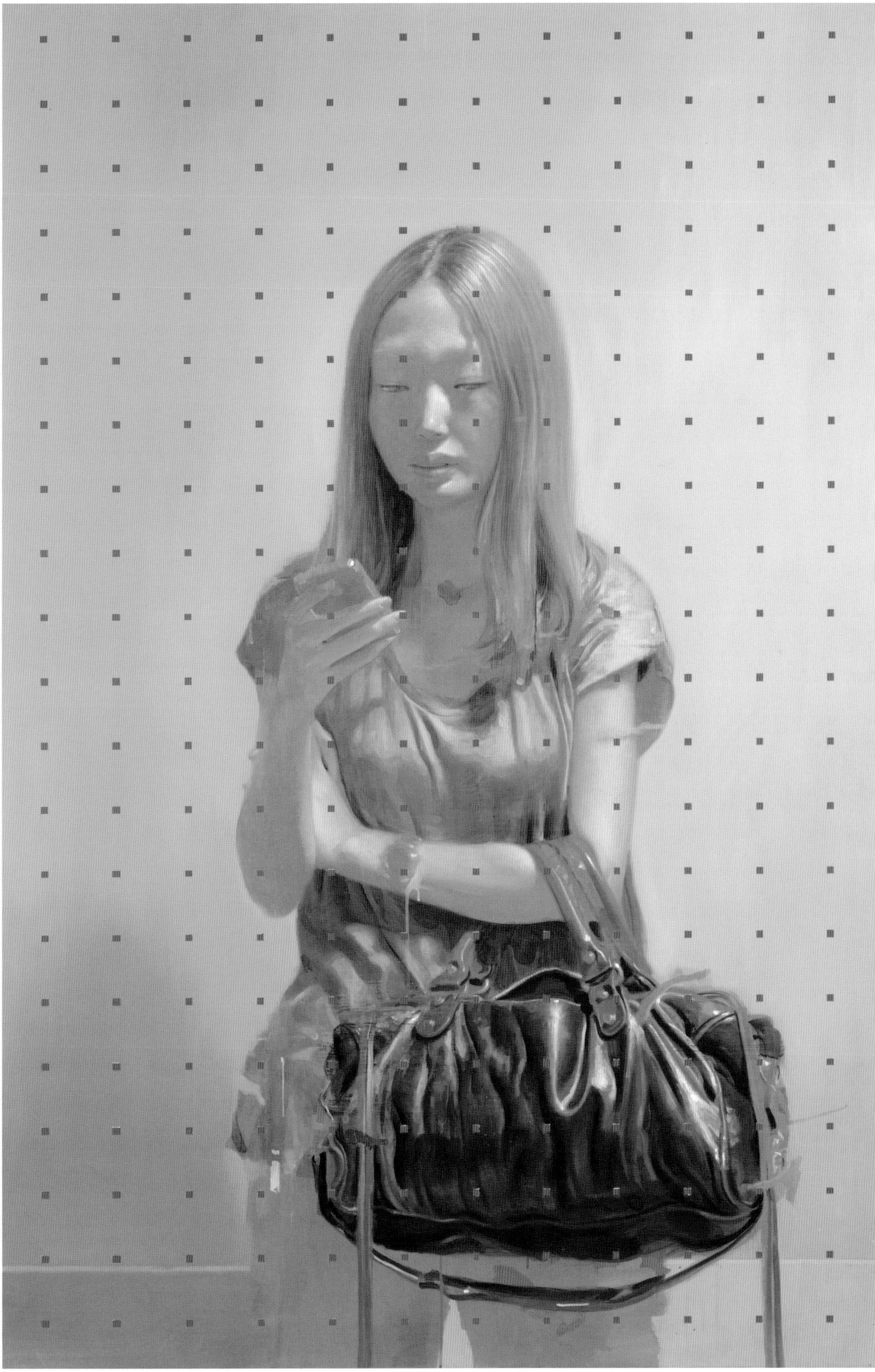

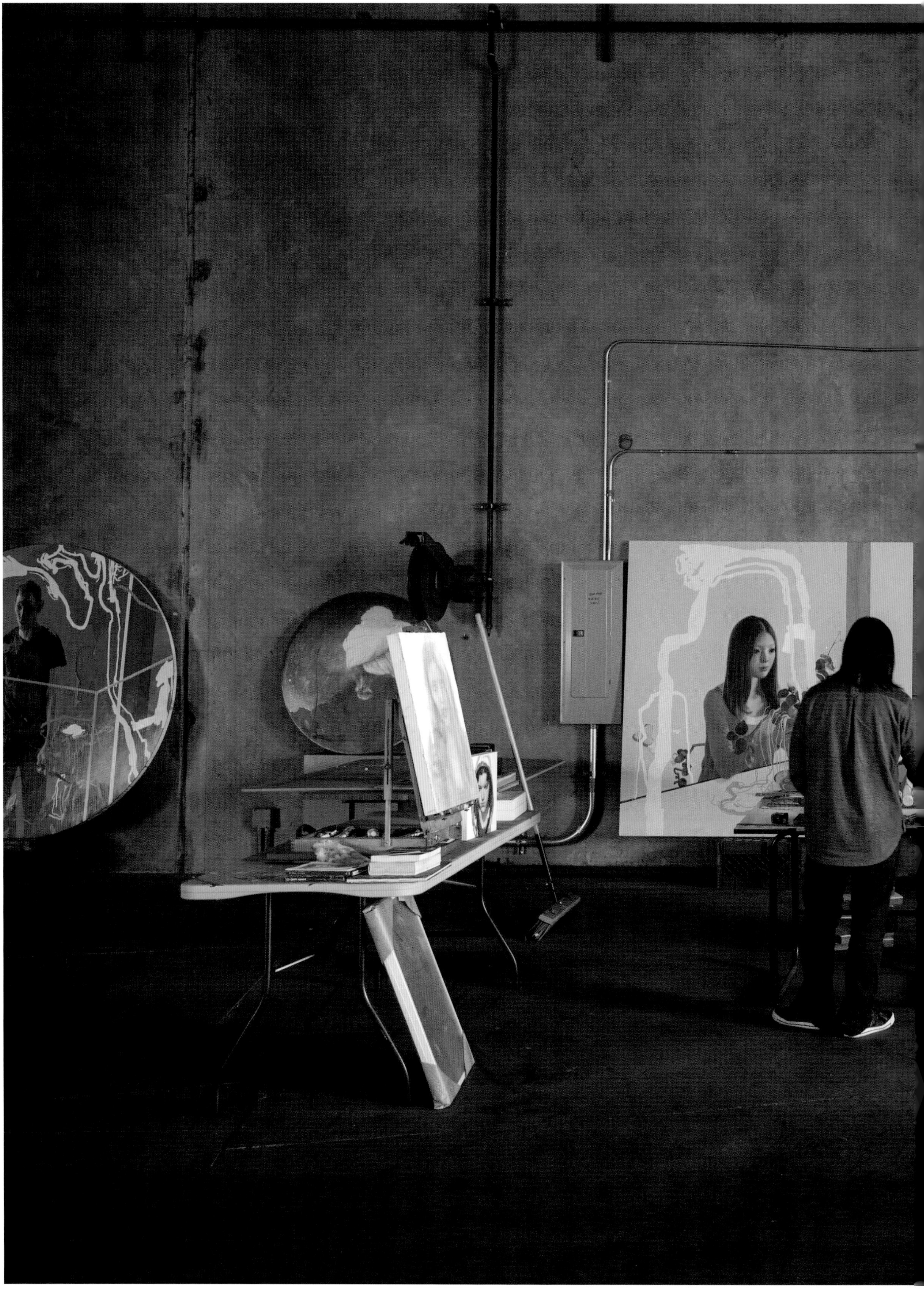

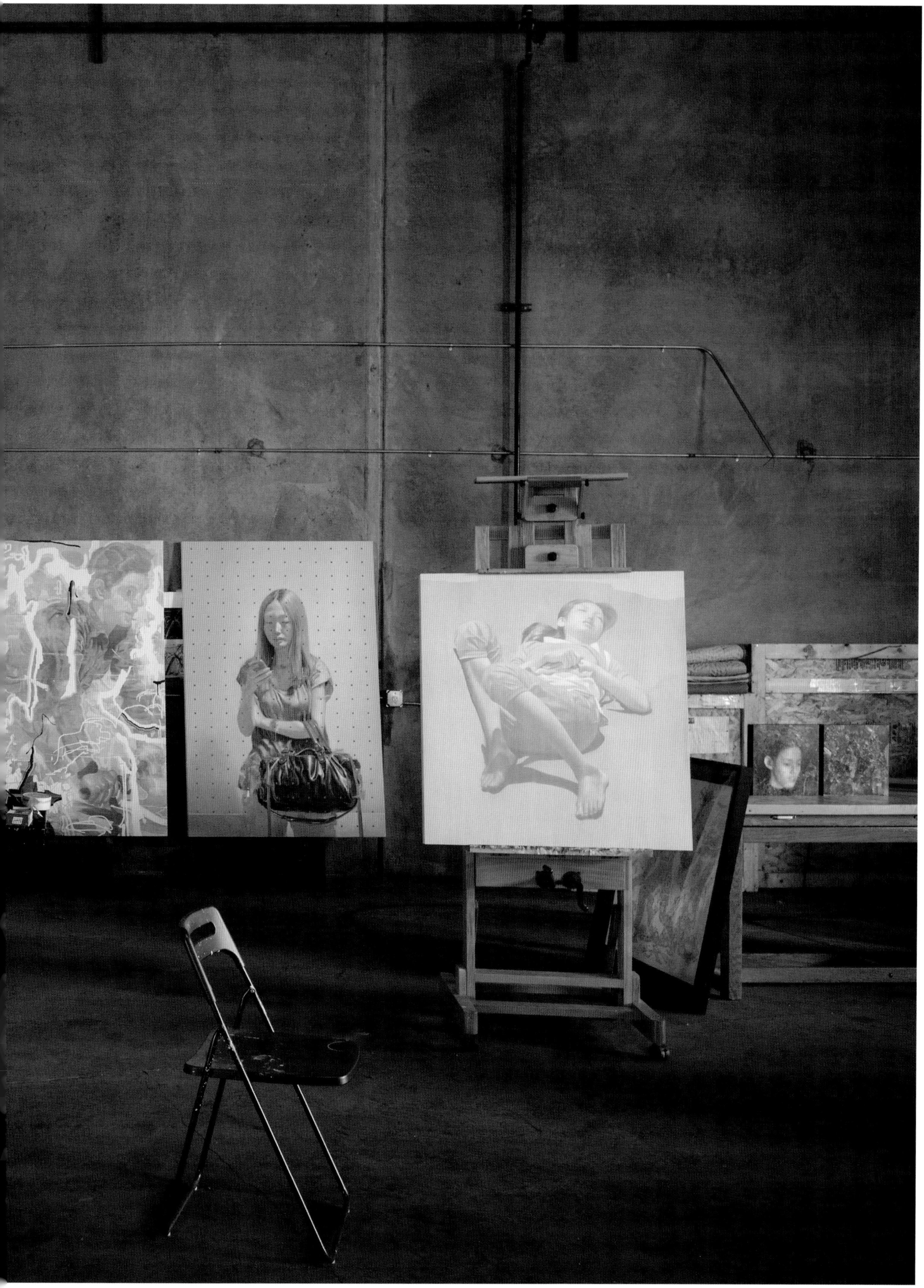

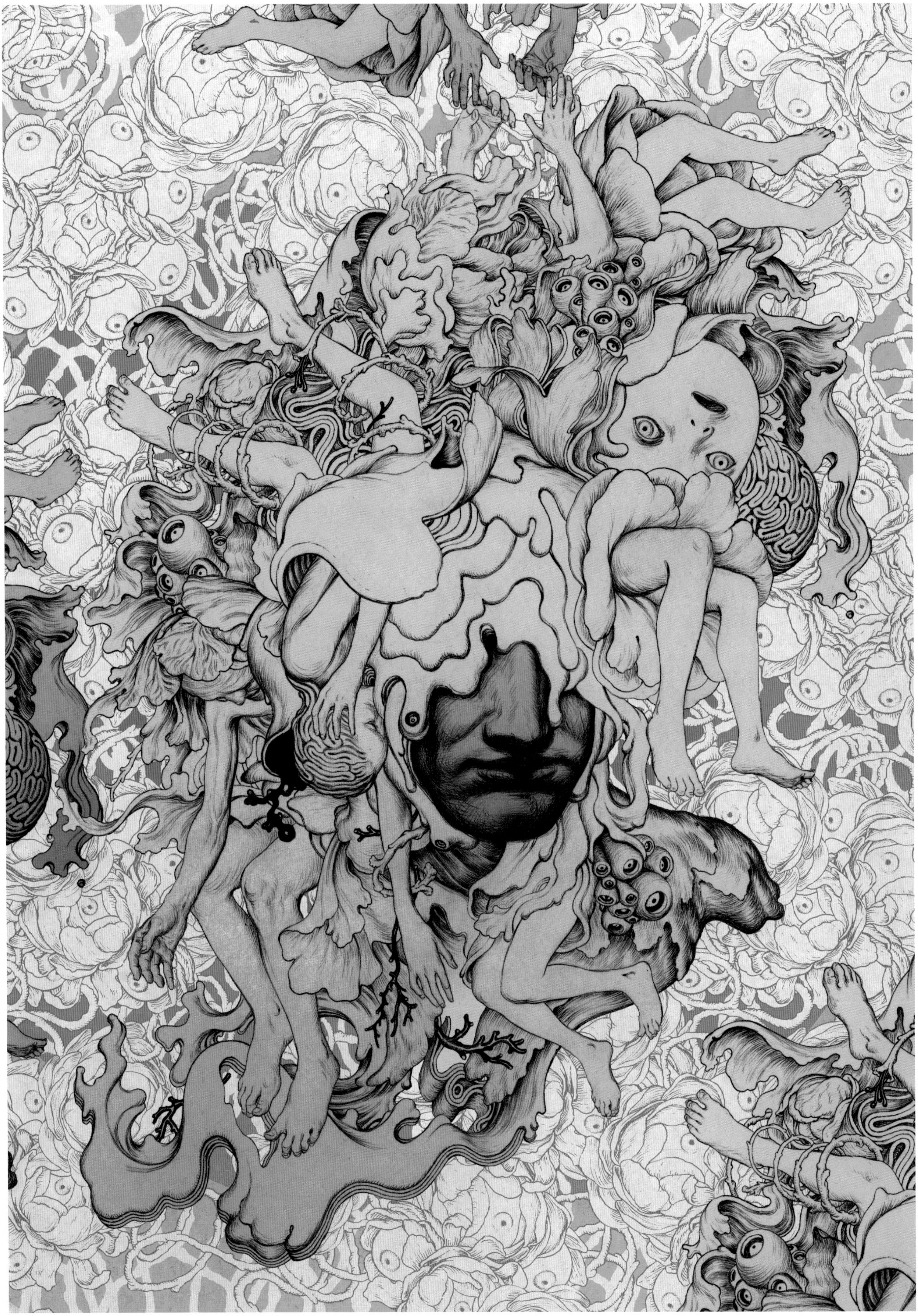

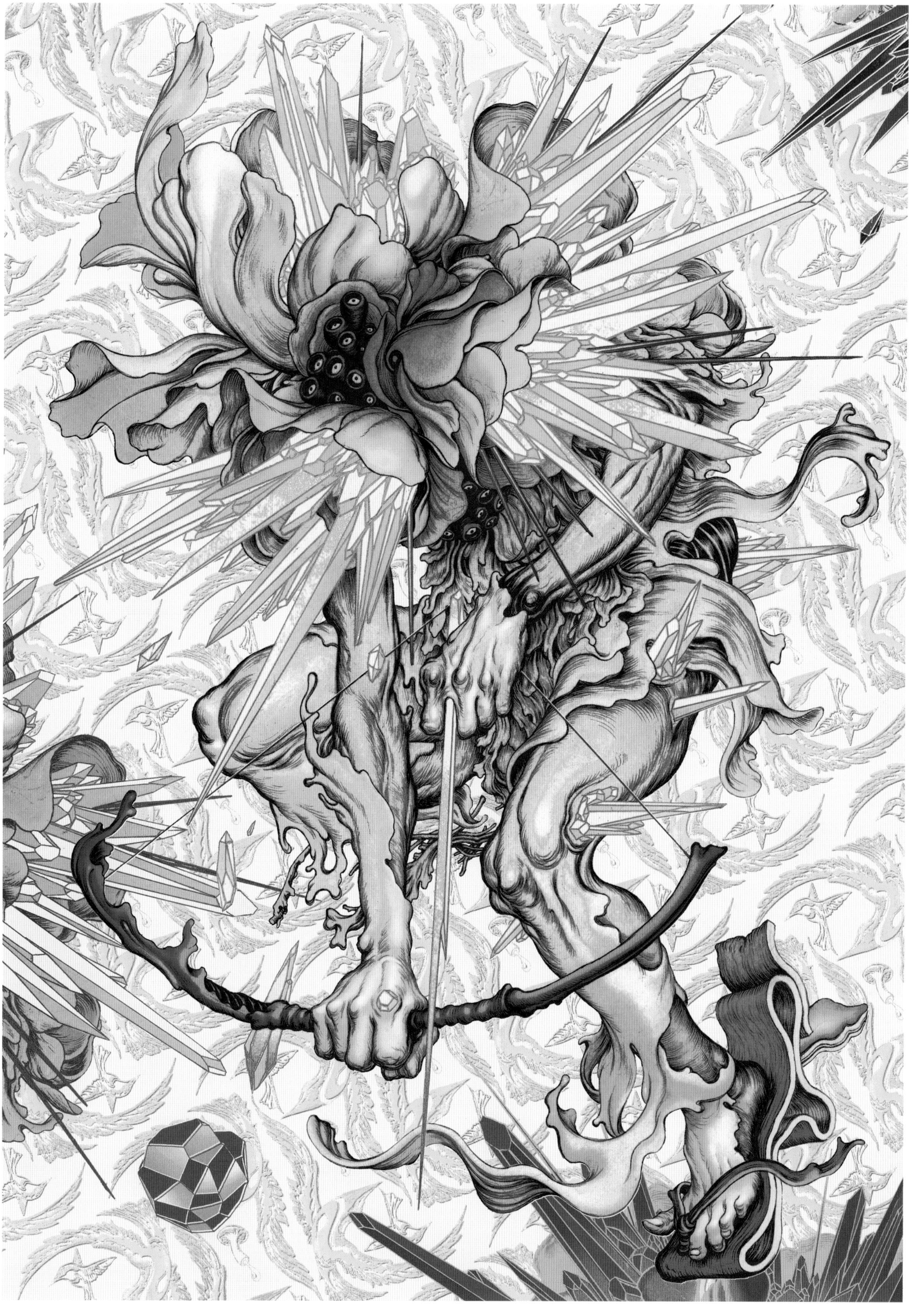

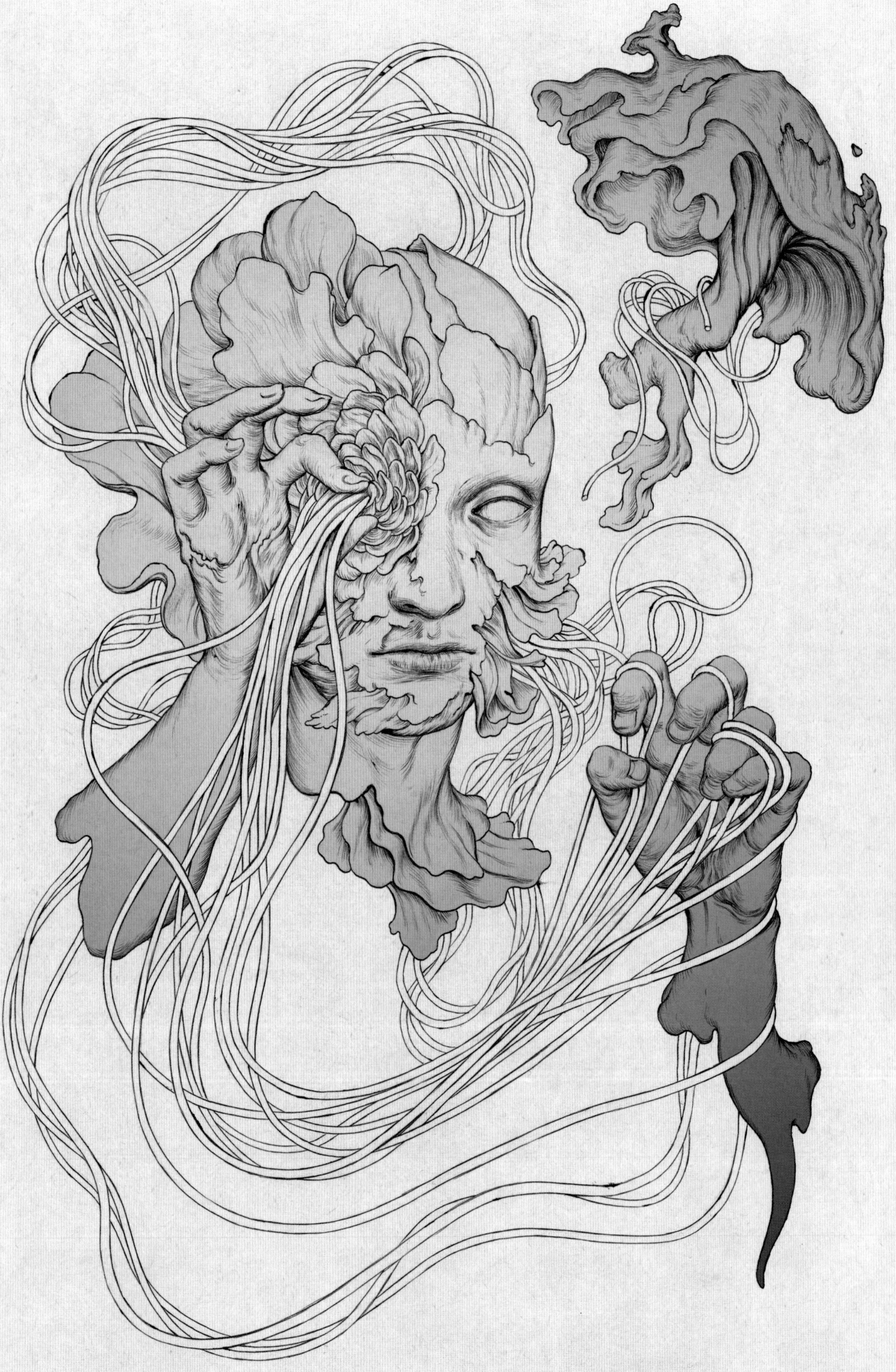

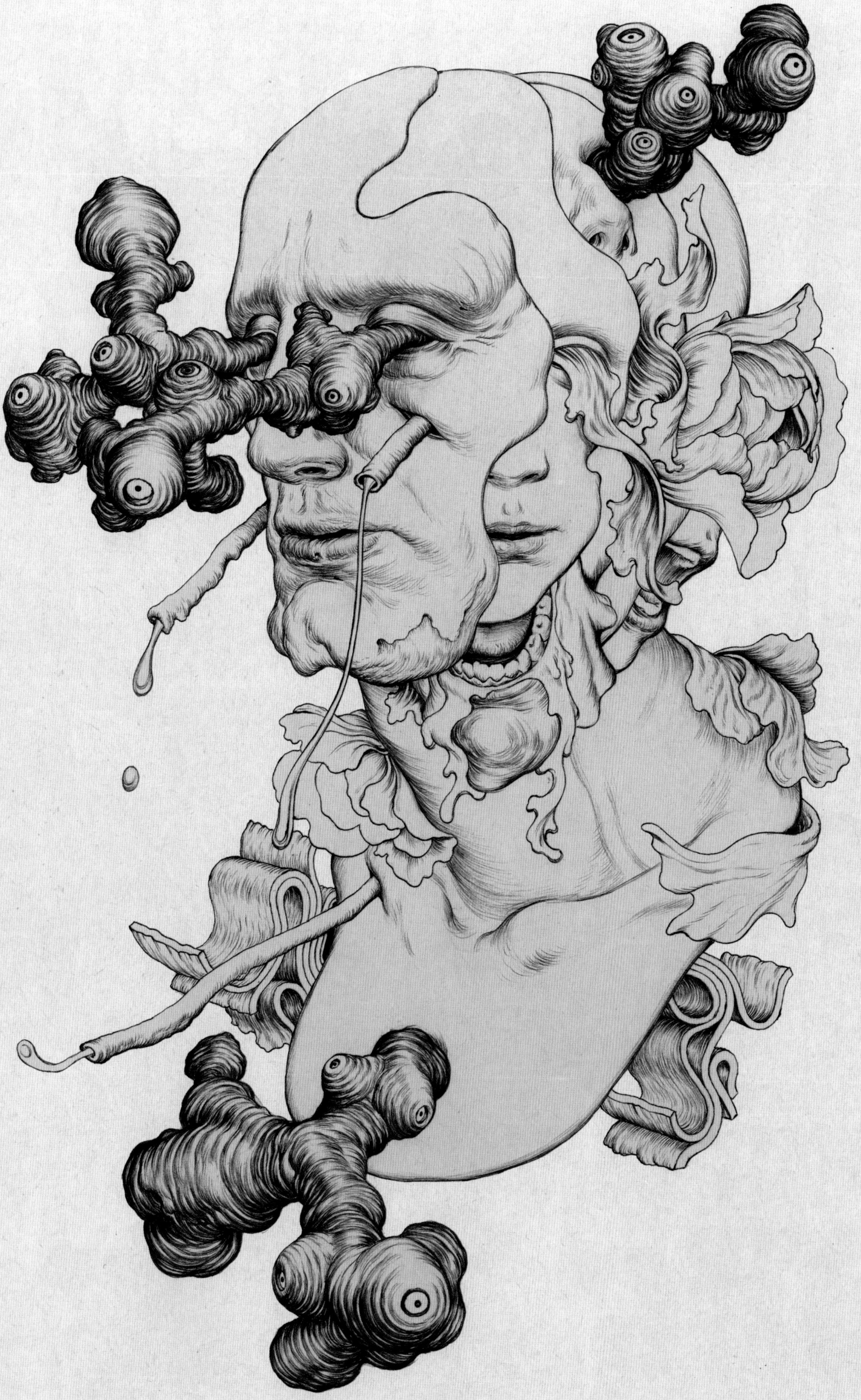

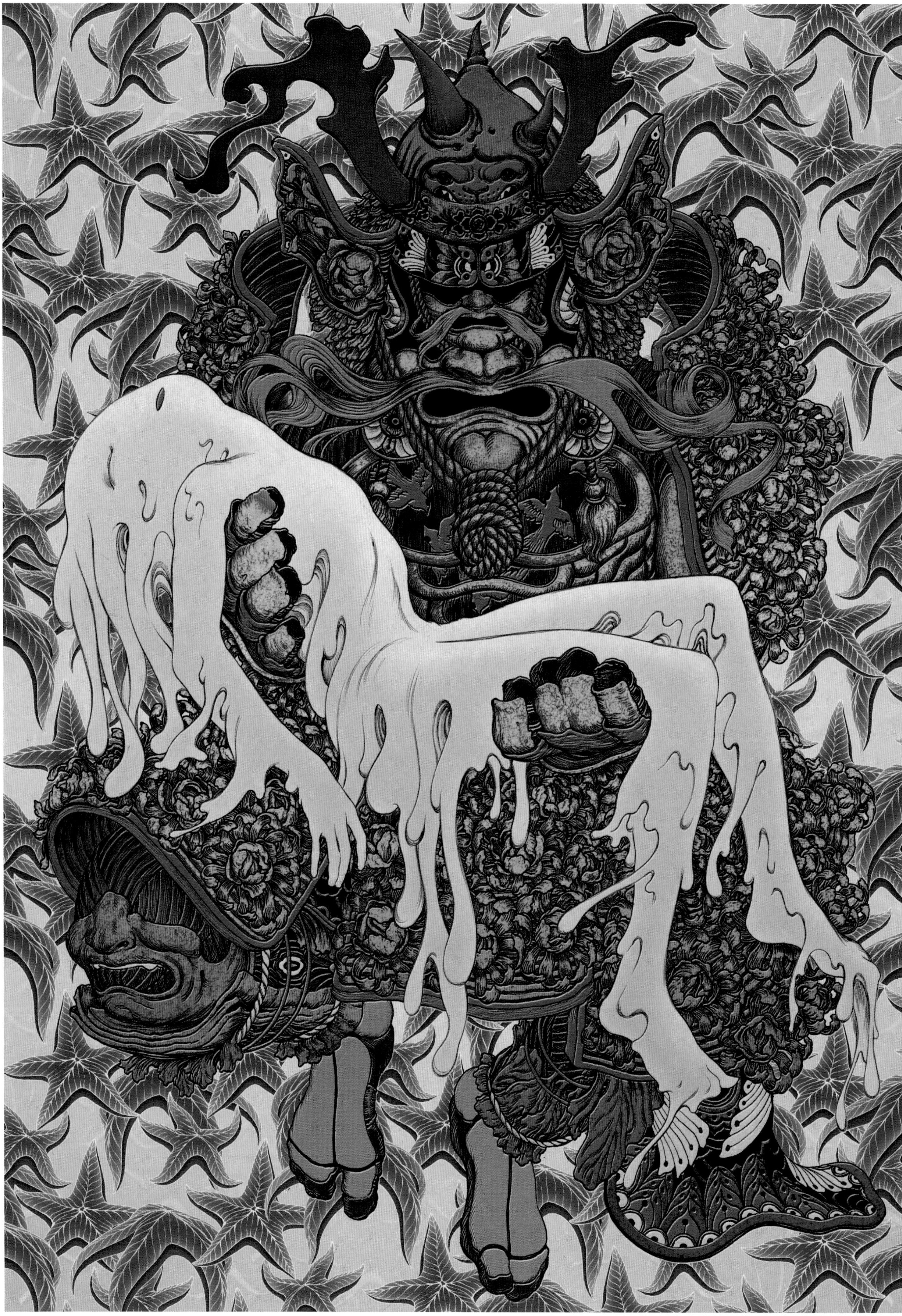

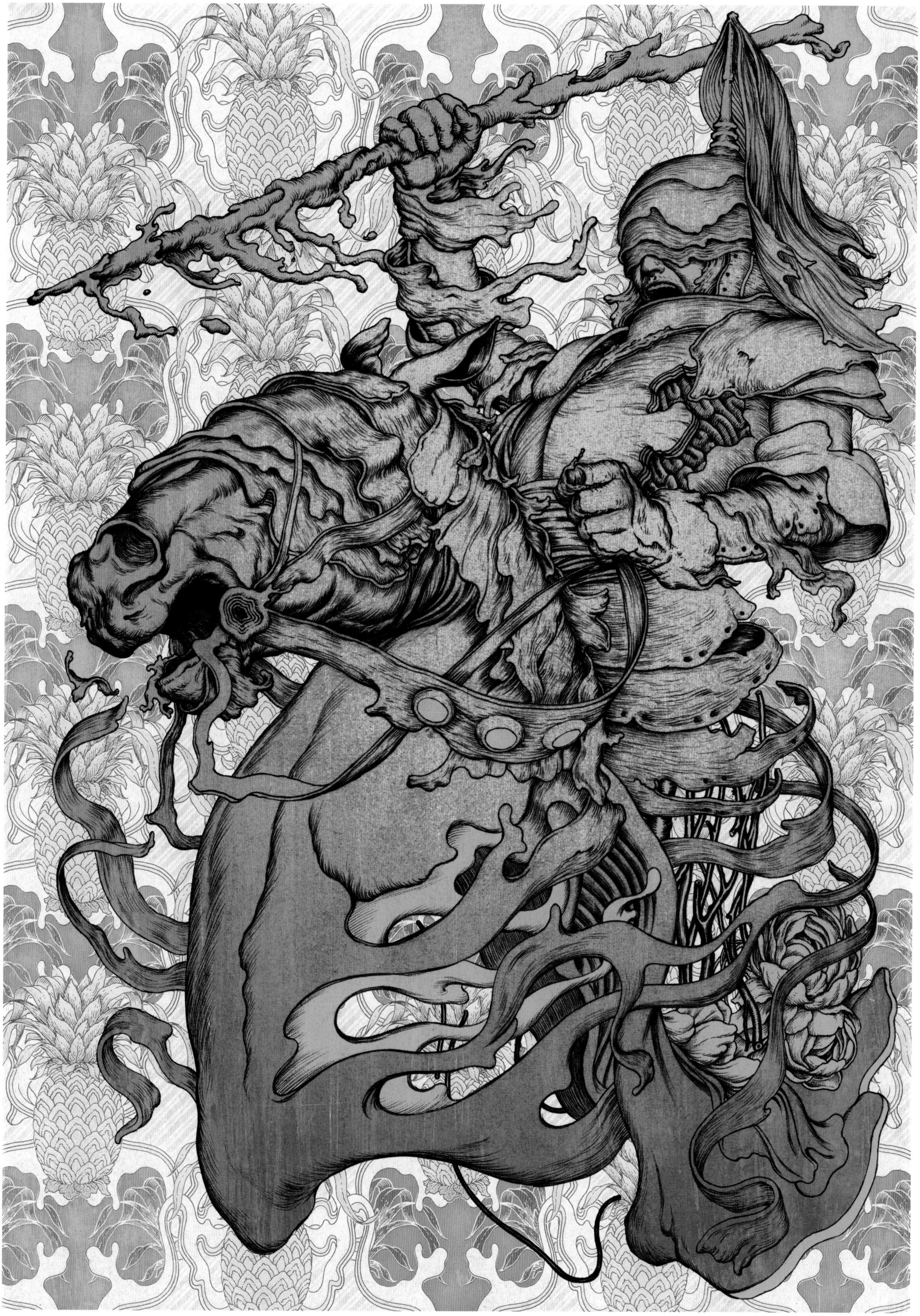

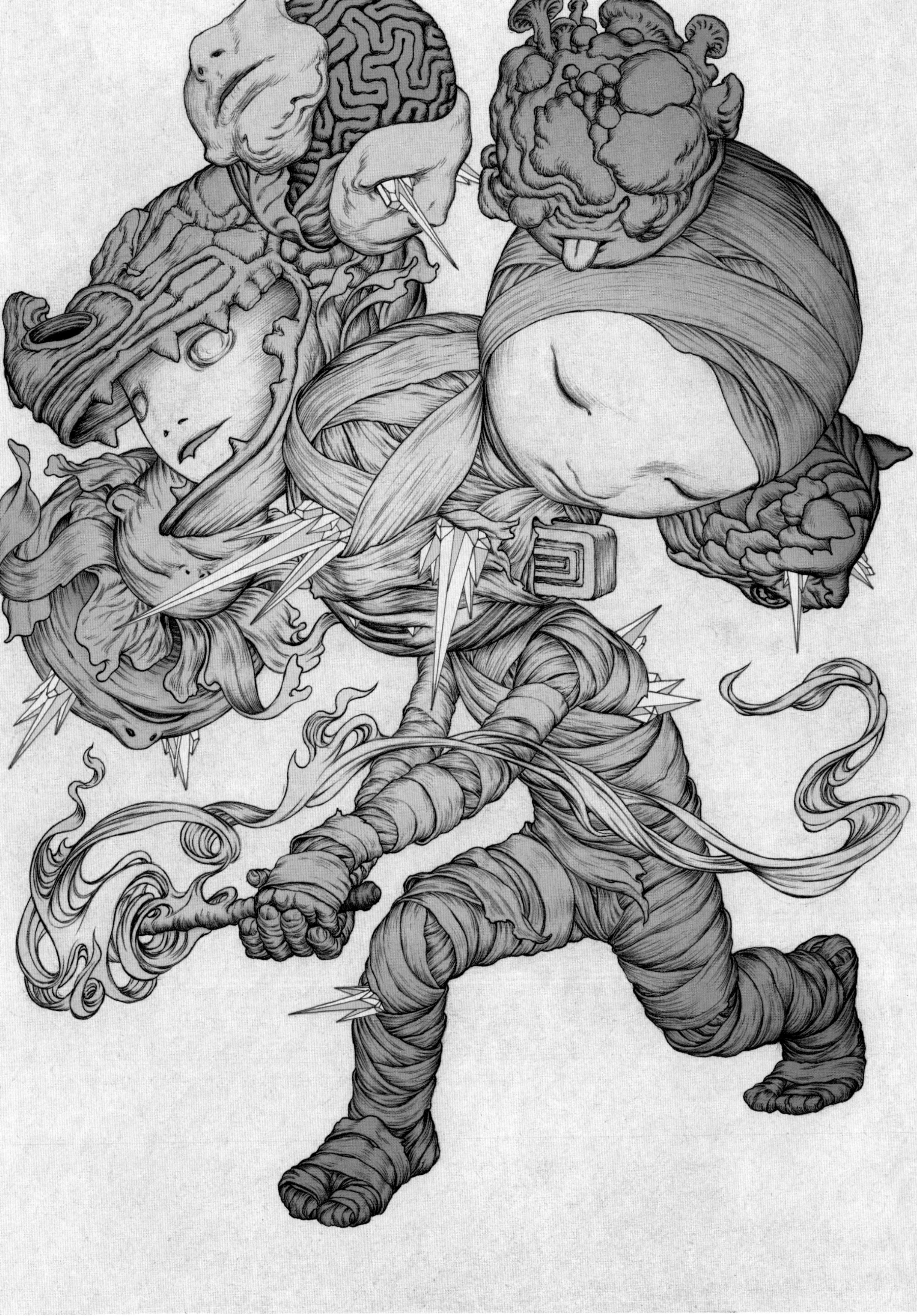

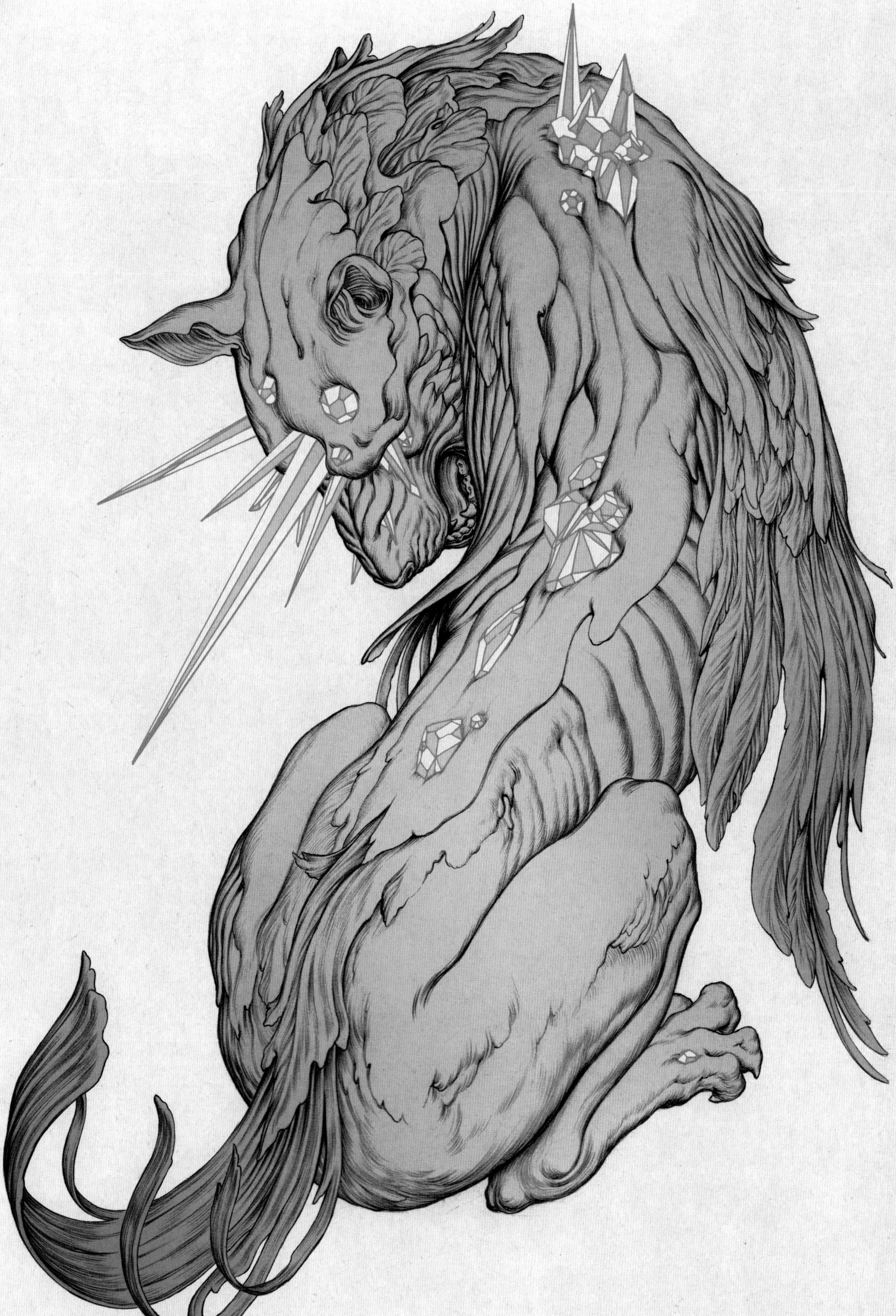

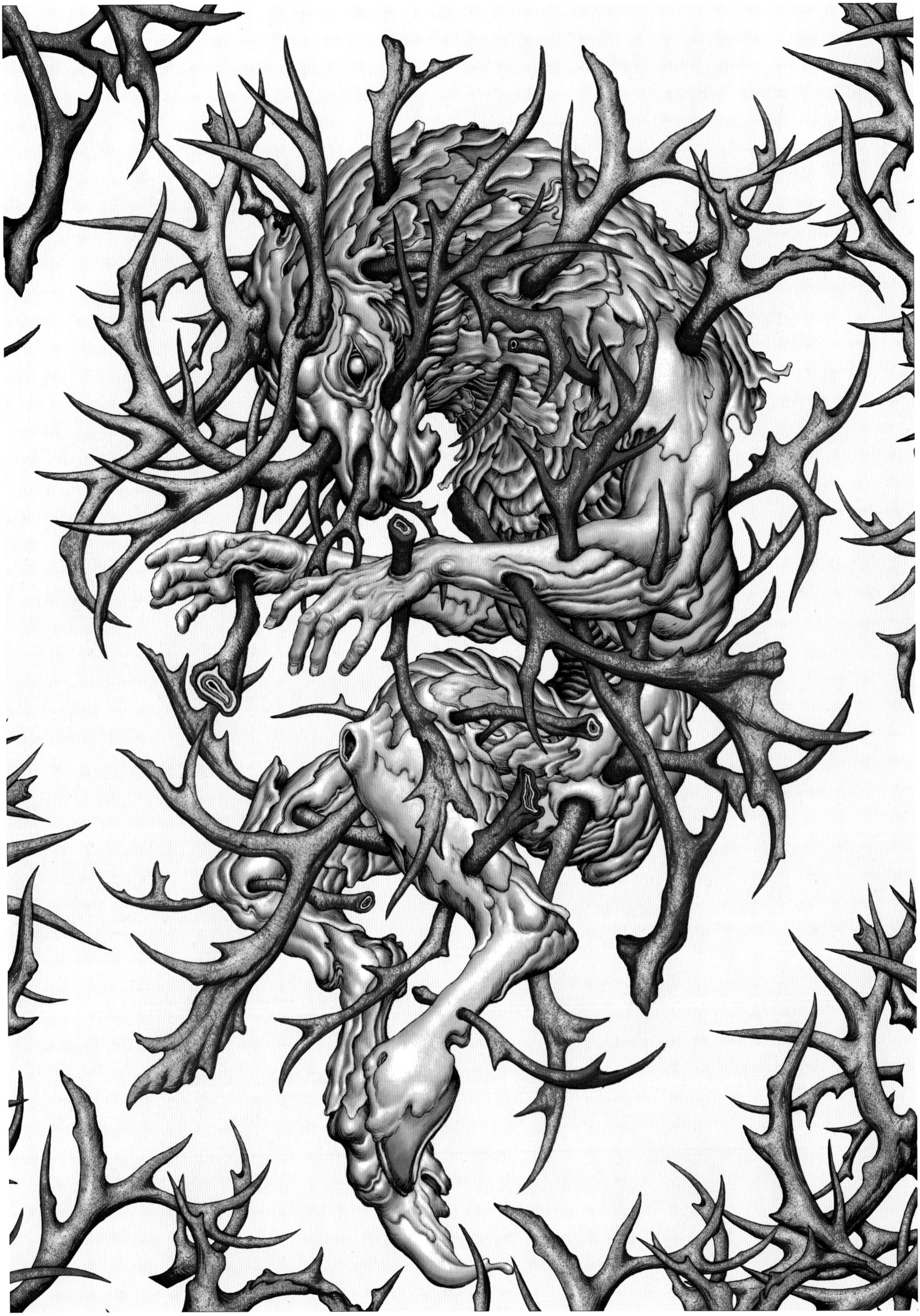

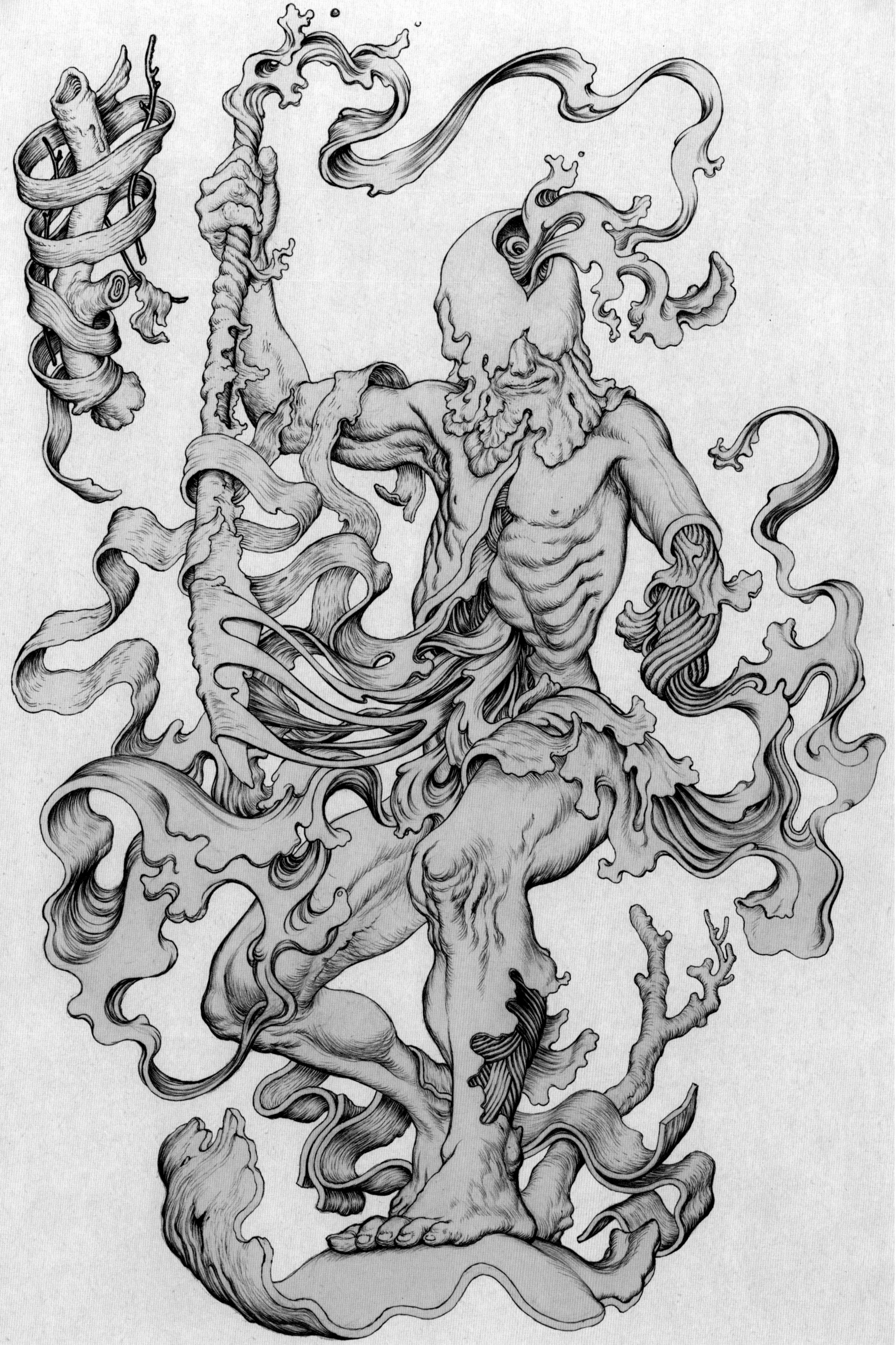

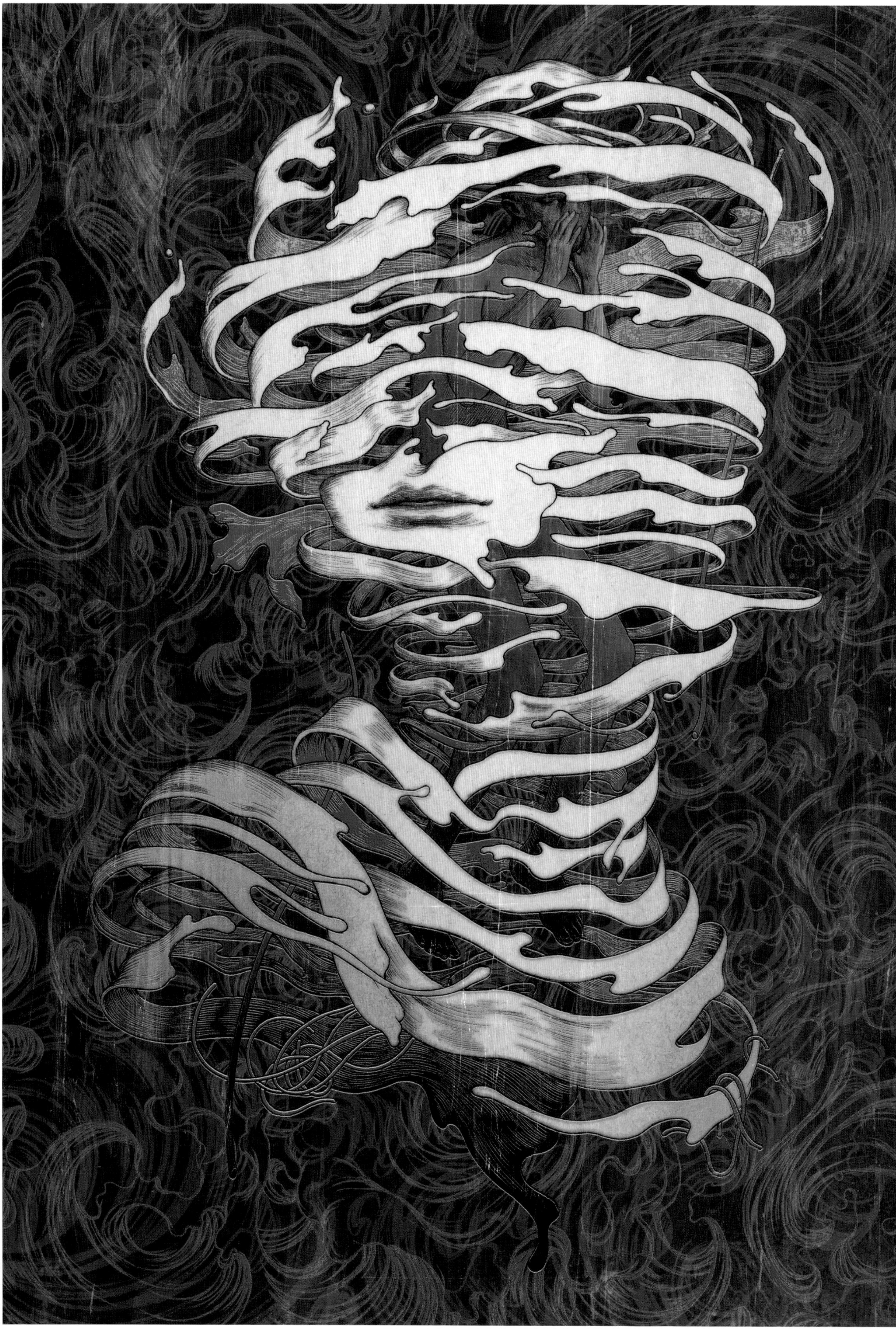

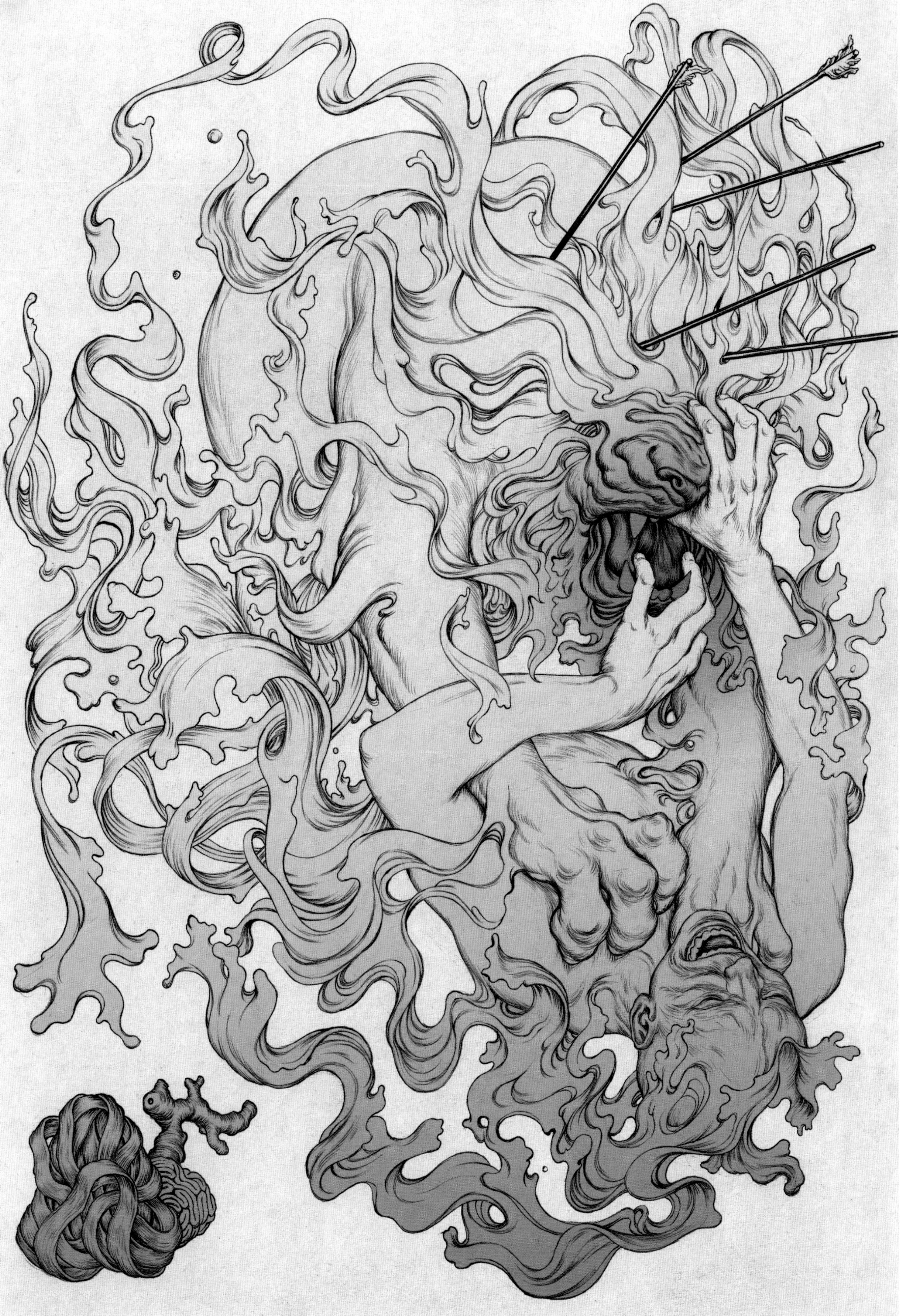

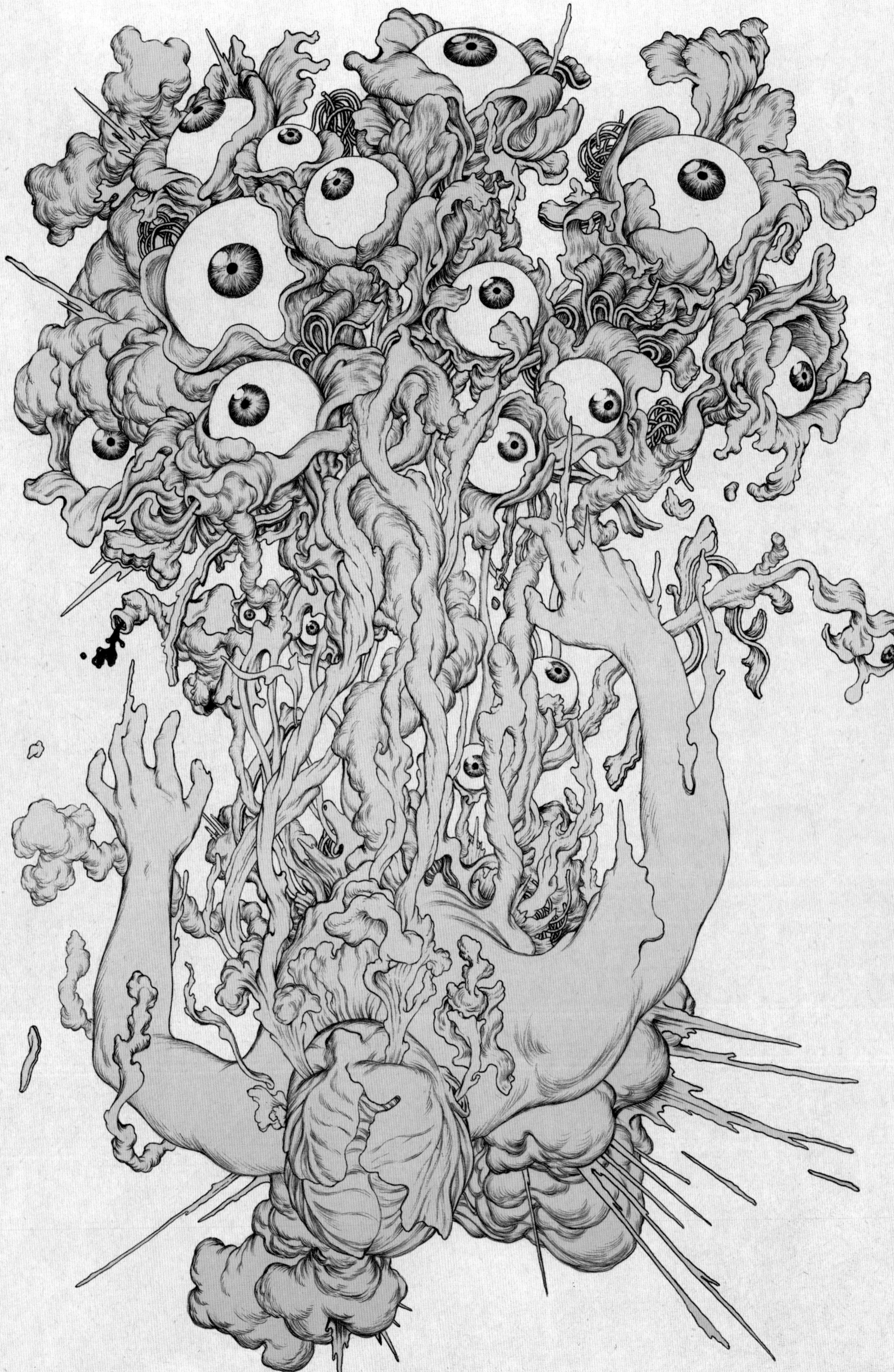

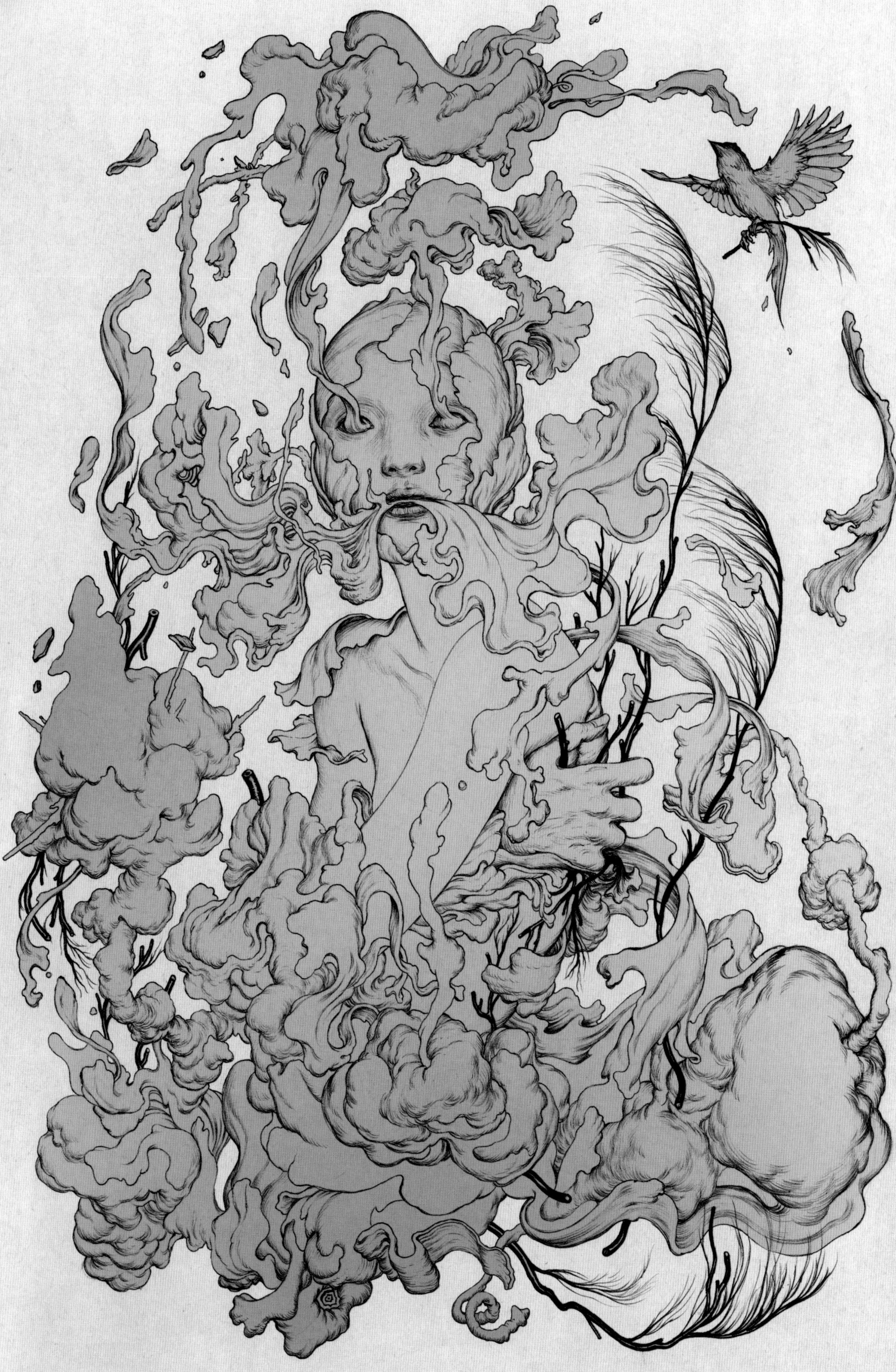

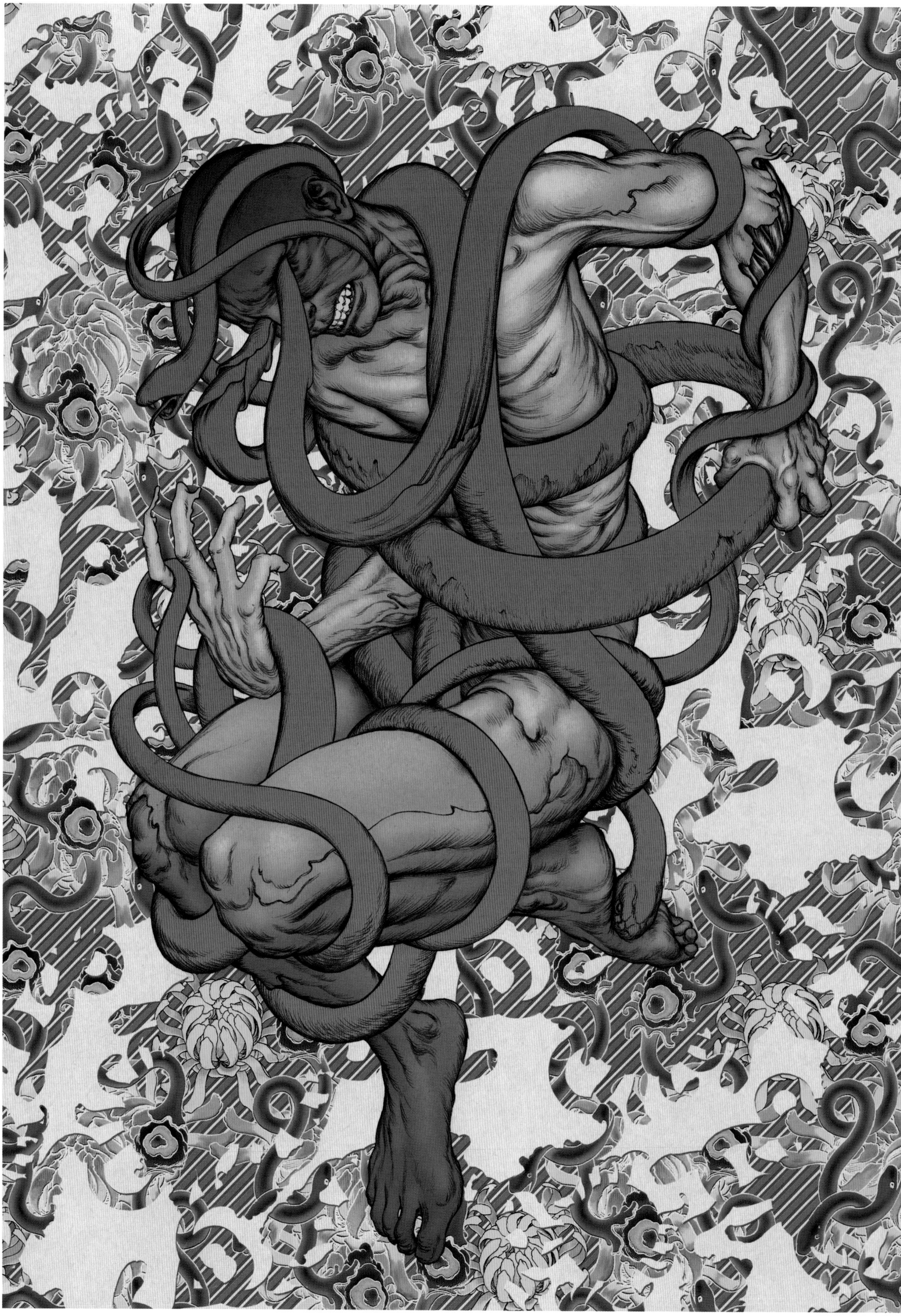

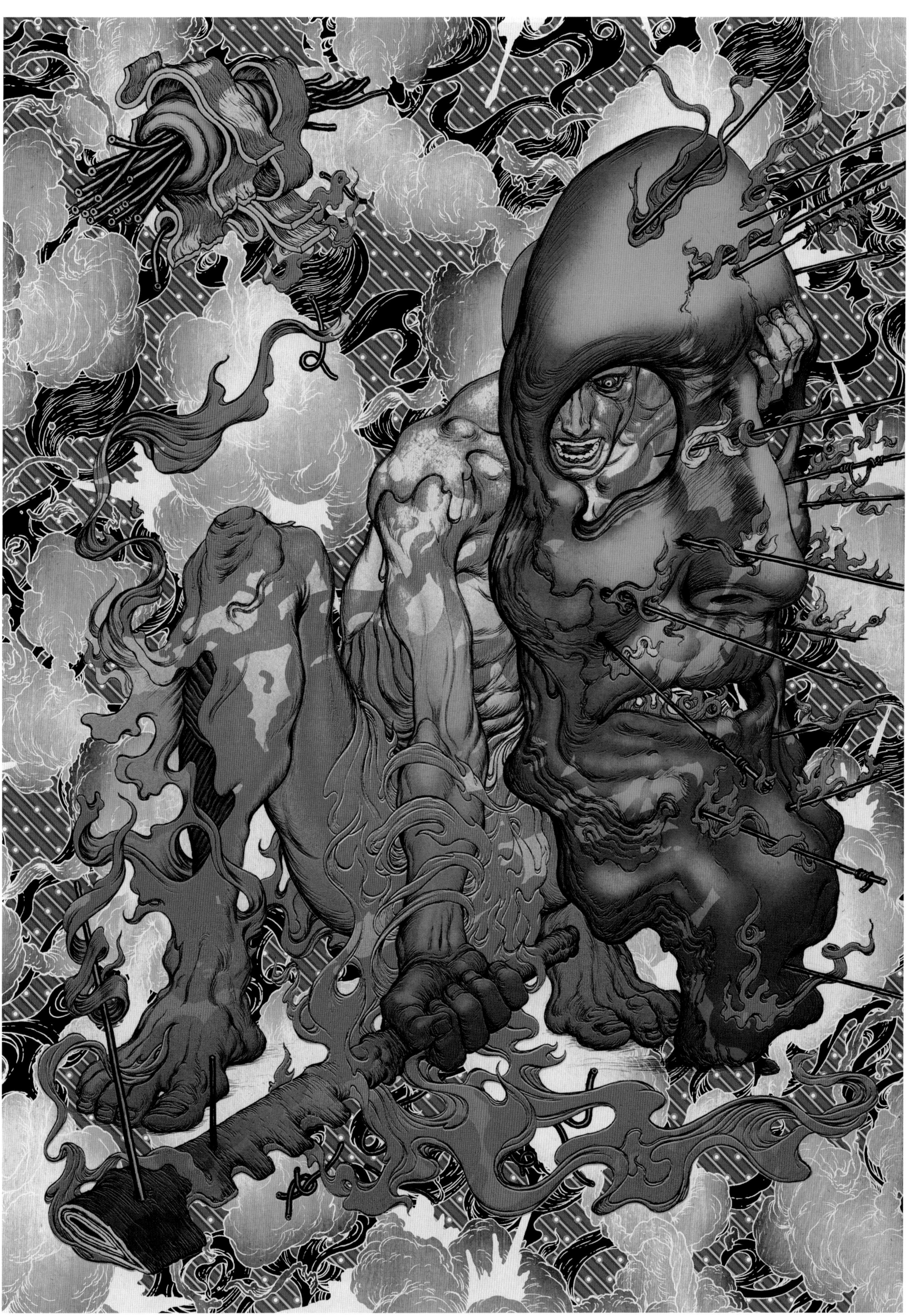

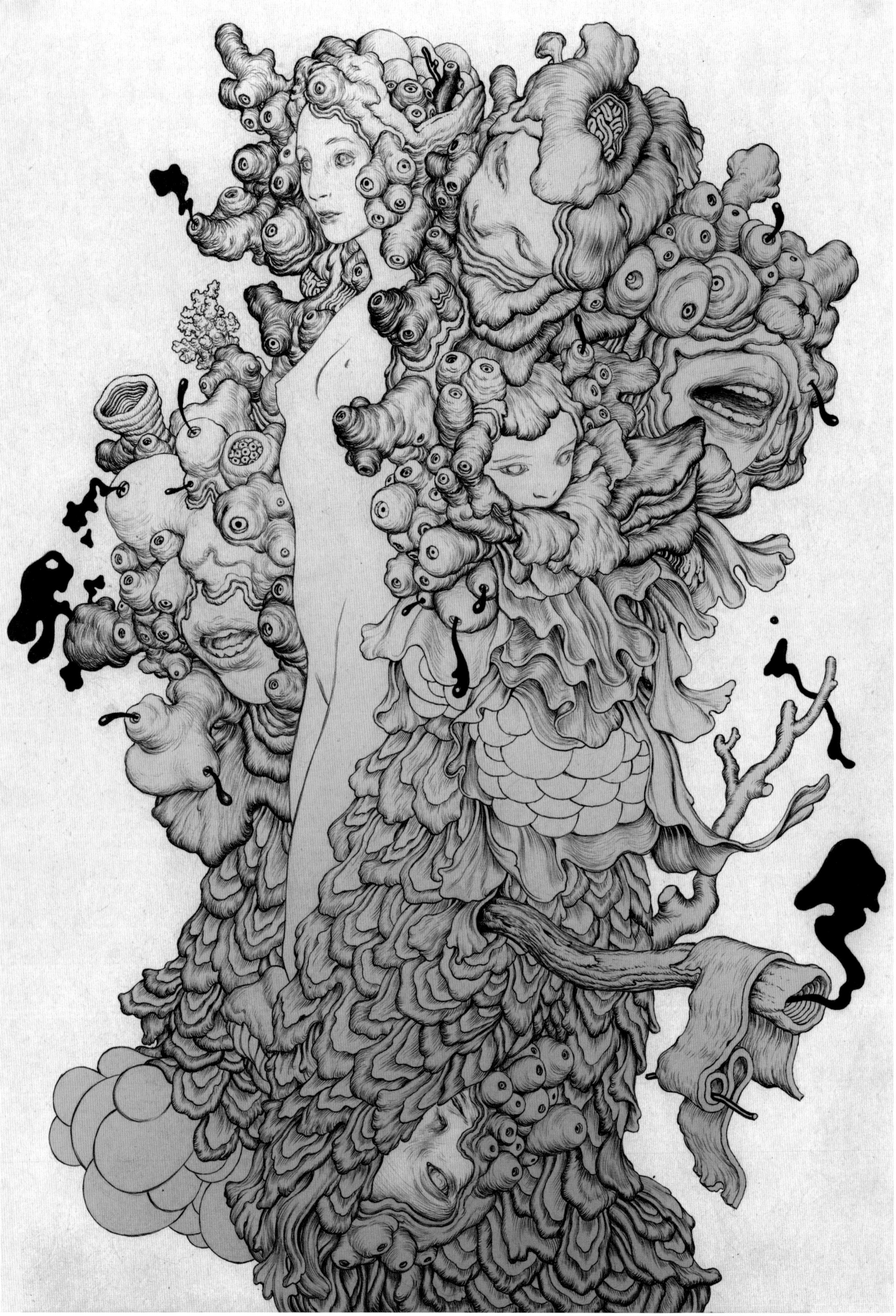

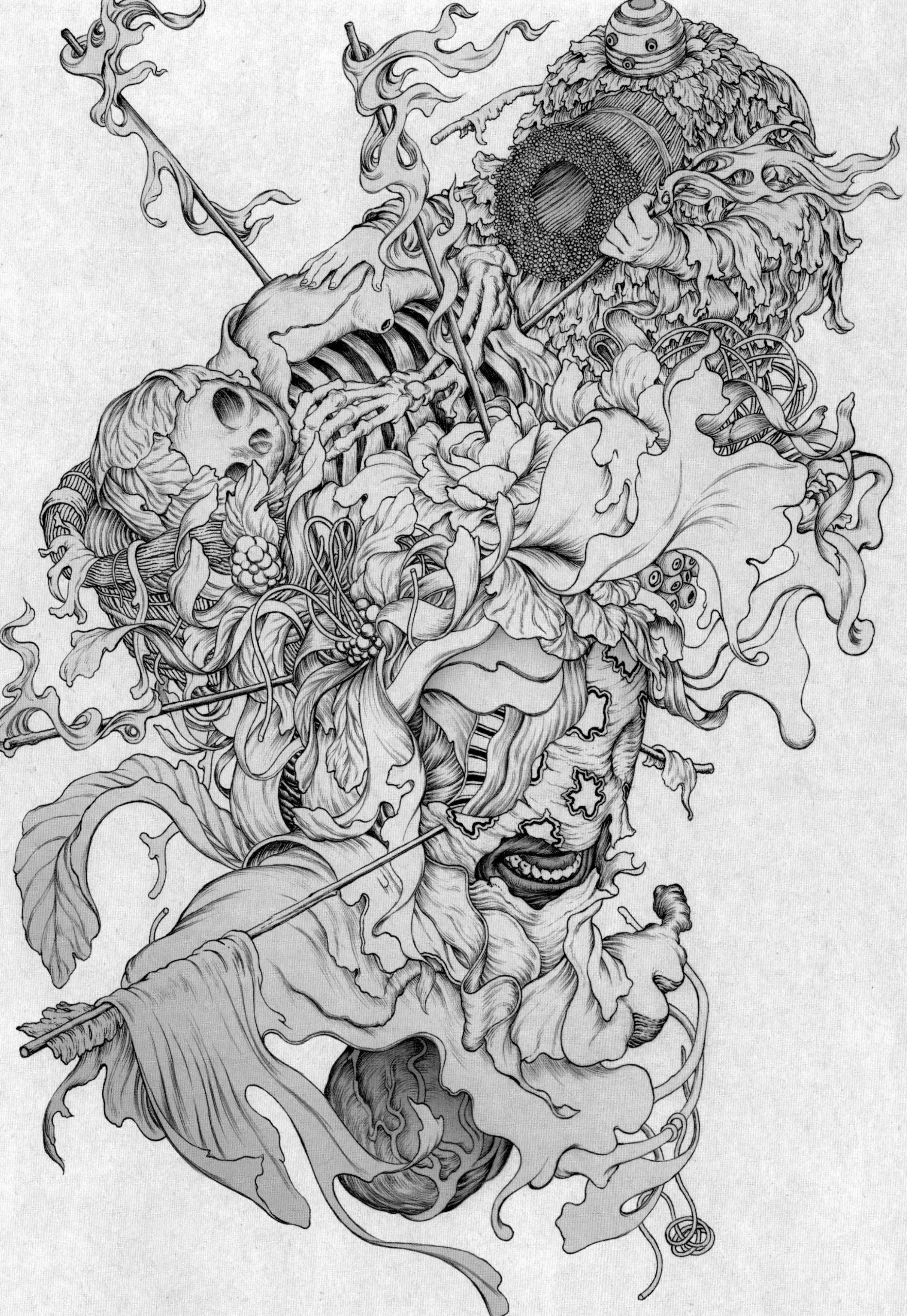

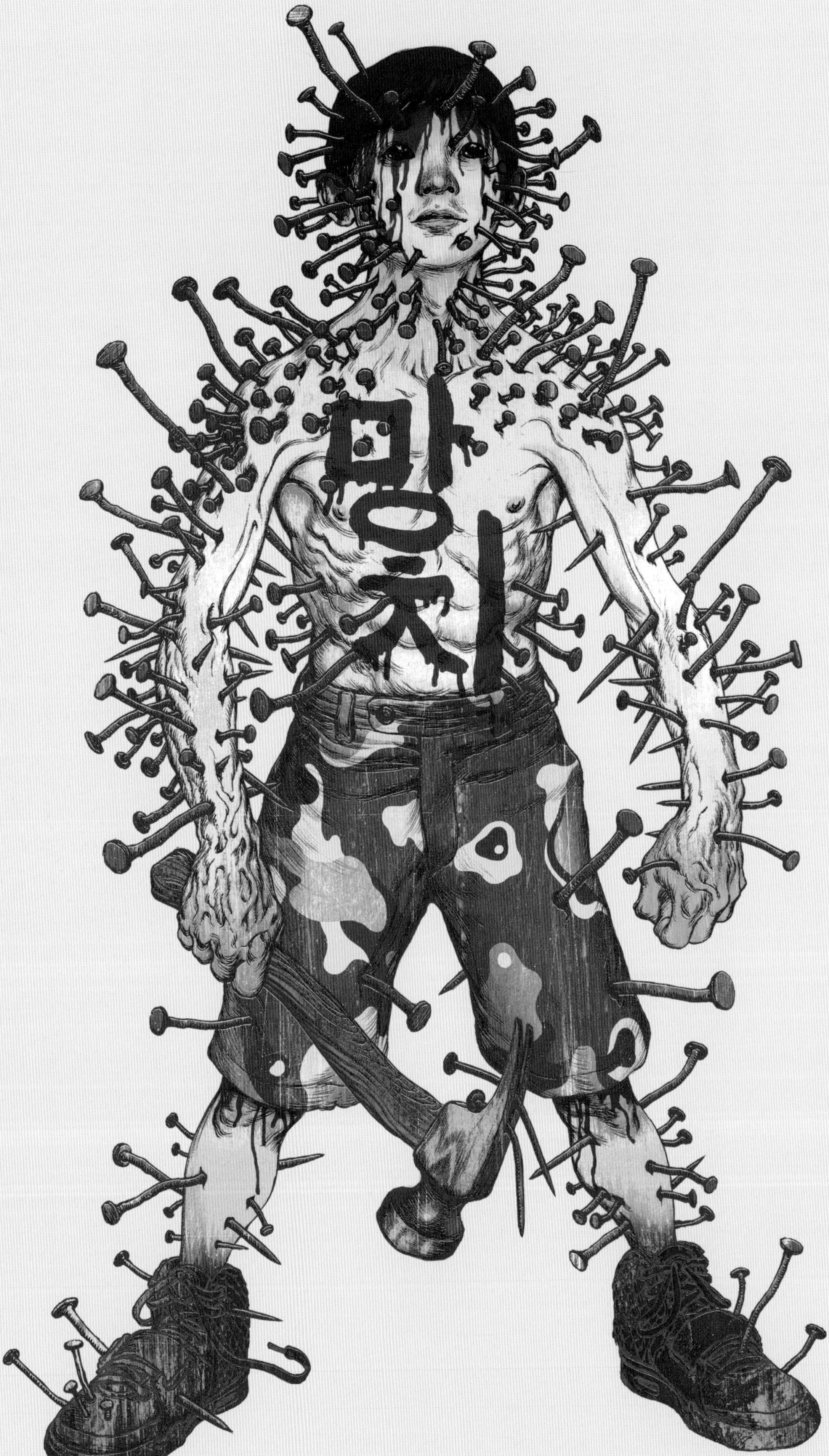
망치

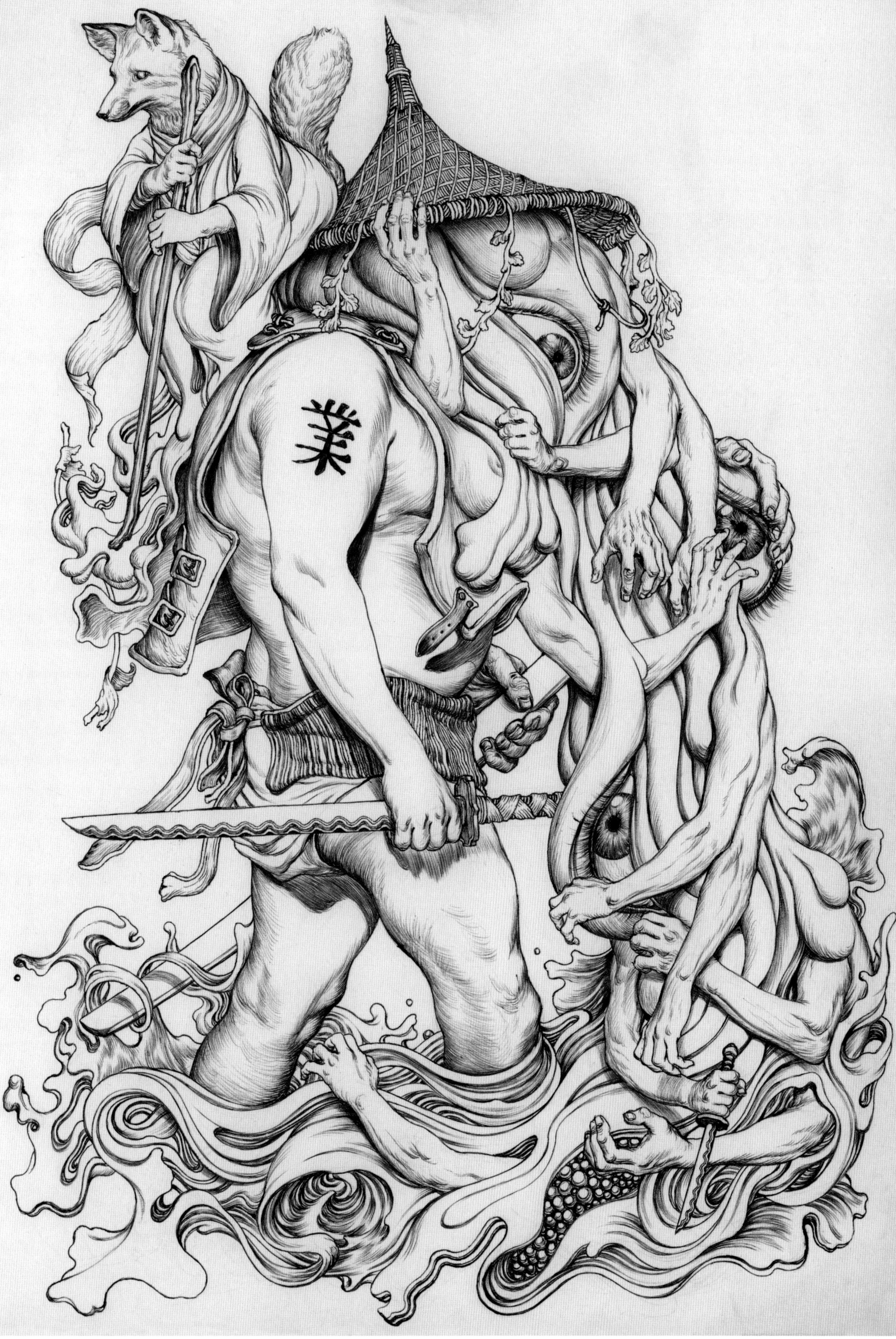
業

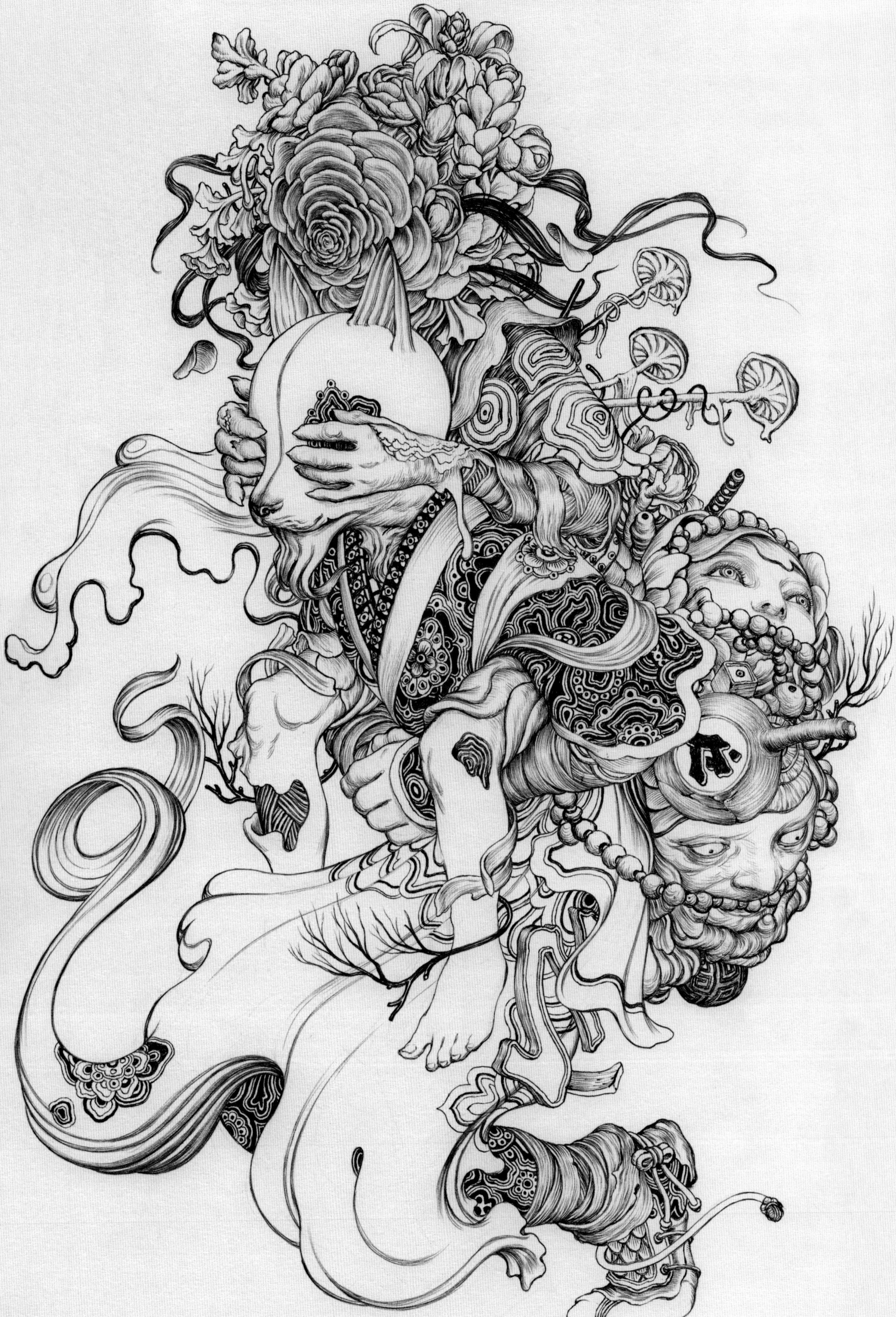

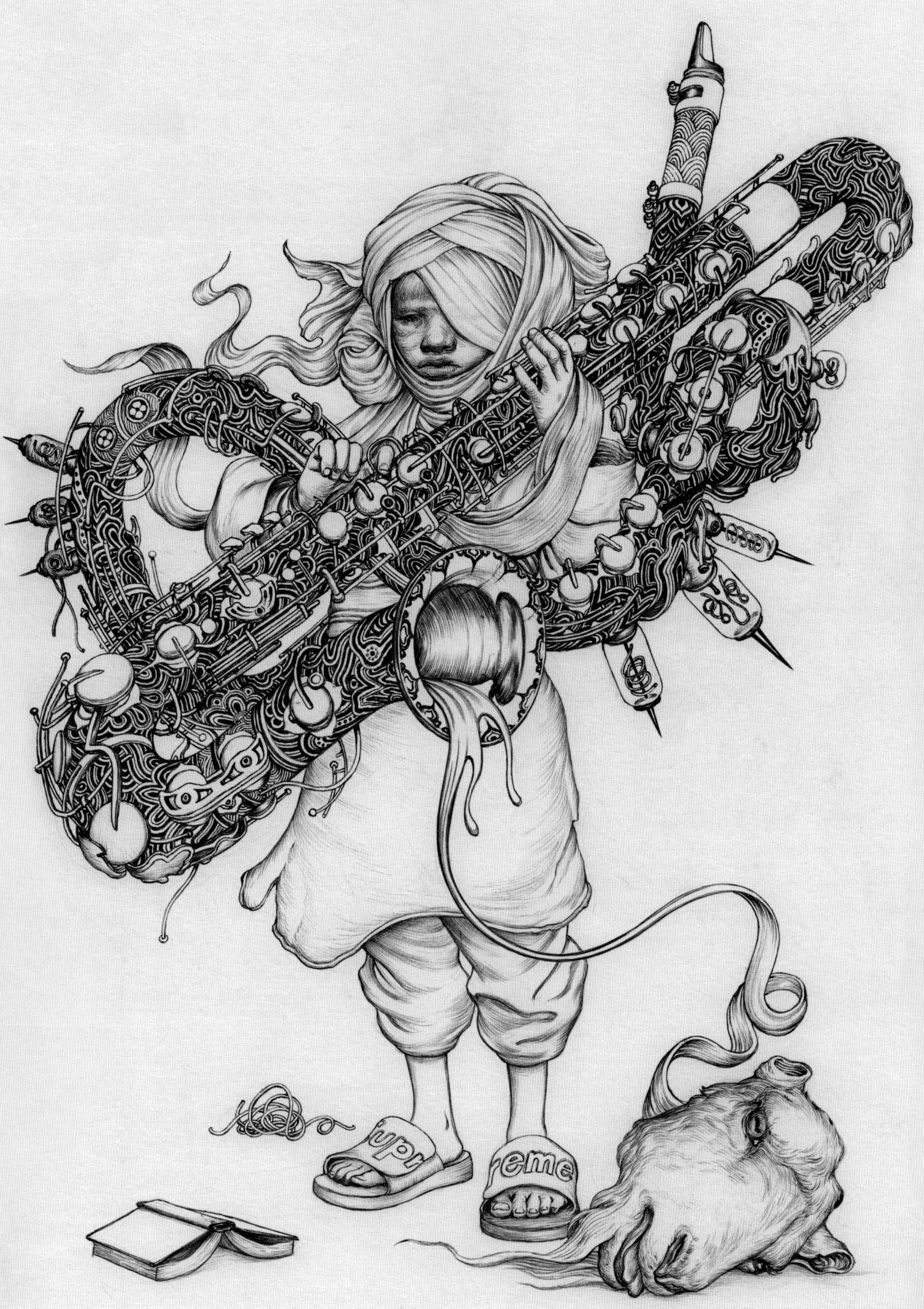
upr
eme

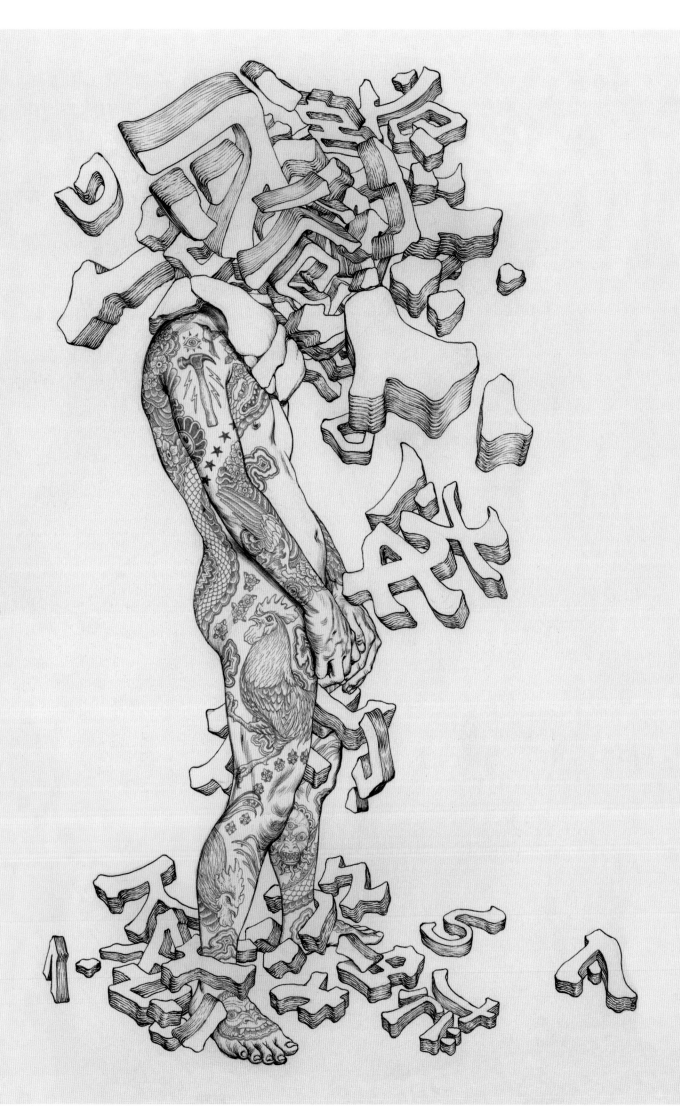

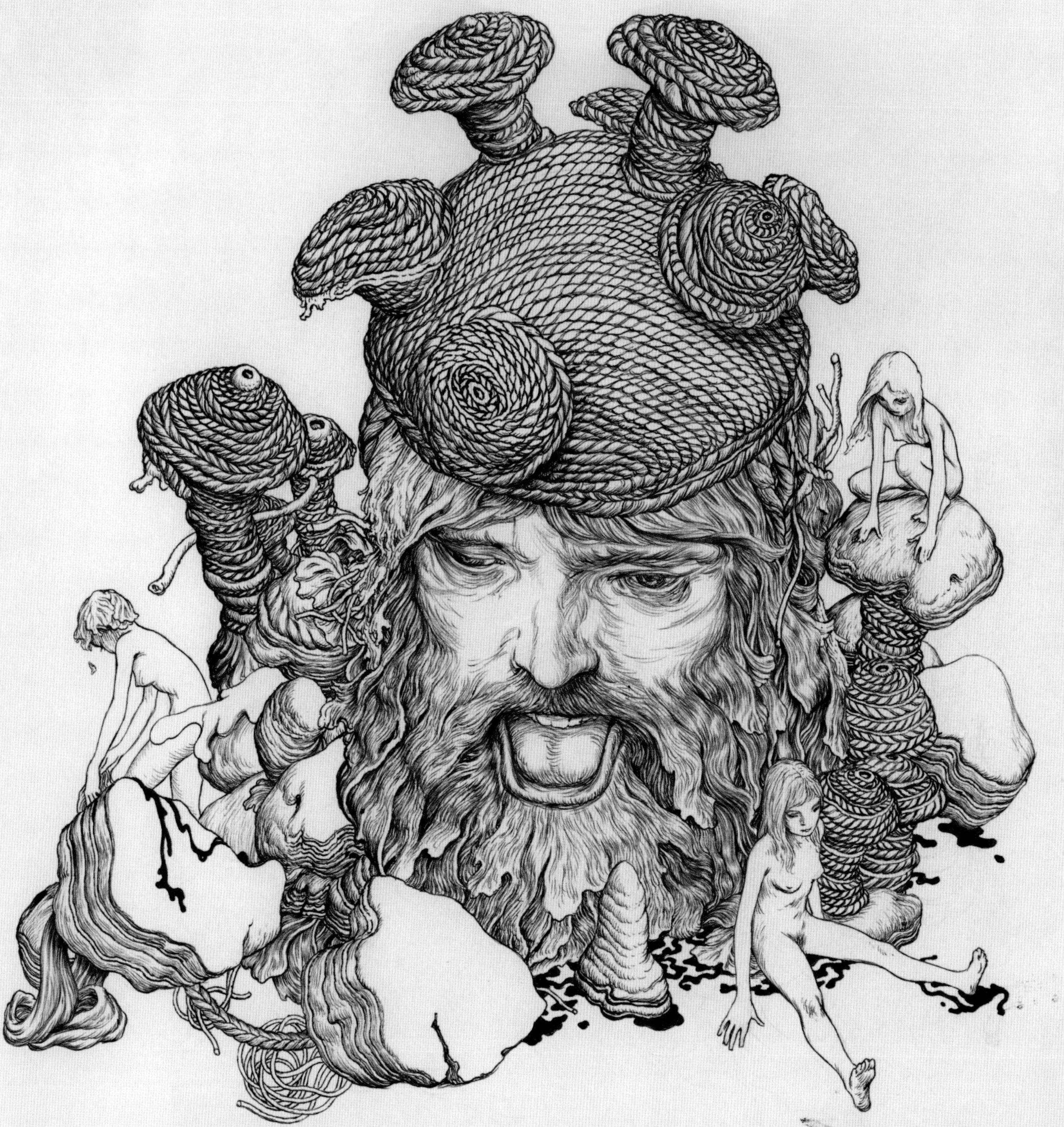

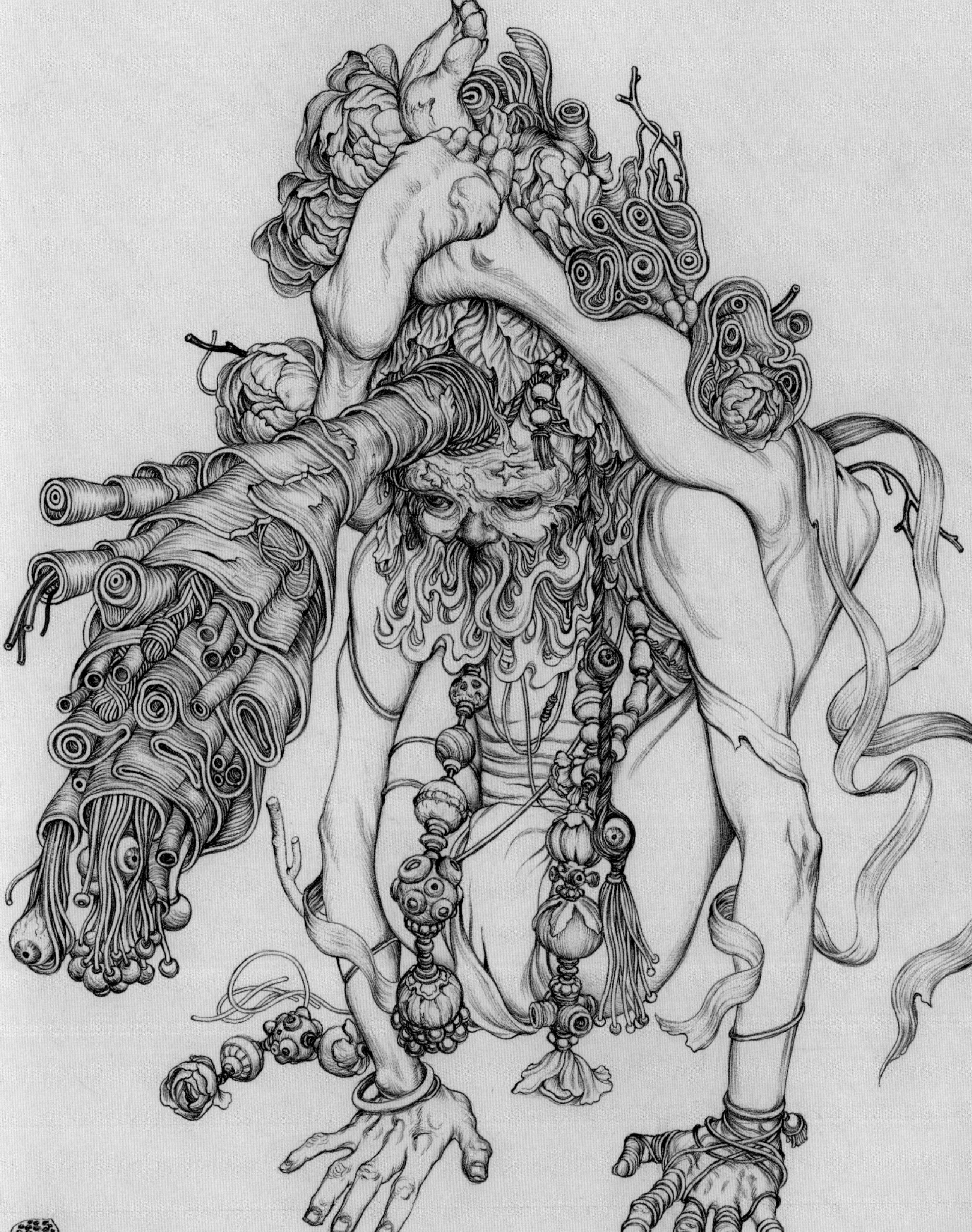

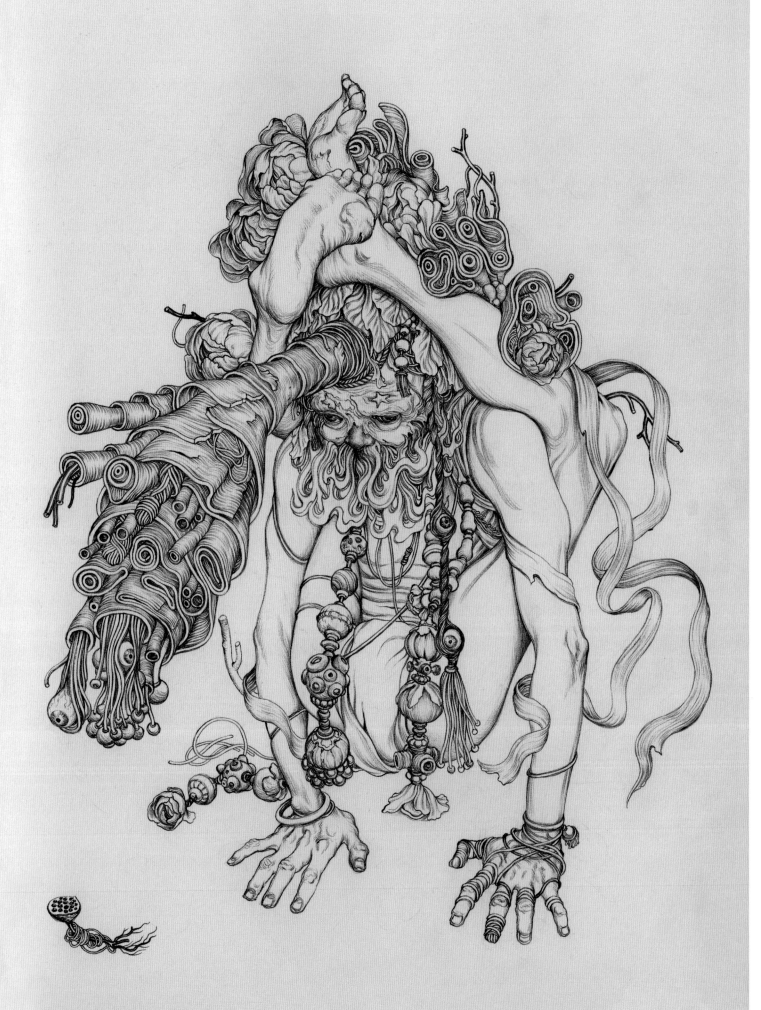

1979 Born in Taipei, Taiwan.

EDUCATION

1997-2001 B.F.A. The School of Visual Arts, New York, NY B.F.A

SOLO EXHIBITIONS

2013 Parallel Lives, Jack Tilton Gallery, New York, NY

2011 Rebus, Martha Otero Gallery, Los Angeles, CA

2009 Kindling, Jonathan Levine Gallery, New York, NY

GROUP EXHIBITIONS

2014 Masterworks, Long Beach Museum of Art, Long Beach, CA

2014 SuperAwesome, Oakland Museum of Art, Oakland, CA

2013 Vitruvius, Martha Otero Gallery, Los Angeles, CA

2012 City of Fire, Stephen Webster, Beverly Hills, CA

2012 Gin & Juice, Ivory & Black Soho, London, UK

2011 Rebus Book Release, Art Catalogues, Ahmanson Building, LACMA, Los Angeles, CA

2011 Oniomania, Martha Otero Gallery, Los Angeles, CA

2010 L.A. Secret Studio: David Choe & James Jean, Parco Factory, Tokyo, Japan

2009 GR Biennale, Japanese American National Museum, Los Angeles, CA

2008 Just In: Recent Acquisitions from the Collection, Leonard Dobbs Gallery, Architecture
and Design, The Museum of Modern Art, New York, NY

2008 Beyond Baby Tattooville, Members Gallery, Riverside Art Museum, Riverside, CA

2006 Panelists 2, Giant Robot Gallery, San Francisco, CA

2006 Black and White, Compound Gallery, Portland, OR

2006 Unforgiving, The Changing Room, New York, NY

2005 Idols of Perversity, Bellwether Gallery, New York, NY

2005 Soothsayers, Scion Installation Space, Culver City, CA

2005 Characters, Scene II, Silvermine Guild Arts Center, New Canaan, CT

2005 Characters, Scene I, Shore Institute of Contemporary Art, Long Branch,NJ

2001 International Printmaking Competition, SoHo20 Gallery, New York, NY

PUBLICATIONS

2011 San Francisco, CA. Chronicle Books. Rebus.

2010 San Francisco, CA. Chronicle Books. Rift.

2009 San Francisco, CA. Chronicle Books. Kindling: 12 Removable Prints.

2009 Richmond, VA. AdHouse Books. Process Recess: The Hallowed Seam, vol. 3.

2008 San Francisco, CA. Chronicle Books. XOXO: Hugs and Kisses.

2008 New York, NY. DC/Vertigo Comics. Fables: Covers by James Jean.

2007 Richmond, VA. AdHouse Books. Process Recess, vol. 2.

2005 Richmond, VA. AdHouse Books. Process Recess, vol. 1.

SPECIAL PROJECTS

2012 Velum, Installation at Lane Crawford, Hong Kong, China

2010 Birds and Boys, Installation at 3.1 Phillip Lim, Los Angeles, CA

2008 Trembled Blossoms, Animated Film for Prada S/S 2008 Collection

2007 Wallpaper & Fabric Prints for Prada S/S 2008 Collection

MUSEUM AND PUBLIC COLLECTIONS

Asian Art Museum, San Francisco, CA

Long Beach Museum of Art, Long Beach, CA

1979　台湾の台北市生まれ

学歴

1997-2001 ニューヨークのスクールオブビジュアルアーツで美術学士号取得

個展

2013 「Parallel Lives」 ジャック・ティルトンギャラリー、ニューヨーク（ニューヨーク州）

2011 「REBUS」 マーサオテロギャラリー、ロサンゼルス（カリフォルニア州）

2009 「Kindling」 ジョナサン・レヴィンギャラリー、ニューヨーク（ニューヨーク州）

グループ展

2014 「Masterworks」 ロングビーチ美術館、ロングビーチ（カリフォルニア州）

2014 「SuperAwesome」 オークランド美術館、オークランド（カリフォルニア州）

2013 「Vitruvius」 マーサオテロギャラリー、ロサンゼルス（カリフォルニア州）

2012 「City of Fire」 ステファン・ウェブスター、ビバリーヒルズ（カリフォルニア州）

2012 「Gin & Juice」 アイボリー＆ブラック ソーホー、ロンドン（イギリス）

2011 「Rebus Book Release」 アートカタログ、LACMA アーマンソンビル、ロサンゼルス（カリフォルニア

2011 「Oniomania」 マーサオテロギャラリー、ロサンゼルス（カリフォルニア州）

2010 「L.A. Secret Studio: David Choe & James Jean」 パルコファクトリー、東京（日本）

2009 「GR Biennale」 全米日系人博物館、ロサンゼルス（カリフォルニア州）

2008 「Just In: Recent Acquisitions from the Collection」 レオナルド・ドブスギャラリー、
ニューヨーク近代美術館「建築・デザイン」コレクション、ニューヨーク（ニューヨーク州）

2008 「Beyond Baby Tattooville」リバーサイド美術館メンバーズギャラリー、リバーサイド（カリフォルニ

2006 「Panelists 2」 ジャイアントロボットギャラリー、サンフランシスコ（カリフォルニア州）

2006 「Black and White」 コンパウンドギャラリー、ポートランド（オレゴン州）

2006 「Unforgiving」 ザ・チェンジングルーム、ニューヨーク（ニューヨーク州）

2005 「Idols of Perversity」 ベルウェザー・ギャラリー、ニューヨーク（ニューヨーク州）

2005 「Soothsayers」サイオン・インスタレーション・スペース、カルバーシティ（カリフォルニア州）

2005 「Characters, Scene II」 シルバーマインギルドアートセンター、ニューケナン（コネチカット州）

2005 「Characters, Scene I」 ショア現代美術研究所、ロングブランチ（ニュージャージー州）

2001 「International Printmaking Competition」 SoHo20 ギャラリー、ニューヨーク（ニューヨーク

出版物

2011 「REBUS」 クロニクルブックス、サンフランシスコ（カリフォルニア州）

2010 「Rift」 クロニクルブックス、サンフランシスコ（カリフォルニア州）

2009 「Kindling: 12 Removable Prints」 クロニクルブックス、サンフランシスコ（カリフォルニア州）

2009 「Process Recess: The Hallowed Seam, vol. 3.」 アドハウスブックス、リッチモンド（バージニア

2008 「XOXO: Hugs and Kisses」 クロニクルブックス、サンフランシスコ（カリフォルニア州）

2008 「Fables: Covers by James Jean」 DC コミックス・ヴァーティゴ、ニューヨーク（ニューヨーク州）

2007 「Process Recess, vol. 2」 アドハウスブックス、リッチモンド（バージニア州）

2005 「Process Recess, vol. 1」 アドハウスブックス、リッチモンド（バージニア州）

スペシャルプロジェクト

2012 「Velum」レーン・クロフォードでのインスタレーション、香港（中国）

2010 「Birds and Boys」 3.1 Phillip Lim でのインスタレーション、ロサンゼルス（カリフォルニア州）

2008 「Trembled Blossoms」プラダ S／S 2008 コレクションのアニメーションフィルム

2008　プラダ S／S 2008 コレクションの壁紙とファブリックプリント

作品が所蔵されている美術館

サンフランシスコアジア美術館、サンフランシスコ（カリフォルニア州）

ロングビーチ美術館、ロングビーチ（カリフォルニア州）

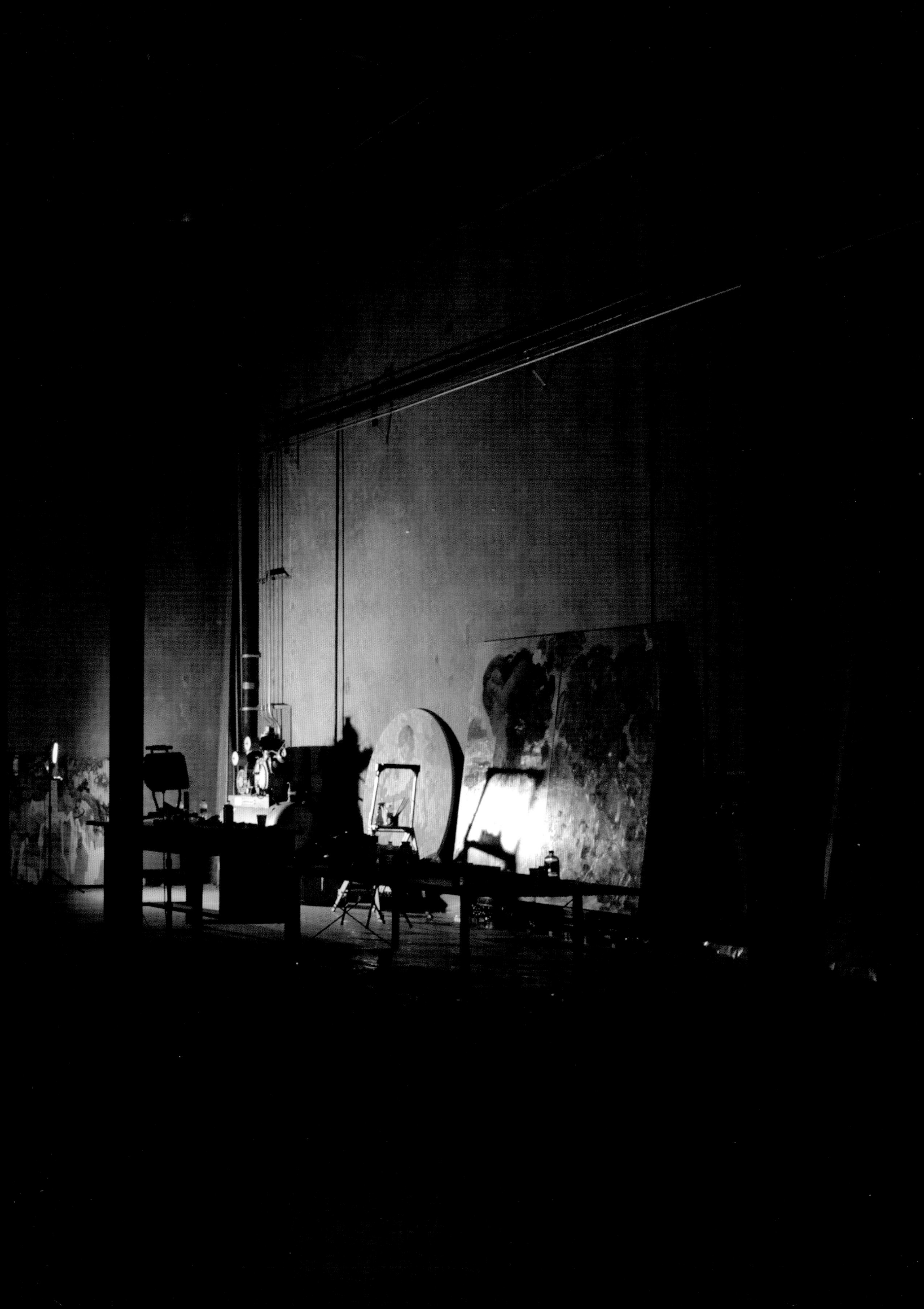

INDEX

76: LUCK. ACRYLIC ON CANVAS, 48 X 60", 2013.

77: HORSE V. ACRYLIC ON CANVAS, 48 X 60", 2013.

78: CRICKETS. ACRYLIC ON WOOD, 18 X 18", 2008.

79: MAZE II (MEMU). GRAPHITE AND DIGITAL, 7 X 8", 2013.

80: YOLK. ACRYLIC ON PAPER, 22 X 15", 2007.

81: RSA BLACK DOG. GRAPHITE AND DIGITAL, 2012.

82: CORMORANT. INK AND DIGITAL, 9 X 12", 2014.

83: SMOKE SIGNAL. GRAPHITE AND DIGITAL, 10 X 16", 2011.

84: PARCHED SAUCER. GRAPHITE AND DIGITAL, 5 X 5", 2009.

85: WAVE (BURIED). GRAPHITE AND DIGITAL, 2012.

86: WAVE (CRANE). GRAPHITE AND DIGITAL, 2012.

87: WAVE (SKULL). GRAPHITE AND DIGITAL, 2012.

88: THE HOST. GRAPHITE AND DIGITAL, 2006.

89: WAVE. GRAPHITE AND DIGITAL, 6 X 11", 2004.

90: WAVE II. ACRYLIC ON PAPER, 25 X 30", 2009.

91: FLIP. GRAPHITE AND DIGITAL, 10 X 13", 2006.

92: ABOVE: HOMEOPATHIC. GRAPHITE AND DIGITAL, 15 X 11", 2003.
BELOW: FLUSH. GRAPHITE AND DIGITAL, 15 X 11", 2003.

93: ABOVE: CHEMISTRY. GRAPHITE AND DIGITAL, 15 X 11", 2003.
BELOW: PICKUP. GRAPHITE AND DIGITAL, 15 X 11", 2003.

94: ABOVE: CONFECTION. GRAPHITE AND DIGITAL, 15 X 11", 2003.
BELOW: MASCOT. GRAPHITE AND DIGITAL, 15 X 11", 2003.

95: EDEN. COLOR PENCIL, INK, AND DIGITAL, 30 X 36", 2009.

96: WEEP. GRAPHITE AND DIGITAL, 11 X 15", 2004.

97: JUMP. GRAPHITE AND DIGITAL, 17 X 11", 2003.

98: SEESAW. GRAPHITE AND DIGITAL, 7 X 5", 2013.

99: SWING. GRAPHITE AND DIGITAL, 12 X 16", 2002.

100: QBERT. GRAPHITE, COLOR PENCIL, AND ACRYLIC ON PAPER, 22 X 30", 2007.

101: ABOVE: POOR THING. CHARCOAL AND DIGITAL, 19 X 12", 2007.
BELOW: DIDELY BOW. COLOR PENCIL AND DIGITAL, 19 X 12", 2007.

102: DANCERS. ACRYLIC ON TWO WOOD PANELS, 24 X 12", 2010.

103: REBUS INSTALLATION. MARTHA OTERO GALLERY, LOS ANGELES, CA, 2011.

104-105: TIGER. ACRYLIC, OIL AND PASTEL ON TWO CANVASES, 105 X 60", 2010.

106-107: HOUNDS. ACRYLIC AND OIL ON THREE CANVASES, 72 X 150", 2010.

108: CHOIR. OIL AND ACRYLIC ON SYNTHETIC TEXTILE, 48 X 60", 2012.

109: SIKH. ACRYLIC AND OIL ON CANVAS, 40" DIAMETER, 2012.

110: BRAID II. OIL AND PUMICE ON WOOD, 12 X 12", 2012.

111: STUDENT. ACRYLIC AND PUMICE ON WOOD, 24 X 24", 2011.

112: BOWS. ACRYLIC ON WOOD, 12 X 12", 2011.

113: SLEEPER. OIL ON WOOD, 37 X 39", 2012.

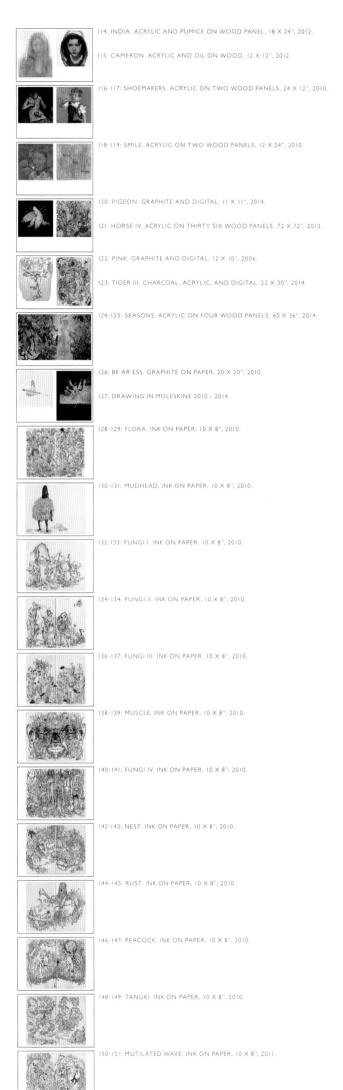

114: INDIA. ACRYLIC AND PUMICE ON WOOD PANEL, 18 X 24", 2012.

115: CAMERON. ACRYLIC AND OIL ON WOOD, 12 X 12", 2012.

116-117: SHOEMAKERS. ACRYLIC ON TWO WOOD PANELS, 24 X 12", 2010.

118-119: SMILE. ACRYLIC ON TWO WOOD PANELS, 12 X 24", 2010.

120: PIGEON. GRAPHITE AND DIGITAL, 11 X 11", 2014.

121: HORSE IV. ACRYLIC ON THIRTY SIX WOOD PANELS, 72 X 72", 2013.

122: PINK. GRAPHITE AND DIGITAL, 12 X 10", 2006.

123: TIGER III. CHARCOAL, ACRYLIC, AND DIGITAL, 22 X 30", 2014.

124-125: SEASONS. ACRYLIC ON FOUR WOOD PANELS, 60 X 36", 2014.

126: BE AR ESS. GRAPHITE ON PAPER, 20 X 20", 2010.

127: DRAWING IN MOLESKINE 2010 - 2014.

128-129: FLORA. INK ON PAPER, 10 X 8", 2010.

130-131: MUDHEAD. INK ON PAPER, 10 X 8", 2010.

132-133: FUNGI I. INK ON PAPER, 10 X 8", 2010.

134-134: FUNGI II. INK ON PAPER, 10 X 8", 2010.

136-137: FUNGI III. INK ON PAPER, 10 X 8", 2010.

138-139: MUSCLE. INK ON PAPER, 10 X 8", 2010.

140-141: FUNGI IV. INK ON PAPER, 10 X 8", 2010.

142-143: NEST. INK ON PAPER, 10 X 8", 2010.

144-145: RUST. INK ON PAPER, 10 X 8", 2010.

146-147: PEACOCK. INK ON PAPER, 10 X 8", 2010.

148-149: TANUKI. INK ON PAPER, 10 X 8", 2010.

150-151: MUTILATED WAVE. INK ON PAPER, 10 X 8", 2011.

152-153: YEAR OF RABBIT. INK ON PAPER, 10 X 8", 2011.

154-155: PHILOSOPHER. INK ON PAPER, 10 X 8", 2011.

156-157: ENOKI. INK ON PAPER, 10 X 8", 2011.

158-159: ARSON. INK ON PAPER, 10 X 8", 2011.

160-161: VISCERA. INK ON PAPER, 10 X 8", 2011.

162-163: WASPS. INK ON PAPER, 10 X 8", 2011.

164-165: GUANO. INK ON PAPER, 10 X 8", 2011.

166-167: CARNAGE. INK ON PAPER, 10 X 8", 2012.

168-169: DOUBLE MASTECTOMY. INK ON PAPER, 10 X 8", 2012.

170-171: TUMOR. INK ON PAPER, 10 X 8", 2012.

172-173: SLUDGEBOY. INK ON PAPER, 10 X 8", 2013.

174-175: WAR HORSE. INK ON PAPER, 10 X 8", 2013.

176-177: PUPPET. INK ON PAPER, 10 X 8", 2013.

178-179: GRID. INK ON PAPER, 10 X 8", 2013.

180: OTTOMAN. INK ON PAPER, 5 X 8", 2011.

181: FUNGI V. INK ON PAPER, 5 X 8", 2013.

182: HANNYA. INK ON PAPER, 5 X 8", 2011.

183: CARRIER. INK ON PAPER, 5 X 8", 2011.

184: GOURD. INK ON PAPER, 5 X 8", 2011.

185: NERVOSA. INK ON PAPER, 5 X 8", 2012.

186: PEARLS. INK ON PAPER, 5 X 8", 2013.

187: NUMBER ONE. INK ON PAPER, 5 X 8", 2013.

188: FROG LICKER. INK ON PAPER, 5 X 8", 2013.

189: PESCADOS. INK ON PAPER, 5 X 8", 2013.

190: DRAWING IN MOLESKINE 2010-2014.

191: EXCERPT FROM MOLESKINE 2010 - 2014.

192-197: RIFT PROCESSION. GRAPHITE AND DIGITAL, 50 X 11", 2009.

198-204: PRADA EPICENTER. GRAPHITE AND DIGITAL, 2007.

198-199: HAAZ SPRING. GRAPHITE AND DIGITAL, 2008.

200-204: PRADA MILAN. GRAPHITE AND DIGITAL, 2007.

205: PRADA INSTALLATION. NEW YORK - TOKYO. 2007-2008

206: PRADA SKETCHES, 2007.

207: PRADA S/S 2008 ADVERTISING.

208: PRADA, TREMBLED BLOSSOMS CONCEPT ART, 2007-2008.

209: PRADA, TREMBLED BLOSSOMS CONCEPT ART, 2007-2008.

210-211: PRADA, TREMBLED BLOSSOMS CONCEPT ART, 2007-2008.

212-213: ADRIFT. MIXED MEDIA ON FOUR CANVASES, 180 X 88", 2015.

214-215: PARALLEL LIVES INSTALLATION. JACK TILTON GALLERY, NEW YORK, NY, 2013.

216-217: PAGODA. MIXED MEDIA ON EIGHTY FOUR WOOD PANELS, 192 X 112", 2012.

218-219: PAGODA. DETAIL VIEW.

220-221: PAGODA. DETAIL VIEW.

222: TUBA. INK ON PAPER AND PLEXIGLASS, 16 X 16", 2012.

223: HORSE II. INK ON PAPER AND PLEXIGLASS, 16 X 16", 2012.

224: RICKSHAW II. INK ON PAPER AND PLEXIGLASS, 16 X 16", 2012.

225: FOUNTAIN III. INK ON PAPER AND PLEXIGLASS, 16 X 16", 2012.

226: JELLY. INK ON PAPER AND PLEXIGLASS, 16 X 16", 2012.

227: CHROME. INK ON PAPER AND PLEXIGLASS, 16 X 16", 2012.

228-229: TIGER II (SCHEMA). GRAPHITE AND DIGITAL, 23 X 16", 2013.

230-231: WAVE III (SCHEMA). GRAPHITE AND DIGITAL, 23 X 16", 2013.

232-233: CORAL BIRD (SCHEMA). GRAPHITE AND DIGITAL, 23 X 16", 2013.

234: CORAL HOUND. COLOR PENCIL, GRAPHITE, ACRYLIC, AND DIGITAL, 40 X 30", 2011.

235: BRAID. ACRYLIC, GOUACHE, AND COLOR PENCIL ON PAPER, 20 X 30", 2011.

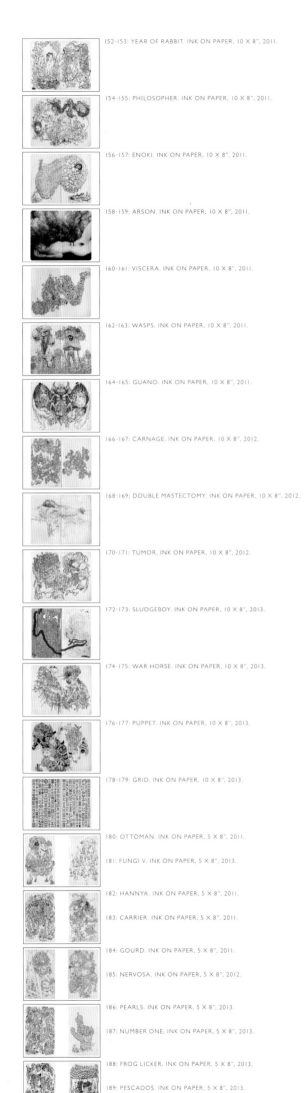

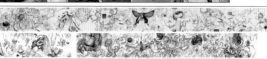

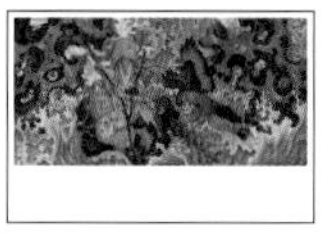

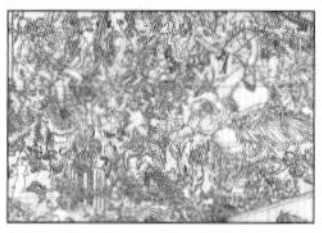

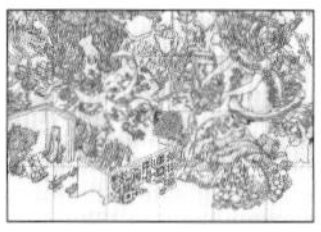

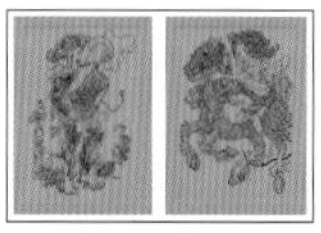

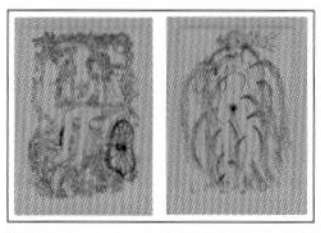

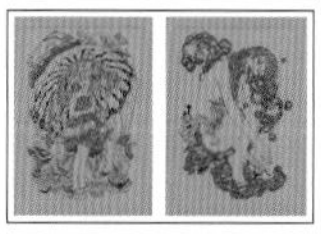

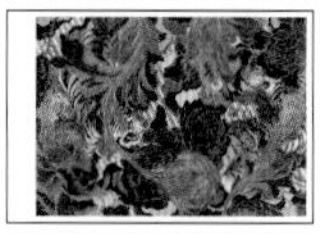

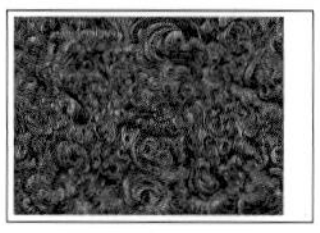

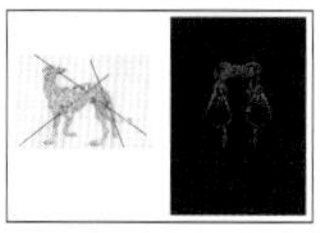

236: TALIB KWELI. GRAPHITE, INK, AND DIGITAL, 20 X 23", 2012.

237: LOTUS WAR PYRAMIND. GRAPHITE AND DIGITAL, 35 X 40", 2011.

238: LOTUS WAR ARCHER. GRAPHITE AND DIGITAL, 2011.

239: LOTUS WAR S/S COLOR. DIGITAL AND INK ON SILK, 36 X 36", 2011.

240-241: LOTUS WAR DAY. GRAPHITE AND DIGITAL, 2011.

242: ESCAPE. GRAPHITE AND DIGITAL, 36 X 36", 2011.

243: DUELISTS. INK AND DIGITAL, 36 X 36", 2012.

244-245: DUELISTS. DETAIL VIEW.

246: BEAUTY KILL. DIGITAL, 36 X 36", 2011.

247: SIRENS. GRAPHITE & DIGITAL, 36 X 36", 2011.

248: RECLAMARE. INK AND DIGITAL, 36 X 36", 2012.

249: THE HORN. ACRYLIC AND METAL ON WOOD, 70 X 76", 2012.

250-251: THE HORN (DRAWING). DETAIL VIEW.

252-253: RECLAMARE (DRAWING). DETAIL VIEW.

254: VELUM LYRICAL S/S. DIGITAL AND INK ON SILK, 40 X 40", 2012.

255: VELUM CASCADE S/S. DIGITAL, AND INK ON SILK, 40 X 40", 2012.

256-257: VELUM MURAL. GRAPHITE, INK, AND DIGITAL, 80 X 26", 2012.

258-259: VELUM MURAL. GRAPHITE, INK, AND DIGITAL, 80 X 26", 2012.

260: FLASH I. GRAPHITE AND DIGITAL, 2014.

261: FLASH II. GRAPHITE AND DIGITAL, 2014.

262: RAVENS. INK AND DIGITAL, 12 X 13", 2014.

263: FLASH PATTERN. GRAPHITE AND DIGITAL, 2014.

264: POMEGRANATE. GRAPHITE AND DIGITAL, 11 X 16", 2014.

265: THORN. OIL AND SPRAYPAINT ON SYNTHETIC TEXTILE, 48 X 72", 2012.

266: BIKER. ACRYLIC, OIL, AND LACQUER ON SYNTHETIC TEXTILE, 48 X 72", 2012.

267: TXT. ACRYLIC ON SYNTHETIC TEXTILE, 48 X 72", 2014.

268-269: LOS ANGELES WAREHOUSE STUDIO, 2012.

270: CORAL HEAD. INK AND DIGITAL, 8.25 X 11.5", 2014.

271: ARCHER. INK AND DIGITAL, 8.25 X 11.5", 2014.

272: SUCCULENT. INK AND DIGITAL, 8.25 X 11.5", 2014.

273: GINGER. INK AND DIGITAL, 8.25 X 11.5", 2014.

274: SAMURAI. INK AND DIGITAL, 8.25 X 11.5", 2014.

275: KNIGHT I. INK AND DIGITAL, 8.25 X 11.5", 2014.

276: TORCH. INK AND DIGITAL, 8.25 X 11.5", 2014.

277: CHIMERA. INK AND DIGITAL, 8.25 X 11.5", 2014.

278: ELK. INK AND DIGITAL, 8.25 X 11.5", 2014.

279: KNIGHT II. INK AND DIGITAL, 8.25 X 11.5", 2014.

280: CHAMBER. INK AND DIGITAL, 8.25 X 11.5", 2014.

281: LION. INK AND DIGITAL, 8.25 X 11.5", 2014.

282: VISCERA II. INK AND DIGITAL, 8.25 X 11.5", 2014.

283: CLOUD. INK AND DIGITAL, 8.25 X 11.5", 2014.

284: UNAGI. INK AND DIGITAL, 8.25 X 11.5", 2014.

285: MASK. INK AND DIGITAL, 8.25 X 11.5", 2014.

286: CORAL QUEEN. INK AND DIGITAL, 8.25 X 11.5", 2014.

287: NEST II. INK AND DIGITAL, 8.25 X 11.5", 2014.

288: MANGCHI II. INK AND DIGITAL, 8.5 X 11", 2014.

289: GANESHA. INK ON PAPER, 8.5 X 11", 2014.

290: PIGGYBACK. INK ON PAPER, 8.5 X 11", 2015.

291: OBOE HARAM. INK ON PAPER, 8.5 X 11", 2015.

292: MANGCHI III. INK ON PAPER, 8.5 X 11", 2015.

293: CRITTER. INK ON PAPER, 8.5 X 11", 2014.

294: SADHU. INK ON PAPER, 8.5 X 11", 2015.

295: MOLESKINE 2014-2015. TOKYO, JAPAN, 2015.

296: LOS ANGELES WAREHOUSE STUDIO, 2012.

297: CURRICULUM VITAE

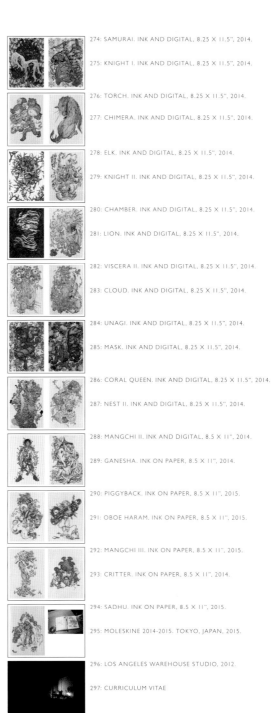

ジェームス・ジーン画集

パ レ イ ド リ ア
PAREIDOLIA

JAMES JEAN

2015 年 9 月 16 日 初版第 1 刷発行

著者　　ジェームス・ジーン

アートディレクション　ジェームス・ジーン

サブデザイナー　佐々木弥生
編　集　　天野昌直
制作進行　　大場義行

発 行 人　三芳寛要
発 行 元　株式会社パイ インターナショナル
　　　　　〒 170-0005　東京都豊島区南大塚 2-32-4
　　　　　TEL 03-3944-3981
　　　　　FAX 03-5395-4830
　　　　　sales@pie.co.jp

制作　　　PIE BOOKS
印刷・製本　株式会社廣済堂

© James Jean/ PIE International
ISBN978-4-7562-4713-1 C0079
Printed in Japan

Pareidolia
James Jean

A Retrospective of Beloved and New Works by James Jean

PIE International Inc.

2-32-4 Minami-Otsuka, Toshima-ku, Tokyo 170-0005 JAPAN

sales@pie.co.jp

©James Jean/ PIE International
ISBN978-4-7562-4713-1
Printed in Japan